Deng Xiaoping

Deng Xiaoping

A Revolutionary Life

—◆◉◆—

ALEXANDER V. PANTSOV

with

STEVEN I. LEVINE

OXFORD
UNIVERSITY PRESS

OXFORD
UNIVERSITY PRESS

Oxford University Press is a department of the University of
Oxford. It furthers the University's objective of excellence in research,
scholarship, and education by publishing worldwide.

Oxford   New York
Auckland   Cape Town   Dar es Salaam   Hong Kong   Karachi
Kuala Lumpur   Madrid   Melbourne   Mexico City   Nairobi
New Delhi   Shanghai   Taipei   Toronto

With offices in
Argentina   Austria   Brazil   Chile   Czech Republic   France   Greece
Guatemala   Hungary   Italy   Japan   Poland   Portugal   Singapore
South Korea   Switzerland   Thailand   Turkey   Ukraine   Vietnam

Oxford is a registered trademark of Oxford University Press
in the UK and certain other countries.

Published in the United States of America by
Oxford University Press
198 Madison Avenue, New York, NY 10016

Cataloging-in-Publication data is on file at the Library of Congress
ISBN 978–0–19–939203–2

1 3 5 7 9 8 6 4 2
Printed in the United States of America
on acid-free paper

To the memory of my parents,
Vadim Georgievich Ehrenburg (1924–1979)
and
Nina Stepanovna Pantsova (1929–2011),
I dedicate this book with love

—Alexander V. Pantsov

Contents

Acknowledgments

IT GIVES US great pleasure to express our deep appreciation to those persons without whose attention and friendly assistance this work would never have seen the light of day. We want to express our thanks to Kirill Mikhailovich Anderson, Nikolai Sergeevich Arinchev, Daria Aleksandrovna Arincheva (Spichak), Richard Ashbrook, Peter W. Bernstein, Ekaterina Borisovna Bogoslovskaia, Denvy Bowman, Christopher Buckley, Chen Yung-fa, Georgii Iosifovich Cherniavskii, John Garnaut, Tamara Ivanovna Illarionova, Liubov Spiridonovna Kaliuzhnaia, James DeGrande, Liudmila Konstantinovna Karlova, Mikhail Vladimirovich Karpov, Elizaveta Pavlovna Kishkina (Li Sha, a widow of Li Lisan), Liudmila Mikhailovna Kosheleva, Boris Iosifovich Koval', Madeline G. Levine, Li Danhui, Inna Li (the daughter of Li Lisan), Li Yuzhen, Lin Liheng (Doudou, the daughter of Lin Biao), Lin Yin (Lena Jin), Dimon Liu, Liu Wei (a secretary of Deng Xiaoping's daughter Deng Rong [Maomao] and a daughter-in-law of Deng Xiaoping's secretary Wang Ruilin), William H. Magginis, David McBride, Nina Stepanovna Pantsova, Svetlana Markovna Rozental', John Sexton, Valintina Nikolaevna Shchetilina, Shen Zhihua, Valerii Nikolaevich Shepelev, Irina Nikolaevna Sotnikova, Evgeniia Aleksandrovna Tobol' (a granddaughter of Igor Vasilievich Yurchenko [Yuzhin]), Yurii Tikhonovich Tutochkin, Ezra F. Vogel, Wang Fuzeng, Wang Jianjun (a secretary of the Guang'an Municipal CCP Committee), Wei Jingsheng, Xiao Jing Wang (a grandson of Wang Zekai), Yu Minling, Zi Zhongyun (one of the interpreters for Deng Xiaoping, Mao Zedong, Liu Shaoqi, and Zhou Enlai), Vladislav Martinovich Zubok, and to many citizens of the People's Republic of China who shared their reminiscences of their lives under Deng Xiaoping but who prefer to remain anonymous.

Cast of Characters

Andropov, Yuri Vladimirovich (1914–1984). Secretary of Soviet Communist Party Central Committee, 1962–1967 and 1982. Chairman of KGB, 1967–1982. General secretary of Soviet Communist Party Central Committee, 1982–1984.

Bao Tong (1932–). Secretary of Zhao Ziyang, 1980–1989. Head of CCP Central Committee research group of reform of political system. Arrested, 1989, and imprisoned. Released, 1996.

Bo Gu (real name: Qin Bangxian) (1907–1946). General secretary of CCP Central Committee, 1931–1935. Deng's antagonist.

Bo Yibo (1908–2007). China's finance minister, 1949–1953. Deputy premier, 1956–1975 and 1979–1982. Vice chairman of the Central Advisory Commission, 1982–1992. Member of Deng's powerful veteran circle.

Braun, Otto (alias Li De, Hua Fu) (1900–1974). Military adviser to CCP Central Committee, 1932–1935.

Brezhnev, Leonid Ilich (1906–1982). First (general) secretary of Soviet Communist Party Central Committee, 1964–1982.

Brzezinski, Zbigniew (b. 1928). U.S. national security advisor, 1977–1981.

Bukharin, Nikolai Ivanovich (1888–1938). Soviet Communist Party Central Committee Politburo member, 1924–1929. Member of the Presidium of Comintern, 1919–1929. Editor-in-chief of *Pravda (Truth)* newspaper, 1917–1929. Main theorist of the Bolshevik New Economic Policy.

Cai Hesen (1895–1931). Leader of the Chinese students in France, 1920–21. Member of CCP Central Executive Committee, 1927–28, and Politburo, 1931.

Carter, Jimmy (b. 1924). President of the United States of America, 1977–1981.

Chen Duxiu (1879–1942). Founder of the Chinese communist movement, leader of CCP, 1921–1927.

Chen Shaoyu (alias Wang Ming) (1904–1974). Deng's classmate in Moscow, 1926–27. De facto head of the CCP, 1931. Head of the CCP delegation to Comintern, 1931–1937.

Chen Yi (1901–1972). Commander of the Third Field Army, 1946–1949. Deputy premier, 1954–1972. Foreign minister, 1958–1972. PLA marshal from 1955.

Chen Yun (real name: Liao Chenyun) (1905–1995). Deputy premier, 1954–1965, 1979–80. Deputy chairman of CCP Central Committee, 1956–1966 and 1978–1982. First secretary of the Central Commission for Discipline Inspection, 1982–1987. Chairman of the Central Advisory Commission, 1987–1992. Economic specialist. Member of Deng's powerful veteran circle.

Chiang Kai-shek (1887–1975). Commander in chief of Guomindang National Revolutionary Army from 1926. Head of Guomindang regime from 1928.

Dan (1884–1926). Deng's mother.

Deng Lin (b. 1941). Deng's first daughter.

Deng Liqun (b. 1915). Victim of Cultural Revolution. Deng's close assistant since 1975. Vice president of the Chinese Academy of Social Sciences, 1978–1980. Head of the CC CCP Propaganda Department, 1982–1987.

Deng Nan (b. 1945). Deng's second daughter.

Deng Pufang (b. 1944). Deng's first son.

Deng Rong (alias Maomao) (b. 1950). Deng's third daughter.

Deng Wenming (1886–1936). Deng's father.

Deng Xiaoping (1904–1997). Deputy premier, 1952–1968, 1973–1976, 1977–1980. Central Committee general secretary, 1956–1966. Purged in Cultural Revolution, but returned to power in 1977 and reversed Mao's policies. Chairman of Central Military Commission, 1981–1989. China's paramount leader, 1978–1997.

Deng Yingchao (1904–1992). Zhou Enlai's wife. Member of Deng's powerful veteran circle.

Deng Zhifang (b. 1951). Deng's second son.

Feng Yuxiang (1882–1948). Marshal, commander in chief of Nationalist Army, the 2nd Army Group of the Guomindang National-Revolutionary Army and Northwest Army, 1924–1930.

Gao Gang (1905–1954). Chairman of Northeast regional government, 1949–1952. Deputy premier, 1949–1954. Head of State Planning Commission, 1952–1954. Expelled from CCP, 1955.

Gorbachev, Mikhail Sergeevich (b. 1931). General secretary of Soviet Communist Party Central Committee, 1985–1991. President of the Soviet Union, 1989–1991.

Gu Mu (1914–2009). Deputy premier and secretary of the CC CCP Secretariat, 1975–1988. Economic reformer.

He Long (1896–1969). Third secretary of the Southwest CC CCP bureau, 1949–1952. Deputy premier since 1954. PLA marshal from 1955. Committed suicide during the Cultural Revolution.

Hu Qiaomu (1912–1992). Mao's secretary since 1941. Deng's close assistant since 1975. President of the Chinese Academy of Social Sciences, 1977–1982 and 1985–1988. Secretary of the CC CCP Secretariat, 1980–1982.

Hu Qili (b. 1929). Secretary of the CC CCP Secretariat, 1982–1989. Member of the CCP CC Politburo Standing Committee, 1987–1989.

Hu Yaobang (1915–1989). First secretary of Communist Youth League of China, 1953–1966. Victim of Cultural Revolution. Deng's close assistant, 1978–1987. Chairman of CCP Central Committee, 1981–82. General secretary of CCP Central Committee, 1982–1987. Economic and political reformer. Sacked by Deng for excessive liberalism.

Hua Guofeng (1921–2008). Mao's successor, 1976. Chairman of CCP Central Committee, 1976–1981. Premier, 1976–1980. Deng's opponent.

Jiang Qing (1914–1991). Mao's fourth wife. Head of the Central Cultural Revolution Group from 1966. Member of the extreme leftist Gang of Four. Deng's main antagonist. Arrested, 1976, and imprisoned.

Jiang Zemin (b. 1926). General Secretary of the CCP Central Committee, 1989–2002. President of the PRC, 1993–2003.

Jin Weiying (1904–1941). Deng's second wife.

Kang Sheng (alias Zhao Yun; real name Zhang Zongke) (1898–1975). Mao's chief spymaster. Deputy chairman of CCP Central Committee, 1973–1975. Deng's antagonist.

Khrushchev, Nikita Sergeevich (1894–1971). First secretary of Soviet Communist Party Central Committee, 1953–1964. Chairman of the Soviet Council of Ministers, 1958–1964.

Kissinger, Henry A. (b. 1923). U.S. national security advisor, 1969–1975. Secretary of state, 1973–1977.

Li Fuchun (1900–1975). Deputy premier and head of State Planning Commission from 1954. Politburo member, 1956–1969.

Li Lisan (1899–1967). A leading organizer of the Chinese labor movement from 1921. De facto head of CCP, 1928–1930. Instigated the so-called Li Lisan adventurist line, 1930.

Li Mingrui (1896–1931). Guangxi warlord. Commander of the Guangxi Peace Preservation Forces, 1929. Commander in chief of the combined forces of the 7th and 8th Corps of the Chinese Red Army, 1930–31.

Li Peng (b. 1928). Acting prime minister and prime minister, 1987–1998.

Li Weihan (1896–1984). Head of the CCP Central Committee Organization Department, 1933–34. Deng's antagonist. Head of CCP Central Committee United Front Department, 1948–1964.

Li Xiannian (1909–1992). Deputy premier, 1954–1980. Deputy chairman of the CCP Central Committee, 1977–1982. Chairman of the PRC, 1983–1988. Member of Deng's powerful veteran circle.

Lin Biao (1907–1971). PLA marshal from 1955. China's minister of defense, 1959–1971. Deputy chairman of CCP Central Committee, 1969–1971. Mao's designated successor, 1969–1971. Deng's antagonist. Tried to escape to the Soviet Union but died in a plane crash, September 1971.

Liu Bocheng (1892–1986). Commander of the 129th division of the Communist 18th Army Group, 1937–1945. Commander of the Second Field Army, 1946–1949. Second secretary of the Southwest CC CCP bureau, 1949–50. President and commissar of the PLA Military Academy, 1950–1959. PLA marshal from 1955.

Liu Shaoqi (1898–1969). A leading Chinese communist. Deputy chairman of CCP Central Committee, 1956–1966; chairman of the PRC, 1959–1968; and Mao's designated successor, 1961–1966. Main victim of the Cultural Revolution.

Luo Fu (real name: **Zhang Wentian**) (1900–1976). General secretary of CCP Central Committee, 1935–1943. China's deputy foreign minister, 1954–1959.

Mao Yuanxin (b. 1941). Mao Zedong's nephew; collaborated with the Gang of Four. Deng's antagonist.

Mao Zedong (1893–1976). Cofounder of CCP, 1921. Leader of the Chinese Communist movement from 1935. Chairman of CCP Central Committee from 1945; Chairman of the PRC, 1954–1959.

Mao Zetan (1905–1935). Mao Zedong's younger brother.

Nie Rongzhen (1899–1992). Deputy premier, 1954–1975. PLA marshal from 1955.

Peng Dehuai (1898–1974). Commander in chief of China's troops in Korea, 1950–1953. Minister of defense, 1954–1959. PLA marshal from 1955. Criticized Great Leap Forward, 1959.

Peng Zhen (1902–1997). First secretary of Beijing Municipal Committee, 1949–1966. Mayor of Beijing, 1951–1966. Deng's deputy in the CCP Central Committee secretariat, 1956–1966. Member of Deng's powerful veteran circle.

Qu Qiubai (1899–1935). De facto head of CCP, 1927–28. Head of CCP delegation to the Comintern Executive, 1928–1930.

Rao Shushi (1903–1975). Head of CCP Central Committee Organization Department, 1953–54. Purged with Gao Gang, 1955.

Ren Zhuoxuan (1896–1990). Leader of the Chinese Communists in France, 1923–1925. Secretary of the CCP Moscow branch, 1925–26.

Stalin, Joseph Vissarionovich (1879–1953). General secretary of Bolshevik party, 1922–1934. Secretary of Bolshevik party from 1934. Chairman of USSR Council of People's Commissars from 1941.

Sun Yat-sen (1866–1925). Father of the Chinese republic. Founder of Guomindang, 1912. Formed a united front with the communists.

Suslov, Mikhail Andreevich (1902–1982). Secretary of Soviet Communist Party Central Committee, 1947–1982. Member of Politburo, 1952–53 and 1955–1982. Soviet ideologue.

Tan Zhenlin (1902–1983). Deputy premier, 1959–1975. Deputy chairman of the Standing Committee of the National People's Congress from 1975.

Thatcher, Margaret (1925–2013). Prime minister of Great Britain, 1979–1990.

Wan Li (b. 1916). First secretary of Anhui Party Committee, 1977–1980. Deputy premier, 1980–1988. Chairman of the Standing Committee of the National People's Council, 1988–1993. Economic reformer.

Wang Dongxing (b. 1916). Mao's bodyguard, 1968–1976. Director of the Central Committee General Office, 1966–1977. Deputy chairman of the CCP Central Committee, 1977–1980. Deng's opponent.

Wang Hairong (b. 1938). Mao's grandniece. Deputy chief of Protocol Department, Ministry of Foreign Affairs, 1971–72. Deputy foreign minister, 1974–1976.

Wang Hongwen (1935–1992). Shanghai rebel chief and member of the extreme leftist Gang of Four during Cultural Revolution. Deputy chairman of CCP Central Committee, 1973–1976. Mao's designated successor, 1972–1976. Deng's antagonist. Arrested, 1976, and imprisoned.

Wang Jiaxiang (alias Communard, Zhang Li) (1906–1974). Opponent of Mao in Central Soviet Area, 1931–1934. Supported Mao during Long March and Zunyi Conference, 1934–35. Director of CCP Central Committee International Liaison Department, 1951–1962.

Wang Jingwei (1883–1944). Leader of "Left" Guomindang. Head of Wuhan government, 1927.

Wang Ruilin (b. 1930). Deng Xiaoping's secretary, 1952–1967 and 1973–1992. Deputy head of the General Political Administration of the People's Liberation Army from 1992.

Wang Zhen (1908–1993). Deputy premier, 1975–1983. Deputy chairman of the Central Advisory Commission, 1985–1987. Deputy chairman of the PRC, 1988–1993. Member of Deng's powerful veteran circle.

Wei Baqun (1894–1932). Communist guerrilla leader in Guangxi, 1925–1932.

Wei Jingsheng (b. 1950). Leader of the Chinese dissident movement from 1978.

Wu Han (1909–1969). Playwright and deputy mayor of Beijing. Criticism of his play *The Dismissal of Hai Rui from Office,* 1965, ignited the Cultural Revolution.

Xia Bogen (1899–2000). Deng's stepmother.

Xiang Zhongfa (1879–1931). General secretary of the CCP Central Committee from 1928. Executed by Guomindang police.

Yang Shangkun (1907–1998). Director of the Central Committee General Office, 1949–1966. An early victim of the Cultural Revolution, 1966. Deputy chairman of the Central Military Commission, 1982–1992. Chairman of the PRC, 1988–1993. Member of Deng's powerful veteran circle.

Yao Wenyuan (1931–2005). Shanghai party journalist and member of the extreme leftist Gang of Four during the Cultural Revolution. Deng's antagonist. Arrested, 1976, and imprisoned.

Yao Yilin (1917–1994). Deputy premier, 1979–1993. Economic reformer.

Ye Jianying (1897–1986). PLA marshal from 1955. Deputy chairman of Central Military Commission, 1966–1985. Deputy chairman of CCP Central Committee, 1973–1985. Minister of defense, 1975–1978. Deng's mentor, 1977–78. Chairman of the Standing Committee of the National People's Congress, 1978–1983.

Yu Guangyuan (1915–2013). Deng's close assistant since 1975. Vice president of the Chinese Academy of Social Sciences and director of the Institute of Marxism-Leninism, Mao Zedong Thought, 1979–1982. Economic reformer.

Yu Zuobai (1889–1959). Chairman of the Guangxi Provincial government, 1929–30. Warlord.

Yu Zuoyu (1901–1930). Yu Zuobai's younger brother, communist from October 1927. Commander of the 8th Corps of the Chinese Red Army, 1930.

Yudin, Pavel Fedorovich (1899–1968). Stalin's envoy in China, who reviewed Mao's Marxist credentials, 1950–1952. Soviet ambassador in China, 1953–1959.

Zhang Chunqiao (1917–2005). Member of the extreme leftist Gang of Four during Cultural Revolution. Deng's antagonist. Arrested, 1976, and imprisoned.

Zhang Xiyuan (1907–1930). Deng's first wife.

Zhang Yunyi (1892–1974). Commander of the 7th Corps of the Chinese Red Army, 1929–1931.

Zhao Ziyang (1919–2005). First secretary of Sichuan Party Committee, 1975–1980. Deng's close assistant. Premier, 1980–1987. General secretary of the CCP Central Committee, 1987–1989. Economic reformer. Backed protesters at Tiananmen Square, 1989. Sacked by Deng. Stayed under house arrest from 1989.

Zhou Enlai (1898–1976). Leading Chinese communist who often opposed Mao, 1927–1934, and then became Mao's right-hand man and staunch supporter. Premier from 1949. Mao's designated successor, 1972. Deputy chairman of the CCP Central Committee from 1956. Deng's mentor from 1923.

Zhu De (alias Danilov) (1886–1976). Mao's closest associate during the civil and anti-Japanese wars, 1928–1945. Commander in chief of the Red Army, 18th Army Group, and People's Liberation Army. Deputy chairman of the CCP Central Committee from 1956.

Zhuo Lin (1916–2009). Deng's third wife.

Note on the Spelling of Chinese Words

THE ENGLISH SPELLING of Chinese words and names used in this book is based on the pinyin system of romanization (use of the Latin alphabet) to represent the pronunciation of Chinese characters. We follow the modified pinyin system used by the Library of Congress, which replaces an older system with which readers may be familiar. Thus, for example, we spell the name of the subject of this biography as Deng Xiaoping, not Teng Hsiao-p'ing. (Both romanizations yield the same pronunciation: *Deng Siao-ping.*) For the same reason we spell the name of China's capital as Beijing, not Peking. Following accepted practice, however, we use the traditional English spelling of the names Sun Yat-sen and Chiang Kai-shek and the city Canton, as well as the names of famous institutions such as Peking University and Tsinghua University.

The pronunciation of many pinyin letters is roughly similar to English pronunciation. However, some letters and combinations of letters need explanation. These are listed in the chart below.

Vowels:

A   like *a* in *father*

AI   like the word *eye*

AO   like *ow* in *cow*

E   like *e* in *end*

I   like *i* in *it*

IA   like *ye* in *yes*

O   like *o* in *order*, except before the letters *ng*, when it is pronounced like the two o's in *moon*

U   like the second *u* in *pursue* when it follows the letters *j, q, x,* and *y*; otherwise, like the double *o* in *moon*, except in the vowel combination UO the *u* is silent

Ü   like the second *u* in *pursue*
YA   like *ya* in *yacht*
YE   like *ye* in *yet*
YI   like *ee* in *feet*

When two separately pronounced vowels follow each other, an apostrophe is inserted to indicate the syllable break between them. Thus, *Xi'an*, for example, is two syllables while *xian* is just one.

Consonants:

C   like the letters *ts* in *tsar*
G   like the hard *g* in *get*
J   like *j* in *jig*
Q   like the letters *ch* in *cheese*
R   in initial position, like the *s* in *vision*; at the end of a word, like the double *r* in *warrior*
X   like the *s* in *soon*
XI   like the *shee* in *sheet*
Z   like the letters *dz* in *adze*
ZH   like the *j* in *jockey*

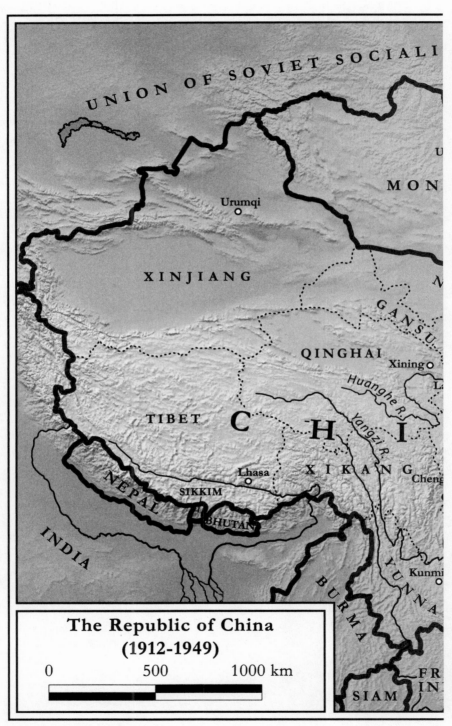

The Republic of China
(1912-1949)

0   500   1000 km

MAP I   Republic of China (1912–1949).

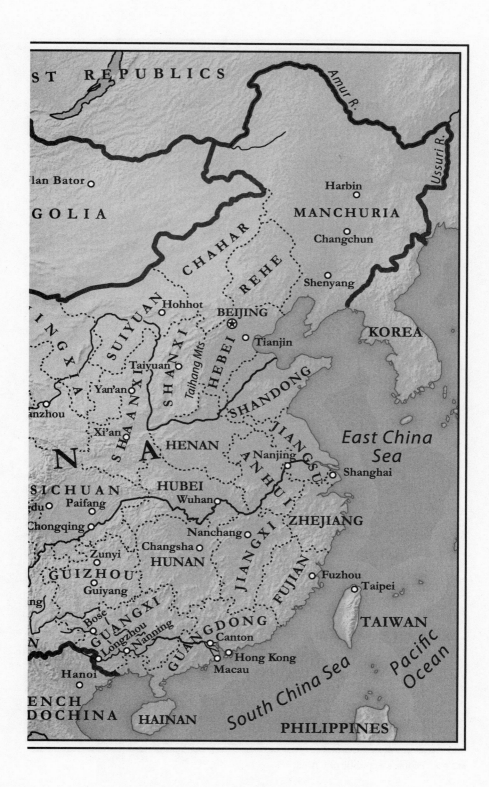

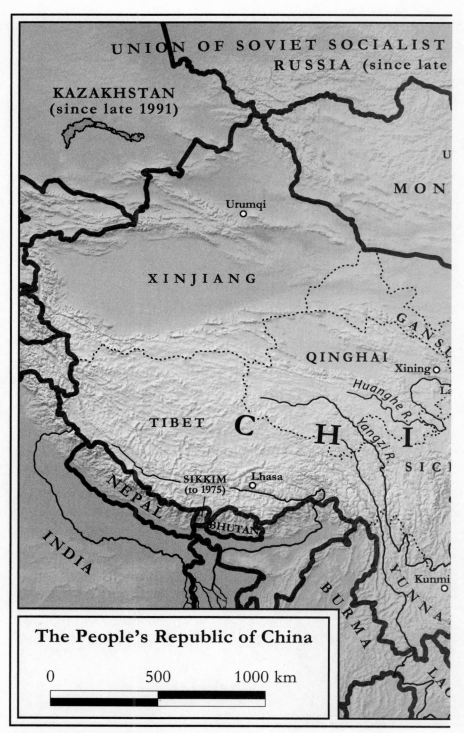

UNION OF SOVIET SOCIALIST

RUSSIA (since late

KAZAKHSTAN
(since late 1991)

MON

Urumqi

XINJIANG

GANS

QINGHAI

Xining

Huanghe R.

La

TIBET

C   H   I

Yangzi R.

SIC

SIKKIM
(to 1975)

Lhasa

NEPAL

BHUTAN

INDIA

Kunmi

BURMA

YUNNA

LAO

The People's Republic of China

0   500   1000 km

MAP 2 People's Republic of China.

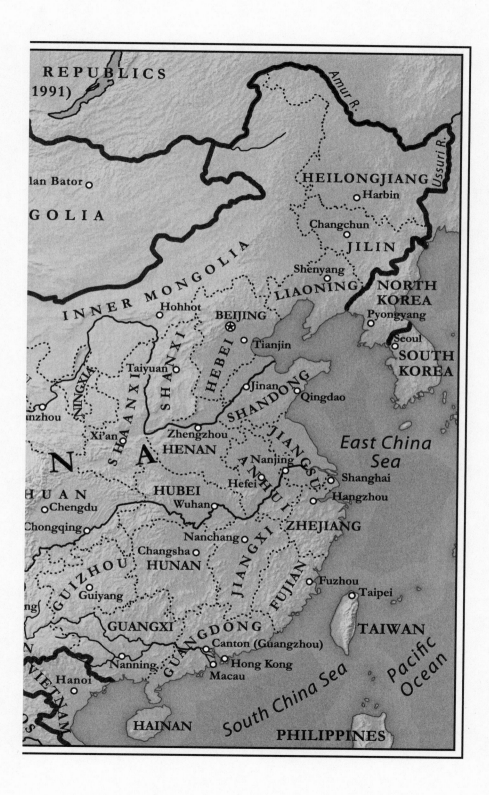

Introduction

IN THE SUMMER of 1989, TV channels around the world transmitted pictures of a lone young man, carrying grocery bags, standing his ground in front of a column of tanks heading along Chang'an Avenue near Tiananmen Square in the Chinese capital Beijing. He took several steps to the left, and then to the right, blocking the way of the powerful machines while his odd bags swung defenselessly in the air.

These close-ups were shot on June 5, after the Chinese leadership, headed by the paramount leader Deng Xiaoping, had begun to "restore order" in the capital with the help of the army. The ongoing demonstrations by students and other city dwellers that had begun in mid-April, demanding true democracy, civil liberties, and the stamping out of corruption, threatened the absolute power of the bureaucracy. The liberal movement gripped not only Beijing but many other large cities as well. Despite numerous pleas to return home, the rebellious youths did not want to abandon their protests, so the leaders of the nation had to choose between employing force and making concessions. And they made their choice, turning the streets leading to Tiananmen red with blood.

Most likely, the young rebels thought that "weak overcomes strong," but in June 1989 this ancient concept of Lao Zi[1] turned out to be unviable. China's totalitarian regime crushed the opposition, accusing it of attempting a counterrevolutionary revolt. Then, as a mark of symbolic and desperate protest, those who survived began to scatter fragments of glass bottles on the streets of Chinese cities. It so happens that when the "ping" in Deng's given name—Xiaoping ("Small and Plain") is written with a different character the meaning changes to a "small bottle."

This final spurt of protest, however, was short-lived. Life went on. Those who had been shot or crushed under tanks were buried; those who had served their terms were released. The rebels who remained at liberty returned to their schools, completed their higher education, and began to work. After the passage of twenty-six years, the young people of China know very little about what happened back then on the streets leading into Tiananmen Square and on the square itself. No one dares speak publicly about the carnage; it is dangerous to do so. The Tiananmen incident is one of the three taboo Ts in modern China, along with the Taiwan and Tibet issues.

Anyway, some say, why dredge up the past? After all, China is developing now by leaps and bounds, the consumer market is chock full of goods, and it seems that the modernization of the enormous country is close at hand. The majority of Chinese look to the future, not the past. Thirty-seven years of economic reforms—for which the very same Deng was the architect, initiator, and guide for market socialism—led to a situation in which the whole world began to speak of the "Chinese miracle."

So perhaps the Chinese leader was right to crush the liberals. After all, China is not the United States. Is it not so that during thousands of years of despotism, the population of All-under-Heaven—the ancient term for the country we know as China—apparently became accustomed to the absolute power of the leadership?

It is certainly true that witting or unwitting apologists for despotism invoke such arguments. However, for some reason the very same Lao Zi supposed that in China "when people no longer fear the power of governments, a far greater empowerment appears—the Great Integrity—which never needs to enforce itself."[2] Around the same time Confucius said, "A gentleman seeks harmony, but not conformity. A vulgar man seeks conformity, but not harmony." By the same token Confucius also believed that one of the four evils in the world is "terror, which rests on ignorance and murder."[3]

So was Deng mistaken? Could China have reached the economic heights without its leadership having desecrated the streets of the capital with the blood of its own youth?

Despite the ever-present temptation to make snap judgments, answering these questions is not easy. After all, the answers do not lie just in the recent history of China; they are linked with our understanding of the path that the Middle Kingdom has traversed throughout the twentieth century—a path that was difficult, tortuous, and dramatic, that took it from a semicolony of the West to a world power, from a backward, archaic monarchy to a socialist republic.

Naturally, they are linked as well with our assessment of the personality of the main Chinese reformer, Deng Xiaoping. What sort of person was he? How did he come to power? What role did he play in the revolution and in the building of socialism? What were the sources and essence of his unusual reforms, which transformed China into a symbiosis of socialism and capitalism? And why finally did he send the army to suppress the protesting youths?

People who knew him, including major world political figures, related to him in different ways, although they all acknowledged his unique abilities. Among them were Nikita S. Khrushchev, Mikhail S. Gorbachev, Gerald R. Ford, Jimmy Carter, Ronald Reagan, and George Bush. Even Mao Zedong, capricious and suspicious, who twice drove Deng from the Politburo, still valued him and therefore allowed no one to crush him, even during the terrible years of the Cultural Revolution (1966–1976).

How should we characterize Deng Xiaoping? He was a revolutionary who lived a very long life, from the beginning of the past century to its end; he became both a witness to and an active participant in myriad events in Chinese history and world history; and he rose to the front rank of leaders of the Chinese Communist Party under Chairman Mao and was then able to win out over all the heirs of the Great Helmsman. Perhaps most remarkable of all is that after following a long and winding path of reconsidering his basic beliefs, he not only broke free from the clutches of the Maoist socio-economic utopia himself but also helped his people see clearly. Yet he retained his firm conviction about the necessity for dictatorship in the form of the unchallengeable rule of the Chinese Communist Party. When confronted by a vision of democracy, he could only see the specter of chaos. He dug in his heels and would go no further. In the final analysis, he did not trust the Chinese people in whose name he and his comrades professed to rule. He refused to hand over the leadership of the state to society as a whole.

Ultimately, he was a man of his times who could only accomplish what he was capable of conceiving. Unlike Gorbachev in the Soviet Union, Deng was unable to overcome entirely his totalitarian worldview. He was called on to be the reformer of Chinese socialism, not its gravedigger.

The present book is dedicated to deciphering this intricate phenomenon that was Deng Xiaoping. It is based on formerly secret archives of the Chinese Communist Party, the Communist Party of the Soviet Union, and the international communist movement. The core of the archival sources consists of previously unexamined extensive personal dossiers of Deng Xiaoping—there are two such files—as well as of his family members, from the Russian State Archive of Social and Political History (the former Central Party Archive of the CPSU Central Committee Institute of Marxism-Leninism) in Moscow. Additional new documents from other Russian archival files that were also consulted include more than thirty-three hundred personal dossiers of leading Chinese Communists such as Mao Zedong, Zhou Enlai, Zhu De, Chen Yun, and others. *We are the first biographers of Deng to make use of all these materials.*

Documentary sources from other collections that became accessible thanks to the efforts, above all, of Chinese historians as well as their Russian, American, and West European colleagues are likewise important and were used. These include the texts of speeches, articles, letters, and telegrams of Deng Xiaoping and of other Chinese leaders; stenographic reports of sessions of the higher organs of the Chinese Communist Party, the People's Republic of China, and the Communist Party of the Soviet Union; documents of the American government and the governments of other countries; and protocols of conversations between Deng and world leaders at the highest level. No less important are the numerous reminiscences of persons who knew Deng both at home and at work: his wives, daughters, sons, brother and sisters, colleagues, secretary, bodyguard, and other members of his entourage. The primary author, Alexander V. Pantsov, has also interviewed many Chinese people with personal knowledge of Deng, people who worked with him or who were affected by Deng's policies and actions. Among the latter is the well-known Chinese dissident Wei Jingsheng, a leader in the Democracy Wall movement of 1978–79. Unique material was also gathered by Pantsov during his numerous trips to China to Deng's native place, the province of Sichuan, and to other places connected to his life in China and Europe. The book also makes use of practically all the extant secondary sources in Chinese, Russian, English, and French.

The biography is an objective study written in the same style as our widely acclaimed previous book *Mao: The Real Story* (Simon & Schuster, 2012). The same balanced approach to its subject is employed, one that neither exalts Deng as a paragon of reform nor dismisses him as merely one of the "butchers of Beijing."

Deng's importance in modern Chinese history merits such a detailed and objective assessment. Our book is not a political pamphlet but rather the result of many years of painstaking scholarly research presented in a narrative style that is meant to be accessible, interesting, and absorbing to a general reader. In attempting to recreate the concrete historical situation in which Deng, Mao, and all their friends and foes operated, we purposefully tried to avoid being biased by political prejudices of the right or the left. It is the only way to understand the people who have lived before us correctly, and it is the only way to respect history. If one starts writing history from one's political point of view, it will never be an objective historical record but rather a political accusation.

Are we lacking a "moral compass" if we write objectively? Not at all. History is full of blood. When we turn over its pages, we feel blood on our fingers. One cannot find an ideal historical figure. Consider Julius Caesar, Peter the Great, and Napoleon. Ponder the lives of Martin Luther, Jean Calvin, and Henry VIII. Think of Oliver Cromwell, Vladimir Lenin, and Chiang Kai-shek. In an American context, reflect on men like President Andrew Jackson, who deliberately persecuted millions of Native Americans, to say nothing of the numerous eminent figures who justified the enslavement of African Americans. Were all of them just one-dimensional fanatics or oppressors? Hardly. They were all controversial figures. Even the lives of Adolf Hitler and Josef Stalin, certainly extreme cases, should be researched objectively. Of course, their biographers must keep in mind that these two despots were both responsible for igniting the most devastating world war in history. Nor should Hitler's guilt for perpetrating the Holocaust ever be forgotten. Still it is obvious that only multifaceted pictures of all these people—even the most odious—can help us decipher the complex historical reality. It is we, not these long-dead leaders, who require the truth.

Our meticulous research helped us present Deng as a man of many contradictions. Like other people he had his positive and negative sides, strengths and weaknesses. Contrary to the conventional view that characterized Deng as a "moderate" who opposed Mao's leftist policies since the early 1950s, we show that until the early months of 1976 Deng was a true disciple of Mao Zedong, extremely loyal to the Great Helmsman notwithstanding the persecution he himself suffered during the Cultural Revolution at the hands of Mao. Deng had wholeheartedly supported Mao since the early 1930s, when they first began to collaborate. He enthusiastically backed Mao's 1950–53 land reform, Stalinization of the PRC, socialization of the economy, and the Great Leap Forward. Deng did begin to make some critical remarks regarding leftist policies starting in late May 1961, but only shortly before Mao's death in 1976 did he manifest disobedience.

Like Mao, Deng was a multifaceted individual whose portrait cannot be painted in just black and white. Among his positive achievements was reduction of poverty in China by 50 percent. He also set China on the path toward greater integration into the international system and was responsible for making China what it is now. But he was by no means a liberal, and by the end of his life he had even become as capricious and intolerant of different views as Mao. Although in the late 1970s he began to demolish the Maoist Utopia by raising the slogan of "seek truth from facts," by the late 1980s he had started considering himself the ultimate source of truth. It was this metamorphosis that caused his conflict not only with some of the closest members of his entourage but also with the significant part of Chinese society that believed in his early liberal programs.

We show Deng as someone who throughout his entire career was not only a devoted Communist party member but also a true party bureaucrat who always believed that the end justified the means—during the revolutionary years, the land reform period, the struggle for socialism, and the Cultural Revolution. People were important to him only as instruments for achieving his goals.

Until Mao became really decrepit, Deng served him slavishly. He abased himself before the Great Helmsman numerous times, especially during the Cultural Revolution, and he finally plumbed the depths of self-humiliation in expressing his loyalty to his own tormentor. His devotion to Mao did not waver despite the fact that his eldest son had become physically disabled as a result of the Cultural Revolution, his wife was suffering from high blood pressure, and his younger children were subjected to moral and physical hardships in remote rural areas. Such fundamental virtues as human dignity, pride, and principle meant nothing to him. They had ceased to exist for him from the time of his youth, when he cast his lot with the communist movement. From that time on, fidelity to the organization trumped all other feelings. To be sure, in this respect he was no different from others who rejected the traditional foundations of society. A hypocritical fickleness became a part of his character during the long years of his political life. It is not astonishing that Mao considered him a great talent and his best disciple even though Deng periodically offended and frustrated him. Deng did so inadvertently, since he was sometimes unable to fathom Mao's secret desires. Deng was in fact a better Marxist than Mao, who tried to build communism at a breakneck speed in defiance of economic laws. Yet Deng still believed that the Chinese Communist Party (CCP) had successfully constructed socialism in a backward China, a notion that Marx would have scorned. Like Mao, Deng acknowledged that he did not really understand economics; yet also like Mao, he still imposed his economic views on the party and society. The theory of reform and opening that Deng developed several years after Mao's death, in the late 1970s and early 1980s, did not originate with him. It was rooted in the Russian Bolshevik Nikolai I. Bukharin's interpretation of Lenin's New

Economic Policy aimed at developing a market economy under the control of the Communist Party. Deng studied this concept in the mid-1920s in Moscow during his sojourn as a student at a Comintern school and began implementing it as soon as he solidified power. At the same time, we show that Deng did not initiate division of communal land among the peasants. Credit for this radical break with the most onerous form of Maoist collectivism belongs to the peasants themselves, who began to divide the land. A cautious Deng swung around to support this development only a year and a half after the beginning of this reform.

Deng was tough, purposeful, ambitious, and cruel. But he was also cautious and patient. In this respect, Deng and Mao were two of the same breed. Deng could easily abandon friends and colleagues as soon as they ceased to satisfy him politically, and never bring them to mind thereafter. He had the same strong will as did Mao, and of course charisma as well. He was a master at manipulating people, engaging in intrigues, and luring people with beautiful slogans. Without these skills he would have been unable to become the leader; he would have been unable to triumph over the other pretenders to succeed Mao and to establish his own dictatorship in the party and the country.

All of the aforementioned features make this biography significantly different from the previous biographies and studies of Deng Xiaoping. With two exceptions, all of these works are out of date, and therefore not always reliable; several are little more than biographical sketches. Even the best-known study of Deng, by Ezra F. Vogel, *Deng Xiaoping and the Transformation of China*, despite its heft and detail, diverges from our book in several vital respects. First, it is not a complete biography of Deng Xiaoping. In fact, it is really not a biography at all. Vogel focuses on only the last twenty-seven years of a life that spanned ninety-two years. He has little interest in the first six and a half decades of Deng's life and provides just a sketchy account of Deng's formative years, his development as a revolutionary, and his rise to power and activities as a core member of Mao Zedong's inner circle (just 32 pages out of 835). Vogel writes as a policy analyst, not as a biographer or historian; he is interested only in Deng's post-Mao reforms. Second, Vogel lacked access to the unique Russian archival sources on which our study is based, sources that are extremely important for understanding Deng's political career and private life. Third, and perhaps most important, Vogel's book is quite uncritical and lacking in objectivity. Deng himself said that his life should be assessed as a fifty-fifty balance of good and bad. That is much closer to the mark than Vogel's sunny perspective. Like Mao, Deng committed many serious crimes and bears responsibility for the death of millions. In the early 1950s, even Mao tried to stop Deng from massacring so many counterrevolutionaries. In the late 1950s Deng persecuted intellectuals, and in the 1970s and 1980s he arrested and even killed dissidents, to say nothing of his responsibility for the June 4, 1989, Tiananmen massacre. It is revealing that in the China studies community, the response to Vogel's book was lukewarm. It was justly criticized on the grounds that Vogel took an uncritical and unrealistically positive approach to Deng Xiaoping.[4] The former editor of *China Economic Review*, Pete Sweeney, expressed a common view in saying: "We look forward to a more critical work on his [Deng's] political ideas."[5]

Ours is that work. *Our book is the only complete and objective biography of the most important political leader in the late twentieth-century history of China.*

In sum, our task as historians was to create a vivid and lively picture of Deng Xiaoping and the country he radically changed. We do not explicitly praise or blame Deng, just as we did not explicitly praise or blame Mao. Thoughtful readers without a political axe to grind can be trusted to reach their own conclusions on the basis of the voluminous evidence we present. We have tried to understand Deng, as we tried to understand Mao, in all his complexity. We hope our book will also help readers comprehend more clearly the past, the present, and the future of China, a country whose mysteries can be deciphered if we take the trouble to do so. In this book, our approach has been through close examination of Deng Xiaoping, the distinctive revolutionary and reformer whom China gave birth to, and who in turn reshaped China during the long years of his political career.

PART ONE

The Bolshevik

I

Born in the Year of the Dragon

A GRAY TOURIST bus comes to a stop in a small square and an energetic female guide announces, *"Deng Xiaoping tongzhi guli! Daole!"* (Comrade Deng Xiaoping's birthplace! We've arrived!) Outside the window graceful green bamboos sway, wide-spreading banana palms bristle, and mighty rows of evergreen oaks, magnolias, and maples tower along the narrow road leading to a nearby complex that was constructed on the site of the hamlet of Paifang in Sichuan province, leaving only the house of the deceased leader in the newly designed park.

The air-conditioned coolness of the motor coach yields to the enveloping heat of the street. Midsummer is not the best time to travel in China's southwest. The thermometer tops 86 degrees, and the humidity is almost 100 percent. One yearns for a refreshing breeze. We walk quickly through the red and white gates into the park; climb aboard a long string of small, open cars hitched to an electric tractor; and soon arrive at an immense one-story farmhouse under a curved brick roof. It is built on a low hill in the traditional Chinese style, a rectangular inner courtyard and buildings along three sides. This is the home of the Deng family. It is enormous, more than 8,600 square feet. In front lilies and lotuses float in a beautiful pond, and behind the main building is a bamboo grove in whose shade sits a low, round well with the purest water. The neighboring people call this estate the "Old Household of the Deng Family."

Stepping into the seventeen-room brick farmhouse, we finally encounter some long-awaited coolness. The energetic female guide quickly leads us to the fourth room, where a massive lacquer-wood bed on four stout legs, its tall canopy incised with the finest carving, hulks in the corner. The bed is covered with a simple mat woven of bamboo splints. "Ladies and gentlemen," the guide announces solemnly, "Here on this bed Comrade Deng Xiaoping was born!"

A chill runs down your spine even though you know very well that the guide is twisting the truth. The actual bed that belonged to Deng's wealthy parents, along with all their other possessions, was distributed to the peasants after the Communist party took power in 1949.[1]

The "white lie" about the bed does not diminish the overall impression. The estate itself has been well preserved. Everything looks as it did on the twelfth day of the seventh month of the Year of the Dragon according to the lunar calendar (August 22, 1904), when the house rang with the piercing cry of the newborn. Father and mother were unable to conceal their joy. They already had a daughter, but like all Chinese they desperately wanted a son as the heir and successor of the family. Among a son's responsibilities was caring for his parents in their old age and, after their deaths, regularly performing the graveside ceremonies prescribed by tradition.

The ecstatic father gave his son an auspicious name: Xiansheng ("Surpassing the Sage"), a reference to Confucius (551–479 BCE). To declare to the world that the infant Deng was wiser than Confucius was the highest degree of imprudence. Deng's father, however, must have consulted with the local Daoist fortuneteller, who thus shares a responsibility for the choice of an "immodest" name.

Up to a point, Deng's father could claim that his son's name had to correspond to his clan's genealogical tradition, that is, of all the Dengs living in the district now called Xiexing, but was then Wangxi. In old China, no one was an individual; every person was merely a part of a whole—the large group of close and distant relatives who traced their descent from a single shared ancestor. In every clan, scribes annually noted the births and deaths of relatives and also recorded other activities of their fellow clan members. In every chronicle, a specific Chinese character was assigned to every new generation of males, a character that had to be used in personal names. The personal names usually consisted of two characters, one of which signifying that of the generation. In Deng's generation—the nineteenth of his clan—the character was *xian* ("surpass" or "be first"), thus his father's choice was restricted. Of course, it did not follow that the character *sheng* ("sage", "holy person") should come after the character *xian*, but Deng's father, born in 1886 and called Deng Wenming (Deng "The Civilized One") by everyone in the village, was an unusual man. As the Chinese saying goes, he "was not afraid to stroke the tiger."

Many years later, Deng Xiaoping referred to his father as a "small land-owner" (*xiao dizhu*),[2] and sometimes even a "middle peasant" (*zhongnong*).[3]

Deng Xiaoping's daughter Deng Maomao notes that her grandfather engaged "some farmhands" to work for him.[4] Deng Xiaoping's younger brother Deng Ken recalls that his father had "40 *mu* of land," or just under seven acres.[5] In 1967, however, Chinese Red Guards, implacably hostile to Deng Xiaoping, claimed that Deng Wenming owned about 20 acres of land and hired many laborers, making him a large landowner, what poor peasants and paupers called *tuhao* or bloodsuckers.[6] Most likely, as one of Deng's biographers has written, "the truth . . . lies somewhere between these two extremes."[7]

For his time, Deng's father was very progressive and fairly well educated. He studied not only in a local old-style primary school but also in a modern College of Juridical and Political Sciences in Chengdu, the capital of Sichuan province, where he encountered nationalist ideas and wholeheartedly sympathized with the late-nineteenth-century reformers.[8] Returning home after graduation, Deng Wenming taught in his township school, which he himself had founded along with his well-to-do neighbors. He joined a secret society, Paoge (Robed Elder Brothers), whose goal was to overthrow the alien Manchu (Qing) Dynasty and restore the Chinese Ming Dynasty that had been toppled in the seventeenth century. After several years he became "Elder Father, Custodian of the Banner," the de facto leader of the organization.[9]

Many members of the Deng clan, several of whom had held positions in the county, district, and even provincial administrations, shared a passionate preoccupation with politics. The founder of the clan, the revered Deng Haoxuan, a native of western Jiangxi province, had moved to Sichuan in 1380 while serving in the War Department. He came there with the imperial troops of Zhu Yuanzhang, the founder of the Ming Dynasty.[10] Among Deng Haoxuan's descendants were many degree holders, including a certain Deng Shimin. He became a member of the famous Hanlin Academy, the cultural center of the country, served as chief official of the Marble Palace (the Supreme Court), and mentored an imperial prince.[11] Perhaps, then, Deng Wenming inherited his thirst for knowledge and political activity.

He was married at thirteen to a young girl who turned out to be barren. Therefore, two years later Deng Wenming had to bring another girl into the house in the hope of obtaining a son. According to law, she was considered a concubine until the death of his official wife. Deng Wenming wanted just one thing from her, namely, to help him continue the lineage. Therefore, the massive lacquer-wood bed brought to the house as the new spouse's dowry was quickly put to the test. Nine months later, in 1902, their first child, a daughter, was born. Still he needed a son. And now he had appeared! "A round face, wide forehead, light eyebrows, white skin, small eyes, plus a rounded nose

tip that is typical of our family and has been handed down from our ancestors," wrote Deng Xiaoping's daughter.[12] To his father and mother, he was the
most beautiful baby in the world. *"Xianwa!"* ("Wonderful boy!"), his mother
exclaimed, pressing him to her.

The father and other members of the household beat gongs furiously and
smashed crockery to drive off evil spirits. For the same purpose, the attending midwife placed Buddhist sutras and Confucian texts at the newborn's
sides. Then the father lighted a torch, and two of the farm laborers grabbed
the young mother, who had not managed to cover herself, and carried her
through the flame in order to purify her. Ceremonial candles, placed on sau-
cers heaped with rice, were lighted before the ancestral altar, and a messenger
was sent to the new mother's family. He presented a rooster to the mother's
parents to announce the birth of a boy.

On the third day, the relatives were invited, and only then was the baby
bathed. Each of the guests placed a single white or red hard-boiled egg into
boiled water that had been poured into a copper basin that served as a font.
The red egg signified the guest wished boundless happiness for the newborn,
and white signified longevity. In addition, unwashed onions and ginger were
put into the basin, symbolizing intelligence and health, along with coins and
ornaments that, with the eggs and the rice, after the infant's bath were presented to the midwife for her efforts.

That same day, efforts began to arrange a match for the infant. "The birth
of a son occasions the wish that he should have a wife; the birth of a daughter
occasions the wish that she should have a marital home. As parents, all human
beings have this mind," said the great Confucian thinker Mencius (391–308
BCE) who is revered in China almost on a par with Confucius.[13] Relatives
and acquaintances vied with each other in proposing brides, either the same
age as Wenming's newborn or somewhat older. A list was compiled, and with
the help of a local geomancer they began to compare the horoscopes of the
groom and bride. After prolonged arguments, they finally chose a girl from
the wealthy Tang clan.[14] Her horoscope was the most appropriate. A match-
maker was sent to the girl's home, and soon everything was arranged. After
exchanging gifts and engagement certificates written on red sheets of paper
decorated with images of dragons and phoenixes, the Deng and Tang families became related. As an infant, however, the girl continued to live in her
parents' home until the couple reached marriageable age.

Tradition and the social status of the Deng clan dictated all these prac-
tices. Even an enlightened man like Deng Wenming could not always evade
the strict bounds of traditional morality. The mother of the family, neé Dan,

was likewise quite traditional. By the time her first son was born, she had already become the official wife of Deng Wenming. Mama Deng was known for her good sense, thriftiness, and ability to prepare delicious Sichuan dishes. She had a special knack for making pickled cabbage that, like all Sichuan cuisine, was spiced with a large amount of hot red pepper. This dish remained the favorite food of her adored son, who, like all Sichuanese, disliked bland food. Mama Deng also raised silkworms and sold silk thread at the market. Deng Xiaoping recalled that his family had a large number of mulberry trees[15].

Little Deng grew up in a loving and caring environment.[16] His parent's home lacked for nothing; the surrounding fields and mulberry trees generated a stable income, the table was always loaded with rice, meat, and vegetables, and the chests filled with beautiful clothing.[17] The Dengs bred hogs, cattle, and buffalo; ducks swam in the pond in front of the house, and poultry and geese strutted about in the courtyard.[18] From the bamboo that grew everywhere, household members and hired hands crafted everything needed in the home, including furniture, mattresses, pillows, and rope. Fresh bamboo shoots, peppered and pickled, were used as food, and tea was decocted from bamboo leaves. The Deng family's income from their bamboo groves was no less than that from rice or silkworms.

Deng Wenming was strict, but he did not beat his son. As a religious man, Deng Xiaoping's father regarded the welfare of his family as of paramount importance. When his little boy was barely five years old, his father sent him to a private old-style primary school in his native village. During the imperial reform of education between 1901 and 1909, such schools were shut down everywhere, but this one survived in Paifang. There Deng Junde, a relative of Deng Wenming, taught children the rudiments of Confucianism and literacy. He was strict and demanding, often caned his pupils, and forced the most obstreperous among them to kneel for hours before a portrait of Confucius. He also prevailed on Wenming to change his son's name from the ambitious Xiansheng to the modest Xixian ("Aspiring to Virtue").[19] This was the name the younger Deng would use until the summer of 1927, when, by then a communist, he would change it to the more prosaic Xiaoping ("Small and Plain"), following the rules of revolutionary conspiracy.[20]

Meanwhile, the boy continued to study and a year later entered Beishan Primary School, the township school his father had just founded in 1910.[21] There, in addition to the classics, the school also imparted the fundamentals of mathematics and literary Chinese. The classics remained the primary subject; therefore, every day along with his schoolfellows, little Deng repeated after his teacher excerpts from the Analects, Mencius, The Great Learning,

and the Doctrine of the Mean as well as from an anthology of Chinese literature. He tried to memorize them but found them mostly incomprehensible.
The moral-ethical precepts of ancient Chinese philosophy did not resonate in
his soul, just as they failed to with many other future Chinese revolutionaries, including the young Mao Zedong.[22]

Deng's school years (1910–1915) coincided with tumultuous events in
China. An antimonarchical revolution had long been brewing, and repeated
attempts by the Manchus to shore up the outmoded system of absolutism
failed. The Manchus even promised to introduce a constitution, but events
overtook them. Anti-Manchu organizations, including the Revolutionary
Alliance led by the well-known democrat Sun Yat-sen, mounted rebellions in
one city after another. The Manchus were condemned by increasing numbers
of their subjects for conniving with foreigners who had forcefully imposed
unequal treaties on the decrepit regime, yielding control over China's tariffs,
granting leaseholds on parts of China's territory as well as exemptions from
Chinese laws and from taxes on internal trade.

In May 1911, the Manchu court's decision to finance railroad construction with foreign loans ignited a firestorm of opposition on the part of many
small Chinese investors, who went bust. A broad patriotic movement arose in
Sichuan and other southern provinces. Everywhere protesters wrote petitions
to the government, boycotted foreign goods, and held meetings and strikes.
Provincial governor Zhao Erfeng dispatched troops against protesters, which
led to bloodletting in early September 1911. Deng Wenming set off for the
county seat, where he took part in the protest movement. Like many educated contemporaries, he concluded, "This society is really choking. It needs
a revolution."[23]

Soon Sichuan, like the country as a whole, was shaken by momentous
news of an uprising of troops on October 10, 1911, in Wuchang in central
China. Thereafter uprisings rolled across the country. A real revolution had
begun in China, and in a month Manchu power was overthrown in most of
the empire's eighteen provinces. As usually happened during revolutions, pillaging occurred everywhere. In Sichuan power soon passed into the hands of
the military, and political life in Sichuan became sharply militarized.[24]

Meanwhile, in Nanjing, delegates from the rebellious provinces convened a meeting of the National Assembly on December 29, at which Sun
Yat-sen, the head of the Revolutionary Alliance, was chosen provisional president. On January 1, 1912, he took office and proclaimed the establishment
of the Republic of China. The Manchus refused to surrender, however, and
entrusted General Yuan Shikai, prime minister of the imperial government

and army commander in North China, with suppressing the rebellion. Yuan, a consummate politician, soon took advantage of the confused situation to put himself forward as the man who could bridge the divide between monarchists and revolutionaries. In mid-January 1912, he delivered "favorable conditions" for the abdication of the six-year-old emperor to the regent, and one month later, on February 12, the monarchy fell. Three days later, Yuan Shikai, supported by the great powers, replaced Sun Yat-sen as president. Lacking his own armed forces, Sun was unable to oppose the ambitious general. Abandoned by the National Assembly, he stepped down.

Meanwhile, Deng's father, who had become involved in revolutionary activities, was appointed commander of the county defense force, joined the party in power, the so-called Progressives, and soon became head of the township administration. By then three more children had been added to his family. Five children required a lot of attention and effort, but their father's only interest was politics, which brought him nothing but trouble. In 1915 or 1916, his failed attempt to capture a local bandit surnamed Zhang garnered him a mortal enemy. When Zhang made peace with the authorities and was appointed commander of a division, Deng Wenming fled for his life. He abandoned his wife and children and took refuge in the city of Chongqing, where he remained for four or five years.

Naturally, during his absence the family's financial situation worsened. According to Deng Xiaoping's reminiscences, mother and children were on the verge of bankruptcy. Deng's younger brother confirmed this. According to him, they had to borrow money all the time just to make ends meet.[25] Before taking flight, however, Papa Deng was able to marry off his eldest daughter and place his eldest son in higher primary school in the county seat, Guang'an. (There were three levels in Chinese primary school: lower, middle, and higher. Having studied in the township school for five years, Deng completed the first two of these.)

By this time (1915), the youthful Deng, like many educated Chinese youths, had already begun to entertain heroic ideas of struggling for the freedom of the Chinese nation, whose degradation they keenly felt. Undoubtedly, news and rumors of revolutionary events in the wider world and the examples of his father and revolutionary teachers at the Beishan school impressed the juvenile Deng. The lectures of Deng Junde, who shared with his pupils the history of the Chinese people's struggle against numerous aggressors, lodged in his mind, and he also began to grasp the basics of contemporary politics. Deng was moved by his teacher's patriotic tales, and he even memorized a heroic poem by the patriotic general Yue Fei (1103–1142), "The River Is Dyed

Red." In his poem, the famous general of the Southern Song called on his countrymen to eradicate all foreign enemies of the Chinese people.[26] Like his fellow pupils, Deng was indignant at President Yuan Shikai's acceptance, on May 7, 1915, of Japan's Twenty-one Demands, which presaged the transformation of the Middle Kingdom into a Japanese colony. Concern for the fate of the country flooded the hearts of all patriotic citizens.

Deng's character gradually took shape. From his mother he inherited firmness and will, from his father a hot temper. (That was why in the Communist party he was called "Peppery Napoleon" and "The Little Cannon.") Yet he did not hold grudges. It was said that in his early childhood he already possessed a keen sense of justice. Thus, on one occasion, wishing to help a poor fellow classmate, he stole five yuan (equal to five silver dollars), at the time a very substantial sum, from his father. When his father began to look for the guilty party, Deng tearfully but silently handed his father a switch. On questioning his son, Deng Wenming concluded that by helping his friend, he had acted properly. He did not beat him but merely wondered why his son was ready to submit to punishment without complaining. To this the little "criminal" replied, "A thief must always receive what he deserves. This is the law."[27]

Deng never sought to be the leader among his classmates, but he would not tolerate insults although he was always very small compared to others his age. In his adolescence, when he stopped growing, he was just under five feet tall.

In his new school in Guang'an, he remained even-tempered and independent. Because of the distance from home, he was able to see his relatives only once a week. The rest of the time he lived in a dormitory in town. At the time, the city of Guang'an still had a medieval appearance, with narrow alleys and cobblestone roadways. The only sign of modernity was the two-story, European-style, gray brick building where Deng was taught arithmetic, geography, history, natural sciences, literary Chinese, music, art, and physical culture. A Catholic church was located nearby. French priests, the first foreigners Deng saw, officiated there.

Deng studied there until his graduation in the summer of 1918. In accordance with the instructions of his father, who was still living in Chongqing, Deng continued his education in a Guang'an middle school. Deng Wenming apparently wanted his son to become an important official. Yet Deng remained at the Guang'an middle school for just one year. In the summer of 1919, his father informed him that a preparatory school for students wishing to study and work in France had opened in Chongqing. Papa Deng believed that his son should not pass up such an opportunity, and therefore the younger Deng left Guang'an for Chongqing. Deng Shaosheng, his uncle, just three and a half years older than Deng, set off with him and a fellow countryman and distant relative who also aspired to travel to Europe.

The work-study program for Chinese youth in France was the brainchild of two French-educated anarchists, Li Shizeng and Wu Zhihui, who viewed France as a democratic and industrially advanced nation. Believing that education and revolution were connected, in 1912 they organized the Chinese Society for Frugal Study in France on the premise that Chinese students would be self-supporting, working in French enterprises according to the principle of "one year of diligent work, two years of frugal study." The result of the superior Western system of education would be a "new" person—a worker-intellectual—who could revive China.

After China's entry into the First World War in August 1917, the Chinese government sent 140,000 laborers to France, mainly to dig trenches.[28] This inspired Li Shizeng and Cai Yuanpei, the rector of Peking University, to organize a massive movement of Chinese youth to study and work in France. Soon they established a joint Sino-French study society. Preparatory schools for those wishing to travel to France were opened in several Chinese cities enrolling students from fourteen years old and up.[29]

In Sichuan the first such school was opened in March 1918 in the provincial capital Chengdu. By August, many patriotic citizens of Chongqing, similarly inspired, had collected more than 20,000 yuan to open a school like the one in Chengdu in January 1919. It was located downtown in the former municipal Confucius temple. It was there that Deng, his uncle, and his friend from back home enrolled in mid-September 1919.[30]

Deng was excited by the idea of seeing the world and receiving a European education. A school comrade, a year older than Deng, recalled, "Comrade Deng Xiaoping enrolled in the preparatory school just a bit later than me. He seemed very cheerful and energetic, was rather laconic, and always studied very diligently and seriously."[31] Deng enjoyed studying and viewed this unprepossessing school as the best in Chongqing.[32] The main subject was French language as well as Chinese literature, mathematics, and physics, along with a smattering of technical knowledge that might help the students find work in France.

Discipline in the school was lax. Students attended classes as they pleased. Deng, like the others, took advantage of this freedom, spending a lot of time wandering around Chongqing with his friends, eating in small restaurants, climbing the hills, and admiring the remarkable panorama of the great city located at the confluence of two mighty rivers, the Yangzi, which Chinese call the Changjiang (Long River), and her tributary the Jialing. Pressed on two sides by these streams, the city itself was squeezed along a narrow peninsula that resembled a parrot's beak. On and along the river there was constant activity all day. By then Chongqing was one of the largest river ports in the country.

This ancient city, founded in the eleventh century BCE, had long been an important trading center. In March 1890, according to an Anglo-Chinese treaty, Chongqing became an open international port, and foreigners, including missionaries and traders, streamed in. The city, with its population of almost half a million, boasted several new-style schools, banks, and numerous shops with every conceivable commodity, among them foreign goods, as well as an American hospital, but no modern industry.

The distinctive feature of the city was a huge number of coolies who supplied water to the inhabitants by carrying it up the steep hills from the river below. The coolies lived along the banks of the rivers, outside the city gates, in filthy hovels. But when the rivers flooded every summer, the water washed away their pitiful dwellings, and thousands of homeless people filled the city streets. The municipal authorities did nothing to improve their situation.

Walking about the city, Deng and his comrades could not help but notice social injustice. But the sufferings of ordinary people bothered them less than the problem of China's national revival. After the death in June 1916 of Yuan Shikai, the powerful politician and military commander who had kept the provincial and local warlords governing China on a tight leash, the country fragmented into numerous autonomous territories headed by military governors. A bloody civil war commenced. Deng's native province of Sichuan also splintered. The provincial government collapsed, and various parts of the province passed into the hands of military cliques that clashed incessantly with each other.[33]

After the First World War ended in November 1918, China's international situation became much more complicated. At the peace conference in Paris, the victorious Entente powers, bound by secret treaties with Japan, brushed aside Chinese objections and awarded the German colony in Qingdao and the area around Jiaozhou Bay in China's Shandong peninsula, seized by the Japanese at the start of the war, to Japan. This imperial high-handedness touched off a huge anti-Japanese movement in China. On May 4, 1919, students in Beijing organized massive demonstrations and were quickly supported by patriotic citizens throughout the country, including Chongqing, where most students took to the streets. They promoted boycotts of Japanese goods, ransacked shops, and confiscated and later publicly burned Japanese wares. Groups of students patrolled the Yangzi and Jialing rivers day and night, preventing ships carrying Japanese cargoes from docking. A large demonstration occurred on June 3, when students from twenty municipal schools protested simultaneously.[34]

Deng, too, participated in the May 4 Movement. For two days and nights, he and other students from the preparatory school held a mass meeting in front of the barracks of the Chongqing garrison, demanding that the officers and men support them. Returning triumphantly to school, they lighted a bonfire and threw into it everything Japanese they had: Japanese-made clothing, tins of tooth powder, and wooden wash basins. Their feelings of pride and consciousness of their own political significance persisted for a long time.[35] Disturbances throughout China continued until June 28, 1919, when news came that members of the Chinese delegation had refused to sign the unjust Versailles Treaty between the Entente and Germany.

Participation in the patriotic movement aroused Deng's interest in politics. Like other students, he began reading revolutionary democratic publications, among them the Beijing newspaper *Chenbao* (*Morning*) and *Xin qingnian* (*New Youth*), the journal that was then popular among young liberals, published by Professor Chen Duxiu, one of the leaders of the May 4 Movement.[36]

Meanwhile, he neared the end of his studies. In mid-July 1920, Deng passed his exams. He did not do brilliantly, however, since French, which was the main subject, did not come easily to him. Nevertheless, he was considered fit to study and work in France, but he had to pay two-thirds of the cost of the journey out of pocket, unlike his uncle, who, on the basis of his exams, was awarded the 300 yuan required for the trip.

Deng was not despondent. He returned home, knowing that his supportive father would give him money. By then Papa Deng was again living in Paifang. Power had changed hands in the county, and his enemy Zhang was no longer a threat. Needless to say, despite the family's financial difficulties he gave his son the required sum. He did so by selling part of his arable land and even borrowing money from his father-in-law and mother-in-law. Before Deng's grandfather and grandmother as well as his maternal uncle, Wenming painted an optimistic picture of the prospects that the trip abroad would open up for their grandson and nephew. He said that after Deng received a foreign education he would inevitably get rich and would then be able to care not only for his father and mother but also for his other close relatives.[37]

Deng's mother, however, initially refused to release her son to the "hairy foreign devils," as the Chinese called foreigners. With tears in her eyes she reproached her husband: "The child is so small, and you are sending him to the other end of the world to study and work! What heartlessness!" "Our mother loved Xiaoping passionately," Deng's younger brother recalled. "She hoped that when he grew up he would attend to the family farm." But father and son were implacable. Deng Xiaoping even went on a hunger strike. Ultimately, his mother grudgingly acquiesced.

At the end of August 1920, Deng said farewell to his family and returned to Chongqing. Before parting, his youngest sister, Xianzhen, who was not yet eight, cried bitterly, saying, "Don't go!"

"What's the matter with you?" Deng asked. "I'll be back soon!"

He squatted, took her hands in his, and added:

"Little sister! You must wait for your elder brother. Don't get married without me!"[38]

Then he arose and departed. It was a long journey to Chongqing, his departure point for France, and he did not want to waste a moment. Before him lay a long life, full of danger and great accomplishments, ascents, falls, and ultimate triumph.

2

From Paris to Moscow: The Lessons of Bolshevism

ON THE AFTERNOON of August 27, 1920, Deng, his uncle Shaosheng, and the other preparatory school graduates left Chongqing on the steamship *Jiqing* (Prosperity).[1] Heading downstream on the Yangzi, they sailed for Shanghai, the transfer point for a vessel bound for Marseilles. There was a festive send-off. The port workers killed a rooster, and stirring the blood of the unfortunate bird with its own feathers, they thickly daubed the prow of the boat. Then deafening explosions of fireworks were set off to appease the fearful God of the great river as well as the souls of river men who had drowned in its turbulent waters. Without such a ceremony, not a single schooner sailed out of Chongqing.[2]

The travelers, most of whom had never been outside of Sichuan, faced a long journey. They congregated on the deck, and their excitement peaked when the ship approached the famous Three Gorges that separated Sichuan from the rest of China. Squeezed on two sides by majestic mountain ridges, the Yangzi surges forward with irrepressible force, narrowing from a deep half-mile wide river to a boiling 175 foot torrent. But after about five miles it broadens out again, and then, sharply and quickly twisting between mountain cliffs and seething over rapids, it narrows once again. And not just once.

Beyond the gorges the current of the broad Yangzi now flowed smoothly again, all the way to the tri-cities of Hankou, Hanyang, and Wuchang, known collectively as Wuhan. Wuhan itself was of unusual interest. They had barely disembarked when Deng and his comrades hurried over to the Hankou railroad station. None of them had ever seen a steam engine, a marvel of Western technology. At the very moment they stepped onto the platform, a train, enveloped in puffs of smoke, pulled into the station. Bewitched, they gazed

at it for a long time with growing conviction they had made the right decision to set out for France. They had to go to Europe to acquire knowledge
so that they could devote themselves wholeheartedly to the industrialization
of China.

Past Wuhan, after another five hundred miles, the ship entered the
Huangpu River, a tributary of the Yangzi, and soon docked in the port of
Shanghai. There were still several days until the departure of the liner *André
Lebon* bound for Marseilles, so Deng and his friends decided to have a look
around the city.[3]

Shanghai, the largest industrial and commercial center in China, and in
all of East Asia, with a population of some million and a half at that time,
must have impressed them. The most striking phenomenon throughout the
city was the dominance of foreigners, who controlled more than twelve of
the territory's thirty-five square miles. The International Settlement and the
French Concession bisected the center of the city, squeezing the Chinese
districts between them. Foreign laws held sway in the foreign concessions.
Foreign troops and police were stationed there, and foreign enterprises,
banks, and a casino operated as well. There was much to delight European
travelers. But Deng and his comrades had a different reaction to Shanghai.
They were incensed that the Sikh policemen at the border of the International
Settlement subjected them to a humiliating search, and that on the gates of
the English parks a sign was posted saying "Chinese and dogs not allowed."
"This is Chinese territory!" they seethed with indignation.[4]

Still seething, early on the morning of Saturday, September 11, they took
their places on the *André Lebon,* the pride of the French passenger fleet. The
ship could carry almost 1,100 passengers, including 200 in first class and 184
in second.[5] But the Sichuan students had the cheapest tickets, in the dirty,
stuffy, and crowded hold. On the open ocean many of them became severely
seasick, but Deng and most of his comrades were not dispirited. They dreamed
of faraway France and how they would combine intensive study with noble
work. After traversing more than eight thousand nautical miles in thirty-nine
days, on the morning of Tuesday, October 19, 1920, the *André Lebon* docked
in Marseilles.[6]

The new arrivals were met on shore by representatives of the Sino-French
Study Society. From Marseilles the entire group was immediately bused to
Paris, or to be more precise, to the northwestern suburb of La Garenne-
Colombes. Here at No. 39 Rue de la Pointe were three organizations respon-
sible for greeting and assigning participants in the Diligent Work and Frugal
Study program: the Sino-French Study Society, the Sino-French Guardians

Council, and the Sino-French Association of Friends of the Guardians Council. All of them worked closely with, and regularly received small subsidies from the Chinese embassy in France.

By the time Deng and his comrades arrived, there were thirteen hundred Chinese students in France, including twenty-one women.[7] Some had completed the highest level of primary school, others (like Deng) preparatory school, and only about ninety had university diplomas. Almost all were under thirty, although several were older. Among them was forty-three-year-old Xu Teli, a former teacher at the Provincial First Normal School in Changsha, and fifty-five-year-old Ge Jianhao (Ge Lanying), the mother of Cai Hesen and Cai Chang, two activists in the Diligent Work and Frugal Study movement. Most of them attended colleges and lycées in France, where they studied French.[8]

Deng and his uncle were assigned to a private college in the small town of Bayeux, 170 miles from Paris, in northern France. Their first trip by train was so enjoyable it made them forget their fatigue. On the evening of October 21, they were given places in the college dormitory, and the following morning, even though it was the weekend, they were already at their desks.

Soon, however, Deng felt disappointed. As in Chongqing, the main required subject was French, for which he had no aptitude. Therefore, during the five months that he spent in Bayeux, in his own words, he "learned nothing." Naturally, he blamed not himself but the college authorities. He and the other Chinese were not only taught poorly, but "the diet was very poor" and they were treated like "children," forced "to go to bed very early every day."[9]

Moreover, by the spring of 1921, despite his extreme frugality, Deng had spent all the money brought from home. His tuition was substantial, more than two hundred francs per month,[10] and he also wanted to spend his time more pleasurably on what the ancient Normandy town had to offer. Bayeux was a well-known French tourist center with many museums, including one housing the famous Bayeux tapestry, and the Cathedral of Notre Dame de Bayeux, as well as a large botanical garden. Its quiet, narrow streets were paved with cobblestones and lined with two- and three-story medieval-style stone houses. There were also countless cafes. Tasting coffee for the first time, Deng acquired a lifelong love as well as a fondness for flaky croissants.

By late winter of 1921, however, the impoverished Deng could no longer visit cafes. On March 13, he, his uncle, and most of the Chinese students quit the college and returned to La Garenne-Colombes. There the staff of the Sino-French Study Society found them work and also staked the students to some spending money. On April 2, Deng and his comrades traveled to the city of Le Creusot in Burgundy, where they became unskilled laborers in the Schneider metallurgical works, one of the giants of French industry. Deng and his uncle began to work in the steel-rolling shop. (From the outset, for some reason the profession of steel worker was what Deng wanted to master in France. As early as August 1920, while filling out a questionnaire for the French embassy to receive a visa, he put "steel worker" in the column "Profession."[11])

Ten hours a day of grueling work, pitiful wages, poor food in the factory cafeteria, and abuse by masters all made a terrible impression on the sixteen-year-old Deng, who was unaccustomed to physical labor or moral humiliation.[12] Like many other young Chinese intellectuals, Deng, for the first time, experienced the burdens of industrialization. "Soon after entering the factory," wrote one of Deng Xiaoping's co-workers at Schneider, Chen Yi, who would eventually become the minister of foreign affairs of the PRC, "I quickly lost all my empty dreams about glory . . . I understood that . . . diligent work did not guarantee frugal study . . . Is it possible to transform society when a person is overwhelmed with work and lacks the strength to live and breathe?"[13] It was while working at Schneider that Chen Yi began to ponder the reason for his unhappy situation and soon concluded that it was due to "the imperfection of the social order."[14] But such ideas did not yet occur to Deng. Of course, he understood that French society was not ideal. Yet for now he still did not think that the "defects of the system" had grown to such "terrible dimensions" in the French Republic itself, the "Fatherland of Liberty."[15] He was still inexperienced and poorly educated. He was simply having a hard time getting by. Moreover, he always felt inferior: because of his youth he was considered a student and therefore was paid less than the other Chinese, while the French workers constantly insulted him for his inability to fulfill his work quota. Of course, it was not just Deng whom these hard workers despised, but all "yellow men."[16]

In the end, Deng could not stand it, and he quit after three weeks. He had neither money nor a place to live, so he returned to the Sino-French Study Society in La Garenne-Colombes. More than five hundred unemployed young Chinese who could also not bear the "horrors of capitalism" were already gathered there. The staff at the society began to disburse five francs a day to each of them, housing them in the basement, the attic, in one of the two stories of the building they owned, as well as in a tent city that they pitched outdoors. One can hardly imagine what No. 39 Rue de la Pointe turned into. The secretary of the Study Society tried to order the lives of his uninvited guests; he commanded them to clean the toilets, take out the garbage, and keep down the noise, but he didn't do very well. The students resented him and called him a "militarist."[17]

This, then, is where Deng took refuge. The spring of 1921 was the apogee of France's postwar economic crisis; the staff of the society was unable to find work for Deng or any other of the Chinese students. In 1921, 55 percent of the Chinese in France were unemployed.[18] Deng later said, "Upon arrival in France, I learned . . . it was hard to find jobs . . . [and] impossible to support study through work . . . all those dreams of 'saving the country by industrial development,' 'learning some skills,' etc. came to nothing."[19]

Naturally, such a life was depressing. Fights occurred more and more often in the house at No. 39; five persons died from knifings, beatings, and accidents.[20] Rumors circulated among the unemployed students that the five franc daily dole would end and that all the hangers-on would be ousted. No one wanted to return to China even though the embassy had offered to pay for tickets. An inglorious return would signify a "loss of face." The only alternative was to stay put and gripe.

Then at the beginning of September, the staff of the society finally declared that they would stop providing for the students. In mid-September the tenants of No. 39 were deprived of their last source of support. Although just then a new Sino-French Institute had opened at Lyons University, its newly appointed co-directors declared that the institute was intended only to train the elite of Chinese society; unemployed and homeless students would not be admitted.[21]

In response, Cai Hesen, along with other activist rebels, including Chen Yi, drafted an angry letter to the rector of Peking University, Cai Yuanpei. It was signed by 243 persons, including Deng, who for the first time took part in a political action.[22] Soon after, 125 of the activists arrived in Lyons and tried to break into the building of the institute but were arrested and soon deported by the French police.[23]

Deng did not participate in storming the institute, and therefore, despite his signature on the letter of the 243, he was not deported. Of course, he sympathized with his older comrades, but soon new events pushed this episode into the past.

At the end of October 1921, he and his uncle finally found work in the Chambrelent fan and paper flower factory. But after just two weeks they were fired, and they could only make ends meet with odd jobs. Not until the beginning of February 1922 did they both receive long-term work, this time in the Hutchinson rubber factory in the town of Châlette-sur-Loing on the outskirts of Montargis. This was a stroke of good luck. The pay wasn't bad, the dormitory was free, and the food, which the Chinese workers prepared for themselves, was cheap and tasty.[24]

Deng spent eight months there, from February 14 to October 17, 1922. He made galoshes in the rubber footwear shop. The work was not too onerous, although he worked a fifty-four-hour week. During his free time, he strolled around Châlette-sur-Loing, visited Montargis, a small, charming city known for its numerous canals as the "Venice of the Gâtinais region" (the medieval name for this part of France), or chatted with his dorm mates. Among his thirty-odd new acquaintances were some interesting personalities, including Yin Kuan, Li Weinong from Anhui province, and Wang Zekai from Hunan. All of them were distinguished from their co-workers by their unusual perspectives. The young Chinese traced their own problems to the "defects of the social order" and started to call themselves communists. Deng joined in. Zheng Chaolin, a new friend from Fujian, reminisced later about Deng: "There was an eighteen-year-old fellow from Sichuan, short and chubby. He cracked jokes here and then made fun there."[25] "Deng was the youngest," Zheng continued. "We all loved him, and treated him like a child. We liked to talk, joke, and play with him."[26]

In this way, Deng, with the help of his older friends, began to absorb novel communist ideas. Soon he began reading the formerly liberal but now Bolshevik journal *New Youth*, published by Professor Chen Duxiu, the founding leader of the Chinese Communist Party (CCP), and established in July 1921 in Shanghai as the organ of the newly born CCP.

Of course, news of communism, Bolshevism, and the October Revolution in Russia must have reached Deng earlier. When he lived in Chongqing the well-known Sichuan newspapers *Xingqiri* (*Sunday*) and *Guomin gongbao* (*The Nation*) published a number of articles about the Russian Bolsheviks and their ideology.[27] In France in the early 1920s, every newspaper wrote about Lenin and Trotsky; some were very sympathetic toward the Russian revolutionaries. Many Chinese students, including Zheng Chaolin, subscribed to these publications.[28] In December 1920, Chen Duxiu sent his liaison, Zhang Songnian, a member of the Beijing communist circle, to Paris where the next spring he organized the first Chinese communist group in Europe, initially consisting of just three members: Zhang himself; his wife, Liu Qingyang; and Zhou Enlai, a young native of Jiangsu province.[29] Subsequently, Zhang attracted two more students to the group.[30] In Paris in late 1921, Chen Duxiu's eldest son, Chen Yannian, who was then an anarchist, began publishing a mimeographed journal, *Gongyu* (*Free Time*), the first such publication among

Chinese students, which, among other things, devoted attention to Marxism and Bolshevism.[31]

Deng must have heard about the new radical leftist movement, but until he met up with the young communists he really knew nothing about it. Even after listening to the stories of Zheng Chaolin and other comrades and reading *New Youth*, he still lacked a clear picture of communism.[32] But one thing he would learn quickly: a strongly unified revolutionary organization could turn the world upside down.

Soon just such an organization was founded. In late June 1922, twenty-three Chinese supporters of communism, including almost all of Deng's acquaintances, gathered in the Bois de Boulogne in Paris. They announced the founding of the Communist Party of Chinese Youth Living in Europe and decided to publish a Bolshevik journal, *Shaonian* (*Youth*). A Sichuanese, Zhao Shiyan, was chosen as head (secretary) of the party.[33] At the end of 1922, the Central Executive Committee of the CCP decided to merge the French, German, and Belgian branches into a new communist organization of Chinese in Europe, namely, the European Branch of the Chinese Communist Party. Zhao Shiyan and Zhou Enlai were among its collective leadership.[34]

The founding of these groups was kept secret and therefore Deng's friends did not inform him. They simply continued to carry on propaganda work, casually chatting him up and supplying him with communist literature. In October 1922, Deng's hope of receiving an education in France was rekindled. He saved up a bit of money and wrote home asking for sufficient funds to attend college. Deng's father sold yet another parcel of land, despite the fact that he and his family, as Deng's daughter writes, were "experiencing great financial difficulties then," and sent his eldest son a remittance.[35]

Unfortunately, when Deng arrived in the small town of Châtillon-sur-Seine, where he intended to enroll in the local college, the tuition turned out to be higher than he supposed and he had to abandon his plans. He made no further efforts to receive a diploma. Many years later, he noted sarcastically that living in France he studied nowhere and only worked.[36] Obviously his failure to receive a French education disappointed and embittered him.

He resumed working at Hutchinson, but after a month he quit once more, proudly informing the shop foreman of his "refusal to work."[37] He now had some money. Even though it was not enough for tuition, he could live on it for a while, especially since no one evicted him from the dormitory.

Dissatisfaction with a society that had no place for him accelerated Deng's move toward the left. Finally, by the summer of 1923, he embraced communism, although he still did not understand its theoretical fine points. He joined the Bolshevik movement not because he had undergone a profound evolution in his ideas, but because he had become disillusioned with capitalism and was ready for anything that would help redress the insults and injuries inflicted on him by the capitalist world. "I acquired class consciousness then when the capitalists and their tools—the foremen—slighted and exploited me," he wrote.[38] "Your capitalists," Deng said many years later to French Foreign Minister Roland Dumas, "taught me a [good] lesson, they taught me and my friends [everything], and pushed us onto the path of communism and propelled us toward a belief in Marxism-Leninism."[39] In other words, unlike Mao Zedong and many other Chinese Communists, the young Deng did not arrive at communism through an ideological struggle. His knowledge of the social sciences and political ideology was still insufficient for him to choose among alternatives. "In general, I was never exposed to the influence of other ideas," he wrote subsequently. "I came to communism directly."[40]

On June 11, 1923, he returned to Paris and joined the European branch of the Chinese Socialist Youth League (CSYL), the new name for the Chinese Communist Party of Youth Living in Europe.[41] He took the ceremonial oath along with Cai Hesen's younger sister, Cai Chang, who was four years older than Deng. He would be lifelong friends with her and her future husband, Li Fuchun, who was then one of the leaders of the European branch of the CSYL.[42]

From then on Deng devoted himself to dangerous Bolshevik work. Soon he wrote a letter to his father and mother terminating his relationship with them. He declared that he did not want to marry the "uneducated and unknown" girl from the Tang clan to whom he had been betrothed, and he asked his parents to abrogate the marital obligation. Moreover, he informed them that he would not be returning home and, therefore, would be unable to take care of the family.[43] For Deng Wenming and Mama Dan, who had sacrificed everything they could for their beloved son, this was a mortal blow. Their son not only turned out to be ungrateful but also threatened to disgrace them before the whole village. His actions violated tradition; their entire clan could "lose face." Deng's father quickly dispatched an angry letter accusing his son of "filial impiety and betrayal" and threatened to break all relations with him unless he reconsidered. But Deng was stubborn, and in another letter he repeated what he had already written. The result, in his own words, was that he himself "in fact . . . broke off relations with [his] family."[44]

Deng's mother immediately took to her bed while old Wenming went to settle things with the head of the Tang clan, whose daughter had been rejected for no reason. The two men agreed that Deng's bride would come as a "widow" to the house of the groom who had rejected her. Several years later Wenming married her off with a large dowry as if she were his own daughter.[45] Unlike his revolutionary son, he believed that firm observance of a marital obligation was a matter of honor.

Thereafter Deng ignored his family. His correspondence with his father ended. For a long time Deng Xiaoping did not know that his younger sister passed away soon after receiving his letters, and that several years later (in 1926) his mother, too, died from tuberculosis. One can hardly blame Deng for the death of his sister, but his mother's health seems to have been undermined by the separation from her son who had abandoned her.

Meanwhile, in the summer of 1923, soon after joining the socialist youth league, Deng began to take part in very important revolutionary affairs: initially in publishing the journal of the European branch of the CSYL, *Youth*, and then, starting in January 1924, the new journal *Chiguang* (*Red Light*). The editorial offices of both of these publications were located in a tiny forty-four-square-foot room in a small hotel not far from Place d'Italie, on the third floor of 17 Rue Godefrois. This was the lodging of Zhou Enlai, who in February 1923 had taken over the post of secretary of the European branch of the CSYL. It was in that room one summer day in 1923 that Deng and Zhou first met. Could Deng have intuited that this well-mannered young man—dressed in a baggy jacket buttoned to the top and trousers that were too short—was destined to play an extremely important role in his life?

Zhou was six and a half years older than Deng. He was born on March 5, 1898, in Jiangsu province into the family of a rural intellectual. He was orphaned at an early age and cared for by relatives. When he turned fifteen, he moved in with an aunt in Tianjin, a large commercial city about seventy miles east of Beijing. There he graduated in 1917 from the prestigious Nankai Academy. He then went to Japan to continue his education, but instead of seriously studying he was attracted to radical leftist, including socialist, literature and began reading *New Youth*. In Tokyo in 1918, he joined the patriotic Chinese organization Xin Zhonghui (New China society). At the end of April 1919, he returned to Tianjin.[46] There he actively participated in the May 4 Movement, quickly making his mark among the urban youth with his brilliant articles in the patriotic press. In Tianjin in September 1919, with nineteen like-minded fellows, he founded the secret Awakening Society, whose aim was to save the fatherland.

Despite this fevered political activity, Zhou did not abandon his desire to receive a higher education. Toward the end of 1919 he was admitted to the Humanities Department of Nankai University. Four months later, however, in January 1920, he was arrested and subsequently expelled from the university for organizing a patriotic anti-Japanese student demonstration. Released from prison in the summer of 1920, Zhou decided to travel to Europe.

He arrived in Marseilles in mid-December 1920 and was soon immersed in revolutionary work. Choosing Paris as his base, he traveled frequently to Germany, Belgium, and England, where he began organizing Chinese students. He was very sociable and lively, and he radiated an innate intelligence combined with an indisputable talent for leadership. In 1923, when Deng and Zhou met, all their thoughts were directed toward distributing communist propaganda among the Chinese diaspora in Europe. Cai Chang recalled:

> We took turns editing the journal *Youth*. Comrades Deng Xiaoping and Li Changying transferred the text to the stencil, Comrade Li Fuchun ran it through the mimeograph . . . Later the name of the journal was changed to *Red Light* . . . Comrades Deng Xiaoping and Li Fuchun worked during the day [at French enterprises], and at night were busy with party affairs, but Comrade Zhou Enlai was a liberated party worker.[47]

Over a period of two years, Deng and Zhou saw each other almost daily; they became close and established a fast friendship. "I had all along regarded him as my elder brother, and we had worked together for the longest period of time," Deng Xiaoping reminisced subsequently.[48]

Demonstrating his talent as a "capable and businesslike" comrade, in socialist youth league circles Deng soon was given the sobriquet "Doctor of Publishing Sciences."[49] But unlike Zhou and several other leaders, he engaged in purely practical work and did not tackle theoretical problems. This is evident from three short articles he published in 1924–25 in two issues of *Red Light*. They were sharp, and rather crude in tone and written in a journalistic style, but bore no comparison with the profound theoretical articles of Zhou or another leader of the European branch of the CSYL (from the beginning of 1925 the CCYL, the Chinese Communist Youth League), Ren Zhuoxuan. Deng's were slashing topical commentaries rather than subtle analyses.

Meanwhile, extraordinary events were occurring in China. Starting in late August 1922, the CCP and the CSYL began organizing a national united front with the Nationalist Party (Guomindang or GMD), founded by Sun Yat-sen, the former provisional president of the Chinese Republic in 1912. They did so under pressure from the Communist International (Comintern), which was supporting them ideologically and financially.

The Comintern was an international organization of communists that the Russian Bolsheviks established in March 1919 to promote world revolution. The Bolsheviks figured that by uniting all anti-imperialist and anti-feudal forces in China under their leadership, they could deal a crushing blow to world imperialism. The united front took the form of individual Communist party and Youth League members joining the Guomindang. While collaborating with the GMD, the Chinese Communists were supposed to preserve their complete independence inside the GMD and remain within it only until the CCP developed into a mass political organization.[50] In other words, Moscow instructed the Chinese Communists to make use of the Guomindang, which exerted considerable influence in south China, not only to struggle for the national independence of China but also to strengthen its own mass base.

In the summer of 1923, Chinese young socialists and communists in Europe were ordered to join the Guomindang. Soon all the members of the European branch of the CSYL, more than eighty, including Deng, joined the Guomindang.[51] The Chinese Communists in France also joined the GMD.

In January 1924, the First All-China Congress of the Guomindang in Canton, where Sun Yat-sen had headed the Chinese government since February 1923, officially approved admission of all Chinese Communists and Socialist Youth League members into the GMD. Sun adopted Moscow's policy because since 1923 the Soviet Union had been providing him material aid, including enormous sums of money, and sending him dozens of military and political advisers. In May 1924, the Russians established a military academy to train the officer corps of the armed forces of the GMD near Canton, in Whampoa district. With Bolshevik help, Sun hoped to use military force to unite the country, which disintegrated after the death of the former president, Yuan Shikai.

After forging a united front, the Chinese young socialists, communists, and Guomindang members in France engaged in joint anti-imperialist actions, holding demonstrations and distributing propaganda materials. They became particularly active in the spring of 1925 when a real nationalist revolution began to unfold in their homeland.

By this time, Deng, an active Socialist Youth League propagandist, had already begun his political ascent. In January 1924, in addition to his editorial work he began to function as technical secretary in the league's office. In mid-July, at the Fifth Congress of the European Branch of the CSYL in Paris, he was elected to the Executive Committee and became one of its three secretaries. In early 1925 Deng set out for Lyons as one of the leaders of the local cell of the Chinese Youth League. There, in April 1925, he was admitted into the CCP,[52] or more precisely, into its European branch.[53]

Soon after, in June 1925, the leaders of the European branches of the CCP and GMD held mass meetings and demonstrations in Paris to protest the French presence in China. These events were inspired by a new anti-imperialist upsurge back home, the so-called May 30 Movement, triggered by the killing of a worker-communist in Shanghai by a Japanese. By then Sun Yat-sen had already passed away (he died on March 12, 1925). The new Guomindang chieftains, including Wang Jingwei, leader of the Guomindang leftists, took advantage of the situation to mobilize all party forces in China and abroad to launch the nationalist revolution. They were supported by the communists in this endeavor. Naturally, the French police would not tolerate demonstrations by Chinese in France. Therefore, many young socialists, communists, and Guomindang members were imprisoned and subsequently deported. In this context, Deng quickly returned to Paris to help fill the vacuum created by the catastrophic shortage of leading cadres. He joined the provisional Executive Committee of the European branch of the Chinese Youth League. At the same time, Deng became a candidate (nonvoting) member of the Executive Committee of the European branch of the CCP.[54] Both of these organs had few members; the provisional Executive Committee of the Chinese Youth League organization, for example, comprised just three persons, including Deng.[55]

In this way, Deng became one of the leaders of the Chinese communists in Europe. The organization, however, was on its last legs. Deng settled in Billancourt, a western suburb of Paris, lodging in Room 5 of a small hotel located at 3 Rue Casteja, adjacent to the Renault factory, where he found employment as a metal worker. Sharing the same room were two other comrades, including the head of the executive committee of the European branch of the CYL, Fu Zhong, and CYL member Yang Pinsun. Throughout the second half of 1925, the three of them tried their best to continue the anti-imperialist struggle that had begun in June. They convened meetings of the Chinese community and published proclamations and appeals. French police archives contain numerous secret reports on these activities.[56] Ultimately, thick clouds gathered above them, and in December 1925, by decision of the organization, Fu Zhong and Deng Xiaoping began preparations to leave France. Their road led toward Moscow, where they were supposed to enroll in a special Comintern university that had been established in April 1921, the Communist University for the Toilers of the East (KUTV in Russian abbreviation). Deng's uncle Shaosheng, who like his nephew had joined the CCP in 1925, also joined them, as did seventeen comrades. Only Yang Pinsun, who had hurriedly left the hotel on Rue Casteja for a safe house, and a few others remained in Paris for several more months to gradually wrap up all of the party and youth league work of the Chinese in France.[57]

On January 7, 1926, Deng, his uncle, Fu Zhong, and the others settled into their seats on the train, which chugged slowly out of the station. The urban neighborhoods were soon left behind and through the windows of their compartment they could see the fields and meadows of this beautiful country that played such a large role in the political coming-of-age of the future great reformer of China. Prior to departure they all received expulsion notices from the French police. The following day the Billancourt police carried out a search in 3 Rue Casteja and in two other hotels where the departing Chinese lived. A secret police report spoke of what had been discovered in Room 5 of 3 Rue Casteja:

> Many important brochures in French and Chinese were found (*Chinese Worker, Sun Yat-sen's Testament, The ABCs of Communism* and others), Chinese newspapers, in particular *Progress* [*Qianjin bao*; the correct translation is *Forward*], a Chinese newspaper published in Moscow, as well as equipment needed for two printing presses, printers' ink, printing plates, rollers, and many packages of typographical paper . . . To all appearances . . . the Chinese [who lived here] were communist activists.[58]

The French police were surprisingly shrewd, but it no longer mattered. The express train was swiftly carrying Deng and his friends to the motherland of the October Revolution, to the country of triumphant Bolshevism whose experience Deng passionately desired to study.

THEY ARRIVED IN Moscow on Sunday, January 17, 1926, after passing through Germany and Poland. At the Byelorussian-Baltic station, they were joyfully greeted by representatives of the Moscow branch of the CCP, who whisked them off to the former nunnery on Strastnaia Square that now housed the Communist University of the Toilers of the East (KUTV). All of them were given student ID cards as well as pseudonyms. Deng received the surname Krezov, a pseudonym that was likely chosen arbitrarily.[59] The chief concern of officials in the cadre departments of Comintern schools was to maintain secrecy.

They were then all moved into the dormitory of KUTV, which was under the Eastern Department of the Comintern. (KUTV now bore the name of

J. V. Stalin, general secretary of the Bolshevik Party Central Committee.[60])
When Deng arrived, KUTV was one of the largest universities in Soviet
Russia, numbering 1,664 students from all over Asia, including more than
100 Chinese, the majority from Europe.[61]

In Moscow Deng ran into many of his acquaintances from France,[62]
among them the former head of the European branches of the CCP and
the CCYL, Ren Zhuoxuan (pseudonym Rafail). Ren, who had already
been in Moscow for two months, was immersed in politics rather than
his studies. His appointment as secretary of the Moscow branch of the
CCP went to Ren's head. On January 19, he enrolled all the new arrivals
in the organization and, to the surprise of many, enforced a military-style
discipline.[63]

Moscow's ways differed from those of Paris. Ever since the Chinese
Communist Party and Youth League branches had been established in
Moscow in December 1921, their members lived a spartan existence. Chinese
leaders wanted to expunge the "old concepts and ideas" their subordinates
had supposedly inherited from the "backward patriarchal society." Zheng
Chaolin, who arrived in Moscow in the spring of 1923, recalled that the members of the Moscow branch of the CCP

> were divided into leaders and masses. . . . The leaders behaved not like
> the masses' fellow students but like their teachers. . . . The Moscow
> students' view of leaders was completely alien to us. . . . They not only
> submitted publicly but also dared not express their dissatisfaction in
> private. . . . We were divided into several cells, each with four or five
> members. . . . Each cell met once or twice a week, and there were ple-
> nary sessions and other sorts of meetings. . . . The atmosphere at them
> was tense, excited, and ardent. . . . Most of the time was given over to
> "individual criticism." . . . You're too individualistic, you're too arro-
> gant, you're too petit bourgeois, you have anarchistic tendencies, and
> so on. The ones who were criticized would think up similar criticisms
> to hurl back against their critics. The result was that . . . seeds of hatred
> were sown in people's hearts.[64]

Ren, who had come from the much more relaxed atmosphere of France,
quickly adopted the Moscow style. Justifying his policy, he later wrote: "Our
method was the Leninist principle of party self-criticism. . . . Since all the students were intellectuals . . . we considered it necessary to transform their petit
bourgeois consciousness . . . the students had to undergo a total makeover . . .

if they did not do this, we criticized them, sometimes severely, until they had remade themselves."[65]

Just a week after his arrival, Deng too had to make a self-criticism. As a loyal member of the party, he submitted a written statement: "Although I arrived here only recently, the organization has already subjected me to a completely justified critique so that I may know my shortcomings and advance along the path of self-improvement and successful transformation into a real communist."[66]

The headquarters of the Moscow branch of the CCP was located at another Comintern school that had opened two months prior to Deng's arrival, the Sun Yat-sen University of the Toilers of China (UTK). UTK was intended solely for Chinese, including members of both the Communist Party and the Youth League as well as the Guomindang.[67] It was the educational incarnation of the united front.

Just twelve days after arriving in Moscow, Deng was transferred to UTK. On January 29, 1926, he received his UTK student ID card, no. 233, in the name of Ivan Sergeevich Dozorov.[68] The following day, Saturday, January 30, he began his studies.

The two-year course was extremely demanding. Deng studied Russian, Marxist theory of historical materialism, Chinese and foreign revolutionary history, the history of the Bolsheviks, economic geography, political economy (from *The Economic Doctrines of Karl Marx,* by the German socialist Karl Kautsky, a book beloved by Lenin), party construction, military affairs, and journalism.[69] Students were in class eight hours a day six days a week, from 9:00 a.m. to 7:00 p.m. with a two-hour meal break.[70]

Deng absorbed the new material like a sponge. In his own words, he had come to Moscow "to find out just what communism is." "When I worked in the organization in Western Europe," he wrote in his autobiography upon entering UTK,

I constantly felt insufficiently prepared and consequently often made mistakes. Therefore, I had long since resolved to study in Russia. However, at that time, I had no money for the trip, so I could not accomplish what I had hoped for . . . I [always] keenly felt that my knowledge of communism was superficial. Others also understood this to be so. . . . Therefore, as long as I am in Russia, I will study persistently so that I can receive more knowledge about communism. I also think that we, the youth of the East, strongly yearn for liberation, but it is difficult for us to systematize our ideas and our actions. It goes without saying that this circumstance greatly inhibits our work in the future. Therefore, I have come to Russia, above all, determined to wholly communize my thoughts and actions after learning to maintain iron discipline, and receiving my baptism in communism. Since arriving in Moscow, I have resolved unequivocally to devote myself to our party, to my class. From now on I shall wholeheartedly accept party education, submit myself to party leadership, and unfailingly fight for the interests of the proletariat.[71]

Deng was assigned to Instructional Group No. 7, nicknamed the "Theoreticians' Circle," which contained the most promising CCP and Guomindang students, including Chiang Ching-kuo who was the eldest son of Chiang Kai-shek, the commandant of the Whampoa Military Academy and simultaneously commander of the First Corps of the National Revolutionary Army (NRA) of the Guomindang; and relatives of other prominent Chinese leaders. Lectures were delivered in Russian with consecutive interpretation into Chinese that was not always accurate. There was no instruction in Chinese, and Deng could not join the French group, because although he had lived in France for five years he had not learned French.

Deng remained upbeat, however. He applied himself assiduously to his studies, sitting in the library for many hours. Although he did no better with Russian than he had with French, he got high marks in the social science disciplines, including the history of the Bolsheviks, Marxist theory, and Marxist economics. Deng focused on the university's Chinese translations of the works of Marx, Engels, Lenin, Stalin, and Bukharin.

The environment in Moscow bolstered his good mood. In 1926 throughout the USSR the New Economic Policy (NEP) was in full bloom. Aimed at developing a market economy under the control of the Communist party, its results were visible everywhere. The economy was booming; markets were increasingly filled with goods produced by state and private enterprises. New stores, restaurants, and cafes were opening all the time. "We were never short of chicken, duck, fish, and meat," recalled one of Deng's classmates.

For breakfast there were given eggs, bread and butter, milk, sausages, black tea, and occasionally even caviar. I do not think rich people anywhere enjoyed a more abundant breakfast than we did. . . . When we students grew tired of Russian food, they [the officials] hastened to accommodate us by employing a Chinese chef . . . we had a choice of either Russian or Chinese food.[72]

The students' free time was also well organized. They visited museums, exhibitions, and theaters. In the summer of 1926, they even went on an excursion to Leningrad.[73]

This life differed greatly from Deng's half-starved existence in France. The evident superiority of NEP-style socialism was confirmed by his reading of Marxist-Leninist books and articles as well as contemporary speeches by Stalin and Bukharin, which made a deep impression on Deng's worldview.

"Right can never be higher than the economic structure of society and its cultural development which this determines," Marx stated.[74] "To try to prohibit entirely, to put the lock on all development of private, non-state exchange, i.e., trade, i.e., capitalism, which is inevitable with millions of small producers . . . such a policy would be foolish and suicidal for the party that tried to apply it," Lenin asserted.[75] "NEP is a special policy of the proletarian state aimed at permitting capitalism while the commanding positions are held by the proletarian state," opined Stalin.[76] "We must say to the entire peasantry . . . enrich yourselves, accumulate, develop your farms. Only an idiot can say the poor will *always* be with us. We must now implement a policy whose result will be the disappearance of the poor," Bukharin exhorted.[77]

Party-political work occupied much of Deng's time. He was soon elected to the university branch of the Chinese Communist Youth League. The students in Group No. 7 also chose him as their party organizer.[78] Therefore, he was drawn involuntarily into the sharp factional struggle unfolding in the university. What was at issue was that in early 1926 Ren Zhuoxuan had proclaimed the slogan "Meetings first, studies second; practice first, theory second."[79] Students who paid more attention to their studies than to party meetings were openly stigmatized for "academicism" and "individualism," and those who could not endure the lengthy meetings but went off to eat were criticized as "petit bourgeois" and "egoists." Many teachers were dissatisfied; the dining hall staff also voiced their disapproval.[80] UTK rector Karl Radek himself expressed the greatest indignation. Although he was a member of the Leninist Old Guard, he valued personal freedom above everything else. On February 18, 1926, he censured the leadership of the Moscow branch of the CCP at a general party meeting at UTK.[81] Afterward he personally drew up a work plan for the branch in which he appealed to the student members of the CCP to study Marxism-Leninism and Sun Yat-senism, strengthen their spirit of mutual assistance, and stop blindly submitting to the authorities. He demanded that Ren Zhuoxuan stop interfering with the students' freedom to think and discuss any problems connected with the Chinese revolution.[82]

Radek's call fell on fertile soil. Many of the energetic young Chinese who dreamed of making a party career in Moscow spoke out openly against the Moscow branch. Their leader was Chen Shaoyu, a twenty-two-year-old native of Anhui province and CYL member who had branded the theoretical and practical directives of Ren Zhuoxuan as "Rafailovism," after Ren's pseudonym Rafail—a term that sounded like a verdict. The upshot was that in the spring of 1926, education almost ground to a halt. Fortunately, the holidays began in June, and the students, including Deng, went off to Tarasovka, outside of Moscow. There, too, however, Chen and his comrades were loath to end their polemics. In June or July they convened a tumultuous general meeting directed against Ren Zhuoxuan and other "bosses" of the Moscow branch. It dragged on for four days until rector Radek, arriving in Tarasovka, in the name of the Bolshevik Party Central Committee, the Comintern Executive, and the university administration, dissolved the Moscow branch of the CCP. In the summer of 1926, Ren Zhuoxuan returned to China.[83]

Afterward, the Russian Bolshevik authorities decided that all the Chinese communists, including Deng, would become candidate or nonvoting members of the Russian Communist Party, a move that stripped them of their independence. Candidate members could not serve in elected positions, so they were unable to compete with regular members of the party, let alone with the leaders of the party committee at UTK. Moreover, the Russian party leadership, unlike rector Radek, adhered to the same views on party building as the bosses of the CCP Moscow branch and did not permit any autonomy. Thus, ironically, the methods of party work in UTK remained unchanged. All members of the party and the Communist Youth League were still obliged to attend lengthy party meetings as well as other events, such as group discussions and sessions on current politics where they were forced to publicly express their loyalty to the party leadership.[84] Sednikov, the secretary of the UTK party committee, tirelessly drilled into the Chinese students the idea that it was forbidden to speak about democracy in a party that was engaged in a single-minded struggle for the victory of the revolution.[85]

None of this bothered Deng. Despite his excitable character, he sought to avoid any deviations and accepted the views of the majority. Wanting to become an obedient soldier of the party, he observed iron party discipline. Therefore, he subordinated himself to Ren Zhuoxuan when the latter was secretary but opposed him when Ren began to lose power. On August 12, 1926, expounding the orthodox view, he wrote in one of his class compositions: "Centralized power flows from the top down. It is absolutely necessary to obey the directives of the leadership. . . . Democracy is not always an unchanging concept. The expansion or contraction of democracy depends on changes in the surrounding environment. For example, in pre-revolutionary Russia and contemporary China, it is impossible to expand democracy."[86]

It was no accident, therefore, that the university party committee regularly gave him positive assessments. Thus in one of them, dated June 16, 1926, it was noted in question-and-answer form:

> *Are all his behaviors compatible with his status as a CPC* [CCP] *member?* Yes. He has no non-Party tendencies. *Does he observe discipline?* Yes. . . . [He] pays great attention to the Party's discipline. He has shown great interest in the general political issues. . . . *Does he attend the Party's conferences and group meetings?* He was never absent [from party meetings]. . . . *Does he accomplish the work assigned by the Party?* He can do so earnestly. *Is he interested in his lessons?* Very much. *Can he set an example for others?* He studies hard, and that has influence on others. *Is he suitable for putting the Party's views into practice within the Kuomintang* [Guomindang]*?* Yes. . . . *What job is most suitable for him?* Propaganda and organizational work.[87]

Another assessment, dated November 5, 1926, said:

> Very active and energetic party member and CYL member (cand[idate] of the All-Union Communist Party). One of the best organization workers in the CYL bureau of the university. As someone who is both disciplined and consistent, as well as capable in his studies, Comrade DOZOROV has accumulated a lot of experience from his organizational work in the CYL bureau and greatly matured. He takes an active part in political work. He acts like a comrade in his relations with others. He is among the best students. His party training is good (worked individually in cultivating Guomindang members—only the best trained party members were assigned this work.) Perhaps could best be employed in organizational work.)[88]

On October 9, 1926, a general meeting of Group No. 7, in which Deng was the party organizer, considered it "appropriate and useful" to switch him from candidate membership to full membership in the All-Union Communist Party, "since he is good and does his work conscientiously and well."[89]

According to party norms Deng also stood out in a moral sense. There were only two or three dozen women in the university compared to several hundred men, but unlike the majority of his peers who constantly pestered the women, Deng behaved very modestly. He was fond of a certain girl who went by the pseudonym Dogadova. She was attractive, slim, her hair cut short, with fine black eyebrows and rather sensual lips, but Deng made no moves to get close to her. He spent all his time on his studies and party work. He knew only that the girl's real name was Zhang Xiyuan, that she had been born in a workers' family (her father was a railroad worker) at Liangxiang Station in Fangshan county of Zhili Province on October 28, 1907, and had come to UTK from China on November 27, 1925, together with Chen Shaoyu. She had joined the Communist party in Moscow a month later. Zhang was initially enrolled in Group No. 3 and then in Group No. 4.[90] She was a rather mediocre student, usually earning Cs, and not always attentive to her party work. Once she was even reprimanded for "failing to carry out a party assignment." Therefore, she too was not interested in romance; she had to regain the trust of the organization.

Meanwhile, events in China were unfolding rapidly. After Sun Yat-sen's death, the leftist faction headed by Wang Jingwei came to power in the Guomindang, and the nationalist revolution accelerated. The Chinese communists in Canton, following directives from Moscow, adopted an aggressive policy aimed at seizing power in the Guomindang and transforming it into a so-called people's party according to Stalin's theoretical formulation in the spring of 1925.[91] By March 1926, many in Moscow and Canton believed that the triumph of the CCP in the Guomindang was within sight. But on March 20, the commander of the First Corps of the National Revolutionary Army, Chiang Kai-shek, executed a military coup against the leftists, compelling Wang Jingwei and several Soviet military advisers who had antagonized Chiang Kai-shek to leave China. Thereafter he demanded that the CCP curtail its political and organizational autonomy within the Guomindang. Chiang gathered all the threads of political and military power in his own hands. Most important, he was proclaimed the commander-in-chief of the National Revolutionary Army.[92]

Forced to accept this fait accompli, Moscow directed the CCP to slow down the tempo of its offensive inside the Guomindang in order to regroup forces.[93] The united front was preserved, and Chiang Kai-shek was satisfied with the concessions. In early July 1926, with the help of the chief Soviet military adviser, Vasilii Bliukher, Chiang commenced the Northern Expedition, a military campaign to subdue the militarists and unite the country. At that time the National Revolutionary Army numbered some 100,000 soldiers and officers. Facing it were the armies of three northern militarists with total forces of 750,000 men. The 150,000-man Nationalist Army, commanded by Marshal Feng Yuxiang and deployed in northwestern China, was objectively an ally of Chiang Kai-shek. Feng had declared his support for Sun Yat-sen in October 1924, when he occupied Beijing and requested assistance from the USSR. Moscow soon dispatched several dozen Soviet military advisers. Three and a half months before the Northern Expedition, however, Marshal Feng suffered a terrible defeat at the hands of the northern Chinese militarists and departed with his family to Moscow in search of expanded Soviet military aid.[94] Nevertheless, Chiang successfully launched the expedition. On July 11, 1926, his troops, inspired by the ideas of the nationalist revolution, scored their first major victory and then occupied Changsha, the capital of Hunan province.

Naturally, the Chinese students in Moscow were enthusiastic about the triumphant development of the Northern Expedition. They were also drawn to the personality of Feng Yuxiang.[95] When Feng and his family arrived on May 9, 1926, at Yaroslavl Station in Moscow, Feng was greeted by an honor guard of Red Army infantrymen and cavalry, numerous Chinese students (Deng very likely among them), and many Soviet and foreign reporters. Over the next three months plus, a full program was arranged for him, but Feng spent most of his time at UTK, meeting with the Chinese students, including Deng Xiaoping, who responded fervently to his calls for revolution and for the overthrow of imperialism.[96] Everyone knew that on the day he arrived in Moscow, Feng, standing in front of Lenin's sarcophagus, announced that he had joined the Guomindang.

During his Moscow sojourn, Feng was promised additional financial assistance, and his group of Soviet advisers was beefed up with new cadres. Feng departed for China along with these reinforcements.[97]

The day after Feng's departure from Moscow, August 17, Chiang Kai-shek resumed the Northern Expedition, proceeding from Changsha to Wuhan. By the autumn of 1926, the National Revolutionary Army had entered the Yangzi River valley. In October, Marshal Feng on his part dispatched a division from Gansu into neighboring Shaanxi province, where on November 18 they lifted the siege of Xi'an, the key city in the region. In the meantime, Chiang took Wuhan and on January 1, 1927, it was proclaimed the capital of Guomindang China.[98] Preparing an expedition to Henan to link up with troops of Chiang Kai-shek's National Revolutionary Army, Feng requested that Moscow send him additional advisers.[99]

The Comintern responded by sending Feng a group of more than twenty outstanding Chinese students from Moscow. Among them was Deng Xiaoping, who had not even finished the two-year-long course of study. The Northern Expedition had entered its decisive phase, and Comintern officials correctly believed that "to set aside . . . the work and curtail it until such time as several comrades in Moscow completed their studies would be absurd."[100]

On January 12, 1927, Deng was removed from the student roster of Sun Yat-sen University and departed that same day for China. His sojourn of more than six years abroad was over. The final report on him by the university party committee said, "Very active and energetic, one of the best organization workers. Disciplined and consistent. Outstanding in his studies. Well trained."[101] The resolution of the general meeting of Group No. 7 promoting him from candidate to full membership in the All-Union Communist Party, however, had to be rescinded.[102] Deng returned to China, where he again became an official member of the Chinese Communist Party. The young and able communist surfed the waves of revolution. On their crest he and his comrades hoped to come to power.

3

From Xi'an to Shanghai

BY THE TIME Deng left Moscow, Marshal Feng had already moved to Xi'an where Deng and his comrades were headed. The train ran only as far as Verkneudinsk (now Ulan Ude), from where they proceeded across the Mongolian steppe and through the city of Urga (Ulan Bator) in Soviet trucks transporting weapons to Feng's army. Then they crossed the Gobi desert on camels and finally rode horseback from Yinchuan to Xi'an. It was a difficult journey—cold on the steppe and hot in the desert, where the dust storms blinded them and choked their mouths and noses with sand. Finally, at the end of March, the tired and bedraggled students from Moscow arrived in Xi'an. Deng's daughter, Maomao, recorded her father's observation that "the more than twenty comrades were dressed in rags when they arrived in Xi'an."[1]

They were housed in the barracks and then presented to Feng Yuxiang. The forty-four-year-old marshal radiated self-assurance.[2] He was tall, solidly built, with a fleshy face and broad shoulders. Feng dressed simply in a villager's padded cotton jacket and baggy trousers, moved deliberately, and spoke softly as if afraid he might "spill the cup of wisdom."[3] He immediately appointed the new arrivals to head the political departments of his army units and other institutions.

Deng was assigned to the Sun Yat-sen Xi'an Military Academy, which enrolled more than seven hundred cadets, mostly former students of local civilian schools who were studying military and military-technical subjects and taking courses in the social sciences. It was located downtown at the edge of the Muslim district, near the famous clock or bell tower and the drum tower that had been constructed in the 1480s.[4]

The academy had been founded shortly before Deng's arrival by the Guomindang leftist Yu Youren whom Feng Yuxiang had appointed commander-in-chief of Nationalist Army units deployed in Shaanxi. Yu in turn appointed Shi Kexuan, a thirty-seven-year-old Shaanxi native, to head the academy. Shi was a former brigade commander with some prior administrative experience who had just recently joined the CCP.[5] Shi's deputy director was a communist named Li Lin, a graduate of KUTV whom Deng knew well from his years in France. Many other Communist party members also worked in the academy.

As chief of the political department, Deng was primarily responsible for conducting party propaganda work in the academy as well as teaching political subjects such as History of the Chinese Revolution, History of the Guomindang, and Principles of Bolshevism. Other subjects included Contemporary Problems of the Chinese Revolution, Leninism, Agrarian and Peasant Problems, and Fundamentals of Army Political Work. For the roughly one hundred cadets who were members or candidate members of the CCP, special courses were offered: What Is the Communist Party? The ABC of Communism, and *Das Kapital*. Deng was able to share the knowledge he had acquired in Moscow. He recalled, "The main subject of political education was the revolution and Marxism-Leninism. In Xi'an, it was a red school."[6]

Deng proved to be an engaged and energetic lecturer. Therefore, the leadership soon assigned him to teach as well in the Sun Yat-sen Academy, intended to train political cadres, and in the Department of Security Instructional School.[7] For a while, he was concurrently one of the secretaries of the academy's communist organization[8], and in May–June 1927 he joined the executive committee of the special Guomindang cell at the academy.[9] He often delivered reports to the cadets and instructors on China's political and international situation, and on conditions in Soviet Russia, and he even took part in amateur talent shows, where he played roles in simple plays on patriotic themes that the audience loved.[10]

He was paid little, but the nearby Muslim Quarter housed numerous culinary temptations in the little eating places that Deng and his comrades frequented. The air of its main street, Beiyuanmen, and adjacent alleys and lanes was filled with spicy aromas. One dish, a thick spicy beef soup with noodles, was particularly tasty. Deng was so fond of it that he often goaded his boss to take him and other party members to eat out on the academy's tab.[11]

Xi'an, the densely populated capital of Shaanxi province, with some eight hundred thousand inhabitants, was one of the largest commercial and cultural centers of China, straddling the border between China Proper and the wild steppe. City markets displayed piles of traditional Chinese handicrafts, including silk and cotton fabrics, porcelain, tea, rice, lacquer ware, and jade ornaments that were exchanged for the goods of the nomadic herders of the steppe. Surrounded on four sides by an impressive fortress wall, Xi'an had always played an important role in Chinese history, serving as the capital of the empire for eleven centuries and through thirteen dynasties. The abundance of prosperous shops on its bustling streets invariably impressed visitors, as did the luxury and splendor of its ancient pagodas and palaces.

But Deng had no time to see the sights of Xi'an. He was able to visit even the Muslim Quarter only once a week. The situation in China and in Xi'an itself was rapidly changing. On April 12, terrible news arrived from Shanghai that Chiang Kai-shek, commander-in-chief of the National Revolutionary Army, had unleashed a bloody White Terror in Shanghai and other cities of Eastern China directed against the communists. Chiang did so because in the course of the unfolding Northern Expedition and the concomitant mass movement of landless peasants, paupers, and rural riffraff, Stalin once again had ordered the CCP to take the political offensive inside the Guomindang. In early spring 1927, the CCP received a directive from the Soviet Politburo "to squeeze out the Guomindang rightists ... to pursue a policy of occupying important positions in the army ... strengthening the work of Guomindang and communist cells in the army ... pursuing a course of arming the workers and peasants, *and transforming the peasant committees in the provinces into real organs of power with armed self-defense.*"[12]

Thereafter the movement of landless peasants, paupers, and rural riffraff against the "rural bloodsuckers" reached a "stage of madness."[13] In several cities, including Shanghai, the Communist party's armed workers' pickets even began violently attacking the well-to-do relatives of influential Guomindang and communist leaders.

This is why Chiang Kai-shek finally dissolved the united front and announced the formation of a new Nationalist government in Nanjing. The result was that two hostile centers of power arose on the territory occupied by the National Revolutionary Army: the anticommunist Nanjing center, headed by Chiang Kai-shek; and the Guomindang leftist Wuhan center, headed by Wang Jingwei. Now much depended on which side Marshal Feng would support. Deng Xiaoping and the other Guomindang leftists and communists immediately launched an anti–Chiang Kai-shek propaganda campaign among Feng's troops. In Xi'an on May 5, a grand fifteen-thousand-person demonstration took place in front of Feng Yuxiang's residence, which was named the Red Castle; not only military servicemen but also many urban residents participated.[14] Chiang was loudly denounced and accused of "betrayal."[15]

Apparently influenced by all this activity, Feng Yuxiang renamed his armed forces the 2nd Army Group of the National Revolutionary Army and advanced into Henan to link up with the army of the Guomindang leftists. On June 1, his troops captured Kaifeng and met up with the 1st Army Group of the Guomindang leftist general Tang Shengzhi.[16] On June 10, the Wuhan leaders, headed by Wang Jingwei, arrived in Zhengzhou to meet with him. During the talks, Feng voiced anti–Chiang Kai-shek sentiments, openly calling Chiang a "wolf-hearted, dog-lunged, inhuman thing."[17] It seemed he was ready to fight Chiang to the death.

At the same time, as he privately informed the Wuhan leaders, he had accumulated numerous complaints against the Communist party, which appeared to be challenging the marshal for control of his own army. The communists were directing a mass movement of the poor, enrolled in peasant unions, worker, women, and youth organizations, and it was creating chaos in the provinces formally under Feng's control. Marshal Feng, who valued order, could not tolerate this.[18] What particularly outraged him was the emancipation of women. "[After] the Women's Associations were established, women in the T'ung-kuan [Tongguan] region [on the Shaanxi-Henan border] went to meetings every day, and paid no attention to the children or to cooking meals," he said angrily. "When their husbands spoke about this, the women said that the care of children is not the work of the women alone, but should be evenly divided; only that was equality. Thus disorder was created in the households."[19]

The Guomindang leftists listened to him courteously but took no action. Then, on June 19, Feng met with the "inhuman" Chiang Kai-shek in Xuzhou to coordinate action against the CCP. There he sent an ultimatum to the Guomindang leftists demanding that they also break with the communists. "The people," Feng asserted, "wanted to suppress such [communist] despotism."[20]

Unlike Chiang Kai-shek, Feng had no desire to execute communists within his ranks. After returning to Kaifeng on June 21, he courteously explained to his chief Soviet military adviser why he was unable to collaborate with the CCP any longer. Then he presented him and the other advisers gifts and money for the road and bade them farewell.[21] Deng later recalled, "During the 1927 purge, while Chiang Kai-shek was mercilessly killing communists in the south, Mr. Huanzhang [Feng Yuxiang] instead just politely dispatched us away."[22] Meanwhile, via Shaanxi governor Shi Jingting, Feng ordered all the communist officials in the Xi'an Military Academy to report to Zhengzhou "for study"; but the Shaanxi committee of the CCP ignored the order.

Two more weeks later, after forming a battalion composed of teachers and cadets from the Xi'an Military Academy, Shi Kexuan launched a short-lived struggle against those who had "betrayed the revolution." Two weeks later, Shi was taken prisoner and executed by the Guomindang.[23] At the end of June, Deng and deputy academy head Li Lin set out for Wuhan on orders from the provincial CCP committee.[24]

A dangerous assignment awaited them in Wuhan, where the situation had reached a critical point. In Changsha, which was another leftist stronghold, the local military commanders and political leaders turned against the trade unions and attacked the communists. In Wuhan itself, the economy ground to a halt amidst expectations that Tang Shengzhi, a purportedly leftist general, was about to throw his support to Chiang Kai-shek.[25]

Arriving in Wuhan in early July 1927, Deng was horrified by the terrible scenes of collapse that he saw. He was immediately assigned work as the lone secretary of the Central Committee (CC) and had to assume the workload of seven other secretaries who were unable to come to Wuhan.[26] His duties included taking the minutes of Politburo meetings, preparing draft CC resolutions, corresponding with local organizations, and establishing links with communists who were going underground. His boss, the director of the secretariat, Deng Zhongxia, a thirty-three-year-old native of Hunan with a long neck and a thick head of hair, was constantly busy with other matters as a member of the Central Committee and a high-ranking leader. He turned the paperwork over to Deng, who managed it quite well.

Deng was not involved in the political and organizational struggle unfolding in the party leadership. He lacked the time, strength, and experience. No one considered him a politician or a theoretician, of which there were plenty in the CCP. At leadership meetings, which usually took place in Hankou, Deng, who took the minutes, witnessed many stormy quarrels. The united front was unraveling literally in front of their eyes, and the leaders of the Communist party as well as the Soviet advisers could think of nothing to stop it. Ignorant of the actual balance of forces in China, Stalin demanded that the communist leaders carry out an agrarian revolution, seize power in the Guomindang, and eliminate the Guomindang's dependence on "unreliable generals."[27] But the members of the Politburo of the CCP had no real power in Wuhan. At the end of June, Chen Duxiu bitterly told Borodin, the political adviser to the Guomindang Central Executive Committee, and

Rafael Khitarov, representative of the Communist Youth International, "I do not understand the directives from Moscow and cannot agree with them. Moscow simply doesn't understand what is going on here. . . . Moscow is demanding the confiscation of land which we are unable to do." As soon as he was informed about Chen Duxiu's comment, Comintern representative M. N. Roy immediately informed the political secretary of the Comintern Executive Committee: "On June 26, the Politburo of the CCP openly contravened the directive of the Comintern. Chen Duxiu said that Moscow does not understand the situation and is sending directives that are impossible to implement. . . . There are open divergences between the Chinese Communist Party and the Comintern."[28]

On July 8, an irritated Stalin demanded that the members of the CCP Politburo "correct the fundamental errors of the party leadership on the basis of the directives of the Executive Committee of the Communist International [ECCI]."[29] Instead, on July 12, Chen Duxiu resigned. He sent a letter to the Central Committee saying in part: "There is really no way out. I actually cannot continue with my work."[30] Three days later, the leader of the Guomindang left, Wang Jingwei, broke with the communists and, emulating Chiang Kai-shek, unleashed a White Terror in Wuhan. The communists responded with a citywide general strike, but it failed. An eyewitness wrote that it was due to their "complete lack of any base among the Hankou workers."[31]

In sum, the united front collapsed, the workers' movement evaporated, and Deng, along with the other communists in the city, had to go underground, just as communists in Shanghai, Canton, and elsewhere had already done. On July 24, the new leaders of the Communist party, including Deng's old friend Zhou Enlai, directed the entire party to switch to an illegal footing and observe strict secrecy in their work. Party organizations had to relocate to new places, masquerading as private homes, stores, and hospitals. All key party personnel had to change their names and appearance, and stay on heightened alert.[32] Implementing this directive, it was at this time that Deng changed his name (Xixian) to Xiaoping and, along with the CC secretariat, moved across the Yangzi River from Wuchang where he had lived to Hankou.

At the end of July a new Moscow emissary arrived in town: Vissarion Lominadze, an old Bolshevik and close associate of Stalin, and one of the ECCI leaders. Informing the Chinese that he had been sent "to correct the numerous errors committed in the past by Comintern officials and the CCP Central Committee in the course of the Chinese revolution," Lominadze demanded that an emergency party conference be convened as soon as possible, the party leadership reorganized, and new tactics worked out in place of those that had failed. Then he emphasized that "the CC CCP had committed the serious error of right opportunism and violated the Comintern's directives."[33]

Just a few days earlier, the newly organized Provisional Bureau of the Central Committee had decided to spark armed mutinies in the Guomindang army as well as rural uprisings in Hunan, Hubei, Guangdong, and Jiangxi. They intended to incite the poor peasants to carry out an agrarian revolution during the period of the autumn harvest when the tenants had to settle accounts with the landlords, by the simple expedient of refraining from paying their debts. Lominadze ardently supported this line. On the night of July 31 to August 1, in the city of Nanchang (Jiangxi province), communist leaders launched the first uprising. The insurgents, numbering a little more than twenty thousand officers and men, were able to seize Nanchang, though they had no intention of holding it. When they launched an attack southward with the aim of establishing a revolutionary government in Guangdong, they suffered a devastating defeat in late September and early October near the port of Swatow in eastern Guangdong, where they had gone to receive arms from the USSR. Afterward, the army simply disintegrated.

In Hankou, meanwhile, on August 7, 1927, the new CCP leader, Qu Qiubai, and Lominadze convened an emergency conference of the CC. It took place in the apartment of one of the former Soviet advisers to the Wuhan government, on the second floor of a large three-story European-style house in the former Russian concession. Twenty-five people participated in the conference. Deng Xiaoping attended the meeting as secretary. He sat in the corner by the window at a small table and took minutes. He did not take part in the discussion, but there really wasn't any discussion.

Lominadze did most of the talking, severely criticizing the Chinese communists. In the name of the leadership of the party, Qu Qiubai made a self-criticism. It was better not to quarrel with an emissary from Moscow. With the Communist party in crisis, financial infusions from the Comintern were needed more than ever. Only five persons took the floor, including, on two occasions, a tall, thirty-four-year-old Hunanese named Mao Zedong, whom Deng saw for the first time. He spoke passionately and persuasively, criticizing the former leadership for "mistakes" with regard to the military and peasant questions. He argued that the CCP should urgently form an army composed of bandits, the dispossessed, paupers, and rural riffraff, who could be attracted to the side of the communists only by confiscating not just the land of the landlords (*dizhu*) but also that of the peasants.[34]

To a certain degree these ideas, hardly trivial, sounded non-Bolshevik. At that time no one in the leadership of the party or the Comintern had posed so directly the question of the decisive role of the military factor in the revolutionary movement or of an alliance between the communists and riffraff and bandits against the peasants. Thus, Deng could hardly fail to remember the speaker. In Moscow he had been taught something entirely different. As for Mao, he himself paid no attention to the diminutive CC secretary, who barely came up to his shoulder. Deng was still an insignificant figure who sat quietly in the corner taking the minutes. "People later said that we met in Wuhan," Mao recalled in 1960. "But I don't remember at all. Perhaps we did meet, but we definitely didn't talk!"[35] Mao was already a very well-known communist, one of the founders of the party and organizer of the Hunan party branch. In the CCP he was called the King of Hunan in recognition of the great authority he enjoyed among Hunanese communists, and he was also considered an expert on the peasant question.

Lominadze immediately criticized the speaker for excessive leftism, but shortly after the meeting Qu Qiubai, the acting general secretary, directed the King of Hunan—who was elected a candidate member of the Provisional Politburo[36] at the August 7 Emergency Conference—to return to his native province to lead the Autumn Harvest uprising.[37]

In late September or early October, Qu Qiubai left Wuhan and moved to Shanghai along with the CC staff, including Deng Xiaoping. Before they moved, in mid-September, Qu Qiubai received via the Russian consul in Hankou Comintern directives to announce the beginning of a struggle by the communists to establish soviets in China.[38] In a number of rural districts, the blazing Autumn Harvest uprisings began to be called the Soviet ones, although soon they were all defeated. The remnants of the insurgent troops fled into the inaccessible, often mountainous, regions where they switched to guerrilla warfare. Mao Zedong and his detachment of fifteen hundred battle-weary troops also retreated to the mountains, to Jinggang, located on the Hunan-Jiangxi border. In April 1928, he was joined by troops under the command of Zhu De, which had participated in the Nanchang uprising and came to this area following the communists' defeat at the port of Swatow.[39]

The Provisional Politburo and Secretariat of the CC remained in Shanghai. Following the classical dogmas of Marxism, the leaders of the Comintern and the Chinese Communist Party continued to view the working class as the main motive force of revolution, and therefore they tried to revive the proletarian movement that had been extinguished in the summer of 1927. To begin with, on December 11, 1927, they organized an uprising in

Canton under the leadership of the Comintern emissary Heinz Neumann. Naturally, this bloody affair, known in history as the Canton Commune, also ended in defeat. But the leaders of the CCP did not give up. They paid particular attention to Shanghai itself despite the worsening situation in the urban underground and the constant mortal risk. Secret police terror was merciless; their top priority was the pursuit of communists and other leftists. On March 7, 1928, the Guomindang government declared a state of national emergency. Disseminating ideas incompatible with Sun Yat-sen's Three Principles of the People[40] was deemed a "political offense" punishable by fifteen years' imprisonment. Those who "disturbed peace and order," "incited disturbance of peace and order," "collaborated with bandits," or "conducted propaganda campaigns against the state" were subject to the death penalty.[41] From mid-April to mid-December 1927, more than fifty-six hundred persons were arrested in Shanghai and neighboring Jiangsu province, of whom two thousand were executed.[42] During that time the Communist party shrank from almost fifty-eight thousand to ten thousand persons.[43]

Everyone tried their best to disguise themselves. Two top communist leaders, Zhang Guotao and Li Lisan, tried to pass themselves off as brothers who had come to Shanghai from the provinces in search of a good doctor. Zhang had a very pale face and therefore pretended to be sick, while Li, in the presence of strangers, was always asking about his health. They lived in a luxurious six-room apartment in the International Settlement (wealthy people aroused less suspicion).[44]

Deng Xiaoping also played at being a rich man. In the very heart of the International Settlement, in one of the alleys off busy Wuma Street, he initially "owned" a small shop, and then an antique store.[45] He dressed in luxurious Chinese gowns, wore fashionable hats, and smoked expensive cigarettes. In fact, by then he had become a person of some significance, at least in underground circles. His secret office was located on the west side of the International Settlement, in the small dead-end alley Bodeli, not far from Tongfu Avenue, in a two-story stone house behind no. 700 (now no. 9 in Alley 336 on Shimenyi Street).[46] This was the office of the Central Committee of the CCP. It was there that Deng came every day to "deal with CC administrative issues and questions of a technical nature."[47] Recognizing his diligence and capacity for work, in mid-November 1927 Qu Qiubai appointed Deng secretary of the Provisional Politburo, and one month later he promoted him to director of the Secretariat of the Central Committee.

Deng Xiaoping's immediate boss now was Luo Yinong, who had also studied in Moscow, but earlier than Deng Xiaoping, in 1921–1924. On April

15, 1928, however, he was arrested, and executed six days later, after which Zhou Enlai took over.[48] During both Luo Yinong's and Zhou Enlai's tenure, Deng maintained files about the addresses, aliases, and secret passwords of all the party organs and leading cadres, and he was responsible for documentation, financial matters, and preparing and conducting conferences of higher-level party organs. In addition, he maintained links with local organizations and branches of the Central Committee and arranged transportation under the CC's purview. Moreover, he prepared the agendas for Politburo meetings. In other words, he did everything he had done before, only now he was no longer a simple secretary but the head of the entire secretarial apparatus. Furthermore, he could participate in all the leadership meetings and express his own views. Meanwhile, he continued to take the minutes of the sessions of the Provisional Politburo, only occasionally entrusting that task to someone else.

In the spring of 1928, another important event occurred in Deng's life. He married Zhang Xiyuan, the same attractive girl with bobbed hair, fine black eyebrows, and full lips whom he had befriended in Moscow. She returned to China in the fall of 1927 and was soon assigned to the Secretariat in Wuhan, where Deng, who became her boss, began to court her. He was young, and Zhang was not only pretty but also good-natured, cheerful, pure-hearted, and utterly devoted to the party. She moved to Shanghai with him in the fall of 1927, and after a while they began living together. They had a luxurious wedding with more than thirty guests in an expensive Sichuan restaurant in downtown Shanghai; after all, Deng was posing as a wealthy merchant. Zhang looked irresistible with a carefully coiffed and elegant hairdo, high-heeled slippers, and a long silk qipao with slits up to her thighs. She was "a rare beauty," Deng Xiaoping recalled many years later.[49]

The banquet cost a fortune, but very few knew it was paid for by Deng's father, whom Deng had gotten in touch with after moving to Shanghai.[50] Papa Wenming, who respected tradition, could not "lose face" by not covering the cost of the wedding of his son, who may have been a good-for-nothing but was still beloved. Soon enough the son repaid the father with base ingratitude. Learning that his father had gradually recouped his financial situation and was involved in business—along with several fellow villagers Wenming had opened a silk-weaving factory in Paifang that began supplying silk filament to Shanghai—in his father's name Deng asked for a loan from his father's urban partners. They complied. It never occurred to them that the wealthy merchant, the eldest son of a man they respected, was an ordinary swindler.

After receiving a handsome sum, Deng gave it to the party and soon, without compunction, changed his residence.[51]

He did so although he knew very well that his father's family was not flush with money. Papa Wenming had plenty of dependents to support. After the death of Deng's mother in 1926, he took a new wife, née Xiao. She gave birth to his fourth son, whom he named Xianqing. But several months later his wife took ill and soon passed away. The unlucky Wenming married for a fourth time, now to a widow who had a nine-year-old daughter from her first marriage. His new wife's name was Xia Bogen, and she came from a rather poor barge hauler's family. She was only five years older than Deng Xiaoping, but unlike him she had known need and suffering since early childhood. Thus her marriage to Wenming was her salvation, especially since Wenming brought up her child as his own.

Therefore, in addition to himself, Deng Wenming also had to feed and clothe his own mother (that is, Deng's grandmother, who was still living), his wife, three sons (two of whom were already being educated at his expense), and two daughters. He also continued to support his prodigal and eternally ungrateful son. The elder Deng was an eminently respectable citizen. Esteemed in his home county, in 1928 he was even appointed commander of the Guang'an County peacekeeping force and commander of the six or seven hundred men in the county self-defense battalion.[52] On market days, his commodious teahouse, which he had opened across the street from Deng's Beishan School, was always packed. People came to socialize, shoot dice, and listen to the wise man: Lao Deng (Honorable Deng) settled disputes, dispensed advice, and often helped out unfortunates.[53] According to the recollections of his fellow villagers, "this man with long, drooping whiskers" invariably earned "the respect of those around him as a good host, military commander, public figure, and judge."[54] Could that be why Deng Xiaoping treated his father so abominably? Was he manifesting proletarian class feeling? Perhaps he simply felt that he had a right to part of his father's property.

Meanwhile, after their wedding the young couple moved to a small, two-story house that Zhou Enlai and his wife, Deng Yingchao, had rented on the west end of the International Settlement on Zunyi Lane, a narrow alley just off a lively thoroughfare. Zhou and his wife lived on the second floor and Deng Xiaoping and Xiyuan on the ground floor. The political situation in the city continued to deteriorate daily since, in addition to Chiang Kai-shek's secret police, the police of the International Settlement and the French Concession—where the main CC offices were located—were also ferreting out communists. Underground became increasingly dangerous. Deng recalled,

> We did secret work in Shanghai under very difficult conditions. . . . I
> never got arrested. . . . That was rare. Nevertheless, there were quite a
> few risky occasions, of which two were quite bad. . . . I went to have a
> secret contact with Luo Yinong. As soon as we finished talking, I left
> through the back door just before the policemen came in through the
> front door. Luo Yinong was arrested. . . . It was a matter of less than
> one minute. Luo Yinong was shot later. The other happened when I
> was living with Premier Zhou, elder sister Deng, and Zhang Xiyuan
> in the same house. . . . The policemen had found out Zhou's residence
> and were coming to search the place. . . . I did not know this as I was
> away from home at the time. I knocked on the door when the police-
> men were searching the house. Luckily, we had a [Communist party]
> member . . . infiltrating the enemy secret service who was inside and
> answered that he was coming to open the door. I found it was not the
> right voice and immediately left, thus avoiding a disaster. I didn't even
> dare to walk in that lane in the following six months. . . . The differ-
> ence of even a few seconds could have had grave consequences."[55]

The overall situation in China varied. In most cities, as in Shanghai, the Guomindang police raged unchecked, but on the Hunan-Jiangxi border, in Hubei, Shaanxi, and several other rural areas, the movement to establish sovi-ets gathered strength. In June and July 1928, the Sixth Congress of the CCP was held to assess the political situation and work out the party's long-term line. Because of the White Terror in China, the congress took place in the USSR, not far from Moscow, with 118 delegates taking part, among them top party officials. Deng Xiaoping, along with Li Weihan and two other important party cadres, Ren Bishi and Luo Dengxian, remained in Shanghai, entrusted with the daily conduct of CC business.[56] It is evident that in this period Deng had already begun to play a rather important role, not only in the party's organizational but also in its political affairs. Most important, he held his own in the narrow circle of the highest party leadership. He was respected and also consulted.

After the Sixth Congress delegates returned to Shanghai; however, Deng's role in party affairs was now somewhat diminished. The new general secretary of the Central Committee, forty-eight-year-old Xiang Zhongfa, an important leader of the workers' movement, replaced Qu Qiubai, who had been severely criticized in Moscow for the defeat of the uprisings in 1927. Xiang was uninterested in Deng's opinions. Instead he relied on the energetic and effective Li Lisan, a talented and well-educated intellectual, who from November 1928 headed the Department of Propaganda and Agitation in the new Central Committee. Zhou Enlai continued to wield considerable influence as leader of the Organization Department. It was this trio that led the party. Deng reverted to carrying out purely secretarial functions, working directly under Zhou, but he was no longer involved in political questions.

Soon, in May 1929, news reached Shanghai that leftist-oriented generals had come to power in Guangxi province in southwest China as the result of a struggle between Chiang Kai-shek and local militarists. These were the cousins Yu Zuobai and Li Mingrui, who had helped Chiang defeat the Guangxi reactionary clique. In this war they followed their own policy and, although assisting Chiang Kai-shek against the militarists, did not endorse his struggle against the communists. Moreover, they actually collaborated with the Communist party via Yu Zuobai's brother, Zuoyu, who had been a member of the CCP since October 1927. After seizing power in the province with the support of Chiang Kai-shek, who was ignorant of their ties with the CCP, they asked Xiang Zhongfa to send them a contingent of capable party workers.

The Politburo decided to dispatch several dozen communists to Guangxi, including military and political cadres experienced in underground struggle. On the advice of Zhou Enlai, they sent Deng Xiaoping as the main emissary of the Central Committee. On August 27, Deng turned the directorship of the Secretariat over to a secretary of the Organization Department and set out. It was time for the young and talented organization man to show what he could do in a new setting. With the help of Yu Zuoyu and other communists who were already in Guangxi, he was supposed to organize an anti-Guomindang uprising among the troops of Yu Zuobai and Li Mingrui, and thereby encourage the swiftly developing soviet movement in other regions.

This new assignment was gratifying. For the first time, Deng was the boss on a regional scale, able to make independent decisions on which the success of the communist movement in all of southwest China would depend. Of course, he could be independent only within certain limits, namely, those prescribed by the Sixth Congress of the CCP in June–July 1928, subsequently confirmed by the CC and the Politburo. The Sixth Congress had taken place under the guidance of Nikolai Bukharin, the most important theoretician of the New Economic Policy, one of the leaders of the Comintern, and the second-ranking leader of the Russian Communist party and the Soviet government after Stalin. On his instructions, the congress had adopted a declaration saying that the present stage of the Chinese revolution was "bourgeois-democratic," despite the "defection of the national bourgeoisie to the camp of the imperialist-landlord counterrevolution." This was Marxist-Leninist jargon for the coups of Chiang Kai-shek, Feng Yuxiang, Wang Jingwei, and other Guomindang leaders. Therefore, in "semifeudal" China, it was not possible at present to implement a socialist policy. Instead, they understood, one should aim to curtail the power of the "landlords," rural gentry, and officials in the countryside; arm the peasantry; establish soviet power; confiscate landed property of "landlords," clans, and temples without compensation and redistribute it among landless and land-poor peasants; annul usurious loans; cancel land and other burdensome contracts and arrangements, both oral and written; and replace all taxes and extortionate fees levied by militarists and civil authorities with a single, progressive, agricultural tax.[57]

The Politburo continued to follow this line even after receiving a written Comintern directive on the peasant question in mid-August 1929, which, contrary to the decisions of the Sixth Congress, stated that because "kulaks" (wealthy peasants) frequently played an "openly or covertly counterrevolutionary role in the movement, therefore, one had also to struggle against them resolutely."[58] This letter reflected a radical change in the Soviet political situation where Stalinist collectivization was unfolding, accompanied by criticism of Bukharin's "rightist pro-kulak" views. Identifying peasant-proprietors as the main target of struggle in the USSR led the Comintern to advance a new slogan in other countries as well, namely, "down with kulaks." This new line replaced the spirit that had animated the New Economic Policy: the appeal to liquidate only "landlords'" land ownership. On August 17, 1929, with Deng taking the minutes, the members of the Politburo timidly voiced their disagreement with the new Comintern policy, and for a time they actually delayed execution of the directive. [59] It was not because they were moderates; they simply did not understand what to do since the letter from the Comintern had not formally revoked the resolution of the Sixth Congress regarding the "bourgeois-democratic" character of the Chinese revolution. So how could they reconcile these two diametrically opposed documents?

In general, however, Deng was not worried because he had firm guidelines: base all work on the decisions of the Sixth Congress. He did worry about his wife, who was in her fourth month of pregnancy. Zhou Enlai, Deng Yingchao, and Zhang Xiyuan's younger sister Xiaomei, who was also in Shanghai with her husband, calmed him down, promising they would look after her. Bidding his beloved goodbye, with a light heart Deng boarded a ship sailing for Hong Kong. From there he intended to slip through Hanoi and arrive in Guangxi, which shared a border with French Indochina. He was accompanied by a modest fellow in horn-rimmed glasses, a certain Gong Yinbing, a native of Hunan and former worker in the Accounting Department of the Party Secretariat. Gong was supposed to work as a courier who would henceforth travel regularly back and forth between Guangxi and Shanghai to keep the Politburo informed about the activities of Deng and his comrades and to transmit the Politburo's latest directives to them.[60]

The huge ship slowly departed the wharf, and the skyscrapers of Shanghai receded further and further. Finally, they disappeared into the hot and humid air. A new page had turned in Deng's life. But he did not yet know just how important it was.

The Moloch of revolution demanded sacrifices. The time had come for Deng to place his own fleeting family happiness on its bloody altar. Five months later, in January 1930, after a difficult birth, Zhang Xiyuan would die along with her newborn infant, a daughter, whom they had not even managed to name. At that time, Deng would be in Shanghai again for just a few days on party business.[61] He managed to see his dying wife and baby, but could do nothing for them.

After many years, the pain of his loss dissolved amidst new events, and the image of his first wife faded into the past. When, in March 1979, representatives of the Revolutionary Committee of the Bureau of Civil Affairs in Shanghai asked him to talk about the death of Zhang Xiyuan, he had only an approximate recollection of the date of her passing. "Zhang Xiyuan," he said, "passed away in Shanghai in the winter of 1929 (around November or December)."[62] Against the background of great revolutionary events, which were etched deeply in memory, the death of rank-and-file persons, even those near and dear, paled in significance.

4

The Guangxi Experiment

DENG AND GONG arrived in Hong Kong in early September 1929. Disembarking on Victoria Island, they hired a rickshaw to take them to their hotel, located on the northern end of the island. The leaders of the Guangdong Committee of the CCP, Nie Rongzhen and He Chang, who also directed the work of communists in Guangxi, lived close by. Deng went to see Nie and He for a briefing on the situation there.

He learned that in January 1928, the Guangdong Committee had sent several groups of Guangxi comrades, who took part in the failed December 1927 Canton uprising, back to their native province.[1] Most of them settled down in Nanning, the Guangxi capital. They were led by Yu Zuoyu, the brother of General Yu Zuobai, who, in 1929, would become one of the masters of Guangxi; Chen Haoren, Zhang Yunyi, and Gong Chu. The Guangdong committee was linked with them via an agent who traveled back and forth between Nanning and Hong Kong.[2]

The Nanning communists were trying to bring local military leaders Yu Zuobai and Li Mingrui over to their side, establish CCP control over the provincial armed forces, and infiltrate the military government of Guangxi in the hope of seizing power and eventually establishing a new Soviet region. These ambitious goals were pursued in a conspiratorial manner under the flag of the "united front" that had operated during the Northern Expedition.[3] Meanwhile, in the high mountain district of Donglan in northwestern Guangxi, inhabited overwhelmingly by national minorities, guerrilla detachments under a local native son, Wei Baqun, were active. (The Zhuang minority constituted 80 percent and the Yao 12 percent of the local population, while Han Chinese were just 8 percent.) Wei Baqun, himself a Zhuang, had extensive landholdings, yet after reading Sun Yat-sen, Lenin, and Chen Duxiu he sponsored "peasant movement courses" in November 1925 near

his village. The graduates, mostly fellow tribesmen, assisted Wei in organizing an "antifeudal struggle." In the autumn of 1926, Wei, known locally as
Elder Brother Ba, armed local Zhuang poor peasants and seized the county
seat, where he established a revolutionary committee. The CCP Guangxi
Committee then dispatched several communists to him, including Chen
Mianshu, whom Wei appointed as county head.[4] After Chiang Kai-shek's
coup in April 1927, the Guangxi militarists succeeded in driving Wei Baqun's
troops into the mountains, but on the advice of the communists Yu Zuobai
began to help Elder Brother Ba with arms and ammunition.[5] In August 1929,
Wei joined the CCP.[6]

This was what Deng learned from his briefing. The next day Deng and
Gong left Hong Kong together with He Chang.[7]

They reached Nanning a week later. General Yu Zuobai, a portly
middle-aged man dressed in a handsome white full-dress uniform, greeted
them cordially. Since June 1929, he had been the chairman of the Guangxi
government. Deng, who introduced himself by the fictive name Deng Bin
(Deng "the Refined"), accepted Yu's offer to serve as a secretary in his chan-
cellery. In that position it would be easier for him to win Yu over. He recalled,
"I met with Yu Zuobai several times and did some united front work. . . .
Meanwhile, I carefully assigned those cadres sent by the Central Committee
to suitable posts in Yu's government."[8]

In mid-September, the first congress of communists took place in the province. According to Deng's daughter Maomao, in words probably taken from
Deng himself, at the congress he "spoke about the current situation and tasks."[9]
It is difficult to confirm this; more likely, either Deng's daughter or Deng himself got things mixed up. The same Maomao asserts that "on the instructions
of the Central Committee, and according to his experience in secret work
over the years, Father did not appear in public in Guangxi. He worked only
in the Party and maintained contact with only a very few people."[10] How then
could he have given a speech at a well-attended provincewide forum? Apropos
of this point, in the report of the Guangxi Special Party Committee to the
Guangdong committee, no mention was made of any speech by Deng, only of
a report by a representative of the Guangdong committee (that is, He Chang),
a work report of the Guangxi Special Party Committee, and speeches by
county representatives.[11] The first congress unanimously endorsed the Central
Committee line and chose a new, seven-person Special Committee headed by
Lei Jingtian, who was the same age as Deng.[12]

Naturally, Lei had to defer in all matters to the CC representative, namely
Deng, the de facto head of the Guangxi party organization as he himself later

recalled.[13] For now, however, he covered his links with the leadership of the Special Committee, meeting with individual comrades in a safe house on the second floor of a small dilapidated store named Bright Lights, which sold gas lamps.[14] At one such meeting a decision was taken to form the Guangxi Action Committee, headed by He Chang, Deng, and Gong Chu, for the purpose of organizing a future uprising.[15]

Meanwhile, in mid-September, General Yu Zuobai was preparing to wage war against Chiang Kai-shek himself. Considering this sheer folly, Deng and the other communists tried to dissuade Yu lest his almost certain defeat undo all their efforts to establish communist control over the Guangxi troops. But Wang Jingwei, former leader of the Guomindang leftists and again a rival of Chiang Kai-shek, was egging on General Yu, who shared Wang's views and paid no attention to the communists. On September 27, 1929, General Yu proclaimed an anti–Chiang Kai-shek campaign. On October 1, his close comrade-in-arms General Li Mingrui, commander of the Guangxi Peace Preservation Forces, invaded Guangdong and General Yu followed suit. Happily for the communists he appointed Zhang Yunyi, a member of the CCP from 1926, commander of the garrison forces in Nanning.[16]

Apparently after consulting with other members of the Action Committee, Deng made what was the only correct decision in this situation. He issued an order that if the forces of Yu and Li were defeated, Zhang Yunyi should immediately launch an uprising among the troops remaining in Nanning, the 4th and 5th Guard detachments under the command of Zhang Yunyi and Yu Zuoyu respectively. These units contained many communists, for example more than one hundred in command positions in the 4th Detachment.[17] The Combined Cadet Detachment deployed in the city was almost entirely "red." It, too, was to rise in rebellion. With Nanning threatened by Chiang Kai-shek's forces, the goal was to remove all the troops loyal to the CCP from the city. The 4th and the Combined Cadet Detachments were to be redeployed three hundred miles to the northwest along the upper reaches of the Youjiang River (Right River), and the 5th Detachment one hundred miles to the southwest along the upper reaches of the Zuojiang River (Left River). This was feasible since Nanning is located along the riverine artery of Guangxi, the Yongjiang River, formed by the confluence of these rivers, all navigable, making it easy to transport troops and equipment. The county seat of Bose located in the upper reaches of the Youjiang, with a population of more than sixty thousand, would be the base, and located in the upper reaches of the Zuojiang was the county center of Longzhou, which was only slightly smaller.

These cities were carefully chosen. Bose was one of the largest Chinese staging posts for the opium trade, and Longzhou was the main provincial customs post, close to the Indochina border. Seizure of the Bureau to Combat the Opium Trade, located in Bose, promised substantial profits to the communists. The bureau openly engaged in collecting a semilegal opium tax from the traders who shipped in narcotics from neighboring provinces, and in selling it through countless opium dens and stores. "The communists planned to collect this tax for a certain time just as the previous authorities had done despite the harm it brought to the people. That way we could resolve our own economic problems," Gong Chu wrote.[18] Seizure of the Longzhou customs post, which was managed by the French, promised similar profits. They could also "borrow" substantial sums of money from the wealthy landowners (*dizhu*) who lived in these two cities.

Bose was especially wealthy. Caravans consisting of hundreds of horses laden with opium arrived periodically from Guizhou and Yunnan, filling the streets. Commercial agents from Hong Kong, Shanghai, and Canton "are said to purchase opium here. . . . Hundreds of horses throng the streets and within the stores the black, flat shaped cakes of opium are rigidly inspected by agents."[19]

After receiving his orders, Zhang Yunyi quickly dispatched one battalion each from the 4th and 5th detachments to the regions of Youjiang and Zuojiang to prepare for the retreat, while Deng contacted the center via underground radio and informed Shanghai of his decision. The Central Committee approved.[20]

Meanwhile, after suffering a crushing defeat, Generals Yu Zuobai and Li Mingrui returned to Nanning, in time to sail immediately for Longzhou along with the remaining battalions of Yu Zuoyu's 5th Guard Detachment. From there General Yu Zuobai left for Hong Kong, explaining to his associates that he had to pay urgent attention to his health. His "treatment" lasted almost ten years. He returned to China only after the beginning of the anti-Japanese war in 1937.

After the departure of the 5th Detachment, Deng and Zhang Yunyi withdrew the roughly two thousand men of the remaining battalions of the 4th Detachment and the Combined Cadet Detachment from Nanning. They set sail for Bose accompanied by all members of the Guangxi Special Party Committee.[21]

During the eight-day journey, there floated before Deng's eyes an unbelievably beautiful but wild and tropical country, which one of his contemporaries, who had visited these places five years earlier, described very well:

Landscape . . . teems with fantastic rock peaks with strata at curious angles. . . . Labyrinths of this stratified black rock, evidently volcanic and filled with cavities caused by air bubbles in the molten mass from which they came, disclosed constantly varying forms. . . . Where Shantung [Shandong] is credited with 680 and Kiangsu [Jiangsu] with 620 people to the square mile, Kwangsi [Guangxi] is guessed to have only sixty-six, fewer than any other province of China proper. Nothing could be a greater contrast than the intense fertility and excellent transportation of nearby French Indo-China and this Kwangsi neighbor, with the same husbandry, the same tools, the same slow and uncertain means of transport, even the same banditry, as three thousand years ago. . . . Remnants of aboriginal races . . . still occupy infertile regions in the southwest.[22]

In this area the rich commercial city of Bose looked like the center of the universe. Located at the foot of a mountain ridge where a small tributary joined the Youjiang, which then turned sharply from south to east, the city must have made a considerable impression on the poor mountain dwellers. A typical medieval Chinese city, surrounded by a fortress wall with iron gates, it received its name in 1723 from the Zhuang village Bosezhai, which once occupied the site. In the Zhuang language this means "good place to wash clothes." It contained many tile-roofed stone houses belonging to the local nobility as well as family temples, stores, markets, restaurants, and, as already noted, opium dens.

Arriving on October 22, Deng lodged at a local hostel for Cantonese, a very beautiful early eighteenth-century private house built in traditional south Chinese style and picturesquely located downtown on the river bank. The furnishings in the windowless second floor room that Deng shared with Zhang Yunyi were spartan, two wooden benches covered with plain mats and two small tables with kerosene lamps.

On arrival, Deng convened a meeting of the party committee, which decided to expose the troops and local population to communist propaganda only gradually. They also urgently needed to organize armed detachments from among the urban poor and handicraftsmen, which, together with the communists, would confront the "counterrevolutionaries." (In Bose and throughout Guangxi there was no modern industry.)

No one knew what else to do since the radio link with Shanghai had been lost as soon as they left Nanning and they had failed to restore it. Hoping to receive instructions in Hong Kong, they dispatched the courier, Gong

Yinbing, who, in addition to a detailed oral report, was supposed to deliver a letter to the party leadership from the Guangxi Special Committee regarding the events of September and October.[23] While awaiting his return, they opted to maintain the united front, presenting themselves as representatives of Yu Zuobai, to refrain from proclaiming soviet power, as well as maintain the old *yamen* (office) and collect taxes at the same rate as before, and merely replace the *duban* (ruler) of the Upper Youjiang River Region with Zhang Yunyi.[24]

During the following purge of "counterrevolutionary elements" from the troops, they shot only one officer, the commander of the 3rd Battalion. The other politically unreliable officers were "escorted with honor" outside the boundaries of the region, which embraced eleven counties. Local township and county chiefs who manifested "reactionary inclinations" were treated the same. Only one of them was executed.[25]

In late October, a special messenger from the Zhuang communist leader, Wei Baqun from Donglan county, who had heard that party comrades had come to Bose, arrived to pay respects to Deng and *duban* Zhang. He gave them money seized during the "antifeudal" revolution. In return, Deng provided Wei Baqun (Elder Brother Ba) with secret instructions to further expand the struggle against *dizhu* (landlords) regardless of the formal conditions of the united front.[26] To this end, he presented him with two or three thousand rifles.[27] Deng could be blunt with Wei and his emissary: only in the old guerrilla region of Donglan, some seventy miles northeast of Bose, did the communists enjoy popular support. There was almost no communist activity in other counties of Upper Youjiang, and the peasants regarded the communists either with suspicion or hostility.

Part of the difference was that Wei had been the first to organize the masses, as far back as the mid-1920s. More to the point was that in Donglan county and its environs the local revolutionary struggle was greatly influenced by interethnic contradictions between the Zhuang and the Han Chinese. The overwhelming majority of peasants there were Zhuang. They were basically the ones who took part in Wei's guerrilla movement, joining its ranks not from class but rather from anti-Chinese sentiment. Divided along clan and tribal lines, they found common ground in their historically rooted hatred of the Chinese. Their ancestors had been the masters of Guangxi prior to the advent of the Chinese, who settled there beginning in the seventh through tenth centuries. The new settlers forcibly chased the Zhuang into the mountains, seized the fertile valleys, and levied excessive taxes. The result was that "relations between the Han and sinicised Chuang [Zhuang], and the tribal people approached a state of permanent warfare."[28] Having lost the land of their forefathers, but preserving their language and culture, the Zhuang struggled against the Han generation after generation. In the mid-nineteenth century, for example, many of them joined the Taiping Rebellion (1851–1864), which aimed to overthrow and replace the ruling Manchu (Qing) dynasty. The rebellion was led by members of the poor Chinese Hakka clans (the so-called guest people), who resettled in Guangxi, mostly in the eastern and some in the northern and southern regions,[29] after the first wave of Chinese migrants. As latecomers, they, like the Zhuang, were forced to settle on infertile lands. Naturally, the members of the wealthy Chinese clans (*bendi*, i.e., core inhabitants) who had seized the valleys exploited the newcomers by renting them land on crushing terms. The result was a colossal rebellion, in which all the dispossessed like the Hakka as well as the Zhuang and many paupers and rural riff-raff gathered together. More than twenty million people died in the resulting firestorm of war that swept through south and east China at the time.

It was this burning antipathy toward the Han that motivated the Zhuang to take up arms in the mid-1920s, especially since their lives had continued to worsen in recent times. With the establishment of militarist rule, tax rates in Guangxi exploded. In addition to the basic land tax, there were dozens of others—on irrigation, to combat natural disasters; on commerce, contracts, purchases of butter, tobacco, tea, kerosene, coal, cloth, and even straw sandals; on raising and slaughtering pigs; on maintenance of soldiers and police; as well as on construction of military barracks. Moreover, these taxes had to be paid several years in advance. Those unable to settle their accounts were thrown into prison and beaten mercilessly.[30]

To be sure, there was considerable inequality of property within the Zhuang tribes and clans themselves. Clan chiefs along with other Zhuang landholders in Donglan county alone owned 60–70 percent of the land. Fellow tribesmen had to rent fields from them.[31] However, the overwhelming majority of ordinary Zhuang, linked to chiefs and landholders by family ties, did not think to rebel against their wealthier tribesmen. It was quite another thing to attack the Han, living in towns whose "fantastic luxury" dazzled the poor Zhuang. In the mid-1920s Wei Baqun's rebels began to "expropriate the expropriators," killing not only wealthy Han but all of the hated Han people in their rage. Before launching their missions, they performed a traditional martial ritual of severing the heads of a dozen chickens, filling vessels with their hot blood, and greedily draining them.[32]

The several dozen local communists, led by Wei,[33] who had been active prior to the arrival of Deng's and Zhang Yunyi's troops, tried their best to infuse the movement with a class character, but generally they failed.[34] The Zhuang guerrillas respected Elder Brother Ba, but they did not grasp his Bolshevik ideas, not only because they were unversed in sociology but also because the Zhuang language lacked such key communist concepts as freedom and equality. Therefore, Wei and his agitators often staged performances before the illiterate Zhuang, who did not know spoken Chinese. To explain the meaning of the word *equality*, one of the communists would hoist himself onto the shoulders of another, and then climb down and stand next to him.[35]

Obviously, wild, mountainous Guangxi presented many difficult problems that were hard to solve. For an inexperienced communist outsider, a young semi-intellectual who lacked ties with the masses and had only book knowledge of Marxism, it was almost impossible. Moreover, Deng, a Sichuanese, knew neither Zhuang nor any of the other local tongues, including the Guangxi dialect of Chinese and the language of the Hakka.[36]

None of this fazed Deng. He was just like the CCP leaders who had sent him to Guangxi. He probably thought all the communists had to do was address the same slogans of "brotherhood" of all the oppressed to both the Chinese and the Zhuang. Moreover, from a class point of view, in the final analysis many of the Donglan Chinese that Wei's guerrillas had pillaged and killed were "exploiters."

Meanwhile, in early November the indefatigable Gong Yinbing brought a directive from the Central Committee that called for a "communist coup," the proclamation of soviet power after transforming the 4th Detachment and the Combined Cadet Detachment into the Red Army 7th Corps, with Zhang Yunyi as its commander. The 5th Detachment in Longzhou would be reorganized into the 8th Corps under the command of Yu Zuoyu and soviets established there as well.[37] Gong also gave Deng an October 30 directive from the Guangdong Party Committee, approved by the CC, concerning the creation in Guangxi of a Front Committee—the supreme organ of military and political power in the areas where the 7th and 8th Corps were stationed. Deng himself, who was ordered to report in person to Shanghai, was appointed its secretary.[38]

The Central Committee decreed that the "coup" should start within ten days of Gong Yinbing's return to Bose. But after talking the situation over with Zhang Yunyi and others, Deng decided to wait.[39] Careful preparations had to be made before proclaiming soviet power and reorganizing the army. He proposed launching the uprising on the second anniversary of the Canton Commune, December 11. Gong Yinbing left for Shanghai carrying Deng's letter, which said, "We will carry out the directive of the Central Committee resolutely and finish all preparations in about forty days. Then we will announce the uprising at once."[40]

By this time the "great communist revolution" had already begun in Donglan and environs. After receiving weapons from Deng, Wei Baqun and his Zhuang warriors quickly attacked and seized the cities of Donglan and Fengshan. There and in the neighboring villages they perpetrated a genuine massacre, putting everyone and everything to fire and the sword. An eyewitness wrote, "In every inhabited place seized in the course of the struggle against the *tuhao* ['bloodsuckers'] and the *lieshen* [wealthy rural officials and teachers, literally 'evil scholars'] everything was burned to the ground. No distinction was made between the *tuhao*, *lieshen*, *dizhu*, and the [Chinese] peasants who were living under their yoke. As soon as someone was sighted, he was killed."[41]

Naturally, Chinese peasants living upstream on the Youjiang River were terrified, and "almost all . . . took the side of the *tuhao* and *lieshen*."[42] In any case they were closely linked to the local *dizhu* not only by ethnic ties but also by blood—like other Chinese, they lived in patriarchal clans. Under such conditions, to proclaim soviet power in Bose without "preparation" was truly risky, especially because a majority of rural inhabitants in the district owned land, and there were not many farm laborers on whom the communists could depend.[43]

Nevertheless, the communists believed that, despite the excesses in Donglan, they could attract the poor Chinese peasants with the simple slogan of "Rob the rich!" But they were mistaken. The social bonds between the peasants and the "landlords" trumped class consciousness even though the landlords (*dizhu*), most of whom were medium or petty landlords, exploited them mercilessly. Deng reported to the CC on the social position of the Han peasantry in the upper reaches of the Youjiang River:

> A majority of the land is concentrated in the hands of the medium and petty *dizhu*, therefore, the peasant proprietors are very poor and unable to feed themselves. In these areas land rent is 60 percent (40 percent to the tenant peasant, 60 percent to the *dizhu*). The tenants are reduced to the position of slaves; they work daily for their masters and receive nothing in return.[44]

Deng believed that consciousness of such manifest exploitation, if properly focused by effective propaganda, would inspire poor peasants to rebel. Therefore, even prior to the coup, he ordered his subordinates to "deepen the agrarian revolution and seize the property of the *dizhu*, *tuhao*, and *lieshen*." At the same time, to assure the Han peasants, he prohibited "pointless arson and killing" and replaced the numerous exactions with a single progressive tax. A special resolution was adopted protecting the property of petty merchants even as the big shots were being squeezed hard. These funds, together with opium money, enabled him to purchase the loyalty of the future 7th Corps, whose soldiers were each paid 20 yuan, a considerable sum. Meanwhile, Deng sent instructions to Elder Brother Ba to proclaim soviet power in Donglan without delay. Newspapers launched in Bose a couple of weeks earlier—*Youjiang ribao* (*Youjiang Daily*) and *Shibingzhi you* (*Soldier's Friend*)—began publishing powerful and open communist propaganda. On November 7, he organized a magnificent demonstration in Bose on the twelfth anniversary of the Bolshevik Revolution.[45]

All these measures barely influenced the mood of the Han peasants. "Only an extremely small number got involved [in the struggle]," Chen Haoren, Deng's deputy, admitted later.[46] Deng confirmed that "from beginning to end" the peasant mutinies "were organized exclusively by the Red Army."[47]

Apart from the Red Army, only the masses of urban and rural paupers and riffraff, without families or shelter, and eager to engage in pillage, demanded the blood and the treasure of the very rich or just moderately wealthy. Hungry and ragged, desperate to survive, they formed bands of roving robbers. These people, in addition to Wei's guerrillas, became the chief allies of the communists. Hearing about the 20 yuan bonus, they rushed to enlist in the communist forces.

Soon, in Bose and nearby counties, just as in Donglan, an epidemic of pillaging and killing commenced as the poor peasants and paupers attacked everyone they considered "wealthy," that is, anyone with even minimal property. Before Deng's eyes the bourgeois-democratic revolution was turning into a radical socialist revolution.

The communists, including Deng, had mixed feelings. On one hand, their local party organization expanded rapidly as movement activists sought to join the CCP. Over several months, the number of party cells increased more than tenfold.[48] On the other hand, the escalation of conflict against all the property-owning classes contradicted the line of the Sixth Congress.[49]

But Deng no longer had time to correct anything. In mid-November, obeying the Politburo order, he and two other comrades left Bose for Shanghai, disguising themselves as merchants fleeing the city. Deng intended to stop in Longzhou to inform the Guangxi general Li Mingrui and the Communist Yu Zuoyu of the decision to reorganize their forces into the 8th Corps of the Red

Army. But not far from Bose unexpectedly he ran into General Li himself en route to inform Deng of his intention to attack Nanning. The gallant general was smarting from his defeat in the war with Chiang Kai-shek and therefore sought revenge. He looked exhausted, pale, and emaciated. Deng returned with Li to Bose, where, after lengthy conversations, he finally succeeded in persuading him to return to Longzhou and focus on building up the 8th Corps and the soviets. Speaking in the name of the Front Committee, Deng even offered Li the position of commander-in-chief of the combined forces of the 7th and 8th Corps. Li agreed and soon departed. News had reached him from Longzhou of a mutiny among his troops, so he had to go and restore order.[50]

Deng tarried in Bose for two more weeks and resumed his journey only after word from General Li that the mutiny had been suppressed. He finally arrived in Longzhou at the beginning of December, but stayed just two days. He managed to convene a meeting of *ganbu* (party officials) at which he announced the Central Committee decision to transform the 5th Detachment into the 8th Corps under the command of Yu Zuoyu, and to discuss details of the coming uprising.

By the time he arrived in Shanghai in January 1930, the planned uprising had taken place in Bose on December 11, 1929. At a mass meeting, Zhang Yunyi announced the formation of the 7th Corps of the Red Army consisting of three columns (roughly equal to regiments) with a total force of five thousand men. The 4th and Combined Detachments formed the first column; the poor peasant and pauper units from nearby counties formed the second column, and Wei Baqun's guerrilla troops formed the third column. Zhang himself led the Corps while Chen Haoren, Deng's former deputy, headed the Corps' political department and replaced Deng as secretary of the Front Committee. Gong Chu became the chief-of-staff.[51]

The next day, at its First Congress in nearby Pingma, the peasant, worker, and soldier deputies from eleven counties and five villages first elected a soviet government of the Upper Youjiang River Region under the chairmanship of the communist Lei Jingtian.[52] Then they announced the confiscation of all land belonging to *dizhu* as well as the property of so-called counterrevolutionaries, by which, contrary to the resolutions of the Sixth Congress and responding to pressure from paupers and rural riffraff, they meant "rich peasants" (*funong*) in the first place. Later both Deng Xiaoping and Chen Haoren admitted that lacking a formal communist party order to confiscate the land of the relatively few *funong* in the upper reaches of the Youjiang River,[53] they introduced the euphemism *counterrevolutionary*.[54] The confiscated land was nationalized and transferred to the soviets for subsequent equal distribution among landless and land-poor rural dwellers without the right to buy or sell in the future.[55] The socialist revolution continued to develop in Bose, becoming more radical by the day.

The Politburo also veered increasingly left under continuous pressure from Moscow and the Far Eastern Bureau of the Comintern, which was located in Shanghai. In November 1929, the leaders of the CCP were finally forced to publish the letter from the Political Secretariat of the Comintern Executive Committee on the peasant question, since the head of the Far Eastern Bureau, Ignacy Rylski, was constantly demanding the CCP leaders issue a directive to local communists to arrest "all feudal elements, gentry [shenshi], landlords, kulaks, and generals."[56]

But in December Rylski again expressed his dissatisfaction with the CCP leadership, which, in his words, "often deviates from the Bolshevik line." He excoriated the leaders of the CCP for supposedly giving "unclear and incorrect" directives to the Guangxi Committee with regard to General Yu Zuobai and other "national reformers" with whom he thought it impermissible to unite. In other words, the Far Eastern Bureau basically considered Deng's "united front" work in Guangxi mistaken.[57] Although the CCP Politburo did not agree with these accusations,[58] they could not ignore them, especially because the intensified struggle against "rightists" in the Bolshevik Communist Party had led to the radicalization not only of the Comintern line on the agrarian-peasant question in China but of the Comintern's entire tactical line on the national liberation movement. The Tenth Plenum of the ECCI, held in Moscow in July 1929, made this unequivocally clear, stressing the "rightist danger" that supposedly threatened all communist parties and criticizing the "rightists" for failing to see "symptoms of a new revolutionary upsurge" in the world.

The "accuracy" of the plenum's resolutions was quickly confirmed in late October 1929, when the New York Stock Exchange crashed, leading soon to the Great Depression. This quickened new hopes among communists everywhere that the Marxist-Leninist prophesy of the inevitable collapse of world capitalism was quickly approaching. A new directive from Moscow arrived in Shanghai in mid-December from the Political Secretariat of the ECCI, drafted October 26, just when the world financial markets began to roil. It pointed out that China had entered into "a period of the most profound national crisis," which is why "the main danger inside the party at present is the right opportunist mood."[59]

Deng plunged into this increasingly leftist atmosphere as soon as he arrived in Hong Kong on the way to Shanghai. Overall his work report elicited a positive response, although not without some criticism. The CC representatives instructed him not to harbor illusions about Li Mingrui since he was a member of the Guomindang and a supporter of Wang Jingwei, the perpetual rival of Chiang Kai-shek within the Guomindang; they demanded that Deng "adopt without fail a firm position with regard to the *funong* [wealthy peasants]."[60]

Deng hastened to assure them that in Guangxi they treated the *funong* as counterrevolutionaries and that the communists generally struggled against members of the Guomindang. Yet he noted, "Of course, we should not nourish . . . illusions regarding Li Mingrui, however, in Zuojiang at present we lack sufficient subjective opportunities to get rid of him, therefore, we consider it necessary to make use of our contact with him temporarily."[61] Deng even proposed admitting General Li into the Communist party, saying that he himself and Yu Zuoyu would recommend him. (In the minutes of the discussion of his report there is no mention of this proposal, but the CC discussed and adopted it, so that from this moment commander-in-chief Li Mingrui was no longer considered a "national reformer."[62])

In conclusion, the CC representatives ordered Deng and the leaders of the 7th and 8th Corps to turn Donglan, the guerrilla base of Elder Brother Ba, into the center of the "agrarian revolution." They stipulated that "aimless and disorderly arson and killing should be halted," but "necessary" ones should continue since, generally speaking, "arson and killing play an important role in the destruction of feudal forces." As for the 8th Corps, the Central Committee representatives demanded that after the uprising 8th Corps troops leave Longzhou, link up with Zhang Yunyi's Corps, and then expand the soviet region eastward toward the provincial borders of Jiangxi, Guangdong, and Fujian, where the forces of Mao Zedong and Zhu De were operating.[63] (Deng himself proposed joining the Guangxi soviet regions with Mao and Zhu's soviet region.[64]) Finally, the CC confirmed the membership of the Front Committee of the 7th Corps and appointed Deng Xiaoping secretary as well as to a new, higher position in the 7th Corps as political commissar.

The CC so informed the Guangdong Committee in early March 1930, by which time Deng was already in Longzhou.[65] He arrived there on February 7, six days after Yu Zuoyu had been proclaimed commander at a mass meeting in the city, and two other communists as head of the political department and chief-of-staff of the 8th Corps of the Red Army respectively. The corps consisted of two columns totaling about two thousand men. Meanwhile, Li Mingrui became commander-in-chief of the 7th and 8th Corps.

After arriving in Longzhou, Deng acted in accordance with the situation. Certain sources claim that the Central Committee also appointed him political commissar of the 8th Corps with full authority to give orders.[66] His authority was enhanced because almost none of the commanders remained in town. While Deng was absent, General Li Mingrui, consumed by a thirst for revenge, had decided on his own to attack Nanning, the provincial capital of Guangxi, which was occupied by the Guomindang Guangxi army, and lassoed Zhang Yunyi into his adventure by convincing him that Nanning was poorly defended. (It is true that at this time the main forces of the Guomindang Guangxi army were deployed along the border with northern Guangdong.) Deng was horrified when he was informed that all the communist forces were deployed in the campaign. "From both a subjective and an objective point of view, an attack on Nanning is doomed to failure," he said anxiously. "The 8th Corps is in particular danger. It might be completely destroyed!"[67]

He immediately issued an order to the corps commanders to turn back, but it was too late. On February 9, news arrived that the 7th Corps had been routed at the outskirts of Nanning. The base in Bose was lost. Soon the situation in Longzhou became extremely precarious. Only some of the 8th Corps troops, under the command of Yu Zuoyu, had returned there. The others, under the command of Li Mingrui, had set out to rescue Zhang Yunyi.

On February 12, 1930, two days after the 8th Corps remnants returned, as he had done earlier in Bose, Deng announced the confiscation of all the land of the landlords and its transfer to the soviets, to be followed by equal distribution without the right to buy or sell, and the substitution of a single progressive tax in place of the numerous levies.[68] Again he exacted contributions from Chinese merchants, forbade them from removing money and goods from the city, and also demanded the seizure of all land and property of rich peasants who were helping "counterrevolutionaries."[69]

The ancient city of Longzhou shuddered violently. It had seen its share of massacres over the centuries but had been tranquil for quite some time. In 1886, Longzhou was opened to foreign trade and soon the French, who had colonized adjacent Vietnam, showed up. They and the local inhabitants managed to coexist peacefully. Now everything changed, after Deng published an impassioned appeal to the inhabitants of Longzhou in which he excoriated French imperialism. His démarche was provoked by a note from the French consul that asked the new authorities "to restore order" in the wake of widespread pillaging, arrests, and killing of peaceful inhabitants. Otherwise the consul threatened to accept the proposal by the governor of Indochina to send fifteen French soldiers and an armored vehicle to Longzhou to protect the consulate.[70]

On February 19, at Deng's urging, the urban poor, supported by 8th Corps soldiers, seized the consulate and customs house, torching the latter, and confiscated all French property in Longzhou, including banks, stores, and even the Catholic cathedral. French citizens who resisted, including the consul and missionaries, were sent packing to neighboring Indochina.[71]

This action netted the communists 150,000 yuan in silver,[72] but soon new complications arose for Deng. At the end of February, five French airplanes bombed Longzhou, dropping four-hundred-pound poison gas bombs, and although Yu Zuoyu's warriors shot down one plane and killed two pilots, it was impossible to remain in the city any longer. Moreover, Deng soon learned that the 8th Division of the Guangxi Army was advancing toward Longzhou, and five hundred French soldiers had crossed over the Vietnam-China border.[73]

Deng and Yu Zuoyu decided that some 8th Corps troops should quickly link up with the 7th Corps, the remnants of which, they assumed, were operating somewhere in the Youjiang River region. The others would temporarily remain in Longzhou but would also evacuate in case of a direct threat to the city.[74] Deng promptly set out for the first column, twenty-five miles northeast of Longzhou, intending to lead it to the Youjiang River, but his column was soon engaged in lengthy battles with a superior foe. On March 10, Deng, "lost patience and decided to lead a small company ahead, leaving the main body behind."[75] It is difficult to say if this was justified. In Deng's own words, he had to transmit some important "directives of the CC CCP to the 7th Corps . . . as quickly as possible."[76] Exactly what is unknown. In any case, shortly after Deng abandoned the troops, the first column was totally destroyed.

At the end of March, the second column of the 8th Corps, still in Longzhou, suffered a crushing defeat. In Deng's words, Yu Zuoyu "became obsessed with collecting taxes" and therefore delayed his retreat to the last moment.[77] The city was taken by the enemy, and the Corps commander fled. Yu made it safely to Hong Kong, where his luck ran out. The British police arrested him and handed him over to Guomindang forces, which, on September 6, 1930, shot him in Canton.

Meanwhile, in mid-March, Deng turned up in the upper reaches of the Youjiang. He learned that the remnants of the 7th Corps, along with units of the 8th Corps under the command of Li Mingrui, had long since left for Donglan, so he set off for Wei Baqun's territory along difficult and dangerous paths. At one point he was attacked by armed bandits who drew their swords and demanded "his purse or his life." Deng wisely handed over the twenty yuan he had on him and escaped with his life.[78]

Finally, in early April, he reached the high-mountain village of Wuzhuan, where Wei lived. An eyewitness recalled, "It was drizzling. At dusk, a smart and vigorous young man, who was holding a walking stick, wearing a bamboo hat, having his trouser rolled up over his straw sandals, and followed by a Red Army soldier, came to my door."[79] The stranger introduced himself as Deng Bin and asked to lead him to 'Elder Brother Ba'."

Deng had known Wei since the fall of 1929, in Nanning, where Wei had come to take part in one of the communist meetings. From then on, they had enjoyed very good relations and even called each other brother.[80] Receiving the wet and hungry Deng, Wei Baqun could not conceal his anxiety. He settled him next to his indoor brazier to dry off, fed him,[81] and the next day provided for his use one of the offices of his own soviet government housed in the former temple of the deity Kuixing.

Here Deng spent an entire month. The 7th Corps had vanished to no one knew where, not even Wei. In Wuzhuan Deng dedicated his time to melding Bolshevism with the Zhuang peasant movement. Along with Wei and Lei Jingtian, he drafted several documents on the agrarian question, attempting to convince the patriarchal Zhuang that their society, just like Chinese society, was actually divided up among *tuhao*, *lieshen*, landlords, rich peasants, middle peasants, poor peasants, tenants, and craftsmen. "In All-Under-Heaven poor people are one family, one poor person will not beat another." When it came to stealing and killing there were enough *tuhao*, *lieshen*, landlords, and rich peasants for everyone.[82]

He began to devote attention to propaganda about collective farm life. During his brief stay in Longzhou, the inhabitants in one of the district centers along the Sino-Vietnamese border took up collective cultivation of the land on their own initiative. They had not only confiscated the land of the wealthy, but almost all the land. Afterward they collected grain, livestock, and equipment from all of the homes and turned it over to the village soviet. In the village "one large kitchen was built which was under the management of the Consumer Department [of the village soviet], as well as one large cow-shed. All household buildings, agricultural tools and working livestock were used in common."[83] Deng apparently liked this experiment and drafted special "Theses on Joint Cultivation of the Land" for the Donglan Zhuang in case they decided to do this. However, he did not insist on a universal and swift transition to this type of management, instead proposing it be decided by the village soviets. The Marxists whose works he had read in Moscow in the middle of the 1920s did not advise a hasty transition to collective farms. After Deng's lukewarm attempts at persuasion, only two villages signed up for collective farming. A minority of the others were content with confiscating "landlord-kulak" land; the rest confiscated all the land but subsequently did not work it jointly, instead dividing the sown area equally among all the households, rich as well as poor. (The majority of Donglan Zhuang did not understand how one could completely deprive one's relatives of property, even wealthy relatives; it was quite another matter to take everything and divide it up equally.)[84]

Meanwhile, in early May 1930, Deng finally received news that Li Mingrui and Zhang Yunyi, at the head of their troops, had again shown up in Guangxi, not far from Donglan, approximately twenty-five miles to the east. Deng hurried to meet them. After showering each other with expressions of friendship, they decided to advance to Bose in two columns. They urgently needed money to pay their soldiers, so after capturing the city they unleashed another orgy of pillaging throughout the district.[85] However, this time many city folk and nearby villagers fled before the new communist invasion. All the relatively well-to-do merchants sailed away to Nanning, taking with them enormous stores of opium.[86]

Deng and his comrades were upset that there was little in the city left to plunder. Nor could they tarry long. The Yunnanese general Zhang Chong was advancing on Bose, and the Reds were not ready to take him on. "The Yunnan troops were good at fighting," Deng recalled later.[87] The Reds evacuated quickly to the little town of Pingma, some twenty miles downriver on the Youjiang, where the 7th Corps remained until autumn. Lacking a radio link with Shanghai, Deng was unable to report on his work or receive directives.

In late September Deng Gang, a special representative from Hong Kong, appeared in Pingma, dispatched by the Southern Bureau of the CCP Central Committee, which had been established in early 1930 as the highest organ of party power in China's southern provinces. Deng Gang had recently returned to China from Moscow, where he had studied for a year at KUTK. (In the Soviet Union he bore a strange pseudonym: Don Steele.)[88] Now he informed Deng and the 7th Corps commanders that on June 11, 1930, the Politburo had adopted an extraordinary resolution, "On the New Revolutionary Upsurge and Initial Victory in One or Several Provinces." Drafted by de facto CCP leader Li Lisan, in essence it ordered the communists to launch an immediate revolutionary struggle for power. "The revolution, which will first blaze up in China will touch off the great world revolution," the resolution stated.[89] There can be no doubt that, starting in 1929, the Comintern had pushed the Politburo to such wild adventurism by speaking of China's entry into "a period of the most profound national crisis."

The 7th Corps was tasked with proceeding to northeastern Guangxi and attacking and seizing three cities: Liuzhou, Guilin, and then Canton itself.[90] The plan was insane since the Corps then numbered just over seven thousand fighters and was facing hundreds of thousands of Guomindang and provincial militarist troops. But under pressure from the CCP Politburo, in the summer and autumn of 1930, practically all the communist troops in the soviet areas tried to carry out analogous and equally absurd plans. Mao Zedong and Zhu De, for example, unsuccessfully attacked Nanchang and Changsha, and the forces of another Communist guerrilla, He Long, threatened Wuhan.

Deng and Zhang Yunyi tried to explain to Deng Gang the difficulty of carrying out the plan, but he was unwilling to listen.[91] The Southern Bureau had assigned him the task of commanding the 7th Corps, so any discussion was out-of-place. On October 2, an expanded meeting of the Front Committee adopted a resolution regarding the campaign, and two days later, at a general formation, the troops took a solemn oath to fight to the death.[92]

In the upper reaches of the Youjiang (in Donglan), only Elder Brother Ba's troops remained. Looking forward, we will note that two years later, in October 1932, soviet power in Donglan collapsed under the enemy onslaught. Death overtook Wei Baqun at the hands of his own beloved nephew, who, tempted by a promised Guomindang reward of 1,400 yuan, one dark night stabbed his uncle with a sharp lance while he was sleeping. Afterward he handed over the head to the Guangxi authorities, who preserved it in alcohol in a glass jar. Over the next several months, they hauled it around to towns and villages throughout the province as a warning to would-be rebels. Buried in the village of Wuzhou in eastern Guangxi, the head would be discovered only in 1961. A memorial was constructed on the former site of its interment.[93] The Donglan peasants buried the body of Elder Brother Ba right after his death, at the foot of beautiful Teya Mountain (Big Tooth). In 1951, the new communist authorities transferred Wei's remains to the municipal park of fallen heroes.

All that lay in the future. For now the 7th Corps main forces began to circle around northeastern Guangxi and southwestern Hunan, vainly trying to break through to Liuzhou or Guilin. Along the way they seized and pillaged small towns, and then they fled under the pressure of the numerically superior foe. Finally, in early January 1931, after losing two-thirds of their strength, they reached the remote Guangxi town of Quanzhou, squeezed between snow-covered mountains on the Hunan border, some eighty-five miles north of Guilin. Unable to hold out any longer, Deng and Zhang now spoke out sharply against continuing the adventure. It was a bold step, but many of the troops supported their commanders. Deng Gang, unable to oppose the majority, departed to complain to the Central Committee.[94]

He must have been gravely disappointed when, reaching Shanghai a month later, he learned that the Li Lisan line had long since been repudiated by the CC. Moscow, dismayed by the lunatic plans of the CCP—which, however, its own radical rhetoric had provoked—therefore reversed course. The Comintern apparently had not expected that the leaders of the CCP would in short order attack large cities, bleed the Red Army white, and claim to be igniting the world revolution. By an irony of fate, the ECCI censured Li Lisan at the very time Deng Gang came to Deng Xiaoping, in late September 1930. On November 16, the "ECCI Letter on Li Lisanism" arrived in China, condemning Li's political line as "anti-Marxist," "anti-Leninist," "opportunistic," and "essentially" Trotskyist.[95] At an enlarged CC plenum in Shanghai in early January 1931, the Kremlin's special emissary, former KUTK rector Pavel Mif, reorganized the leading organs of the Chinese Communist Party, strong-arming his own former student, Chen Shaoyu, into the Politburo Standing Committee. After this, Chen began to dominate the leadership of the party, supported by several other fellow KUTK graduates. Including Bo Gu, a newly appointed head of the Chinese Communist Youth League, and launched a frenzied anti-Li Lisan campaign. The old leaders of the party were forced to adopt a new line despite their disdain for "Mif's fledglings."

The heroic efforts of the 7th Corps were in vain. At the end of March 1931, the new Politburo leaders demoted Deng Gang to a minor post in Guangdong, where he was killed a year and a half later at the age of twenty-nine in a battle with Guomindang forces.[96]

Throughout January, Deng, Li Mingrui, and Zhang Yunyi, unable to attack the large cities and unaware that the Li Lisan line had been repudiated, awaited word from the center. Then, on February 1, after much wandering, they entered the small northern Guangdong village of Meihua and were astonished to learn from a local communist that Li Lisan had been deposed. One can only imagine their reaction!

Deng and his comrades now decided on a correct course of action, namely, to break through by any means and link up with Mao Zedong's and Zhu De's forces in southern Jiangxi. By then, October 17, 1930, Mao's soviet region had been named the Central Soviet Area (CSA) and was the communists' main base. It was approximately seventy miles northeast of Meihua. However, the way there was blocked by the Lechanghe (now called the Wujiang), a wide and fast-flowing river. The troops were divided. One part, under the command of Deng and Li, crossed to the other side, but as soon as the remaining units under Zhang Yunyi began to force their way across, they came under enemy artillery fire. The result was that Deng and Li led their troops to Jiangxi alone and soon, after several days, reached the border of the Central Soviet Area on February 8. It was not until April 1931 that Zhang Yunyi and his fighters, after surviving many trials, reached Jiangxi.[97]

By then Deng was back in Shanghai. He had set off for that city on March 10, 1931, to report to the CC. In his own words, when he learned about the elevation of Chen Shaoyu, he was "very disturbed," since he was "not well disposed toward him." (Deng and Chen had studied together in Moscow.) Before departing, he talked things over with Li Mingrui and another member of the Front Committee, Xu Zhuo, who expressed their understanding and approved his decision to go to Shanghai. Moreover, "at this time," as Deng declared, "there was no serious enemy threat [to our troops]."[98] Xu Zhuo replaced Deng as secretary of the Front Committee, and the latter, in the guise of a merchant in medicinal plants, left the army encampment.

Perhaps this is really how it was, although several facts cast doubt on Deng's story. For example, it is reliably known that on the same day Deng left for Shanghai, the enemy attacked Li Mingrui's forces and he had to beat a hasty retreat. Deng, who was nearby in a hospital visiting troops, hearing the gunfire, wrote a note on the spot to Li Mingrui in which he said, "I assumed you have just engaged the enemy and are currently in retreat. As it is impossible for me to catch up with you, please fight your own way through to the Jinggang Mountains and meet the Red Army there. I am going to take this opportunity to report to the Party Center about the Seventh Army [7th Corps] affairs."[99] He handed the note to Xu Zhuo and left immediately.

Doesn't this indicate that a "serious threat" actually existed? Why, then, abandon his old comrades at such a difficult moment and write such a strange note? If Deng himself was afraid that he would be unable to catch up with the 7th Corps, why did he think that Xu Zhuo would be able to? Perhaps, as in February 1930, Deng had simply "lost patience" and decided to get away. It is difficult to say. One of his comrades-in-arms, a future general of the People's Liberation Army, Mo Wenhua, did not believe that Deng had left his troops after receiving approval from the Front Committee.[100] During the Cultural Revolution, Red Guards flat out accused Deng of "fleeing to Shanghai to hide from danger," thereby demonstrating "the true essence of a pitiful coward."[101] Deng then had to defend himself; he delivered a virtuoso performance in his "Autobiographical Notes," written in June–July 1968, and in a letter to

Chairman Mao on August 3, 1972. He acknowledged that in early 1931 under no circumstances "should he have abandoned the 7th Corps of the Red Army. [What I did] was one of the worst mistakes of my life . . . in a political sense." Yet he insisted that his action was "lawful in an organizational sense."[102] (This refers to Deng's having received approval from the Front Committee.) Neither Li Mingrui nor Xu Zhuo was still alive by this time, so the entire episode had to remain on Deng's own conscience.

The Guangxi experiment thus ended in total failure. Li Lisan's adventurism was only partially responsible. The radical policies of the Chinese Bolsheviks did not evoke a response in the hearts of the majority of the population of the province. The result was that agrarian reform took the form of a series of robberies and murders, an orgy of armed banditry on the part of paupers, rural riffraff, and Donglan Zhuang, actively supported by the Red Army. There was no mass movement of peasants. Deng was soon forced to admit this himself.[103]

PART TWO

The Maoist

5

The Spirit of "Five Fearlessnesses"

DENG RECEIVED A cool reception in Shanghai in late March 1931. The new leaders ignored him for a month. He was isolated in a clandestine apartment, where he may have been expected to contemplate his "grave errors," which had led to the defeat of the soviet movement in Guangxi. The Central Committee already knew about the peripatetic wanderings of the 7th Corps from Deng Gang, as well as from the head of the Corps political department, Chen Haoren, who had arrived in Shanghai two months before Deng Xiaoping after abandoning the Corps' encampment in January 1931.[1] On March 9, Chen, no friend to Deng, presented a report to the CC accusing the Front Committee of the Corps (that is, Deng himself) of "not paying requisite attention to mass work," "avoiding confrontation with the enemy," and "lacking an aggressive impulse."[2] A month later, on April 4, new accusations were lodged against the commanders of the 7th Corps by one of the field commanders who arrived in Shanghai in late February.[3] These were all serious charges.

How this issue was resolved is unknown, but since none of the top leaders accused Deng, and he was not forced to confess, we may suppose that a struggle was waged in the Politburo. Apparently, Zhou Enlai, supported by Xiang Zhongfa and Zhang Guotao, who were dissatisfied with the actions of Chen Shaoyu, blocked the passage of a negative resolution. Chen Shaoyu disliked Deng, who was "not well disposed" toward him. On March 27, Zhou, Zhang Guotao, and Xiang Zhongfa attempted to involve the Far Eastern Bureau of the Executive Committee of the Communist International (ECCI) in Deng's case, an attempt to legitimize the need to hear Deng's side of the story.[4] However, another month passed before Deng presented his report to the CC on April 29. He made no attempt to justify himself. After detailing the history of the struggle in Guangxi, he confessed to numerous errors, including following a "left-adventurist Li Lisan line," and committing a "right opportunist kulak deviation." He stated that his "central" mistake was that "in deciding all questions" he relied "exclusively on military power."[5] In brief, he essentially agreed with his critics.

Such conduct was precisely the merciless self-criticism that Chen Shaoyu and some other Politburo members required in accordance with the Chinese tradition that demanded he lose face. They could not brand him a "class enemy" because neither Zhou Enlai nor other veteran party members, linked to Deng by their common revolutionary past, would allow it. Zhou and other veterans had *guanxi* (relations) with Deng, the informal ties that were vital in Chinese society. Deng well understood how *guanxi* worked and used it to his advantage. Later, whenever a dangerous intraparty collision occurred, Deng would follow the tried-and-true tactic of boldly admitting his "sins," thereby losing face, but by relying on his ties, preserve his place in the leadership.

Chen Shaoyu and his comrades generally accepted Deng's self-criticism; the repentant Deng was kept without work in Shanghai for an additional two and a half months before he was given an opportunity to rehabilitate himself. In mid-July, assigned to work in the Central Soviet Area, he boarded a steamship for Swatow in eastern Guangdong, from where he would proceed to southern Jiangxi.

The period of idleness in Shanghai left him feeling depressed, not only because he "suffered setbacks ... in his political career, but because everything in the city reminded him of his late wife Zhang Xiyuan."[6] The previous January, he had not even been able to bury her. This was done for him by others in the party, who, for security reasons, engraved her tombstone with the alias Zhang Zhoushi.[7]

Deng managed to visit the grave several times, even bringing his younger brother Xianxiu, with whom he had been reunited after an eleven-year interval, to the cemetery.[8]

Now, sailing out of Shanghai, Deng could finally relax. His traveling companion turned out to be a beautiful young girl. Promenading on the deck with her, he could not help but admire her tender oval face, just like Zhang Xiyuan's, sensuous lips, and short-cut hair. But most of all, big doe eyes, set off by black eyebrows, that gazed at Deng with such warmth and tenderness! Born in the autumn of 1904, she was only two months younger than him. Her name was Jin Zhicheng (Jin "the Strong-Willed"), a revolutionary sobriquet, but everyone who knew her affectionately called her Ajin, which means "Goldie." (The surname Jin means gold.) Born in a village in Zhejiang province in the family of a petty merchant who gave his daughter a good education, in 1922 Ajin graduated from a pedagogical institute in the city of Ningbo and started teaching at a primary school for girls. She was soon attracted to communist ideas and joined the Communist party in October 1926. After the defeat of the CCP in the National revolution of 1925–27, she moved to Shanghai, where she engaged in party and trade union work with women. In January 1931, she was arrested and spent a month in prison but then was released "in the absence of evidence" by corrupt policemen who had received a bribe from agents of the Communist party. She was unable to remain in Shanghai, and the Central Committee assigned her to the Soviet Area. That is how she wound up on the same steamship with Deng.[9]

A mutual attraction between the two young persons setting out on a dangerous journey soon grew into ardent passion. One evening Deng and Ajin wound up in each other's embrace. From then on he began to call her his wife, and she called him her husband.

In early August they arrived at the high mountain city of Ruijin, the center of Ruijin County in the southeast of the Central Soviet Area. To their great delight, their clandestine life was over. Red flags fluttered everywhere, and one need not fear the Guomindang secret police. Ruijin inspired radiant hopes in them. For the first time, they felt like free citizens in their own country.

"From now on call me Jin Weiying," Ajin happily addressed Deng, "and let the other comrades call me that, too."

They were sitting by the bank of a small mountain stream, and Ajin was admiring her reflection in the frigid water. The character "ying" means "reflection," and "wei" is one of the characters in the word "suweiai" (soviet).

"Good," Deng laughed. "This name sounds really lovely. So I will call you Jin Weiying [Jin "Soviet reflection"]. Although I also like to call you Goldie."[10]

Here in Ruijin they formalized their marriage.

The euphoria, however, quickly passed. Deng again found himself in the center of political struggles. The secretary of the county party committee, with a zeal worthy of a better cause, tracked down "hidden enemies" among his subordinates: social democrats, Guomindang members, and members of a secret "AB League" (AB *tuan*), established by the Guomindang in Jiangxi as far back as 1925–26 to eradicate communists. (The letters A and B indicated different levels of initiation of its members, namely, provincial and county.) The county secretary probably went berserk. During his six months in power (from February to early August 1931), he arrested and executed 435

communists for supposed ties to social democrats, including the former secretary of the county party committee, the chairman of the local soviet government, the head of the trade unions, and more than 80 percent of other
leading cadres.[11] Of course, the leaders of the AB League, social democrats,
and other anticommunists were trying to infiltrate their provocateurs and
spies into the CCP organization in order to disrupt the communist movement. They were particularly active in the early 1930s, during Chiang Kai-
shek's punitive expeditions against the Jiangxi Soviet Area, the first of which
took place in late 1930 and early 1931, and the second and third in April–May
and July–September 1931 respectively. But the secretary of the Ruijin party
committee showed excessive zeal. The purge commission he headed seized
both the innocent and the guilty and could not be bothered with looking for
credible evidence of their crimes. Many others then also acted that way. In the
soviet area of western Fujian, for example, in the same period 6,352 persons
were executed on false accusations.[12] And in December 1930, Mao Zedong's
supporters incited an armed conflict in the party organizations and army
units of southwest and central Jiangxi, known as the Futian Incident. Mao's
envoys organized such cruel purges that their victims rose up and killed their
tormentors. Nevertheless, Mao emerged victorious from this conflict. The
Futian rebels were disarmed and destroyed, and the purges continued. More
than 90 percent of party cadres in southwest Jiangxi were killed, imprisoned,
or cashiered.[13]

Deng had learned of the Futian events in late 1930 and early 1931. Later,
in a report to the Central Committee dated April 29, 1931, he expressed his
disapproval of Mao's actions, which, he believed "in reality strengthened the
AB League." Yet he also condemned the insurgents.[14]

When Deng arrived in Ruijin, Mao Zedong, Zhu De, and other leading
cadres were at the front, far from the city. In the rear region of Ruijin, there
were only a few leading persons, among whom three wholly shared Deng's
views: Yu Zehong, Xie Weijun, and Huo Buqing. Deng's wife also actively
supported him. In mid-August 1931, Yu, Xie, and Huo advanced Deng's can-
didacy for the post of county secretary of Ruijin. In early October, the former
secretary and the chairman of the county soviet government were arrested
and shot for their excessive zeal in pursuing real and imagined enemies. Deng
worked to rehabilitate the victims of political repression. More than three
hundred survivors from among the falsely accused communists were set free.
Later he recalled, "We swiftly punished the counterrevolutionaries, rehabilitated the unjustly arrested cadres, and convened a congress of soviet deputies.
The cadres, almost all of whom were local peasants, and the masses were set

into motion, and the situation throughout the county immediately took a turn for the better."[15]

At the end of September, Mao Zedong, Zhu De, and the headquarters staff of the First Front Army relocated to the village of Yeping in a suburb of Ruijin, following the communists' defeat of Chiang Kai-shek's third punitive campaign. The significance of the county center and the new county secretary grew swiftly.

Nevertheless, Deng still remained a second-rank cadre with limited authority. Yet he now met often with the leaders—Mao Zedong, Zhu De, and other members of the CC Bureau for the Soviet areas.

In early October, he chaired a massive municipal meeting to mark the defeat of Chiang Kai-shek's third punitive campaign, and he spoke after Mao Zedong.[16] Then he threw himself into establishing soviets in villages and hamlets, carried on communist propaganda among the peasants—to that end, he even founded a county newspaper, *Ruijin hongqi* (*Red Flag of Ruijin*)—and devoted great efforts to implementing agrarian reform.[17]

In dividing the land, he followed the leveling principle that Mao had expressed one year earlier in the striking formula, "Drawing on the plentiful to make up for the scarce, and drawing on the fat to make up for the lean."[18] For the communists of southern Jiangxi, this was the only practicable agrarian policy. This was the only way they could attract to their side the numerous paupers as well as the impoverished clans of migrant Hakka that had resettled here many centuries earlier but not become assimilated with the local clans' *bendi* (core inhabitants), who controlled the economy. There were even more Hakka in southern Jiangxi than in Guangxi. The mountainous region where Ruijin was located was generally known as "Hakka country." In this region there had always been few *bendi* clans prior to the advent of the migrants, and none remained after the communists arrived. The Hakka, who were constantly warring with them, destroyed them root and branch. Yet the landholdings confiscated from the *bendi* were insufficient to satisfy everyone. The only recourse was to redistribute all of the land so as to satisfy, to some degree at least, the poor strata of the population who were willing to divide everything or nothing.

In mid-October 1931, however, a letter from the CC leaders in Shanghai arrived in Ruijin, in which this agrarian policy was severely criticized and its chief advocate, Mao Zedong, accused of a "rightist, kulak [wealthy peasant] deviation," meaning that Mao gave the poor, the "kulaks," and the "landlords" equal rights to land. The Shanghai leaders said that the kulaks should be given the worst allotments and the poor the best, while the landlords should generally be given nothing.[19] In response, in early November the CC Bureau for the Soviet areas convened a party conference in Ruijin at which they showered accusations on Mao, who tried in vain to justify himself by referring to local conditions.[20] He was removed from the post of acting secretary of the bureau and labeled an "extreme right opportunist" for his "egalitarianism."[21]

Later that same month, to be sure, under pressure from Moscow, Mao was appointed chairman of the Central Executive Committee (CEC) of the Chinese Soviet Republic and of the Council of People's Commissars.[22] But this did not strengthen his position since party officials, not government officials, made all the decisions. As in all communist systems, party officials outranked government officials, who took their orders from their party superiors. Thus the campaign to unmask the supporters of egalitarianism continued to gather steam.

Deng soon also became a target. In March 1932, a commission of the Central Executive Committee investigated his county and then adopted a strong resolution: "In Ruijin, as before, they are not following the principle of 'no land whatsoever to landlords, only bad land to the kulaks.' . . . There are even places where up till now good parcels are being allotted to kulaks. . . . This situation has not yet been rectified."[23]

This criticism was dangerous, especially since by then Ruijin had become the capital of the Chinese Soviet Republic. The central authorities began to scrutinize everything that went on there. The Sword of Damocles again was suspended over Deng, but once more he was saved by an old acquaintance, this time Li Fuchun, his comrade from Paris and by now the secretary of the Jiangxi Province Party Committee. Li rescued his friend from harm's way by transferring him to the remote county of Huichang, some thirty miles southwest of Ruijin, which had just recently been conquered by the Red Army. This may have happened with the agreement of Zhou Enlai, Deng's guardian angel, who now headed the CC Bureau for the Soviet areas.

In May 1932, Deng moved to Huichang, where he remained until March 1933. A small, ancient town, it is located in a narrow valley surrounded by steep mountains that make it extremely picturesque. Deng probably took little notice of the beauty of this place. As soon as he arrived he plunged headlong into his work, which soon increased. In June 1932, the Jiangxi Party Committee appointed him secretary of the united party committee of three counties, Xunwu and Anyuan in addition to Huichang. In July he was appointed concurrently political commissar of the newly established Third Subregion Military District of the Jiangxi Military District, which included Wuping County in Fujian. His workload was staggering. He had to deal with agrarian reform so as neither to offend the poor peasants nor irritate the leadership,[24] and also to establish party organizations, soviets, and self-defense forces. He succeeded in recruiting 13,528 persons into the militia in several months, an impressive result.

But again he ran into bad luck. In early 1933, he was embroiled in a new intraparty struggle, this time between the CCP Central Committee leadership and Mao Zedong on tactical questions of how to conduct the war against Guomindang punitive campaigns. From the time of their guerrilla warfare in the Jinggang mountains in 1928–29, Mao and Zhu De had followed the tactics of people's guerrilla warfare, the basic principles of which Mao expressed in this way:

(1) Divide our forces to arouse the masses, concentrate our forces to deal with the enemy; (2) The enemy advances, we retreat; the enemy camps, we harass; the enemy tires, we attack; the enemy retreats, we pursue; (3) To extend stable base areas, employ the policy of advancing in waves; when pursued by a powerful enemy, employ the policy of circling around; (4) Arouse the largest numbers of the masses in the shortest possible time and by the best possible methods.[25]

Comintern officials, however, considered Mao's tactics "dangerous," "passive," and "deviationist."[26] They were convinced the only correct tactics were those of the Soviet Red Army, whose commanders firmly believed in the magical power of offensive warfare. Genuflecting before Moscow's authority, Chen Shaoyu and his comrades—the foremost of which was Bo Gu, who became head of the CCP at the end of 1931 after Chen left for the Soviet Union to represent the CCP on the Executive Committee of the Comintern—considered it imperative to discredit Mao despite the fact that Mao's tactics had enabled the guerrillas in Jiangxi to repulse three enemy offensives. In fact, Mao's successes undermined their own authority.

In early November 1931, at a party conference in Ruijin, Mao was criticized not only for "kulak deviation" but also for "military errors." Deng, who took part in the discussion, offered some words of support for Mao, although he did not develop his point of view. Apart from him, the only others who defended Mao's military tactics were his own younger brother, Zetan, one of the county secretaries in Jiangxi and commander of the 5th Independent Division; Xie Weijun, the secretary of eastern Jiangxi; and Mao's secretary Gu Bo. They were all mocked as the "four uncut diamonds," suggesting that unlike the "cut diamonds," they had not yet been polished.[27]

The struggle against Mao Zedong peaked in the autumn of 1932. At a plenum of the CC Bureau for the Soviet areas, Mao was again subjected to devastating criticism for "right opportunism" and relieved of his post of general political commissar of the First Front Army. Outraged, he sent two indignant telegrams to the CC, but it did not support him.[28]

Soon after, in early 1933, as a result of the huge failures in the Shanghai party organization, Bo Gu, the head of the Central Committee, and his friend Luo Fu, the propaganda chief, were compelled to move to the Central Soviet Area.[29] Since both men hated Mao, a stormy conflict was inevitable.

The occasion for this was three documents from the Fujian Party Committee that very cautiously expressed doubt about the efficacy of the Central Committee's military tactics with respect to the soviet area of southwest Fujian.[30] The party leaders, naturally, were dissatisfied, especially because prior to writing two of the documents their author, Luo Ming, secretary of the Fujian Party Committee, had met with Mao to discuss the need to employ purely guerrilla defensive warfare in the soviet area of southwest Fujian. Afterward Luo Ming convened a meeting at which he not only openly supported Mao's military tactics but also convinced the entire Fujian Party Committee that Mao was correct. This thin, shy-looking youth showed his strong character and apparently was not afraid that disagreeing with the CC's military tactics might bring down on him accusations of "betrayal."[31]

In mid-February 1933, Bo Gu and Luo Fu launched a struggle inside the party against the "Luo Ming line." The obstinate Fujianese and his supporters were removed from their posts,[32] and others who thought like Luo Ming were hunted down everywhere. On February 23, in the journal *Douzheng* (*Struggle*), the organ of the party leadership, an article appeared titled "Just What Is the Offensive Line?" in which Deng Xiaoping was attacked for the first time because "purely defensive" tactics were being followed in his subregion. Deng was targeted not simply because he had tried to defend Mao Zedong at the November party conference. Most importantly, he had actually waged guerrilla warfare, and three months prior to the article, in November 1932, under the blows of the Guangdong army he and his guerrillas had been forced to surrender the town of Xunwu, located near the border of the CSR, to the enemy. From the perspective of Bo Gu and Luo Fu, this act of surrender confirmed they were correct. What other than guerrilla warfare led to defeat?

Five days after the article appeared, the Jiangxi Party Committee sent a written directive to the three county committees that reported to Deng, declaring that Deng's "defensive line" and the "Luo Ming line" derived from a single source. Once again, trying to save his old friend, the secretary of the Jiangxi Party Committee, Li Fuchun, promptly transferred Deng out of Huichang to the post of director of the Propaganda Department of the Jiangxi Committee, thereby taking him under his wing.[33]

Meanwhile, the campaign to criticize Deng continued to grow. In mid-March he was summoned to a meeting of the CCP leadership, where he received a dressing down. Afterward, Deng, true to his practice, wrote a self-criticism in which he acknowledged his "mistakes." He understood that it was better to "lose face" several times than to lose your head once. But his self-criticism did not help. Soon Luo Fu personally arrived in Huichang and pressured party activists to adopt a resolution censuring Deng, this time defining his "mistakes" as an expression of the "Luo Ming line in Huichang, Xunwu, and Anyuan counties."[34] The other three "uncut diamonds"—Mao's brother Zetan, Xie Weijun, and Gu Bo—were also targeted as objects of struggle. The leaders of the party and their underlings intensified their attacks, though everyone understood they weren't after this foursome, but Mao Zedong himself. He was not only the main advocate of guerrilla warfare but the most authoritative opponent of Bo Gu and Luo Fu in the party.

This struggle continued throughout the spring. In the second half of April, an enlarged meeting of the Jiangxi Party Committee took place at which Li Weihan, Deng's old acquaintance from Shanghai, delivered a vicious report attacking all four "uncut diamonds" not only as "the authors of the Luo Ming line in Jiangxi" but also as leaders of an "antiparty faction" that was conducting an "anti-Comintern" policy.[35]

Deng was forced to write a second self-criticism, and then a third. "I myself feel and understand that I made mistakes," he confessed. "There is no question about it. All I want is to engage in practical work as soon as possible."[36] Yet he rejected accusations of "right deviation" and "opportunism" that Bo Gu's especially rabid supporters tried to pin on him.

In early May, Deng received a "final serious warning" and was removed from his post as director of the Propaganda Department of the Jiangxi Party Committee. The other three were also punished, and all four were deprived of the right to bear arms. At one of the meetings, before the eyes of a hushed public, they were demonstratively relieved of their revolvers.[37]

On the whole, however, the four got off rather easily. None of them was arrested or even expelled from the party. In May, Deng was sent to one of the border counties of the Central Soviet Area to conduct an inspection, but he was recalled after ten days. Someone at the top panicked that he might "take off."[38] For a while, it seems, they did not know what to do with him, but just then an influential member of the party leadership, the director of the General Political Administration of the First Front Army, Wang Jiaxiang, intervened. On the recommendation of his deputy, who had known Deng from 1929, Wang took on Deng as director of the Secretariat of the General Political Administration. And in July he appointed Deng, his assistant whose work had proved satisfactory, editor-in-chief of *Hongxing* (*Red Star*), the organ of the Central Revolutionary Council (CRC).

For Deng, the most serious consequence was in his personal life. In early May, believing her husband guilty on the basis of the accusations hurled at him at the time, Jin Weiying deserted him.

Mao Zedong was obviously correct when he once said, "[When defending the truth] one must possess 'a spirit of five fearlessnesses': first, not to fear losing one's position, second, not to fear being expelled from the party, third, not to fear that your wife will divorce you [Mao used the colloquial expression *lao po*—old lady], fourth, not to fear imprisonment, and fifth, not to fear death."[39]

Did Deng then possess this spirit in full measure? Probably not, since betrayal by the person he was closest to left a deep impression on him. Most painful was that several months later Jin Weiying, who had transferred to work in the Organization Department at the party leadership headquarters, began living openly with his worst enemy, the director of the Organization Department, Li Weihan. In January 1934, Jin and Li were married. To the end of his life, Deng could not forgive the person whom at one time he had affectionately called "Goldie." If, in his presence, someone happened to mention her name, he would immediately change the subject.

Yet his wife does not deserve to be severely censured. For both of them the revolution trumped love. From November 1931, they basically had lived apart since Ajin herself had an important party position as a county party secretary in a region far from Deng. Husband and wife saw each other infrequently. When she learned of his "monstrous crimes," his self-criticism, and the resolution of the enlarged meeting of the Jiangxi Party Committee at which she herself had been present, she naturally believed in his guilt. Anything else would have meant opposing the party.

Thereafter, Goldie's life unfolded tragically. In September 1936, she bore Li Weihan's son, but she had no time to look after him since she devoted herself entirely to party work. In March 1938, the Central Committee sent her to study in Moscow. Two months later she was transferred to the secret Chinese party school in the village of Kuchino outside of Moscow. In early 1940, she began to manifest symptoms of derangement and was placed in a psychiatric hospital, where she remained until the beginning of the Soviet war against the Nazis.[40] When Zhou Enlai and his wife, Deng Yingchao, visited her in March 1940, they were struck by her ghastly appearance: "She was completely abnormal, she had a glassy look, her dressing gown hung loosely on her, and we could not make any sense of what she was saying."[41] At the beginning of the war, all the hospital patients without relatives in Moscow were loaded into vehicles for transportation to a safer place, but what happened afterward is unknown. No documents from the evacuation survive. It is quite possible that she died as a result of a German aerial attack on the column of vehicles.[42]

Deng lost a lot because of his disgrace, but he also gained a lot, as time would tell. The criticism aimed at him, as well as his being linked with Mao Zetan, attracted the attention of Mao Zedong himself. The fighting spirit of the little, hotblooded, Sichuanese who had suffered on account of his devotion to Mao's military tactics impressed the leader of the Chinese Soviet Republic, who at the time had been stripped of any real power. Mao would always remember that Deng Xiaoping "had been subjected to criticism in the Central Soviet Area as one of four criminals named Deng, Mao [Zetan], Xie and Gu. He was the chief of the so-called Maoists."[43] Deng also spoke of how in the Central Soviet Area he was considered the "chief of the Maoists." But, he added, "I was able to stand my ground after I had been dealt a blow. And this despite being in a difficult position. There is no secret to it. After all, I am a communist and, consequently, an optimist."[44]

Meanwhile, in October 1933, a new person appeared in the Central Soviet Area destined to play an important role. He was Otto Braun, known in China as Li De and Hua Fu, a German communist sent to China a year and a half earlier by the Comintern and the IV or intelligence Section of the General Staff of the Soviet Red Army as a military adviser to the CC CCP. Prior to coming to Ruijin, he had lived for a year in Shanghai and had very close contact with Bo Gu right up to January 1933. Both tried to be supremely loyal to Moscow, and—incidentally—spoke Russian very well. Braun had also studied in Moscow, at the M. V. Frunze Military Academy. The two men soon became fast friends. Braun considered himself the chief authority on questions of military strategy and tactics of the Chinese Red Army, was intolerant of objections, and was self-assured to the point of arrogance. Much later Braun himself admitted, "I became extremely stubborn and rigid . . . and defended my views without any self-criticism."[45]

He was contemptuous of Mao's military tactics. In the military academy he was taught offensive operations above everything else. With Bo Gu's support, he foisted on the Red Army the senseless tactics of positional warfare under the slogan, "Do not yield an inch of ground!" This was soon reflected in the dismal results of military operations by CCP troops, who, beginning in September 1933, were trying to repel the Guomindang army's fifth punitive expedition.

Busy with his publishing duties, Deng refrained from getting involved in the conduct of military affairs. He spent all his time preparing propaganda articles, editing materials sent to him, and even composing and correcting proofs himself. The journal *Red Star* appeared weekly in an edition of 17,300 copies. Deng had more than enough work to occupy him. Between August 6, 1933, and September 25, 1934, he put out sixty-seven numbers of the journal.[46]

Meanwhile, the situation at the front deteriorated. Guomindang forces advanced everywhere, erecting a chain of blockhouses—powerful stone forts at a distance of one to two miles from each other—along the borders of the Chinese Soviet Republic. They tightened the ring of the blockade. Finally, Bo Gu, Otto Braun, and Zhou Enlai, who was serving as general political commissar in place of Mao, decided to abandon the Central Soviet Area. This decision was taken by the Secretariat of the Central Committee in May 1934 and ratified by the Comintern in early June.[47]

By this time new disagreements had arisen within the ruling group of the CC. Wang Jiaxiang and Luo Fu, who had replaced Mao in January 1934 as chairman of the Council of People's Commissars, began to express dissatisfaction with the authoritarian methods of Bo Gu and Otto Braun. Mao sensed an opportunity to overthrow the two by joining with Wang and Luo, along with the field commanders and commander-in-chief Zhu De, who were dissatisfied with the continuous defeats. Mao had already established good working relations with Wang Jiaxiang, and now he succeeded in winning over Luo Fu.[48]

The conspirators engaged Bo Gu and Braun in the decisive battle three months after the main forces of the Red Army in October 1934 embarked on the famous Long March from the Central Soviet Area to the west.[49] During the march, Mao, Luo Fu, and Wang succeeded in winning over a majority of the party leadership. Almost all the army commanders supported them.

Naturally, Deng, who set out with his editorial staff on the Long March in the transport field column bearing the secret code name "Red Order," was wholly on their side.

Many years later, replying to his daughter's question of what work he performed during the Long March, Deng responded humorously, "Just followed."[50] In fact during the march he continued to edit and publish *Red Star,* producing multiple copies via stencil on a duplicating machine. He sought to raise the morale of the retreating warriors and inspire faith in future victory. From October 20 to mid-December 1934, he managed to publish six numbers of the journal.

But in mid-December 1934, he was suddenly reassigned to important work on the CC staff again as head of the Secretariat. This was most likely connected to the fact that Mao, Luo Fu, and Wang Jiaxiang were just beginning to prepare their decisive blow against Bo Gu and Braun. On the eve of Deng's appointment, Bo Gu agreed to convene an enlarged leadership conference to discuss the experience and lessons of the struggle against the fifth punitive expedition. It was arranged to hold it in Zunyi, a city in Guizhou, toward which the Red Army was quickly advancing. As head of the Secretariat, Deng would be the one to take the minutes of the historic conference.

Zunyi was taken on January 7, 1935, and two days later, Bo Gu, accompanied by Otto Braun, entered the city along with Zhu De, Zhou Enlai, Deng, and a large part of the other members of the party and army leadership, with the exception of Mao, Luo Fu, and Wang Jiaxiang, who stayed in a suburb of Zunyi. All the others bivouacked in the center of town, in several spacious private houses, not far from a very beautiful Catholic cathedral built of white and gray stone with long semicircular windows decorated with marvelous stained-glass and a curved red brick roof. The architecture combined two styles, traditional Chinese and European Gothic. The communists, incidentally, commandeered the cathedral for the General Political Administration and used it for mass propaganda activities.[51]

Twenty persons participated in the conference, which began on January 15 and lasted three days. It was crowded and noisy in the small room on the second floor of the recently constructed residence where they met. Luo Fu, Mao, and Wang Jiaxiang destroyed all the arguments of Bo Gu and Zhou Enlai, who had delivered a report and supplementary report in which they laid all the blame on objective conditions. Then the trio blamed Bo Gu and Zhou as well as Braun for the retreat from the Central Soviet Area. Mao labeled their military tactics a "childish game of war." "Finally," he "turned his attack on leadership techniques" of Bo Gu and Otto Braun.[52] Deng sat in the corner and diligently took minutes. He himself did not speak; nor was there any need for him to do so. The outcome of the conference was predetermined. Otto Braun also did not speak. He considered the proceedings a kangaroo court, and he was suffering an attack of malaria. As for Zhou Enlai, as soon as he saw which way the wind was blowing he reversed himself and, taking the floor for the second time, wholly acknowledged the truth of what Mao and his associates said.[53] Obviously, he had "lost face" in the eyes of many. The result was that Mao, Luo Fu, and Wang triumphed. Luo drafted a resolution that was adopted, calling Bo Gu's report "basically incorrect," and identifying mistakes by the military leadership and in the tactical line as the main reason for the loss of the Central Soviet Area.[54]

Following the conference, the members of the Politburo held a separate organizational meeting at which Mao was co-opted onto its Standing Committee. Next he was appointed assistant to the general political commissar, Zhou Enlai, who no longer represented a threat to him.[55] Early in February, at a meeting of the Standing Committee, Luo Fu suddenly demanded that Bo Gu yield the post of general secretary to him. Mao immediately supported him. The discombobulated Bo Gu capitulated. A month later, on March 4, the new party leader appointed Mao front political commissar.[56] Thus, Mao became the main figure in the army, and it was his opinion that all the members of the Politburo began to heed.

From then on, the Chairman (as Mao, the chairman of the CEC CSR was respectfully called, often without his family name) became Deng's main teacher and protector in place of Zhou Enlai. For many years, Deng would gaze up at Mao from below, wholly acknowledging his boundless authority. Zhou, who had "lost face," would remain merely a senior comrade, one of many leaders whom, of course, it was impossible not to respect, but whom one need not worship.

Meanwhile, the Long March continued. At the end of June 1935, with Mao's agreement, and possibly on his initiative, Deng was transferred to work in the army as chief of the Department of Propaganda of the Political Administration of the First Army Group commanded by Lin Biao, one of the persons closest to Mao.[57] This was a promotion given the fact that political power in China, including, as Mao observed, in the Communist party itself, came from the barrel of a gun. Typically, later on when Deng's daughter asked her father why he had been transferred to the Department of Propaganda of the First Army Group, he replied, "In those days they were marching every day without anything to do [in the CC]." In Mao Zedong's words, Deng was "need[ed] on the front."[58]

Deng rejoiced at his new assignment. At this time he generally radiated optimism. Several days earlier, he had had a joyful reunion with another old friend, Fu Zhong, the very person with whom he had lived in Paris and then studied together at UTK. In the intervening years Fu Zhong had become a professional soldier and in the spring of 1930, after coming to Shanghai, began to work in the Military Committee of the CC. In the summer of 1931, Fu went to the soviet area on the Hubei-Henan-Anhui border north of

Wuhan. There, from April 1931, all the work was directed by Zhang Guotao, one of the leaders of the party, and Fu held the post of head of the Political Department in Zhang's Fourth Front Army. In October 1932, the army suffered a defeat at the hands of Guomindang forces and was compelled to abandon the Hubei-Henan-Anhui area. A month later, it founded a new soviet in northwestern Sichuan, which is where in mid-June 1935, after completing the first stage of the Long March, Deng encountered his old friend, now terribly thin and also matured.

Deng was overjoyed, especially because Fu Zhong, who possessed considerable authority among his troops, presented Deng with "three precious gifts: a horse, a fox-fur coat, and a pack of dried beef." "These three things were of great use indeed!" recalled Deng, who had just lost his horse. Unable to withstand the rigors of the march, it had fallen by the wayside.[59]

The trek from Jiangxi to Sichuan taxed everyone, including Deng, to the outer limit of their strength. Of the eighty-six thousand who had commenced the march in the Central Soviet Area, only slightly more than twenty thousand made it to Sichuan.

Yet the greatest hardships still lay ahead. After meeting up with Zhang Guotao's forces, the now-united Red Army, unable to remain in northwestern Sichuan, continued the march, this time toward the Sichuan-Gansu-Shaanxi border. The wild and backward inhabitants of these high mountains exhibited a visceral hatred toward the communists, and the conflicts that regularly flared up threatened to grow into a protracted war.

In July the united Red Army was reorganized and Deng's Army Group became the 1st Corps of the First Front Army. But then a conflict for power erupted between Mao and Luo on one side and Zhang Guotao on the other. In early August the troops divided into two columns, the left headed by Zhang and the right headed by Mao. They marched north in separate columns. Deng and Fu Zhong also had to part; each of them went with his own troops.

Before the communists, there stretched an enormous swampy plateau with no way around. Zhang Guotao's column marched along the left margin of the swamp and Mao's column along the right, intending to link up beyond the plateau some eighty-five miles from the border of southern Gansu.

The left column, however, got stuck in a stinking, marshy bog and was unable to cross one of the broad mountain streams that flooded across its path. It retreated to the south. Mao's column, which included Deng, reached Gansu in mid-September. Zhang Guotao demanded they return, but Mao and Luo Fu refused. The split in the leadership of the Communist party and the Red Army was not overcome until the very end of November 1936, when Zhang Guotao, who had lost his army in battles with Guomindang forces, finally turned up at Mao's headquarters to bury the hatchet. A year and a half later, Zhang fled from communist-controlled territory and openly announced he had quit the CCP.[60]

By then the Chairman had settled into a new soviet area on the Shaanxi-Gansu-Ningxia border. On October 22, 1935, in the north Shaanxi hamlet of Wuqizhen, he declared the Long March over. He announced that the Red Army had traversed twenty-five thousand *li*, that is, more than eight thousand miles. Actually it was twelve thousand *li*, itself an impressive accomplishment, but twenty-five thousand sounded more heroic.[61] No more than five thousand officers and soldiers who had managed to reach there were on hand to celebrate this event. Deng was among them. In November 1935, he again became chief of the Department of Propaganda in the Political Administration of the First Army Group, and soon he took part in extended battles with Guomindang troops that were attacking the soviet area. In one of these he barely escaped being wounded. His fox-fur coat, a present from Fu Zhong "received several bullet holes,"[62] but he himself was lucky.

In January, he went east to Shanxi province along with the main forces of the Red Army, but after the offensive sputtered out he returned to the soviet area. There, in May 1936, he was promoted to deputy chief of the Political Administration of the First Army Group, responsible for party organizational and propaganda work. Several days later he was thrown into a new military campaign in northwest Gansu, this time against Gansu militarists who were allies of Chiang Kai-shek. There he spent several months in endless battles and campaigns, earning the respect of his subordinates and the favor of the commanders. But in November he suddenly contracted typhoid, his temperature soared, he became semiconscious, "He could not eat anything. . . . So he had to be fed with some rice water."[63] During the marches and withdrawals, he was now carried on a stretcher. He recovered full consciousness only in early January 1937, by which time his army group had already returned to Shaanxi. To his surprise, he learned that in mid-December 1936 he had again been promoted, this time to chief of the Political Administration of the First Army Group.

There in Shaanxi he received another bit of news, this time sorrowful, about the tragic death of his father, Deng Wenming, to whom just a year earlier another daughter had been born. Wenming had died a mile or two from his home at the hands of a bandit who waylaid him on a narrow path as he returned from the capital of Sichuan. Deng's second brother, Deng Xianzhi, eldest of those remaining in the household, observing the time-honored traditions, buried the body of the head of the family.

During the burial, according to villagers' stories that reached Deng, something extraordinary occurred. After the grave was already excavated, a long snake, reddish-gold in color, such as no one had ever seen before, suddenly crawled out of it. Coiling itself and rustling quietly, it hid itself in the green grass. Those present interpreted it as a divine omen: everyone knew that the appearance of a snake with a diamond-shaped head, golden skin and four red dots over its eyes assumes the spirit of the Yellow River Dai Wang (King of the Yellow River). Therefore, no one doubted that this signified the appearance in the Deng family of a great man, the very one who would overturn Heaven and Earth and carry out a great revolution.[64] Perhaps they were right.

Master of the Taihang Mountains

DURING DENG'S ILLNESS momentous events were occurring that transformed the political landscape of China. In Xi'an on December 12, 1936, Chiang Kai-shek was arrested by order of the commander of the Northeast Army, Marshal Zhang Xueliang. Zhang demanded that Chiang end the civil war against the communists and lead nationwide resistance to Japanese imperialism.

By this time, the question of Japan had become the main one for a majority of Chinese. Starting from the fall of 1931, the Japanese had been pursuing a policy of steadily encroaching on Chinese territory, first occupying Manchuria, then the adjoining North China province of Rehe, and then eastern Hebei as well. In 1935 they came right up to Beiping (as Beijing had been called since June 1928[1]). Chiang Kai-shek, involved in military operations against the Chinese Soviets, was unable to offer any resistance to the Japanese incursion. However, the Chinese communists, with the aid of patriotic propaganda and demagogy and riding a wave of popular anti-Japanese sentiment, slowly but surely gained the support of many Chinese citizens indignant at Japanese aggression and Chiang Kai-shek's passivity. On Mao's initiative, on April 15, 1932, the Chinese Soviet government officially declared war against Japan.[2] Of course, the communist armies were operating far from Manchuria. Therefore, this act was purely symbolic, but in the eyes of many patriots the Communist party was turning into an authentic nationalist force.

The policy of the CCP was in line with that of Moscow. In the summer of 1935, Stalin himself, fearing German and Japanese incursions into the USSR, sharply altered the tactics of the Comintern and its constituent parties. From then on all communists were to bend their effort to organizing a new united front, in the West anti-fascist and in the East anti-Japanese. Soon the Politburo of the Central Committee of the CCP changed the name of the

Chinese Soviet Republic into the Chinese Soviet People's Republic.[3] In the meantime, a powerful anti-Japanese movement developed throughout China.

Dissatisfaction with the conciliatory policy of Chiang Kai-shek's government toward the blatant aggressors also manifested itself among Guomindang troops, particularly among the two hundred thousand officers and men of the Northeast Army of Marshal Zhang Xueliang, the former Manchurian militarist who had retreated from Manchuria under the pressure of the Japanese and redeployed to southern and central Shaanxi province. That is precisely why Zhang had come out against Chiang Kai-shek, calling on him to reconcile with the Communist party on a common anti-Japanese platform.

Soon, to be sure, Zhang Xueliang, facing the prospect of a full-scale war against the superior Guomindang army, released Chiang Kai-shek, and Chiang himself took the marshal into custody. Nevertheless Chiang finally understood that further concessions to the aggressor were impermissible.

In late March he negotiated directly with CCP representatives headed by Zhou Enlai in Hangzhou. The resulting agreement allowed the CCP to retain control over its own armed forces, consisting of three divisions totaling just over forty thousand troops, as well as to maintain the government of their own region. But they would now be subject to orders from Nanjing.[4] In early April the CCP Politburo approved this decision, which however they did not intend to implement fully.[5] Communist forces numbered more than a hundred thousand, and no one in the Communist party leadership wanted to curtail them by more than half.

As they prepared to battle the Japanese, the CCP strengthened its party organizations in North China. During May and June, Mao and Luo Fu convened a number of meetings in Yan'an in Northern Shaanxi, where the CC and Red Army Headquarters had relocated in January 1937. Liu Shaoqi, a talented party functionary who was serving as secretary of the Northern Bureau, delivered several reports. Deng had known him since 1929, initially in Shanghai and then in Ruijin. In Zunyi in 1935, they had both supported Mao.

Liu was born on November 24, 1898, in Hunan. Like Deng, he had studied in Moscow and joined the party there in December 1921. Tall, gaunt, and pale-complexioned, he was very reserved, which made him appear sullen and secretive, quite unlike Deng and many other Chinese communists, including Mao Zedong.[6] But he was decisive and courageous, and Mao's equal as an organizer and expert on Bolshevik theory.[7]

Liu called for an all-out effort to "defend North China," especially Beiping and Tianjin, which faced the direct threat of a Japanese attack.[8] On June 10, a Politburo Standing Committee resolution assigned Yang Shangkun, then serving as deputy director of the General Political Administration of the Red Army, to help Liu, and it appointed Deng Xiaoping to replace Yang and serve concurrently as deputy director of the Political Administration of the Main Front Command. (Seventeen days later the Political Administration of the Main Front Command was renamed the Department of Political Education, and Deng was elevated to its head.[9])

Thus, during these past two years Deng's career had made great strides. From June 1935 to June 1937, he had rapidly ascended the ladder of power, rising from the relatively insignificant position of head of the Propaganda Department of the Political Administration of the First Army Group to deputy director of the General Political Administration of the entire CCP army and chief of the Department of Political Education of its fighting units. Obviously, he continued to please Mao, without whose support such a trajectory would have been impossible.

And why wouldn't Mao value Deng? Deng was an efficient and dependable commissar, the heart and soul of any campaign, a man who did not strive to become a leader or engage in theorizing. He behaved modestly and demonstrated his exceptional devotion, openly acknowledging the Chairman as the undisputed leader. Eleven years younger than Mao, the diminutive Deng, with a childlike face and sparkling eyes, was known among his friends as a tireless chatterbox, cracking jokes and telling stories. The Chairman also must have liked Deng's peasant background, his easygoing manner, his passion and devotion to the party's cause. Mao was just like that himself: a sharp-tongued peasant lad from the back-of-beyond who had made his way in the world by force of his intellect, his will, and his devotion to communism. They even shared a love of spicy food, flavored with large amounts of red pepper! And what of the fact that Deng, unlike the homegrown revolutionary Mao, had once studied in colleges in France and universities in the Soviet Union? Very few communists in China had studied abroad. Most important of all was that Deng had retained his Chinese core; he had not become a dogmatist like Bo Gu; therefore he was able to grasp the Chairman's ideas.

In sum, in June 1937 Mao brought Deng into the top Yan'an leadership. Soon after, on July 7, Japanese troops launched large-scale military operations in North China. On July 29, they took Beiping, the next day Tianjin. Two weeks later, on August 13, they began to bomb Shanghai, the center of Chiang Kai-shek's economic interests and those of Anglo-American investors.

At the time, Deng was in Nanjing, at a conference organized by the military council of the Guomindang government along with a CCP delegation. As he said later, he worked "behind the scenes," drafting basic documents.[10]

Returning to Yan'an, he learned on August 22 that the generalissimo, whom the Japanese had pushed to the end of his rope, had concluded a non-aggression treaty with the Soviet Union, which promised to help China in its struggle against Japanese aggression. That same day, Chiang Kai-shek ordered that the Chinese Red Army be absorbed into the National Revolutionary Army, which he commanded. Three days later, communist troops in the Shaanxi-Gansu-Ningxia region were designated the 8th Route Army,[11] consisting of three divisions (each comprising two brigades) under the command of Lin Biao (115th Division), He Long (120th Division), and Liu Bocheng (129th Division). Zhu De was appointed commander of the army, and then of the army group, with Peng Dehuai as his deputy and Ren Bishi head of the Political Department.[12]

Deng was appointed deputy director of the Political Department of the 8th Army (18th Army Group). In essence, he continued his previous duties. Moreover, at the end of September, he began to represent the 18th Army Group on the Committee for Mobilization at the headquarters of the commander of the Second War Zone, Yan Xishan, the governor of Shanxi.[13] On September 21, with Zhu De, Ren Bishi, and deputy chief-of-staff of the 18th Army Group Zuo Quan, he traveled to Taiyuan, the capital of Shanxi. There, on September 23, he learned that an anti-Japanese united front of all Chinese political parties had been formed. Stalin could celebrate. If only formally, China had now joined the struggle against Japan, thereby significantly lowering the chances of a Japanese attack against the USSR.

Four days later, all four of them—Zhu, Ren, Zuo, and Deng—were already fifty-five miles northeast of Taiyuan, in Wutai county, very close to the front, where the situation continued to deteriorate catastrophically. Seizing one population center after another, the Japanese Imperial Army was rapidly moving south along three lines toward Nanjing, Wuhan, and Taiyuan.

Just then, in the northern and northeast regions of Shanxi, the main forces of all three divisions of the 18th Army Group were on the march.[14] At the end of August, the Politburo had ordered them to engage in mobile guerrilla warfare together with other Chinese units in the Second War Zone in order to gain the trust of the Nanjing government and the approbation of public opinion. In case of a Japanese breakthrough along the front, CCP forces were enjoined to switch to independent, guerrilla actions ("sparrow warfare," as Mao called it), and to expand the sphere of military operations to all of Japanese-occupied North China.[15] Mao Zedong insisted on waging guerrilla war behind enemy lines, calculating that this method would not only enable the Communist party to gain the trust of the people abandoned to the mercy of fate by Chiang Kai-shek but also to preserve, and possibly expand, its armed forces. He demanded that despite the united front with the Guomindang, which, understandably, he did not trust, the communist troops should conduct "independent and autonomous" military operations against the Japanese in mountainous terrain, husband their forces, and under no circumstances become puppets in the hands of Chiang Kai-shek, the former mortal enemy of the communists. The anti-Japanese war would be protracted, he explained, and therefore one had to be patient and wait until the Japanese Army had exhausted its forces.[16] "The enemy advances, we retreat; the enemy camps, we harass; the enemy tires, we attack; the enemy retreats, we pursue," he continued to advise his comrades, insisting that no more than 75 percent of the main forces of the former Red Army be devoted to fighting the Japanese; the other 25 percent should remain in Yan'an to defend it against a possible attack by Chiang Kai-shek.[17] Luo Fu wholly shared his views.[18]

Mao's position made sense. Like any other militarist, he understood perfectly that his power, and even his very existence, depended entirely on the strength of his army. Therefore, he was not serious about the united front and did not wish to submit to Chiang Kai-shek's orders. "Pursuing a joint resistance [with the Guomindang] against Japan, we need to unite it with national and social revolution," he said.

> During the prolonged period of the united front, the Guomindang will exert systematic and all-around pressure on the Communist party and the Red Army, in an effort to win them over to its side. We must increase our political vigilance. . . . Inside the Guomindang are some elements that are vacillating between the GMD and the CCP. This creates favorable conditions for us to win the Guomindang over to our side. The question of who will win over whom will be settled in a conflict between the two parties.

Mao's ultimate goal remained a socialist revolution. Therefore he considered the main danger within the party to be that of "right opportunism," in other words "capitulation" to the Guomindang and refusal to struggle for a socialist revolution.[19]

Waging a protracted guerrilla war was unthinkable without creating base areas in the Japanese rear. At the end of October, that is precisely what the 18th Army Group set out to do. On October 23, 1937, after the Japanese broke through on the northeastern Shanxi front, Nie Rongzhen, the deputy commander of the 115th Division, received orders from the Central Committee to remain at the head of a small force of some two thousand troops behind the lines of the Japanese Army in the Wutai mountains, which stretched in a series of lofty ridges for 175 miles from north to south along the Shanxi, Chahar, and Hebei border. On November 7, a day before the Japanese took Taiyuan, a military region command headed by Nie Rongzhen and embracing a number of enemy-occupied districts was established there. Its center was the small county town of Fuping, high in the mountains in northwestern Hebei, close to Shanxi.[20]

In early November, Mao Zedong repeatedly declared that in North China regular army actions led by the Guomindang had ended, and that guerrilla warfare led by the Communist party was now primary.[21] In this connection the 18th Army Group began to redeploy new subunits and units behind the front line. The 120th Division, headed by He Long, was ordered to engage in guerrilla warfare in northwestern Shanxi, and the 129th Division, headed by Liu Bocheng, to infiltrate individual battalions and companies into southeastern Shanxi, into the Taihang Mountains region.

At this time, Deng was engaged in propaganda work in southwestern Shanxi. At the end of December he returned to the headquarters of the 18th Army Group, which had been relocated to the southeastern county of Hongdong, located in the western spur of the Taiyue Mountains, an extension of the Taihang Mountains. There he celebrated the New Year, not knowing that it would bring him a new appointment.

On January 5, 1938, the Central Revolutionary Military Council decided to transfer Deng to the 129th Division as political commissar and head of the Political Department.[22] This was Deng's finest hour. Granted political power in one of the three CCP army divisions, Deng became one of the most powerful figures in the territory under Communist party control. In essence he was now a regional militarist with enormous military power concentrated in his hands. His future career depended on how skillfully he would be able to make use of this power.

On January 18, 1938, he arrived in the Taihang region, in the village of Xihetou, Liaoxian County, where Liu Bocheng's headquarters was located, surrounded by lofty mountains. Their snow-covered flanks, covered with pines, spruce, and fir trees, glistened in the sun. Stretching along the borders of Shanxi, Hebei, and Henan, from the Wutai Mountains in the north to the Yellow River in the south, the Taihang massif was a natural barrier between the north China plain and the Shanxi plateau. Steep mountains, rising to thirty-five hundred feet, stretched out to the horizon, ridge after ridge.

"Door after door; gate after gate; mountains on the outside; mountains on the inside," local inhabitants say.[23]

Deng paid no heed to the intense cold. He was in an elevated mood. An eyewitness recalls, "Deng Xiaoping arrived at headquarters. He is not tall, and when he saw us, he often smiled."[24]

He quickly found a common language with divisional commander Liu Bocheng. They had been acquainted a long time, since January 1932. Like Deng, Liu was Sichuanese and almost a neighbor. Born in Kaixian County, half-way from Guang'an to the county seat of Yilong, Liu was twelve years older than Deng, both born in a Year of the Dragon. This, however, was the extent of their resemblance. "Our characters and passionate interests did not entirely coincide," Deng said.[25]

A professional military man, during the 1911 Revolution Liu had served in a student army and then studied in the Chongqing military academy. He joined Sun Yat-sen's party in 1914, fought many battles, was wounded nine times and during one battle had lost his right eye. He first contacted the communists in 1924, but only two years later, after convincing himself that the Communist party could save China, did he join the party.[26] In 1927, he fled to Hong Kong after taking part in the unsuccessful Nanchang Uprising. Then he was sent to the Soviet Union and studied for two years at the M. V. Frunze Military Academy. After returning to Shanghai in the summer of 1931, he worked on the Military Committee of the CC under Zhou Enlai, later moving to the Central Soviet Area, where initially he served as rector and political commissar of the Military Academy. Beginning in October 1931, he headed the General Staff of the Central Revolutionary Military Committee. In 1933, like Deng, he was dismissed for supporting Mao's guerrilla tactics, but in December 1934, during the Long March, with the support of Mao and Luo Fu, he was restored to his former post. In January 1935, Liu supported Mao at the Zunyi Conference, served for a time in Zhang Guotao's Fourth Front Army, and arrived in Shaanxi in October 1936 with the remnants of those defeated troops. The 129th Division was formed in 1937 from Zhang Guotao's surviving troops. Mao appointed Xu Xiangqian, former commander of the Fourth Front Army, as deputy divisional commander. The Chairman did not implicate this old veteran in the mistakes of Zhang Guotao. Mao understood he was simply executing the orders of his political leader.

His subordinates called Liu Bocheng "the One-eyed Dragon," but this sobriquet did not suit him: the divisional commander was gentle and mild. "From our first meeting I was deeply impressed by his goodness, sincerity, and benevolence," Deng recalled.[27]

In Taihang, Deng immediately became engaged in organizational, mobilizing, and political work in the division and the surrounding territory.
He devoted his greatest attention to communist propaganda.[28] He made
a profound impression on Evans F. Carlson, an unofficial representative of
President Franklin D. Roosevelt, who visited the Taihang region in July 1938.
"[Deng Xiaoping] was short, chunky and physically tough, and his mind was
as keen as mustard," recalled Carlson.[29]

To increase the impact of their propaganda on poorly educated audi-
ences, Deng and his subordinates staged patriotic performances; sang songs;
posted *dazibao* (big-character posters) on walls, homes, and temples; gave
fiery speeches at mass meetings; and held heart-to-heart talks with fighters
and local inhabitants. They used simple language "to explain to the masses
about the current situation and the way for them to survive, and to expose
the cruelty of the enemy."[30]

But their appeals did not always evoke a response, even though many refugees from cities and towns seized by the hated Japanese had crowded into
the mountains. At the time the divisional command, "economically, did not
adopt any measures to speak of. . . . The people lived in destitution and the
army experienced extreme difficulties in obtaining supplies." Moreover, the
officers and men viewed the "enemy-occupied areas" as their "colonies." "In
enemy-occupied areas we did no work among the people except asking them
for supplies [in other words, pillaging those who lived outside the boundaries of the base area]. . . . This was a period of extreme poverty for us (worst in
the Taihang area)," Deng wrote. Thus, the communist troops "left a very bad
impression on the people there" and "seriously damaged" their own "political
prestige." As a result their authority was almost nonexistent.[31]

The poor inhabitants of the surrounding villages, basically small proprietors, were extremely destitute even by Chinese standards and thanked
their fate only for the fact that the communists did not encroach on their
minuscule landed property (if they had even that). In November 1935, the
CCP Politburo and the Central Executive Committee of the Chinese Soviet
Republic had changed tactics with regard to the working peasantry, abandoning the equal division of land.[32] This reflected the transition to the policy
of an anti-Japanese united front, but also, to a certain degree, the fact that
in northern China, the number of large landlords and rich peasants could
be counted on one's fingers; there were no Hakka, and the standard of living of the paupers differed little from that of the small peasants. Even had
there been an equal division of land, they would have received almost nothing. In northern Shaanxi and throughout Shanxi, rural inhabitants balanced

on the knife edge of starvation. In Shanxi, for example, on the eve of the communists' arrival, in 1933 there began a terrible drought that lasted for several years, and just before the war it was followed by flooding. Many people died of famine, while those who survived dragged out a miserable existence. A particularly difficult situation developed in the Taihang Mountains, where only a million and a half people remained alive in 1938.[33]

There was really nothing to pillage from such people. That is why initially the 129th Division encountered difficulties. Instead of regulating agricultural production and lightening the burden of the peasantry, Liu Bocheng, relying on military force, basically engaged in enlarging his region and establishing new bases in Shanxi, Hebei, Henan, and Shandong, while Deng was stepping up the propaganda effort. By mid-spring of 1938, the 129th Division had succeeded in establishing several bases behind enemy lines. In this effort they were assisted by the first and third columns of the local so-called New Shanxi Army as well as the Shanxi Sacrifice League for National Salvation, formed on the initiative of Yan Xishan back in September 1936.[34] At a conference of the Military-Political Council of the 129th Division in late April 1938, convened by Deng on orders from Mao Zedong and Liu Shaoqi, it was decided to establish a Shanxi-Hebei-Henan military region.[35]

Four months later, Deng returned to Yan'an for a CC plenum. This was the first time he had been invited to such an important party conclave as an actual participant, even though he was not a member of the Central Committee. The meeting, from September 29 to November 6, was an enlarged plenum: only eighteen of the fifty-six participants were CC members or candidate members.[36] The others were important military officers or, like Deng, important party functionaries. The plenum was vital both for the party and for Deng personally. Over three days Mao, who had established full control over the CCP, delivered an extensive report. He made it clear to his audience that, now that the CCP had united around him, it was necessary to review the party's history, separate "truth" from "falsehood," and evaluate everyone in accordance with whether they had supported the correct line. It was necessary to reject dogmatism decisively and to "sinicize" the teachings of Marx, Engels, Lenin, and Stalin.[37]

In his concluding remarks at the end of the plenum, Mao returned to the history of the CCP. Unexpectedly, as if in passing, he said, "We need to reject the blow that was struck [by the dogmatists] in 1933 in the Central Soviet Area against Comrade Deng Xiaoping."[38] His audience welcomed these words, and immediately after the plenum, Deng was inducted into the North China Bureau of the Central Committee by decision of the Politburo.[39] He was given the floor at the plenum on October 6, but his brief speech merely noted the need to strengthen the military regions of North China by all means, "from the bottom up," by relying on the masses.[40] Yet it would be a long time before Deng himself and Liu Bocheng would begin seriously to do this. Not until October 1939 did they move in this direction, establishing a bank in the southern Hebei base area and printing paper money that was widely circulated in all the communist regions of North China.[41]

But this would come after Deng, along with Liu Bocheng, returned to Yan'an for a series of top-level meetings between July 3 and August 25, 1939, focusing, among other questions, on the Communist party's perspective on Sun Yat-sen's Three Principles of the People [Nationalism, Democracy, the People's Livelihood]. Mao prescribed the new guidelines concerning Sun Yat-senism:

> The CCP's view on the Three Principles of the People. . . . First, at a theoretical level, we recognize them. Second, on a practical level, we implement them. In their work the 8th Army, the New 4th Army,[42] the border regions and the party all follow the general program of the Three Principles of the People. We need to propagandize and explain the Three Principles of the People openly, otherwise it will be impossible to form a bloc with the leftists [in the Guomindang] or to win over the masses. The point of departure in this whole policy is the following: We must not antagonize the majority of the Guomindang.[43]

By this time, Mao, on Stalin's initiative, had begun to develop a new conception of the revolutionary movement in China; armed with this theory, the Communist party should be able to gain victory in the future, postwar struggle for power against Chiang Kai-shek.[44] The CCP now had to advocate so-called New Democracy instead of the radical leftist, socialist path. New Democracy differed from "old Western democracy" because it was to be implemented under the leadership of the Communist party. From a political incarnation of the working class, the party now reinvented itself as an organization of the revolutionary united front seeking to unite "all classes and strata of the population with revolutionary potential." Hence Mao's support for social reforms in the spirit of Sun Yat-sen's Three Principles of the People, the party's new emphasis on national sentiment rather than class interests in appealing to Chinese compatriots. Mao promised to guarantee private property rights after the revolution, stimulate national entrepreneurship, and pursue a protectionist policy, that is, to attract foreign investors under strict state control. He called for lowering taxes, developing a multiparty system, establishing a coalition government, implementing democratic freedoms, and swiftly correcting all "leftist errors" that communists had committed in the past.[45] Such tactical maneuvers enabled the Communist party to expand its mass base significantly by attracting moderate Chinese who were opposed to any sort of dictatorship, whether communist or Guomindang.

Embracing the Chairman's new ideas, Deng and Liu returned to the Taihang region in early September 1939, ready to implement them. After opening the bank, in 1940, they devoted increased attention to the development of production, jettisoning their previous policy of viewing enemy-occupied regions as "their colonies." In March 1941, on orders from the North China Bureau they convened a legislative assembly of the Shanxi-Hebei-Henan border region, which, in July, expanded its jurisdiction to Shandong province. A month later, in the newly united Shanxi-Hebei-Shandong-Henan guerrilla region, with a population of twenty-three million people, they founded a government as the highest organ of executive power.

Naturally, the party continued to run everything. In early September 1942, the Politburo established a Taihang Sub-bureau of the North China Bureau in the area where the 129th Division was deployed. Mao appointed Deng to head it. As divisional political commissar, he had already been directing the work of local party organizations.[46]

In the spring of 1943, throughout the territory of the 129th Division, taxes were lowered to between 30 and 35 percent, rent by 25 percent, and interest rates to 15 percent and below.[47] "These policies are all designed to promote development of the economy while restricting feudal exploitation," according to an article Deng Xiaoping wrote for the central organ of the CCP *Jiefang ribao* (*Liberation Daily*).

> This is the path that Dr. Sun Yat-sen pointed out to us. . . . The taxes levied by the government on industry . . . [are] minimal. . . . We . . . mediate between landlords and tenants and between employers and employees . . . the government has been granting low-interest and interest-free loans every year, ranging from several million to ten million yuan. . . . During busy farming seasons men in army uniform toil alongside civilians across hill and dale.

And further, "Without the correct policies, there can be no economic development to speak of; these policies must be shaped in the light of the well-being of the people."[48]

These sensible ideas were merely of a tactical, not a strategic, character. Following their seizure of power throughout China, the communists quickly abandoned Sun Yat-senism. But for the time being in Taihang and other districts of Shanxi, Hebei, Shandong, and Henan where the 129th Division was operating, from the late 1930s to the mid-1940s implementation of Mao's new ideas had a positive impact not only on the regional economy but also on the image of the Communist party, whose popularity grew rapidly. This occurred despite the onset in Shanxi and surrounding areas of a terrible drought in 1941–1943, accompanied by an invasion of locusts. Paradoxically, despite their voracious appetites, the insects actually saved people from starvation. Soldiers and peasants alike caught the locusts, smashed them with their hands, and then roasted and greedily devoured them.[49]

In the early autumn of 1939, Deng brought not only new ideas from Yan'an but also a new wife. She was Zhuo Lin (Zhuo "Dear Little Thing"), from Xuanwei county in northeast Yunnan. They were introduced by Deng's friend Deng Fa, who had arrived in Yan'an in August 1939 from Xinjiang. In Yan'an Deng Fa became the rector of the Party School, and since he, like Deng Xiaoping, was not married and loved to talk and have a good time, the two Dengs soon got together and even began to live under one roof. "At that time, Deng Fa and your father strolled happily everywhere every day in Yan'an," Luo Fu's wife, Liu Ying, told Deng Xiaoping's daughter. "And people were saying they looked like two roving gods!"[50]

"Under one roof" is a bit misleading since most party and military officials in Yan'an were living in caves dug into the steep slopes of the loess mountains outside town. These caves were lined up for miles north of the city along the shallow and rocky Yan River, and from a long distance they looked like the nests of swallows or bats.[51] It was in one such "nest" that the two Dengs lived.

The simplicity of their circumstances did not bother them, especially since they spent all their free time outside their cave dwelling, in Yan'an itself, a comparatively large city with shops and eating-houses, noisy markets and crowded streets that afforded many diversions. Although Japanese aircraft inflicted serious damage on it, destroying many houses and the massive fortress wall that towered along its entire perimeter, the city continued to seethe with life, and it was really possible to enjoy oneself. Since the beginning of the anti-Japanese war many patriotic youths had flocked there, including many attractive women devoted to the party's cause. Deng Fa, two years younger than Deng, was something of a ladies' man.

He persuaded his comrade to accompany him to the Yan'an Security Department, where he had made the acquaintance of some young female colleagues. A big-hearted man, Deng Fa loved to arrange matches for his unmarried friends. He was eager to marry off Deng, who at that time was rather dashing (if the word is suitable for Chinese guerrillas): thin, very youthful-looking despite his thirty-five years, with a fine but masculine-featured face. He shaved his head, which enhanced his manly look.

Deng was immediately attracted to Zhuo Lin, who was working in the Security Department. She was petite, even shorter than him, with a round face, thick eyebrows, and mischievous eyes. He was also attracted by her character: lively, energetic, and independent. They began to see each other, drop in on each other's friends, often in the company of Deng Fa and Zhuo Lin's friend, and talk about many things. Deng learned that she was born in April 1916, and was twelve years younger than him, so like Deng himself and Liu Bocheng, she was born in a year of the Dragon. He also learned that her real name was Pu Qiongying (Pu "Jade Flower") and had chosen the pseudonym Zhuo Lin for herself in 1938, when she enrolled in courses in the Security Department. All the students were preparing for possible underground work in the Japanese or Guomindang rear areas and therefore changed their personal and family names. Her father was known through-out China as the "King of Smoked Ham" because in 1920 he had discovered a method of preserving ham and founded his own company, Xuanhe. A liberal who had long supported Sun Yat-sen, who even awarded him the rank of major general, he ultimately lost interest in the revolution, his business collapsed, and he became thoroughly disillusioned. Nevertheless, he provided Zhuo Lin and his six other children with excellent educations. Zhuo Lin graduated middle school with distinction, and matriculated in the physics department at the elite Peking University. In Beiping in December 1935, she was attracted to communist ideas and took part in the anti-Japanese student movement. After the Japanese occupied Beiping, she abandoned her studies and fled to Yan'an with her older sister and a girl friend. There, in November 1937, she enrolled in a cadre training school, joined the party in early 1938, and took short-term courses in the Security Department, where she worked after graduation. An intelligent and cultured woman, she had little interest in being courted by soldiers and officers of the 18th Army Group, most of them raw village youths.

She was initially reserved with Deng. Later she recalled,

> I did not know if he had any intentions toward me. Not until he asked
> my girl friend, the one with whom I had come to Yan'an, to speak with
> me. She told me that he wanted to marry me, and asked if I would

consent. I replied that I was still young and had no desire to marry early. In general, I refused him. Since all of the old *ganbu* [cadres] who arrived in Yan'an after the Long March were workers and peasants, we [the intelligent girls] were afraid of marrying them, not because we despised them, but because they were uneducated, and we would have nothing to talk to them about. . . . Afterward he came twice to speak with me. The first time he spoke about himself and his aspirations. I listened and listened and suddenly felt, that he was something, he had some education, and was an intelligent man. The second time I fell to thinking, "Sooner or later I will get married, and here I am, twenty-three already." So I said to myself, "Enough, I'll do it!" So . . . I agreed.

She "stipulated one condition: to leave Yan'an soon after the wedding." She was afraid that her friends would laugh at her for marrying a "villager."

Deng Xiaoping pretended that he understood her anxieties, but he said, "I have only one drawback: I am several years older than you. Otherwise, I hope I can still catch up with you."[52]

At the end of August the wedding took place. Mao Zedong and his lover, Jiang Qing, played an active role in organizing the festivities. The nuptial tables were set up in front of their cave. Three months later, on November 19, Mao and Jiang Qing also got married, despite the even larger difference in age—twenty-one years!

Almost the entire party leadership, including Luo Fu, Bo Gu, Liu Shaoqi, Li Fuchun, and others, came to congratulate them. Only Zhou Enlai and his wife, who were in the Soviet Union, were missing. The guests made merry all night long, eating and drinking. According to Chinese custom, they tried to get the bridegroom drunk. But at the end of the evening Deng still was looking hale and hearty.

"Xiaoping can drink a lot of liquor" Luo Fu's wife told her husband.
    He smiled.
    "There was a trick to it."

As true friends, Deng Fa and Luo Fu, unknown to the others, had provided Deng a bottle of water from which he drank the entire evening.[53]

A couple of days later, Deng took his wife off to the Taihang Mountains, not to his base but to the headquarters of the 18th Army Group, which by then had also relocated to this region. On meeting them, Peng Dehuai exclaimed, "Just look at you! Deng Xiaoping! You've really found yourself your old woman till the end of your days. You look so alike—like brother and sister!"[54]

Working with Peng, Deng left Zhuo Lin alone to focus on women's courses. But she began to feel sad. When Deng visited her after a while, she complained of loneliness.

"You could at least have written me," she said in a hurt tone.
"Written you? About what?" Deng said in surprise.
"Well, about what you do every day."
Deng shrugged his shoulders.
"Okay. I will order my secretary to prepare several copies of a letter for me, and every month I'll send you one."
Then Zhuo Lin could no restrain herself.
"That's it! Enough! You need not write me letters! Then we'll live together in order to understand each other."

From then on they never parted—for fifty-eight years. All those years, Zhuo Lin remembered the words of a Central Committee official (she never identified him) who had summoned her to his office before she and Deng left for the Taihang. He said, "Your task is to take good care of Deng Xiaoping."[55] It sounded like a party mission.

On September 11, 1941, Zhuo Lin presented Deng with a daughter, whom she gave her own name, Lin. (Written differently, this Chinese character means "grove," which is how Deng Lin would subsequently write it.) Alas, the young mother was unable to nurse the infant for long. Just a week later Deng's and Liu's forces had to retreat from the village in which the infant had been born, and Zhuo Lin had to hand the baby over to a peasant family. She later said she didn't want the troops to be distracted by having to defend her and the child.[56] Restraining her tears and not looking back, Zhuo Lin departed with her husband. "Lin Er, Lin Er [Grove, Grove] my poor little one," she kept repeating.

Happily, the child was not lost. In October 1943, Zhuo Lin reclaimed the little girl and entrusted her care to the wife of Cai Shufan, a member of the Taihang Bureau of the CC CCP, who along with her husband went to study in Yan'an. Cai and his wife doted on Deng Lin, and with Deng's and Zhuo's permission they adopted her. However, they too were unable to keep her and therefore placed her in a children's home in Yan'an, located in one of the loess caves. This, naturally, was not an ideal shelter for an infant; once, when no one was watching her, Lin Er almost died. She went too close to the hearth that was burning in the cave and an errant spark set the sleeve of her cotton jacket on fire. The governess, who was outside with the children, did not immediately hear the child's cry, and by the time she came running, the two-year-old's arm was engulfed in flames. It was a miracle that Lin Er was saved, but she was left with a big scar from the burn.[57]

Busy with their own affairs, her parents knew nothing of this. On April 16, 1944, Zhuo Lin gave birth to a son. The parents were ecstatic. First Zhuo and then Deng began calling him affectionately and jokingly Pang Pang ("Little Fatso"); the infant was born quite plump, so he deserved his nickname. But Zhuo Lin was unable to keep this child with her. This time she had no milk at all, so she and Deng also had to hand their son over to a peasant family as well, but only for a while.

In October 1945, another child was born, a second daughter, whom Zhuo Lin poetically named Nan ("Laurel sapling"). (She named all the children; Deng did not interfere.) At home the girl was called Nan Nan, a name given her by her older brother who, as soon as he saw the infant, held out his little hands to her and babbled "Nan Nan, Nan Nan." No one understood what he was trying to say. Pang Pang was just beginning to talk, but Deng and Zhuo liked the name.[58] Unfortunately, they had to part with Nan Nan too for a time, also entrusting her to strangers.

By then the anti-Japanese war was over. On August 15, 1945, the Japanese surrendered, but CCP troops began preparing for new battles, this time against the Guomindang for power in China. On the eve of Deng Nan's birth, units of the 129th Division had already conducted several successful operations against Guomindang troops that were intruding into their territory, but the major, decisive battles still lay ahead.

Two months earlier, in June, at the Seventh CCP Congress in Yan'an, Deng, as one of the main regional party leaders, was elected to the Central Committee. According to the tabulation of votes, he was twenty-eighth of the forty-four CC members.[59] (Incidentally: as far back as the spring of 1940, Moscow had advised Mao to include Deng in the leading organs of the party at the Seventh Congress.[60])

Deng himself was absent from the congress, since, on Mao's instructions, from October 1943 to July 1945 he was in charge of the North China Bureau of the CC and the Front Headquarters of the 18th Army Group in Taihang. At this time he implemented the so-called rectification campaign (*zhengfeng*) in all party organizations within his territory. This was a broad-scale intraparty "purge," aimed at reexamining party history to boost the cult of the leader, namely, Chairman Mao. All the other leading cadres of North China and the army, including Luo Fu, Bo Gu, Zhu De, Peng Dehuai, and Liu Bocheng, were in Yan'an, where they underwent an analogous indoctrination under the personal control of Mao and the special commission he had established, headed by Kang Sheng, the party's secret services chief. That Mao left Deng in charge in the Taihang and entrusted him with conducting the campaign in the Shanxi-Hebei-Shandong-Henan region demonstrates the enormous trust reposed in him by the Chairman.

This is confirmed by the fact that Mao personally congratulated Deng on his election to the CC and invited him to Yan'an to participate in the First Plenum of the Seventh Central Committee as the congress approached its conclusion.[61]

From Deng's perspective Mao embodied a great strategist, tactician, and theoretician, and a wise leader and teacher who was leading the party to one victory after another.[62] Mao's triumph in the party was complete and decisive. His cult truly became all-embracing. The party's statutes adopted by the Seventh Congress—presented by Liu Shaoqi, whom Mao had placed in the second position in the party leadership—stated that "the Communist Party of China guides its entire work by . . . the Thought of Mao Tse-tung [Mao Zedong]."[63]

Most likely, Deng was well aware that it was Mao who had included his name on the list of CC members. [64] Sitting in the hall where the plenum was held, decorated with portraits of Marx, Lenin, Stalin, Mao Zedong, and Zhu De, Deng, like everyone else, applauded the "Great Helmsman," who had been chosen at the plenum as chairman of the Central Committee, of the Politburo, and of the Secretariat of the CC. Deng believed that Mao and the Chinese revolution were indivisible.

7

At the Forefront of the New Democratic Revolution

ON AUGUST 25, 1945, Deng flew back to Taihang from Yan'an, accompanied by political cadres and commanders of the 18th Army Group, including Liu Bocheng. The plane and crew were provided by the Americans, who, since the end of July 1944, had a liaison mission attached to CCP headquarters.[1]

China's allies were overjoyed by the end of the anti-Japanese war: both the Americans who entered the war against Japan on December 7, 1941, and the Russians, who had declared war against Japan on August 8, 1945, and then routed Japan's Kwantung Army in Manchuria. Neither the Americans nor the Soviets wanted a new conflict in China that might escalate into a Third World War, for which Truman and Stalin were unprepared.[2] Truman wanted his soldiers home to satisfy American public opinion, while Stalin sought a compromise in China given the U.S. nuclear weapons monopoly. The secret protocols of the Yalta Agreement as well as the Soviet-Guomindang treaty of friendship and alliance, signed respectively on February 11 and August 14, 1945, likewise restrained Stalin's initiative. Both were stacked in favor of the Soviet Union, giving the USSR vital economic, political, and territorial concessions in the Far East. Soon after the war, Stalin began expressing doubts about the CCP's ability to take power. He did not want to risk what he had already gained from the United States and China by providing unconditional support to the CCP. Thus he advised Mao Zedong "to come to a temporary agreement" with Chiang Kai-shek, insisting that Mao travel to Chongqing for a personal meeting with his sworn enemy. His lame justification was that a new civil war might lead to the destruction of the Chinese nation.[3] Shortly after the end of the war against Japan, the Central Committee of the Soviet Communist Party sent a telegram to Mao: "We consider the policy of unleashing a civil war inimical to the cause of the revival of China. . . . We consider it expedient for you to meet with Chiang Kai-shek and come to an agreement with him."[4]

But Mao and Chiang could not come to an agreement. The profound antagonism between their parties made another civil war inevitable. Armed clashes between CCP and Guomindang troops even occurred behind Japanese lines during the war against Japan, notwithstanding the formal existence of a united front.

New "frictions" between the troops had already begun in August 1945 over which side would accept the Japanese surrender as well as where and when. On August 11, four days before Emperor Hirohito announced Japan's surrender, Zhu De ordered CCP troops to launch a general offensive on all fronts so as "to be prepared to accept the surrender."[5] Generalissimo Chiang responded by commanding the communists "to remain where they were until further orders."[6] General Douglas MacArthur, commander-in-chief of American forces in the Pacific Theater, ordered Japanese armies in China and north of the 16th Parallel in Indochina to surrender only to Chiang Kai-shek's forces.[7] On August 16, Mao and Zhu De demanded that Chiang "revoke" his order and "acknowledge his mistake."[8] Soon the 18th Army Group occupied the major city of Kalgan, located 120 miles northwest of Beiping. In response, He Yingqin, commander-in-chief of Chinese government ground forces in charge of overseeing the Japanese surrender, demanded that Japanese troops retake the city and hold it until Guomindang forces arrived.[9] In sum, the seeds of a new bloody slaughter had been sown, and the antagonists began feverish preparations for a large-scale war.

Troops under Deng's political leadership were destined to play an enormous role in this conflict. They were stationed in places that, in the words of Liu Bocheng, were "the main gates to the liberated areas of North China through which the enemy [Guomindang troops] would first have to pass."[10] (The communists referred to their bases in the Japanese rear as "liberated areas.")

In September and October 1945, the 129th Division, just before being redesignated the Field Army of the Shanxi-Hebei-Shandong-Henan military region, conducted a successful operation against Guomindang troops entering Taihang to take the Japanese surrender. This operation in fact touched off the civil war.[11] Many years later, Deng recalled with pride, "We had just a little over 30,000 troops, and if one speaks of the staff we had no full-strength regiments. Our weapons were poor; we had few artillery shells. . . . Under such conditions . . . it was not easy to destroy the enemy completely."[12]

Meanwhile, Mao and Chiang Kai-shek were negotiating in Chongqing about how to promote peaceful construction on the basis of equality for all political organizations. Neither believed the negotiations would succeed. "I was compelled to go [to meet with Chiang] since Stalin insisted upon it," Mao Zedong said later.[13] Meanwhile, American pressure forced Chiang Kai-shek to the negotiating table, but, as one of Chiang's biographers observed, "There was no way the Kuomintang [Guomindang] would 'abdicate to a loose combination of parties.'"[14] Thus, the victory that Liu's and Deng's troops achieved over the Nationalists in October 1945 was enormously significant. "Our policy . . . was set long ago—to give tit for tat, to fight for every inch of land. This time we gave tit for tat, fought and made a very good job of it," said an overjoyed Mao.[15] After all, the more such victories the sooner would Stalin abandon his caution on the China issue and give Mao the green light for war.

Yet Stalin was in no hurry to do this. He categorically forbade communist troops from occupying the cities of Northeast China until after the Soviet army had withdrawn. He even repeatedly expressed his hope that the National Government would establish its power in Manchuria. Nevertheless, Moscow had no objections to the communists' secretly infiltrating the rural districts of Manchuria, organizing a clandestine Northeast Bureau of the CC CCP, and even establishing a Northeast Autonomous People's Army under the command of Lin Biao.[16]

Striving to consolidate their success, Mao ordered Liu Bocheng and Deng Xiaoping to mount another operation against Guomindang troops moving north.[17] Again, Liu's and Deng's army were victorious. Generally, as Deng himself later acknowledged, "after the victory was achieved in the anti-Japanese war, our field army never stopped fighting for one day. We could only receive training for a week at most, and it was hard for us to have ten days to spare."[18]

Ultimately, even Stalin began to waver. In October 1945, he decided to transfer some Japanese arms seized by Soviet soldiers to CCP troops in Manchuria. Although he did not want to advertise his participation in the Chinese civil war, he had recognized it was a reality. "All of our liaison officers and others must be withdrawn from Yan'an and other operational zones of Mao Zedong's forces as soon as possible," he suggested to his subordinates at this time. "The civil war in China has taken a serious turn, and I'm afraid that our enemies will later accuse our people in these regions, who are not in control of anything, of being the organizers of civil war in China. The sooner we get them out of there the better."[19]

In February and March 1946, ironically, Chiang Kai-shek himself, under pressure from rightists, pushed Stalin toward unconditional support of the Chinese Communist Party. The Guomindang and the Chinese public began expressing dissatisfaction with Soviet army conduct in the Northeast. There is no doubt that the occupation forces of the USSR engaged in inexcusable pillaging: they dismantled and shipped major industrial enterprises and other property to the Soviet Union. Manchurian industry incurred a loss of US$858 million.[20] On March 6, the Ministry of Foreign Affairs of the Republic of China lodged a protest in this connection, demanding the swift evacuation of the Soviet army.[21] Did Chiang Kai-shek understand then that the Chinese communists would replace the Russians? Probably not; he figured on occupying the cities the Soviets evacuated, relying on the help of the United States. But he miscalculated.

On March 13, Stalin began withdrawing his troops and completed this on May 3, 1946. Meanwhile, infuriated with Chiang Kai-shek, he called on his Chinese comrades to act decisively and even criticized them for being too polite toward the United States. He thereby allowed CCP troops to enter Manchurian cities and insisted that Lin Biao's army occupy them as quickly as possible. He commanded the Red Army to facilitate Chinese communist seizure of the lines of communication.[22]

Then Mao struck a third blow against the Guomindang. In March 1946, he ordered Lin Biao to attack GMD troops in Manchuria advancing on Changchun, the capital of Jilin province. Again victorious, they occupied Changchun and Harbin and began to transform Manchuria, rich in iron and coal, into their military base.[23]

These initial victories and the new Soviet policy in China inspired Mao, Deng, and the entire CCP leadership. At the end of April 1946, Mao wrote to Lin Biao, "Every thing is decided by victory or defeat on the battlefield[;] do not put any hope on negotiations."[24] Two months later, he telegraphed the same message, in different words, to Liu Bocheng and Deng, "If we can achieve several military victories after the start of the war, we will be able to obtain peace. If the number of our victories will be equal to the number of our defeats, we will still be in a condition to obtain peace. But if they [the Nationalists] win, there will be no hope for peace."[25]

Unfortunately for the Chinese communists, the first year of the war, which officially began in the spring of 1946, was generally unsuccessful. The 4.3 million Guomindang troops greatly outnumbered the communist army of barely 1.2 million. The communists were forced to abandon 105 cities and towns. Chiang Kai-shek conducted a broad offensive from Shaanxi province in the west to the Pacific shore on the east; he also fought in Manchuria. The Americans, however, considered Chiang's action "over-ambitious," threatening economic chaos and the very survival of his government. By lengthening the front, Chiang was subjecting his "communications to attack by Communist guerrillas," forcing his soldiers either "to retreat or to surrender their armies together with the munitions which the United States has furnished them."[26] But for the time being the communists were losing.

Like everyone else, Deng was going through tough times. His field army was engaged in intensive guerrilla warfare in accordance with the old and time-tested principle: "The enemy advances, we retreat; the enemy halts, we harass; the enemy tires, we attack; the enemy retreats, we pursue." His troops were annoying the enemy with numerous attacks from the rear and on the flanks. "Our method of fighting is strange," Liu Bocheng said. "We pay no attention to the enemy's stretching hands, keep clear of them, pass through their small strongholds and hold their waists in our arms at one swoop, pulling out their hearts and hitting their vulnerable points."[27]

Such tactics worked, especially since apart from its numerical superiority Chiang Kai-shek's army was inferior to Mao's forces in other respects, particularly morale. Unlike the officers and men of the CCP, the Guomindang forces had little will to fight. As a matter of fact, long before the new civil war, the Guomindang "began to lose the dynamism and revolutionary fervor which had created it."[28] This was the root of Chiang Kai-shek's disaster. Despite his numerical superiority, his generals often avoided engagements so as not to risk their units, which were the source of their political influence and their own enrichment. Corruption and local particularism flourished, and the vestiges of militarism were also strong. Closely observing the situation in China, Truman felt compelled to declare to the members of his cabinet, "Chiang Kai-shek['s troops] will not fight it out. [The] Communists will fight it out—they are fanatical. It would be pouring sand in a rat hole [to give aid] under present conditions."[29] He was fully supported by his secretary of state, George Marshall: "He [Chiang Kai-shek] is losing about forty percent of his supplies to the enemy. If the percentage should reach fifty percent he will have to decide whether it is wise to supply his own troops."[30] Nonetheless, given the Cold War, the Americans continued to support Chiang Kai-shek. Up to the end of 1949, they provided him credits and loans worth around $2 billion (more than to any country in Western Europe after the Second World War), and sold him $1.2 billion of weapons.[31]

From the beginning of March 1946, the staff headquarters of the Shanxi-Hebei-Shandong-Henan region was located in the city of Handan, nestled in the eastern spurs of the Taihang mountains in southern Hebei province. Deng, Zhuo Lin, and all their children lived in this ancient city with its narrow paved streets and solitary Buddhist temples. The family had reunited in December 1945, prior to their arrival in Handan. Deng was overjoyed, but Zhuo Lin was terribly anxious. At this time, their elder daughter looked emaciated, did not speak at all, and barely ate. Their son suffered from diarrhea, and Zhuo Lin had no milk for their youngest, a nursing infant. But gradually everything worked out, and by spring 1946 the children were stronger. Deng's daughter Maomao writes,

> To the children, Handan was the first big city they had experienced. Everything was different from the countryside, and everything was new to them. There was a flush toilet in the bathroom of the house. My elder brother was just over three years old then. [Actually, he was a little over two, but Chinese count the nine months spent in the womb as the first year of life.] He had never seen such a thing before and found it strange, so he often went to the bathroom to let water out of the flush toilet for fun.

The families of the top commanders lived near each other, and the women took turns preparing food. Only Zhuo Lin was not asked to cook; no one could eat her dishes. "Mother has still not learned how to cook," Maomao concluded her account.[32] (Incidentally, Deng had learned to cook in France. Throughout his life during his free time he liked to prepare Sichuan dishes as well as dumplings.[33])

Deng spent his days in meetings, helping Liu Bocheng to draw elaborate plans for military operations, mobilizing communists, and directing agrarian reform, which, with the start of the civil war, became extremely radicalized. From mid-June 1946, in accordance with a Central Committee resolution of May 4, 1946, Deng and his cadres began, as previously, to egg on the poor peasants, rural riffraff and paupers against the wealthy landowners, to organize village meetings at which they compelled them to "settle accounts" with the "exploiters," expropriate the land from those labeled landlords, and redistribute it equally.[34] They ignored the fact that in the Taihang region, as generally in North China, peasant holdings were the norm and landlords few. They selected the objects of struggle arbitrarily.

Only rarely did Deng find time to spend with his family, but he was too exhausted to enjoy his wife's company or play with his children. Within his family, he was a man of few words. Zhuo Lin had to reconcile herself to this situation. "It was quite impossible to talk about domestic affairs with these old cadres," she wrote. "They had no views on such questions. . . . Little by little we got used to each other, and adjusted our relationship."[35]

During free time, Liu Bocheng and his family often came to visit Deng's home. His wife, Wang Ronghua, was well matched with Zhuo Lin. She was equally energetic and just one year younger. They usually sat around one big table, drank tea, and talked while the children played on the floor. During one such visit, Zhuo Lin asked Deng to give their son an "adult" name:

"Are we going to call him Little Fatso all the time?"

Deng thought for a while and said, "Let's call him Taihang. He will be Deng Taihang."

But Zhuo Lin disagreed. The eldest son of Liu Bocheng and Wang Ronghua already bore this glorious name.

"Commander!" she turned to Liu Bocheng. "You have already appropriated our name. Please be so kind now and think of a name for Pang Pang!"

Liu laughed, "Such matters should be dealt with by the political commissar. This has no bearing on the commander."

But Deng objected, "Everyone knows that Liu and Deng are inseparable. So come on, think of something!"

So Liu wrote on a scrap of paper the expression, *"pushi fangzheng"* meaning "simple and neat," selected the two characters "pu" and "fang" and said, "Okay. This child was born simply and neatly. Let him be Pufang. What do you think?"

Everyone liked this very much. Zhuo Lin said to Pang Pang, "Go and thank Uncle Bobo right away. [This is what the children called Liu Bocheng.]

Hearing this, Taihang, Liu Bocheng's and Wang Ronghua's son, walked toward Pang Pang and bowed his head before his father. Everybody laughed.[36] The banality of family life contrasted sharply with the high drama of the civil war.

Meanwhile, the war continued. After Chiang Kai-shek's broad offensive in 1946 against all the "liberated areas," in the spring of 1947 he focused his attack in two directions: against Yan'an in the northwest and CCP bases in Shandong in the northeast. In mid-March Mao was forced to abandon Yan'an, and for the remainder of the year he led the exhausted units of the Yan'an garrison and his personal guard detachment along the mountainous roads of northern Shaanxi. Communist troops in Shandong, led by Chen Yi, also began to suffer defeats. Then Mao executed a brilliant plan: to use Liu's and Deng's troops, which were temporarily immobilized between the "claws" of the enemy, for a deep penetration to the south, via the Yellow River, into Chiang Kai-shek's rear, to establish a new base area in the high mountain region of Dabie on the central plain. This diversionary maneuver was aimed at forcing Chiang Kai-shek to redeploy military units from the northwestern and northeastern fronts to defend the major cities of the central plain, namely, Wuhan, Jiujiang, Nanchang, Shanghai, and the capital Nanjing itself. This ruined the generalissimo's strategic plans.

Mao had first conceived this operation in the summer of 1946 and broached it with Liu Bocheng and Deng, who, naturally, enthusiastically supported the Chairman. In Deng's words, "The position of the Central Plains is of great strategic importance. It is like the gate opposite the enemy, and the Dabie Mountains are right at the gate."[37] Liu and Deng assured the Chairman they could move forty-five to fifty thousand troops south and complete a "small Long March" in ten days. Mao said that first everything had to be carefully considered.[38]

In mid-May 1947, he revived the idea on seeing that the situation on the fronts was extremely serious.[39] On May 15, on his initiative, a Bureau of the Central Committee for the Central Plains was established, with Deng as secretary.[40] At the end of June, Liu Bocheng's and Deng's troops crossed the Yellow River. On the eve of the crossing, which may justly be called "the most spectacular military operation of the civil war,"[41] Deng made a passionate speech to the soldiers, he said,

> The war should be carried into the areas controlled by Chiang Kai-shek and . . . the enemy should not be allowed to smash our pots and pans. . . . The Shanxi-Hebei-Shandong-Henan Liberated Area was like a shoulder pole carrying the two battlefields of northern Shaanxi and Shandong. . . . The heavier the load might be after pushing the war into the enemy-occupied areas, the more favorable the overall situation will be.[42]

The operation, which was accomplished in a single night, marked the start of a counteroffensive by CCP forces,[43] which at the end of March 1947 were renamed the Chinese People's Liberation Army (PLA). Tens of thousands of officers and soldiers on the front, ninety-odd miles wide, crossed the river and launched operations on the south side. The army of Liu and Deng was ready to advance toward the Dabie Mountains. Mao gave the order at the end of July, and on August 7 it set out on a forced march of more than three hundred miles.[44]

The going was tough. The troops had to pass through a marshy bog stretching many miles south of the Yellow River, formed as a result of a recent flooding. They had to destroy their heavy equipment: neither motor vehicles nor artillery could be dragged across. But the warriors still faced their main obstacle in the form of another great river—the Huai—which divides north from south China and which blocked their path to the mountains. To ford it seemed impossible, and the soldiers had no improvised means available. People began grumbling, but at dawn on August 27, the water level in the river suddenly began falling. A true miracle! Liu gave the order to begin the crossing, and with sinking hearts the troops entered the water. After fording the river they looked back; to their utter astonishment the water was rapidly rising where they had just crossed!

What comes to mind is:

And Moses stretched out his hand over the sea; and the Lord caused the sea to go back by a strong east wind all that night, and made the sea dry land, and the waters were divided. . . . And the Lord said unto Moses, Stretch out thine hand over the sea. . . . And Moses stretched forth his hand, and the sea returned to his strength when the morning appeared.[45]

Who played the role of Moses in this case—Liu Bocheng or Deng—is hard to say, but that Heaven was favorably disposed toward the Chinese communists appears to be true. Even Deng, an atheist, acknowledged, "In crossing the Huai River, we were greatly helped by the Heavenly Master."[46]

The twenty-day march was basically completed; the troops arrived in the Dabie Mountain region and on August 27 Deng informed the Chairman and the CC of the completion of the "historic mission." Deeming "the wise leadership of the Central Committee and Chairman Mao" as the key to success, he figured on establishing a stable "liberated area" in the new territories in just over half a year.[47]

But new problems confronted Liu Bocheng, Deng, and their warriors. Deng recalled, "Northerners had quite a tough time in the south. When we crossed the Huai River, many developed diarrhea."[48] Northerners were unaccustomed to southern cooking, preferring noodles to rice. Their stomachs rebelled against spicy food. The northerners did not understand the local dialect, were ignorant of local ways and customs, and had a hard time getting their bearings.

Moreover, Deng initially pursued a leftist agrarian reform in the new territories, which undermined the trust of the population in the newcomers. Naturally, Deng was strictly following the party line, which became even more radical in autumn 1947. On September 13, the All-China Agrarian Conference, convened in Xibaipo, some 190 miles southwest of Beiping, adopted a "Fundamental Proposition on the Agrarian Law of China," which openly proclaimed, "Annul the property rights of landlords [*dizhu*] to land . . . equal distribution . . . among the entire population. . . . Small land parcels will be compensated at the expense of large ones, and poor ones at the expense of better ones."[49] In other words, the communists returned to Mao's old formula approved back in the period of the soviet movement in Jiangxi, "Drawing on the plentiful to make up for the scarce, and drawing on the fat to make up for the lean."

The explanation for this "zigzag" was that from the start of the new civil war, promoting the slogan "Down with Chiang Kai-shek" engendered a feeling within the party of a "return to the political slogans and political practice of the 'soviet movement'."[50] Even the usually sober Liu Shaoqi became impatient with the pace of solving social problems. It was Liu who was responsible for drafting the secret resolution of May 4, 1946, and leading the All-China Agrarian Conference.

Soon, however, Mao realized that the leftist agrarian reform contradicted the tactical policy of New Democracy. In early December 1947, he consulted with his entourage, and then several members of the Central Committee expressed doubts to him about the leftist policy.[51] Liu Shaoqi himself began to say that the line was mistaken.[52]

On January 14, 1948, Mao brought Deng into the discussion. He was the only party leader engaged in establishing a military base on a newly acquired territory where communist guerrillas had last been active many years earlier. Local people were reacting very unfavorably to the twists and turns in communist agrarian policy. Probing Deng's views, Mao sent Deng a list of six questions, among them, "Should land in the newly liberated areas be divided equally or, for the time being, should the rich peasants be left alone as well as the weaker and petty landlords?"[53] This was the first time the Chairman had invited Deng to discuss socioeconomic problems, but Deng was initially confused. On January 22, he wrote to Mao, "If, in the agrarian reform, we do not touch the rich peasants, it will be impossible to satisfy the demands of the poor peasants and laborers." But he immediately noted the reservation that in the Dabie Mountains his troops were confiscating the land and property of landlords and rich peasants only on the territory of the stable base area where approximately six million persons lived. In the other places, that is, where guerrilla warfare was being waged and where an additional six million persons lived, they "were temporarily not touching either the small landlords or the rich peasants."[54] But Mao was dissatisfied. "The strategy of struggle and the forms of organization in the new regions, established after the beginning of the counteroffensive, should differ accordingly from those we have in the old regions, established prior to the surrender of Japan, as well as those we have in the semi-old regions established between the surrender of Japan and the counteroffensive," he wrote to Deng on February 6.[55] Now Deng understood, and he hastened to agree. "For the time being, we will not take the property of the rich peasants. . . . And we will leave the landlords alone, especially the small ones; we will not destroy them down to the root."[56] The Chairman valued this prompt response; on February 17, on the back of Deng's last radiogram, he wrote, "The experience [of struggle] in the Dabie Mountains, described by Xiaoping, is especially rich; I hope it will be applied by all the troops."[57]

Then, in late April 1948, for the first time Deng sharply criticized the leftist line in agrarian reform: "The 'Left' tendency is manifested in the course of differentiating classes in land reform, where rich peasants [*funong*] are treated the same way as landlords [*dizhu*], the interests of middle peasants [*zhongnong*] are infringed upon and middle peasants are rejected."[58]

In early June, in the name of the CC Bureau for the Central Plains, to which he had been appointed first secretary one month earlier, Deng drafted a directive on agrarian reform that Mao praised. It merits quoting at length,

> We are guilty of having been too impetuous . . . alienating ourselves from the masses, isolating ourselves, and creating many difficulties in our struggle against the enemy and in our efforts to establish base areas. . . . Our guidelines and plans were not formulated on the basis of reality in the new liberated areas, but out of our wishful thinking. When we arrived in the new liberated areas, we did not investigate and study the situation, but simply planned to complete land reform in six months. . . . In most cases land was not truly redistributed. In some cases its redistribution was controlled by landlords and rich peasants. In others, the masses who had obtained land returned it secretly to the landlords and rich peasants and then rented it from

them. . . . In still others, a handful of reckless persons (many of whom were riffraff or persons who had connections with landlords) seized the fruits of land reform. . . . In still other cases, the peasants were only brave enough to take the land of small, weak landlords and rich peasants and of middle peasants, avoiding the land of powerful land-lords and rich peasants. These things happened nearly everywhere. . . . Believing we could solve every problem with guns plus land reform, we made severe "Left" errors. . . . We [also] . . . made mistakes in pur-suing the policy concerning . . . industry and commerce . . . and made mistakes of beating people and making arrests and conducting execu-tions indiscriminately. . . . The middle peasants were victimized by all the mistakes we made . . . and we even harmed the interests of poor peasants. . . . Unstable social order and anarchy gravely under-mined the economy, which then came to a standstill. Depression in the market and the closure of industrial and commercial enterprises were prevalent. . . . Large numbers of the people . . . lost their means of livelihood. . . . In both town and country we seriously damaged nearly all public buildings, factories, workshops, schools, cultural under-takings, churches and temples, as well as houses, furniture and trees owned by landlords and rich peasants. It was our troops, in particu-lar, who did the most serious damage, arousing strong repugnance among the masses. People said, "The Communist Party can handle its military affairs well, but not its political affairs!" Up to now, only a few of our leading comrades have truly realized that this kind of agricultural socialism is destructive, reactionary and evil and that it is causing incalculable losses to the interests of the people and the Party's political influence.[59]

What a remarkable admission of error and failure!

On June 28, to Deng's text the Chairman added just two paragraphs prais-ing his troops for "drawing off a large number of enemy troops, thereby wholly destroying their counterrevolutionary plan to bring the war to the liberated areas." Then he sent this document in the name of the Central Committee to all CC bureaus and sub-bureaus as well as to the front committees.[60]

Meanwhile, the situation of the Guomindang in 1948 had become critical, not only because of the actions of Liu's and Deng's forces. The Guomindang army had begun a hasty retreat, and Chiang Kai-shek was powerless to reverse the situation. Dean Acheson, who had replaced George C. Marshall as U.S. secretary of state in early January 1949, noted,

The long struggle had seriously weakened the Chinese Government not only militarily and economically, but also politically and in morale. [During the war against Japan] they [already] had sunk into corruption, into a scramble for place and power, and into reliance on the United States to win the war for them and to preserve their own domestic supremacy.... The mass of the Chinese people were coming more and more to lose confidence in the Government.... [The year of 1947 and the first half of 1948] revealed ... that their seeming strength was illusory and that their victories were built on sand.[61]

The Chinese government's inability to stimulate economic development or manage the economy became evident. Inflation took off in 1946. From September 1945 to February 1947, the value of the yuan collapsed. In 1947, monthly inflation was 26 percent. Guomindang leaders were hopeless in the face of the deepening crisis.[62] The strike movement rose sharply; in Shanghai alone in 1946, there were 1,716 strikes. In the spring of 1948, the government introduced ration cards for basic provisions in all major cities, as well as compulsory purchases of grain at artificially low prices to increase the grain reserves.[63] The low prices—a form of financial coercion—enabled the government to purchase more grain than it could have done at market prices. However, this latter measure alienated the Guomindang's natural ally, wealthy peasants.

In sum, Chiang Kai-shek's "troops had lost the will to fight, and its Government had lost popular support," Acheson concluded, emphasizing that "the Communists, on the other hand, through a ruthless discipline and fanatical zeal, attempted to sell themselves as guardians and liberators of the people. The Nationalist armies did not have to be defeated; they disintegrated. History has proved again and again that a regime without faith in itself and an army without morale cannot survive the test of battle."[64]

On April 25, 1948, the communists retook Yan'an. By June 1948, the Guomindang army had shrunk to 3.65 million men while the armed forces of the CCP had grown to 2.8 million.[65]

By this time, in late February 1948, Deng and his army, having completed their mission, had left the Dabie Mountains and returned north of the Huai River. The PLA was now ready to begin a broad-scale offensive against Chiang Kai-shek's forces.

By the fall of 1948, changes in CCP agrarian policy also were evident. Everywhere New Democracy garnered the sympathy and support of the population. Well-to-do peasants, disillusioned with the Guomindang, responded

positively to the CCP's repudiation of leftism. The Communist party succeeded in uniting diverse political forces around itself. It played a decisive role.

From September 8 to 13, 1948, Deng participated in an enlarged Politburo
meeting in the village of Xibaipo, which, after Mao's forces arrived there in
May 1948, had become the new capital of communist China. The conclave
resolved to basically destroy the Guomindang regime within about three
years.[66] From September 1948 through January 1949, communist forces conducted three major strategic operations: the first in Manchuria, the second in
East China, and the third in the Beiping-Tianjin region. More than 1.5 million enemy officers and soldiers were destroyed, and several major cities,
including Beiping itself, were taken.

Deng, along with Liu Bocheng and Chen Yi (commander and political
commissar of the East China forces neighboring Deng's field army), made
a great contribution to the planning and execution of the second operation,
the Huaihai (named after the Huai River and a town Haizhou on the Yellow
Sea coast) Campaign, carried out from November 1948 to January 1949. On
the eve of the battle, the Central Military Commission established a General
Front Committee to unite the command on this front, consisting of five
men: Deng, Liu Bocheng, Chen Yi, and Chen Yi's deputies Su Yu and Tan
Zhenlin. Deng was the secretary of the committee.[67]

The troika of Deng, Liu, and Chen made the major decisions. They had
known each other for a long time and got along very well. Moreover, all
three were from Sichuan, spoke the same dialect, and loved loud table talk
and jokes, but when it got down to serious matters they were decisive and
purposeful. They differed only in appearance—the lanky Liu Bocheng, the
massive Chen Yi, and the diminutive Deng, who played the main role in the
triumvirate, as the troops understood very well. Everyone knew that Mao
himself, after appointing Deng secretary of the front committee, told him, "I
give you the power to command."[68] Most soldiers and commanders treated all
three members of the troika with respect, but it was Deng whom they feared.
With the Chairman's support he had concentrated enormous power in his
hands and was not afraid to use it. He was extremely demanding of all his
subordinates and merciless toward those who violated discipline. Moreover,
he proved to be not only a strong party organizer but also a skillful military strategist. From his long association with Liu Bocheng, he had already
become rather good at parsing the fine points of military science. Staff officers sought his directives with regard to all operational matters.[69]

Victory in the Huaihai campaign foreordained the collapse of the
Guomindang regime. In March 1949, Deng participated in the Second

Plenum of the CC CCP in Xibaipo. Mao, anticipating the triumph of the revolution, set the course on destroying the national bourgeoisie as a class.[70] Deng was unconcerned about this change. He believed so strongly in the Chairman that he was ready to support any of his policies, whether rightist or leftist. At that time Mao really was oscillating from side to side. During an enlarged Politburo meeting as far back as September 1948, Deng could not help noting that the Chairman, who himself had just decried excessive leftism on the agrarian question, asserted that in the period of New Democracy the socialist sector would become the leading sector in China's national economy since bureaucratic capital as well as large independent industrial, commercial, and banking enterprises would become state property after the revolution. He said, "We must speak about the socialist character [of the national economy], despite the fact that [it] will be New Democratic on the whole."[71] Evidently, he was trying to transcend New Democracy, and only Liu Shaoqi tried cautiously to remind Mao and his comrades that the CCP "must not pursue socialist policies prematurely."[72] Everyone else, including Deng, kept silent.

And not by chance. The rectification campaign of 1942–45 (*zhengfeng*) had transformed the CCP into a leader-dominated party just like the Stalinist Soviet Communist Party. Deng supported this metamorphosis heart and soul. He was certain,

> We must consolidate the Party; otherwise, the Party will become decadent. . . . All comrades in the Party, without exception, should subject themselves to Party consolidation. . . . Those who are really incorrigible should be expelled from the Party. . . . Whether the Party leadership is good or not and how well the Central Committee's line and policies are carried out depend on whether Party members measure up to the qualifications for membership. Chairman Mao gives us correct instructions, but if we practice liberalism and always contravene them, we shall fail all the same. If, through Party consolidation, we can unify our will . . . we shall succeed in the cause of the people's liberation. . . . We want to achieve unity of thinking and organization in the Party.[73]

The Second Plenum also discussed the PLA's further advance south, including crossing the Yangzi River. That task was assigned to the armies of Liu Bocheng and Deng Xiaoping, and Chen Yi, which, on January 15, 1949, received the new designations of the Second and Third Field Armies respectively.[74]

After the plenum a meeting of the Secretariat was convened at which, by prior agreement, Mao gave Deng the first word. At Mao's request, Deng presented the candidates for the leading posts in the new regional military-party administrations that the communists intended to establish after the fast-approaching victory. "Deng Xiaoping took out a name list. As he read it, he made explanations," wrote his daughter Maomao.

> The East China Bureau of the CCP Central Committee was to consist of ... Deng Xiaoping, Liu Bocheng, and Chen Yi, with Deng serving as first secretary. The East China Region had jurisdiction over ... Shandong, Jiangsu, Zhejiang, Anhui, and Jiangxi provinces. The East China Region was to have two million troops [of four million in the PLA]. Chen Yi was to serve as the mayor of Shanghai. Liu Bocheng was to serve as the mayor of Nanjing.... Mao Zedong readily agreed to Deng's detailed and comprehensive report. He said, "Now personnel arrangements are thus decided upon. If there are changes in the future we can do that."[75]

On March 31, Deng drafted the plan of military operations, including forcing the Yangzi River and advancing toward Nanjing, Shanghai, and Hangzhou. He sent it to the Central Military Commission, which approved it on April 3. On the night of April 20, along a three-hundred-mile-wide front, the Second and Third Field Armies crossed the great river, which was about three-quarters of a mile wide. "We did not encounter a stiff resistance anywhere," Deng reported. "Nearly all 300,000 men crossed the river in a twenty-four hour period, plunging the enemy troops into chaos. With just one thought on their minds—breaking out of the encirclement—they [Guomindang troops] fled southward helter-skelter. The People's Liberation Army immediately took up pursuit, launching a wide frontal attack, until it took Nanjing in the process, on April 23."[76]

The Guomindang government moved to Canton. In May 1949, the Second and Third Field Armies attacked Shanghai. Crushing the two hundred thousand enemy defenders in one week, they occupied the country's largest metropolis on May 27. Three weeks earlier, Hangzhou, the capital of Zhejiang, had fallen.

The Guomindang was beyond salvation. PLA troops streamed south in a mighty torrent. In early September, the Guomindang government again retreated to Chongqing, as it had done during the anti-Japanese war.

Like all communists, during these heroic days and months Deng experienced incomparable joy. He felt triumphant. The taste of victory intoxicated him. Entering Nanjing on April 27, he visited Chiang Kai-shek's palace with Chen Yi. "Did you sit on President Chiang Kai-shek's presidential throne?" his daughter later asked him. "Yes, we did," he said smiling.[77]

In early May, Zhuo Lin and the children joined him in Nanjing. Together they moved to Shanghai, where they settled into one house with Chen Yi and his family. (The new mayor also had a wife and three children.) Deng soon brought the ashes of his first wife, Zhang Xiyuan, to this same house. He and Zhuo Lin had had great difficulty in locating her grave, since during the Japanese occupation the cemetery in which her ashes had been interred was destroyed. Now her ashes were placed in an urn on the first floor. Deng intended to rebury them, but he never got around to it and ultimately forgot. He didn't even remember when he left Shanghai. Nor did Zhuo Lin remember the ashes of her husband's former wife. Not until 1990, when he was an old man of eighty-six, did Deng, while visiting Shanghai, suddenly remember. He asked one of the local party cadres what had become of the ashes, which he now desired to have buried in the cemetery of revolutionary heroes in Beijing. But the Shanghai official happily informed him that the "orphaned" ashes had long since been buried in the equivalent cemetery in Shanghai. That same evening he brought Deng a photograph of the grave. Several days later, apparently at Deng's request, the official, accompanied by Deng's daughter Maomao and Deng's secretary Wang Ruilin, laid flowers on Zhang Xiyuan's grave. Deng himself did not visit the cemetery.[78]

In the summer of 1949, scarcely settled into Shanghai, Deng received an order from Mao to report to Beiping. In mid-July, at Mao Zedong's villa Shuangqing in the picturesque Fragrant Hills northwest of Beiping, he conversed twice with the Chairman and then made a report to the Central Committee. From Beiping he sent a letter to the members of the East China Bureau of the CC, conveying important news:

> Chairman Mao stressed the need for a swift military occupation of Guangdong, Guangxi, Yunnan, Guizhou, Sichuan, Xikang [Eastern Tibet], Qinghai, and Ningxia provinces, and an early occupation of the offshore islands and Taiwan. At the same time, the sooner we carry out our foreign policy of leaning to one side [i.e., the USSR], the more favorable it will be for us. . . . As regards our domestic policy, we must stress the need for conscientiously relying on our own efforts.[79]

On August 4, he spoke before the preparatory conference of the Chinese People's Political Consultative Conference, the highest organ of the communist-controlled united front. He told them about the completion of the Nanjing-Shanghai-Hangzhou campaign; "Politically," he concluded, "our victory spells the end of the reactionary Nanjing government."[80] Afterward, he went to Nanjing, the site of the East China Bureau of the CC and the staff headquarters of the Second Field Army, both of which he directed, rather than to Shanghai.

At the end of September he again returned to newly renamed Beijing, which again became the national capital. This time his orders were to rest up and recover his health since recently he had suffered from severe headaches, evidently brought on by overwork.[81] The Chinese People's Political Consultative Conference was in session in Beijing. On September 30, it selected him as a member of the Central People's Government (CPG). Mao became the chairman of the CPG; his chief deputies were Liu Shaoqi, Zhu De, and Sun Yat-sen's widow Song Qingling, who was fanatically devoted to the CCP.[82]

There in Beijing, on Tiananmen Square on October 1, 1949, Deng, along with Liu Bocheng and other comrades in the common struggle, took part in the ceremonies dedicated to the founding of the People's Republic of China. He stood, not far from Mao, under the arches of the palace tower that rose above the entrance to the Forbidden City, and eagerly imbibed the Chairman's every word. Mao proclaimed, "Today the Central People's Government of the People's Republic of China has been established."[83] Deng listened as the loudspeakers broadcast the heroic song "March of the Volunteers," the hymn of the new country, and watched as Mao slowly raised the red flag with its five yellow stars in the upper left corner. He knew that the large star in the center symbolized the Communist party, and the smaller stars framing it in a semicircle to the right represented the four main classes of New Democratic China: workers, peasants, urban petty bourgeoisie, and the national bourgeoisie. The jam-packed square went wild. Above thundered the roar of artillery: twenty-eight salvos signifying the twenty-eight year struggle of the CCP.

The revolution had triumphed in most of the country. Deng was in the forefront of those who had made a decisive contribution to this victory.

Chief of the Southwest Region

ON OCTOBER 21, Deng and Liu Bocheng returned to the Second Army, which was facing a new campaign in their home province of Sichuan. The area was defended by several hundred thousand Guomindang troops determined to wage a decisive battle against the communists. The Second Army was also tasked with bringing the southwest provinces of Guizhou, Guangxi, Yunnan, Xikang, and the state of Tibet under communist control. After the fall of the Qing dynasty, Tibet had declared its independence from China in July 1913, but no country recognized it. In July 1922, the CCP had passed a resolution declaring one of its main tasks to "reunite Mongolia, Tibet, and Turkestan (Xinjiang) into a Unified Republic of China based upon the principle of federation."[1]

The Central Military Commission had outlined the forthcoming operation in May 1949, and Mao had personally discussed this operation with Deng in mid-July.[2] On August 1, the CC established a Southwest Bureau, naming Deng as first secretary, Liu Bocheng as second secretary, and He Long as third secretary. It took almost three months to work out the details of the military plan.[3] Finally, on October 22, the Second Army launched its campaign, chasing Chiang Kai-shek from Chongqing, which fell to the communists in late November. On December 8, Deng entered the city in a blaze of glory. None among the welcoming crowds would have recognized in the strong-willed commander the local preparatory school graduate, the shy sixteen-year-old youth, who long ago had set out from Chongqing for distant France.

Zhuo Lin and the children joined Deng in Chongqing. "They [Deng and Liu Bocheng] had not intended to take their families with them when they set out on the campaign to the southwest," she recalled, " . . . but I said [to Deng]

'You are always 'losing' us, paying us no attention, it just won't do! This time I will definitely go with you. I am a member of the Communist party. You may cut off my head, but still I will go with you.' [After this] he had no choice but to let us accompany him."[4] It was useless to quarrel with Zhuo Lin, who went despite being almost seven months pregnant. An equally strong-willed woman, she got whatever she wanted.

Liu Bocheng's wife and her four children joined Zhuo Lin and her three children in the journey to the southwest. They traveled in two American jeeps along a bumpy, dusty road. The children were acting up and constantly saying they had to pee. "Well, the boys could just pee while the jeeps were driving, but how about the girls?" Zhuo Lin said. "We found a pot in a temple somewhere, and in that way the girls were able to manage."[5]

Meanwhile, the Second Army, supported by other units, surrounded Chengdu, where Chiang had moved to, and on December 10 they forced Chiang Kai-shek to escape to Taiwan, where he was followed by other members of his collapsing government. Having lost the battle for mainland China, Chiang and his comrades-in-arms were determined to continue the fight against communism from Taiwan.

On December 27, Chengdu fell. The civil war in China was nearly over. The victorious communists now occupied almost all the provinces. All that remained to be taken were Xikang, the island of Hainan, Tibet, and Taiwan. But the Americans determined the fate of Taiwan by sending their Seventh Fleet into the Taiwan Strait at the end of June 1950, just days after the outbreak of the Korean War. The presence of the Seventh Fleet prevented the PLA's Third Field Army from launching an invasion of Taiwan and enabled Chiang Kai-shek, with the assistance of the United States, to transform the island into an anti-communist bastion.

In Tibet the Americans were powerless. Both Chiang Kai-shek and Mao considered Tibet part of China, and there was no possibility of international intervention to support Tibetan independence. The Dalai Lama later acknowledged, "The Tibetans, I think unrealistically, expected too much from America. . . . [And if Chiang Kai-shek had] come forward to support Tibetan independence [then] in the eyes of millions of Chinese [Chiang and his political party would have been] a national disgrace."[6]

England, which had granted independence to India and Pakistan—Tibet's southern neighbors—in 1947, recognized the People's Republic of China in January 1950, soon followed by its former colonies. Thus Mao's hands were untied. "Right now after England, India, and Pakistan have recognized us a favorable situation has been created for us to enter Tibet," he telephoned

Deng on January 10, 1950, from Moscow, where he was negotiating with Stalin. He ordered the Southwest Bureau to "liberate Tibet."[7]

But the Chinese leader was in no hurry to apply force. The Dalai Lama was widely respected in China and throughout the world. Therefore, on the basis of the formal principles of New Democracy and the united front, Mao insisted on the unification of Tibet through peaceful means, with force as a supplementary measure to be used only in case the Tibetan government refused negotiations. In late November 1949, he had suggested that "resolving the question of liberating Tibet should be put off until the autumn or fall of next year,"[8] a position he maintained even after the victories on the diplomatic front.

Following his orders, by the end of March 1950 Liu and Deng's troops "liberated" only the eastern part of Xikang province, situated between Sichuan and Tibet in an operation that began in December 1949. For a time the Jinsha River (as the upper reaches of the Yangzi River were called) became the border between Tibet and the PRC. The ten thousand or so poorly armed Tibetan troops were deployed in the western part of Xikang.

Special representatives of Mao and Premier Zhou Enlai held talks with emissaries of the Dalai Lama in New Delhi over a period of several months. But with the negotiations going nowhere, Mao gave Deng and Liu the green light to attack.

On October 7, 1950, units of the Second Field Army, numbering forty thousand officers and men, crossed the Jinsha River. Their objective was to crush the Tibetan army, which they accomplished easily in two weeks of bloody battles. More than fifty-seven hundred Tibetan fighters perished.[9] Then the diplomats took over again. The PLA halted its advance seventy-five miles east of Lhasa and focused on propaganda work among the Tibetan POWs. They were lectured on socialism and the foreign devils "with long noses, round blue eyes, and light skins" who "have sat" on their "necks" and kept them "apart from the motherland."[10] Then they were released to return home and even given travel money. The Chinese army tried to win the favor of the local population by acting courteously and paying for everything they took from the peasants and town folk. They did not rob anyone or defile the monasteries. They even repaired the roads. "The Chinese were very disciplined," the Dalai Lama acknowledged. "They carefully planned."[11]

Meanwhile, the Tibetan government attempted without success to gain international support in its resistance to Chinese aggression. Appeals to the United Nations, the United States, England, and India went unanswered.

The Fifth Session of the UN General Assembly unanimously refused to discuss the Chinese invasion. The world turned its back on Tibet.

Isolated and defenseless, the Tibetans submitted to the bitter reality that confronted them. They sent a delegation to Beijing, where, on May 23, 1951, Chinese representatives presented to them a seventeen-point text, "Agreement on Measures for the Peaceful Liberation of Tibet." The document said, "The Tibetan people shall unite and drive out imperialist aggressive forces from Tibet; the Tibetan people shall return to the big family of the Motherland—the People's Republic of China."[12] By its terms the Dalai Lama would formally retain his authority in religious and domestic affairs (with the exception of defense) and PLA troops would enter Tibet, supposedly to assist in implementing the agreement. The Chinese representatives demanded that the Tibetan delegation sign the agreement, although they had not been authorized to do so. Then the document was "authenticated" with the official seal of the Dalai Lama—which had been forged in advance by craftsmen in Beijing.

The Americans, who had done nothing to assist Tibet, now tried to dissuade the Dalai Lama from ratifying the agreement and even offered him asylum. The Dalai Lama, who was then only fifteen years old but already well versed in politics, accepted the document via a telegram he sent to Mao Zedong at the end of October 1951. "What is burned by fire should be healed by using fire," he wisely decided. This meant that "trouble comes from the East, from the Chinese. The only way to deal with that is to go there, to have talks, with dialogue."[13]

Meanwhile, units of the First Field Army quickly occupied southwestern Tibet, and the Liu-Deng forces entered Lhasa without firing a shot. The "peaceful liberation" of Tibet was accomplished.[14] Deng had not taken part in the expedition, but he had planned and directly controlled the entire operation with Liu Bocheng and He Long. Thus he could also celebrate the victory.

By this time he was juggling several important positions. He was not only a member of the Central People's Government, political commissar of the Second Field Army, and first secretary of the Southwest Bureau but also a member of the highest military organ of the republic, the People's Revolutionary Military Council, and political commissar of the Southwest Military Region. Starting in December 1949, he was the mayor of Chongqing as well. In July 1950 he became deputy chairman of the Military Administrative Committee (MAC) of southwest China, the highest governmental organ in the region embracing the four provinces of Sichuan, Guizhou, Yunnan, and Xikang.[15] The total area of the region was more than

347,000 square miles, larger than Texas and Oklahoma combined. Its total population according to a number of estimates was between 70 and 150 million people.[16]

The PRC was then divided into six regions, in four of which—East China, Central-South, Northwest, and Southwest—the governing organs were called military-administrative committees.[17] This division corresponded to the directives of the Common Program of the Chinese People's Political Consultative Conference, which had been adopted on September 29, 1949, as the provisional constitution of the PRC.[18] Liu Shaoqi defined this form of rule as "merciless, direct military dictatorship."[19]

In China, as in all communist dictatorships, the government was subordinate to the party. Thus, even though Deng was only deputy chairman of the MAC, his position as first secretary of the regional party bureau made him the regional boss. Moreover, Mao, fearing regions might become too powerful (as they had become after the fall of the Manchu dynasty in 1912), divided the party, military-administrative, and purely army powers among the three most powerful figures of the Southwest. He Long headed the military region, Liu Bocheng the Military Administrative Committee, and Deng the Southwest Bureau. But Deng, who alone among them reported directly to the Chairman, enjoyed virtually unlimited power. As he recalled subsequently, "In the first few years after the founding of the People's Republic of China, the Central Committee gave the local organizations extensive powers to deal with problems independently."[20]

After the "liberation" of Tibet, Deng's Southwest Bureau and the Southwest China Military Administrative Committee extended their control over it as well.[21] Now an enormous territory of more than 849,000 square miles was under Deng's control. The one million Tibetans joined an already diverse regional ethnic minority population of between ten and thirty million, with their own traditions and beliefs. Nobody really knew the actual number, or even how many distinct ethnonational groups there were. Deng, for example, thought there were more than seventy national minorities in Yunnan, whereas according to the most recent data there are twenty-four or twenty-five.[22] Some of them were at the stage of matriarchy and clan-tribal relations. Slavery existed in several districts. Among some tribes living in the jungles along the borders with Burma and Laos, cannibalism was practiced. Almost all these peoples hated the Han.

The overwhelming majority of both the Han and the national minorities were illiterate and desperately poor. The mortality rate was sky-high. There was no electricity in the villages and hamlets, and no good roads. Much of the arable land was used to grow opium poppies. Unemployment in the cities was rife and the financial system, like everywhere in the country, chaotic.

In sum, the region that Deng took over was enormous, overpopulated, and economically backward. The CCP leaders had no doubt that coercion, spiced with a healthy dose of propaganda, was the only way to jump-start progress toward a brighter future.[23] Karl Marx's words that "force is the midwife of every old society that was pregnant with a new one" rang in their ears.[24] Before them stood the example of the socialist Soviet Union, the "elder brother" as it was respectfully called, whose path they intended to follow.

Widespread resistance by remnant Guomindang forces throughout the region increased the communists' inclination toward employing "Red" terror. Bitter rearguard battles were fought in the Southwest, especially in Sichuan and Yunnan, the last strongholds of Chiang Kai-shek's forces. Armed struggle intensified in 1950, after the communists ousted local elites and established their own power at the local level. Various forces that had stayed on the fence during the civil war now attacked the Communist party. Just how many insurgents there were is difficult to say. Mao Zedong asserted that in 1950, in China as a whole, there were more than four hundred thousand "bandits scattered in remote regions."[25] According to official data from the Ministry of Public Security, there were several hundred thousand in the Southwest alone.[26] He Long and Deng gave a much lower figure, reporting several tens of thousands of bandits active in the region.[27] Yet He Long and Deng also reported that "wide spread" military operations against the PLA were taking place, "embracing all the region of southwest Sichuan, Xikang, Yunnan, and Guizhou." Later, Deng recalled that ninety thousand officers and men of the regular Guomindang army and ninety thousand stubborn "bandits" were fighting against the communists.[28] Whatever the precise figures, the forces of counterrevolution were numerous and persistent.

In March 1950, the CCP Central Committee adopted two resolutions: "On the Elimination of Banditry and the Establishment of New Revolutionary Order," and "On the Suppression of Counterrevolutionary Activity." Liu Shaoqi was then in charge as Mao was on leave, recovering from the strain of his meetings with Stalin in Moscow in December 1949 through February 1950.[29] When Mao returned, he said these resolutions were not tough enough, and he accused his colleagues of committing the rightist error of "excessive leniency."[30] Bending under his pressure, on October 10, 1950, the CC issued a new directive increasing the penalties for "counterrevolutionary crimes."

Deng, the thirty thousand party cadres and about two hundred thousand non-party local cadres in the Southwest region responded enthusiastically to the CC resolutions.[31] After October 10, they indulged in an orgy of executions. Regional security organs, army units, poor peasant-pauper militia, court employees, and procurators all took part in this prolonged bloodbath.[32] The scale of executions that took place between late 1950 and early 1951 in western Sichuan demonstrates the extreme to which they went. In November 1950, 1,188 persons were executed there; in December, 942; in January 1951, 1,309; in February, 3,030; in March, 1,076; in April, 844.[33] In six months a total of 8,389 were killed, or on average 46 persons every day. (During this same period only 700 people were executed in Beijing.)[34] In February 1951, Deng, along with Deng Zihui from South China, asserted that it would be good to execute between one-half and two-thirds of all counterrevolutionaries, and on March 13 Deng sent a report to Mao informing the Chairman that almost 90 percent of the local cadres in some parts of Yunnan were "spies, landlords or other bad elements." The situation in Sichuan also disturbed him.[35]

The wave of public executions that engulfed Deng's region was so large that the Chairman himself felt compelled to intervene. "We should not kill too many people," he wrote to Deng on April 30, 1951. "If we kill too many, we will forfeit public sympathy and a shortage of labor power will arise." He issued a new order: in the countryside execute no more than one in a thousand, and in the cities even less.[36]

Once the Chairman had spoken, everyone fell into line. In accordance with Mao's system of rationing executions, Deng and his subordinates gradually curtailed the shootings. In the same region of western Sichuan, for example, in May and the first ten days of June, 403 persons were executed.[37] The "daily norm" was reduced to 9–10 persons, a reduction of more than three-quarters.

During the massive campaign to suppress counterrevolutionaries, in the country as a whole by the end of 1951 according to conservative official figures more than two million people had been killed. Another two million were imprisoned or sent to labor camps.[38] Many victims were not even opponents of the CCP, but executed on false accusations.[39]

In the Southwest as well as throughout China, numerous excesses characterized the implementation of the agrarian reforms following publication of the new Agrarian Reform Law, of June 28, 1950. Over the next two and a half years, the Southwest Bureau diligently implemented this measure, which, in Mao's words, was supposed "to topple the entire landlord class."[40] The reform was an agrarian revolution from above. Since most peasants

remained passive, special brigades of party activists were sent into the countryside to organize "peasant unions" consisting mostly of paupers and landless agricultural workers. Their mission was to deal violently with everyone
they viewed as landlords. The new law formally prohibited confiscating the
land of rich peasants, since Mao considered it necessary "to defer the solution
of the problem of the semi-feudal rich peasants for several years."[41] Where
landlord holdings alone did not satisfy the land hunger of all the poor peasants, however, even the smallest property owners were robbed. This occurred
almost everywhere; including Sichuan where the share of landlord holdings
constituted 60 percent of the total.[42] The rich peasants whose land was expro-
priated were conveniently labeled "counterrevolutionaries," since the law
allowed taking their land. Communist actions flagrantly contradicted their
own policy pronouncements. The number of rich peasants actually shrank.
Land belonging to temples, including clan temples, monasteries, churches,
schools, and clans, as well as to industrialists and merchants, was also confiscated. Rough-and-ready "people's tribunals" authorized to pronounce death
sentences were set up in the villages. Many who had resisted the communist
takeover were either shot or exiled to concentration camps.

As early as May 1951, Deng reported to Mao that the first stage of reform
was completed. By then communists in the Southwest region had distributed
land to more than 13.5 million landless peasants and paupers, "punishing
law-breaking landlords [dizhu], arousing poor peasants and farm laborers [to
the struggle] . . . and suppressing the counter-revolutionaries."[43] In a "very
acute struggle, unprecedented in history" (as Mao characterized the division
of landed property in China[44]), a turning point had occurred and Mao was
ecstatic. He scribbled comments on Deng's report: "Everything is very good!
Deserving congratulations! In places where it's not been done, it should be
done just like this. . . . Everything is correct, we need to do this everywhere."
He informed his colleagues, "Comrade Xiaoping's report is very good!"[45] Not
all the regional leaders received such an assessment. For example, Mao criticized Ye Jianying, the chief of South China, for "being too soft" on the local
landlords.[46]

Mao Zedong also lauded Deng's approach to solving the agrarian question
among national minorities. Following Mao's injunction to proceed cautiously
with regard to national minorities, Deng oversaw a process of gradual transformation in the minority regions despite grumbling from some party cadres.
In Tibet, agrarian reform was on hold. "Some comrades are worried that if
they do it this way, they might lose their class stand, not understanding that
class stand is manifested differently there," he said. "What is the correct class

stand? It is at present not launching class warfare, instead achieving unity of the nationalities."[47] Deng and the Southwest Bureau welcomed a large number of national minorities into educational institutions in the Southwest, including a new Nationalities Institute. By October 1952, twenty-five thousand nationality cadres had received Bolshevik-style training.[48]

In the second stage of agrarian reform, launched in June 1951, twenty-five million additional farm laborers were given land, and by the summer of 1952 a further forty-five million landless peasants received plots of land in the third stage. "One may say," Deng reported to Beijing, "that agrarian reform in the Southwest is basically completed."[49] By the spring of 1953, when the fourth stage of the agrarian reform was completed, ten million of the remaining sixteen million peasants became so-called middle peasants with their own plots of land.[50] The remaining six million, all members of national minorities, did not go through the reform until the mid-1950s.

Next as grist for the grinding stone of revolution were the urban bourgeoisie. In the first year of the PRC, thanks to the rational and moderate policy of New Democracy, they had increased the value of their production by one and a half times and received what were record profits.[51] Instead of rejoicing at the leap in production, Mao was disturbed that the bourgeoisie was flourishing. Therefore, he decided to deal them a severe blow. Such was the logic of class conflict: "With the overthrow of the landlord class and the bureaucrat-capitalist class, the contradiction between the working class and the national bourgeoisie has become the principle contradiction in China."[52] Deng, who always made sure to be in line with the Leader's "wise directives," agreed.

In late 1951 and early 1952, Deng launched repressive campaigns in the Southwest against "bourgeois elements."[53] The "Three Anti's" campaign was directed against the corruption of officialdom by the bourgeoisie, and the "Five Anti's" targeted private entrepreneurship.[54] The communists began to extort immense contributions from the bourgeoisie, thereby undermining their economic position. Targeted individuals were hauled before hostile crowds and publicly humiliated, and many were shot after trials that were a mockery of justice.

The other regional leaders acted no differently from Deng. Ultimately, Mao himself felt compelled to order a change of course. At a Politburo meeting in the spring of 1952, he asserted,

> We still have New Democracy [it seemed that he had long since forgotten this term, but now suddenly remembered it] and not socialism. We

are in favor of weakening the bourgeoisie, but not liquidating them. We need to beat them up for several months, and then drag them into the light again, but we should not beat them outright, not destroy them.[55]

Nevertheless, by September 1952 the share of state capital in industry rose to 67.3 percent, and in trade to 40 percent. The socialist sector already dominated the Chinese economy.[56]

Following Mao's lead, Deng also achieved success in the financial-economic field. "The regional rate of inflation," writes Richard Evans, "fell with the national rate, which declined from one in the hundreds of thousands to 20 percent in 1951 and to well below 10 percent in 1952."[57]

Deng also supported Mao wholeheartedly when, in May 1950, Mao ordered a verification and reregistration of Communist party members. The object was to purge supposedly "alien" elements that had infiltrated the party. Deng explained to communists in Chongqing that the movement "means primarily to check on ideology and work style, to see what attitude our comrades have towards the Party's revolutionary cause and whether or not . . . they performed their work well and acted in conformity with Mao Zedong Thought. The purpose is to overcome confusion and achieve unity in matters of ideology and politics."[58] By 1953, 10 percent of party members in the country had been expelled. Deng had a hand in achieving this impressive result.

His speeches to party activists also stressed that communists must set a high standard by their own moral example: "A Party member should have a correct work style . . . acting and living plainly."[59] He, however, meant these words for others, not himself. During the two and a half years he lived in Chongqing, Deng, like many other party leaders, traded in guerrilla puritanism for urban comfort. He and his family initially occupied an entire floor of a two-story building that had previously belonged to the Guomindang. The other floor was first occupied by Liu Bocheng's family and later by He Long and his family. Deng and Zhuo Lin quickly established very friendly relations with the convivial He Long and his household. Soon, however, Deng and his family moved to the spacious, newly constructed offices of the Southwest Bureau, which were equipped with air conditioning, then a rare luxury. Deng loved to eat well, but Zhuo Lin was a mediocre cook. Therefore, special chefs prepared the Deng family's meals. During Deng's free time he enjoyed playing billiards, even hiring an instructor to tutor him in the fine points of this game. Many years later, during the Cultural Revolution of the late 1960s, the

Red Guards, who loathed Deng, charged that, "He ate special foods, lived in special lodgings, and enjoyed the finest things."[60]

To be sure, this was an exaggeration when it came to material goods. Apart from a Swiss Rolex watch and a high-quality brown woolen sweater, Deng owned no luxury items. During the civil war he had come into possession of a Parker fountain pen as a sort of trophy, but a pickpocket stole it from him in Shanghai in the summer of 1949. Deng regretted its loss to the end of his life, and every time he visited Shanghai he would mutter, "The pickpockets in Shanghai were terrible."[61]

Deng dressed modestly in what was in effect the party uniform. Like Mao and all the other top leaders, he wore a drab-colored jacket (cotton in the summer, padded in the winter), buttoned at the throat, with four pockets, and loose-fitting trousers. Deng's headgear was an ordinary soft worker's cap.

His entire family dressed the same way, his children no differently from their ordinary peers. Zhuo Lin, too, preferred the unadorned party style. From the time they settled in Chongqing, she served as headmistress of a boarding school she had founded. Ostensibly open to anyone, in reality it was intended only for the children of high-ranking cadres of the Southwest Bureau and the Military Administrative Committee. Zhuo Lin oversaw everything: the curriculum, training, the rest periods of the ninety pupils, provision of clothing, nutrition, and so on. Because of a shortage of teachers she herself taught several subjects: Chinese language, arithmetic, and even music, although she had a tin ear. Her own children—Deng Lin, Pufang, and even five-year-old Deng Nan—were among her pupils.

Deng and Zhuo had more children in Chongqing. On January 25, 1950, their third daughter came into the world, called Maomao ("Hairy One") because of the light, downy hair on her head. Many Chinese parents affectionately called their newborns by this name. Following the family tradition of naming daughters after beautiful trees, Zhuo Lin bestowed on her the formal name of Deng Rong (Deng "Ficus"). This name had profound meaning. It was while sitting under a ficus that Siddhartha Gautama became Buddha; therefore, ficus in Buddhism is the Boddhi (Enlightenment) tree. Although Deng and Zhuo Lin were hardly Buddhists, Buddhist symbolism meant something to them as Chinese. A year and a half later, in August 1951, a second son was born, Zhifang. As long as he remained a child, however, everyone in the family called him Fei Fei ("Fidgety") for his rather lively character.

Zhuo Lin did not want this last child, as she was very burdened. She had begun working in the school one month after she had given birth to Deng Rong. She asked the head of medical services in the Second Army to perform an abortion. But he said, "Maybe it is a boy!" In China, it will be recalled, sons were always preferred over girls, so, "thanks to his words," Maomao wrote, "my younger brother Fei Fei came into this world."[62]

At this time, Deng Xiaoping's stepmother, his father's widow, Xia Bogen, was also living in Deng's house along with her youngest daughter Xianqun. The latter was a likable and modest girl whom Deng sent to middle school. Mama Xia was five years older than her stepson. Soft-spoken, good-hearted, and hard-working, Mama Xia and Zhuo Lin hit it off at once, and Zhuo was comfortable leaving her in charge of the house and the children when she left for work.

In 1950, several other relatives took shelter "under Deng's wing." He himself invited those living in Paifang.[63] Others came on their own. He took proper care of them all. He took on his brother Xianxiu (Deng Ken), who had worked for the CCP, as his deputy in the municipal administration of Chongqing. He sent his stepsister Xianfu to study in the Southeast Military-Political Academy, and later gave her a job in the party organization.[64] He initially sent his brother Xianzhi, an opium addict, who had long managed the family finances, to recover at a drug treatment clinic. Then he secured a position for him as a county official in Guizhou. Deng also looked after his stepbrother Xianqing and found him a good position.

In sum, he acted warmly to all the members of his family, perhaps making up for his long years of inattention toward them. But there was more to it as well. He was rescuing his family from likely danger. During the agrarian reform begun in 1950, the poor peasants of Paifang would undoubtedly want to "settle accounts" with the landlord Deng Xianzhi, despite his being the brother of the head of the Southwest Bureau. They also would have targeted Xia Bogen and the rest of the Deng family who were living in "the old manor." The ricochet might even strike Deng Xiaoping. Someone might even think to inform Mao. (Incidentally, when sending Xianzhi to the drug treatment clinic, Deng insisted that he change his family and personal names. Xianzhi was not only considered a big landlord in Paifang but had served as head of the district office under the Guomindang.)

Of course, many years later, during the Cultural Revolution, the Red Guards exposed all of Deng's actions. "Deng Xiaoping relocated his step-mother/landlord and his landlord relatives to new lodgings in Chongqing," they said indignantly. "Deng Xiaoping is truly the filial son of the landlord class who has lost any sense of shame."[65]

But the fearsome wave of massacres that swept across rural China spared Deng's relatives. He had skillfully solved his family's problems.

Meanwhile, on July 1, 1952, the thirty-first anniversary of the founding of the CCP, Deng participated in the ceremonies inaugurating the rail link between Chongqing and Chengdu that he had initiated. He was extremely proud of this project, which his own late father, Wenming, had dreamed of. Standing on the platform, Deng smiled broadly as the large black locomotive chugged into the Chongqing railway station. An industrializing China had set out on the path of profound transformations.

A portrait of Mao framed by sheaves of grain adorned the front end of the locomotive. It was as if the Leader himself had come to Chongqing to congratulate his faithful pupil. In truth, the head of the party and the state was obviously satisfied with Deng, who up to now had faithfully followed his course.

9

The Beijing Hippodrome

AT THE END of July 1952, Mao transferred Deng to Beijing and gradually brought him into his circle of intimates. The Chairman became increasingly fond of the energetic and still rather youthful Sichuanese. (Deng was forty-eight.) On August 7, Mao appointed him one of five deputies to Zhou Enlai, premier of the State Administrative Council. Until then, two of the four deputies were noncommunists. By appointing Deng, another communist, as the new deputy Mao was signaling that the period of New Democracy was coming to an end. Soon the country would enter a new stage of constructing socialism. Mao also included Deng on the twenty-one-name list of top Chinese leaders whose biographies were scheduled for publication in a new edition of the Soviet encyclopedia, a considerable honor in the communist world.[1]

Deng left for the capital with Zhuo Lin and the children, Grandma Xia Bogen, and half-sister Deng Xianqun. They settled into a cozy house not far from Zhongnanhai, the residence of the top leadership. Only members of the Politburo, of which Deng was not yet one, lived in Zhongnanhai itself, part of the old imperial palace complex, adjacent to the former imperial Forbidden City.

Deng's new neighbor was his fellow provincial and old comrade-in-arms Nie Rongzhen, then deputy chairman of the General Staff of the PLA and commander of the North China Military Region. Nie Rongzhen was very hospitable, and his cook prepared excellent Sichuan cuisine. Therefore, Deng and his family were frequent visitors, "to enjoy food there for 'free'" and to down a shot of hard liquor which he enjoyed. He was not an alcoholic, but he made it a rule to enjoy a shot glass before dinner.[2]

With so many of his old friends now gathered in Beijing, Zhou Enlai above all, Deng was in his element. A festive atmosphere reigned in the revolutionary capital. Crimson flags fluttered, martial music rumbled from loudspeakers, slogans and posters hung on the walls of houses. But the streets were almost empty of motor vehicles since China as yet lacked an auto industry and relatively few cars and trucks were imported from the USSR.

In the second half of 1952 and the first half of 1953, Mao transferred to Beijing several other regional leaders whom he also appointed to high positions in the state and party apparatus. Politburo member Gao Gang, the head of the Northeast Bureau, was made director of the State Planning Commission; Rao Shushi, director of the Organization Department of the Central Committee; and Deng Zihui, director of the Rural Work Department. Earlier, in September 1950, Mao had transferred Xi Zhongxun to Beijing, initially as director of the Propaganda Department, and later appointed Xi secretary of the State Administrative Council. With the exception of Xi Zhongxun, Deng knew all of these people very well. In the corridors of power, the quintet of Deng, Gao, Rao, Deng Zihui, and Xi Zhongxun were referred to as "the five horses galloping into the capital." Gao was called "the horse galloping in first place," since he had received the greatest power of the five.[3]

Soon the Chairman, fearing excessive regionalism, a familiar phenomenon throughout Chinese history, abolished all of the military administrative committees and regional party bureaus. He strengthened the central leadership with the former regional leaders whom he obviously preferred to keep close at hand.

By this time, a rift had appeared within the leadership of the Chinese Communist Party between the newly promoted Gao Gang, who favored a swift transition to socialist construction, and Mao's current deputy in the party, Liu Shaoqi, who favored gradualism. Premier Zhou, responsible for economic development, leaned toward Liu while Mao balanced between Gao on one hand and Liu and Zhou on the other.

Mao, of course, was a leftist, so Gao Gang's views rather than those of Liu Shaoqi were closer to his. But Stalin, whose material and political assistance Mao was interested in, would not allow him to jettison New Democracy and make a quick transition to socialism. Stalin's caution was visceral. He instinctively realized that an industrialized communist China could pose a threat to his leadership in the communist world. Therefore, the Kremlin dictator, who was providing indispensable if limited aid to his ally, bound Mao to himself. The tactical course of the Chinese Communist Party was subordinated to Stalin's political line.[4] Mao acted inconsistently in the late 1940s and early 1950s, oscillating between his own innate leftism and the moderation imposed on him from Moscow.

Accordingly, by turns he criticized Gao, then Liu, then Zhou. Thus, in May 1949 he supported Liu Shaoqi, launching a sharp criticism of Gao Gang for his leftist adventurism.[5] But two and a half years later, Gao convinced Mao to launch the struggle against China's domestic capitalists.[6] Mao also supported Gao Gang's leftist report advocating acceleration of the agricultural cooperative movement in Manchuria and sharply rebuked Liu Shaoqi for taking the opposite line.[7] Then in the spring of 1952, Mao appeared to reverse himself and reaffirmed the need for "the further utilization of private capital in the interests of developing the economy and well-being of the people."[8]

Mao had always been a good actor. Now playing the role of the People's Emperor, he enjoyed toying with his subordinates, who found it difficult to fathom his moods. He affected the style of a Daoist sage who periodically uttered inscrutable philosophical maxims and spiced his revelations with quotations from the ancient classics. He deliberately obfuscated the issues, and often asserted that the time had come for him to retire. In talking about retirement, Mao was following the example of Stalin. The Soviet dictator, in turn, had modeled himself on Ivan the Terrible, who feigned retirement as a means to gauge the reaction of his courtiers.[9] Of course, none of their colleagues would allow either Stalin or Mao Zedong to retire. The entourages of the "great leaders" quickly grasped their cat-and-mouse game but could not anticipate what the aging dictators would come up with next.

It was in such a charged atmosphere that Deng worked in Beijing. He now had almost daily contact with Mao, or to be more precise, every evening or every night, since the Chairman usually awoke around 4:00 or 5:00 p.m. and worked until morning. Mao usually received Deng and other "party comrades" in Zhongnanhai. In his private quarters, lying on his enormous bed, piled high with books, he listened to their reports, worked on documents, and periodically uttered portentous words. He sometimes held meetings in a neighboring pavilion, where he would breakfast or dine while listening to reports. Scorning both etiquette and linguistic clarity, he would express his Delphic opinions on a variety of subjects.

Deng's main task, therefore, was to guess what the Boss really wanted at any given moment. Such was the art of politics in totalitarian China, the Soviet Union, and everywhere that powerful personalities dominated the state. Deng could not attach himself to any leader other than Mao among the contending chieftains—not to Gao Gang, or Liu Shaoqi, or Zhou Enlai—but he had to maintain good relations with them all. He had to sniff which way the wind was blowing and tack in the direction that the Great Helmsman indicated. For now Deng understood this very well. It was not by chance that en route from Chengdu to Beijing, to his daughter Deng Nan's question, "Papa, in Sichuan, everyone called you 'the head,' but what will they call you in Beijing?" he replied, "The foot."[10] That was precisely what the Chairman now required him to be forever: his strong foot.

This was impressed on Deng in the fall and winter of 1952. In September Mao sent a delegation headed by Liu Shaoqi to the Nineteenth Congress of the Soviet Communist Party. Liu's mission was to determine whether Stalin thought it was time to begin constructing socialism in China, now that capitalism there was on its last legs. The answer Liu returned with in October could not have satisfied Mao. Although Stalin finally agreed socialist construction in China could begin, he insisted on the need to act "gradually." He advised Mao "not to rush cooperativization and collectivization of agriculture, since China is in a more advantageous position than the USSR in the period of collectivization."[11]

The ambiguity of the recommendation allowed Liu Shaoqi and Zhou Enlai to interpret it as they pleased, accenting the words "gradually" and "not to rush." Mao then transferred the leftist Gao Gang to Beijing as chairman of the State Planning Commission, complained to Gao about the "conservatism" of Liu and Zhou, and instigated him to launch a campaign against "right opportunism" in the party.[12]

The occasion for the latter was the publication in the main party newspaper, *People's Daily*, on December 31, 1952, of the draft of a new tax system prepared by Bo Yibo, the minister of finance, adopted five days earlier at a meeting of the State Administrative Council.[13] The law levied uniform taxes on all forms of property, thereby depriving state and cooperative enterprises of their tax privileges, and providing favorable conditions for competition to the private capitalist sector. This was in keeping with the principles of New Democracy.

Deng, who knew Minister Bo very well, had reason to believe that Mao too supported this moderate approach. Just recently, Deng himself had proposed to the Chairman that a halt be called to the Three Anti and Five Anti movements, which had been targeting the bourgeoisie, and Mao had expressed complete support.[14] But reading the draft, Mao suddenly grew indignant. The document had not been cleared with the CC staff, and he personally had known nothing about it. On January 15, 1953, he sent an irate letter to Zhou Enlai, Deng, Chen Yun, and Bo Yibo, expressing his opposition to the revival of private entrepreneurship.[15] He believed that its drafter manifested "bourgeois ideas," committing a "right opportunist error."[16]

Not expecting such a reaction from the Chairman, Zhou, Deng, Chen, and Bo were upset. Who would have supposed that Mao's mood would change so abruptly? As premier, Zhou assured Mao of his loyalty and promised to take care of the situation.[17] But Mao remained irate. On February 16, 1953, he published in *People's Daily* his private letter to Gao Gang containing a critique of "right deviation."[18] In March, Mao reshuffled the government, removing eight key industrial ministries from Zhou's control and assigning them to Gao Gang, whose stock soared as a result. Several departments were also put under Deng's wing: the People's Control Commission, the Commission on Nationality Affairs, as well as the ministries of railroads, post, communication, and cadres, though these were of secondary importance.[19] In the summer of 1953, Mao began planning for a nationwide conference on financial and economic work, at which he intended to unmask all of the "rightists," including Liu Shaoqi, the most powerful of them all.

Mao assigned Gao Gang to preside over the conference, along with Zhou and Deng.[20] At a Politburo meeting on June 15, 1953, the Great Helmsman set the general ideological tone of the forum by criticizing Liu Shaoqi and other party officials for striving to "firmly" establish "the new-democratic social order."[21] At the closed-door conference itself (June 13 to August 13), a stormy discussion developed not only as to the taxation system but the overall political strategy of the CCP. After hearing several reports, including the main report by Gao Gang, everyone took part in criticizing Bo Yibo.

Gao Gang, who aspired to become the leader of the Communist party after Mao retired to the "second line" of leadership, was the most active. By then he had begun badmouthing both Liu Shaoqi and Zhou Enlai and hinting that he enjoyed the support of Stalin himself.[22] He assumed that he also had Mao's backing for his ambitions. Launching a vicious attack against Bo Yibo, his actual target was Liu Shaoqi (whom, however, Mao had forbidden him from criticizing directly). Yet everyone, including Liu himself, understood what Gao was doing. He accused Bo of making "mistakes of principle," that is, of struggling against the party line, virtually a capital offense in the Chinese communist movement.[23]

Since no one knew whether Gao Gang had acted on Mao's instructions, the situation for the "moderates" was threatening. On July 7, Zhou wrote a letter to Mao Zedong asking for instructions. Grasping that Liu and Zhou were terribly frightened, Mao, who had no desire to remove them from their positions, stepped forward as peacemaker. He had simply wanted to remind them who was the master in the house. Having made his point, he could now savor his victory. After being informed of Gao Gang's actions, Mao replied to Zhou, "One must conduct the struggle openly and resolve the issues. . . . It is improper to hold your tongue in front of someone and then chatter behind their back, engage in innuendo, and not point to people directly, but make covert hints."[24]

Zhou immediately conveyed this "revelation" to Bo, Liu, and Deng, who understood what had to be done. They took the floor at the conference and openly confessed their errors.[25] For his part, Zhou, while summing up the discussion and confessing his own "political and organizational errors," censured Bo Yibo severely and extensively.[26]

Deng, who could have skipped making an apology since he was less "guilty" than the others, spoke with great artifice. On August 6, he declared,

> Everyone is criticizing the errors of Comrade Bo Yibo. I approve of this. [However] anyone can make mistakes; I myself have made not a few, and other comrades present cannot say they are without sin. Bo Yibo has made many mistakes, not just one or two *jin* [a measure of weight equal to 1.1 lbs.] but one or two tons. But no matter how many there may be, one cannot say these are mistakes in line [that is, political mistakes]. If one says that these or those mistakes that he committed over several years of work are mistakes in line, I would not agree.[27]

In sum, Deng sharply criticized Bo Yibo, engaged in self-criticism, and at the decisive moment supported his penitent comrade. Mao was satisfied that Deng had understood him correctly. At a Politburo session on August 9, Mao even criticized Gao Gang.[28] On August 12, Mao spoke at the conference and called it "a success." He praised Liu and Deng for having acknowledged "some mistakes," and unequivocally supported Zhou. Clearly he viewed the conference as a turning point in the ideological-political development of the CCP rather than a forum aimed at overthrowing Liu Shaoqi and Zhou Enlai. He called for firm and consistent criticism of Bo Yibo while warning his overly zealous critics such as Gao Gang, "Opinions are welcome, but to undermine Party unity would be a most shameful thing." Categorizing in fact Bo Yibo's "errors" as "mistakes in line", he said that the "new tax system . . . if allowed to develop, would have led inevitably to capitalism, in contravention of Marxism-Leninism." In sum, from his perspective the conference had helped to deflect this threat from China and stripped away what he considered

New Democratic illusions. The path to socialist development now lay open. Afterward, the Chairman accelerated collectivization of the peasantry on the basis of the new general line for construction of socialism in fifteen years or a little longer.[29]

Although on this occasion Mao had expressed himself quite clearly, Gao Gang persisted in his effort to win several important party leaders, including Chen Yun, Lin Biao, Peng Dehuai, and Huang Kecheng, over to his side. He even offered several of them high positions in a revamped party leadership.[30] Meanwhile, he continued badmouthing Liu Shaoqi and Zhou Enlai.

Gao also tried wooing Deng Xiaoping, as Deng later recalled:

He [Gao Gang] tried to win me over . . . he said that Comrade Liu Shaoqi was immature. He was trying to persuade me to join in his efforts to topple Comrade Liu Shaoqi. . . . Gao Gang also approached Comrade Chen Yun and told him that a few more vice-chairmanships should be instituted with himself and Chen each holding one of them. At this point, Comrade Chen Yun and I realized the gravity of the matter and immediately brought it to Comrade Mao Zedong's attention.[31]

Deng was twisting the truth slightly. Although Gao Gang had spoken with Deng in September, it was not until December that Deng told Mao.[32] It was a delicate question and haste was inadvisable. There was no telling if, perhaps, Mao was having another change of heart and Gao Gang was actually speaking in his name. One aspect of Deng's "recollection" is open to serious doubt, namely, that he flatly told Gao Gang "Comrade Liu's position in the Party was the outcome of historical development," adding that Liu was a good comrade on the whole, and that it was inappropriate to try to oust him from such a position.[33] More likely, Deng took time to think it over while trying to fathom the mood of the mercurial Great Helmsman.

Despite all that happened, Mao maintained normal working relations with Liu Shaoqi, Zhou Enlai, and even with Bo Yibo. Although Bo was dismissed as minister of finance, he remained one of the deputy chairmen of the Financial-Economic Council, whose chair was Chen Yun. Meanwhile, Deng's stock continued to rise. Four days after the conference, in addition to the deputy premiership, Mao made him first deputy chairman of the Financial-Economic Council and concurrently minister of finance in place of Bo Yibo. The Chairman conferred with Deng throughout September on various official matters.[34]

In October he again made it clear that he did not want to have anyone repressed. This assurance occurred in the context of an All-China Conference on Organizational Work at which the new director of the Organization Department, Rao Shushi, lambasted his own deputy, An Ziwen, who had previously directed the department's daily work. Like Gao Gang, Rao Shushi was actually attacking Liu Shaoqi. As CC secretary, Liu supervised the Organization Department. As a friend of An Ziwen, Liu invariably took his side in An's numerous conflicts with Rao, who believed that Liu was undermining his authority. Moreover, in the spring of 1953, calculating that Gao Gang might become Mao Zedong's successor, Rao Shushi established close ties with him.[35]

Liu Shaoqi was not pleased. He immediately informed Mao Zedong, who exploded. Rao, quite unlike Gao Gang, was not acting under the Chairman's directions. Mao wanted to unmask Rao at the conference, but Zhou Enlai prevailed on him not to. The Great Helmsman made it known that he approved the work of the Organization Department under its previous leadership. Following this, at the conference Zhu De and Deng, who was evidently acting with Mao's approval, spoke approvingly of the work of the Organization Department. Deng assured the assembled, "[The department's achievements are] indivisible from the leadership of Chairman Mao and especially of Comrade [Liu] Shaoqi."[36]

Rao Shushi and Gao Gang had been warned, but inexplicably they stubbornly continued to engage in factional activity. They even began to divide up posts in the future leadership among themselves. Chen Yun and then Deng finally told Mao about their machinations. Mao was furious. Meeting with Deng, he asked his views and solicited his advice. Knowing the Chairman's fondness for classical aphorisms, Deng quoted the words of Confucius, "If a gentleman forsakes humanity, how can he make a name for himself?"[37] Mao agreed.

At a Politburo session on December 24, 1953, Mao attacked Gao and Rao, accusing them of "splittist" activity. Gao Gang sat there, red as a lobster, and when Mao turned and asked whether his victim agreed with the verdict, Gao barely squeezed out: "Agree."[38] Mao then declared he was going on leave, appointed Liu Shaoqi as acting chairman, and instructed him to oversee the next enlarged CC plenum in February, at which a resolution "On the Strengthening of Party Unity" was to be adopted. Liu demurred regarding Mao's suggestion, made in a private conversation, that he assume leadership of the Central Committee. Instead Liu suggested that Deng Xiaoping for the third time be put in charge of its daily work as head of the CC Secretariat.

Most likely, it was Liu's way of thanking Deng for his support during what had been a critical moment.[39]

Mao liked the idea but delayed making the appointment until he returned from his holiday in Hangzhou. While he relaxed on the shores of beautiful West Lake, he left Gao Gang and Rao Shushi to be torn apart by Liu, Zhou, and Deng.

The main report at the CC plenum (February 6–10, 1954) was delivered by Liu Shaoqi, who criticized "comrades" who had undermined party unity, become conceited, and considered themselves "the best and the brightest." Apparently according to an agreement with Mao, he did not mention Gao Gang and Rao Shushi by name.[40] Everyone else, including Deng, who even engaged in self-criticism, followed Liu's lead. However, Gao Gang and Rao Shushi apparently failed to grasp what was going on and did not criticize themselves.

Then the plenum established two commissions, one on "the Gao Gang Affair" (headed by Zhou Enlai) and the other on "the Rao Shushi Affair" (headed by Deng, Chen Yi, and Tan Zhenlin). Several weeks later, the two commissions presented reports to the Politburo accusing both Gao and Rao of "sectarianism," "factionalism," establishing "independent kingdoms" in their regions, and plotting to seize power. The charges piled up like winter snowdrifts. Zhou Enlai reported that Gao Gang was not only a "bourgeois individualist careerist," "a de facto agent of the bourgeoisie within our Party," a "plagiarist," a "sectarian," an "amoral decadent," disseminator of "many lies and rumors, attacking others and glorifying himself," but also a traitor to the motherland.[41] The top leaders of the CCP seemed to be stunned.

The facts were scandalous. Everyone learned that Gao had shamelessly curried favor with the Russians in Manchuria and repeatedly sacrificed Chinese national interests while flattering the Soviet Elder Brother. For example, during the civil war, he distributed portraits of Soviet leaders throughout the region rather than images of CCP leaders. Speaking to Stalin while visiting Moscow in the summer of 1949, he suddenly proposed an increase in the number of Soviet troops in Dalian, suggested that the Soviet navy be brought into Qingdao, and, most important, that Manchuria be admitted into the USSR as its seventeenth republic. Moreover, Gao Gang repeatedly denounced CCP leaders, including Liu Shaoqi, Zhou Enlai, Peng Zhen, Li Fuchun, Bo Yibo, and others, to Stalin and Stalin's representative in China, Ivan Kovalev, for "rightist deviation," "overestimation of the Chinese bourgeoisie," and other "sins." He even informed Stalin that Mao himself was guilty of anti-Soviet, "right Trotskyist" activity. But Stalin did not believe these accusations, and during one of their meetings in Moscow he handed Mao Zedong a report he had received from Kovalev on December 24, 1949; it summed up these accusations[42] as well as a stack of secret telegrams from Kovalev and Gao Gang.

At the time Mao swallowed his anger because Stalin remained the head of the international communist movement. He dared not punish Gao Gang for being excessively pro-Soviet. That was then. But by the time Zhou, Deng, and others addressed the matter of the splittists, Stalin's embalmed body lay next to Lenin's in the Mausoleum on Moscow's Red Square. Gao faced the storm alone.

So, too, did Rao Shushi. The report by Deng's commission denounced Rao for a multitude of "crimes": "anti-Party alliance with Gao Gang," "extreme individualistic bourgeois careerism," struggle against "some . . . leading comrade of the Center [i.e., Liu Shaoqi]," and others. The only charges missing were "betraying the homeland" and "moral turpitude." Everyone knew that unlike the lady-killer Gao, Rao Shushi was exceptionally modest and a model family man. He was also circumspect in his contacts with foreigners, including the Elder Brothers.[43] Nonetheless, what Deng's commission had dug up was sufficiently damning to earn Rao a severe censure.

The material uncovered by Zhou's commission was literally deadly. It led to tragedy. While the commission was still gathering information, Gao Gang snapped. On February 17, 1954, he tried to shoot himself, but his bodyguard intervened. Several months later, on August 17, he made a successful attempt at suicide by swallowing a large dose of sleeping pills.[44] He felt that Mao, whose tacit support he believed he possessed, had betrayed him.[45]

Meanwhile, in April 1954, after returning from vacation, Mao appointed Deng head of the Central Committee Secretariat, and concurrently head of the Organization Department, Rao's old post. Clearly Deng was a major beneficiary of the Gao Gang–Rao Shushi Affair. He was truly first among the steeds "to gallop into the capital."

In September 1954, at the opening session of the newly convened national parliament, the National People's Congress (NPC), Deng was confirmed as deputy premier of the State Council, the new organ of executive power headed by Zhou Enlai. Mao occupied the new and highest position in the state—chairman of the PRC—and Liu Shaoqi became chairman of the Standing Committee of the NPC. Deng also became one of fifteen deputy chairmen of the State Defense Council and one of twelve members of the party's Central Military Commission. These latter appointments were a great honor, as Mao and Deng were the only civilian leaders in these organizations, which were otherwise staffed by leading military commanders. A year later these worthies were bestowed the rank of marshal of the PRC. Mao had also offered Deng the rank of marshal, but he modestly declined.[46]

The first session of the NPC adopted the Constitution of the PRC, which confirmed that for now China was a "people's democratic state led by the working class and based on the worker-peasant alliance."[47] By then, however, socialism was already being constructed throughout the country, the peasantry was being forcibly collectivized, and private property in the cities had been taken over by the state. New Democracy was past its expiration date.

As a deputy premier, Deng, of course, also took part in socialist construction, but his main duty was heading the Central Committee Secretariat. In March 1955, Mao entrusted Deng with reporting on the "crimes" of Gao Gang and Rao Shushi at a national conference of the CCP that summed up the "affair." Deng severely criticized Gao and Rao, fully justifying the Chairman's great faith in him. The conference expelled the splittists from the party and, supporting Mao Zedong's political line, called for the eradication of all his enemies.[48] Soon after, on April 1, 1955, Rao Shushi was arrested;[49] in March 1975, he died in his prison cell from pneumonia.

Meanwhile, Deng continued his rapid ascent. In early April 1955, at a regular plenum of the Central Committee, he was chosen as a member of the Politburo along with Lin Biao, another of Mao's favorites. He now stood on the summit of power, close to the Chairman, who could not do without him. Mao admired Deng's exceptional capacity for work, organizational talent, and energy. "Whether politics or military affairs, Deng Xiaoping is good at everything," the Chairman had noted sometime in the early 1950s.[50] Since then, he had not changed this assessment.

"Critique of the Cult of Personality"
and Its Consequences

IN EARLY FEBRUARY 1956, Mao appointed Deng deputy head of the delegation that was supposed to represent the CCP at the Twentieth Congress of the Communist Party of the Soviet Union (CPSU). He made Zhu De its head, and the members included Tan Zhenlin (from December 1954, Deng's deputy in the CC Secretariat), Wang Jiaxiang (director of the International Liaison Department of the Central Committee), and Liu Xiao (PRC ambassador to the USSR).

This was the first forum following Stalin's death of the main fraternal party, convened by Stalin's successor, Nikita S. Khrushchev, who evoked mixed feelings on the part of Mao, Deng, and other Chinese leaders. During his visit to China on the fifth anniversary of the founding of the PRC in the fall of 1954, Khrushchev considerably amused and entertained them all, but he also perplexed them.

Nikita Khrushchev was no diplomat, and where reason was called for he was guided by emotions. Throughout his time in China, he was in a euphoric mood. Disregarding protocol, he hugged and kissed Mao, scandalizing the Chinese; played the buffoon; promised a lot; and distributed goods like a merchant. During talks at the summit level, in which Deng Xiaoping took part, he signed a number of agreements by which the Soviet side gave China a long-term loan of 520 million rubles and pledged assistance in construction of a large number of industrial projects. He even agreed to help China train nuclear specialists.[1] Khrushchev's attempt to ingratiate himself with the Chinese leadership backfired. Mao, Liu, Zhou, Deng, and all the other Chinese pupils of Stalin viewed Khrushchev's conduct as a sign of weakness rather than generosity. Now Deng would encounter this unusual Soviet leader on his home ground.

Deng left no record of his thoughts as he prepared to revisit Moscow, the Red Mecca. It was the city of his youth, where he had first encountered Zhang Xiyuan, his first love, where he had immersed himself in the study of Marxism-Leninism and nurtured his revolutionary hopes. He had first come here thirty years ago as a youthful twenty-one-year-old. How quickly the years had passed! Where was UTK now? The Executive Committee of the Comintern? The former nunnery on Strastnaia Square where KUTV had been located? Unsentimental as he was, his thoughts must have gone back to the past as he anticipated his trip.

This time he flew into Moscow. With stops for refueling, the flight took three days. Departing on February 9, Deng, accompanied by Tan Zhenlin and Wang Jiaxiang, touched down in the capital of the USSR on February 11. Prior to departure he had twice discussed with Mao, Liu Shaoqi, Zhou Enlai, and Chen Yun how the delegation should conduct itself at the congress. It was decided that the Chinese communists would not display any excessive respect toward the Elder Brother since Khrushchev and company, unlike the late Stalin, were unsuited for the roles of "Leaders and Teachers."

Soon after arriving in Moscow, Deng explained this approach to the venerable Zhu De, then in his seventieth year, who had arrived in the capital of the USSR several days earlier after a tour of Eastern Europe, as well as to Ambassador Liu Xiao. Requesting the draft of Zhu De's welcoming speech at the forthcoming Twentieth Congress, Deng made two observations in the spirit of the party's new course. "First," he said, "one must not speak only of the support and assistance of the Soviet Union to China; the support and assistance were reciprocal. Second, speaking of Soviet assistance, one should know when to stop and not exaggerate."[2] Accustomed to accepting party leadership directives, the venerable Zhu at once made these corrections.

After this, in the several days before the congress, which was scheduled to begin on February 14, Deng, Zhu, Tan, Wang Jiaxiang, and Liu Xiao had an enjoyable time taking outings around Moscow. Three of them—Deng, Zhu, and Wang—had memories from the past. Zhu, like Deng and Wang, had also studied there, around the same time as Deng, from the summer of 1925 to the summer of 1926, not at UTK but at KUTV. Wang Jiaxiang had not only pursued studies at UTK/KUTK in 1925–1930, but in 1937–38 he had worked in the Executive Committee of the Communist International and from October 1949 to January 1951 he had served as the first PRC ambassador to the Soviet Union. Only Tan Zhenlin was in the Soviet capital for the first time, and therefore his comrades were happy to show him around town. Deng and Zhu took in many new sights: the Exhibition of National Economic Achievements, the Metro, the Exhibition of the Peaceful Atom, as well as Moscow University in the Lenin Hills. They were all feeling very upbeat.

On February 15, Zhu De greeted the congress in the name of the Chinese Communist Party and then read a letter from Mao Zedong in which he sang the praises of the late Stalin. In his message Mao spoke of the invincibility of the "Communist Party of the Soviet Union created by Lenin and fostered by Stalin together with his comrades-in-arms."[3] The delegates rose to their feet and greeted the messages from the CCP with a stormy ovation. Everything, it seemed, was going well.

Then, unexpectedly, on February 19, during a reception at the Kremlin, Khrushchev informed Zhu De that he wanted to meet with the Chinese delegation tête-à-tête after the congress. "To speak about Stalin," he said enigmatically.[4] Zhu naturally agreed, although he did not understand what the leader of the CPSU had in mind. He, Deng, and the other Chinese delegates began to realize what was afoot only the next day, when they heard the speech of Anastas I. Mikoyan, one of the leaders of the CPSU and deputy chairman of the USSR Council of Ministers. To their profound surprise, he criticized Stalin for violating the principles of collective leadership. Then they recalled that the other speakers, too, "in their speeches only spoke about Leninism and quoted Lenin exclusively, not citing Stalin even once." They immediately informed Beijing and suggested they take this position: "Not to express an opinion regarding the merits and mistakes of Stalin, but to emphasize the importance of collective leadership in the struggle against the cult of personality."[5] Mao did not object.

Then Zhu De suddenly recalled that on February 6, five days prior to the arrival of Deng and the other Chinese comrades, Khrushchev, receiving him at the Kremlin and speaking about the collectivization of agriculture, which in China was then nearing completion, observed that in the USSR after the achievement of cooperativization, production of foodstuffs long remained below the level of 1913. "The fault lay with the leadership which did not understand the peasantry," he explained. "After Stalin traveled though Siberian villages in 1928, he never visited the countryside again. He knew it only through films. Other members of the Politburo had no better understanding [of agrarian problems.]"[6] The naïve Zhu had paid no heed to these words, but in light of what was going on at the congress, they suddenly took on a special meaning. The members of the delegation quickly informed Mao.

But the Chinese learned of the main event only after the congress. On the evening of February 27, a special messenger from the Kremlin told Zhu De that on instructions from the Central Committee of the CPSU it was his duty to inform him of Khrushchev's secret report, delivered on the night of February 24–25 "On the Cult of Personality and Its Consequences." The report accused the late dictator of innumerable crimes, including the destruction of many honest Soviet citizens.[7] Deng Xiaoping pointed out,

> During the congress we did not hear the secret report against Stalin. On the evening of the second day after the congress had concluded, the CC [CPSU] Department on Relations [with Foreign Communist Parties] sent a person who brought the report. . . . The members of the delegation conferred and decided that since Commander Zhu De was old, I should be the one to listen to the message. In reality, it was not any sort of message, but an [entire] secret report that the interpreter Shi Zhe set forth. Our interpreter partly read [the report] and partly summarized it. After he finished, the special messenger immediately retrieved the report and departed. [Shi Zhe] read it only once.[8]

It was perhaps more than a curious coincidence that the messenger came literally the day after Deng Xiaoping and Tan Zhenlin, in the name of the Chinese Communist Party, had laid wreaths at the Lenin-Stalin Mausoleum.

Deng imparted this "earthshaking news" to Zhu De and the other members of the delegation, saying that "the report was confused and illogical," but one could tell that Khrushchev had stunned him. Zhu De replied, "Everything they said is their own business. We are here as guests." But Deng disagreed. "Stalin is an international figure. To speak of him this way is disgraceful. It is impermissible to insult a revolutionary leader like Stalin in this fashion." Tan Zhenlin tried to reconcile Zhu and Deng: "We should not meekly agree with their point of view; we have to have our own position. However, this is their domestic politics, and there is no way we can influence it." Wang Jiaxiang and Liu Xiao kept silent. Then Deng said, "This is a matter of enormous significance. We need to inform the Central Committee and we will not express our own position." They then collectively composed a cablegram and dispatched it to Beijing.[9]

The news from Moscow naturally shocked Mao, despite the fact that as far back as April 1954 he had received a dispatch concerning a definite change of attitude toward Stalin in the Soviet Union from his ambassador to the

USSR, who at the time was Luo Fu.[10] But a change in tone was one thing, and outright condemnation quite something else. It was incredible!

It was not that Mao was particularly fond of Stalin, who, we may recall, treated him condescendingly during their meetings in Moscow, but he respected him greatly and viewed him as a great teacher and brilliant Marxist. Therefore, his initial reaction was one of revulsion. But after further reflection, he suppressed this initial unpleasant feeling. Be that as it may, the condemnation of the Kremlin's ex-dictator liberated him ideologically.[11] Now Mao could undertake any revision of Marxist theory he pleased without looking at the Soviet experience.

At the same time, he and the other Chinese leaders were naturally angered by how absurdly the Soviet chieftains were handling the matter of informing them of the report: the representatives of the CCP were not even allowed to take the text to Beijing. Khrushchev acted the same way with the other major communist parties, of which there were twelve, in addition to the CCP—those of the socialist countries plus the French and Italian parties. The leaders of their delegations were likewise only shown the report and hastily acquainted with its contents, after which it was taken away. Delegations of other "fraternal" parties were generally told nothing at all. Such negligence was unforgivable.[12]

On that same evening, February 27, the Soviet Communist Party invited the Chinese delegation to a small meeting of representatives of selected communist parties at which Khrushchev spoke to explain his report. The following day, Khrushchev paid a visit in person to the Chinese at the state guest house in a Moscow suburb where they were staying. Again he disparaged Stalin and asked for their support.[13]

Returning to Beijing on March 3, Deng reported on what had happened to Mao, Liu Shaoqi, and Zhou Enlai just three hours after his arrival. In the hastily called meeting in Zhongnanhai, several other leaders of the PRC also took part. Deng had to summarize the text of Khrushchev's report from memory.

In March, Mao held four meetings with members and nonmembers of the Politburo and Secretariat of the CC, at which the unmasking of Stalin was discussed repeatedly. One could tell that the matter stung him to the quick. How could it be otherwise? After all, it was not just a question of the deceased "Father of Nations," but of Stalinist socialism itself, the construction of which was nearing completion in the PRC. Khrushchev's reckless speech destroyed the foundations of the model, dealing a heavy blow to the authority of all communist parties of the socialist countries, including the

PRC, since none of these organizations could exist without the cult of personality. All of them were leader-type parties constructed on the Leninist principles of extreme centralism that characterized the structural matrix of the totalitarian systems. Khrushchev's report directly undermined the cult of the Great Helmsman, which was no less inflated in China than the cult of Stalin in the USSR.

Mao found this last circumstance particularly troubling. Various thoughts, each more disturbing than the one before, must have invested his mind: How would Liu Shaoqi, Zhou Enlai, and other colleagues perceive the critique of the cult of personality? Might they not make use of Khrushchev's report to discredit the Chairman? Would one of them turn out to be a perfidious person such as Khrushchev who would betray his own leader and teacher?

On the surface, all the members of the top leadership were solidly behind Mao Zedong, but who knew what was going through their minds? Khrushchev had also hung on Stalin's every word when he was alive. Learning that in Moscow Zhu De had not grasped the essence of Khrushchev's report, Mao became furious. "Zhu De is an ignorant man. . . . Khrushchev and Zhu De are both unreliable," he said.[14]

On the evening of March 17, Mao convened an enlarged meeting of the Secretariat at which Deng once more reported on the Twentieth Congress—this time to all the members of the leadership along with several other important officials.[15] By this time the leaders of the CCP had been able to acquaint themselves with the text of the report, which had been specially translated and printed for them by staff members of the New China News Agency (Xinhua) using the English translation published in the *New York Times* on March 10. That translation had been based on the Russian text that CIA agents procured from their channels in Warsaw. Khrushchev had stirred up a hornet's nest; the whole world was hankering after his report.

At the enlarged Secretariat meeting, Mao declared:

On one hand, by making the secret report denouncing Stalin, Khrushchev took the lid off [to release the steam]. This is good. But on the other hand, he made a lot of trouble so that the whole world shook. . . . It was wrong not to consult with all the parties regarding such an important question regarding such an important international figure. Facts demonstrate that chaos has arisen in communist parties throughout the world. . . . Earlier I thought that Khrushchev was not an ordinary person, that he was rather clever. . . . But now I see that he suffers a little from empiricism. Coming to power, he needed our support, [and that is why] he improved Soviet-Chinese relations.

Everyone present agreed, and Deng added: "The CPSU in essence has not renounced its great power complex. They made a secret report, but prior to it turned to no one [for advice], and then made it known [to everyone] just once and then considered the matter closed." Wang Jiaxiang and Luo Fu, who was now the first deputy foreign minister of the PRC, likewise accused Khrushchev of possessing a great power complex.

At the end of the meeting, Mao asked everyone to ponder once again how to deal with such an important question as the critique of the cult of personality.[16] He began the next meeting, on March 19, with these words, "Overall my impression is rather confused, and what you think about it I don't know." Then he began listening attentively to the speakers while slurping rice congee from a porcelain cup since he hadn't yet had breakfast. "I read Khrushchev's secret report from 'head to tail,' but didn't lose my appetite," he joked.[17]

Taking the floor, Deng declared, "The report basically focused on Stalin's character, but it's impossible to assert that in such a large country, in such a large party, over such a long period of time, that a series of mistakes occurred because of the character of one person."[18] Obviously, Deng was skillfully rescuing Stalin from attack, and Mao Zedong as well. In his words, the Leader in general did not bear personal responsibility for errors and crimes he had committed; the entire party and its leadership did. Naturally, Mao could not help but note the efforts of his protégé. Deng's approach must have impressed him.

The speeches by Wang Jiaxiang, Luo Fu, and especially by Zhou Enlai also turned out well for Mao. Once again they sharply criticized the CPSU for its great power complex. To be sure, unlike Deng, they aired quite a few grievances against Stalin personally, mostly for mistakes in directing the Chinese revolution from Moscow. Wang, for example, said the "Li Lisan line and the policy of Wang Ming,"[19] namely, "adventurism," and "capitulationism" respectively, came from Stalin, and Zhou declared that earlier

when speaking of numerous mistakes of the party, we did not refer to the USSR, but only blamed ourselves. In reality, however, many of the errors were not ours, but those of the Soviet communists or the Comintern that was led by the CPSU [inasmuch] as the Chinese party was previously dependent. Now, speaking of Stalin's errors, it must be said that the CPSU bears definite responsibility for the defeats of the Chinese revolution.[20]

Mao agreed with all of this, observing that Stalin's achievements and mistakes were in a ratio of 70:30. Afterward he gave a long speech in the form of reminiscences of what "he had kept in his heart over the course of six years." He spoke of the bitter insults Stalin had inflicted on him during his visit to Moscow in late 1949 and early 1950. Stalin had not received him for a long time and kept him in a dacha almost like a prisoner, and during the negotiations he had slighted him to such a degree that Mao's nerves were completely shot. Then he announced, "Rain will fall from the skies, girls will get married. What can we do?" He added:

> There is also some good in Khrushchev's denunciation of Stalin. Khrushchev struck off some hard fetters, emancipated consciousness, and helped us to think over problems. It is not necessary to build socialism wholly relying on the Soviet model; we can begin from the concrete situation in our own country, and set a course and policy that corresponds to the national characteristics of China.[21]

It seemed that everything was turning out well. But the next speaker was Liu Shaoqi, who probably put Mao Zedong on his guard. He asserted that from his perspective, among other errors, during collectivization Stalin had forced the pace of cooperativization.[22] It is unlikely that Liu did this without an ulterior motive. Everyone knew just how sharply Mao himself had recently criticized Liu for "conservatism" and "moderation" regarding questions of socialist transformation. So was Liu Shaoqi now trying to cast suspicion on the Chairman?

By this time, in the course of just two and a half years—from 1954 to the first half of 1956—110 million peasant households, or about 92 percent, had entered production cooperatives, yielding to violence on the part of the CCP. To be sure, the scale of rural resistance was in no way comparable with that which occurred during the Bolshevik collectivization. The well-to-do peasants (*funong*), after losing their property, entered the collective farms rather than being physically eliminated.[23] Nonetheless, collectivization occurred at an accelerated pace, and its economic consequences were also harmful for China.

The Great Helmsman was easily offended, but at the moment Liu Shaoqi was obviously not thinking about this. Possibly he was just taking a principled stand since at heart he was an opponent of an unwarranted rapid pace of socialist construction, and perhaps he simply paid no heed to the Chairman's moods. Be that as it may, his speech evidently increased Mao's suspicions of him as well as of his like-minded colleagues.

Of all of Mao's entourage, apparently Deng alone thought that Liu had "gone out on a limb." At the end of the meeting he therefore began to spread the word that there had never been a cult of personality in China or the CCP, because Mao himself supposedly always fought against its appearance.[24] This had a false ring to it, but Deng's lie was intended to save Liu, for whom Deng had ever greater respect since their common struggle against Gao and Rao.

The Chairman, however, ignored Deng's words and instructed his secretary, Chen Boda, along with officials of the Xinhua News Agency and the CC Propaganda Department, to draft an editorial on the question of the cult of personality in the USSR. It was completed by April 5 and published the same day in *People's Daily* under the title "On the Historical Experience of the Dictatorship of the Proletariat." It was edited by Mao himself, assisted by several other members of the leadership, including Deng.[25] It was aimed at a wide audience and consequently did not contain excessive criticism of the former communist idol even regarding the Chinese revolution. The leaders of the CCP, Mao in the first instance, did not want anyone to oppose their own dictatorship under an anti-Stalinist banner. Later, at an enlarged Politburo meeting on April 28, Mao Zedong admitted, "We do not intend to write for the masses in the newspapers . . . about the bad things that Stalin and the Third International did. (If we have so much as a single sentence in such an article, it would 'arouse an unhealthy interest.')"[26] As Mao wanted, Stalin's merits and mistakes were summed up in the article in a ratio of 70:30, but the Soviet Union, nonetheless, was praised for its "selfless criticism . . . of past mistakes."

After this, on April 25, at an enlarged session of the Politburo, Mao delivered a speech, "On the Ten Major Relationships," that had far-reaching consequences. In essence, this speech marked the most important turn in Mao Zedong's worldview, reflecting the new atmosphere of emancipation then developing in the CCP. For the first time, the Chairman openly called for advancing to the bright future along a shorter path than that taken by the Russians, according to the principles of "more, faster, better, and more economical," although he did not present a detailed program for constructing Chinese-style socialism.[27]

The Chairman's ideas struck many Chinese leaders, including Liu Shaoqi, Zhou Enlai, and Chen Yun, as adventurist. At this time, Zhou Enlai, Chen Yun, and other economists were engaged in preparing the Second Five-Year Plan, and they did not welcome Mao's leftist ideas. Neither Liu nor Deng grasped the revolutionary significance of Mao's speech.

Mao was offended. "It seems that I was dizzy with success, that I engaged in 'blindly rushing forward,'" he said sarcastically. At the end of the summer he told his "associates" that he intended to give up the post of chairman of the PRC for "reasons of health," keeping only the chairmanship of the Central Committee of the CCP.[28]

Meanwhile, the main event of 1956 was approaching: the Eighth National Congress of the CCP. At this forum, according to Mao's proposal made as far back as March 1955, Liu Shaoqi was supposed to deliver the political report on the work of the CC, Deng Xiaoping the report on changes in the Party Statutes, and Zhou the report on the Second Five-Year Plan. Mao himself no longer intended to make any major speeches. There was nothing unusual about this. Stalin, too, at the Nineteenth Bolshevik Party Congress in 1952, had basically kept silent, instructing the CC secretary, Georgii M. Malenkov, to deliver the main report. But just like Stalin, Mao scrutinized the numerous drafts of all the congress documents.

It seemed that he was satisfied with them, but that was only on the surface. In reality, he was simply concealing his thoughts skillfully, and by giving his colleagues free rein he was testing them while indulging his own mounting suspicions. It was as if he was saying to them, "Let's see what cards you have."

Indeed, they fell into his trap. Even Deng made a series of blunders, including omitting the term *Mao Zedong Thought* from the Party Statutes as well as from his own report on changes in the statutes. This occurred during the congress itself, at one of the meetings of the Politburo, right on the eve of Deng's speech. Until then, Mao Zedong Thought had been preserved as the ideological foundation of the CCP in the many variants of the statutes and the report.[29] Now the old warrior Peng Dehuai, apparently under the influence of the condemnation of the cult of personality in the Soviet Union, suddenly took it into his head to suggest "deleting" it from the statutes. At once Liu agreed with him.[30] Deng likewise did not object, most likely because at the time Mao did not express dissatisfaction.[31] Moreover, Deng knew that starting from the late 1940s the Chairman himself had repeatedly made clear his disinclination to overemphasize this term. Thus, in January 1949 he himself had removed it from the statutes of the New Democratic Youth League (the former Communist Youth League), substituting instead "combining the theory of Marxism-Leninism with the practice of the Chinese revolution." He also excised this term from several other documents, including the new edition of volume three of his own *Selected Works*, which appeared in April 1953.[32] Mao himself, however, had not proposed deleting this expression from the statutes of the party, so it is incomprehensible how such an experienced party operative as Deng could have failed to orient himself in a timely fashion. But facts are facts. Deng made a mistake. And Mao, as the future would show, remembered it. In November 1967, Mao would share with several of his closest colleagues his grievances against Deng and Liu Shaoqi for supposedly ignoring his opinion during the Eighth Party Congress.[33]

Meanwhile, in the Party Statutes, in place of the sentence that the Chinese Communist Party "guides its entire work" by Mao Zedong Thought was this: "The Communist Party of China takes Marxism-Leninism as its guide to action."[34] Presenting his report "On Changes in the Party Statutes," Deng placed special stress on the need to struggle against "the deification of the individual." In this connection, he praised the Twentieth Congress of the CPSU for having showed to everyone "what serious consequences can follow from the deification of the individual."[35] Subsequently, he tried to justify himself: "Several persons were involved in drafting this report. I did not write this section. As far as I can remember, it was written on the basis of the article 'On the Historical Experience of the Dictatorship of the Proletariat.'"[36]

Deng's excuses were pathetic. He bore responsibility for the report, which, it should be noted, also contained ingratiating words sure to please Mao. In particular, Deng's thesis that Mao Zedong himself had supposedly played a big role in the struggle against the cult of personality in the CCP was probably intended to preempt criticism of the Chairman. Moreover, Deng declared, "Marxism never denies the role that outstanding individuals play in history" and generally speaking "love for the leader is essentially an expression of love for the interests of the Party, the class and the people, and not the deification of an individual."[37] In other words, playing it both ways, he let everyone know that love for the Chairman, who supposedly eschewed hero worship, was conducive to the building of socialism in China.

Mao could hardly disagree with this sentiment, of course. Overall his relations with Deng remained quite good, despite being somewhat clouded by his suspicious nature and resentment that Deng had not grasped the essence of his speech "On the Ten Major Relationships" and had casually agreed to the deletion of "Mao Zedong Thought." It was on Mao's own suggestion, made on the eve of the Eighth CCP Congress in September 1956, that the delegates elected Deng general secretary of the Central Committee. This position, which, incidentally, had been abolished at the Seventh Congress, was much more important than the post of head of the Secretariat since the general secretary not only discharged party organizational functions, but also played an important role in making political decisions. It implied that he would enter the innermost elite of the party leadership: in the newly established Politburo Standing Committee. "I think that Deng Xiaoping is very honest," Mao declared.

> He is like me. That doesn't mean he is without faults, but he is rather upright. He has a number of abilities, and he handles matters rather well. Do you think he is good at everything? No, he is just like me. He makes mistakes on many issues, and not a few of his judgments are incorrect. But in general he stands out and he gets things done. He is quite meticulous, an honest and good fellow. People are not too afraid of him. Today I am showering quite a bit of praise upon him. . . . I think he is suitable [for this work]. Whether he is worthy or not everyone will decide, but I think he is more or less worthy. There are also persons who are dissatisfied with him, just as there are with me. [Yes], some are dissatisfied with me; I'm a person who causes injury to many. But today these people have chosen me, because they have put the general interest above their personal interest. Would you say that Deng Xiaoping harms nobody? I don't believe it. But overall, this is a worthy man, a rather good man who solves problems more or less fairly and is strict about his own mistakes. . . . He has been tempered in intraparty struggles.[38]

One needs hardly add that Deng was very pleased with his promotion, although he modestly declined it when his name was put forward, "I am unworthy, unworthy, no, I cannot, I have a sinking feeling."[39] But he could hardly do otherwise: such was the well-worn Chinese tradition. It was considered immodest to accept an appointment right away.

The result was that Deng was almost unanimously elected a member of the Central Committee, trailing only Mao, Liu Shaoqi, and the veteran party member Lin Boqu in the number of votes cast for him. Then, at the CC's First Plenum on September 28 he was made a member of the Politburo and general secretary. He joined the Standing Committee and became the sixth-ranked person in the party hierarchy after Mao, Liu Shaoqi, Zhou Enlai, Zhu De, and Chen Yun (the latter four all became deputy chairmen).

Now he was no longer in Mao's shadow. He stood side by side with the Great Helmsman. But, as before, he never dreamed of being on an equal footing with the Chairman. Totalitarian power implied the dictatorship of a single undisputed Leader.

"A Great Growing Force"

AS GENERAL SECRETARY, Deng settled in with his family at one of the elite houses in Zhongnanhai, Hanxiuxuan (Pavilion of Hidden Beauty), behind the high walls that separated the elite from the people. The house was located not far from the hall used for ceremonial sessions of the Central Committee and the government—Huairentang (Pavilion of Abundant Humaneness)—and was constructed in the traditional style with a four-sided interior court yard and one-story buildings around the perimeter. It was allotted to Deng by the director of the CC General Office, Yang Shangkun, a forty-eight-year-old veteran of the Chinese Communist Party whom Deng had known since November 1926, when Yang began studying in Moscow at Sun Yat-sen University. In 1927 their paths diverged, but in 1933 in the Central Soviet Area they intersected again. Later, in the initial period of the anti-Japanese war, Deng actively collaborated with Yang Shangkun, then the secretary of the North China Bureau, which is to say, Deng's direct party superior. "Yang's family and ours had been quite close," recalled Deng's daughter Deng Maomao.[1]

In the new home, under a gray brick roof, Deng and Zhuo Lin occupied one wing on the north side of the perfectly symmetrical courtyard planted all around with graceful cypress trees. Their children and Grandma Xia Bogen lived in the west wing, and Deng's secretary, Wang Ruilin, a twenty-five-year-old Shandong native with big, round eyeglasses who had worked for Deng since September 1952, in the east wing. (In addition to Wang, secretarial duties for Deng were carried out by only one other secretary, Zhuo Lin herself.) Deng's young bodyguard, Zhang Baozhong, a peasant orphan from Heilongjiang who turned twenty-two in 1956 and had been with Deng since 1954; the cook, Yang Weiyi; and servant Wu Hongjun were in the house almost all the time. Deng's neighbors were his old friends Li

Fuchun and Chen Yi, also deputy premiers, as well as one additional friend, Tan Zhenlin, Deng's former deputy in the Central Committee Secretariat. Li and Chen were chosen for the Politburo at the Eighth Party Congress, and Tan would become a member of this highest organ in 1958 and, a year later, a deputy premier as well.[2]

Mao lived literally a two-minute walk from them, in the Pavilion of Chrysanthemum Fragrance in the Garden of Abundant Reservoirs, which was also near Huairentang. The residences of Liu Shaoqi, Zhou Enlai, Zhu De, Chen Yun, and other top party and state officials were nearby. Deng now met frequently with them and with Mao. The socioeconomic and political situation in the country and the world, as well as conditions in the party, required unremitting attention.

In the fall of 1956, right after the Eighth Party Congress, the leaders of the Chinese Communist Party again became seriously concerned about international affairs, this time the situation in Eastern Europe. In early October 1956, the former Polish communist leader, Władysław Gomułka—who had been removed as general secretary in 1948, not without Stalin's intervention, had languished three years in prison (1951–1954) and had only just returned to the party—began demanding that Soviet officers serving in the Polish armed forces be withdrawn. His prime target was a member of the Polish Politburo, the deputy chairman of the Council of Ministers, and the minister of defense, Marshal Konstantin Rokossowski, who had been appointed to these posts by Stalin. Khrushchev panicked and, without thinking, on October 19 ordered Soviet troops stationed in northern and western Poland under provisions of the Warsaw Pact to commence a gradual movement toward Warsaw. That same day, he suddenly showed up in Warsaw for talks, accompanied by three members of the Presidium of the Central Committee of the Communist Party of the Soviet Union and the commander of Warsaw Pact troops, Marshal Ivan Konev. But the talks with the Poles went nowhere since many Polish leaders supported Gomułka. They mobilized their domestic security forces and began organizing people's armed militias. The USSR and Poland seemed on the verge of the first war between socialist countries. Khrushchev took fright and ordered a retreat; Soviet forces halted their advance. The temporary lull, however, could fool no one. The Kremlin boss still wanted to "settle the situation in Warsaw" by all possible means.[3] Meanwhile, on October 21, a plenum of the Central Committee of the Polish United Workers' Party elected Gomułka as first secretary.[4]

The crisis of socialism in Poland, naturally, was provoked in the first instance by Khrushchev's speech about Stalin. His adventurous military actions toward an independent country merely exacerbated the situation. Clearly understanding this, Mao began to express dissatisfaction with the head of the CPSU. Observing this, other Chinese leaders, including Deng, who had earlier considered Khrushchev's struggle against the cult of personality "disgraceful," also began to express indignation toward Khrushchev.

On the evening of October 20, before news arrived in Beijing of Khrushchev's decision to halt his troops, Mao convened an enlarged session of the Politburo at which, for the first time, he criticized the Soviet Union for "great power chauvinism." Just before, he had received a letter from the Polish leadership asking for help, so he felt he was a legitimate arbiter.[5] "In the old society it was the norm for the teacher to thrash a pupil if the pupil did not behave," he reminded the assembled. "But the relations between the USSR and Poland are not those of teacher and pupil. They are relations between two [independent] states and parties."[6] Everyone agreed and resolved to warn Khrushchev not to resort to the use of force against Poland under any circumstances.

After the session, Mao summoned Soviet ambassador Pavel Yudin, whom he received in his bedroom in a dressing gown, contrary to all protocol. "We resolutely condemn what you are doing," he declared in extreme irritation. "I request that you immediately telephone Khrushchev and inform him of our view. If the Soviet Union moves its troops, we will support Poland." A witness reports that "during the entire meeting Yudin was extremely tense. The embassy counselor [Nikolai] Sudarikov, who accompanied him as protocol officer, felt the same way. Sweat was dripping from Yudin's face and, constantly wiping his brow with his hand, he repeated, 'Yes, yes'."[7]

Khrushchev panicked after receiving this information from Yudin, and on October 21 he decided, "in view of the situation . . . to refrain [entirely] from armed intervention. And to show patience." He invited representatives of several communist parties from socialist countries, including China, to come to Moscow for "consultations."[8]

Mao, Liu, Zhou, Chen Yun, and Deng decided to assist the Soviet leadership in managing the situation. On October 23, around 1:00 a.m., the unfortunate Yudin was again summoned to Mao's bedroom, where, sitting on his bed, the Chairman told him so. Then he gave vent to his profound dissatisfaction with Khrushchev's anti-Stalin policy. "It was proper to criticize Stalin, but we have a different view regarding the methods of criticism," he declared.[9] Liu Shaoqi, Zhou Enlai, Chen Yun, and Deng Xiaoping, arranged in a semicircle on chairs near the bed of the Great Helmsman, maintained a servile silence.

Early on the morning of October 23, a Chinese delegation flew to Moscow on a Soviet plane. In the delegation Mao included Liu Shaoqi, Deng Xiaoping, Wang Jiaxiang, and Hu Qiaomu. (The last was a member of the Secretariat of the Central Committee and one of the Chairman's personal secretaries.) By the time the delegation met with Khrushchev at 11:00 p.m. that same day, the situation in another East European country, Hungary, had sharply deteriorated. The Hungarian people, who since the spring had shown increasing dissatisfaction with the Stalinist policies of the Hungarian Workers' Party, erupted into a genuine popular uprising on October 23. Thousands of demonstrators on the streets of Budapest and other cities, rallying under the slogans of "national independence and democracy," recited the lines of Sándor Petöfi, the famous poet and hero of the 1848 Hungarian Revolution, who fell in battle with tsarist Cossacks: "By the God of the Magyars / we now swear, / we swear we never shall be now / the slaves we were."[10] As a result of the democratic revolution, power passed into the hands of the popular, liberal communist Imre Nagy.[11]

Hungary was the core of the discussions, lasting nine days, between representatives of the Communist Party of the Soviet Union and the Chinese Communist Party. Liu, Deng, and the others negotiated with Khrushchev as well as Vyacheslav Molotov and Nikolai Bulganin at Stalin's former dacha in Lipki near Moscow. On several occasions, Khrushchev invited Liu Shaoqi, Deng, and other delegation members to sessions of his own Presidium.[12]

Liu immediately conveyed Mao's view regarding the Soviet Union's "improper methods of criticizing Stalin" to Khrushchev, who could merely nod his head. Khrushchev was extremely anxious and unable to conceal his interest in securing Chinese support. After blasting Khrushchev, Liu assured his Soviet comrade that the Chinese Communist Party was on his side, at least with respect to Poland (having in mind the refusal to employ force). Deng said the same thing.[13]

The following day, October 24, at a meeting of Khrushchev's Presidium, Liu Shaoqi again emphasized that he "considers the CC CPSU's measures with regard to Poland to be correct."[14] Khrushchev was satisfied. "Liu Shaoqi was a pleasant man, with whom you could talk on a human basis; you could examine problems with him and solve them," he recalled subsequently. "Liu Shaoqi as a person impressed me the most. . . . When we conversed, I felt that we thought in the same way, that we understood each other right away, without everything having to be spelled out, even though we were speaking through an interpreter." Deng also made a "very strong impression" at the time on Khrushchev.[15]

But the situation was rapidly evolving, and Liu Shaoqi was constantly consulting with Mao. Mao initially disagreed with the view of Khrushchev and other Soviet leaders who believed that Soviet troops should swiftly be deployed into Budapest. Instead, he recommended a peaceful approach as in Poland.[16] Suddenly, in the afternoon of October 30, after receiving information from his ambassador in Hungary as well as from Liu Shaoqi about lynchings of state security officers that were taking place in Budapest, Mao lost patience. He immediately called Liu Shaoqi, who informed Khrushchev and the other members of the Soviet Presidium of Mao's new point of view. Now Mao believed that "[Soviet] troops should remain in Hungary and Budapest."[17] This signaled his approval of the suppression of the Hungarian democratic movement.

Ironically, on that very day, Khrushchev and other Soviet Presidium members concluded that Soviet troops should be withdrawn from Hungary and all the socialist states, and that the Hungarian events should be settled through peaceful means. In other words, they finally embraced the previous Chinese viewpoint. Bulganin told the Chinese they now had an "incorrect conception,"[18] but Deng parried:

> First [you] need to grasp the political situation and not allow political power to fall into the hands of the enemy. The Soviet troops must return to their prior positions and defend people's power. . . . The Soviet army must not withdraw from Hungary, it must do everything to help the Hungarian communists reestablish political control and order along with the Soviet army.

He also noted that the forces of the USSR should "play a model role, demonstrating true proletarian internationalism."[19]

Deng's speech was rather pointed, and Liu, trying to soften the impression, joked, "Well, yesterday we advised you to withdraw troops from Hungary, and you were against it, and today we advise you not to raise the question of not withdrawing troops."[20] Some of those present laughed, but the overall atmosphere remained tense. Liu and Deng promptly informed Mao, who of course remained dissatisfied, believing that Khrushchev was vacillating from left to right.

He was correct. Khrushchev was completely tied up in knots. It was only on the morning of October 30, as a concession to the Chinese, that the Presidium adopted a "Declaration on the Foundations and Further Development of Friendship and Cooperation between the Soviet Union and

Other Socialist States," which said in part, "The countries of the great community of socialist nations can base their mutual relations only on the principles of . . . non-interference in each other's domestic affairs."[21] And now what? Attack Budapest?

Khrushchev was unable to calm down. All night he thought things over and the next day, in essence accepting the Chinese thesis, he declared at a meeting of the Presidium that "the troops will not be withdrawn from Hungary and Budapest and will take the initiative in restoring order in Hungary."[22] At the airport that evening, seeing off the Chinese delegation, he informed Liu Shaoqi that the Presidium of the Central Committee of the CPSU had decided to "restore order in Hungary."[23]

On November 4, the Soviet army entered Budapest and other Hungarian cities, encountering desperate resistance everywhere. The freedom fighters hurled Molotov cocktails at the armored vehicles and even dashed under the tank treads. Although Khrushchev succeeded in drowning the Hungarian revolution in blood (more than 2,500 Hungarians were killed and more than 20,000 wounded), the permanent losses of Soviet troops were also horrendous: 720 dead, or more than two and a half times more than during the entire Korean War (1950–1953). More than 1,500 soldiers were wounded or injured.[24]

By this time Deng had been back in Beijing for a while. Returning around midnight on November 1–2, the members of the Chinese delegation hastened to Zhongnanhai, where they presented a detailed report first to Mao and then to the entire Politburo. "The great power chauvinism of the Soviets," they asserted,

> has very deep roots and evokes strong dissatisfaction on the part of the fraternal parties. Although the leadership of the CPSU feels that past approaches are not working, it has not yet realized that it needs "to shift directions." The nationalist sentiment in the East European countries also has deep roots, and right now nationalism is flourishing. Each one exaggerates their own national characteristics at the expense of internationalism; a tendency has arisen to reject everything that is connected with the USSR, including the October revolution.[25]

Mao then spoke of the need to prepare a new article about Stalin, "especially in view of the Hungarian events."[26] Such an article would be published in *People's Daily* on December 29; its criticism of Stalin was significantly attenuated.[27]

Meanwhile, on November 6, Deng spoke before the members of the Secretariat of the CC about what had happened in Eastern Europe, declaring,

"After the events in Poland and Hungary, ideological confusion could be observed among [our] youth, members of the democratic parties, and even some of our party's cadres, and [therefore] it has become necessary to conduct purposeful class and international education everywhere and in a timely fashion."[28] Thus, after supporting the suppression of the popular uprising in Hungary, Deng, with renewed energy, turned to rooting out ideological counterrevolution in his own homeland once and for all.

He applied his efforts in two directions: preparing another "purge" of the party in the framework of a new rectification campaign (*zhengfeng*), as well as a national movement under the slogan "Let a Hundred Flowers Bloom, Let a Hundred Schools of Thought Contend." The latter was aimed against ideological enemies among the intelligentsia by means of provoking scientists and cultural figures as well as members of the "democratic parties" to express their views freely. Naturally, the prime mover of both campaigns was Mao; Deng was their main executor.

The second campaign was the broader one in scope; Mao had conceived it in December 1955 and first proclaimed it in May 1956, but at the time it had not received the support of the intelligentsia, which rightly feared falling into a trap.[29] Since that time Mao had returned to the theme more than once, but only during the Polish and Hungarian crises, which revealed the real danger of capitalist restoration in socialist countries, did he begin to implement this idea. On October 17, he discussed the question with Liu, Zhou, Deng, and other members of the leadership,[30] and a month later, at a meeting with an international youth delegation, Deng declared, "although Marxism-Leninism is our guiding ideology, in matters of science let 'a hundred schools contend'. Our line is one of free discussion. The truth will out if we are not afraid of controversy. If Marxism-Leninism winds up defeated, that will mean that Marxism-Leninism is untrue."[31]

Afterward, what appeared to be an ideological thaw occurred in China. Party control in educational institutions was somewhat relaxed, and articles expressing liberal ideas appeared in the press. But soon one could notice that Mao, Deng, and other party leaders were not taking to liberalization. They did not oppose it openly, but sometimes they were unable to disguise their irritation. Thus, on January 12, 1957, on visiting Tsinghua University in the capital, Deng warned those who were acting too freely that if they continued in the same spirit, the methods of dictatorship would be applied to them.[32]

Nevertheless, at the end of February, making a public speech "On the Correct Handling of Contradictions Among the People" at an enlarged meeting of the Supreme State Conference, Mao called for accelerating the

Hundred Flowers Campaign.[33] Deng, naturally, supported him. "It would be wrong, just because mistakes are made in criticism, not to dare and speak up. This would be a return to the past when a deadening spirit of silence and despondency reigned."[34]

In early May 1957, the Chairman called for complete ideological and political pluralism within the framework of the party purge announced at the end of April. Nonparty citizens and especially members of the "democratic" parties[35] and other intellectuals were called on to criticize Marxism and the members of the Chinese Communist Party, make bold and honest assessments of party policy, and help to eliminate the "three intraparty evils" of bureaucratism, subjectivism, and sectarianism. For almost a month, all Chinese newspapers and means of mass propaganda were open to anyone wishing to express critical views on a variety of political issues. In May in Beijing, a series of conferences took place under Deng's leadership with participation of well-known, noncommunist public figures.

Many liberals, however, began criticizing not "individual errors" but the entire system of communist dictatorship. Then, on June 8, at Mao's initiative, the CC issued directives to undertake a counteroffensive against "rightist elements." Freedom of speech was eliminated, and the communists returned to their previous methods of political and ideological terror.

The wide-scale political provocation succeeded. Now the communists were able forcefully to uproot all the weeds and destroy other "nasty things."[36] "The big fish was already in the net," Deng observed in conversation with Petr Abrasimov, counselor of the USSR in the PRC. "Without encouragement from the CCP, they [the rightists] would not dare to open fire and begin to act on such a broad scale. The rightists . . . resemble a snake which has slithered out of the earth, scented danger, and wants to slither back in, but has been strongly seized by the tail," he explained cynically.[37] It is unlikely that Abrasimov was surprised: the CC of the Chinese Communist Party had informed Moscow about the real goals of the campaign in advance in a secret letter. This is what Ekaterina Furtseva, then the secretary for ideology of the CC CPSU said to a journalist from *Novoye Vremia* (*New Times*), Valentin Berezhkov: "The formula 'Let a Hundred Flowers Bloom' is calculated to uncover the opponents of people's power, and then deprive them of the opportunity to slow socialist development in China."[38]

Now Mao entrusted Deng with leading a repressive campaign against the intelligentsia, appointing him head of a newly formed group within the CC to carry out the counteroffensive and to "squeeze the pus out of the abscess."[39]

Deng took on the job with relish. Thanks to his actions, for the first time in the history of the People's Republic of China the label of "rightist bourgeois elements" was affixed to millions of educated people, about half a million of whom were confined to "reeducation through labor camps." Not all of them had criticized the regime; many had remained loyal to the new authorities but fallen victim to intrigues and the "logic of class struggle." It was enough to be overheard saying, for instance, that "American-made shoe polish is really good" to be arrested and sent to a labor camp.[40] Deng was not bothered by this. He had never been a liberal and could not tolerate pluralism. He participated in the Hundred Flowers Campaign only because Mao wanted him to.

At the end of September 1957, at the Third Enlarged Plenum of the Eighth Central Committee, Deng delivered the main report, on the struggle against "rightist elements" and on the party's rectification campaign. Summing up the results of the campaigns, he demanded an intensification of Marxist-Leninist propaganda and political education after uprooting the "poisonous weeds." He also assured everyone that the decisive battle against "rightists" would continue on an even broader scale, explaining that what was at stake was "a socialist revolution on the political and ideological fronts," that is, resolving the antagonistic, irreconcilable, and fatal contradictions between the people and the bourgeois "rightist" intelligentsia. He pointed out the need to employ "methods of exposing, isolating, and breaking up—and in certain cases punishing and suppressing" the enemy, and he warned ominously that the intelligentsia's demands for "so-called 'independence' and 'freedom': the so-called 'freedom of the press,' 'freedom of publication,' and 'freedom for literature and art' were absolutely unacceptable."[41]

To the end of his life, Deng never doubted that the struggle against "rightists" via such a cynical provocation was justified, although from the time when he himself and his family suffered intense and unjust persecution during the Cultural Revolution (1966–1976), he regretted the sufferings of those who were innocent. In February 1980, at the Fifth Plenum of the Eleventh Central Committee he confessed, "I . . . made mistakes. We were among the activists in the anti-Rightist struggle of 1957, and I share the responsibility for broadening the scope of the struggle—wasn't I General Secretary of the Central Committee then?" A month later he gave a more balanced assessment:

The necessity for the anti-Rightist struggle of 1957 should be reaffirmed. . . . I've said on many occasions that some people really were making vicious attacks at the time, trying to negate the leadership of the Communist Party and change the socialist orientation of our

country. If we hadn't thwarted their attempt, we would not have
been able to advance. Our mistake lay in broadening the scope of the
struggle.[42]

Deng's regrets came too late. An enormous number of innocent persons who
suffered on account of his actions had died by then.

Deng's efforts did not go unnoticed. In November 1957, Mao took Deng
along with him to Moscow for the celebration of the fortieth anniversary
of the October revolution. He introduced him to Khrushchev with these
words: "See that little fellow over there? He's a very wise man, sees far into the
future." Then he pulled out all the stops, praising Deng as "the future leader
of China and its Communist Party." "This is the future leader," he said, "he
is the best of my comrades in arms. A great growing force. . . . This is a man
who is both principled and flexible, a rare talent."[43] Khrushchev himself had
taken note of Deng a year earlier. "Yes," he agreed. "I also [during the negotiations over Poland and Hungary] felt that this is an impressive person."[44]
Mao's praise was particularly remarkable since he spoke to Khrushchev about
other leaders of the CCP "in gloomy terms . . . even . . . he besmirched them."
Of Liu Shaoqi, for example, he said that his "virtue consists in being a man
of high principles, but his defect is his lack of necessary flexibility." He said
that Zhu De was "very old and although he possessed high moral qualities
and was widely known, one could not entrust him with leading work. Age
has not been kind to him." He even found flaws in Zhou Enlai (true he didn't
name any), although he added that Zhou "was able to engage in self-criticism
and is a good man."[45]

In Moscow, Deng and Mao took part in two international conferences: of representatives of communist and workers' parties of the socialist
states, and of representatives of communist and workers' parties of more than
sixty countries from around the world. It was Deng who, in the name of the
Chinese Communist Party, responded to the draft of the final document of
the first conference, the Declaration, which was supposed to put an end to
the ideological-political crisis that had shaken the socialist camp by affirming
its "indestructible unity."

It had been Mao's idea to convene a conference of ruling parties of the
socialist states; he feared new cataclysms in the socialist camp. In early
February 1957, Khrushchev endorsed the idea, and on October 28 he sent
a Soviet draft declaration to Beijing, but neither Mao nor other members of
the top Chinese leadership liked it.[46] Their main objection was to the thesis
about the possibility of "peaceful transition from capitalism to socialism."

First enunciated by Khrushchev at the Twentieth Congress,[47] this thesis immediately irritated the Chinese, who did not openly object but only expressed their disagreement at closed sessions.[48] In late October 1957, before flying to Moscow, Mao explained to Ambassador Yudin, "We are not going to discuss the question publicly . . . because this would not be in the interest of Comrade Khrushchev, whose leadership should be reinforced. That we refrain from discussing our views doesn't mean that they are not truth."[49]

CCP leaders were also displeased with other Twentieth Congress theses contained in the draft: "On the peaceful coexistence of two systems," and "On the possibility of preventing war in the current epoch."

Mao decided it would not be a bad idea to prepare a draft themselves, and to do it in Moscow where he could lobby for it with his Soviet comrades. He found the question of "peaceful transition" particularly irksome, and he explained this to the director of the Central Committee Propaganda Department, Lu Dingyi, and his secretaries, Chen Boda and Hu Qiaomu, requesting the three of them to compose a draft. Yang Shangkun would help them. Deng was in charge overall.[50]

The group set to work on the draft the day after arriving in Moscow, November 3. After completing a draft, they began to coordinate with Soviet comrades headed by the CC secretary for ideology, Mikhail A. Suslov, a dyed-in-the-wool party apparatchik. The negotiations lasted for several days, and Deng conducted them so skillfully that he succeeded in getting Suslov to accept the Chinese text in essence. Suslov did not agree to delete the thesis about "peaceful transition," but Deng and the other Chinese argued that the bourgeoisie would never yield power to the working class peacefully and armed force would be necessary.[51] By decision of the Great Helmsman, Deng proposed including both theses in the draft: peaceful transition and non-peaceful transition. Khrushchev instructed Suslov to accept this version, and Deng, with Mao's approval, agreed to include in the draft a sentence of great importance to Khrushchev about the "historic decisions" of the Twentieth Congress that not only had "great significance for the CPSU and the construction of communism in the USSR" but also signified the beginning of a new stage in the international communist movement facilitating "its further development on the foundation of Marxism-Leninism."[52] Thus a compromise was reached about which Deng informed the Politburo Standing Committee on his return to Beijing.[53]

On November 19, Mao with other delegation chiefs signed the declaration. "This time you have succeeded in observing the principle of equality," he remarked portentously to Khrushchev, in Deng's presence. "The Declaration has turned out well. Before there was talk about fraternal parties, but those were empty words. In reality the parties were fathers and sons, cats and mice."[54] Khrushchev forced a smile. Of course, the Chairman's arrogance displeased him, but he pretended not to notice.

In those days Khrushchev tried to ingratiate himself with Mao. Several months earlier, he had smashed the "antiparty" group headed by Stalin's former right-hand man Molotov; Mao was displeased and now Khrushchev wanted very much to win Mao over to his side. Therefore, he had Mao and the other Chinese, including Deng, housed in the Kremlin, where the czar's own quarters were allotted to Mao. (The majority of delegations from the other communist parties were lodged in dachas outside of Moscow.) Every morning Khrushchev visited Mao, showered him with gifts, escorted him to cultural sights, and held "intimate friendly" conversations with him.[55] But he failed to win Mao's respect. Following the Polish and Hungarian events, Mao lost all respect for Khrushchev and the Chairman even criticized him to his face. "You have a bad disposition," Mao told Khrushchev during one of the banquets. "You wound people easily. There can be various points of view among the fraternal parties, so let them be expressed, and don't be in hurry to discuss them. There's no need to worry about this."[56]

Deng, naturally, paid close attention to the excellent lesson in diplomacy that Mao taught him in Moscow. By the end of the visit, Deng's reverence toward the "Elder Brother" vanished forever. Meanwhile, his admiration for the Great Helmsman reached its apogee, especially since he could not help but notice Mao Zedong's special attention toward him. Of course, he had not heard Mao praise him to Khrushchev since the leaders were sitting apart from their comrades-in-arms at the time, but it was obvious that the Chairman treated him as his de facto deputy in the delegation. It was with Deng that Mao set off for private conversations with Khrushchev and with Deng that he discussed the most delicate details of the negotiations.[57]

Therefore, to his own surprise, it was on this visit to Moscow that Deng finally became privy to Mao's innermost thoughts regarding Chinese-style socialism according to the principle of "more, faster, better, and more economical." These were the ideas contained in the Chairman's speech "On the Ten Major Relationships," which Deng had earlier not understood. When, on November 18, at the conference of representatives of communist and workers' parties Mao suddenly announced that in fifteen years China would overtake Great Britain in the production of steel,[58] Deng applauded enthusiastically.

Of course, Mao made his declaration under the influence of the brag-gart Khrushchev, who several days earlier, at an anniversary session of the Supreme Soviet of the USSR on November 6, had loudly proclaimed that in the coming fifteen years the Soviet Union would not only catch up to but overtake America.[59] But an inclination toward adventurism always character-ized the Chairman.[60]

After returning to China, Deng began following the new line with genu-ine enthusiasm. Other top leaders, some of whom had been quietly nurturing doubts about the pace of the transition to socialism, also chose to believe the Great Helmsman around this time. Deng recalled,

> Comrade Mao got carried away when he launched the Great Leap Forward, but didn't the rest of us go along with him? Neither Comrade Liu Shaoqi nor Comrade Zhou Enlai nor I for that matter objected to it, and Comrade Chen Yun didn't say anything either. We must be fair on these questions and not give the impression that only one individual made mistakes while everybody else was correct, because it doesn't tally with the facts. When the Central Committee makes a mistake, it is the collective rather than a particular individual that bears the responsibility.[61]

In January 1958, Mao convened conferences of high-level cadres in Hangzhou and Nanning, where he severely criticized those who opposed "haste" and "blindly rushing forward." "Ideology and politics are in command," he pronounced in Hangzhou, and in Nanning he caustically criticized Zhou, warning him and several other "comrades," that they were "only fifty meters distant from the rightists themselves."[62] The premier was upset and made a self-criticism. Later he explained to his secretary that the main case of his mistakes was that he had "fallen behind Comrade Mao Zedong." "I must carefully study Mao Zedong Thought," he said sadly.[63] But Mao proposed replacing him, and appointing the well-known leftist Ke Qingshi, head of the East China (Shanghai) Bureau of the Central Committee of the CCP, as premier. After a while, however, when Zhou requested permission to retire, Mao magnanimously forgave him.[64]

On January 31, Mao summed up the results of both conferences in an important document, "Sixty Theses on Work Methods," in which he set forth the line of the Great Leap in the economy, putting forward the slogan of "Three Years of Persistent Work." He again expressed determination "to catch up to and overtake England in fifteen years," though on this occasion he did not deny that it might take "a somewhat longer period" to achieve this. "We need to exert ourselves to the maximum," he appealed.[65]

Deng did not participate in the January conferences, but he closely followed their progress. And he was inspired by them. "In 1958 . . . I experienced real joy," he recalled.[66] Captivated by Mao's powerful charisma, it seems that his will was totally paralyzed and he was no longer able to critically assess either China's economic conditions or the plans of the Leader. He believed in the Great Helmsman as in God and blindly subordinated himself to Mao. In this, he was just like the other members of the top leadership.[67] An eyewitness wrote, "Everyone was hurrying to jump on the utopian bandwagon. Liu Shaoqi, Deng Xiaoping, Zhou Enlai, and Chen Yi, men who might once have reined the Chairman in, were speaking with a single voice, and that voice was Mao's. . . . Everyone was caught in the grip of this utopian hysteria."[68]

In Sichuan in mid-February, Deng told local cadres:

> Regarding questions of constructing socialism, a struggle is going on between two methods: to build socialism faster or to build socialism more slowly. The method of Chairman Mao and the Central Committee of the party, proceeding from objective conditions, is to accelerate construction. In leading construction one also needs to be a revolutionary, one needs to actively create conditions for acceleration. . . . Such is our correct approach.[69]

At this time, Mao, radiating energy, urged on the "laggards." Constantly rushing around the country, with incredible energy he compelled the party cadres to bring his adventurist plans to life. He had a weak grasp of economics, but a superabundance of enthusiasm, will, and faith in his own infallibility. He proposed nothing concrete, because he himself essentially had no idea how to overtake England; he simply had a passionate desire to do so. He was particularly obsessed with the idea of sharply increasing production of such indicators of economic growth as steel and grain. For some reason he saw these as fundamental. He demanded that the leading cadres experiment, promising not to "beat up on them" for "leftism" or "subjectivism."[70] He understood one thing: China had an enormous advantage in comparison to other countries, namely, a gigantic supply of cheap labor on which it must depend.

In March 1958, in Chengdu, the capital of Sichuan, at a conference of leading party cadres, Mao accused them of conservatism and of blindly imitating the USSR despite the fact that almost all of them were already blindly following after him. Deng, who was among the participants this time, engaged in self-criticism. "Struggling against rushing blindly forward is not good," he acknowledged.

> This dampens the enthusiasm of the masses and the cadres. For a short time, my thinking about this struggle was chaotic. I did not understand there were certain differences between two lines, and on several questions I shared the view of several comrades who thought that with regard to capital construction and several things, it was better to act more slowly and cautiously.[71]

In April he observed to the Soviet ambassador Yudin, "We . . . are thinking about how to present . . . the following task to our people in some form: to catch up with the United States of America in 25 years or more." In his view, such a slogan would help the masses rush forward.[72]

Mao could forgive his comrades if they admitted their "faults." Thus, he was satisfied with Deng's conversion from a conservative to an energetic proponent of the Great Leap.

Meanwhile, in May 1958, on the initiative of the Great Helmsman, the Second Session of the Eighth Congress of the CCP was convened in Beijing to reconsider the "Proposals for the Second Five-Year Plan for Development of the National Economy (1958–1962)," adopted by the Eighth Congress two years earlier. The rate of growth of the national economy stipulated in the proposals no longer suited the Chairman since, according to it the amount of steel to be produced in 1962 would only be 10.5–12 million tons. In order to overtake England, a really giant spurt was needed, especially because by this time Mao had concluded that China would be able to overtake England in steel production in seven years rather than fifteen, and in the mining of coal in just two or three years.

Liu Shaoqi, who had fully aligned himself with the leader of the party, delivered the main report. On Mao's instructions, Deng made the report on the Moscow conferences.[73] Naturally, the delegates at the Second Session enthusiastically supported both reports and then approved a new general line for the CCP in the formula "Make every effort, strive forward to construct socialism more, faster, better, and more economically."[74]

Thus the main party forum gave a green light to the Great Leap. Soon Mao joyfully pronounced that in the future year, that is, in 1959, England would be left behind. This meant that in 1958, the PRC would have to produce 10.7

million tons of steel, doubling its output, and in 1959, 20–25 million. A bit
later he reviewed the figures: now he wanted 30 million tons of steel in 1959.
And in fifteen years, that is, by the mid-1970s, Mao figured on an annual
output of 700 million tons, or twice as much steel per capita as Great Britain.
In 1958 he wanted to double the grain harvest to 300–350 million tons even
though the initial plan envisioned a grain harvest in 1962 of barely 250 million tons.[75]

The plans were defined and the cadres and the people set to work. Deng
was extraordinarily active, daily discussing problems of economic development with Mao and other members of the Politburo and the Secretariat.

At the same time, on the instructions of the Chairman, who was well
satisfied with the role that "the future leader of China and its Communist
party" played at the Moscow negotiations, Deng began to devote more time
to international affairs—in the first instance, to the increasingly complicated
relations between the CCP and the CPSU. (In the Secretariat until then,
in addition to overall leadership, he had been directly involved only in the
fields of propaganda and agriculture; the ties with the Soviet communists
and other international affairs were overseen by Wang Jiaxiang.)[76]

The new round of discussions with the Kremlin leadership drew Deng
into its orbit in the summer of 1958. On the evening of July 21, Mao summoned Deng and explained that Ambassador Yudin, who had just returned
from leave, had requested an urgent meeting. Along with Deng, other
members of the Standing Committee also arrived, and soon Yudin himself
appeared, escorted by two embassy officials. After greetings and some general
talk, he presented Mao with a proposal by the Soviet leadership for the USSR
and the PRC to establish a joint Pacific Ocean naval fleet. Mao asked who
would control the fleet, but the ambassador did not know since Khrushchev
had not said. Mao became incensed, especially since four months earlier the
Chinese leadership had received a letter from Soviet Minister of Defense
Rodion Malinovsky containing a Soviet proposal to construct jointly in the
PRC a radio location station to track the ships of the Soviet Pacific fleet. Mao
and other Chinese leaders, including Deng, saw these proposals as encroaching on China's sovereignty.[77]

The following day, with Deng and other Chinese leaders present, the
Chairman lectured Yudin for five and a half hours. "I was unable to sleep
after you left yesterday, nor did I eat anything," he said. Yudin diplomatically
suggested that Mao discuss these questions directly with Khrushchev, but
Mao said that a summit meeting "might not be held."[78]

Yudin was so upset that after several days he had to take to his bed with a severe brain aneurysm and temporary paralysis of his right side. On July 31, Khrushchev himself suddenly flew to Beijing, deciding to negotiate personally with Mao. His intentions were honorable. He was simply worked up, having been "exaggerating," as he later said, "the international interests of the Communist parties and socialist countries."[79]

Mao met him, listened to his explanations ("I apologized as much as I could," Khrushchev would say later),[80] but would not forgive him right away. Instead he spat out all the insults and anger accumulating from the time Stalin had humiliated him.

Of all his comrades-in-arms, he invited to his first meeting with Khrushchev only Deng, now the chief expert on Sino-Soviet relations. Before the start of the conversation, either forgetting that he had already introduced Deng to Khrushchev or not counting on the latter to have remembered, he said, "This is Deng Xiaoping, our general secretary." And he added, "Don't look at him as small, he was the commander-in-chief of our Huaihai battle, secretary of the Front Committee, and he is in charge of the daily work of the CC, therefore, today he will take the lead in talking with you."[81] However, as the stenogram of the meeting shows, Mao did most of the talking and Deng only made a couple of timely rejoinders.[82] Only in the following days did he give evidence of his temperament and his brilliant ability to engage in polemics. According to interpreter Yan Mingfu, at a certain point Mao stepped aside and unleashed Deng to attack Khrushchev. Deng, "relying on facts, unmasked the efforts of the CPSU to undermine . . . the sovereignty [of China] and to control . . . [the Chinese] party."[83]

The visit exhausted the Soviet leadership. One day Mao shifted the negotiations to a swimming pool, where it might seem one could relax, but this brought Khrushchev no relief. Cleaving the smooth surface of the water, the Great Helmsman demonstrated his proficiency to his guest while the head of the CPSU, a poor swimmer, helplessly floundered. Khrushchev could not even unwind at night, because the villa where he was staying was plagued by mosquitoes. "Now that we are in China even the mosquitoes are trying to help you," he said to Mao.[84] Before flying home, trying to "put a good spin on a bad game," pointing to Deng Xiaoping, he joked to Mao, "Your little guy has frightened me most of all!"[85] Perhaps the diminutive Deng reminded him of the voracious blood-sucking insects that had spitefully bitten him during the humid Beijing nights.

It was like "sticking a needle up his ass," said the Chairman to one of his retinue about how he had treated Khrushchev.[86] He instructed Deng to brief the first secretaries of the CCP provincial party committees on the current state of Soviet-Chinese relations.[87]

However, neither Mao nor Deng could focus on Khrushchev for long. By the fall of 1958, the Great Leap had reached its apogee. To maximum the effective use of labor and mobilize the masses to construct various irrigation projects, large cooperatives or people's communes that encompassed ten thousand households or more were established in the countryside and the cities. Animated by the prospect of near-term abundance, people not only worked but also established communist relations. Wages and private plots were eliminated, and a changeover occurred to the principle of "from each according to their abilities, to each according to their needs." Domestic fowl and even utensils were collectivized. In an attempt to maximize the productivity of labor, collective dining halls serving free food were established in place of family kitchens. Mao was pleased by this initiative. "In both the countryside and in the cities we must infuse communist ideas into the socialist order everywhere," he declared.[88]

Deng, too, was ecstatic about the people's communes. "The people's communes possess an enormous and valuable power, and the peasants say they 'would not collapse even if a thunderclap strikes them'," he wrote. "In our country the people's communes are a powerful instrument for accelerating socialist construction in the countryside as well as the optimal form of social organization in the future transition of the countryside from collective property to state property, from socialism to communism."[89]

In August 1958, Mao thought that "the food problem had been solved," and he decided that it was time to focus on metallurgy.[90] An epidemic of building primitive blast furnaces broke out throughout the country. Citizens from small to large began to smelt iron from anything they had at hand: scrap iron, door handles, shovels, household utensils.

Deng spent almost the entire fall of 1958 on the road, inspecting communes, industrial enterprises, educational institutions, and other sites. At the time, the top leaders were tirelessly traveling all over the country. Mao himself set the example. In September Deng studied the situation in the Northeast, in October he inspected Tianjin city and Hebei province, and in late October and early November toured his native Southwest. He met with party cadres, commune members, workers and students, teachers and physicians; made speeches; and discussed problems. Following Mao's line, he asserted enthusiastically,

We must not only build socialism, but carry out the transition to communism. To smelt steel . . . means to achieve communism; this is our strategic task. . . . We need to experiment. . . . We need to pay most attention to organizing the people's communes. . . . Most of all we need to think boldly, carry out a revolution in ideology. Without an ideological revolution there can be no technological revolution. . . . The public dining halls in the communes must be improved so that peasants will eat better there than they did earlier at home. Only thus can the communes and collectivization demonstrate their superiority.

He sketched an impressive picture of a near future when all citizens would have sixty-six pounds of pork annually, and five pounds of grain and a half pound of apples daily; and all women would walk around in high-heeled shoes and use lipstick. "We can have as much as we want!" he exclaimed.[91]

People nodded in agreement. A model peasant who announced that he had produced thirty-five metric tons of rice per *mu,* or one-sixth of an acre, at a time when in China only about half a ton was harvested from two and a half acres, made a special impression on Deng.[92]

Such were the times. Mao himself was the boaster-in-chief, so it was not surprising that everyone assumed obligations they were unable to fulfill. An eyewitness said, "People were bursting with unbelievable enthusiasm, and it seemed that, with just a bit more, they could move mountains. I was able to play the piano a bit, and therefore I undertook to write an opera in two months."[93]

Only rarely during his travels did Deng have any doubts. "In order to equalize wages we need to eliminate the distinctions [between workers and peasants, the city and the countryside, mental and physical labor], but we don't have to achieve leveling," he advised district chiefs in Hubei. "It is a bit premature to advance the slogan 'From each according to their ability, to each according to their needs'. We need to give people freedom of choice," he told party cadres in Guangxi. "Let there be a large collective, but let there be small freedom."[94]

There in Guangxi, he began to express dissatisfaction with the quality of the metal smelted in the primitive blast furnaces.[95] This was understandable. After all, who better than someone like Deng, who had worked, however briefly, in the Schneider steel mill in France, would know that the small primitive furnaces were unable to produce any sort of real steel?

In November 1958, Mao himself began to worry. The "battle for steel" had diverted the Chinese leadership's attention from the grain problem, and the task of harvesting rice and other grain had fallen on the shoulders of women, old men, and children. Although they worked incessantly, they were unable to gather all of an unusually rich harvest. A shortage of grain developed, and Mao gave the command to decrease the pace of the Great Leap. Later Deng would say, "It did not take him [Mao] long—just a few months—to recognize his mistake, and he did so before the rest of us and proposed corrections."[96]

The Chairman now instructed Deng to draft a plan for the fifteen-year construction of socialism, and he demanded that caution be used with regard to the transition to communism.[97] Soon, at the Sixth Plenum of the CC, convened in late November, on Mao's initiative a very moderate "Resolution on Several Problems Regarding People's Communes," which Deng also drafted, was adopted.[98] Explicating it, Deng said,

> We need to distinguish between collective and state property, social-ism and communism. In the present, commune property is basically collective, and one cannot say that there is state property; there are only a few elements of state property. Our task is to build socialism, gradually strengthening the communist factors and preparing condi-tions for the transition to communism. . . . In the period of socialism the principle of distribution according to work plays an active role; one may not reject it.[99]

At this same plenum, Mao submitted his official request to retire from the post of chairman of the People's Republic of China and recommended Liu Shaoqi in his stead. The plenum unanimously accepted his proposal, empha-sizing that it "is a wholly active request since, no longer serving as Chairman of the state, Comrade Mao Zedong can fully devote himself to the work of Chairman of the Central Committee of the party."[100]

At this time, neither Mao nor Deng nor other leaders were eager to publicly admit mistakes. Therefore, all the obligations to ship grain abroad (mostly to the East European socialist countries) were fulfilled, even though only 200 million tons of grain were harvested in 1958 rather than the planned 300–350 million. The result was that through taxes and compulsory grain purchases at rock-bottom prices practically everything was taken from the peasants. Zhou openly admitted, "I would rather that we don't eat or eat less and consume less, as long as we honor contracts signed with foreigners," and

Deng proposed that if everybody could just save a few eggs, a pound of meat, a pound of oil, and six kilos of grain, the entire export problem would simply vanish. The other leaders did not object.[101]

The result was that famine took hold in the country. According to various figures, in the winter of 1958–59, 25 million peasants were starving, and from 70,000 to 120,000 died from hunger.[102] For Deng, who keenly felt what was going on, the time had come to make a choice: either oppose the Chairman or follow him to the end, in spite of the millions of innocent citizens whose lives had become miserable.

12

Being and Consciousness

INSIGHT DID NOT come at once. Throughout 1959 Deng continued to follow the Chairman, who still thought that the difficulties were temporary.
In mid-February, Mao, despite the obviously worsening economic situation,
asserted, "If one speaks overall, then our achievements in 1958 were enormous, while the shortages and mistakes were secondary, not more than one
finger out of ten."[1] He began to press for a continuation of the Great Leap.

With spring approaching, Deng too had a burst of enthusiasm that
eclipsed his doubts. He persistently emphasized the "great successes," the
"overall unity," and the "correctness of the general line," repeating, "Last year
we observed a Great Leap everywhere; there was rapid development in all
areas."[2]

Yet, another, more critical, tendency began appearing in his speeches from
late 1958. "Chaos has arisen in industry," he acknowledged in January 1959,
"evidently the entire state plan is puffery." "Now we clearly see," he added
in April, "in working up the plan if we do not proceed from objective possibilities, it will be difficult to avoid certain disproportions in the process
of achieving it. Certain man-made difficulties may arise." He identified the
main reason for the failures as an "epidemic of boasting" that flourished in
the party in 1958.[3]

But such speeches did not arouse the Chairman's dissatisfaction at the
time since he himself expressed indignation at local cadres who had deluded
him about the grain harvest.[4] This what he said: "Right now we need to
restrain our ardor. . . . Would it not be an international mistake if we strive to
outperform the Soviet Union? We need to adhere to the dialectical method,
consider mutual interests, the dialectic develops rapidly and has already
neared a resolution of this problem."[5]

Deng likewise spoke in general terms, acknowledging that it was unnecessary to strive to break "international records," and following Mao, he
suggested improving methods without changing the line: to bring about "regulation by industrial branch," restore the "former good system" of managing
enterprises and payment for work, strictly observe the eight-hour work day,
and promote criticism and self-criticism. In this connection, like the Leader,
he continued to assert that the Great Leap would continue in 1959.[6] There
were no disagreements between him and the Chairman in this period.

In the spring of 1959, Deng directed the New China News Agency to
gather information about problems regarding establishment of the people's
communes. Neither Mao nor he believed reports from the localities any
longer. Then he and Zhou dispatched five inspection groups to regulate
the work of smelting steel. They were supposed to investigate the situation
and, if necessary, shut down some of the blast furnaces and transfer their
personnel to agricultural production.[7] In February, Deng personally investigated the situation in East China with Peng Zhen, Li Fuchun, and Yang
Shangkun, visiting Shanghai, Suzhou, and Jinan. In Shanghai he reminded
the party economic activists of Mao's almost forgotten words spoken at the
opening of the Eighth Congress in 1956: "A modest heart leads to success;
pride to failure."[8]

Such behavior served to strengthen his position in the upper echelon of
power. In early April 1959, at the Seventh Plenum of the Central Committee,
Mao declared:

> Power, of course, is concentrated not only in the Standing Committee
> and the Secretariat, but we must always have a central organ which con-
> stantly pays attention to problems. I am the Chairman of the Central
> Committee, I am also the Chairman of the Standing Committee,
> so that, like Mao Sui, who put himself forward,[9] I propose myself
> as commander-in-chief. The general secretary of the Secretariat is
> Deng Xiaoping, so that you [Mao addressed Deng] are the deputy
> commander-in-chief. Isn't that so? Mao Zedong is the commander-in-
> chief and Deng Xiaoping the deputy commander-in-chief. Do you
> agree? [Mao looked at the participants in the plenum.] If we agree,
> then that's what we'll do. And as they say, "as soon as power is in your
> hands, you start issuing orders at once." That's what they said during
> the Tang Dynasty. Deng Xiaoping! You have become a commander,
> power is in your hands, so start issuing orders right away! Are you bold
> enough?[10]

Deng must have beamed at these words, but as a cautious person, naturally he did not hurry to throw his weight around. He continued to listen attentively to what the Chairman said about the situation in the country and the world. He also was not deaf to the opinions of other comrades: Liu Shaoqi, Zhou Enlai, and Chen Yun. But those men, too, had nothing particularly wise to say and, like Mao, preferred to curse the local cadres for serving up inflated statistics, complain about temporary difficulties, call for investigations, and prophesy a gigantic upsurge in the economy in the near future.

Only one voice sounded like thunder in a clear sky: that of the minister of defense and Politburo member Marshal Peng Dehuai. Three and a half months after the Seventh Plenum, on July 14, 1959, the courageous Peng sent a personal letter to the Chairman criticizing the Great Leap. The letter disavowed the slogan of "Politics in Command" and condemned the "petty bourgeois fanaticism," " 'Left' deviation," and " 'Left' tendencies of subjectivism" that were prevailing in the party.[11] The marshal acted alone. Later he would say that he did not seek support from anyone else in the top leadership (Liu Shaoqi, Zhou Enlai, Chen Yun, Zhu De, Lin Biao and Deng Xiaoping), because none of them had the courage to condemn the mistaken course openly.[12]

Deng remained a bureaucrat and did not play in games that involved directly opposing the Chairman. But even had he suddenly been unfaithful to his principles, he would still have been unable to render assistance to Peng Dehuai. At the time the gallant marshal was composing his letter, by a twist of fate Deng was out of commission. In early July, while playing billiards in an elite club not far from Zhongnanhai, he slipped, lost his balance, fell on the stone floor, broke his right femoral bone, and was hospitalized. "This was a well-deserved punishment for the dissolute Deng Xiaoping," Red Guards, who disliked both Deng and the Western game of billiards, wrote several years later.[13] The pain was horrific. He was operated on immediately and remained hospitalized for three months. Judging by hints from Mao's physician, who was overseeing Deng's case at the time, apart from his leg Deng had thoughts only of the young nurse who was taking care of him. The upshot was that the girl became pregnant, was relieved of her duties, and was forced to have an abortion.[14] The doctor's words, however, may be doubted. While Deng was getting about on two legs he did not chase after girls. But who knows? Perhaps the hip fracture had the effect of changing his Puritanical relationship toward women.

Cooped up in the hospital, Deng missed the enlarged session of the Politburo and the plenum of the CC that took place in July–August 1959 in the resort town of Lushan (Jiangxi Province), at which Mao viciously attacked Peng Dehuai. The Chairman regarded the marshal's letter as "a program of right opportunism," which, supposedly, was "purposeful in design and organization." Following the plenum Peng was expelled from the Politburo and relieved of his post as minister of defense. (Lin Biao was appointed as the new minister.) Those who supported Peng were likewise cashiered: Zhou Xiaozhou, first secretary of the Hunan Provincial Party Committee; Luo Fu, first deputy minister of foreign affairs; Huang Kecheng, chief of the General Staff of the PLA; and Li Rui, one of the Chairman's secretaries.[15]

From his sick bed Deng sharply criticized Peng Dehuai and his "confederates." Mao could expect nothing less from him. Recently, as we have seen, Mao had been very pleased with Deng. At the end of September, on the reorganization of the Central Military Commission, Deng was made a member of its Standing Committee, the supreme organ for directing the armed forces.[16] After this, in an article dedicated to the tenth anniversary of the PRC, Deng came down hard on "a small number of right opportunists" who "do not see the great successes of the Great Leap and the movement to establish people's communes begun in 1958, and try their utmost to exaggerate several short-comings in the mass movement that have already been overcome in order to negate the party's general line for the construction of socialism."[17] This article appeared in the main print media of the Soviet Communist Party and the CCP—(*Pravda*) and *People's Daily*—almost simultaneously.

At the same time, late September and early October, Deng returned to practical work on a limited basis. The doctors advised him not to overdo it (to work no more than four hours a day), so until the end of 1959 he only rarely visited official organizations. He mostly stayed at home, played cards (especially bridge, which a Sichuanese friend had taught him in 1952), frequented the theater in Zhongnanhai with his family, and, accompanied by Zhuo Lin and his bodyguard Zhang Baozhong, walked a lot, exercising his leg. During these walks, he was gloomily silent as usual. Leaning on a cane, he paced the path. But Zhuo Lin and Zhang Baozhong noticed that he was thinking intensely about something all the time.[18]

We can only guess what he was thinking. The year 1959 witnessed crop failures, partly on account of natural disasters. Only by dint of inhuman efforts did peasants in the people's communes manage to harvest just 170 million tons of grain, which was 15 percent less than in 1958. However, the agricultural tax was increased by 18.6 million tons. As a result there was widespread famine on the scale of a nationwide disaster. The country was on the edge of a humanitarian catastrophe; the Great Leap had failed.

This failure and Peng Dehuai's bold démarche forced Deng to reconsider the situation over and over again. Was this the "bright future" he was striving for? No, Mao's theoretical and practical directives did not accord with the Marxism that the general secretary had studied in Moscow. Marx had asserted that "being defines consciousness," but Mao had demonstratively placed ideology and politics first. There was no way to reconcile these opposing positions.

Deteriorating Soviet-Chinese relations also troubled Deng. The personal factor played an enormous role in the polemics with the leadership of the CPSU, but in this case Deng was convinced that the fault lay with Khrushchev. Understandably, Mao's arrogant behavior fueled Deng's nationalistic reaction, while Khrushchev's clumsy performance evoked resentment and indignation. For too long, foreigners had oppressed China, and this latest dispute increased the sense of nationalistic grievance among the Chinese. The weak Khrushchev seemed like a convenient target to compensate for more than a century's worth of insults. But at some point Khrushchev felt that enough was enough, and he realized that Mao simply did not respect him. So he also took offense. He was especially humiliated by the swimming pool negotiations, which were indeed "politically incorrect." Generally speaking, Mao's behavior, which was never calculated to conceal his contempt for the head of the CPSU, finally evoked a response.

On October 30, 1958, at the Presidium of the CC CPSU, Khrushchev insisted on "cutting back trade, not sharply, with the PRC,"[19] and on December 1, in a marathon conversation with U.S. Senator Hubert Humphrey in the Kremlin, he clearly condemned the domestic policies of the Chinese leadership.[20] Mao learned this at once through his own channels; he had never expected such a gambit from the "big fool" Khrushchev, as he characterized the Soviet leader to his wife, Jiang Qing.[21] But the head of the CPSU did not calm down. In January 1959, in a report to the Twenty-first Congress of the CPSU, he criticized "egalitarian communism," comparing it with "war communism," the harsh system that Lenin and the Bolsheviks had instituted during the Russian civil war of 1918–21. (Later he claimed that he had done this "in passing," but he had actually devoted an entire theoretical section to this theme.[22]) Although he spoke in general terms without specifically censuring China, Zhou, Kang Sheng, and other Chinese delegates attending the congress understood and were outraged. This was Khrushchev's intention. He recalled, "After they had heard my remarks and read the text of my report, there was no need to explain to them further that we had a negative view of the 'great leap forward.' This circumstance also, apparently, did not contribute to a deepening of our friendly relations. On the contrary, it caused a cooling-off."[23]

On June 20, Khrushchev administered an even more palpable blow; he suddenly annulled the October 15, 1957, agreement, signed in Moscow, promising to furnish China with the technology to produce a nuclear weapon.[24] "They were denouncing us so hard . . . and at a time like that supply them with an atomic bomb, as though we were unthinking, obedient slaves?" he would say subsequently.[25] On July 18, while in the Polish city of Poznań, he openly and sharply criticized the "communes," saying that those who were playing with this idea "had a poor understanding of what Communism is and how it is to be built."[26]

Mao, of course, reacted irritably to all of this, but for the time being he did not respond to Khrushchev. He even adopted a special resolution at an enlarged Politburo session to give the appearance (for now) that nothing had happened.[27] But on September 30, 1959, Khrushchev flew to Beijing for talks in conjunction with the tenth anniversary of the People's Republic of China. Conflict became inevitable.

Deng was ailing at the time, so he did not take part in the new summit. He merely shook hands with Khrushchev and his old acquaintance Suslov, who was also in Beijing, on the eve of the October 1 festivities. (Despite his broken hip, Deng came to review the parade and demonstration on Tiananmen Square.)[28] Naturally, he learned right away that the talks that took place on October 2 were unusually tempestuous. Two questions were at the center of the discussion: Soviet and Chinese relations with the United States, including the Taiwan issue; and Moscow's reaction to the conflict along the Sino-Indian border, which had flared up at the end of August 1959. The first question arose in connection with Khrushchev's visit to Washington in September to meet with President Eisenhower, whom the leaders of the Chinese Communist Party naturally viewed as their main enemy. The second came up with the fact that Khrushchev, wishing to avoid complications prior to his meeting with Eisenhower, had not supported the fraternal PRC in its clash with India. The TASS statement of September 9 on the situation along the Sino-Indian border clearly indicated the Soviet Union's neutrality. The issues essentially involved the policy of peaceful coexistence proclaimed at the Twentieth Soviet party congress that the Chinese considered mistaken.

No previous meeting of two leaders of socialist countries had produced such incandescent passions. Neither Khrushchev nor Mao wanted to understand the other. Marshal Chen Yi, PRC minister of foreign affairs since 1958, voiced the Chinese position in the frankest way. He asserted that the policy of the USSR was one of "opportunism and time-serving." Khrushchev flared up and began shouting, "Look at this lefty. Watch it, comrade Chen Yi, if you turn left, you may end up going to the right. The oak is also firm, but it breaks." Mao supported Chen Yi: "We . . . attached to you one label—time-servers. Please accept it." Khrushchev: "We do not accept it. We take a principled communist line." His little eyes blazed.

Why may you criticize us, and the senior brother may not censure you? At one meeting with comrade Yudin you, comrade Mao Zedong, very sharply criticized the CPSU, and we accepted this criticism. . . . It turns out that you may censure us, and we may not. . . . You do not tolerate objections, you believe you are orthodox, and this is where your arrogance reveals itself. Chen Yi attached a label to us, and it is a political label. What ground does he have to do this. . . . Take back your political accusations; otherwise we will downgrade relations between our parties.

Mao tried to reason with him, but Khrushchev carried on. "If, as you say, we are time-servers, Comrade Chen Yi," he shouted, "then don't extend your hand to me. I will not shake it!" Chen Yi did not yield an inch, but in a conciliatory tone Mao said, "Chen Yi speaks about particulars, and you should not generalize." Wang Jiaxiang added, "The whole matter is about wrong translation. Chen Yi did not speak of time-serving as some kind of doctrine."[29]

But it was impossible to calm Khrushchev down. He decided to cut short his visit, and the next day he flew out of Beijing. At the airport prior to his departure, he continued his shouting match with Chen Yi, but Mao no longer intervened. Only at parting, as if he had just remembered Khrushchev's remarks in Poznań about people's communes did Mao say, "I must explain something to you. Our people's communes were not created from above; they are the result of the spontaneous action of the masses. We had to support them."[30] But Khrushchev was uninterested in an explanation. Arriving in Moscow, after briefing the members of the Presidium, he demanded that "the record of the discussions with Chinese friends should not be preserved in the archives, but destroyed."[31] The split between the leaders of the CPSU and the CCP had become a fact.

By referring to the communes, Mao had simply been trying to save face. These cooperatives had failed and the Great Helmsman had no desire to enter into polemics in the economic realm. In his dispute with the CPSU, he felt

confident only in the sphere of politics, on questions of international relations, peaceful coexistence, peaceful transition, and the like.

It was precisely in this arena that he decided to wage an open battle against
Khrushchev, whom since early October he had begun to speak of as a person
"inclined toward revisionism." In early December at an enlarged Politburo
meeting in Hangzhou, Mao even asserted that

> Khrushchev is a poor Marxist. . . . His world view is empirical, his
> ideological method is metaphysics, he is a great power chauvin-
> ist and a bourgeois liberal. . . . Meeting with Khrushchev on many
> occasions, I observed that this is a man who doesn't understand
> Marxism-Leninism, whose knowledge is superficial, who does not
> understand the method of class analysis, and is like a correspondent
> of a news agency: whichever the way the wind blows, he turns in that
> direction.

Mao also noted that Khrushchev sometimes spouted whatever first came into
his head, and that he was an "extreme subjectivist-idealist." Yet he expressed
the hope that the Soviet leader would mend his ways: "If not, then perhaps
the CPSU will muster the strength to correct him. . . . In eight years or so
he will be totally bankrupt."[32] In January 1960, at a new enlarged session of
the Politburo meeting in Shanghai, Mao called for open polemics against the
CPSU in the press.[33]

Meanwhile, Khrushchev was also not sitting idly by. In early February
1960, at a banquet during a Moscow meeting of the Warsaw Pact Political
Consultative Committee, Khrushchev, stinking drunk, began cursing Mao
in the presence of Kang Sheng, the Chinese observer. "If the old man is a fool,
then he is no better than a pair of torn galoshes. He should be put in the corner
like defective products that are good for nothing."[34] Kang Sheng immediately
informed Mao, who assigned his propagandists to prepare articles against the
"modern Soviet revisionists," timed to coincide with the ninetieth anniversary of Lenin's birth (April 22, 1960). Deng and other Mao loyalists, wishing to apply balm to the spiritual wounds of the Great Helmsman, proposed
reviving what had seemed to be the forgotten term *Mao Zedong Thought*.
This, evidently, was also intended to irritate Khrushchev. In late March at
a meeting of high-level cadres, Deng said, "Inside the country we would be
able to speak everywhere of 'Marxism-Leninism, Mao Zedong Thought.'
Thus these two terms will be unified, not two things. We will place a comma
between them, joining them together." Also, "Mao Zedong Thought not only

corresponds to the general truth of Marxism-Leninism, but also adds much that is new to Marxism-Leninism."[35]

Liu Shaoqi likewise spoke in favor of Mao Zedong Thought, and ultimately the Great Helmsman agreed to use the term in propaganda.

A month later *Hongqi* (*Red Flag*), the theoretical organ of the CC CCP, and the party newspaper *People's Daily* published two polemical exposés, "Long Live Leninism!" and "Forward along the Path of the Great Lenin!" respectively. Both were well buttressed with quotations from Lenin, Marx, and Engels, and aimed against Khrushchev's policy of "peaceful coexistence of the two systems" and his thesis of the possibility of "peaceful transition from capitalism to socialism." The Russian response was flabby. The ideologues of the CPSU could not find weighty quotations from the classics on which to base the foreign-policy course of the Twentieth Congress.[36] Nevertheless, the starting gun for open polemics had been fired. By the late summer of 1960, members of the U.S. National Security Council who were closely following the course of events began to consider seriously whether the Soviet Union might not resort to the same measures it had used against Trotsky, namely, assassination, in order to rid itself of Mao Zedong.[37]

In early June, prior to a session of the General Council of the World Federation of Trade Unions in Beijing, Deng, whom Mao had again sent to battle with the CPSU, subjected "Soviet revisionism" to a savage criticism for more than an hour and a half at a banquet in honor of several foreign delegations, including the Soviet one.[38] Ironically, at the very same time, at a meeting of the Soviet Presidium, Khrushchev had raised the question of "asking [the Chinese] to come and exchange views on a series of questions" to ease the tension.[39] Deng's speech torpedoed this intention. Three weeks later, Khrushchev himself replied to Deng by attacking CCP representative Peng Zhen at the Third Congress of the Romanian Communist Party in Bucharest. He shouted at him, "If you want Stalin, you can have him in a coffin! We'll send him to you in a special railway car!"[40] At the same congress, the Russians distributed a sixty-eight-page document censuring the domestic and foreign policies of the CCP, after which they organized a two-day discussion at which a majority of the delegates—except the Albanians, the North Vietnamese, and the North Koreans—attacked the Chinese.

Back in Moscow, Khrushchev maliciously observed to his companions, "When I look at Mao Zedong, I simply see Stalin. He is an exact copy."[41] On July 16, he ordered the withdrawal of all Soviet specialists from China, demanding the return of all technical documents needed to construct the projects in China being built with Soviet aid. Over the course of a month, from July 28 to September 1, 1,390 Soviet engineers and technicians, scientists, designers, and other experts returned to the USSR. The construction of more than 250 large and medium-size Chinese industrial enterprises either ground to a halt or was suspended.

The blow was precisely aimed and very painful, especially at a critical moment for the Chinese economy. In early August, after consulting Mao and Zhou, Chen Yi summoned the new Soviet ambassador, Stepan Chervonenko, and asserted that the decision to withdraw all the Soviet specialists was "a big event that shook all of China." Nevertheless, he added diplomatically that "it is impossible to think that our countries could become unfriendly," and warned that a break between friends was serious business.[42] With the help of the Vietnamese leader, Ho Chi Minh, who offered himself as a go-between, the leaders of the CCP and the CPSU held new talks and by mid-September had succeeded in taking a step toward each other. On August 15, the Soviet side invited the Chinese to discuss bilateral relations "in order to eliminate differences and hold the conference of fraternal parties successfully in November in Moscow." Mao graciously accepted and decided to send Deng to Moscow again. Yet he did not back off from a principled struggle, and on September 12 he instructed Deng to present Chervonenko with the Chinese response to the sixty-eight-page document received in Bucharest—a response that was twice as long.[43] On top of the previous accusations, it piled up new ones concerning the withdrawal of Soviet specialists and included disagreement with the CCP on the agenda for general discussion by the fraternal parties in Romania. (The latter was obviously contrived; after all, Deng Xiaoping himself had publicly attacked the "Soviet revisionists" three weeks prior to the conference in Romania, on the eve of the meeting of the General Council of the WFTU in Beijing.) To resolve differences and achieve unity, Mao advanced five propositions focused on the need to follow the Moscow Declaration of 1957.

On September 16, Deng flew to Moscow heading a nine-person delegation, including Peng Zhen, Yang Shangkun, Kang Sheng, Chen Boda, and Liu Xiao, China's ambassador to Moscow. Prior to departure Deng briefed the delegation. "We need to base ourselves on the general world situation," he said, "to guard the unity of the international communist movement and Soviet-Chinese friendship. But it is impossible to retreat on questions of principle. It is imperative that we explain our position. We need to rebut the mistaken propositions of Khrushchev who is imposing his views about a united CPSU family onto others."[44] Deng fully shared Mao Zedong's position, but the mission was doomed from the start.

The delegation was housed in the Soviet party-state dacha in the Lenin Hills district, near the PRC embassy. Everyone, including Deng, liked it. The quiet location was surrounded by woods. But the delegates only slept there; their working sessions took place in the embassy, linked to Beijing by phone and farther from the listening devices that, they logically assumed, were installed in the dacha. In a combative mood, they met the Russians in the Kremlin. "We have positions on all the issues, therefore, we will not be afraid to dash boldly into battle," Yang Shangkun wrote in his diary.[45]

Over the next six days (September 17–22), the Chinese met five times with Suslov and his comrades. An eyewitness recalls, "At that time Deng Xiaoping was 56, but looked very young. Short but broad-shouldered, he had a sturdy physique and was full of energy."[46] Deng expounded the claims set forth in the September reply to the sixty-eight-page CC CPSU document, and Suslov followed his party's line. Suslov asserted that the Soviet specialists had returned home only because they were unable to work in the atmosphere created by the Great Leap, therefore, the Chinese were at fault for their departure. Deng replied that relations with the specialists were excellent, but in turn he went on the attack "in an entirely calm but tough manner": "You unilaterally annulled agreements. And what have you achieved in the end? Not only have you inflicted enormous damage on our national economy, but you have seriously dampened the feelings of the Chinese people. You should not be shortsighted with regard to this question; you need to adhere to an historical approach!"[47] During Deng's speech, all of the Soviet delegates noisily expressed their indignation. Suslov deserves credit for finally offering to terminate the polemics "without any conditions." Deng, lacking instructions from Mao, replied, "This is possible. Stopping is possible, but there is one condition: you must first admit that you were mistaken. You reviled us every which way, and we made no reply to you. Do you think this is just?"[48]

A mutual understanding was not achieved. After the talks, however, the CPSU arranged a first-class reception in the Kremlin's Catherine Hall. One of the interpreters, Li Yueran, said,

I remember . . . Khrushchev was there and other members of the Presidium. Khrushchev sat next to Deng Xiaoping. . . . Although Khrushchev had his usual smile on his face, he had a stern look in his eyes. In fact, during the break, beginning with Albanian affairs [as we know, the Albanians were among those who did not support the Soviet sixty-eight-page anti-Chinese document], he attacked the CCP, though not directly. Deng Xiaoping was a straightforward man, therefore, staring right at Khrushchev, he said: "The Albanian Party of Labor is a small party, but it can safeguard its independence and autonomy. You should respect others more; there's no need to exert pressure on anyone." "This is not simply a question of disagreements between the CPSU and the CCP," Khrushchev said, raising his voice, his face turning red. "They took our gold and our grain, and cursed us in return." "Providing aid is a proletarian international obligation. Aid is provided not so that one may control and interfere in domestic affairs. You help them, and they help you," Deng Xiaoping answered firmly.[49]

But the irate Khrushchev continued to attack Deng ferociously. Downing one drink after another, he said the Chinese were inconsistent with respect to the question of Stalin. Initially they supported the struggle against the cult of personality, but not now; he brought up the subject of Gao Gang. "Gao Gang was our friend, and you destroyed him, this was an unfriendly act toward us, but he still remains our friend!" Then he switched over to Molotov. "You like Molotov, don't you? Well, then, take him, we'll give him to you." Finally, dead drunk, shifting his glazed eyes, he went after Kang Sheng, "From our perspective the article 'Long Live Leninism,' published in China, was ultra-leftist. These pieces came from your pen! You are the one pushing leftist dogmatism!" The reptilian and irritable Kang Sheng smirked contemptuously, "You labeled me a left dogmatist. I present you the label of right opportunist." Khrushchev was taken aback, but then raised his shot glass: "All right then! Let's drink to our mutual health. Bottoms up!"[50]

On September 23, the Chinese delegation returned home. Deng reported to Mao and the other members of the Standing Committee.

The question of relations between the PRC and the USSR is neither big nor small. It's not big because the sky is hardly likely to fall on account of it, and it's not small, because it really touches upon a number of principled elements. . . . If they will take steps [toward us], then we will, too, but if they take only one step, under no circumstances will we be the first to take the next step.[51]

On September 30, he flew to Moscow again to take part in the editorial commission of representatives of twenty-six communist and workers' parties engaged in drafting a final document for the conference of eighty-one parties scheduled for Moscow in November. But the inability of Deng and Suslov (in reality Mao and Khrushchev) to overcome their differences had an impact on the work of the editorial commission, whose members, the CPSU and the CCP above all, disagreed on almost every word. Deng was not despondent. Precisely following the instructions of his leader, he remained absolutely calm.[52] He even cracked jokes, cheering up the members of the delegation.

"Eh, Zhang Yi," he addressed the wife of Ambassador Liu Xiao, "Do you know the story of how 'The Rabbit Ate the Hen'?"

"What?" said Zhang in surprise. "A rabbit?"

"Yes," said Deng. "This happened in the '30s with Lu Dingyi." [Head of the CC CCP Propaganda Department.]

"In Yan'an?" someone asked.

"We did not raise rabbits in Yan'an, in Yan'an we made reports. So Lu was giving a talk about Trotsky [Tuoluociji in Chinese], what kind of person he was. But he was speaking in Wuxi dialect [a city in Jiangsu province], what a disaster! All the time it came out as 'Tuzi chi ji.' [The rabbit ate a hen.] After the report, several of us comrades, simply couldn't believe that a rabbit ate a hen, just like Zhang Yi right now, and coming out of the hall, we were asking each other, 'How could it be that a rabbit ate a hen?'"[53]

Hearing this and similar stories, everybody laughed and after such conversations they were ready to do battle again with the insufferable Suslov.

Finally, after Herculean efforts, the twenty-six member commission was able to agree more or less on a "Declaration of the Moscow Conference," to be signed in November by representatives of eighty-one parties. On October 23, Deng left for Beijing to report on the situation and, on November 5, along with Liu Shaoqi, whom Mao had appointed to head the Moscow conference delegation, returned to Moscow, this time as Liu's deputy. They were housed in the same dacha in the Lenin Hills. Liu, not feeling well, was obviously unprepared for an exhausting polemic with Khrushchev. The rapid deterioration of Soviet-Chinese relations touched him personally. From the age of five, his eldest son Liu Yunbin had lived, studied, and worked in the Soviet Union and had then married a Russian girl. Liu, who was fond of children, had a granddaughter in Moscow and was anxious about her fate. That is why on this trip he paced for a long time in the woods near the dacha and chain-smoked. He was a reserved man, and now he became very gloomy.

But Deng remained level-headed and seemed energized by the polemics. He was utterly absorbed by the discussions with the "elder brother" in which he tangled again with Suslov and Khrushchev. Only rarely did Liu Shaoqi interject a comment. The outcome of the conference was a compromise document in which the Soviet side accepted the Chinese theses concerning the immutable nature of imperialism and the equality of all communist parties, and the Chinese agreed to include in the declaration theses about the significance of the Twentieth Congress of the CPSU and peaceful transition. After Liu Shaoqi affixed his signature, Deng and the other members of the CCP delegation returned to China on December 2 with clear consciences, while Liu remained in Moscow on official business for one more week.[54]

Mao considered the results of the conference and Deng's work a success, and he observed that the twenty-six-member commission had "worked fruitfully; this was good, there were disputes and discussions."[55] After returning from Moscow, Deng plunged into dealing with economic problems.

By the summer of 1960, China was in severe crisis. In June, Zhou informed Mao that the agricultural economy was ruined,[56] following which, in July, the head of the State Planning Commission, Deng's old friend Li Fuchun, proposed adopting a new economic policy, one of "adjustment, consolidation, and improvement." Zhou added "filling out."[57] The goal of the new course, he said, was to "liquidate certain disproportions which came into existence as a result of the Great Leap."[58] Even Mao realized that the situation was scandalous, although he felt no personal responsibility for the failure of the Great Leap, unlike the gentleman of antiquity of whom Confucius said, "A gentleman would be ashamed should his deeds not match his words."[59]

In September 1960, Mao requested that the Politburo Standing Committee make the brigade, or in other terminology the production team, consisting of two hundred or so persons, the basic accounting unit. His dearly beloved people's communes would remain only as basic administrative units, as well as a constituent element of a tripartite system of property in the countryside. (An enlarged Politburo meeting in February and March 1959 divided the people's communes, embracing forty to fifty thousand persons, into "large production brigades" with about six thousand people in each, and at the lower level into "production brigades" or "teams." Each level of property corresponded to a particular level of collectivization.) He did not intend to retreat any further, and not until early November 1960 did he approve Zhou's initiative, endorsed by the CC, allowing commune members to have small personal plots and to engage in sideline production on a small scale.[60]

But none of this broke the back of the crisis. People were dying of hunger daily by the tens of thousands. In Beijing there was an acute shortage of foodstuffs. The monthly ration there for peanut oil was no more than 330 grams (for party workers the norm was 500 grams) and, if one was particularly lucky, one pound of meat per person. The rice ration was thirty pounds. Just over one pound of sugar was allotted to a family of three.[61] Many party leaders, including Deng, together with their wives, began growing vegetables in the inner courtyards of their luxurious private homes, going out to the countryside to collect wild grasses and edible roots, and drinking tea brewed from the leaves of trees.[62]

At the end of the year, it became known that the grain harvest had decreased to 143.5 million tons, while the population in comparison to 1959 had shrunk by 10 million persons.[63] Subsequently, specialists calculated that from 1958 to 1962, as many as 45 million persons died from famine in the PRC.[64]

In January 1961, at a regular plenum of the CC, Mao called on everyone "to conduct investigations and to study how things actually are" and added, "We must proceed from practice in everything. . . . We, Marxist-Leninists cannot rob the toilers."[65] Evidently, this was quite an original thought.

In March 1961 Deng took part in two high-level cadre conferences in Beijing and Canton on the problems of communes. At the Canton conference, on the Chairman's initiative, a document was adopted, drafted by the Great Helmsman's secretaries, the so-called Sixty Points on Agriculture, which again noted the need to "change course." Mao was then repeating everywhere that the "epidemic of communism" had brought no good, but he continued to blame local cadres and called on the members of the leadership to conduct investigations. In early April, Deng set out for areas around Beijing.[66]

Zhuo Lin accompanied him. Over nearly a month they met with the leaders of local party organizations and commune members and inspected fields, industrial enterprises, and communal mess halls. They were shaken by what they saw and heard. It seemed as if the countryside had long been under enemy occupation. The commune members had nothing: no pots, no cups, no buckets, no dishes. Their homes had neither doors nor locks. Everything combustible had been burned in the backyard blast furnaces; everything that could be turned into cast iron had been smelted. The communal mess halls were disastrous, and commune members were dragging out a miserable existence. Yet people were afraid to express dissatisfaction. They looked hungry, worn out, and indifferent to anything but food. Deng asked over and over again, "Are you eating well in the communal mess halls?" The peasants replied, "Yes, it's OK. It's all right." Finally, Deng said sternly, "The communal mess halls are a big issue. The masses are discussing it widely at present.

Let's all consider it." Then Zhuo Lin, who had just returned from one village, stood up. "In Shangnian village," she said, "the communal mess hall is not working. The local commune members divide the grain and cook at home. That's the only way to go!" Hearing this, Deng was very pleased and, turning to the Shangnian villagers who were present at the meeting, he said, "Your cadres are acting properly in opposing the 'epidemic of communism' and 'egalitarianism.' They have not confiscated your pots, cups, buckets, and dishes, they have not broken off your locks, not removed your doors from their hinges. This is good."[67] The commune members were confused, unable to keep up with the rapidly changing party line.

Returning to Beijing, in early May, Deng, along with Peng Zhen, who had investigated a neighboring district, presented a report to Mao that he had actually been awaiting:

> For the further and all-around upsurge of the [productive] activity of the peasants, we must continue to improve the system of state supply, purchase of foodstuffs and distribution of surplus grain. . . . The question of purchasing foodstuffs, and distribution of surplus grain . . . is causing the greatest anxiety at present among both the cadres and the masses. Basically, there are two points of view: The majority of production brigades approve [the system] in which the surplus of grain [above the taxed portion] established by the plan is distributed in a ratio of nine-tenths to the state and one-tenth to themselves, while production above and beyond the plan is distributed in a ratio of four-tenths to the state and six-tenths to themselves. [Only] a small portion of production brigades don't like this. At present commune members tremble over grain as if it were pearls . . . it's necessary that most of the surplus grain be distributed among themselves according to their work and the amount of fertilizer each commune member has provided. They must be induced to work as hard as they do on their private plots in order to carefully cultivate the collective land and fertilize it actively.

The report laid particular stress on the harm of egalitarianism that undermined the material interest of the peasants in the results of their labor. At the same time, it noted that "the question of communal mess halls is rather complicated," and it should be resolved by the commune members themselves.[68]

Obviously, Deng and Peng proposed nothing particularly revolutionary; they did not demand liquidation of the communes and merely advised Mao to return to the socialism of the mid-1950s, with its higher-stage cooperatives. Others, including both Zhou Enlai and Zhu De, gave Mao essentially the same advice, stressing the need to restore distribution according to labor, but they were more explicit regarding the communal mess halls. "All commune members, including women and bachelors, want to cook at home," Zhou asserted. "The question of how to shut down the communal mess halls must be decided and how to restore commune members to their home kitchens."[69] Neither Zhou nor Zhu suggested eliminating the communes as a form of administrative organization.

By this time Mao himself had concluded that the communal mess halls should be shut down.[70] Thus the reports of his colleagues merely confirmed that once again he was right. At a loss what to do next, he decided to retreat to what he called the "second line," ceding the day-to-day management of state and party affairs to his subordinates while himself focusing on weightier matters. Liu, Zhou, and Deng could try to straighten things out.

They began to investigate the problems in greater depth. Just a month later, at a CC work conference at the end of May 1961, Liu Shaoqi unexpectedly spoke critically of Mao in the Chairman's presence. Naturally, he did not mention the Great Helmsman by name, but everyone understood whom he had in mind. "The peasants in Hunan have a saying," he said, " 'three-tenths of misfortune is from Heaven, but seven-tenths is from man.' Overall there are places in the country where the main cause [of difficulties] is natural disasters, but I'm afraid there are not many such places. In the majority of places the main cause is deficiencies and mistakes in our work." He continued, "There are comrades who think this is a matter of one finger and nine fingers. But I'm afraid it is already evident that . . . if one speaks all the time about nine fingers and one finger and does not change this equation, this will not conform to reality."[71]

Everyone knew that it was Mao who compared the achievements and failures of the Great Leap according to the principle of "nine healthy fingers and one sick one." Those present held their breath, and Mao felt insulted. Zhou, ever cautious, remained silent, but suddenly a miracle occurred. Deng unequivocally supported Liu:

> Can we use the methods of the past to solve current problems? I think not. In the sphere of relations of production tension exists not only in the countryside, but also in the cities. Here, too, is the question of property. In the final analysis, does misfortune come from Heaven or from man? Comrade Shaoqi has also said that in a number of districts,

I'm afraid, mistakes in our work (including several political directives) were primary and natural disasters secondary.[72]

Mao was shaken. Several days later, evidently concealing his resentment, he declared that for a long time "he had not understood very well how to construct socialism in China."[73] To his physician he added bitterly, "All the good party members are dead. The only ones left are a bunch of zombies."[74]

Where had Deng's flexibility, which had so impressed Mao Zedong, gone to? Is it possible that his investigation of the communes had made such a profound impact on him that even after he had presented his moderate report to the Great Helmsman, he continued to agonize over the sources of misfortune? Like Liu, had he finally grasped the reason for the economic collapse, and could not restrain himself? Most likely. "We acted in direct contradiction of objective laws, attempting to boost the economy all at once," he would say subsequently. "As our subjective wishes went against objective laws, losses were inevitable."[75]

After traveling this hard path of learning, Deng came to the conclusion that the Utopian Maoist model of socioeconomic development had to be reformed. Accordingly, he now confronted a new problem that lasted right up until the death of the Chairman, namely, how to oppose the Leader without compromising his own position in the party. He did not want to suffer the fate of the rebellious Peng Dehuai, but he was no longer able to follow blindly after Mao.

"*Yellow Cat, Black Cat*"

DENG'S MAY 1961 speech supporting Liu Shaoqi, which so irritated Mao, was the first sign of his disobedience. As an experienced bureaucrat he must have known he was playing with fire, but that did not stop him.

A year later, in the summer of 1962, he enraged the Chairman even more by approving the expansion of household production, the so-called family contract system, which was then spreading in the countryside. In so doing he was following the example of Chen Yun and Liu Shaoqi.

The transition to the contract system had begun spontaneously in the eastern province of Anhui in late 1960. According to the contract, peasants were obliged to turn over to the collective (that is, the brigade, but in fact the state) a specified amount of the harvest from the parcel of land that, in essence, was leased to them, in return for "workdays," a measurement for a number of days' work with food or grain. Everything they grew above the plan they could keep for themselves, or turn over to the same brigade but for a separate payment. The system varied with the place. They could not decide what to grow; they were given orders by the brigade leaders, who prior to the start of work provided them with tools, fertilizer, and seeds. There was nothing antisocialist about this; the household contract system did not go as far as the Bolsheviks' New Economic Policy since in the PRC the peasants lacked the right to sell their surplus on the market. Nevertheless, the household contract system, which stimulated the material self-interest of the commune members, quickly began to bear fruit. By the autumn of 1961, the grain harvest had increased by 4 million tons. Everything, it seemed, was going very well, but in the latter half of 1961 Mao, who initially had not objected that people were "experimenting," began expressing dissatisfaction with the revival of "individual peasant farming." In September, the Central

Committee issued a directive condemning household contracts.[1] At the end of December, Mao asked the First Secretary of the Anhui Party Committee, "Production has been restored, are we going to change the 'system' of [household] responsibility?"[2] But the secretary, who had been lobbying for the contract system since the spring of 1961, replied to the question with a question, "The masses have just tasted sugar, may we perhaps let them work a while longer?"[3]

Mao became indignant and soon fired the Anhui official who had dared to contradict him. However, he did not abolish the contract system, which continued to spread across China.

In early 1962 the Great Helmsman was dealt a new blow at an enlarged CC meeting in Beijing, the largest in the entire history of the party. Seven thousand leading cadres participated in the meeting, which lasted from January 11 to February 7. Since Deng was in charge of convening and running the forum, Mao had reason to be dissatisfied with him once again. Mao had supposed that the forum "would do a good job of analyzing the experience and lessons of the past and work out a unified position," but he encountered the most serious criticism he had been subjected to for quite some time.

Even had he wanted to, there was little Deng could have done; the situation had simply slipped out of his control. His own deputy in the CC Secretariat, Peng Zhen, openly attacked Mao for the first time. Initially, Peng blamed the entire Politburo Standing Committee for the failure of the Great Leap, but then he focused his criticism on Mao, who, he recalled, had insisted on an accelerated transition to communism and agitated in favor of the communal mess halls. Everyone listened with bated breath. Then Deng addressed the audience: "We were recently at the Chairman's and he said, 'You have made me . . . into a saint, but there are no saints. Everyone has shortcomings and makes mistakes. The only question is how many. Don't be afraid to talk about my shortcomings; the revolution was not made by Chen Duxiu and Wang Ming, but by me with all the others'."

Nobody understood if Deng wanted to relieve the tension or encourage Peng to continue his critique. But Peng Zhen, throwing caution to the wind, declared:

Even if Chairman Mao's authority is not as high as Mt. Everest, still it reminds us of Mt. Taishan, so much so that even if we remove several tons of earth from this mountain, it still remains lofty. It is also enormous like the East China Sea—even if you withdraw several truckloads of water, a lot still remains. There is at present a tendency in the party—people dare not express their opinions, they're not bold enough to criticize their own mistakes. They seem to think, if you speak out you will suffer a calamity. But if Chairman Mao committed even one percent mistakes or even one-thousandth of one percent and failed to engage in self-criticism, this would be bad for our party.

The next day, the leftist Chen Boda, a Mao loyalist, tried to make Peng Zhen see reason, but the latter added, "Let us clarify the question of Chairman Mao. Most likely Peng Zhen's statement that one may criticize Chairman Mao is not popular. I [only] wanted to refute the notion one can criticize everybody except Chairman Mao. This notion is wrong."[4]

Recently Peng had repeatedly displayed obstinacy. After the catastrophic Great Leap, this native of the north China province of Shanxi, a tall, burly man just two years older than Deng, had lost his self-control. Starting in 1960, he periodically expressed his skepticism toward the Leader, publicly doubting the greatness of his Thought: "Is the Thought of Mao Zedong a 'doctrine'? This is something to be discussed." And even of the Chairman himself: "Who is Number One?—let our descendants say. Our work is not yet done!"[5]

For now Mao tolerated this, but his irritation was accumulating. Not only against Peng, but also against Deng, who was Peng's boss. Several days after Peng Zhen's performance, Liu Shaoqi spoke once more about a topic Mao found unpleasant, namely, the "relationship among fingers":

Earlier we invariably considered the relationship between shortcomings, mistakes, and successes as one to nine. Now, I'm afraid one must speak of three fingers and seven fingers. There are [even] some regions where one may say that the shortcoming and mistakes constitute more than three fingers. . . . There still exists the notion that "left" is better than right. . . . I think this concept is incorrect, is mistaken.[6]

After such words Mao could only demonstratively fling his "self-criticism" into the faces of Liu, Peng Zhen, and all the others. He did this by acknowledging what many already suspected, "I don't understand many issues of economic construction. . . . I have devoted comparatively more attention to problems of the social order, problems of the relations of production. As regards the forces of production, there my knowledge is minuscule."

After purging himself in this fashion, Mao proceeded to counterattack, demanding that his other "comrades" engage in self-criticism: "Speak openly about what's on your mind, take an hour, or two hours at most, but lay it all out."[7]

This demand evoked a response, and the party leaders, trying to outdo each other, began confessing their sins, among them Deng, who, sensing that Mao was seething with indignation, decided to calm things down. His speech could serve as an example of the bureaucratic art. On one hand, he divided responsibility for the Great Leap among the members of the party, placing the lion's share of the blame on himself and the Secretariat that he headed. On the other hand, he praised the "self-critical" Mao Zedong and his ever-victorious Thought. Then, summing up, he said that overall, despite some shortcomings and mistakes, everything was good in China—the ideology, the party, the Central Committee "with Comrade Mao Zedong as its leader," the cadres, the traditions, the style of work, and even the popular masses. In recent years the party had departed from its "fine traditions" only because "more than a few of our comrades have not studied Mao Zedong Thought hard enough or acquired adequate understanding of it."[8]

Speaking after Deng, Zhou Enlai likewise conducted himself diplomatically and, like Deng, placed most of the blame on himself. He rattled on about his mistakes so much and abased himself to such a degree that even Mao, interrupting him, said, "Good enough. You have already repented. Once is enough."[9]

But neither Zhou nor Deng succeeded in improving the Chairman's mood. Peng Zhen's and Liu Shaoqi's arguments poisoned his soul.[10] Right after the conference an aggrieved Mao left Beijing for Hangzhou on a long holiday. One of his favorite retreats was on the shore of the enchanting and tranquil West Lake. He again entrusted management of the party's daily affairs to Liu Shaoqi and other members of the Politburo Standing Committee, including Deng, but he no longer trusted any of them.[11]

As before, he "intentionally" relinquished power. In this case he followed the tactic of luring "the poisonous snake" from its hole. "Let everything repulsive crawl out completely, since if they come out only half-way they can hide again," he loved to say.[12] He was certain that the tried-and-true tactic of the Hundred Flowers campaign would also work well with respect to the party leadership.

As always, he was right. It is simply amazing that such experienced bureaucrats as Liu, Deng, Zhou, and Chen Yun were unable to see through him. Mao had scarcely departed when they convened a working meeting on economic problems under the chairmanship of Liu Shaoqi at which they acknowledged the existence of an economic emergency.[13] They found no better way to address it than to support development of the household contract system, despite the Great Leader's dissatisfaction with the growth of individual peasant proprietors. In Anhui by the summer of 1962, 80 percent of the peasants were already working under the household contract system; in a number of districts in Sichuan, Zhejiang, and Gansu the figure was 70–74 percent; and in several counties in Guizhou, Fujian, and Guangxi it was from 40 to 42.3 percent. In China overall almost 20 percent of peasants were enrolled in the contract system.[14]

Moreover, beginning in March, Liu Shaoqi and Deng started in earnest to rehabilitate those who had fallen under the wheel during the purge of the late 1950s. Although they didn't dare broach rehabilitating Peng Dehuai and his "confederates," more than thirty-six hundred rank-and-file rightists were vindicated.[15]

In the first half of 1962, many other leading figures in the Central Committee, the government, and provincial party committees lobbied to expand the household contract system, notably the State Planning Commission chairman, Li Fuchun, and the heads of the Rural Work Department, Deng Zihui and Wang Guanlan. Deng Zihui was especially persistent. At a Politburo Standing Committee work conference in May, he said, "In several mountainous districts we must allow them [the peasants] to engage in individual farming. We can also call this the household contract system. These will be socialist individual peasants. If they fulfill the task of raising [the level of] production, there's nothing wrong with this."[16] Many of those present supported him.

From his splendid isolation Mao continued to view this method of running the economy with ever growing dissatisfaction. "Things are getting complicated now," he said to his physician.

Some people are talking about a household contract system, which is really nothing but a revival of capitalism. We have governed this country for all these years, but we are still able to control only two thirds of our society. One third remains in the hands of our enemy or sympathizers of our enemy. The enemy can buy people off, not to mention all those comrades who have married the daughters of landlords.[17]

Mao did not say whom he had in mind when referring to "sympathizers of our enemy," but his interlocutor surely knew that Wang Guangmei, the wife of Liu Shaoqi, was the daughter of a wealthy landlord who had held important positions in the Beijing military administration in the 1920s. And Deng's wife, Zhuo Lin, was also not from a poor family.

On February 25, 1962, Mao instructed his secretary, Tian Jiaying, to establish a small commission to investigate the situation in the countryside and go to places in Hunan where Liu Shaoqi had recently been, as well as visit Mao's own native village, Shaoshanchong. He knew that Tian shared his own negative feelings toward the household contract system. He was astonished when his honest secretary returned two months later and informed him that the peasants "persistently demanded that the commission 'give them all-around help in dividing up the land by household'." Mao made a wry face: "We follow the mass line, but sometimes one cannot listen to everything the masses say. For example, it's impossible to listen to what they say about the household contract system."[18]

But Tian, at his own risk, reported the results of his investigation to Chen Yun, and then to Liu Shaoqi, who in turn acquainted Deng with them. All three fervently supported the conclusions of Mao's secretary. Deng wrote just one word on the commission's report: "Approved!" Liu said to Tian, "We need to give the household contract system the force of law."[19] Chen Yun composed a special report to Mao Zedong and the Politburo Standing Committee, in which he emphasized, "In a number of districts one may again [as in the early 1950s] apply the method of dividing the land and strengthening assignment of tasks by households in order to stimulate the production activity of peasants to accelerate the restoration of agricultural production."[20]

At the end of June 1962, at a session of the Secretariat examining a report on rural work by the East China Bureau, Deng also openly said, "In districts where the life of the peasants is difficult, we can use various methods. The comrades from Anhui said, 'It doesn't matter if the cat is black or yellow, as long as it can catch mice it is a good cat.' These words make good sense. The system by which tasks are assigned by household is a new thing, we can try it, take a look."[21]

We don't know if that expression was actually used in Anhui, but it is certain that in Deng's Sichuan peasants loved this pointed proverb about different-colored cats. Perhaps Deng simply used it, ascribing it to Anhui. In any case, his sentence about cats became his most famous expression. In popular lore the yellow cat turned into a white one, probably for greater contrast. He said it then because cadres of the East China Bureau sharply criticized the household contract system, labeling it a "mistake in line" and pointing out that it was intended to revive the individual peasant economy. Chen Yun and Deng Zihui, who took part in the session, defended the household contract, and the opinions of the members of the Secretariat were split in two.[22]

For some reason, Deng dropped his guard. Perhaps he thought that Mao had sincerely confessed his "mistakes"; more likely, he sincerely believed there was no other way to revive China's economy. Ultimately, he was not the only one at the time who rushed forward to attack windmills. Could it be that these romantics seriously thought they could change Mao's mind?

It is difficult to say. On July 7, at a plenum of the Central Committee of the Communist Youth League, Deng repeated his seditious sentence about cats, this time giving it a profound theoretical meaning and presenting it as a Sichuanese saying. He cloaked it with the authority of his old friend Marshal Liu Bocheng:

> We must . . . arouse the peasants' enthusiasm for increased agricultural production. . . . When talking about fighting battles, Comrade Liu Bocheng often quotes a Sichuan proverb—"It does not matter if it is a yellow cat or a black cat, as long as it catches mice." The reason we defeated Chiang Kai-shek is that we did not always fight in the conventional way. Our sole aim is to win by taking advantage of given conditions. If we want to restore agricultural production, we must also take advantage of actual conditions. That is to say, we should not stick to a fixed mode of relations of production but adopt whatever mode that can help mobilize the masses' initiative.[23]

For Mao, who was closely following everything that his disobedient younger colleagues were saying and doing in Beijing, Deng Xiaoping's words meant only one thing: even his loyal comrades-in-arms like Deng were ready to restore capitalism in the country. After all, the general secretary of the Central Committee had affirmed that all forms of production relations were good as long as they paid off.

Of course, Deng did not intend to restore private ownership of land. All forms of the production relations he referred to were socialist. At the plenum of the Young Communist League, he even emphasized, "Generally speaking, we must consolidate the collective economy of the country, that is, consolidate the socialist system. That is our fundamental orientation."[24] But Mao paid no attention to this.

Mao returned to Beijing in July, infuriated against Deng and all the other proponents of the contract system. The first person he received was Liu Shaoqi, who dropped by to tell Mao that Chen Yun and Tian Jiaying wanted to speak with him. But Mao, who was swimming in his pool, became enraged. Emerging from the water, he unleashed thunderbolts at Liu, "Now land is being divided up again just the way it used to be in the bad old days. . . . What have you done to resist this? What's going to happen after I'm dead?"[25] After this he received Chen Yun, who, not suspecting the Great Helmsman's foul mood, began discussing the expediency of a rather long coexistence of individual and collective property. Infuriated, Mao shouted, "'Individual peasant proprietors dividing up the land,' this is the downfall of the collective economy, this is revisionism."[26] On the margins of Chen Yun's report he wrote, "This man, Chen Yun, came from a small businessman's background. He cannot get rid of his bourgeois character. He leans consistently to the right."[27]

Chen Yun took fright.[28] Soon he wrote a letter to Deng in the expectation that Deng would pass it along to Mao. In it he requested a leave for reasons of health. He returned from this "leave" only after the Chairman's death fourteen years later.

After "dismantling" Chen Yun, in the presence of Liu, Zhou, Deng, and the leftist Chen Boda, Mao turned on Tian Jiaying and Deng Zihui. He requested that Chen Boda, then editor-in-chief of the *Red Flag*, prepare a draft resolution about strengthening the collective economy of the people's communes and developing agricultural production. Bowing to his pressure, the CC swiftly issued a circular prohibiting publicity regarding the household contract system,[29] and soon the fanatically loyal Chen Boda prepared a draft resolution that was reviewed and approved at the next (Tenth) Central Committee plenum in September 1962.[30]

The cautious Zhou, who always avoided talking about politically sensitive topics and did not indicate whether he was for or against the contract system, immediately supported the Great Helmsman. For their own good, Deng and Liu, too, no less frightened than Chen Yun, approved everything the Leader demanded. An eyewitness recalled, "After Chairman Mao's position became known, no one could fail to realign their own position with his."[31]

Deng hurriedly called Hu Yaobang, first secretary of the Communist Youth League Central Committee, requesting that he quickly delete a sentence about yellow and black cats from the stenographic report of his speech.[32] Liu, meeting with cadres being sent to grassroots-level organizations, criticized the household contract system, asserting that, unfortunately, both higher- and lower-level cadres had "lost faith in the collective economy."[33]

But Mao continued his offensive. Apparently during his vacation he had thought everything through in detail, and now he took revenge for the

humiliation he had been subjected to at the seven-thousand-cadre conference. No matter how efficient the household contract system was in economic
terms, he could not accept it, because he did not want to allow restoration of
capitalism.

Over the next month, in July and August, in the resort town of Beidaihe
near Tianjin, he "brain-washed" leading cadres from all over the country
whom he had summoned for a new work conference. On the eve of the
conference, meeting with the first secretaries of the provincial party committees, he bellowed, "Are you for socialism or capitalism?! . . . Now some
persons are in favor of introducing the contract system throughout the
country, including dividing up the land. Does the Communist party favor
dividing up the land?"[34] At the same conference, more calmly, he suggested
to his cowed comrades, "Individual peasant proprietorship inevitably leads
to polarization, and this will not take two years, stratification will begin in
just one year. . . . Khrushchev himself did not dare openly to dissolve the
collective farms."[35]

The reference to Khrushchev was no accident. By the time of the Beidaihe
conference, total discord reigned in Soviet-Chinese relations. After the
Moscow Conference of 1960 and following a brief warming, a fierce feud
resumed in the spring of 1961, this time linked to the further deterioration of
relations between the CPSU and the CCP's ally, the Albanian Party of Labor
(APL). Enver Hoxha, the Stalinist leader of the APL, after routing his intraparty pro-Khrushchev opposition in early 1961, sharply escalated his attacks
against the USSR and against Khrushchev personally, whom he began to
accuse of revisionism just as the Chinese had done. The Albanian leader had
a long list of claims against Khrushchev. He condemned him for his struggle
against Stalin's personality cult, for the theories of peaceful transition and
peaceful coexistence, and especially for severing economic aid to his country after an APL delegation had failed to support Khrushchev's attack on
the CCP during the congress of the Romanian Communist Party. At the
Moscow Conference in November 1960, Hoxha even vented his grievance
against Khrushchev publicly: "While the rats could eat in the Soviet Union,
the Albanian people were starving to death, because the leadership of the
Albanian Labor Party [i.e., the Albanian Party of Labor] had not bent to
the will of the Soviet leadership."[36] Hearing this, Dolores Ibárruri, head of
the Spanish Communist Party, compared Hoxha to "a dog biting the hand
that feeds it."[37] In May 1961, the Presidium of the CC CPSU adopted new
anti-Albanian measures that ended the supply of weapons to Albania and
withdrew eight Soviet submarines from the naval base at the Albanian town

of Vlorë.[38] Naturally, Mao supported the Albanians and an exchange of letters featuring mutual reproaches commenced.

Suddenly Mao received news of Khrushchev's intention to adopt a new program for the CPSU in place of the one that Lenin had proclaimed in 1919. The draft program was unveiled in the Soviet Union in late July 1961. The leadership of the Soviet Communist Party was evidently renouncing the cardinal Bolshevik idea of the dictatorship of the proletariat. The draft proclaimed that the social order of the USSR and even of the Communist Party itself was one of the whole people.

The Great Helmsman simply choked on Khrushchev's impudence. At a Politburo Standing Committee session he said, "This 'Draft Program of the CPSU' is like the bandages that Mama Wang uses to bind her feet—just as long and stinking."[39] He sent the faithful Zhou to head the CCP delegation to the Twenty-second Congress of the CPSU, convened in October 1961 to adopt the new program for the Soviet Union. Zhou did not conceal his indignation, which only intensified among the Chinese after Khrushchev read his reports concerning the activity of the CC and the party's new program. The head of the CPSU not only reiterated his old theses from the Twentieth Congress that the Chinese considered revisionist ("peaceful transition" and others) but also renewed his criticism of the Stalin cult. As a mark of protest, the Chinese laid wreathes at the Lenin-Stalin Mausoleum. On the one intended for the Generalissimo was written, "To J. V. Stalin, the great Marxist-Leninist." Afterward Zhou met with Khrushchev to reiterate the CCP's position on all the contentious issues. But Khrushchev, flaring up, said, "We in the past needed very much your help; at that time the CCP's opinion carried weight for us. But now it is different."[40]

Zhou cut short his visit eight days before the end of the congress and flew back to Beijing, where over more than ten hours he indignantly reported to Mao and other leaders what had transpired. He declared, "The ideological differences between the CCP and the CPSU are a matter of principle ... in the ideological struggle between the two parties stands the question of who will defeat whom."[41] At this time, by resolution of the Twenty-second Congress the Soviets removed the coffin containing Stalin's body from the Mausoleum and buried it near the Kremlin wall. Adopted unanimously by the congress, the resolution said, "Stalin's serious violations of Lenin's behests, his abuse of power, massive repression against honest Soviet people and other actions in the period of the cult of personality make it impossible to leave the coffin containing his body in the V. I. Lenin Mausoleum."[42]

Mao understood this as the "traitor" Khrushchev's complete repudiation of Marxism-Leninism. At Mao's behest, at a CC work conference in December 1961 on the international situation, Deng reported on the struggle against Soviet revisionism. "The international communist movement faces the threat of a split," Deng said. "This is primarily about a split within the socialist camp, mainly a split in Soviet-Chinese relations."[43]

From the Chinese side, of course, the motive force for the split was Mao himself, without whose approval Deng could not have trumpeted such a far-reaching conclusion. Zhou, Chen Yi, Peng Zhen, Kang Sheng, Yang Shangkun, and the overwhelming majority of members of the Chinese Central Committee supported this splittist mood. Only Liu Shaoqi and especially Wang Jiaxiang, who headed the CC's International Liaison Department, supported a conciliatory position. In February 1962, after enlisting Liu's support, Wang even sent Zhou, Deng, and Chen Yi a letter, followed by several reports, counseling reconciliation with Moscow.[44] But they were not enamored of the idea. Hearing of Wang Jiaxiang's proposal and Liu's compromising position, Mao simply exploded. For now he did not touch Liu, but he removed Wang from his position, replacing him with Kang Sheng.

"The Soviet Union has already existed for several decades," he told participants in the working meeting at Beidaihe, "and still revisionism has appeared there; it serves international capitalism and is essentially a counterrevolutionary phenomenon. . . . The bourgeoisie may revive. This is what happened in the Soviet Union."[45]

The same danger of capitalist restoration could occur in China, he believed, and therefore at the Tenth Plenum of the CC he placed before the party a most important task: "From today on we must speak about class struggle every year, every month, every day, speak at meetings, at party congresses, at plenums, at every session, so that we have a more or less clear Marxist-Leninist line on this question." As Chinese and world experience have shown, "classes exist in socialist countries, and class struggle undoubtedly arises from this." Consequently, restoration is possible as well, just as happened after the victories of the bourgeois revolutions in England and France, when these revolutions "went into reverse."[46]

The participants in the work conference and the members of the plenum wholly supported their Teacher. Deng, too, enthusiastically applauded him. But who can tell if he was being sincere? Mao himself was no longer convinced of Deng's straightforwardness. This was dangerous. Thus the general secretary, who had tilted at windmills, had to regain the trust of the Great Helmsman.

Just then a good opportunity arose. The Chairman, who no longer believed in Deng's ability to deal with economic problems, decided to deploy him once more in the battle against Soviet revisionism. On that front, Deng had distinguished himself from the other Maoist "hawks" by his exceptional energy and ability to engage in witty and tough-minded polemics with the Russians. Therefore, despite his profound dissatisfaction regarding the matter of Deng's cats, Mao again entrusted Deng with leading the struggle with the external enemy.

After again chasing his opposition into the corner, Mao felt back on top. Now he wanted to challenge Khrushchev, whom he thought continuously stirred up "waves of dirt and lies,"[47] to a final and decisive battle. This was reflected in the decisions of the Chinese Politburo and new letters addressed to the CC CPSU.[48]

Deng hastened to justify the Chairman's faith. On July 5, 1963, executing Mao's assignment, he arrived in Moscow for what turned out to be the last time. In the seven-member delegation that he headed were Peng Zhen, Yang Shangkun, and Kang Sheng; their main opponents were Suslov, Ponomarev, and Andropov. In the words of an eyewitness, these "strange" negotiations, which it was "difficult even to call negotiations," were like a dialogue of the deaf.[49] Over the next fifteen days, eleven meetings were held in the recently constructed Reception Hall of the CC CPSU. The antagonists took turns delivering lengthy and "drawn-out"[50] declarations that were no longer aimed at normalizing relations. Both sides were simply dotting the i's, summing up their final conclusions, and rudely criticizing their opponent in order to provoke him to break relations first. Neither wanted to take responsibility for the break.

Prior to and during the negotiations, hysterical campaigns were conducted in both countries in the press and on the radio. On June 14, Chinese citizens, and a month later Soviet citizens, first learned of the profound ideological differences between the two "fraternal" parties and countries. On June 27, the USSR expelled three Chinese diplomats and two ordinary Chinese citizens who were publicly distributing CCP materials that defamed the CPSU. They were greeted as heroes in China.

Parallel with the Soviet-Chinese negotiations in Moscow, Soviet-American-British meetings were taking place for a treaty banning nuclear tests in the atmosphere, in outer space, and underwater. The Chinese regarded these negotiations as a blatant anti-China stunt intended to pressure China to forswear nuclear tests, since it was known that China was working on developing its own nuclear weapons. Therefore, they supposed that Khrushchev was selling them out yet again in order to cozy up to the imperialists.[51]

All of this naturally influenced the atmosphere of the Sino-Soviet negotiations in Moscow. The war of nerves was exhausting. The suspicious Chinese believed they were being followed constantly and their conversations bugged, and that they were even being fed poorly. Once after dinner, in the car on the way back to the dacha, Peng Zhen, convinced that the automobile itself had been bugged, complained loudly about the quality of the food, after which their cuisine actually improved.[52]

Deng spoke at the second session on July 8, and the fourth on July 12. His first speech, including translation, took five hours, and the second took four. He also made a short, summary speech at the final session on July 20. Otherwise, he was basically silent, only rarely interjecting a sarcastic or caustic remark.

His first speech outlined the history of the conflict in chronological order, starting with the Twentieth Congress of the CPSU. He accused his opponents of departing from Marxism-Leninism on questions of war and peace, of conducting great power and adventurist policies during the Polish crisis of 1956 and of capitulationist policies during the Hungarian events, of besmirching Stalin, of attempting to place China under their military control, of attacking PRC domestic and foreign policy, of cutting off aid to the Chinese people for military and peaceful economic construction, and of making accommodations with American imperialism. He also recalled Khrushchev's shameless utterances about both the CCP and Mao.

In reality, he said nothing new. His speech, categorical and accusatory, left the Russians no room to compromise. In conclusion, Deng repeated the well-worn thesis that Khrushchev had revealed to members of the international communist movement the interparty disagreements between the CPSU and the CCP. He was referring to the Soviet leader's conduct at the congress of the Romanian Communist Party in late June 1960. "Fortunately, Comrade Peng Zhen went to the Bucharest meeting," Deng quipped. "He weighs about 175 lbs., therefore, he held firm, but if I had done, since I weigh only about 110 lbs., I wouldn't have been able to." To this Ponomarev justly retorted,

> But Comrade Grishin [chairman of the All-Soviet Council of Trade Unions who participated in the Beijing session of the General Council of the World Federation of Trade Unions in June 1960, during which it was Deng who first made the disagreements public] weighs 155 lbs. This began prior to Bucharest, in Beijing. This was the beginning of and the reason for the Bucharest conference.

But Deng did not care about "details." "I understood you," he snapped.[53]

Suslov replied to all of Deng's accusations the next day, focusing on the colossal assistance the USSR had provided China in the 1950s. Deng heard him out and asked quietly, "Perhaps we should take a break tomorrow?" Evidently Suslov, who spoke in a monotone for five hours, had tired him out.

On July 12, a reinvigorated Deng again criticized the CPSU, this time for its "nonrevolutionary" line regarding the national liberation movement in Asia, Africa, and Latin America. The next day Ponomarev responded, and then a day later Peng Zhen spoke. After another one-day break, it was Andropov's turn and, finally on July 19, Kang Sheng's. The latter read a text prepared earlier in Beijing about how "good" Comrade Stalin was and how "incorrectly" Khrushchev acted in repeatedly calling him a criminal, a bandit, a gambler, a despot like Ivan the Terrible, the worst dictator in the history of Russia, a fool, a piece of shit, and an idiot. The Chinese had extracted all these words and expressions from Khrushchev's own speeches.[54]

Suslov lodged a firm protest "against the distortions, falsifications, and slander directed against the leadership of our party and Com[rade] N. S. Khrushchev, against our party and the decisions of its congresses."[55] But Deng, Kang, and the other Chinese ignored him. "Com[rade] Suslov made some kind of protest," Deng noted derisively, and he suggested breaking off the session till some future meeting.[56] After consulting with Khrushchev, Suslov agreed on the following day, July 20. In accordance with Mao's directive, Deng invited a delegation from the CPSU to make a reciprocal visit to Beijing at a date to be decided later. "Our current meeting has served as a good start," he concluded. "It is essential that we continue our meetings."[57] Neither Suslov nor Deng, however, believed they would ever meet again.

Later a farewell banquet was held at the Kremlin attended by Khrushchev. He lifted his glass to propose that in the future all disagreements be eliminated, but his words were devoid of sincerity. Deng likewise spoke of striving for solidarity and friendship, but he was equally hypocritical.

That same evening Deng and his comrades departed Moscow. Mao insisted they go by train, fearing that the Russians would blow up the plane. But Deng bravely replied, "No, we'll fly." At 10:00 p.m. the airship carried him away forever from the capital of "world revisionism."[58]

Mao was philosophic about the rupture of relations between the one-time fraternal parties. "Prolonged unity leads to rupture, prolonged rupture leads to unification," he said, paraphrasing the famous opening of the novel *Romance of the Three Kingdoms*.[59] The situation with regard to the CPSU was actually to his advantage. Attempting to avert the restoration of capitalism

in China, in early 1963 he launched a new mass campaign of socialist education during which a propaganda movement was unfolded of *fan xiu fang xiu*
(oppose revisionism from abroad, guard against revisionism at home). Thus,
the courageous conduct of Deng's delegation, which dealt a rebuff to the
Soviet "revisionists," dovetailed perfectly with Mao's aims.

On the afternoon of July 21, Mao himself, accompanied by Liu, Zhou,
and other members of the inner circle of power, came to the airport to greet
the "heroes." Prior to this, only twice had he gone to greet comrades arriving
from abroad: in November 1960, Liu Shaoqi after the Moscow Conference;
and October 1961, Zhou Enlai after the Twenty-second Congress of the
CPSU. More than five thousand cadres and members of the public took part
in the triumphal ceremony. Among them was Deng's daughter Maomao.[60]

Deng was happy. It seemed that the clouds hanging over him had dis-
persed and once again he enjoyed the unlimited trust of the Chairman. But
it only seemed that way. After the battles of 1961–62, Mao was not prepared
simply to forgive him, especially since with the passing of the years the Great
Helmsman was increasingly suspicious. Chinese Khrushchevs, ready to
betray him just as the perfidious Khrushchev had betrayed Stalin, haunted
him everywhere. Deng and his multicolored cats also fit this role.

But Mao was in no hurry to deal a blow; in general he was not impatient,
especially in the case of Deng. He continued to require the services of the
energetic general secretary, although Mao, of course, was now constantly on
guard, just as he was with Liu Shaoqi, Peng Zhen, and other comrades who
seemed "inclined toward right opportunism."

In late July 1964, on Mao's instructions, Deng oversaw a commission
drafting articles unmasking international revisionism—Soviet-style in the
first instance, of course. The chairman of the commission was Kang Sheng,
and its members included the head of the Xinhua News Agency, Wu Lengxi,
and a number of other propagandists. These articles were in response to the
"Open Letter from the Central Committee of the Communist Party of the
Soviet Union to Party Organizations and All Communists in the Soviet
Union," published in the Soviet press on July 14 during the last round of
negotiations.[61] The articles were published in the name of the editors of the
main organs of the CC CCP, the newspaper *People's Daily* and the journal
Red Flag. There were nine articles in all; a tenth one had been planned, but
Mao decided that nine was enough to take care of Khrushchev. In China, it
was said, "We dished out nine criticisms for just one of theirs."[62]

Soviet leaders responded irritably to the criticism ("The Chinese are block-
heads," the members of the Presidium of the Soviet Central Committee said

among themselves[63]), but Mao was very satisfied. He almost forgave Deng for supporting the household contract system, but new events compelled him once again to suspect the general secretary of "right deviation." This time his indignation was so profound that it took him almost ten years before he magnanimously bestowed a new pardon on his "foolish" pupil.

14

Number Two Capitalist Roader

STARTING IN 1963, the Chairman battled energetically against domestic "counterrevolution." In May the Central Committee even adopted a special document, the so-called First Ten Points, defining the goals, motive forces, objectives, and scale of the Socialist Education movement in the countryside, which by then had become the main arena of struggle against the restoration of capitalism in connection with the spread of the contract system. This document was drafted under the direct supervision of Mao, who pointed it against a certain "new bourgeoisie," in which the Leader mainly included unreconstructed "landlords," "rich peasants," and other inveterate exploiters who, from his perspective, had infiltrated the leadership of a number of communes and brigades to mount counterattacks against the party and divide up the land.[1] It is difficult to say just what sort of landlords and rich peasants existed in the PRC after collectivization, communization, famine, and the struggle against household contracts, but Mao insisted on such a view of the problem.

The struggle against Soviet revisionism also took a new turn. The Great Helmsman finally triumphed over the hapless Khrushchev, whom a plenum of the CC CPSU put out to pasture on October 14, 1964, no thanks to Mao, but the Chairman had not yet succeeded in routing his domestic "enemies." The danger of restoration impelled him to suspect the evil intentions of an enormous number of his comrades in the party, especially since the Socialist Education Movement constantly revealed scandalous facts about "bourgeois degeneration" in the party organizations. The reliable leftists in the party leadership—Lin Biao, Kang Sheng, Chen Boda, and others—frequently reported the alarming situation to him. Many provincial officials did not lag behind, sending up the chain of command only the information he wanted to hear. It became clear that in at least half of the party cells "class enemies" had seized power.

As general secretary, Deng also took an active part in the struggle against "restoration." But Mao, who valued him as the person who had unmasked Khrushchev, was less satisfied with his work on the domestic front. From the start it was clear that Deng, unlike the leftists, was unwilling to pursue class struggle recklessly at the expense of economic development. Later, in the summer of 1968, Deng himself acknowledged,

> During the Socialist Education Movement that began in 1963, under the leadership of the Chairman himself, a document, The First Ten Points, was drafted that clearly gave primacy to class struggle, the two-line struggle. . . . There was absolutely no need to compose a second Ten Points . . . but I took part in drafting this document in Hangzhou, and I must bear chief responsibility for the errors in it.[2]

The Second (or Later) Ten Points that Deng referenced was adopted by the Politburo in November 1963. Its primary author was Tian Jiaying, Mao's secretary, who in 1962 had supported the family contract system. This document stressed: "At no stage of the Movement should production be affected."[3] Liu Shaoqi as well as Deng supported it.

Outwardly Mao did not react at all, but he could hardly have failed to pay attention to the "moderates'" attempt to weaken the campaign. A year later, in January 1965, he would let everyone know that he had simply been biding his time, again resorting to his favorite tactic of luring the "poisonous snakes" from their holes.[4]

Meanwhile he began pondering the sources of foreign and domestic "revisionism" and ultimately concluded that the major contradiction in Chinese society was no longer between the poor laboring classes and the unreconstructed exploiting classes, but between the politically conscious masses on one hand and the bureaucrats at the helm of power on the other hand who had not reformed their worldview. These greedy party cadres, who were walking the capitalist road, were the main source of restoration since they were trying to take society along with them. How could they be made to listen to reason? Should they be removed from their leading posts and ejected from the party? Of course, but this alone would not suffice as others just like them would come in their stead. Therefore, it was necessary to change the very worldview of people, to purge them of all vestiges of the past, to create a new person, a genuine builder of communism. In other words, a cultural revolution was required, that is, class struggle in the sphere of culture directed at the total destruction of traditional morals, habits, ideas, and other cultural values of the Chinese people and their replacement with new communist ones. Following the revolutionary transformation of the economic base, all aspects of the superstructure had to be radically transformed as well. (Later he would emphasize that "struggle against those in power in the party who were taking the capitalist road is the main task, but by no means the goal. The goal [of the cultural revolution] was to resolve the question of worldview, to exterminate the roots of revisionism."[5])

Neither Liu Shaoqi nor Deng nor many other Chinese leaders, of course, had hit on this idea. Therefore, concerned with questions of socialist education, they continued to implement the Leader's old notion, namely, that in China "the main contradiction was that between the poor peasants and lower middle peasants on one hand and the well-to-do strata on the other."[6] (Thanks to Mao, Liu even had the good fortune to bear the title of "commander-in-chief of the Socialist Education Movement.") But they had obviously fallen behind Mao.

In the summer of 1964, he launched an attack on the cultural front, asserting on June 27 that the creative associations and most periodicals "over the past fifteen years ... have basically not implemented the policies of the party."[7] If in the future things were allowed to slide and a class purge of the creative associations was not carried out, then "one fine day ... [they] would turn into organization of the type of the Petöfi Club," referring to the association of intellectuals who had agitated for political reform in Hungary. On July 2, he demanded that the members of the Politburo Standing Committee organize a new *zhengfeng* (rectification campaign) in the Ministry of Culture and all creative associations for which a special Five-Member Cultural Revolution Group should be established in the CC.[8] He appointed Peng Zhen as its head, Lu Dingyi, director of the Department of Propaganda of the CC as deputy; and as its members Kang Sheng, Zhou Yang, who was Lu Dingyi's deputy, and Wu Lengxi, who was director of the Xinhua News Agency as well as editor-in-chief of *People's Daily*.[9]

Mao soon became dissatisfied with the actions of Peng Zhen's group since Peng proceeded in an extremely cautious fashion, striving to limit party interference in the sphere of culture to academic discussions while Mao desired to set the cultural front ablaze with the flames of class struggle.

Liu Shaoqi and Deng also continued to irritate Mao by their disinclination to fathom his mood. Apparently they were stubbornly refusing to notice that he no longer considered the party's first priority to be inciting "the poor and lower middle peasants" against "the well-to-do strata of the countryside."

In September 1964, under the leadership of Liu Shaoqi, the CC drafted a new guiding document regarding Socialist Education. The Revised Later Ten Points, based on materials collected by Liu's wife, Wang Guangmei, during her five-month investigation of a people's commune in Hebei province. This document elevated the concept of the old struggle of the poor peasants against the landlords to an absolute.[10]

Mao immediately suspected something wrong: it turned out that Liu had consciously diverted the struggle from the new main enemies—the highly placed party members ("capitalist roaders")—onto the small fry.

In mid-December 1964, a Politburo work conference was convened to discuss and adopt the document drafted by Liu's team. It was prepared by Deng, who, hearing that Mao was feeling indisposed, committed another blunder. Apparently acting out of concern, he suggested to Mao that he skip the sessions since no serious discussion was expected. But Mao, again taking offense, showed up anyway and listened to Liu's report. Several days later he openly clashed with him, declaring,

> The landlords and rich peasants are the directors standing in the wings. Right now the rotten cadres are stage center. They—degenerates—comprise the group that is now in power. If you organize a struggle only against the landlords and rich peasants, you will not get support from the poor and lower middle peasants. The most urgent question is that of the cadres, for the landlords, rich peasants, counterrevolutionaries, and bad elements are not in power.

Liu Shaoqi tried to object, "Some do not approve that way of formulating the question." But Mao cut him short, "Now we don't need to pay attention to any sorts of classes or social strata, we need to go after 'those in power,' the communists, the 'big shots' in power and those who follow after them."

Naturally, Zhou immediately supported the Chairman, but Deng, who apparently feared that the struggle against capitalist roaders in the party would get out of hand, proposed to concentrate the attack against only a small number of "particularly inveterate degenerates." Mao ignored him and simply restated his point: "First we need to catch the wolves, and only then the foxes. That's how we have to tackle the problem, if you don't begin with those in power, nothing will come of it." Liu again tried to object, but Mao no longer listened to him.[11]

This quarrel occurred on December 20. Six days later, Mao invited his old comrades to a banquet at the Great Hall of the People to celebrate his birthday. The more than forty persons attending, including Liu and Deng, were in a festive mood until Mao unexpectedly delivered an ill-tempered speech. "I want to continue the criticism of several erroneous concepts and judgments that appeared during the course of the Socialist Education campaign," he said. Without referring to Liu by name, he suddenly asserted that his views were un-Marxist, after which he averred that some organs of the CC had turned into "independent kingdoms" (he had in mind Deng's Secretariat). He concluded with an ominous warning that "there is a danger in the party of a resurgence of revisionism."[12] While he was speaking, a deathly silence reigned in the hall.

The following morning, returning to the work conference, Mao declared, "There are at least two factions in our party: one is the socialist faction, and the other the capitalist faction."[13] The next day he began waving two texts in front of the assembled—the Constitution of the PRC and the Party Statutes—and shouted that the former gave him rights as a citizen, and the latter gave him rights as a party member. He also said that "one of you" (that is, Deng) had not allowed him to come to the conference, and another (Liu Shaoqi) would not let him speak.[14]

Mao gained the support of the majority, following which the Revised Later Ten Points was rejected and a new document, referred to as the Twenty-three Points (Articles), drafted by Chen Boda under Mao's direction, was adopted in January 1965. It stated, "The key point of this movement is to rectify those people in positions of authority within the Party who take the capitalist road."[15]

It was then, in January 1965, that Mao decided to replace Liu, because he "had strenuously opposed" the struggle against "those in the Party in authority" who were "taking the capitalist road," meaning the struggle that was unfolding during the course of the Socialist Education Movement.[16]

For now he had not reached this conclusion regarding Deng, although he was still angry at his general secretary. But soon his relations with him were ruined, as Deng came into sharp conflict with an individual whom neither he nor anyone else in China should cross, namely, Jiang Qing, the vindictive and perfidious wife of the Great Helmsman.

In 1964, this frail but exceptionally strong-willed woman enjoyed great influence among the Chinese leadership, and not because Mao loved her passionately. Over the twenty-five years of their marriage he had cooled toward her and satisfied his sexual needs with a clutch of lovers, chief among whom was the strikingly beautiful, twenty-year-old train attendant Zhang Yufeng ("Jade Phoenix"). But the Chairman valued Jiang Qing's fanatical loyalty and needed her as an expert in the realm of culture. In the early 1930s, she had performed on the Shanghai stage and in the movies, and in late September 1962 Mao had given her control over both CC and government agencies dealing with cultural affairs. His militant spouse began zealously inculcating principles of class morality into "rotten" literature and "degraded" art. Under her leadership, new operas and ballets, a species of propaganda wretched in form and primitive in content but incredibly revolutionary, began to appear on the Chinese stage.

The theater, however, was too small a stage for the energetic Jiang Qing. She craved political power. Therefore, she soon clashed with many members of the leadership who had disliked her ever since she had become Mao Zedong's wife. Most veterans retained warm memories of the Leader's previous wife, He Zizhen, from whom the Chairman had separated two years prior to his new marriage. The malicious Jiang could never forgive them this. Only a few of them were on good terms with her, including Kang Sheng, her former lover, who incidentally had introduced her to the Chairman in 1938.

Until the fall of 1962, however, Jiang had only been a housewife and Mao's secretary and therefore was unable to harm Deng or anyone else in the Politburo. But after the Great Helmsman placed her at center stage in the class struggle, she felt empowered and began to intervene in the affairs of many Chinese leaders, although she was a member of neither the Politburo nor the Central Committee.

Naturally, her behavior irritated the old cadres. But strangely, almost none of them, Deng Xiaoping included, thought it necessary to conceal their feelings. It was unpardonable behavior for a seasoned bureaucrat.

Thus, in the summer of 1964, after watching one of the "masterpieces" approved by Jiang Qing, in everyone's hearing Deng proclaimed,

> Because of the movement [to reform operas] many no longer dare to write articles. At present the Xinhua News Agency only receives about two articles a day. Only the roles of soldiers are performed in the theater and only battles are depicted. And let's look at films. How can one achieve perfection when they're not allowed to portray this and not allowed to portray that?[17]

There is no doubt that Jiang Qing quickly inscribed Deng's name on her enemies list and hammered into Mao's head the idea that Deng was untrustworthy. For a while Mao seemed to ignore her calumnies, but ultimately he began to ponder what she was saying.

Meanwhile, in early 1965, the cunning Jiang Qing succeeded in winning her spouse over to the view she wanted him to have of Deng's close friend, Wu Han, the deputy mayor of Beijing and one of China's leading playwrights and historians. Deng really loved this liberal professor, even though he was not a CCP member. He valued Wu Han's profound knowledge of Chinese history, especially of the Ming dynasty. Deng would meet with him almost weekly in one of the elite party clubs for a hand of bridge. They would be joined by the first secretary of the Central Committee of the Communist Youth League, Hu Yaobang, who also loved this Western game. They enjoyed conversing with each other over cards.[18]

Old man Wu's knowledge of Ming history proved his undoing. Back in January 1961, he had written a play about a courageous and noble sixteenth-century official named Hai Rui, who had dared to tell the truth to a Ming dynasty emperor besotted with sin. Although the subject was well known, Jiang Qing figured that Wu Han was consciously drawing a parallel between the cases of Hai Rui and Peng Dehuai. She brought up the matter of the play as soon as it was staged, but at the time neither Mao nor anyone else in his entourage supported her. Mao Zedong liked the figure of Hai Rui, in whom he saw himself, "an honest and upright revolutionary," a fighter against all the sins of the rotten classes.[19]

But the situation changed at the beginning of 1965. Mao Zedong, furious at Liu Shaoqi, began to see enemies everywhere. Jiang Qing now succeeded in convincing him of Wu Han's "double dealing," and soon afterward of Deng's disloyalty. She was helped by her old friend Kang Sheng, who was no less vile than she. Initially, when Jiang Qing raised a question about the play, Kang Sheng also responded skeptically to her undertaking, but later on—sometime in the latter half of 1964—he understood that he could extract quite a bit of political capital from this. He also began whispering into Mao's ear that Wu Han was a "counterrevolutionary," acting at the behest of an entire "gang" that was trying to rehabilitate the former minister of defense. "We criticized Peng Dehuai, while they [Kang hinted at Liu, Deng, and others] are embellishing Peng Dehuai. Is this not oppositionist activity?"[20]

Mao finally came around to Jiang Qing's and Kang Sheng's conclusions, after which the idea of a "conspiracy" among the leadership of the Communist party gripped him and struck him as entirely logical. Wu Han was directly subordinate to the mayor of Beijing, Peng Zhen, who, it will be recalled, was one of the closest comrades-in-arms of Liu Shaoqi and Deng as well as the latter's deputy in the very same "independent kingdom" that was how Mao now viewed the Secretariat of the Central Committee. In the Chairman's fevered brain, all four—Wu Han, Peng Zhen, Liu Shaoqi, and Deng Xiaoping—were united in one "black gang," which from his perspective had seized "a great deal of power . . . over propaganda work within the provincial and local party committees, and especially within the Peking [Beijing] Municipal Party committee." Therefore, he decided, it had become necessary "to reveal our dark side openly, comprehensively, from bottom to top" and strengthen the cult of personality even more "in order to stimulate the masses to dismantle the anti-Mao Party bureaucracy."[21]

In February 1965, Mao decided to commence criticism in the press of Wu Han's play. Here is what he himself said later about it,

> A number of departments and several regions of our country were in the hands of revisionists; indeed, they filled everything, they had crawled into every crack. At that time I proposed that Comrade Jiang Qing arrange the publication of an article criticizing the play "The Dismissal of Hai Rui from Office," but in this "red" city [Beijing], I turned out to be powerless. Nothing could be done, [Jiang Qing] had no recourse but to go to Shanghai to take care of this matter. The article was finally written; I reviewed it three times and found it suitable. Entrusting it to Comrade Jiang Qing, I suggested that other leading officials of the CC read it, but Comrade Jiang Qing said, "Better to publish the article as is. In my opinion, it's just as well that Comrades Zhou Enlai and Kang Sheng not read it." Otherwise, Jiang Qing added, both Liu Shaoqi and Deng Xiaoping will also want . . . to read it.[22]

The article Mao referenced was published on November 10, 1965, in the Shanghai newspaper *Wenhui bao* (*Literary Reports*). Its author was the thirty-four-year-old journalist Yao Wenyuan, who was working for the local party newspaper *Liberation Daily*. The article took a lot of work. Eleven drafts were prepared, which Jiang Qing and another Shanghai leftist, Zhang Chunqiao, secretly dispatched to Mao Zedong by courier to Beijing. The manuscripts were put in boxes with tape recordings of Beijing opera.[23] These increased security measures were taken because Mao wanted to deliver a surprise blow to the "moderates." He did so.

The final test of the loyalty of Deng, Peng Zhen, and the other "rightists" (with the exception of Liu Shaoqi, of whose "revisionism" Mao had no doubt) was at a CC work conference in September and October 1965 at which the Chairman suggested that Wu Han be criticized. As might be expected, neither Deng nor Peng nor the others passed the test. Just for the sake of appearance, Deng began an investigation of the professor's activities and soon declared that "Wu Han is a leftist [that is, reliable] element."[24] Peng Zhen, who had earlier shown himself to be loose-tongued, in late September at a meeting of cultural officials in the Central Committee headquarters declared, "In truth, all persons are equal, regardless of whether they are on the Party Central Committee or [are] the Chairman."[25]

Mao could not forgive this. He flung a challenge at the participants in the work conference, "I call for a rebellion, like the rebellion against Yuan Shikai who proclaimed himself emperor." Then he added, "Soon I will see Marx. What will I pass over to him? I dare not [pass over to him] the revisionist tail that you leave to me."[26] After this he signaled Yao Wenyuan to publish the article labeling Wu Han's play a weapon in the bourgeoisie's struggle against the dictatorship of the proletariat and the socialist revolution.

Naturally, the Beijing leadership reacted negatively to the publication of the article. Wu Han was not only a professor and a playwright, but also a deputy mayor. The first response of Peng Zhen, who had no inkling that Mao himself was behind the article, was not to allow it to be republished in the central press. He turned to Deng for support. Suspecting nothing, Deng said,

> I saw that play. Ma Lianliang [a famous actor] played Hai Rui. There's nothing wrong with it. Some people try to climb on others' shoulders. They have only half-baked understanding, but they nitpick and squawk, hoping to make a name for themselves. I can't stand that sort. Tell the professor there's nothing to it. We'll still play bridge together. Political and academic matters should be kept apart. It's dangerous to mix them. It blocks free expression.[27]

Peng Zhen took heart and together with Professor Wu attempted to repel Yao Wenyuan's political attack by switching the discussion of the play onto an academic track. On November 15, in a supplement to the newspaper *Guangming ribao* (*Enlightenment Daily*), Wu Han published a response to the criticism of the Shanghai journalist, pointing out several factual inaccuracies in the publication in the *Literary Reports*. "I am not afraid of Yao Wenyuan's criticism," Wu Han wrote, "but it seems to me that such pseudo-criticism, accompanied by affixing of erroneous labels, that such behavior is wrong. Who [after this] will dare to write anything, who will dare to take up the study of history?"[28]

After reading this reply, Mao was unable to sleep all night. Peng Zhen and the Beijing Municipal Party Committee, which controlled the central press, evidently did not wish to surrender. The struggle was heating up. "It was impossible to do anything with the Beijing Municipal Party Committee," Mao subsequently recalled.[29]

Deng, unaware of who he was actually picking a fight with, continued to play bridge with his friend. The poor professor, however, was unable to concentrate on the game and sighed pitifully all the while. But Deng tried to calm him: "Professor, don't be so gloomy. What are you afraid of? Is the sky going to fall? I'm sixty-one this year. From the time I joined the revolution to this day I've survived plenty of storms. I've learned two things . . . be optimistic. Take the long view. When you do that you can cope with anything. You have my support, so relax."[30]

Five days later, the Chairman was dealt an even stronger blow: the Beijing leaders counterattacked. The same supplement to the *Enlightenment Daily* declared, "Yao Wenyuan's outrageous opus does not accord [with the spirit of the movement] 'Let a Hundred Flowers Bloom, Let a Hundred Schools of Thought Contend'."[31] Then the director of the Department of Propaganda of the Beijing Municipal Party Committee, responding to a question from the editor-in-chief of the municipal newspaper *Beijing ribao* (*Beijing Daily*) on how to reply to a *Literary Reports* correspondent wanting to know why their article on Wu Han had not been reprinted in Beijing, laughed, "Just tell him what the weather is like today, ha-ha-ha."[32] What striking political blindness!

Jiang Qing wanted to meet with the general secretary, and seeing Zhuo Lin at a reception for some foreign delegation, she approached her. "It has been many years," she said, "that the line pointed out by Chairman Mao has been ignored in literary and artistic circles. I hope to meet Deng Xiaoping and discuss the serious problems existing in literary and artistic circles." Zhuo Lin told Deng, but he didn't think to invite Jiang Qing to see him. Moreover, he observed in one of his conversations, "Since there are only a few good new shows, the old ones can also run. I vote with both hands for the reform of classical drama, however, I myself don't like it."[33]

Finally, Zhou Enlai intervened. On November 26, he phoned Peng Zhen and told him of Mao's role in the publication of Yao Wenyuan's article.[34] On November 29 *People's Daily* finally published this vile libel. To be sure, it did so with its own commentary referring to the developing scholarly polemic rather than to the explosive political implications of Yao's article.

Thereafter, Wu Han, crushed by the criticism, stopped coming to the club, but Deng still hoped that the storm would blow over. That is why he sometimes talked about old man Wu with his other bridge partners. "The professor's dismissal has not yet been revoked," he wisecracked. "When it is revoked, he will be able, thank God, to return to playing cards." And, "Wu Han shouldn't necessarily be linked with Peng Dehuai. That does not relate to the Wu Han affair."[35] Peng Zhen likewise had no intention of surrendering. In December 1965, he said to Wu Han, "Where you're wrong, criticize yourself, and where you're right, persist."[36]

But Mao would not calm down. He made use of the article about Wu Han to elevate the Socialist Education Campaign to a new level: in his own words, this article served as "a signpost toward the Great Proletarian Cultural Revolution."[37]

Two days after publication, he departed the hated city of Beijing, which was in the hands of the "black gang" of Liu, Deng, and Peng Zhen, for Shanghai, the stronghold of the leftists, where the very air seemed infused with radicalism. Several days later, by now in a good mood, he set out for cozy Hangzhou, where on the shores of peaceful West Lake he could finally relax: now everything was developing according to his plan.

Ten days later, however, he was on the road again. He couldn't sit still. He needed to be fully engaged. He returned to Shanghai, where he convened a new enlarged meeting of the Politburo Standing Committee, then backtracked for several days to Hangzhou, where Chen Boda, Kang Sheng and other intimates awaited him to discuss further plans for the campaign against Wu Han. Then he visited several other places before returning to Hangzhou after New Year's. In early February 1966 he arrived in Wuhan.[38]

At this time, Deng, Liu Shaoqi, and Zhou Enlai, all three of whom were members of the Politburo Standing Committee, took their equivocating political stand on the "Outline Report Concerning the Current Academic Discussion," drafted by the Five-Member Cultural Revolution Group. The compromise document said on one hand that "the critique of Comrade Wu Han's play 'The Dismissal of Hai Rui from Office' . . . represents a mighty battle of Marxism-Leninism and Mao Zedong Thought against bourgeois views in the field of ideology"; on the other hand, it noted that

> the problems involved in the scholarly discussion are rather complex, and it is not easy to sort them out in a short stretch of time. . . . We must adhere to certain principles while searching for the essence of the phenomena in actual facts; everyone is equal before the truth; one must convince with arguments; it is impermissible to decide things categorically in the manner of scholarly satraps and dictate one's will

to others. . . . Both destruction and creation are necessary (without creation there can be no real and definitive destruction).[39]

Afterward, Peng Zhen and three other members of the group (Kang Sheng, Lu Dingyi, and Wu Lengxi) took their report to Mao in Wuhan. Mao received them in the East Lake Hotel on the shores of East Lake on February 8. He was not pleased with the report, but for the time being he did not want to show his cards. "You people work it out," he said, "I don't need to see it."[40] Then after a moment's silence, he added, "We'll return to these questions in three years or so."[41]

This was a trap, but Peng, Lu, and Wu supposed that the Chairman had approved their theses. After the conversation with the Chairman, with light hearts, and accompanied by their secretaries and bodyguards, they set off for the antiquarian bookstores in Wuchang and Hankou, which were famous throughout China.[42] Several days later the CC adopted the "Outline Report Concerning the Current Academic Discussion." Classified top secret, it was approved for limited dissemination.

Now Mao swung into action. In Hangzhou in mid-March he convened an enlarged meeting of the Politburo Standing Committee to which he invited Liu Shaoqi and Zhou Enlai (Deng at the time was on an inspection tour in the Northwest) as well as the first secretaries of the provinces, autonomous regions, and province-level cities under central government supervision. A number of CC officials also took part in the conference. What they heard surprised many of them. Mao not only came down hard on Peng Zhen, Wu Han, and Wu Lengxi for propagandizing bourgeois culture but also called for launching class struggle in all the higher, middle, and primary schools throughout the country: "At present the intelligentsia, who come from the bourgeoisie, the petty bourgeoisie, and the landlord-kulak class, monopolize the majority of higher, middle, and primary schools. . . . This a serious class struggle. . . . We need to let the young people . . . come to the fore. . . . Let the students . . . make a ruckus . . . we need for the students to overthrow the professors."[43] Wu Lengxi, who was completely demoralized, asked that Zhou Enlai allow him to make a self-criticism: "The Chairman's criticism [of me] was very severe; I must disarm myself completely." The disheartened Zhou replied, "He did not criticize only you, but us, too."[44]

Among other questions discussed at the conference was whether to send a CCP delegation to the forthcoming Twenty-third Congress of the CPSU. Among those present, Peng Zhen alone supported this idea while the Chairman categorically rejected it. "We will not go," he summed up, "we will keep [our] red flag unsullied, there's no point in dragging things out."[45] Peng's "treacherous behavior" deeply irritated him, although it hardly came as a surprise. Soon he renounced the theses in Peng Zhen's report and disbanded the five-person Cultural Revolution group. In April, Peng was put under house arrest, and soon Lu Dingyi was also purged.[46] Afterward they were lumped together with two other officials, head of the PLA General Staff Luo Ruiqing and the director of the Central Committee General Office, Yang Shangkun, who had earlier been removed for entirely unrelated reasons, as part of a supposed "antiparty group."[47]

On May 16, 1966, the Politburo announced the disbandment of the Group of Five and its replacement, on Mao Zedong's orders, with a new Cultural Revolution Group, headed by Chen Boda, under the Politburo Standing Committee. (At the end of August, Chen, overburdened with work, yielded his position as head of the group to one of his deputies—Jiang Qing, the Chairman's spouse.[48]) For the first time the Politburo communiqué called on the entire party to "hold high the great banner of the proletarian cultural revolution."[49]

Several paragraphs of this communiqué were written by Mao himself. The most important was this one:

Those representatives of the bourgeoisie who have sneaked into the Party, the government, the army and various cultural circles are a bunch of counter-revolutionary revisionists. Once conditions are ripe, they will seize political power and turn the dictatorship of the proletariat into a dictatorship of the bourgeoisie. Some of them we have already seen through, others we have not. Some are still trusted by us and are being trained as our successors, persons like Khrushchev, for example, who are still nestling beside us. Party committees at all levels must pay full attention to this matter.[50]

No one understood whom the Great Helmsman had in mind when speaking of persons like Khrushchev. Of course, everyone knew that the Chairman's successor was Liu Shaoqi, but it never occurred to anyone, not even Kang Sheng or the Shanghai leftist Zhang Chunqiao, that Liu might be whom Mao had in mind. Yet Mao considered his thesis about the "Chinese Khrushchev," who had not yet been seen through, to be the main one in the communiqué, as he soon unequivocally informed Kang Sheng and Chen Boda. He very much wanted his report "to detonate" not only the party but society as a whole.

The now enlightened Kang Sheng subsequently explained:

> The Great Cultural Revolution originated from the idea that classes and class struggle still exist in the socialist system. . . . Our experience over the past 20 years in building a proletarian dictatorship, and especially the recent incidents in Eastern Europe where bourgeois liberalism and capitalism were restored, also pose the question of how to conduct a revolution in the context of the proletarian dictatorship and under socialist conditions. To solve the problem, Chairman Mao himself initiated the Great Cultural Revolution in China.

In Kang Sheng's words, from the very outset the Great Helmsman proposed a three-year plan for conducting the revolution. "For a great revolution like this," affirmed Mao's trusty comrade-in-arms, "three years is not a long period of time."[51]

The involvement of the broad masses in the Cultural Revolution, which was its distinguishing characteristic, began with this communiqué. The Chairman empowered people to judge "revisionist party members," including "party big shots." The shock force of the Cultural Revolution was to be youth, who were not burdened by superfluous knowledge or restrained by the "fallacious" humanitarian concepts of Confucian society, which is to say students of higher educational institutions as well as technical colleges, middle schools, and even primary schools. On May 25, the students of Peking University rose in struggle against the capitalist roaders by posting on their dining hall wall the first *dazibao* (large character poster). In it they accused several leaders of the University Work Department of the Beijing Municipal Party Committee, as well as the rector of Peking University (who was simultaneously the secretary of the Peking University party committee), of "carrying out a revisionist line that was aimed against the Central Committee and Mao Zedong Thought."[52] Students from other universities and schools in Beijing as well as from the provinces followed suit, posting thousands of *dazibao* and abandoning their studies. An epic struggle against the capitalist roaders to reform the consciousness of six hundred million inhabitants of the PRC had begun.

For now Deng remained untouched, though information must have reached Mao that his general secretary, deeply shaken by what was transpiring, passively protested from time to time. For example, after Yang Shangkun was taken, Deng sheltered Yang's daughter for a time, and after the arrest of Peng Zhen, he not only failed to condemn Peng but sent him a half-basket of oranges.[53] He could probably do no more than that: the totalitarian system, which he himself had helped create, precluded any kind of open opposition to the Leader. "Under the circumstances that was the best I could do," he subsequently acknowledged.[54]

He could have been punished for the half-basket of oranges, had this been Mao's will. But Mao still did not give the go-ahead. And Deng, perhaps, began to suppose that the bitter cup would pass him by. Like other top leaders, he "had no inkling of the terrible storm that was about to break," and he continued to make one error after another. Evidently, he was "completely unprepared for this sudden insane movement," or perhaps he no longer wished to be the Great Helmsman's "foot."[55] Who knows? In any case, Deng's behavior served only to hasten his downfall. The Chairman, nursing his grievance, was becoming ever more infuriated against him.

At the beginning of June, Deng finally drove Mao out of his mind. Deng and Liu openly favored restricting the student demonstrations by supporting the Beijing Municipal Party Committee, which had sent a work team composed of active Party and Communist Youth League members to Peking University to "restore order."

However, invoking the names of Liu Shaoqi and Deng Xiaoping, Zhou Enlai had telephoned Mao on May 29, asking whether it was all right to send work teams, and the Leader had voiced no objection. Employing his usual tactic, Mao was again testing Deng and Liu, giving them another opportunity to fully reveal themselves. Again they fell into his snare, and after convening an enlarged meeting of the Politburo Standing Committee on June 3, they decided to send similar work teams to other Beijing educational institutions. "It won't do without the work teams," Deng asserted. "The work teams represent the party leadership . . . we need to send the work teams quickly, like a fire brigade to a fire."[56] Mobilized in these groups were 7,329 cadres.[57]

Then on June 9, Deng, Liu, Zhou, Chen Boda, Kang Sheng, and Tao Zhu, the new director of the Propaganda Department, set off for West Lake in Hangzhou to persuade Mao to return to Beijing. But Mao burst out laughing and refused. They then begged permission to dispatch work teams to all the universities throughout the country; Mao said neither yes nor no.[58]

Utterly confused, Deng and Liu returned to Beijing and took two diametrically opposed decisions. On one hand, they suspended instruction in schools and universities throughout the country "temporarily, for six months," and canceled exams. On the other hand, they considered the dispatch of work teams to all universities "to restore order" to be correct. "The Central Committee deems that the measures taken by the work team in Peking University with respect to the disturbances to be correct and timely," they asserted. "In all organizations where similar phenomena arise, the same measures that were applied at Beida [Peking University] may be employed."[59] Soon afterward, more than ten thousand persons were dispatched in work teams from Beijing to other regions of China.[60]

They could not have committed a greater mistake. Mao could now easily accuse them of "suppressing" the masses. Now he only awaited an opportune moment to deal a crushing blow. Meanwhile, Kang Sheng secretly informed Zhou Enlai that "Liu and Deng may not survive," noting that he (Zhou) "should not have anything to do with the work teams, and should take leadership of the movement [the Cultural Revolution] into his own hands."[61] Kang was doubtless speaking to Zhou in Mao's name.

The Chairman himself, pretending that nothing was going on, dropped in to visit his native place, the village of Shaoshanchong, where several years earlier a luxurious country home, Dishuidong (Grotto of Falling Waters), had been constructed that he had not yet visited. Then he visited Wuhan, where on July 16 he performed a ten-mile swim in the Yangzi River, demonstrating to the whole world, including Number One Capitalist Roader Liu Shaoqi and Number Two Capitalist Roader Deng Xiaoping, that he was still strong and in good health. On July 18 he returned to Beijing and finally dealt a blow to Liu and Deng.

He settled into the western district of the city, in Diaoyutai (Fishing Pavilion), the former diplomatic residence, demonstratively refusing to return to Zhongnanhai, where Deng Xiaoping and Liu Shaoqi were living. Liu immediately came to see him, but Mao refused to receive him. "The Chairman is resting from his journey," the Great Helmsman's secretary informed the dumbstruck Liu. Actually, Mao was conversing behind closed doors with Kang Sheng and Chen Boda, who presented Liu's and Deng's actions in the worst possible light.

The next day, the dispirited Liu convened an enlarged meeting of the Politburo Standing Committee to discuss the work teams. This only made things worse. Mao absented himself from the meeting, but Chen Boda, acting on Mao's instructions, demanded that the work teams be recalled immediately. A majority of those present, unaware of Mao's true position, rejected Chen Boda's proposal. Deng, who had obviously lost patience, expressed himself in a particularly pointed manner. Jumping up from his seat and pointing his finger at Chen, he said, "You fellows say we're afraid of the masses. Go and see for yourself!" Then, after taking a breath, he continued, "Pull out the work teams? Nothing doing!" Liu Shaoqi supported him.[62]

Not until the following evening was Liu able to meet with Mao, who finally showed his cards, asserting that "the work teams are good for nothing, the former [Beijing] Municipal Party Committee is rotten, the Propaganda Department of the Central Committee is rotten, the Department of Culture is rotten, the Ministry of Higher Education is also rotten, and *Renmin ribao* [*People's Daily*] is good for nothing."[63] Over the next eight days, Mao held seven meetings during which he demanded that "the work teams be recalled," since they "acted as a brake and were actually aiding the counterrevolution."[64] "Who suppressed the student movement?" he indignantly queried Liu Shaoqi and Deng. "Only the northern militarists . . . We must not hold back the masses. . . . Those who suppress the student movement will end up badly."[65]

Afterward, in response to the Great Helmsman, Deng, Liu Shaoqi, and other Central Committee leaders visited Beijing educational institutions to conduct investigations. But there they came under critical fire. Trying to justify themselves, they looked pitiful. They "spoke to the students and urged moderation. They sounded rather weak and helpless."[66]

Deng and Liu were also humiliated in late July at a meeting of activists of student organizations in the Great Hall of the People on Tiananmen Square. Before more than ten thousand persons, Deng was forced to make a self-criticism, which he did clumsily. "It must be made clear that the dispatch of the work teams to the colleges and middle schools by the Beijing Municipal Party Committee was done in accordance with the decision of the Central Committee. Some comrades say old revolutionaries are faced with new problems. That certainly is the case," he said, evidently feeling out of sorts.[67] Liu also looked depressed, "bewildered, at a loss, adrift in a sea not of his making." He spoke shrilly, almost hysterically, admitting that he did not know how to conduct the Cultural Revolution.[68] To stormy applause in the hall, Li Xuefeng, first secretary of the Beijing Municipal Party Committee, announced that, in accordance with a Politburo resolution, work teams would be withdrawn from all the schools and universities in the city.[69] Deng's daughter, Maomao, who was present at the meeting, cried bitterly.

On May 29, an organization named the Hongweibing (Red Guards) had been established at an elite secondary school attached to Tsinghua University, the leading science and technology school. Mao liked the name very much and praised its members. A massive organization of Red Guard groups followed, to which Mao assigned a concrete task: "To . . . crush those persons in authority who are taking the capitalist road."[70]

On August 5, the Great Helmsman wrote his own *dazibao*, consisting of some two hundred Chinese characters: "Bombard the Headquarters!" He ordered it to be printed and distributed on August 7 to participants in the Eleventh Plenum of the Central Committee then taking place in Beijing. Now everyone understood that the Cultural Revolution was aimed against Liu Shaoqi and Deng Xiaoping as the leaders who were guiding the daily work of the CC. Changing its agenda, the plenum addressed the personal affairs of the head of the PRC and the general secretary of the party.[71] "We have uncovered the Chinese Khrushchevs who have been hiding among us," Kang Sheng recalled.[72]

After the plenum the post of general secretary was abolished, and the Secretariat itself was stripped of power. It no longer met, and its functions were transferred to the Cultural Revolution Group. Deng and Liu remained members of the Politburo Standing Committee, and in the voting Deng received unanimous support, as did Mao and Lin Biao,[73] but his influence was sharply reduced. Mao appointed Lin Biao as his successor in place of the discredited Liu Shaoqi. Lin also became the sole deputy chairman.[74]

At a CC work conference that took place right after the plenum from August 13 to 23, Lin Biao attacked Liu and Deng by name, asserting, in the words of Deng's daughter, that Deng Xiaoping "was to be treated as an enemy."[75] He assumed that the question of Deng as well as Liu was in the category of contradictions between "ourselves and our enemies." After this Deng had trouble sleeping, stopped working after the conference, and handed his duties over to Kang Sheng.[76] Now he sat at home all the time, spoke with no one, and only looked at party materials that were sent to him from time to time.

All of September passed like this. In October, at a new CC work conference, Deng was again subjected to a brutal personal attack. Delivering the main report, Chen Boda asserted that two lines were battling in the Cultural Revolution, the "proletarian revolutionary" line of the party center, headed by Chairman Mao Zedong, and the "bourgeois reactionary line . . . whose representatives were Comrades Liu Shaoqi and Deng Xiaoping. They must bear primary responsibility." (The very term *bourgeois reactionary line* was thought up by Mao, of course, who edited Chen Boda's report.) Then Lin Biao again attacked Deng and Liu Shaoqi by name, charging them with pursuing "a line of repression of the masses and opposition to the revolution."[77]

All that remained was for them to shoot themselves. But neither Liu nor Deng did this, and at Mao's request they again engaged in self-criticism. On October 23, first one and then the other acknowledged that they "bore the main responsibility." Moreover, Deng declared, "I can definitely say that had I been more modest at the time and listened more to the views of others and, in particular, constantly reported to and asked for instructions from the Chairman, I would certainly have received his instructions and help, which would have helped me to correct my mistakes in time."[78] Deng promised to correct his "mistakes and start anew." But according to Maomao, his "self-criticism was also forced.... This was not at all the way he felt but, under the circumstances, he could say nothing else."[79]

In any case, how he felt hardly mattered. Having secured Liu's and Deng's loss of face, Mao now played the role of a conciliator. On the text of Deng Xiaoping's self-criticism, which he had received the evening before, he wrote an inscription:

> Comrade Xiaoping, you can make this speech. After the first line, where you say: "I will correct my mistakes and start anew . . . ," why not add a few more positive words, such as "Through my own strenuous efforts, plus the aid of my comrades, I am confident I can correct my errors. Please give me time, comrades. I will stand up again. I have stumbled after half my life in the revolution. Surely I can recover from this one mis-step?"[80]

Two days after Deng's self-criticism, Mao, summing up, said:

> It's impossible . . . to blame everything wholly [on Liu Shaoqi and Deng Xiaoping]. There is both their fault and the fault of the Central Committee—the Central Committee did not manage things very well. There was not enough time, and we [that's what Mao said—"We!"] turned out to be psychologically unprepared, and we did not do our political and ideological work right. . . . After the conference, obviously, it will be better.[81]

Yet he could not refrain from airing his grievances: "Deng Xiaoping is hard of hearing, but during meetings he always sits far away from me, and beginning in 1959, he never sought me out to report on his work."[82]

That Deng was hard of hearing was true. Sometimes he experienced noise and buzzing in his right ear. This sensation, known as tinnitus, got worse with every passing year.[83] This was precisely why, during meetings of the top leadership in Mao Zedong's bedroom, he purposely sat at the head of the bed on which the Chairman was lying. Thus the Great Helmsman was complaining

about him for no reason. Mao was also twisting the truth when he said that
the general secretary of the CC did not seek him out to report on his work.
One need only look at the *Chronological Biography of Deng*, recently published in the PRC, to be convinced that what Mao said was untrue. He simply
wanted to inflict another wound on his former faithful pupil. After all, he
had trusted him so much, calling him "the best of my comrades in arms," and
"a great growing force," yet Deng had offended the old man after the failure
of the Great Leap. Mao sensed that Deng had stopped delving into his wise
thoughts and no longer tried to catch every word. So he had no intention of
forgiving him or Liu Shaoqi for now. He wanted to savor their humiliation.

Grasping the Leader's mood, the members of the Cultural Revolution
Group struck while the iron was hot. The struggle against Deng and Liu
served as the trampoline of their political careers. At the end of December
1966, at the initiative of one of them, Zhang Chunqiao, several thousand
students and teachers at Tsinghua University held a demonstration during
which they publicly attacked Liu Shaoqi and Deng Xiaoping by name for the
first time, calling for their overthrow.[84] On placards and *dazibao* they wrote
"Down with Liu Shaoqi! Down with Deng Xiaoping!" The names of Liu and
Deng were crossed out in black.

For Deng the most difficult of times was now upon him. And he probably
more than once recalled the words of Confucius: "It is in the cold of winter that you see how green the pines and cypresses are."[85] Like these majestic
trees, he needed to stand his ground in a season of adversity. Not break, not
go down, but preserve his strength and wait for spring to come. Clench his
teeth and bear his ordeal.

15

Arrest and Exile

FORTUNATELY, DURING THESE terrible days Deng was not alone. The devoted Zhuo Lin was there to help him survive his sufferings. Unlike his previous wife, who had betrayed him, Zhuo was at her finest, sharing all of his trials and tribulations. Deng was truly lucky to have married her. One would be hard pressed to find another such friend.

Grandma Xia, Deng's stepmother, knew nothing of politics, but she loved her stepson with all her heart. On one of the wearisome evenings, she said to Zhuo Lin, "You have to look at the situation soberly. Think how many years you've been married. You must understand him very well. If you divorce him, you will be acting foolishly!"

Zhuo Lin looked at her in astonishment.

"Mama! I really do understand him very well. Calm down. I will not divorce him."[1]

"During the period of the Cultural Revolution, our mother supported father with all her strength," recalled Deng's eldest daughter, Deng Lin, "and although everyone around was shouting 'Down with Deng Xiaoping! Deng Xiaoping is the Number 2 big shot in power in the party taking the capitalist road,' he is 'a such and such,' she worried about him most of all, looked after him, shared happiness and grief with him; their hearts beat in unison."[2]

Naturally, Zhuo Lin was very anxious, particularly with regard to the children. They were already being picked on in their schools as members of the "Black family of the No. 2 Capitalist Roader." But she could not discard her husband even for their sake. On the contrary, she inspired in them faith in their father's innocence, telling them about his heroic past. She wanted "her children to know their Papa was clean, he had done nothing wrong."[3]

They also behaved with dignity on the whole, although under pressure from the Red Guards they partook in "criticism and struggle meetings," where, stifling their tears, they formally condemned their father. Deng's daughters were even forced to write a *dazibao* that was posted on a wall in Zhongnanhai in which they clumsily criticized the head of the family for some petty faults. Yet they never said, "We are breaking off relations with our father, the capitalist roader."[4] They did not follow the example of some other children who denounced their own "reactionary" parents as "enemies of the people."

Meanwhile, the Cultural Revolution, rapidly spreading throughout the country, became an increasingly bloody affair. The frenzied Red Guards, whom the Great Helmsman had empowered to smash the capitalist roaders, became intoxicated with terror. A wave of violence engulfed Beijing, and then other Chinese cities. In Beijing alone in the two months of August and September, 1966, 1,772 persons suspected of belonging to the capitalist roaders were killed by the enraged youths. In Shanghai during this same period, 1,238 perished, with 704 taking their own lives, unable to bear the insults of the youthful Red Guards. The security forces did not intervene.[5] "China is such a populous nation, it is not as if we cannot do without a few people," Mao said at the time.[6]

Teachers were the primary targets of the adolescents. In some schools individual classrooms were converted into prisons where the students taunted the helpless teachers whom they had arrested on charges of belonging to the "black gang of bourgeois reactionary authorities." The teachers were tortured, beaten, and humiliated, many to death. One such prison was directly across from the party leaders' residence of Zhongnanhai, in the music classroom of No. 6 Middle School. Written in a teacher's blood on one wall were the words, "Long live the red terror!"[7] This was how the young people understood the slogan put forth in the Central Committee communiqué of May 16, 1966: "In this great cultural revolution, the phenomenon of our schools being dominated by bourgeois intellectuals must be completely changed."[8] How else could they have understood this?

All across China, Red Guards organized show trials in which the main performers were the capitalist roaders they had arrested. Elderly people, frightened to death, were herded along the streets, their arms tied, to the cackling and malicious cries of the crowd. Then kangaroo courts were organized that compelled "such-and-such counterrevolutionary revisionist element" or "so-and-so member of a black anti-party gang" to bow before the revolutionary masses.

At the end of December 1966, revolutionary workers, rebels instigated by Zhang Chunqiao, took the building of the Shanghai Municipal Party Committee by storm. Wang Hongwen, "the head of the general staff" of the Shanghai Rebels (*zaofan*), led the uprising. As a result, the Shanghai Municipal Party Committee "was paralyzed and toppled"; nobody listened to it anymore.[9]

On January 6, the rebels organized a hundred-thousand-person meeting of "criticism and struggle" in the People's Square in Shanghai at which municipal leaders were forced to confess to their "crimes."[10] The rebels, supported by the Shanghai garrison command, then organized new municipal organs of power.

On hearing of the seizure of the municipal committee in Shanghai, Mao called on "the entire country, the entire party, the entire government, all the armed forces and the entire nation to learn from the example of Shanghai."[11] Afterward, throughout the country new organs of power, revolutionary committees, were established in which the positions were supposed to be divided among representatives of three sides: chiefs of the Red Guards and Rebels, PLA officers, and "revolutionary cadres." The Cultural Revolution continued to intensify.

On January 11, 1967, the Politburo adopted a resolution to deprive Liu, Deng, and several other high-ranking capitalist roaders, including Chen Yun, of the right to participate in its meetings.[12] On April 1, *People's Daily* and *Red Flag* published an article attacking Liu and Deng. In it for the first time in the open press Deng was named "the second most important person in power in the party who is taking the capitalist road."

Deng could no longer contain himself. On April 3, he wrote a respectful letter to the Great Helmsman, declaring that since January 12, he had wanted to meet with him to ask for "instructions." "I gather that the nature of my error has already been decided," he humbly noted.[13] And he hit the target. This is precisely what Mao Zedong, who all this time had been nursing his grievances, expected of him. How he loved it when people abased themselves before him.

After making Deng suffer another month, he sent a trusted confidant to him, the new director of the CC General Office, General Wang Dongxing, the head of his bodyguards since 1947. The calm and businesslike Wang conveyed an important directive to Deng: "Don't worry." He explained that Mao was separating the question of Liu Shaoqi from the question of Deng Xiaoping, and giving Deng permission to write to him.[14] This could only mean that the Chairman considered Deng a "comrade."

Why? Who knows? Perhaps because he actually thought Deng was a rather honest man and exceptionally capable to boot. Perhaps he thought Deng had committed errors "inadvertently," unlike Liu Shaoqi, whom he had considered a 100 percent Khrushchevite ever since January 1965. Perhaps he simply feared Deng's enormous popularity among the troops. Almost all of the marshals and generals viewed the former political commissar of the Second Field Army as one of their own. He was also greatly respected among much of the officer corps, none of whom could forget the years of martial brotherhood. Now might not his sudden complete downfall exacerbate the situation within the PLA? Be that as it may, Deng could breathe a sigh of relief.

Several days later, Mao himself wished to speak with Deng and had him awakened during the night and brought to him. They spoke until morning. Mao criticized him again for dispatching the work teams. Deng again begged forgiveness, but then the Great Helmsman asked him what was not an easy question, namely, why had Deng suddenly abandoned the 7th Corps of the Red Army in March 1931? It will be recalled that Deng always claimed he had left the front to report on the current situation to the CC in Shanghai. But Mao, penetrating him with his fixed gaze, awaited a reply. Obviously this is what had moved him to arouse Deng from his bed. If Deng was confused and resorted to evasions, then all of his "rightist eccentricities" of the past years would take on a new significance. From a "comrade" he would be transformed into a "betrayer" of his military friends—and this would sharply alter his relationship with the PLA. But Deng was able to stand up for himself, and looking the Chairman squarely in the eye, he said that he had left the troops after receiving permission from members of the front committee. He repeated what we already know, namely, that he had left to report to party leaders in Shanghai.[15] Apparently the Chairman accepted his explanation, but it only seemed so.

By this time the madness of the Red Guards had extended into Zhongnanhai itself, the inner sanctum where the top leaders lived. The wall of Liu's house was splashed with the inscription, "Down with the Chinese Khrushchev, Liu Shaoqi!" Youthful employees of the Central Committee, all of whom joined the ranks of the rebels, repeatedly dragged the elderly chairman of the PRC to "criticism and struggle meetings," breaking his arms, kicking him, and beating him about the face. On July 18, they did a search of his home, turning everything upside down. In mid-September, they arrested his wife and put her behind bars. The grief-stricken Liu suffered an attack of hypertension and his blood sugar level soared.

On July 19, 1967, the Zhongnanhai rebels came to search Deng's home. Earlier they had taken him and Zhuo Lin out of the house, so that Grandma Xia and the children were the only witnesses to their outrage. To the disappointment of those who had dispatched them, they found nothing. Deng kept no documents or notes from work in his home.[16]

Case closed? Certainly not; their failure only served to infuriate the rebels. They pasted angry *dazibao* demanding the overthrow of the "second most powerful person in the party taking the capitalist road!" on all the walls of the lane on which the Deng family lived. Ten days later they dragged Deng and Zhuo Lin to a "criticism and struggle meeting" at which they were roundly abused and even beaten. They demanded that Deng provide them a written confession in three days and prohibited him and his wife from leaving their house. No one, not even their children, were permitted to visit them.[17] In other words, Deng and Zhuo were placed under house arrest.

Returning home after the meeting, Deng, who was terribly agitated, again wrote to the Great Helmsman. He must have known that the rebels attacked with Mao's consent. Did the Leader find his latest humiliating explanations unsatisfactory? "I am truly at a loss what to do. I sincerely hope for a chance to seek your instructions personally. I know this request may not be appropriate, but I have no other way to express the feelings in my heart."[18] Never before had Deng fallen so low.

This time Mao did not deign to reply, although he certainly received the letter. He was not in Beijing, and Deng's suffering did not really concern him. At the time a real civil war "using firearms"[19] was going on among various Red Guard and anti-Red Guard organizations. As for Deng, Mao played with him like a cat with a mouse. First he gave him hope, then he tormented him. He did not seek Deng's death; nor did he intend to expel him from the party. On July 16, he even let slip to one of his associates, "If Lin Biao's health gets worse, I intend to call Deng back. I'll make him at least a member of the Standing Committee of the Politburo."[20] Following this, he repeatedly declared to Zhou Enlai, Zhang Chunqiao, Wang Dongxing, and several other comrades-in-arms that Deng and Liu were not two peas in a pod.[21] But he needed Deng to pass through at least the first circle of hell so that he would remember it to the end of his days. He would be punished for his various "errors" and "willfulness," so he would no longer try to be clever and would serve him, the Great Man, like a slave. He was still a long way from forgiving Deng; he had to make him suffer still for a certain time.

On August 1, 1967, Deng's loyal secretary and his bodyguard were removed from his house. Four days later, rebels again burst into Deng's dwelling. Over the entrance they stretched out a long red banner, "Criticism and struggle meeting against Deng Xiaoping, the second most important person in the party in power who is taking the capitalist road." Deng's surname and personal name were written in black while the other characters were written in white. Deng's daughter Maomao recalled,

> They took Papa and Mama out to the garden and surrounded them. Rebels pushed their heads down and forced them to bend at the waist, demanding that they confess. Roars of "Down with them!" shook the air. A string of shouted accusations followed, and a babel of voices yelled questions. . . . During the meeting a girl rebel . . . screeched in a voice that was exceedingly shrill. Mama's eyeglasses had been removed. With her head down she tried to steal a glance at Papa, but she couldn't see clearly. Papa was rather deaf. Standing half-bent, he could hardly hear anything, and could answer none of their questions. He tried to offer an explanation, but the words were barely out of his mouth when he was rudely interrupted.[22]

Deng was deathly pale. Returning home, he lay down at once. In the days that followed he remained withdrawn, was sullenly silent, did not smile, and chain-smoked while sitting in his armchair. In mid-September he wrote about his difficult situation to Wang Dongxing, director of the Central Committee General Office. Wang showed the letter to Mao, but the Great Helmsman forbade him from replying.[23] Soon Deng suffered a new blow. Through orders from on high, his children and Grandma Xia were evicted from Zhongnanhai and housed a half-hour walk away in a little two-room apartment on the first floor of a small house. Only the cook and the servant remained with Deng and Zhuo Lin.

Thus Deng and his wife passed two years in almost total isolation. They were forbidden to see their children or even to correspond with them. They knew nothing about them or about other relatives who were persecuted on account of Deng Xiaoping. They were not even informed that Deng's younger brother Xianzhi, who had worked in a county government in Guizhou, did not survive persecution. On March 15, 1967, he committed suicide. Nor did they receive news of the untimely death of Zhuo Lin's brother, Pu Desan, who died in prison.[24]

Yet they were no longer subjected to violence, and they even received their rather substantial monthly pay. As an official in the highest category, Deng was paid 404 yuan per month, while Zhuo Lin received 120, whereas the maximum pay for the majority of workers was only slightly more than 40 yuan.[25] In the mornings, Zhuo Lin, following the regimen of officials of the CC General Office, engaged in physical labor, sweeping her own court-yard. Deng helped her even though no one told him to. The rest of the time they either read, or simply sat silently in the room, listening to the radio and chain-smoking. Zhuo Lin also had taken to tobacco. "I smoke because I'm thinking of the children," she said. "The minute I can see them again, I'll quit."[26] They were both miserable.

Meanwhile, Deng's powerful enemies in the CC and the Cultural Revolution Group, notably Mao Zedong's wife, Jiang Qing; secret services chief Kang Sheng; and Minister of Defense Lin Biao, tried to convince the Chairman to get rid of the former general secretary once and for all. Naturally they did not want to share power with him in the future after Mao forgave him. On November 5, 1967, they pointedly raised the question of Deng at one of their meetings with the Great Helmsman. Mao rehearsed his old griev-ances with them:

> Liu and Deng cooperated. The Eighth Party National Congress reso-lution [on Liu Shaoqi's political report] was adopted without first passage by the presidium and without asking my opinion. As soon as they adopted it, I immediately opposed it. In 1963 they promoted a Ten Provision program [The Second Ten Points]. Only three months later [it was actually almost a year] they both held another meeting and put out a "Post Ten Provisions" [The Revised Later Ten Points], again without asking my opinion. [Mao was dissembling: he had actu-ally read, corrected, and formally approved the document.] I wasn't at the meeting. Deng Xiaoping must be criticized. Let the Military Commission prepare a document.

The members of the group were ready to applaud, but Mao paused and then added, "My idea is that he should be distinguished from Liu Shaoqi. Their cases must be treated separately."[27]

After this fiasco, however, the members of the group did not drop the matter. They persisted in trying to prove to Mao that Deng was no less an "enemy" than Liu Shaoqi, and even worse that he was a "traitor" who deserved if not the death sentence than at least expulsion from the party. With this goal in mind, in May 1968 they established a "Group on the Special Case of Deng Xiaoping," tasked with gathering compromising material on the "number two capitalist roader," especially regarding his "desertion" from the

7th Corps. In June, this group demanded that Deng write something like a critical autobiography. It is difficult to say why. Is it possible they thought that Deng might crack? Mao, learning of the creation of the Special Group on Deng Xiaoping, could not refrain from goading Jiang Qing and those like her:

> One must allow people to make mistakes. When they make mistakes, they must be punished, but can it be that you yourself do not make mistakes? From my perspective this is precisely how we must deal with Deng Xiaoping. Some say that he collaborated with the enemy, but I don't put much store in this. You fear Deng Xiaoping as if he were a monster.[28]

On July 5, Deng presented his almost-seventy-page "confession." He repented of many "sins," since without self-criticism no one would have accepted his report. He even admitted that early in 1931 he had "committed a serious political error" in leaving the 7th Corps. But even a serious political error was not the same as an organizational one, that is, "betrayal" and "desertion." Deng again insisted that he had gone to Shanghai after receiving approval from the front committee. Moreover, he mentioned that in 1933, during the struggle against the Luo Ming line, the CC under Bo Gu had already investigated this matter, and that he (Deng) had also written an explanation.[29] The reference to Bo Gu was rather transparent since Bo Gu had persecuted not only Deng but also Mao himself. Obviously, Deng was defending himself while also skillfully attacking.

But the special group was not just sitting idly by. It was given access to an enormous quantity of archival documents, including Deng's personal dossier in the Organization Department of the CC CCP; it interrogated many witnesses and visited places connected with the life of the enemy. In late July 1968, it drafted a nearly forty-page "Composite Report on 'The Main Errors of Deng Xiaoping—the Second Most Important Person in Authority Taking the Capitalist Road'." The report presented a lot of "evidence" of Deng's "right opportunist activity" during the period of the PRC, but to Jiang Qing and her comrades' disappointment it contained no persuasive evidence regarding his "betrayal."

The members of the group were instructed to dig deeper, but they were unable to unearth anything more. Consequently, in October 1968, at the Twelfth Enlarged Plenum of the Eighth Central Committee, Jiang Qing, Kang Sheng, and the other leftists were obliged to acquaint the delegates with what they had. Nevertheless, they demanded Deng Xiaoping's expulsion from the party. Overwhelmed by emotion, they even crossed out Deng's family and personal names in the "Composite Report" circulated among the CC members. Still, this did not influence the Chairman, since they had few facts at their disposal. "As for this fellow Deng Xiaoping," Mao said at the plenum,

> I always say a few words in his defense. This is because during the anti-Japanese and liberation wars he beat up on the enemy. Moreover, no problems were uncovered in his past. . . . Well, now everyone wants to expel [him], but I am somewhat reluctant to do so. I think that we always have to distinguish this person from Liu Shaoqi; there are really some differences between them. I'm afraid my views are somewhat conservative and not to your taste, but still I speak well of Deng Xiaoping.[30]

That sufficed to keep Deng in the ranks of the CCP. Only Liu Shaoqi was expelled "forever," and branded a "traitor, provocateur and strikebreaker, running dog of imperialism, of contemporary revisionism and Guomindang reaction, who committed a massive number of the most serious crimes."[31]

Deng expressed his fervent support of the plenum's decisions. He could not defend Liu in any case, and his retention in the party naturally was most important for him. In early November he wrote to Wang Dongxing, "I very much hope that I will be able [to continue] to remain in the party as an ordinary member. I ask to be given the opportunity for the most ordinary work or be allowed to engage in physical labor to the limit of my strength."[32] Again he received no reply.

Only in the spring of 1969 did his life change. At the Ninth Congress of the CCP in April, Mao again declared that "we must make a distinction between Deng Xiaoping and Liu Shaoqi."[33] The congress, which summed up the three-year Cultural Revolution period of *Sturm und Drang*, naturally agreed with him. In a new letter to Wang Dongxing, Deng humbly repeated that he wanted only one thing: "In the years remaining to him to work with all his energies wherever the party might send him." He also gave his word that he would "never request a reexamination of his case."[34]

Only then did Mao soften, and soon officials of the CC General Office informed Deng and Zhuo Lin that from now on they could meet with their children once a week, on Saturday afternoons. Their second daughter, Deng Nan, was the first one whom the authorities in Zhongnanhai permitted to see them. Father and mother could not get enough of her. "We've not seen each other for two years," Zhuo Lin exclaimed. "Well, of course, Deng Nan is now all grown up. And how lovely! The older she gets, the more beautiful!"[35] Deng Nan had in fact grown lovelier. Her braid, tied with a short ribbon, added a special charm to her face. Deng's nearly twenty-four-year-old daughter radiated youth and health even though over the course of three months in 1968 she had been subjected to beatings and insults in the Physics Department of Peking University, where she was a student. She and her older brother "Little Fatso" Pufang, also a physics student at Peking University, had been arrested in May 1968, locked up in cell-like rooms, and subjected daily to hours of interrogation aimed at getting them to denounce their father. Their older sister, Deng Lin, was worked over at the Central Institute of Fine Arts, where she was a student. At home, the younger children, Maomao and Fei Fei, along with Grandma Xia, were visited by first one and then another group of rebels. Maomao and Fei Fei were also besieged at school.

Deng Nan was petrified, but she stubbornly affirmed that she knew nothing. In the adjoining room Pufang cried out, "I'm the only one who knows about family affairs. My younger sisters and brother don't know anything. If you've got any questions, ask me!"[36]

Now seeing her father and mother, Deng Nan could not hide her emotions. Deng looked at her in silence and smiled while Zhuo Lin talked nonstop, asking her many questions: "Why did you come alone? Where are the others?" and so forth. Only when her mother asked, "What about Pufang?" did Deng Nan become flustered and quickly go to the bathroom, followed by her mother, who intuited that some misfortune had befallen Pufang.

Her premonition was correct. Deng Nan burst into tears and told them everything. At the end of August 1968, following another interrogation, Pufang snapped. He jumped from the fourth story of the building where he had been held under guard, breaking his spine. Not a single hospital would admit this "loathsome offspring of the black gang" until the Red Guards, unwilling to take responsibility for the death of the son of the former general secretary, arranged his hospitalization. The physicians diagnosed a compression fracture of the eleventh and twelfth vertebrae and of the first lumbar vertebra, but they refused to treat him, also on political grounds. Therefore, Pufang became paralyzed from the chest down. Only many months later was the unfortunate nearly twenty-five-year-old transferred to a special clinic where he was given at least minimal care.[37]

His parents were mortified. "I cried for three straight days," Zhuo Lin recalled.[38] Deng, as always, was silent and smoked, but later wrote a letter to Mao Zedong requesting that Pufang be transferred to a better hospital. Mao showed compassion, which was actually not surprising. This was how he could bend Deng completely to his will. From now on, his subjugated pupil would be eternally grateful to his own tormentor for having saved his son. The Great Helmsman issued an order to Wang Dongxing, who quickly arranged Pufang's transfer to the surgical wing of an elite army hospital, where he finally received real treatment. Deng and Zhuo Lin paid twenty-five yuan monthly for his care.[39]

Meanwhile conditions inside China were deteriorating. Since the end of August 1968, the situation on the border with the USSR had become increasingly tense. By this time, relations between the CPSU and the CCP were completely ruptured, and interstate relations were strained to the limit. After Soviet troops entered Czechoslovakia on the night of August 20–21, 1968, and Soviet authorities proclaimed the so-called Brezhnev doctrine, stating that the USSR had the right to intervene in any socialist country if socialism was imperiled, Chinese authorities sensed a clear and present danger. In October 1968, the Chinese army was put on alert. In March 1969, on the eve of the Ninth CCP Congress, armed clashes occurred along the Far Eastern border between the PRC and the USSR as Soviet and Chinese border guards battled for control of an island in the Ussuri River that the Russians called Damansky and the Chinese Zhenbao. Who fired the first shot is still unknown; most likely it occurred spontaneously. Someone's nerves snapped, but there were dead on both sides. On just the first day of clashes, March 2, twenty-nine soldiers and two officers on the Soviet side and seventeen servicemen on the Chinese side were killed. Forty-nine persons were wounded and one Soviet soldier taken prisoner and tortured to death. From March 2 to 21, the Soviet troops lost fifty-four soldiers and four officers killed and eighty-five soldiers and nine officers wounded. The precise number of losses on the Chinese side is unknown. According to Chinese statistics, twenty-nine troops were killed, sixty-two were wounded, and one went missing in action. According to Soviet statistics, more than eight hundred Chinese were killed.[40]

Mao was so shaken that at the Ninth Congress he declared, "We must be ready to fight, and on our own territory."[41] After the congress he issued a secret directive to prepare for the evacuation of the majority of party leaders from Beijing so that, in case of war, they would be able to organize resistance locally.[42] At the same time, the main capitalist roaders were taken out of the capital. On October 17, Liu Shaoqi was transported to Kaifeng (Henan province), where he was housed in a building belonging to one of the local "revolutionary" authorities. He was already in very bad condition, coughing constantly, his pulse rate accelerated, and his lungs gurgling; he was burning with fever and gasping for breath. A month later, on November 12, 1969, he died.[43]

But a different fate awaited Deng. It was decided to remove him as well, though not alone like Liu Shaoqi; rather, with his wife and stepmother. Moreover, his health was not below par, and the Great Helmsman instructed Wang Dongxing and Premier Zhou Enlai to be in charge of arranging Deng's departure and assuring his well-being. Jiangxi province in southeast China was chosen as his place of residence. There Deng was supposed to undergo "reeducation through labor," in order to rectify himself once and for all. Zhou personally made many calls to the "revolutionary" authorities in the province to ensure favorable treatment for his old friend, his friend's wife, and stepmother: "Of course he [Deng Xiaoping] mustn't work full time. He's . . . not in very good health. The rent should be reasonable . . . you must help them, and appoint people to take care of them." And further,

> He [Deng] is an old man over 60. . . . My idea is that you put him near Nanchang where it will be easy to look after him. The best thing would be for him and his wife to stay in a small two-storey house. They could live upstairs, and a helper live downstairs. It should be a single house in a courtyard. That way they would have space to move around in, and it would be safe.[44]

Then, when everything was ready, on the morning of October 22, 1969, Deng, his wife, and his stepmother, accompanied by two members of the Deng Xiaoping Special Group, boarded an IL-14 jet, with several boxes of books as well as many household goods,[45] and flew from Beijing to Nanchang. They did not know what awaited them, but in any case the departure to the periphery had to be considered "a positive development."[46] Two years of complete isolation had ended. Deng received the opportunity to "expiate his guilt" through labor.

Meanwhile, the authorities in Jiangxi had done everything Zhou Enlai requested of them. They even found the kind of house he wanted: a two-story house with inner courtyard and a tall fence. It was located twenty-six *li* northwest of the provincial capital, on land previously occupied by the former Nanchang Infantry Academy of the Fuzhou Military District, which had been converted into a May 7 School, a special camp for reeducation through labor of cadres, not far from the village of Wangchengang (now Wangcheng) in the suburban county of Xinjian. It was a rather spacious, red brick building with a tile roof and a long carved balcony, surrounded by cinnamon and plane trees. It used to be the house of a head of the academy, which is why it was called the General's House. Deng's and Zhuo's bedroom on the second floor contained two wooden beds placed against the wall, just one chair and a chest of drawers. Grandma Xia's bedroom was also on the second floor, which also housed a study with a desk, a sofa, a bookcase, and a reading table, and even a bathroom. The first floor contained a dining room, a kitchen, and a vestibule. The building was divided into two parts, but only one part was allocated to the prisoners. The other was for the guards who lived below, namely, a staff member of the revolutionary committee of Jiangxi province and a young soldier. Outside twelve soldiers from an artillery regiment kept guard. Deng, Zhuo, and Xia spent three and a half years in this secluded house.

Deng was assigned to undergo three and a half hours daily of "tempering through labor" (from the beginning of 1970 it was two and a half hours) in the tractor repair station of Xinjian County, from whose walls several days earlier all the *dazibao* attacking him had been removed. The workshop was approximately two *li* from the academy. Elder Deng—this is what the leadership decided the workers should call Deng; they were prohibited from calling him "Number Two Capitalist Roader" Deng Xiaoping or Comrade Deng—had to show up every morning at 8:00 a.m. He and Zhuo Lin usually arose at 6:30. Deng did exercises; washed himself with a wet, cold towel; and breakfasted with Zhuo and Grandma Xia. At 7:30 he and Zhuo Lin, who also worked in the workshop—she cleaned the coils of the spark plugs—left home. The twenty-minute walk was not tiring. After two years of seclusion, they were finally able to breathe the pure village air. They walked along a narrow path that looped between rice paddies and houses, in silence, thinking their own thoughts. Behind them trudged the guard. At half past eleven, after knocking off work, Deng, who worked as a mechanic in the workshop just as he had done in his youth in the Renault factory, and Zhuo Lin returned home. They lunched with Grandma Xia, slept for a couple of hours, and then studied the works of the Great Helmsman and read newspapers to elevate their ideological level. Political study was part of their "reeducation." Deng also did some chores at home. He washed the floors, cut firewood, and broke up chunks of coal. Zhuo Lin did the laundry and the sewing, and Grandma Xia the cooking. They raised chickens and grew vegetables in a little garden. They all took their supper at 6:00, and Deng, as was his habit, would sip spirits or local moonshine. At 8:00 they listened to the Central Radio to keep up with the news. Before going to sleep, without fail Deng would walk around the house, and go to bed at 10:00 p.m. He read for an hour and then fell asleep with the aid of a sleeping pill. This is how the days passed.[47]

The secretary of the workshop party committee was a certain Luo Peng, an old communist, a former staff member of the Ministry of Public Security who, by an irony of fate, had been demoted in the late 1950s during the anti-rightist struggle led by none other than Deng. The goodhearted Luo, to be sure, bore no grudges and treated Deng quite well. "We are quite happy," Deng wrote to the CC General Office.[48] Following Mao's instructions, he usually informed Wang Dongxing, the director of the General Office, about his affairs. From November 1969 to April 1972, he sent him seven letters, and only twice, on November 8, 1971, and August 3, 1972, did he dare to disturb the Great Helmsman.[49]

A couple of days after their move, Deng and Zhuo were allowed to see their children again. Now the children could come to see them for long stretches—two or even three months at a time. By then their beloved children, with the exception of Pufang, were in the countryside, working as peasants. Deng Lin was working in Hebei, Deng Nan and Maomao in Shaanxi, and Fei Fei in Shanxi. In 1969–71, all of them visited their parents. In June 1971, Deng succeeded in having Pufang, who was still suffering badly, transferred to their house. "Because Pufang was immobilized, his lower limbs had shrunk somewhat, and his legs and feet felt cold to the touch," Maomao recalled.[50]

Meanwhile, important changes were occurring in China. In the fall of 1970, a frenzied campaign of criticism began against Chen Boda, heretofore one of Mao's closest confidants. Initially Chen Boda headed the Cultural Revolution Group, and from August 1966 he was a member of the Politburo Standing Committee. After the Second Plenum of the Ninth Central Committee, he was suddenly accused of "treason and espionage." Deng could not understand why, but he was heartened by the fall of Chen, one of his main enemies.[51] A year later, in September 1971, Lin Biao mysteriously vanished from the political arena. For a long time, Deng had no idea what had happened to him. The communists in his workshop, including Deng and Zhuo Lin, had not been told of this until November 6, 1971. Deng, naturally was shocked to hear that Lin, his wife, and his son had tried to flee to the USSR. From the new mass campaign of criticism against Lin, who had been declared Mao's successor at the Ninth Congress, he understood that the Great Helmsman had finally begun to see clearly through Deng's old enemy.[52] This cheered him up and inspired high hopes for an imminent change in his own fate. "It would have gone against Heavenly Reason for Lin Biao not to die," Deng said.[53]

Setting everything aside, on November 8 he wrote directly to Mao, bypassing Wang Dongxing. He praised the "brilliant leadership of the Chairman and the Central Committee" who unmasked "the plot" of the deserter in a timely fashion, thanked the Great Helmsman for having sent him (Deng) to Jiangxi, where he had spent "exactly two years now," and informed him that in accordance with instructions, he was "reforming" himself "through labor and study" and was "strictly observing the guarantees" he had "made to the Party." He added,

> I have no requests for myself, only that some day I may be able to do a little work for the Party. Naturally, it would be some sort of technical work. My health is pretty good. I can put in a few more years before retirement. . . . I am longing for a chance to pay back by hard work a bit of what I owe. . . . Chairman, I sincerely wish you long life. Your long and healthy life ensures the greatest happiness for the whole Party and all our people![54]

At this time, in the room next door lay his eldest son, half-paralyzed, and his wife in recent years had been periodically suffering from high blood pressure. Did Deng ever reflect that he was writing a letter of gratitude to the man responsible for his dear Little Fatso's becoming an invalid, for his wife's hypertension, and for his daughters' and younger son's psychological and physical torture in the countryside? Did he understand that blame for everything that had happened to him, to his family, and to the entire country lay not so much with Jiang Qing and Lin Biao but with the "great" Mao? It's difficult to say. He never spoke about this with his family members or with anyone else at this time. No one can say what he felt in his soul.

It seemed that he had long ago scraped the bottom in expressing his loyalty to his own tormentor. However, this missive exceeded all the others. One can easily understand why. Deng was trying to take advantage of the situation to return to the ranks without regard to such basics as human dignity, pride, and principle. A hypocritical shrewdness had become a part of his character during the long years of his political life. Even his doting daughter admitted, "Under the compulsion of the political situation and the times, much against his will, he wrote blaming himself, using the jargon of the Cultural Revolution. . . . He was unable to say what he wanted to say, he was forced to say things he didn't want to say." In general, he "was obliged, reluctantly, to apologize for alleged misdeeds."[55]

The letter was dispatched, but again there was no reply. Mao was also not feeling well. Because of the betrayal by his "close comrade-in-arms" he became depressed, stopped doing anything, was sullen, and shut himself up in his bedroom for days on end. He had become very decrepit, was coughing all the time, complained of headaches and heaviness in his legs. He also had elevated blood pressure, and periodic tachycardia.

But he did read the letter—though not right away—and liked it. He had become sentimental. Lin Biao's flight had so depressed him that he began to feel nostalgic for the friends of his martial youth, many of whom, like Deng, were in disgrace because of him. He was very distressed when he learned that Marshal Chen Yi, who had also suffered considerably early in the Cultural Revolution, had died on January 6, 1972. In poor health and ignoring the protests of his doctors, clad only in a dressing gown over which he had thrown a coat, Mao set out to express his condolences to Chen Yi's widow. To everyone's great surprise, he told her, "If Lin Biao had succeeded in his plot, he would have destroyed all of us veterans." Then he thought of Deng Xiaoping and noted that the question regarding him belonged to contradictions "within the people."[56]

Mao's words were extremely significant. Everyone recalled how in August 1966 Lin Biao had placed the question of Deng in "the category of contradictions between ourselves and our enemies." Thus, Mao's declaration could be seen as a de facto rehabilitation of the number two capitalist roader. Zhou Enlai immediately asked Chen Yi's relatives to disseminate the "revelation" of the Great Helmsman so that it became publicly known.

Yet Deng had to wait another year for his formal pardon. Mao returned him to duty gradually. In February 1972, Deng was informed that his rights as a member of the party had been restored, meaning he was no longer under arrest. In April, his younger children, Maomao and Fei Fei, were allowed to resume study in universities. In May, an old party member, General Wang Zhen, who enjoyed the Chairman's favor, informed Maomao of the words the Leader had spoken at Chen Yi's funeral, "Tell him [your Papa] his question will definitely be solved. . . . Your Papa should come back to work!"[57] Deng understood that he had to take one more step toward the Great Helmsman in order to butter him up once and for all. So he wrote him one more letter, on August 3, 1972.

This time he summed up his self-flagellation, assuring Mao that he had thought everything through and drawn the proper conclusions; "I committed numerous errors," he wrote. "The source of my errors was that I divorced myself from the masses, from practice, and did not fundamentally overcome my petty bourgeois world view." He admitted that "the greatest [error]" he had made in the past was that he had "not held high the great banner of Mao Zedong Thought." The result, was that "I . . . went so far as to put forward a counterrevolutionary bourgeois reactionary line together with Liu Shaoqi. As general secretary, I did my work badly, did not report everything in a timely fashion to the Chairman, and committed the error of establishing an independent kingdom." Deng again regretted that he had supported the household contract system in the early 1960s, and he also declared that he could not forgive himself for believing in Peng Zhen and his ilk. He expressed profound satisfaction that "the Great Proletarian Cultural Revolution had unmasked and criticized him." "This had to be done, and by so doing it [the revolution] saved someone like me."

In general, he explained that he had been bad only in the past, but that now, "having been reformed," he had turned into a politically conscious member of the party. "For now I feel healthy," he repeated what he had written Mao earlier, "I could engage in some kind of technical work (for example, research or study [of the situation in the country]). I have no other desires. I calmly await the orders of the Chairman and the Central Committee. From the bottom of my heart I wish the Chairman eternal longevity!"[58]

Mao was finally satisfied. He either believed Deng or he continued to wax sentimental. After eleven days, he wrote a note on Deng's letter:

> Comrade Deng Xiaoping committed serious errors. However, he must be distinguished from Liu Shaoqi. 1. In the Central Soviet Area he was subjected to criticism as one of four criminals named Deng, Mao, Xie, and Gu. He was the chief of the so-called Maoists. . . . 2. He had no problems in his past. He did not surrender to the enemy. 3. He helped Comrade Liu Bocheng very well, he has military merits. Moreover, it is impossible to say that he did nothing good after we entered the cities. For example, he headed the delegation to the talks in Moscow and did not bow down before the Soviet revisionists. Some of this I spoke of earlier, and now I repeat it again.[59]

After this, even Jiang Qing spoke of the need to restore Deng "in time" to "all his work and prestige," inasmuch as he has been " 'tempered' through the arduous process of struggle-criticism-transformation."[60]

Now Deng's return became a mere formality. Misfortune hastened the event. In January 1973, Zhou Enlai's health sharply deteriorated. In May 1972, he had been diagnosed with bladder cancer, and now doctors detected blood in his urine. There was no one who could replace the premier. Only Deng with his experience and energy, his knowledge and organizational capabilities could do it. At least he could relieve Zhou's burden. So Mao finally gave the order to return the former capitalist roader to power.

On February 19, 1973, Deng and Zhuo Lin, with their children and household members, left the General's House. Workers from the tractor factory saw them off. Zhuo Lin treated them to mandarin oranges and sugared dried fruits.[61]

Deng was already in his sixty-ninth year, but he felt very chipper. Only once in a while did his blood sugar level drop. But he always kept at hand a bottle of sweet water or syrup, and when he felt unwell, he took several sips. The attack would pass. "I'm still good for another twenty years," he repeated happily. "I can last twenty years more. No doubt about it."[62]

New trials awaited him. The path to the summit was not strewn with roses. He would have to struggle, to bide his time, to stick it out.

PART THREE

The Pragmatist

16

"Soft as Cotton, Sharp as a Needle"

ON FEBRUARY 22, 1973, Deng and his family arrived in Beijing, where winter still reigned. The ground was covered with snow. Officials from the General Office of the Central Committee joyfully greeted the former capitalist roader and Zhuo Lin on the platform of the railroad station and drove the whole family to a residence in the western suburbs. It was a new, very spacious, two-story luxury house. "We were delighted," Deng's daughter recalled.[1]

Finally, almost the whole family was together; only Pufang stayed in the hospital. In addition to the three daughters and younger son, three sons-in-law had taken up residence in the house. While their parents were living in Jiangxi, all of the daughters had married. First in 1971, middle daughter Deng Nan married a classmate named Zhang Hong, with whom she worked in a village commune. In November 1972, she gave birth to a little girl who, at the suggestion of Deng's younger daughter, Maomao, was named Mianmian ("Sleepyhead"). This strange name was chosen because the little one had come into the world "during the period of political 'hibernation' of her grandfather." At the time, everyone was politicized.

The newly fledged grandfather was in seventh heaven. "In our family it doesn't matter whether she's the baby of a daughter or a son. She's my grand-daughter, and I'm her grandpa," he said.[2]

Next his youngest daughter, Maomao, married the son of a former deputy minister of health. She was introduced by a woman friend who knew him from Beijing. The young man, He Ping, was a student at the Harbin Military Engineering Institute. His father had also been repressed, so the newlyweds had more than a little in common.

Deng Lin, the eldest, was the last to settle down. Unlike her sisters, she had never been attractive. Overweight, plain-looking, and wearing large, thick glasses, she had never aroused the interest of men despite her exceptional talents as a singer and artist. She first studied in the middle school attached to the Beijing Conservatory and then graduated from the Central Institute of Fine Arts. She was considered the most creative person in the family, and her works, executed in a traditional national style, using ink and water color on silk or paper, even attracted the attention of specialists. But none of this helped in her personal life. Finally, a match was arranged for her with a good man named Wu Jianchang, a technician at the Institute of Nonferrous Metals.

Thus Deng and Zhuo Lin's family expanded. All of the healthy children were employed, Deng Lin working in the Academy of Arts, Deng Nan in the Institute of Automation, Maomao studying at the Medicinal Department of the Beijing Medical Institute, and Fei Fei in the Physics Department at Peking University.

Settling into Beijing, Deng again engaged his previous secretary, Wang Ruilin, who throughout the "time of troubles" also underwent reeducation at one of the May 7 schools in Jiangxi province. His former bodyguard, Zhang Baozhong, and servant, Wu Hongjun, reported back to Deng as well. Life had apparently returned to normal.

Meanwhile, on March 9, 1973, Zhou Enlai informed Mao of Deng's return and requested that Deng be named his deputy. Since Mao himself had decided that Deng should relieve the sick premier of his burdens, this was just a formality.[3]

On March 28 at 10:00 p.m., Deng met with Zhou, for the first time in more than six years, in Yuquanshan, the residence of the CC, in northwest Beijing. The premier was undergoing medical tests in this quiet setting. Deputy Premier Li Xiannian and Jiang Qing came to welcome Deng.

Zhou looked terrible—emaciated, jaundiced, and aged. Jiang Qing, however, radiated energy and looked younger than her fifty-nine years. Slim, with a short coiffure, and wearing horn-rimmed glasses, she was always in a strange state of hysterical excitement. One could hardly say that of Zhou, who had previously been rather expansive and even hot-tempered; or of Li Xiannian, who had once served under Deng during the last civil war. Both of them were calm and laconic. The sixty-four-year-old Li also looked very old: his thinning hair framing his powerful skull was completely white. He had served as a deputy premier since 1954, was minister of finance for many years, and in the early 1970s had become Zhou's virtual right hand.

The meeting was a formality. Zhou and Li had long waged a struggle for Mao's favor against Jiang Qing, who headed the CC's leftist faction, and they could not discuss matters with Deng in her presence. The leftists, who had risen to power during the Cultural Revolution by trampling on the veterans, understood nothing about the economy or diplomacy. All they knew was how to expose "class enemies" and prattle about "revisionists." They were in charge of the mass media and the ideological work of the CC, and frequently organized noisy propaganda campaigns. Zhou, Li, and Marshal Ye Jianying, who was in charge of the daily work of the Central Military Commission, strived to limit the destructive leftist influence on the economy while trying to increase production and modernize the army.

Mao, a skillful politician, balanced between the factions, compelling both Jiang Qing and Zhou to appeal to him as the highest authority and thereby consciously preserving a kind of balance between the contending sides. In fact, he had recalled Deng from exile to strengthen the group of veterans that had been weakened by the premier's illness. Even though he had aged greatly and was physically enervated (in the fall of 1971 his doctors had diagnosed congestive heart failure), Mao still grasped the reins of power. He was in full control of both the party and the nation.

The next morning Mao received Zhou, who informed him that "He [Deng] is in good form both spiritually and physically." Afterward, the Chairman invited Deng in at three in the afternoon. He extended his hand, and looking him straight in the eye asked:

"What have you been doing all these years?"
"I've been waiting," replied the former number two capitalist roader.
"Okay," said the Great Helmsman, "Work hard and stay healthy."[4]

That same evening, at the Chairman's suggestion, Deng attended a Politburo meeting that officially approved him as a deputy premier in charge of foreign affairs. He was also empowered to participate in the work of this highest organ of the party despite the fact he was not even a member of the Central Committee. Such was Mao's wish.

China's international position at this time was steadily improving. In the early 1970s, Mao and Zhou had taken advantage of the new geopolitical situation arising from the exacerbation of Sino-Soviet relations and the catastrophic deterioration of the U.S. military position in Vietnam. They had attracted the Americans by their fervent anti-Sovietism and the prospect of China as a go-between in U.S. negotiations with the Vietcong (the South Vietnamese communist guerrillas) and North Vietnam, Beijing's ally.

In October 1971, the Americans allowed the PRC to occupy its lawful place in the UN, and in February 1972 U.S. president Richard M. Nixon visited Beijing, where he held talks with Mao and Zhou. At the end of his visit, on February 28, when Nixon was touring Shanghai, a joint communiqué was published in which it was emphasized that "progress toward the normalization of relations between China and the United States is in the interest of all countries."[5] Sixteen countries soon established relations with the PRC at the ambassadorial level, prominently Great Britain, Japan, West Germany, and Australia. Although establishment of official diplomatic relations with the United States was delayed over the Taiwan question, the international authority of the PRC rose dramatically.

It was at one of the diplomatic receptions in Beijing that Deng was first openly presented to the public after his disgrace. This occurred on April 12, 1973. According to those present, he looked unsure of himself and tried to stay on the sidelines until Mao's maternal grandniece, Wang Hairong, who was acting deputy minister of foreign affairs, escorted him to the center of the gathering. Only then did Deng smile, and all the guests applauded him.[6]

Deng's circumspect behavior is explicable not only because this was his first social round after so many years of seclusion. After spending a month and a half in Beijing, he probably realized just how dangerous a situation he was now in. Neither Jiang Qing nor her supporters, including Kang Sheng, the head of CCP secret services, as well as the Shanghai "heroes" Wang Hongwen, Zhang Chunqiao, and Yao Wenyuan, would forgive him the slightest misstep. In their eyes he remained a bourgeois degenerate and a capitalist roader even though they could probably not display their true feelings toward him.

Zhou, who specially invited Deng again to Yuquanshan, this time along with Zhuo Lin, enlightened him about Jiang Qing and her comrades-in-arms. They conversed behind closed doors for several hours, and Zhou even advised Deng not to trust unknown doctors (the leftists were capable of anything).[7]

Zhou's general condition continued to deteriorate. But for now he could not remain in the hospital because Mao, afraid to do without him, forbade the doctors from even thinking about hospitalization and operations. He probably supposed that Zhou would not survive surgery. He was mistaken; the physicians thought that in 1972 the premier had a good chance for recovery, but Mao never trusted the doctors. Therefore, Zhou underwent diagnosis and treatment mostly on an ambulatory basis, periodically retiring with his faithful wife, Deng Yingchao, to Yuquanshan, where physicians and other service personnel attended him.[8]

Meanwhile, the time was approaching to convene the Tenth Congress of the CCP, which Mao had set for August 24–28, 1973. Since it would likely select a new leadership, the congress was vitally important both for Zhou and Deng and the leftists. In a paternalistic society such as China, the composition of the Central Committee, the Politburo, and the Politburo Standing Committee would be determined by one man, Mao Zedong. Thus, the intraparty struggle to influence the Chairman reached a critical point.

In May, Jiang Qing's faction achieved a notable victory. They convinced the Great Helmsman to allow the young (thirty-eight-year-old) radical Wang Hongwen, the former "chief of the general staff" of the Shanghai Rebels, to participate in the work of the Politburo, as well as another leftist, the sixty-year-old mayor of Beijing, Wu De, who enjoyed Mao's favor.

A certain Hua Guofeng, former secretary of the party committee of the Great Helmsman's home county, who had created a magnificent memorial in the Leader's native village, also received this right. At fifty-two, he too was relatively young. He had joined the CCP in 1938 and made his career in its ranks. At the start of the Cultural Revolution, Mao appointed him first secretary of the Hunan provincial party committee, and then acting chair of the Hunan revolutionary committee. At the Ninth Congress in 1969, he was added to the CC, in 1971 transferred to work in the State Council, and in March 1972 appointed minister of public security.[9] But neither Mao nor Deng, needless to say, could have imagined that this tall and portly though modest-looking man with gentle manners and a shy smile was fated to play a critical role in Deng's life in the near future. Nor, of course, could Hua Guofeng have supposed this.

Meanwhile, the struggle of Jiang Qing's faction against Zhou continued. In midsummer 1973, the leftists had another stroke of good luck. In late June and early July, the Chairman, who was in a bad mood due to illness, uttered a number of critical remarks about Zhou, on account of his supposed "insufficient firmness" with regard to the Americans. "He [Zhou] doesn't discuss important matters [with me], and he drags out petty matters every day. If the situation does not change, revisionism will inevitably arise," he grumbled.[10] He even demanded that Zhang Chunqiao, who on his instructions was preparing a draft of the political report to the Tenth CCP Congress, include criticism of Zhou in the text.[11] During his conversations with Wang Hongwen and Zhang Chunqiao, Mao mentioned Lin Biao, who had not only "woven the threads of a plot" but in his spare time also been attracted to Confucianism. After the discovery of the "plot," an entire card file of quotations from Confucius was found in the home of the former minister of defense. Mao compared Lin to Guomindang leaders, who, like the former marshal, honored the ancient philosopher.[12] On leaving Mao, Wang and Zhang were satisfied. Soon after, they and Jiang Qing launched a new propaganda campaign against Confucius, which they linked up with the old one against Lin Biao. The campaign was actually directed against the unsuspecting premier, Zhou Enlai.

The reason behind the new campaign was that Confucius, China's greatest philosopher (551–479 BCE), lived during the ancient Zhou dynasty. The character used for the Zhou dynasty was the same as that of the premier's surname. In the time of Confucius, ancient China was in the midst of a profound socioeconomic crisis, the dynasty had lost power, traditional communal relations were rapidly collapsing, and many people were expressing doubt about the cult of ancestors. The humanist philosopher Confucius spoke out in defense of the receding order, which Jiang Qing and her confederates deemed "reactionary." The leftists were lucky that the name of the dynasty coincided with the character for the premier's surname; the constant repetition in a negative context of the character of his surname seemed like a well-disguised attack on the premier. For most Chinese in the 1970s, the character "zhou" in newspapers and magazines evoked the head of the State Council.

In August, however, Jiang Qing and her confederates were deeply disappointed. Mao's mood changed, and he asked the premier to deliver the main report at the Tenth Congress. Thus, Zhou's faction retained considerable influence. At the same time, Wang Hongwen delivered a report on additions and changes to the Party Statutes and was chosen one of the deputy chairmen along with Zhou, Kang Sheng, Ye Jianying, and the chief of the PLA General Political Administration, General Li Desheng. In the main elected organ, the Politburo, the strength of the two factions was roughly equal. A majority of the nine members of the Standing Committee were on Zhou's side.[13] Yet this meant nothing since the major decisions were still made by one man.

Deng participated in the congress, and on Mao's orders he was even elected to the CC.[14] But unlike Wang Hongwen and Hua Guofeng, he was not officially made a member of the Politburo. One of the chief members of Zhou's faction, Marshal Ye Jianying, requested that Mao appoint Deng concurrently to some key post in the army, but the Great Helmsman merely said "this could be considered," as if he were still assaying Deng's soundness.[15]

He put Deng to a decisive test in late November and early December 1973, when he attacked Zhou anew with even greater force. On the evening of November 10, Henry Kissinger, who had just been appointed the U.S. secretary of state, arrived in Beijing on an official visit. Zhou and Ye Jianying received him. Mao also met with him once, on November 12, but basically followed the negotiations by reading stenographic records. After the negotiations had concluded, Mao suddenly suspected that the premier had concealed something from him, some details of his conversation with Kissinger. This accusation was far-fetched, since when Zhou came to report to Mao (according to other sources, he tried calling him) the Chairman, who was not feeling well, was already sleeping and his lover-cum-secretary Zhang Yufeng did not want to disturb him. After awaking, Mao was very dissatisfied and immediately suspected the premier of "intrigues." After reading the stenographic records a bit later, he again felt that Zhou had not been sufficiently firm in his dealings with the imperialists.

Kissinger had tried every way possible to win Beijing over to a military alliance against Moscow, and Zhou indeed had not tried to vindicate the PRC's independent policy with sufficient vigor.[16] The premier had been excessively diplomatic and instead of putting the exceedingly importunate secretary of state in his place, he indicated that his proposal might be acceptable on the condition that "no one feels we are allies."[17] Via his closest collaborators, his grandniece Wang Hairong and Nancy Tang (Tang Wensheng), a department head in the Foreign Ministry, who were serving as his go-betweens with the leadership, Mao immediately informed the Politburo that from his perspective Zhou had leaned in the direction of military collaboration with the United States, agreeing to have the Americans shield the PRC with a "nuclear umbrella." Zhou, of course, had done nothing of the sort, but Mao was incensed: "Some people want to lend us an umbrella," he grumbled, "but we don't want it."[18]

He had been suspicious before, but now that he was ill he stopped trusting anyone at all. At his demand the behavior of Zhou as well as that of Ye Jianying was examined several times in the Politburo, where Jiang Qing and her minions accused the pitiful premier of "treason" and "right opportunism." Jiang Qing even said that the next "two-line struggle" in the party, a principled struggle between right and wrong, was now in progress. Her statement was tantamount to pronouncing a death sentence.

Everyone present had to take part in the persecution; no one could remain silent. One after the other, everyone got up to denounce Zhou and Ye even though many of them were their supporters. Deng's turn came. Without blinking an eye, he joined the chorus. What else could he have done? Such were the rules of party etiquette. He began in a roundabout way, almost as if he was defending Zhou. "One cannot judge international and interstate relations on the basis of a single set of negotiations or a single sentence; one must begin from the overall situation," he said. But then, without pausing for breath, he added,

> As for the current situation, we must speak of a large battle. But neither side is now prepared for it, in particular, neither the U.S. nor the USSR. However, if one really wages the battle, there is nothing to be afraid of. In the past, we overcame the Japanese aggressors, having nothing but "millet and rifles," and now we can defeat [everyone] with the help of the selfsame "millet and rifles."

Then, returning to Zhou, he said, "You're just one step away from the Chairman. For the rest of us, the Chairman is beyond reach although we also can see him. But you not only see him, you can also talk with him. I hope in the future you will remember this."[19]

Thus Deng was also censuring Zhou for his "repudiation" of an independent and autonomous foreign policy; because Zhou supposedly feared the imperialists, he "leaned" to one side, toward alliance with the United States against the USSR, and had not even informed the Great Helmsman in a timely fashion of the results of the negotiations.

Hearing that Deng had not kept silent, and had demonstrated his adherence to party principles, Mao was ecstatic. "I knew he was a good speaker," he said excitedly. "He didn't need any help from me."[20]

Thus Deng passed this most important test. The ordeal had a terrible effect on Zhou. "He was shattered, mentally and physically," writes one of his biographers. "He could no longer eat or sleep."[21] Two years later, after passions had long since subsided and Zhou had not long to live, the deputy minister of foreign affairs, Qiao Guanhua, came to see him in hospital to express his regrets for having taken part with the others in November 1973 in hounding Zhou. Zhou, grown wise from experience, and with one foot in the grave, calmly replied, "The situation was beyond your control. You could not control the situation. Everyone spoke up. You had been working with me for several decades, especially on the American issue. How could you have gotten off the hook without speaking up? Besides, no one is perfect. Why should I be above criticism?"[22]

Zhou understood everything perfectly. He himself "said and did many things that he would have wished not to."[23] What Zhou said to Qiao Guanhua, he might also have addressed to Deng had the latter come to ask forgiveness as well. But Deng did not show up with excuses. He knew, no less than Zhou, that in the CCP there could be only one chief to whose will everyone else submitted. Unequivocal loyalty to the Chairman trumped all other feelings: faithfulness, friendship, love, and decency. So why ask forgiveness?

Moreover, in early December, satisfied with the new working-over Zhou had been subjected to, Mao now attacked Jiang Qing for being too harsh on the premier, saying it was a mistake to assert that a "two-line struggle" was taking place in the party. "One must not speak like that," he observed, adding that Jiang Qing was probably "impatient" to seize power. He also rejected his wife's request to include her and Yao Wenyuan on the Politburo Standing Committee.[24]

Deng's place in the party soon changed drastically. On December 12, 1973, just three days after the Zhou affair was concluded, Mao convened a new Politburo meeting at which he proposed formally bringing Deng into that highest organ. Moreover, he asked that those present confirm Deng as a member of the Central Military Commission. Turning toward Deng, he teased, "Speaking of you, you're someone I like. There are contradictions between us, but in nine cases out of ten there are not, only in one case. [In other words], nine fingers are healthy, and one sick."

A bit later, Mao presented Deng to the members of the Politburo as someone who was already their informal chief of the "General Staff" (since the post of head of the Secretariat no longer existed in the Politburo, Deng would again fulfill these duties). "Some persons are afraid of him," he continued, "but he acts rather decisively. If one assesses his life as a whole, then demerits and merits are in the proportion of 30 to 70. He is your old chief, I have asked him to return." Looking at Deng, he joked again, "Hey you! People are afraid of you. [But] I'll give you my two cents, 'Be firm inside and soft on the outside, hide the needle in the cotton.' Externally be more affable, but inside, hard as steel. Gradually overcome your past mistakes. He who does nothing makes no mistakes. When you work, you always make mistakes. And if you don't work at all, that itself is a mistake."[25]

Naturally, both of his proposals—including Deng in the Politburo and on the Military Commission—were adopted unanimously. At the end of December, Mao presented Deng to the members of the Military Commission:

We had persons in the party who did nothing yet still managed to commit mistakes, but Deng Xiaoping made mistakes while actually doing things; however, he has carried out a self-critical analysis very well during the period when he had an opportunity to think over his actions, and this proves that he was sufficiently bold both to make mistakes and to acknowledge and correct them.

And further, "Speaking of him, I like him. He's still a good man for a fight." In conclusion, Mao repeated his favorite joke, "In my opinion, he appears to be soft like cotton, but he is actually sharp as a needle."[26]

Mao's confidence, of course, encouraged Deng, particularly since the Chairman had just weakened not only Jiang Qing's position but Zhou's as well. All this inspired hope for a new and rapid career trajectory. Deng, we may be sure, was always the Chairman's man and, judging by the testimony of informed persons, he not only never belonged to the leftist faction but also "strictly speaking . . . [never belonged] to Zhou's faction." In reality, Zhou needed him more than he needed Zhou.[27] Deng's closest ties continued to be with the PLA commanders, with Ye Jianying and other generals and officers with whom he had served during the anti-Japanese and civil wars.[28] He maintained businesslike relations with Zhou and his technocrats from the State Council, siding with them basically because neither he nor they saw eye to eye with Jiang Qing and her leftists. Both Deng and Zhou worshiped the Great Helmsman, but they were united in wanting to end the anarchy of the Cultural Revolution in order to guide the PRC into the circle of leading nations. The factional war in the PRC continued to heat up.

Meanwhile, on Mao's instructions, Deng prepared for an important diplomatic mission. On March 20, 1974, the Chairman decided to send him to New York to attend a session of the UN General Assembly in April.[29]

This was a great honor, since from the time the PRC was accepted into the UN in 1971 not a single highly placed Chinese representative had addressed the world body from its high tribune. Participation in the General Assembly was supposed to strengthen Deng's authority as Zhou's presumptive successor both at home and abroad. It would indicate that "his [Deng's] time had come."[30] It would also strengthen the position of the faction of the ailing premier, which had been badly shaken after the working-over Zhou and Ye had been subjected to in November and December.

The leftists, of course, did not want this to happen. Jiang Qing insisted that Deng "was burdened with work at home" and therefore could not go. But Mao was adamant. He would hear no objections from anyone, not even his own wife, who, it seemed, was so involved in the intraparty struggle that she no longer understood her husband's mood. "Jiang Qing!" Mao finally burst out in exasperation, "Comrade Deng Xiaoping's trip is my idea. It would be good if you do not oppose it. Be careful and restrained, do not oppose my proposal."[31]

Jiang had to yield, and on April 6, 1974, Deng left for New York. He was seen off in high style in keeping with the importance of his mission. The entire party leadership, with the exception of Mao, gathered at the airport. More than four thousand representatives of the laboring masses were also rounded up. The send-off was at the highest level. The top leaders knew that Deng was flying to America to carry out a special mission: to present to the whole world from the tribunal of the United Nations the Great Helmsman's new foreign policy doctrine, in which humankind was divided into three worlds. Mao assigned the superpowers—the United States and the USSR—to the first world; Japan, the countries of Europe, Australia, and Canada, to the second; and all other states to the third. According to Mao, the Third World, to which China belonged, must unite in struggle against the hegemonic countries, namely, the United States and the USSR. This doctrine, which Mao first outlined in conversation with the president of Zambia, Kenneth Kaunda, in late February 1974,[32] was the clearest expression of his view that China needed to adhere firmly to the principle of independence in its foreign policy and not lean to the side of either superpower.

On April 10, Deng made a brilliant presentation at a session of the General Assembly. An eyewitness recalls:

My friends and I sat in the balcony reserved for guests. The hall below was packed. . . . When Deng, who seemed especially small to us in the balcony made his appearance . . . he was greeted with a stormy ovation. Everyone arose in order to welcome him. I tried to listen to his speech without the interpreter . . . although his Sichuan accent was very strong. . . . I remember that his speech went over very well. Deng was congratulated and it seemed evident that [on that day] he was the central figure. Of course, the PRC was still a relatively new member of the UN, and this also stimulated interest in Deng's speech.[33]

Naturally, Deng had not written the speech himself. A special group worked on it, but he and Zhou had made some revisions. The text was discussed by the party leadership for a long time and rewritten repeatedly, until Mao finally approved the sixth draft.[34] It provided a very negative assessment of the international actions of both the United States and the USSR, asserting that both countries of the First World were "the biggest international exploiters and oppressors of today" and even "a source of a new world war." However, it emphasized that "the superpower which flaunts the label of socialism is especially vicious."[35]

The minister of foreign affairs of the USSR, Andrei Gromyko, who was present at the assembly, could not hide his irritation, and not wishing personally to deal with the "traitor to the cause of the working class," which is how he undoubtedly viewed Deng, he even asked his American colleague, Henry Kissinger, to respond "on both our behalf."[36]

Meeting with Kissinger four days later for a dinner given in his honor at the Waldorf Astoria hotel, Deng attempted to soften the impression. He joked and tried to be relaxed. Kissinger and Deng conversed all evening, from about 8:00 p.m. to 11:00. Deng smoked a lot; drank maotai (a very expensive and strong Chinese vodka) with Kissinger; reviled the Soviet communists, with whom he "could never reach agreement"; and even said in a burst of forced "candor" that "we work with you to fix the [Russian] bear in the north together with you." (That is, to contain Soviet hegemonism.) But Kissinger could not suppress the unpleasant aftertaste left by Deng's speech at the UN. His interlocutor's "personal style" seemed to him "rather frontal" and even "somewhat acerbic," although Deng also looked insufficiently conversant with historical problems and diplomacy. Moreover, Kissinger observed that Deng, who had only recently returned from exile, did not feel completely self-assured: he was constantly looking for support from those in his entourage and frequently looked at them.[37] (Kissinger would radically change his opinion of Deng after he got to know him better, and ultimately he would develop "enormous regard for this doughty little man with the melancholy eyes who had stuck to his cause in the face of extraordinary vicissitudes."[38])

During his nine days in New York, Deng did not have an opportunity to get well acquainted with this great city. Meeting followed meeting, reception after reception. Deng's view of New York was mostly through the window of his limousine as he was driven down Broadway, Fifth Avenue, and Wall Street. On Sunday, April 14, he was able to stroll about downtown a little. Whether the City of the Yellow Devil, Russian writer Maxim Gorky's appellation for Washington Irving's Gotham, made an impression on him we do not know. Most likely he did not discuss this with his fellow travelers. We only know that he liked the children's toys in Woolworth's very much, including a doll that could cry, nurse, and even pee. The father of Mao's interpreter Nancy Tang, who was accompanying Deng, bought the doll for Deng's granddaughter.[39]

On his way home, Deng stopped in Paris for a day and a half. This was a city he really loved. Here he had spent his youthful years. He asked officials of the Chinese embassy to drive him around the streets, hoping to find familiar places. But everything had changed; he didn't even recognize the hotel on Rue Godefrois where Zhou Enlai had lived and where he (Deng) had printed the journals *Youth* and *Red Light*. Time had passed very quickly. He would soon turn seventy. Almost his whole life had passed, and he still had not become a free man. Confucius had said, "At seventy, I follow all the desires of my heart without breaking any rule."[40] Deng, however, still had to accommodate himself to others.

Before his departure, he made one more request to the ambassador: to buy him croissants and cheese. He wanted to take these with him to Beijing as gifts for his comrades-in-arms with whom he had worked in France. In the Bank of China he had been given some hard currency (US$16) as pocket money, but he had husbanded it and only now decided to spend it. On the spot, embassy officials bought him 200 croissants and a large assortment of cheese. (Obviously, they had surreptitiously topped up his $16 with their own money.[41])

How happy Zhou Enlai, Nie Rongzhen, and other friends of his youth were when Deng, radiating satisfaction, presented them with these bourgeois delicacies! They were probably no less happy than Deng's granddaughter was with her American doll.

A large quantity of these French foods was intended for Zhou, whose life was inexorably moving to a close, and a farewell greeting from his youth could not but touch him. On June 1, with Mao's agreement, he was finally hospitalized in the elite PLA No. 305 hospital, where, on the same day, an operation was performed. His condition improved somewhat, but two months later he again took a turn for the worse, and on August 10 his physicians operated again.[42] However, they were no longer able to help him. Occasionally he went out to particularly important party meetings. The struggle against leftists who threatened to dampen production demanded his constant attention.

Although Mao Zedong declared his love for Deng Xiaoping, he continued to tack between factions. He was also mortally ill. In the summer of 1974 he displayed symptoms of Lou Gehrig's disease, or amyotrophic lateral sclerosis (ALS), which first manifested itself in progressive paralysis of Mao's right arm and right leg, and after a while it spread to his throat, larynx, tongue, and intercostal muscles. It became clear to the doctors that the Chairman had no more than two years to live.[43] But Mao stubbornly clung to life and continued to closely follow the situation in the nation and the party.

He had no intention of forcing Jiang Qing and other leaders of "universal chaos under Heaven" from power, although he intermittently criticized them no less than he did Zhou. Sometimes he would even mutter irritably at Jiang Qing, Wang Hongwen, Zhang Chunqiao, and Yao Wenyuan in the presence of their enemies, "Don't knock together a Gang of Four." He would also declare, "Jiang Qing has a greedy character!" But he would suggest to his comrades-in-arms, "One must apply the principle of one divides into two toward her [Jiang Qing]. One part of her is good, the other not so good."[44] At the same time he consistently promoted the youthful Wang Hongwen. After Zhou was hospitalized, it was Wang whom Mao entrusted with full leadership of the daily work of the Politburo.

Sensing that Mao's criticism of them did not pose a mortal danger, in early September 1974 the leftists launched a new offensive against the veterans. But this evoked a stormy conflict at a meeting of the Politburo. The main antagonists this time were Jiang Qing and Deng Xiaoping. The conflict arose over whether it was better for China to purchase modern ships from abroad or to build them itself. At the end of September 1974, the Chinese ship *Fengqing* had returned from a voyage to Romania that supposedly demonstrated the Chinese were able to build ocean liners successfully. But several officials in the Ministry of Transportation, who reported directly to Zhou, nevertheless asserted that the ship-building industry in China was still insufficiently developed, and so no matter how good the *Fengqing* might be, there was an urgent need to purchase or lease a whole fleet of ships from abroad. Otherwise, the PRC would have no other ships comparable to the *Fengqing*. Hearing this, Jiang Qing took offense at the slight to Chinese power and accused the ministry and the entire State Council of "selling out the Motherland," and "servility to things foreign." At the next meeting of the Politburo, she attacked Deng directly (Zhou was absent), subjecting him to a virtual interrogation. "What is your position regarding the matter of the *Fengqing*? What do you think about 'acting servilely to foreigners?'" Deng exploded. Jiang Qing, playing the role of ill-tempered investigator, really got his goat. "When discussing matters in the Politburo, we must proceed from the principle of equality," he parried. "It's impermissible to treat others that way! How can the Politburo work in a spirit of cooperation if things go on this way?" Blazing with rage, he got up, walked out, and slammed the door.[45]

Jiang Qing immediately accused Deng of rejecting the Cultural Revolution, and the next day she dispatched Wang Hongwen to report to the Great Helmsman, who was resting in Changsha. Wang began whispering into Mao's ear that Zhou Enlai, Marshal Ye Jianying, and Deng Xiaoping were preparing to take the path of Lin Biao. "At a meeting of the Politburo . . . a quarrel erupted between Jiang Qing and Comrade Deng Xiaoping, a very, very serious quarrel," Wang informed Mao.[46] But Mao, who was feeling very bad on account of his advancing paralysis, flared up, and wheezed at the frightened Wang, "If you have an opinion, then you must say it directly to their face, but this way is no good. You need to close ranks with Comrade Xiaoping." Then Mao added, "Go back and spend more time with the premier and Comrade Jianying. Don't act in unison with Jiang Qing. Be careful around her."[47]

Wang conveyed Mao's words to Jiang Qing and the other members of his faction. But the scorned woman continued to rage. She summoned Wang Hairong and Tang Wensheng, who were close to the Great Helmsman; seething with indignation, she insinuated that Deng was treacherous. In this situation, Deng did the right thing. One evening he showed up in person at Jiang Qing's house to speak to her "heart to heart." Yet, as he later told Mao Zedong, their conversation went nowhere. "I came to her, we spoke, but 'steel' clashed with 'steel'." Mao laughed: "That's a good one."[48]

The Great Helmsman then gave greater support to Deng and to Zhou's faction. Recently he was growing troubled by the state of the economy, which suffered a serious blow from the Cultural Revolution he had initiated. He knew very well that industrial production was falling; coal mining and steel smelting in 1974 had declined by 9.4 and 3.07 percent respectively compared to the previous year; all basic consumer goods, including food and clothing, were rationed; and there was unemployment. The situation in the countryside, where 250 million peasants were suffering from hunger, was particularly difficult. There were colossal problems in the transportation system, with 50 percent of the trains not on schedule and numerous serious accidents happening. Enormous quantities of raw materials and goods were not reaching consumers. Workers, engineers, and technicians frequently participated in political campaigns, factional disputes splintered the leadership of factories and mills, and the leftists treated knowledgeable economists as "class aliens," certain that it was better to be "red" than to be expert. More than 30 percent of enterprises were unprofitable; there were chronic budget deficits.[49]

Mao needed a person who was no less pragmatic than Zhou to replace the ailing premier, and Deng, who had demonstrated his devotion, was just such a person. On October 4, 1974, Mao informed Wang Hongwen of his desire to make Deng the first deputy premier, who would discharge the duties of the premier. Several days later, he ordered the inseparable Wang Hairong and Tang Wensheng, his grandniece and English-language interpreter respectively, to tell the Politburo that he had decided to appoint Deng as deputy chair of the Central Military Commission and chief of the General Staff of the PLA. (All three appointments he actually made at the request of Marshal Ye Jianying.)[50] "The French faction is good," he noted, having suddenly remembered that Deng had joined the CCP in France.[51]

Jiang Qing was beside herself but could do nothing. Once again Mao had equalized the competing factions and continued to balance between them.

On October 11, 1974, the CC disseminated a new resolution from the Chairman: "The Great Proletarian Cultural Revolution has been going on already for eight years. Now it is time to calm down. The entire party and the entire army must unite."[52] (Mao had first voiced this unusual thought in August 1974, but only now was it revealed.) To Li Xiannian and Wang Hongwen, who visited him in Changsha in early November, the Great Helmsman declared, "We need to develop the economy."[53] To Deng, who also came to visit him several days later, he said, "There's no other way out, you must carry this load."[54] Later on, at the end of December, he calmly explained to Wang Hongwen that Deng Xiaoping is "strong ideologically, a man of many talents. Much better than you." On the spot he proposed also making Deng CC deputy chair and a member of the Politburo Standing Committee.[55] Yet, apparently recalling Deng's earlier inclination toward the capitalist road, he observed that while developing the economy, one should not forget the serious danger of revisionism. He demanded that everyone study the theory of the dictatorship of the proletariat since "a commodity system presently exists in our country; there is still inequality in the system of pay . . . etc. This can only be limited under the dictatorship of the proletariat."[56]

Naturally, everything that Mao wanted was done. At the Second Plenum of the Tenth Central Committee in January 1975, Deng was unanimously chosen as a deputy chairman of the CC and member of the Politburo Standing Committee. And at a session of the National People's Congress that same month, he was officially confirmed as first deputy premier. At the same time, he headed the General Staff. Simultaneously, throughout the country a massive campaign to study the theory of the dictatorship of the proletariat unfolded. At Mao's request, it was headed by the leftists Zhang Chunqiao and Yao Wenyuan.

From then on, at the center of Deng's attention, in addition to foreign policy matters, was the question of economic development. In 1975 he began actively working to set the army and the economy in order, striving to implement the long-term program of the Four Modernizations—agriculture, industry, defense, science and technology—first put forward by Zhou Enlai in December 1964.

According to this program, by 1980 the PRC should be able to create an independent and comparatively complete system of industry and overall economy. By the end of the twentieth century, it should reach the contemporary level of development of the leading countries. Premier Zhou announced this program again in a government work report at a National People's Congress meeting in January 1975. But he was not its author at that time. The basic features of the program had already been sketched in 1974 in the State Planning Commission, whose leading figures were Li Fuchun and the talented economist Yu Qiuli.[57] Deng also had a hand in its making: he was the author of Zhou's report. "I drafted that speech," he recalled, "We didn't go over 5,000 characters. Zhou was too weak physically. He couldn't have read it all if it was long."[58]

In January, along with Marshal Ye Jianying, who after the January (1975) session of the NPC had become minister of defense, Deng convened a meeting of General Staff officers at the rank of regimental commander and above, at which he announced a struggle against factionalism, first of all among the cadres. In unequivocal terms, he referred to the destructive activity of the leftists who disrupted army discipline with endless campaigns of "criticism and struggle."[59]

Afterward Deng turned to putting railroad transport in order; then he switched to steel production, followed by defense industry, and finally to education, culture, and science. He repeatedly convened meetings, sessions, and conferences and counterpoised his own campaign to uproot factionalism, that is, leftism, to the leftists' campaign of criticizing Lin Biao and Confucius. He bent every effort toward alerting all party cadres that the time had come to switch from revolution to production. "The whole Party must now give serious thought to our country's overall interest," he explained, having in mind the economy. "I am told that some comrades nowadays only dare to make revolution but not to promote production. They say that the former is safe but the latter dangerous. This is utterly wrong."[60] He called for reviving good traditions and not waiting until "persons" who had "wrought havoc with the Party's cause" were restored to reason. "The leadership must be clear-cut and firm in its opposition to factionalism," he asserted. "Those who cling to factionalism should be transferred to other posts, criticized or struggled against whenever necessary. We should not drag things out or wait forever."[61]

At the end of May 1975, he grounded his policy theoretically, relying on three "important" directives from the Leader: "On questions of theory [that is, of the dictatorship of the proletariat], we must struggle against external revisionism and not permit domestic revisionism"; "we must calm down and unite"; and "we must develop the economy." He declared that "these three important directives from now on are the program in all spheres of our work."[62] As we have seen, he put special emphasis on the latter two directives.

To work on the scholarly problems associated with putting things in order, Deng organized a Political Research Office at the State Council. He placed at its head a Deng loyalist, the sixty-three-year-old intellectual Hu Qiaomu, who had formerly served as one of Mao's personal secretaries and as a member of Deng's Secretariat. At the beginning of the Cultural Revolution, Hu, like Deng, had been inscribed on the list of capitalist roaders. He also had been worked over and dragged out at meetings but was finally rehabilitated. Hu assembled a team of six persons, including the well-known journalists Wu Lengxi, Hu Sheng, and Deng Liqun as well as the philosopher-cum-economist Yu Guangyuan. Deng attached the group to the State Council rather than the Central Committee because at that time the everyday work of the CC was being managed by the leftist Wang Hongwen.[63]

Jiang Qing and her comrades-in-arms tried to counterattack. After their sluggish campaign to criticize Lin Biao and Confucius proved bankrupt, they launched a new ideological campaign: against the empiricism and "capitula-tionism" that were supposedly contained in the novel *Water Margin*.[64] All of them were aimed at Zhou, Deng, and other "revisionists," who, from their perspective, were trying to follow "the Liu Shaoqi line without Liu Shaoqi."[65]

But from the beginning of July 1975, at the suggestion of Ye Jianying, approved by Mao Zedong, Deng started playing first violin in the Politburo. He rather than Wang Hongwen conducted the meetings of this highest party organ. And he began to direct the everyday work of the CC. (Mao sent Wang Hongwen to Zhejiang and Shanghai for a while to provide "help" to the local leftists.)[66] Deng was also given the responsibility to supervise the brigade of doctors who were treating the Chairman. Thus he occupied the third position in the party hierarchy after Mao himself and Zhou. But both the Chairman and the premier were mortally ill, and Deng, as always, was in good health.[67]

As early as April 18, 1975, after returning to Beijing from Changsha, Mao Zedong had already said to the visiting head of North Korea, Kim Il Song,

Comrade Dong Biwu [deputy chairman of the NPC Standing Committee] has passed away. The Premier is sick. Comrades Kang Sheng and Liu Bocheng are also sick. I am sick too. This year I am 82 years old. I cannot hold on for very long.... I am not going to discuss politics [with you], but he will [Mao points to Deng Xiaoping who was present at the meeting]. His name is Deng Xiaoping. He knows how to fight a battle; he also knows how to fight against revisionism. The Red Guards purged him, but he is fine now. In those years several [of our leaders] were purged, and they have been rehabilitated now. We need them.[68]

And this is what he said to the head of the North Vietnamese communists, Le Duan, on September 24, 1975, "Our leadership is now facing a crisis. The Premier . . . is not in good health, he had four operations in one year and [the situation] is dangerous. Kang Sheng and Ye Jianying are not in good health either. I am 82 years old. I am very ill. Only he is young and strong," Mao said, pointing to Deng Xiaoping.[69]

Mao's enthusiasm for Deng soon passed, however. Jiang Qing and other leftists succeeded in getting the very ill old man to sing their tune. Mao's nephew, Yuanxin, the son of his younger brother, Zemin, and one of the persons most devoted to Jiang Qing, played the decisive role in this matter. In early October, for some reason the decrepit dictator decided to make Yuanxin his go-between in contacts with the Politburo in place of Wang Hairong and Tang Wensheng. Apparently, he simply missed his nephew, whom he had always treated very warmly. Yuanxin was an orphan; his father was killed in 1943 when Yuanxin was only two. His mother remarried and at Mao's and Jiang Qing's request she allowed her son to live with them in Zhongnanhai. Basically, it was Jiang who brought him up, so it is not surprising that Yuanxin was attached to her.

Becoming one of Mao's intimates, the clever and cunning Yuanxin was able to make skillful use of the situation to strengthen the position of the leftists. "I listen attentively to the speeches of Comrade [Deng] Xiaoping," he whispered to his uncle,

and I have the feeling that he barely touches upon the achievements of the Great Cultural Revolution, and says very little in criticism of Liu Shaoqi's revisionist line. From the slogan of the "Three Directives are the Main Link," in essence only one directive remains: develop production. This year I have not heard that he [Deng] has raised the issue of how to study theory, how to criticize the novel *Water Margin*, how to criticize revisionism.[70]

He went on like this for an entire month, and finally Mao could not hold out. He believed what he had been told. "Just what is 'The Three Directives are the Main Link'?" he asked Yuanxin in his low rumbling voice, obviously displeased.

> Do order and unity negate class struggle? The main link is class struggle, and everything else is the goal.... Some comrades, for the most part old comrades, are still stuck at the stage of the bourgeois democratic revolution; they do not understand socialist revolution, they grumble about it and even reject it. As for the Great Cultural Revolution, on one hand they are dissatisfied [with it], and on the other they are settling scores [with it]. They are settling scores with the Great Cultural Revolution.[71]

Just at this time, Deng committed a big blunder. He forwarded to Mao a letter from a certain Liu Bing, deputy secretary of the Tsinghua University party committee, in which Liu complained about the excesses of other university party leaders who were well-known leftists. Mao viewed Liu Bing's letter as slander directed against honest people, and moreover that the missive was directed against himself since "a matter relating to Tsinghua was not isolated, but reflected the contemporary two-line struggle."[72] Thus Deng in turn was out of favor.

At Mao's request the members of the Politburo began to criticize Jiang Qing's adversary "who had overstepped the bounds," and soon they dismissed him from most of his duties, permitting him only to open and close Politburo meetings and deal with foreign policy matters. A new movement directed against Deng began to gather steam throughout China.

It seemed as if Jiang Qing's faction had triumphed. China entered the new year of 1976 under the banner of struggle against the "Right Deviationist Wind to Reverse Correct Verdicts." But Deng did not lose hope. He seemed to have a premonition that his new fall from grace, the third in his life, would soon end. The arriving new year of 1976, the Year of the Dragon—that is, his year, would be the overture to a new and higher ascent.

17

New Trials

AS ALWAYS, MAO wanted just one thing: for Deng to repent. Fully and irrevocably. Unexpectedly, however, Deng displayed some character. It was not that he struck a pose, but he began to respond strangely. In conversations with Politburo members who were criticizing him at the request of the Great Helmsman, he tried to defend himself, insisting that the policy of restoring order was correct, and citing the Chairman himself, who had supported his policy. He even refused to head a Central Committee task force charged with drafting a resolution pronouncing the Cultural Revolution an overall success. Mao wanted the ratio of successes to failures set at 70:30.[1] But Deng replied that he was "a person who was living at the Peach Blossom Spring who knew neither of the Han dynasty nor the Wei and Jin dynasties."[2] He borrowed this image from the great Chinese poet Tao Yuanming (356–427 CE), author of the famous utopia *Peach Blossom Spring*, which told of a certain tribe that had fled to the ends of the earth during the time of the emperor Qin Shi Huangdi (who happened to be one of the Great Helmsman's favorite historical figures). The tribe was therefore unfamiliar with the history of the following dynasties. Mao understood him very well, especially since in jest he himself called the veterans repressed during the Cultural Revolution "people living at the Peach Blossom Spring." "Away from affairs for six or seven years," Mao said, "there was much they did not know."[3] But Deng, it seems, was not joking at all. He bluntly asserted that, as an exile, he could not say anything good about the Cultural Revolution. How could Mao *not* be angry about it?

Of course, the former number two capitalist roader was swimming against the tide. He could no longer spar with Mao as he had previously. Perhaps he had simply tired of unjust persecutions. Or, understanding that the Chairman would not live much longer, he was no longer afraid of anything. During the two years back in Beijing, Deng had greatly strengthened his position in the party, in the state apparatus, and, what was most important, in the army. He had long enjoyed the respect of veterans from the CCP and the PLA, and now, thanks to his successful handling of the economy, he had gained the sympathy of the majority of cadres. He was admired by Minister of Defense Ye Jianying as well as the overwhelming majority of generals who were tired of the excesses of the leftists. However, none of them would ever cross Mao to support Deng. The Great Helmsman's authority in the party, in the army, and among the people was so much stronger than Deng's that Ye Jianying and all the generals would have unhesitatingly sacrificed Deng had the Leader and Teacher so desired. Thus, Deng could not engage in a direct conflict with the Chairman. He soon understood that he had to restrain himself.

At a Politburo meeting on December 20, he finally made a self-criticism, and at subsequent meetings on January 2 and 3, 1976, he further expanded on it. Moreover, he presented the party leadership with a written self-analysis in which he confessed to a multitude of "errors." He sent a similar letter to Mao Zedong.[4] But the Chairman did not wish to forgive the obstinate one. The nationwide campaign against "The Right Deviationist Wind to Reverse Correct Verdicts," which had begun in November 1975 and was basically directed against Deng, continued to pick up steam.

Now Deng spent a lot of time with his family. He, Zhuo Lin, and the remaining family members now lived in a large house in the center of town, not far from Tiananmen Square. His friend Marshal He Long used to live there, but on June 9, 1969, at the height of the Cultural Revolution, exhausted from the unremitting persecutions and humiliations, He Long committed suicide. After his death the house remained empty for a long time.

Deng liked it there. He loved to sit on the terrace of an evening, stroll about the inner courtyard, and watch his beloved grandchildren playing with their toys. There were two of them by now. In addition to his granddaughter Mianmian, he now had a grandson, Mengmeng ("Little Sprout"), the son of his oldest daughter, Deng Lin. He was born prematurely, weighing only 3.5 pounds at birth, but had grown up quite healthy.[5] At the beginning of 1976 he was just over a year and a half, and his grandfather, naturally, worshiped him.

His grandchildren diverted him, but Deng could not entirely forget his own misfortunes. His wife and children observed that from time to time he "closed his eyes and fell into a reverie." Every night "a single lamp burned in the darkened enclosed porch. Papa sat there alone, often for a long, long time."[6]

Mixed with reflections on his own fate were bitter thoughts about Zhou Enlai, who by early January 1976 had already undergone several unsuccessful operations. Zhou knew that he was dying; lying on his hospital bed, he sang the *Internationale* in a thin voice. His wife, Deng Yingchao, who was by his side, joined in, swallowing her tears. Deng remembered that when he visited the premier on September 20, 1975, on the eve of Zhou's forthcoming operation, Zhou squeezed his hand and said, "You worked well this year, much better than me!" And then, suddenly straining himself, he cried, "I'm true to the Party, I'm true to the people!"[7] Everyone present froze, but Deng understood his old comrade very well. Just at that time a campaign against apologists for "capitulation," supposedly found in the novel *Water Margin*, was taking place, and the leftists, as we know, were aiming it against Zhou, Deng, and other supporters of rectification. At the end of December, Zhou called Marshal Ye Jianying and in a weakened voice asked him under no circumstances to allow power to fall into the hands of the Gang of Four (that is, Jiang Qing, Wang Hongwen, Zhang Chunqiao, and Yao Wenyuan). That, it will be recalled, is how Mao himself had once referred to them.[8]

On January 5, another operation was performed on the premier, but two days later Zhou fell into a coma. The next morning, January 8, at 9:57 a.m., he passed away.

That same day Deng convened a meeting of the Politburo. Agreement was reached on the composition of a commission to organize his funeral, formally headed by Mao himself. Early on the morning of January 9, the masses were informed of Zhou's death.[9]

Many persons mourned the premier. In the memory of most Chinese, he remained a wise, honest, and empathetic person, "a knight beyond fear or reproach" who had tried to restrain the savagery of the Cultural Revolution. This image took root in the consciousness of the masses. On the day of his funeral, January 11, more than a million Beijing residents saw Zhou off on his final journey.

The Politburo decided on January 12 that Deng would give a funeral speech at the memorial meeting for the premier. This was natural. If only formally, it was he who directed the CC's daily affairs. Zhang Chunqiao had proposed Ye Jianying, but the marshal, who invariably supported Deng, firmly resisted.[10] Therefore, in the Great Hall of the People on January 15, Deng read the official text of the funeral speech that had been adopted by the Politburo. In the eyes of the Chinese, immediately this made him the successor to the beloved Zhou. Deng's authority among ordinary Chinese rose sharply.

Late on the evening of January 15, in accordance with Zhou Enlai's testament, his ashes were scattered over the rivers, mountains, and valleys of China.

Five days later, Deng again presented self-critical remarks at a Politburo meeting. One sensed that he was at the limits of his patience. After his brief speech, he asked the members of the party leadership to release him "from all important, responsible work." Not staying to listen to the criticism of the leftists, he stood up, said he needed to relieve himself, and walked out.[11] Jiang Qing, Zhang Chunqiao, and the other radicals were simply choking on their fury.

The next day, January 21, Mao Yuanxin informed Mao of Deng's indecent behavior. But the Chairman only grinned; "The question of Deng Xiaoping is still a question within the people [that is, Deng is not an enemy]; he [Deng] is behaving well and is capable of not going into opposition like Liu Shaoqi and Lin Biao." After a moment's silence, he added,

> There is still a difference between Deng Xiaoping and Liu Shaoqi and Lin Biao. Deng Xiaoping is prepared to engage in self-criticism, but Liu Shaoqi and Lin Biao never were.... We will again discuss the question of Xiaoping's work later. I think we can lighten his burden, but not deprive him of work, that is, we don't need to part company with him at one fell swoop.... I will ask Hua Guofeng to head the State Council. He considers himself insufficiently competent in political matters. Let Xiaoping deal with foreign policy issues.[12]

A week later Mao instructed Hua to direct the everyday activities of the CC in place of Deng, and on February 2 the Politburo unanimously approved the appointment.

Thus Deng was deprived of any power whatsoever. Instead, the star of the quiet-looking Hua Guofeng ascended rapidly. Since January 1975 the minister of public security had been only the sixth-ranking of Zhou's twelve deputies. Suddenly, Mao, with one foot in the grave, blessed Hua and made him acting premier and in charge of the Central Committee. Evidently, Hua himself had not expected this. But Mao's thinking was understandable. Hua Guofeng belonged neither to Deng's faction nor to the leftist faction. He always stood apart, and that is precisely why he suited the Great Helmsman, who was continuing to balance between the factions. Devoted to the Chairman body and soul, but colorless and not too ambitious, he was perfect for the role of intermediary between the warring factions. Both the leftists and the rightists would have to accept him. "They say he has a low profile," Mao reasoned. "That's why I'm choosing the man with the low profile."[13]

Afterward, the CC distributed new "Important Directives of Mao Zedong" to responsible officials regarding criticism of Deng Xiaoping. They said:

> Xiaoping advanced the slogan of "The Three Directives are the Main Link," [but] he did not consider this question with the Politburo, did not discuss it in the State Council, did not inform me, but just spoke out on his own. This person has never paid proper attention to class struggle; it has never been the key link for him. Then there's the business of the "white cat," "black cat"; it doesn't matter whether it's imperialism or Marxism. He does not understand Marxism-Leninism and he represents the bourgeoisie.... [But] we need to help him, criticizing his mistakes means to help him, it's no good to let things slide.[14]

On instructions from the Chairman, on February 25, 1976, Hua Guofeng allowed party leaders of provinces, autonomous regions, central level cities, and military districts to commence criticizing Deng Xiaoping by name for his "mistaken revisionist line." To be sure, it was forbidden to post *dazibao* (big-character posters) and to denounce Deng on the radio and in the press. The revisionist could only be criticized at meetings.[15]

The leftists took immediate advantage of the situation. Jiang Qing was particularly active. Over several days she convened meetings of the leading officials of twelve provinces and autonomous regions, at which she called Deng a "counterrevolutionary double-dealer," a "fascist," and "a representative of compradors, landlords, and the bourgeoisie." She even accused him of "betraying the fatherland," calling him an "agent of international capitalism in China."[16]

This, of course, was too much. Jiang Qing was obviously contradicting the Great Helmsman, who, as we have seen, considered the question of Deng one "within the people." Hearing of her speeches from Hua, Mao was infuriated. "Jiang Qing is interfering too much in many things," he wrote on Hua Guofeng's report. "She convened a separate meeting [of the leaders] of twelve provinces and made a speech."[17]

But even Mao Zedong had a hard time bringing Jiang to heel. Despite the prohibition on mentioning Deng by name in the press, the leftists under her leadership quickly compiled anti-Deng collections, such as *Excerpts from the Speeches of Deng Xiaoping*; *A Comparison of Deng Xiaoping's Speeches with the Teachings of Marx, Lenin, and Chairman Mao*; *A Comparison of Deng Xiaoping's Speeches with the Moral Dogmas of Confucius and Mencius*; and *A*

Comparison of the Speeches of Deng Xiaoping with the Leaders of Opportunism. They even began to shoot a documentary film under the title of *Speak Resolutely Against Deng Xiaoping.* In March, Deng and his family were forced to move from their luxurious house to a more modest dwelling.

The campaign against "The Right Opportunist Wind to Reverse Correct Verdicts" merged with the criticism of Deng into a single propaganda movement. Mass meetings were held in factories, institutions, and people's communes, at which the old capitalist roader was denounced anew. But this time many of the participants in the show got by with mouthing some boilerplate phrases. One sensed that the people were not supporting the new action. After all, Deng had been viewed as the legitimate successor to Zhou. He could not be replaced by the likes of Hua Guofeng. How could one revile a man who had been shielded by the grace of the just-departed, beloved premier? Especially since ordinary Chinese linked Deng's name to restoration of the economy and the struggle against the whole sickening phenomenon of leftist factionalism. Thus the criticism of Deng was doomed to failure.

Soon a large part of the population stopped taking part in it. In Beijing and other cities, rumors spread to the effect that the premier himself had died as a victim of the leftists who despised him. In March, *dazibao* appeared in many places against the Gang of Four. A burst of dissatisfaction followed publication in Shanghai's *Literary Reports* of an article insinuating that Zhou, like Deng, was a capitalist roader, and that Zhou had "helped to elevate" Deng after his downfall. In Nanjing leaflets immediately appeared calling on the people to protest. Almost forty thousand local students staged a demonstration. But the police broke it up. This became known at once in Beijing. Then on Tiananmen, at the Monument to the People's Heroes that towered above it, people began placing bouquets and wreaths in memory of Zhou Enlai and festooning the trees around the entire perimeter of the square with white paper flowers. (White is the color of mourning in China.) *Dazibao* censuring such female rulers as Indira Gandhi and Empress Dowager Ci Xi were brought as well. (Jiang Qing was not referred to by name, but everyone knew exactly whom the authors had in mind.)

This movement developed spontaneously over the course of two weeks, and finally on April 4, the traditional Day of Remembrance of the Dead, the square was packed with people. Everyone was very excited. Here and there shouts were heard: "We will defend Premier Zhou at the cost of our own lives! "Long live the great Marxist-Leninist Zhou Enlai!" "Down with everyone who opposes Premier Zhou!" Many sang the *Internationale.*[18]

Jiang Qing and her close associates were scared of a massive, uncontrolled movement. At an emergency Politburo session on the evening of April 4, they decided to remove all wreaths and flowers and to suppress the unsanctioned meeting. Hua Guofeng supported them. (Ye Jianying and Li Xiannian were not present at the session "because of illness.") "A group of bad people has crawled out," declared Hua who was still minister of public security. Wu De, the mayor of Beijing, added, "This looks like an action planned in advance. In 1974–75 Deng Xiaoping was engaged in cultivating the majority of public opinion.... Deng Xiaoping prepared the current events over a long period.... [Their] nature is clear. This is a counterrevolutionary incident."[19]

On April 5, the police were sent into action against the demonstrators, but they encountered resistance. People became indignant as the police began to collect and destroy the wreaths. Thousands of people were shouting, "Give us back our wreaths!" Fights broke out, and some people torched one of the buildings on the square and set fire to police cars. Only by dint of great effort was the riot suppressed. Dozens of people were arrested.

Yuanxin informed Mao Zedong of the "counterrevolutionary mutiny"— "objectively," of course. He placed all the blame for the popular demonstrations on Deng, comparing him to Imre Nagy, the Hungarian premier at the time of the Hungarian Revolution, and likening the protesters to the participants in the anticommunist uprising in Budapest in 1956. The Great Leader approved suppression of the revolt: "Bold fighting spirit. Good, good, good."[20]

On the morning of April 6, Jiang Qing dropped in on Mao to inform him of the horrible details of the burnt vehicles, the massacres, and so forth. Then she declared, "Their [the mutineers'] chief backstage boss was Deng Xiaoping. I accuse him. I propose that Deng Xiaoping be expelled from the party."[21] Mao raised his eyes and looked at her for a long time, but he made no reply.

The next day, after listening to a new report from his nephew, in a wheezy voice he gave instructions: "On this basis deprive Deng Xiaoping of all his duties; leave him in the party, observe what effect this will have." After lapsing into silence, he continued, "This time [we have] first, the capital, second, Tiananmen, and third, arson and fights. These three things are good. The character has changed. On this basis, drive [him] out."[22]

That same day, he appointed Hua Guofeng first deputy chairman of the Central Committee and officially premier of the State Council. Three weeks later, no longer able to speak, he would write to his final successor, "Go slowly, do not be anxious. Keep on course. With you in charge, I am at ease." Two months later, he would add, "Pay chief attention to the domestic affairs of the nation."[23]

Naturally, the appointment of Hua displeased Jiang Qing and other left-ist radicals, but the dismissal of Deng so overjoyed them that for a while they overlooked this "small" unpleasantness. It seemed it would be easy to deal with a bumpkin like Hua.

Jiang and the other radicals rejoiced; the majority of people in Beijing lamented. As a mark of silent protest people began placing little bottles in the windows of their homes; if written with a different Chinese character the *ping* in Deng Xiaoping's name means "small bottle," and the character *tai* in the word *chuantai* (windowsill) is translated as "top" or "summit." By placing little bottles in the windows of their homes, those who opposed the Gang of Four wanted to say, "Deng Xiaoping is still on top!" At the same time, a short "hedgehog" haircut *(xiao pingtou)* became popular among men, since if one wished this name could be translated as "Xiaoping is the chief." (The character *tou* means "head.")

At least outwardly, Deng himself maintained his composure. From the end of January—that is, from the time Mao decided to relieve him—he spent all his days at home. Naturally, he knew about the events on Tiananmen Square, but most likely he had no connection whatsoever with them. As before, he spent most of his time in his office, chain-smoking and thinking. He barely spoke with the members of his household, trying not to involve them in his own troubles. At 8:00 a.m. on the morning of April 7, he learned from a Central People's Radio broadcast that he had been dismissed from all his posts in and out of the party. The announcement was inconsistent. On one hand, it emphasized that "after discussing the counterrevolutionary incident on Tiananmen Square and Deng Xiaoping's recent conduct, the Politburo of the Central Committee of the CCP believes that the nature of the question of Deng Xiaoping has changed, and [it is now a question of] antagonistic contradictions." On the other hand, it declared that Deng remained in the party.[24] It seemed that, as before, during the time of turmoil, Mao did not want to inflict a bloody reprisal on the "unwise" Deng and, even though overthrowing him, was in no hurry to strengthen the Gang of Four. This was cause for hope. Deng immediately wrote the Chairman a letter of thanks.[25]

Meanwhile, Jiang Qing was spreading rumors among the party leadership that the "masses" were ready "to strike a blow at Deng Xiaoping and seize him," since it was he who had headed "the counterrevolutionary uprising." She even assured them that Deng had personally come by car to Tiananmen Square to lead the mass meeting.[26] Hearing of this, the head of the General

Office of the Central Committee, Wang Dongxing, who was not fond of Jiang Qing, promptly requested permission of the Chairman to convey Deng and his wife to a safe place where it would be easier to guard them. Mao assented. Thus Deng and Zhuo Lin were parted from their children and put under house arrest in their former luxurious home in central Beijing. There they lived in complete isolation (if one doesn't count the relative who came to help with the housework, the cook, and a bodyguard) for three and a half months.

The children were forced to take part in the public denunciation of their father, after which they moved elsewhere. Everyone in the family suffered badly from Deng's disgrace. "A family like ours shouldn't have any babies!" Deng Lin and Deng Nan, not containing themselves, exclaimed in unison. Along with their younger sister Maomao, they began to prepare for the worst.[27]

Meanwhile, a full-throated campaign to criticize the revisionist Deng by name unfolded in China. Exposés were published daily in newspapers and magazines, while radio and television endlessly broadcast news of his "crimes." Among the masses, however, the campaign continued to lack traction. This was so even among the officials and personnel of law-enforcement agencies. The anti-Deng publications, and in particular the documents on restoring order that Deng had prepared in 1975 and that were now being published by Jiang Qing and her confederates to show how "bourgeois" Deng was, evoked an opposite reaction from most readers, not hatred toward the capitalist roader but sympathy for a man who wanted to improve the lives of the people.[28]

A former inmate in one of the prisons recalled:

By 2:00 p.m. I was taken to the interrogation room. . . . There I was confronted by three older cadres who clearly looked to be members of the public security ministry.

"Have you read the papers today?" they asked me.

"Yes," I said. "I have."

"What is your reaction to what they are saying?"

"I read that bad people were making trouble in the square and that they attacked revolutionary army men. But . . . I don't understand how the man behind this could be Deng Xiaoping. . . . I personally cannot believe that Deng would incite hoodlums to attack the People's Liberation Army. He grew up in it. He led it. He lives it."

I expected to be punished. Instead, they all broke into grins.

What the hell was going on? I thought. They did not look as if they were trying to lure me on. They looked happy. . . . I went back to my cell genuinely puzzled.[29]

In July Deng and Zhuo Lin received permission to be reunited with their children. They all gathered again in their old house. "[Father and mother] were reunited not only with their children, but with their adorable grandchildren as well," Maomao wrote.[30]

Here in a small one-story house on the night of July 27–28, they experienced the shocks of a most terrible earthquake. At its epicenter, the city of Tangshan, some ninety miles west of Beijing, its strength measured 7.8 on the Richter scale. Tangshan, a city of one million, was completely destroyed. According to official data, more than 240,000 people died in the ruins and more than 160,000 were injured.

Maomao recalled,

I ran out to the porch, yelling, "Earthquake! Earthquake!" There was a boom! I whirled around. A big piece of the ceiling had fallen in the porch. . . . By then Deng Lin and Deng Nan had come. We looked at each other. "Papa! Mama!" we cried . . . we . . . burst the lock [on Deng and Zhuo Lin's bedroom]. They had both taken sedatives and were fast asleep. We awakened them and helped them walk unsteadily outside. The ground and sky were moving. A deep terrifying roar welled from the bowels of the earth. . . . Deng Lin suddenly cried: "The children!" In the excitement we had completely forgotten them. We ran to their room and carried them out—still sleeping soundly.[31]

Afterward Deng and his family took shelter for a long time in a hastily erected tent near the house. Most residents of Beijing were living on the streets and in courtyards. People were afraid to return to half-ruined houses that had miraculously survived the earthquake.

Under these circumstances, inhabitants of the capital as well as other regions of the country were in no mood to criticize Deng. The only topic of conversation was the earthquake. Thus the massive propaganda campaign flopped.

Soon China was shaken by one more bit of news. On September 9, at 12:10 a.m., Mao Zedong passed away. The entire country was plunged into mourning. On September 18, more than a million gathered on Tiananmen Square at a meeting in memory of Mao. Memorial meetings took place in every city and people's commune. At 3:00 p.m. the whole country paused for three minutes in sorrowful silence; the only sound was the continuous wail of sirens from factories and mills. Hua Guofeng delivered a memorial speech at Tiananmen Square. He declared that "Chairman Mao will live eternally in our hearts" and called on the entire party, army, and peoples of China "to turn sorrow into strength," to fulfill the testament of the Great Helmsman: "Practice Marxism and not revisionism, unite and not split; be honest and straightforward and not engage in intrigues." (Mao had made this testament to party and military leaders in August 1971.[32]) Hua put forward a series of tasks in domestic and foreign policy, stressing the need to continue the revolution under the dictatorship of the proletariat. One was to "deepen and develop the criticism of Deng and the struggle against the Right Deviationist Wind to Reverse Correct Verdicts."[33]

The death of Mao upset Deng himself. Of course, the Great Helmsman had often been unjust toward him, but he had not allowed the Gang of Four to destroy him. And he could have sent him the way of Liu Shaoqi. On September 18, he and his family conducted their own memorial service at home. Wearing black armbands and standing in a semicircle, he and the members of his household silently bowed before a portrait of the deceased.[34] Later Deng would say of Mao, "We must never sully the glorious image of Comrade Mao Zedong in the entire history of the Chinese revolution. . . . Despite the fact that Comrade Mao wanted to 'rectify' anyone who disobeyed him, he still gave some consideration to how far he should go."[35]

Mao's successor, Hua Guofeng, and the Gang of Four continued to apply public pressure on Deng, reviving the massive campaign of criticism against him and continuing to hold him under house arrest. Yet the regimen of confinement was mild: he and Zhuo Lin were simply not allowed out on the street. Since the other family members were free to come and go as they pleased, they were able to act as intermediaries between their father and the outside world. This they did, bringing Deng newspapers and conveying rumors.

On October 7, he learned from He Ping, Maomao's husband, the shocking news, not yet officially released, that the day before Hua Guofeng had arrested the Gang of Four, including Mao Zedong's widow, Jiang Qing, as well as Mao Yuanxin, the Great Helmsman's nephew, in Zhongnanhai. He Ping's parents had been told this in secret by an old wartime comrade who had access to secret information. They immediately shared their joy with their son.

"Come here, come here, quick!" He Ping shouted, flying into his father-in-law's house. "He was streaming perspiration," his wife wrote.

We knew something was up. . . . Because we were wary of planted listening devices, whenever we wanted to talk about anything important we would all go into the bathroom and turn the taps in the tub on full force to drown out the sound. So there we were—Papa, Mama, Deng Lin, Deng Nan, and me. We shut the door and opened the taps wide. We crowded around He Ping and listened to him tell us about the destruction of the Gang of Four.

Papa was pretty deaf, and with the water rushing into the tub, he couldn't hear clearly. The news had to be repeated.[36]

Deng Lin, Deng Nan, and Maomao were jumping with joy, and Deng himself was so excited that he crumpled the cigarette in his hand, forgetting that he had wanted to smoke it.

The news was indeed stunning. Deng understood that the "quiet" Hua Guofeng resolved to arrest the Gang of Four, undoubtedly having allied himself with the highest ranks of the army, that is, with the persons who up to now had attached themselves to himself, Deng. Of course, he knew no details of the coup, but he was no novice when it came to politics. He was ecstatic.

On October 10, he sent a letter to Hua Guofeng, who three days earlier had been unanimously chosen at a Politburo meeting as chairman of the CC and of its Military Commission, in which he expressed his joy:

The Central Committee of the party, under the leadership of Comrade Guofeng, has smashed this group of scoundrels and achieved a great victory. This is a victory of socialism over capitalism that strengthens the dictatorship of the proletariat and averts a capitalist restoration. This is a victory for Mao Zedong Thought and the revolutionary line of Chairman Mao. Together with the whole people, I feel sincere emotions of great joy, and unable to restrain my feelings, I loudly shout, "Long live! Long, long live!" Long live the Central Committee of the party under the leadership of Chairman Hua! Long live the great victory of the party and the cause of socialism.[37]

He learned the details of the coup later on, and again he was convinced that in China it was the army that played the main role. In other words, as Mao himself had said in 1927, "political power comes from the barrel of a gun."

In brief, this is what happened. After the death of the Great Helmsman, Jiang Qing and her supporters did everything they could to isolate Hua. They also prepared a blow against the veterans. Jiang repeatedly demanded that Deng be expelled from the party, and Wang Hongwen called for overthrowing "revisionism" that had appeared in the Central Committee. "The struggle is not yet over," he asserted. Zhang Chunqiao spoke in the same vein.[38] It is no wonder that old cadres in and outside of the army were agitated. Nor did Hua Guofeng feel secure. This laid the foundation for their cooperation.

The minister of defense, Marshal Ye Jianying, to whom Premier Zhou had bequeathed the task of finishing off the Gang of Four, played the key role in the plot. After Mao's death, he enlisted the support of two others from among the living marshals, Xu Xiangqian and Nie Rongzhen, as well as the influential veterans Li Xiannian, Chen Yun, Deng Yingchao, Wang Zhen, and the former chief of the general staff of the PLA Yang Chengwu. As early as September 12, he discussed the question of the Gang of Four with General Wang Dongxing, director of the General Office of the Central Committee and commander of Unit 8341, the guard regiment of the CC. What Wang replied is not known (he probably kept his own counsel), but the stubborn marshal did not retreat and a couple of days later he conversed with Hua Guofeng himself. Obviously, he acted very boldly. Neither Wang nor Hua belonged to the late Zhou's faction; nor were they supporters of Deng. They had no informal ties with other veterans. But Ye Jianying went for broke. "They refuse to quit," he said to Hua. "They can't wait to seize power. The Chairman is gone. It's up to you to fight them."[39]

Hua took some time to think it over and only after a week—realizing that if they delayed it would spell disaster for the party, the country, and all of them—did he ask Li Xiannian to meet with the marshal and ask when and how to solve the question of the Gang of Four.[40] Ye Jianying again visited Hua and discussed the matter in detail. In early October, the marshal again met with General Wang, without whom nothing could be done. Hearing out the marshal, who declared that the "situation is critical, and there is no other option for the party and the state than to remove the Gang of Four," Wang, finally sensing which way the wind was blowing, agreed.[41]

Ye, Hua, and Wang discussed the concrete plan to seize the Gang of Four. It was simple. Under the pretext of discussing the proofs of volume five of the *Selected Works of Mao Zedong* that was being prepared for publication, Hua would invite Wang Hongwen, Zhang Chunqiao, and Yao Wenyuan to a spurious meeting of the Politburo Standing Committee, at 8:00 p.m. on October 6 in the hall for ceremonial meetings of the CC and the government, namely,

Huairentang in Zhongnanhai. There guards from the military detachment, Unit 8341, would seize them. It was planned to arrest Jiang Qing at home (she lived nearby in the same residence in Zhongnanhai, in house number 201). It was decided as well to arrest Mao Yuanxin and several others among the most active supporters of the Gang of Four.

At the very last moment, on October 5, just in case, Ye Jianying placed the top-ranking officers loyal to him on alert.[42] The next evening the plotters implemented their plan. Twenty-nine of the most reliable guard officers were chosen and divided into four groups. One group, under the command of Wang Dongxing's deputy, General Zhang Yaoci, was to arrest Yuanxin and Jiang Qing. The three others were to take Wang Hongwen, Zhang Chunqiao, and Yao Wenyuan into custody.

About fifteen guards concealed themselves behind the massive blinds in Huairentang hall, and when Wang Hongwen, suspecting nothing and arriving first, entered the empty hall and began looking around the sides, suddenly they switched off the lights, jumped out from ambush, and tied him up. They did the same with Zhang Chunqiao, who was second to arrive, and Yao Wenyuan, who arrived late. The latter became so agitated that he collapsed in a heap on the floor. The prisoners were taken one by one to an adjacent room, where Hua Guofeng and Ye Jianying were awaiting the outcome of events. Hua told the detainees they were arrested "for crimes against the party and socialism." At the same time, General Zhang Yaoci, at the head of a group of ten or so men, took Yuanxin into custody at 8:00 p.m. and were in front of Jiang Qing's house thirty minutes later. The gallant general recalled:

> When we entered her study she was sitting on the sofa. I said to her, "Jiang Qing, I received telephonic instructions from Premier Hua Guofeng. The Central Committee of the CCP has decided to isolate you and conduct an investigation of you in connection with your present activities directed toward splitting the Central Committee. . . . You must honestly and sincerely confess to your crimes and submit to discipline. . . ." When I said this, Jiang Qing's eyes blazed with malice, but she did not budge and said not a word. . . . She did not cry out nor did she pace the floor. I finished and Jiang Qing stood up. . . . On the street a passenger car from the Ministry of Public Security was awaiting her, Jiang Qing calmly seated herself inside and was driven away.[43]

The Chairman was barely cold in his coffin when his closest comrades-in-arms, including his wife and nephew, were placed under arrest. An hour and a half later, Hua and Ye convened an emergency Politburo session at Ye Jianying's home at the outskirts of Beijing at which they informed the members of the party's highest organ of "the great victory." Marshal Ye explained that they had only done what "the Chairman had wanted to do while he was alive, but had not succeeded in doing."[44] No one expressed indignation, and even those who had hitherto supported Jiang Qing happily applauded. All of the cadres had long since been accustomed to submit to force.

They met throughout the night to determine what to do next. Meanwhile, forces loyal to Ye Jianying took control of the mass media: the Central People's Radio Station, the New China News Agency, and the editorial offices of the Beijing newspapers and magazines. Toward morning, at 4:00 a.m., wrapping up the session, Hua Guofeng nominated Ye Jianying as chairman of the CC and of the Military Commission, that is, as the new leader. But the marshal modestly declined; he would turn eighty in six months, so it was too late for him to become the chief, and moreover, as everyone knew, before his death Mao had chosen Hua as his successor. Thus, Ye offered the positions to Hua, which is how Hua Guofeng became the new Great Helmsman.[45]

At the time, Hua was by no means a reformer. A party functionary who knew little about economics, he worshiped Mao and knew how to submit to him, but in the new circumstances fealty to the deceased was insufficient, especially because Hua had come to power allied to military leaders and party veterans who were hardly eager to continue the Cultural Revolution.

Not surprisingly, right after the coup sharp contradictions arose between him and the veterans. At the center was the question of what to do about Deng. Marshal Ye, Li Xiannian, and other elders unequivocally demanded that Hua politically rehabilitate their old comrade. But Hua resisted. Two propaganda campaigns were being conducted throughout the country under his leadership: to unmask the Gang of Four and to criticize Deng Xiaoping. Hua was insufficiently bold to stop the latter campaign, which would mean betraying Mao Zedong, who had initiated it. He did not want to go down in history as the "Chinese Khrushchev." "The criticism of Deng and the struggle against the right deviationist wind to reverse correct verdicts" were begun by Chairman Mao, Hua asserted. "[This] criticism is indispensable."[46] He was wholly supported by Wang Dongxing and Wu De, the mayor of Beijing, who were close to him ideologically. They had nothing personal against Deng, but none of them could bring themselves "to betray" Mao. For example, Wang Dongxing, who was blindly devoted to Mao Zedong, said to party ideology cadres, "Deng Xiaoping, just like the Gang of Four, opposed [Chairman] Mao, his ideas, and his revolutionary line. We should not slacken criticism of

Deng while unmasking the Gang of Four. . . . Deng . . . is no good. To this day he does not understand the Cultural Revolution."[47]

Typically, in October 1976, on Hua's initiative, the Gang of Four began to be criticized not for "ultra-leftism" but for "ultra-right opportunism." On October 8, Hua Guofeng decided to build a grandiose Memorial Hall to Mao in the center of Beijing on Tiananmen Square, a mausoleum in which—contrary to the will of the deceased, who wanted to be cremated after death—his embalmed body would be placed. At the end of October, he told officials of the CC Propaganda Department, "Everything that Chairman Mao said and [even] everything to which he merely nodded in assent, we will not subject to criticism."[48]

Such an attitude toward the words and actions of Mao was important to Hua in order to legitimate his own power. The Great Helmsman had appointed Hua several months before his own death, when he (Mao) was already gravely ill. If one granted that he was fallible, especially in a state of illness, then his choice of Hua as the new leader could not be considered indisputable.

In mid-December 1976, however, Hua retreated a bit. Deng suddenly took ill and needed urgent hospitalization. He was developing inflammation of the prostate and could not manage without surgical intervention. Under pressure from Marshal Ye Jianying, who took upon himself the job of supervising the work of the doctors, as well as other veterans who called on Hua Guofeng and Wang Dongxing to show sympathy, they gave approval to a partial excision of Deng's prostate gland. The operation was performed by highly qualified physicians in the same elite army hospital where Deng's son Pufang had once been a patient. Deng was soon on the road to recovery.

Meanwhile, on December 12, Ye Jianying presented Hua Guofeng with irrefutable evidence that the Gang of Four had grossly falsified the facts concerning the events on Tiananmen back in April. He obtained the relevant documents at just the same time. This broke the logjam and opened the way to Deng's political rehabilitation. Two days later, on December 14, at the insistence of Ye Jianying and other veterans, the CC again granted Deng access to its secret documents. He was immediately given the first collection of materials, *On the Crimes of the Anti-party Group of Jiang Qing, Wang Hongwen, Zhang Chunqiao, and Yao Wenyuan*. Deng acquainted himself with the documents and said, "Enough. I will not read the second and third collections. This suffices to establish their guilt."[49]

Several days later, even though Deng was still formally under house arrest, Deng's old comrades came to see him, one after another: Deputy Premier Yu Qiuli, Marshals Xu Xiangqian and Nie Rongzhen, the son of Ye Jianying, and others. They all expressed the hope that Deng would soon be free.

As 1976 drew to a close, Deng no longer doubted that his return to the ranks would occur very soon. He greeted the New Year in the hospital with his family, full of bright hopes and expectations.

1. The house in Yaoping (Paifang) village where Deng Xiaoping was born. Photograph by Alexander V. Pantsov.

2. The room where Deng Xiaoping was born. On the wall there are pictures of his mother, neé Dan, and father, Deng Wenming. Photograph by Alexander V. Pantsov.

3. Beishan Primary School, where Deng Xiaoping studied 1910–1915. Deng's place was at the second table on the right. Photograph by Alexander V. Pantsov.

4. Deng Xiaoping in France, 1920. Image from Associated Press. LIC-00155080.

5. Sun Yat-sen University of the Toilers of China in Moscow, where Deng Xiaoping studied in 1926 and early 1927. Photograph by Alexander V. Pantsov.

6. Zhang Xiyuan, Deng Xiaoping's first wife. Moscow, 1926. Image from the Russian State Archives of Social and Political History (RGASPI).

7. Deng Xiaoping in Guangxi. Image from Associated Press. LIC-00155080.

8. Jin Weiying, Deng Xiaoping's second wife. Image from the Russian State Archives of Social and Political Hsistory (RGASPI).

9. At the 129th Division Headquarters. Deng Xiaoping and Liu Bocheng (second from right). At far left is Li Da, head of the division staff; at far right is Cai Shufan, Deng's deputy. Liaoxian County, Shanxi Province, January 1938. Image from Associated Press. LIC-00155080.

10. At the Kremlin. From right to left: Peng Zhen, head of the CCP CC United Front Department Liao Chengzhi, Deng Xiaoping, head of the Chinese Trade Unions Liu Ningyi, Nikita S. Khrushchev, Yang Shangkun, Liu Shaoqi, the PRC ambassador in the USSR Liu Xiao. Moscow, November 6, 1960. Image from the Russian State Archives of Social and Political History (RGASPI).

11. Zhu De, Zhou Enlai, Chen Yun, Liu Shaoqi, Mao Zedong, and Deng Xiaoping. Beijing, early 1962. Image from Associated Press. LIC-00155080.

12. Deng Xiaoping and his third wife, Zhuo Lin, in exile. Xinjian County, Jiangxi Province, 1972. Image from Associated Press. LIC-00155080.

13. Deng Xiaoping, Hua Guofeng, and Ye Jianying at the Third CC CCP Plenum. Beijing, December 1978. Image from Associated Press. LIC-00155080.

14. Deng Xiaoping and Hu Yaobang. Beijing, September 1981. Image from Associated Press. LIC-00155080.

15. Deng Xiaoping meets Harlem Globetrotters during his visit to the United States. At far right is Zhuo Lin. Second from right is an interpreter, Ji Chaozhu. Washington, DC, January 29, 1979. Image from Associated Press. LIC-00155080.

16. Deng Xiaoping with Mikhail S. Gorbachev and his wife Raisa. Beijing, May 16, 1989. Image from Associated Press. LIC-00155080.

17. Zhao Ziyang addresses student protesters in Tiananmen Square. Beijing, May 19, 1989. Image from Associated Press. LIC-00155080.

18. A lone protester at Chang'an Avenue near Tiananmen Square. Beijing, June 5, 1989. Image from Associated Press. LIC-00044185.

19. Deng Xiaoping's inspection tour in South China. Shenzhen, January 1992. At Deng's right are his daughters Deng Rong and Deng Nan. Image from Associated Press. LIC-00155080.

20. Deng Xiaoping lies in state following his death on February 19, 1997. Deng Nan, Zhuo Lin, Deng Rong, and Deng Lin (from left to right) are in grief. Image from Associated Press. LIC-00155080.

18

Practice as the Criterion of Truth

IN JANUARY 1977, on the first anniversary of Zhou Enlai's death, leaflets and *dazibao* appeared in Beijing demanding a reassessment of the events on Tiananmen Square and the full rehabilitation of Deng. They criticized Wang Dongxing; the mayor of Beijing, Wu De; Kang Sheng (who had died at the end of 1975); and even Mao himself. It could not be determined who was responsible.[1]

Meanwhile, in early February Deng was released from the clinic. On instructions from Ye Jianying, he and his family were settled into an elite house in a housing estate in the Western Hills on the outskirts of Beijing belonging to the Military Commission. The marshal himself lived nearby. Finally, they met again and had plenty to talk about. A new stage in the struggle for power had begun, this time against Hua Guofeng and other dogmatic Maoists.

Hua and Wang Dongxing made an important move in this struggle on February 7. On their directive, the major newspapers and the journal *Red Flag* published an editorial laying out Hua Guofeng's basic ideas, which had been conveyed to officials in the Propaganda Department of the Central Committee. "We will resolutely defend whatever political decisions were taken by Chairman Mao; we will unwaveringly follow whatever directives were issued by Chairman Mao."[2] This line came to be known as the "Two Whatevers."

After reading the article, Deng understood that he needed to act. He met with Deputy Premier Wang Zhen and expressed his profound disagreement with the line of Hua Guofeng and Wang Dongxing. "It does not accord with Marxism-Leninism and Mao Zedong Thought," Deng asserted.[3] Wang Zhen completely agreed. "If this principle [Two Whatevers] were correct, there could be no justification for my rehabilitation," Deng would later explain reasonably. "Nor could there be any for the statement that the activities of the masses at Tiananmen Square in 1976 were reasonable."[4]

The highest-ranking generals also intervened in the struggle over the Two Whatevers. One of the most important military leaders, the commander of the Guangdong Military Region and first secretary of its party committee, General Xu Shiyou, who was a close comrade-in-arms and friend of Deng, sent a critical letter to Hua Guofeng. In the name of his officers and political cadres, he demanded that Hua acknowledge the mistakes Mao had made in the Cultural Revolution and called for the rehabilitation of Liu Shaoqi, Peng Dehuai, and Lin Biao, in addition to Deng Xiaoping. This démarche posed a threat to Hua.[5]

At the March 1977 CC work conference dedicated to criticism of the Gang of Four, Chen Yun, who had just returned to politics after the death of Mao, and who along with Liu Shaoqi and Deng had supported the contract system in 1962, unexpectedly took the floor. Mincing no words, he said,

> Comrade Deng Xiaoping had nothing to do with the events on Tiananmen. I hear that several comrades on the Central Committee, considering the needs of the Chinese revolution and the Chinese Communist Party, believe that Comrade Deng Xiaoping should again be allowed to take part in the leadership work of the Central Committee. [I think] this is absolutely correct and necessary, and I wholly support it.[6]

A number of other veterans—including Wang Zhen, quoting Chairman Mao himself, who had once called Deng a "rare talent"—echoed Chen Yun. But Hua, who was terribly incensed, replied, "If, acting hastily, we let Deng come back to work, we'll fall into the trap of the class enemies.... We need to learn from [the negative example of] Khrushchev."[7]

Nevertheless, Deng's defenders made a strong impression on those at the work conference. That's all they talked about in the corridors. Hua Guofeng could not hold out. After thinking it over, he proposed a compromise. At his request, one of the oppositionists, Wang Zhen, made a self-criticism. For his part, Hua declared:

> An investigation has shown that Comrade Deng Xiaoping was not involved at all in the events on Tiananmen. We need to resolve the question of Comrade Deng Xiaoping. But we must proceed step-by-step;

there must be a process, only then at the appropriate moment can we return Comrade Deng Xiaoping to work. The point of the Politburo is the following: We will officially take the decision at the Third Plenum [of the Tenth Central Committee] of the party [scheduled for July 1977] and the Eleventh Congress [August 1977]. We will return Deng Xiaoping to work. This will be more or less correct.

Hua also said that the mass outpouring of grief on the occasion of Zhou Enlai's death that took place at Tiananmen was "justified."[8]

When he learned of this, on April 10, "after considerable thought," Deng wrote a letter to Hua Guofeng, Ye Jianying, and the CC. Bending under the pressure of the veterans, Hua had to surrender. Deng expressed gratitude to the committee for revoking the accusation that he had been involved in the events on Tiananmen. Then he declared, "I am particularly glad that Chairman Hua affirmed in his talks that the activities of the broad masses of people at Tiananmen . . . were reasonable." At the same time, while in fact criticizing the Two Whatevers, he emphasized that "from generation to generation, we should use genuine Mao Zedong Thought taken as an integral whole in guiding our Party, our army and our people so as to advance the cause of the Party and socialism in China and the cause of the international communist movement."[9] He also made an important strategic move, asking the CC to distribute this letter inside the party along with the letter of congratulations he had written to Hua Guofeng on October 10, 1976.

Hua dispatched Wang Dongxing and a certain Li Xin, who until recently had been Kang Sheng's secretary and was now faithfully serving the new leaders, to speak with Deng. They requested that Deng stop criticizing the Two Whatevers. But he firmly refused, explaining that "Comrade Mao Zedong himself said repeatedly that some of his own statements were wrong. . . . This is an important theoretical question, a question of whether or not we are adhering to historical materialism."[10] (Somewhat later, in conversation with his closest associates Wang Zhen and Deng Liqun, he would express his point of view in a laconic formula: "We should study and apply Mao Zedong Thought as an ideological system."[11])

It was difficult to dispute this. Deng himself felt he had "fired a cannonball" at the "Whateverists," acting "in defiance of Chairman Hua."[12] And he won. Four days later, on April 14, Hua Guofeng felt compelled to approve distribution of Deng's letters, although it was not until May 3 that they were brought to the attention of party and army cadres at and above the county and regimental levels, two days after publication in *People's Daily* of an important article by Hua on the occasion of the April 15 publication of volume five of the *Selected Works* of Mao Zedong.[13] Hua's article again contained an appeal to firmly follow Mao's line "of continuing the revolution under the dictatorship of the proletariat."[14]

Meanwhile, only weeks remained until Deng's complete rehabilitation, which Hua was powerless to stop. On July 1, Deng returned to Beijing, where he settled into a cozy lane not far from the famous artificial Beihai lake (Northern sea), directly behind Gugong, the imperial palace. Fifteen days later, on July 16, hale and hearty, he appeared among the top party leadership as a participant in the Third Plenum of the Tenth Central Committee.

The next day, July 17, the plenum unanimously approved the "Resolution to Restore Comrade Deng Xiaoping to His Posts," notwithstanding the fact that in his report, Hua, as before, insisted on the Two Whatevers. Deng was again a member of the Central Committee, of the Politburo and its Standing Committee, deputy chairman of the Central Committee and the Military Commission as well as deputy premier of the State Council and chief of the General Staff of the PLA.

The last period of disfavor in his life had ended.

At the plenum on July 21, he delivered a short but very significant speech. In this first post-rehabilitation speech, he formulated the central points in the new program of modernization that he had been thinking about during his long years of exile. Like Mao during the period of the struggle for new China, he called on his comrades in the party to renew the struggle against dogmatism. This time he asked not for the "sinicization" of Marxism but for a creative approach to the teachings of the Chairman himself. The bitter experience of reform in 1962 and of restoring order in 1975, both of which had led to Deng's fall, convinced him that overcoming Maoist communism and modernizing the PRC could be done only by "smashing the spiritual fetters," that is, by fully emancipating the consciousness of the cadres, and indeed of the entire nation. Therefore, skillfully cloaking himself in the authority of the deceased Leader, he reminded the assembled of Mao Zedong's old slogan, "Seek truth from facts."

This slogan, which in Deng's words contained "the quintessence of Mao Zedong Thought," Mao Zedong had composed in Yan'an for the Central Committee's party school in December 1943. Now Deng counterposed it to the Two Whatevers. Granted, he did not say who would decide what is truth, but there could be no doubt that without false modesty he presented himself, Ye Jianying, and other veterans as mentors to Hua Guofeng and other "youngsters" to take them along the correct path.[15]

At the same time, just as twenty years earlier during the "Let a Hundred Flowers Bloom, Let a Hundred Schools of Thought Contend" campaign, Deng called on all citizens of China to "fully" develop democracy: "We must create a political situation . . . in which we have 'both unity of will and personal ease of mind and liveliness,' a situation in which we can place all problems on the table for discussion and people can criticize the leading comrades when they think it necessary."[16]

He obviously calculated that an upsurge of democracy would help him overcome the Whateverists completely, unmask the Cultural Revolution, and thereby confirm his own leading position in the party. He did nothing new, acting just like Mao Zedong when Mao wanted to weaken his intraparty enemies: appeal to the masses in the name of democracy. The only cause for surprise is that Deng decided once again to appeal to the masses to express their opinions openly, despite the fact that he himself, and Mao, and other communist leaders in the past had repeatedly deceived the people with pseudo-liberal slogans. Even more puzzling is that many citizens again greeted his words enthusiastically, prepared once more to fall into the trap.

On July 30, Deng appeared in public for the first time. A big fan of soccer, he came to the stadium to watch a match between teams from the PRC and Hong Kong. Catching sight of him, the crowd gave him an ovation. Everyone in the stadium stood up and warmly welcomed the new "liberal." Deng, smiling, stood up and clapped his hands. A charismatic leader had returned to power.

On August 7, he received a foreign representative for the first time, the ambassador from North Korea. "I fell down three times and got back up three times," he noted humorously. "This year I turned 73. The laws of nature spare no one, but my mood is chipper, and I want to work a while longer."[17]

From August 12 to 18, 1977, Deng took part in the Eleventh Congress of the CCP. He was already seen as the third-ranking leader in the party and the state, after Hua Guofeng and Ye Jianying. Li Xiannian was fourth and Wang Dongxing fifth. These five men made up the new Politburo Standing Committee, which was a coalition. In it Deng could rely on Ye Jianying while Hua Guofeng would count on Wang Dongxing. Li Xiannian at the time was playing his own game, and although he apparently remained close to Deng, he was not demonstrating this openly. To some staff members of Zhongnanhai, the seat of CCP power, he seemed "slippery." One of Deng's speech writers even thought that Li "obviously disliked Deng Xiaoping."[18] But who knows for certain? The two veterans were connected not only by the struggle against the Gang of Four under the leadership of Zhou Enlai, but also by their revolutionary past. Most likely Li was simply playing it safe.

At the congress itself, in the presence of more than fifteen hundred delegates, Deng delivered the third-most-important speech, the concluding remarks. Hua Guofeng had delivered the political report, and Ye Jianying the report on changes in the Party Statutes. Deng again appealed to everyone to emancipate their consciousness and seek truth from facts. He also asserted that "deed and word must match and theory and practice must be closely integrated."[19]

His speech contrasted with Hua Guofeng's report. Although Hua declared the Cultural Revolution over—his concession to the veterans—he continued to defend it and affirmed Mao's infallibility. He said that this Cultural Revolution was only the first in a series of many cultural revolutions to follow, and that its "victorious conclusion ... does not mean the end of class struggle." In his words, "this struggle will be protracted and tortuous and at times even very sharp. Political revolutions in the nature of the Cultural Revolution will take place many times in the future." He also called for making "China a great, powerful and modern socialist country before the end of this century," but he did not retreat from Maoist models of economic development. He even demanded that a new "all-around leap forward" be achieved," vowing moreover to "eliminate the bourgeoisie and all other exploiting classes."[20] It seemed this was how Hua Guofeng intended to modernize China.

After the congress, Deng concentrated on practical efforts toward modernization. As deputy premier, he assumed leadership in the field of science and education, which he deemed a priority. On his initiative, the party began to change its relationship with the intelligentsia, which during Mao's time had been treated like "bourgeois rabble." University entrance exams, which had been suspended at the start of the Cultural Revolution, were restarted, and increased attention paid to the development of science and technology. "I play the role of chief of the rear area; my work consists of searching out talent, supporting scholars and teachers, and supplying money and equipment," Deng said.[21]

Meanwhile, the campaign to criticize the Gang of Four continued to unfold in China. The Chinese press let out all the stops. The widow and faithful pupils of Mao were even accused of being fascists and capitalist roaders and of secretly collaborating with the despicable Guomindang. Critical materials and collections of caricatures poured off the presses. Everywhere meetings and demonstrations of indignant citizens took place, covered in the press. Party journalists were in ecstasy from the "great victory." "Beijing is bubbling with joy! All China is astir with excitement!" reported correspondents from the *People's Daily.*

> On both sides of the Great Wall, on both sides of the Yangtze [Yangzi] River . . . the hearts of the people are happy, their fighting spirit soars. With Chairman Hua Kuo-feng [Guofeng] at its head, the Party Central Committee has smashed at one blow the "gang of four. . . ." We must fight the "gang of four" to the end and consolidate and expand the gains of the Cultural Revolution.[22]

But the farther the campaign went, the clearer it became just how phony it was. If Jiang Qing and those like her were guilty of anything, it was in inciting that very same Cultural Revolution to which Hua Guofeng fanatically swore his devotion. And if they were bad people, then it followed that their victims were good. But how, then, could one unmask the Gang of Four and not criticize "complete chaos under Heaven"? The very logic of the struggle against the Gang of Four knocked the props out from under Hua's feet.

Deng and Marshal Ye did not let slip the opportunity to make use of this. In December 1977 they got Hua Guofeng to appoint Hu Yaobang, the former secretary of the Communist Youth League, and a close ally of Deng, to the post of director of the CC Organization Department. Himself a victim of the Cultural Revolution, Hu quickly focused on restoring the honorable names of all the victims of Red Guard terror.

This diminutive and frail-looking party official, even slightly shorter than Deng, was actually exceptionally energetic and efficient. He had turned sixty-two two weeks before his appointment, so from the perspective of Deng, who was seventy-four, and Ye Jianying, who was eighty-one, Hu was quite young. The son of a poor peasant family in Hunan, he had not finished middle school, but he was passionate about learning and reading. He became one of the most educated cadres in the CCP.

Hu joined the party in 1933 in Ruijin, where he worked in a bureau of the Communist Youth League. He took part in the Long March and held a series of posts in the General Political Administration of the Red Army. In late 1937 and early 1938, he attended lectures at the Anti-Japanese University in Yan'an. There he befriended Zhuo Lin, Deng's future wife, who was studying in a cadre training school. During the civil war of the 1940s, he did political work in Nie Rongzhen's and Peng Dehuai's army, and from the founding of the PRC until 1952 he worked under Deng Xiaoping's leadership as secretary of the North Sichuan CCP Committee. Deng's native village fell within his purview at the time. It was Deng who facilitated his transfer to Beijing as secretary of the Central Committee of the New Democratic Youth League, the name of the Communist Youth League after 1949. In 1957, Hu was chosen as first secretary of what again was called the Communist Youth League of China. But in December 1966, like Deng, he was repressed and went through the circles of hell, was tortured at "criticism and struggle meetings," and underwent "reeducation" at a May 7 School in Henan province. He was rehabilitated in March 1973, after which he became one of the most devoted supporters of Deng Xiaoping's restoration of order. Deng sent him to work in the party committee of the PRC Academy of Sciences to reorganize the scholarly cadres, which he did very well. Then in 1976, in tandem with Deng's new fall from power, Hu was cashiered and criticized. Only in March 1977, under new circumstances, was he returned to the corridors of power with the help of Ye Jianying.[23]

Initially he was appointed vice president of the Higher Party School of the CC, which had only just reopened after the many years of the Cultural Revolution. The president of the school was Hua Guofeng himself, and the first vice president was Wang Dongxing, but these were just formalities and Hu actually directed the institution.[24] He immediately launched an open struggle against the Two Whatevers. Toward this end, in July 1977 Hu began to publish a pointed discussion journal, Lilun dongtai (Theoretical Trends), which popularized Deng's ideas about emancipating consciousness from the fetters of Maoist communism.

People who knew Hu justly referred to him as "one of the last intellectual idealists in the Party."[25] In October 1977, at his urging, People's Daily published an article that for the first time raised the question of reexamining the cases of all the victims of the Cultural Revolution.[26]

Now Hu was heading the CC Organization Department, so he was in charge of cadre questions. As early as January 1978, he convened an important conference on the question of rehabilitating the leaders of twenty-six ministries and departments.[27] Repudiation of the Cultural Revolution had begun.

The scale of the task was staggering. In the shortest time possible, direct or indirect accusations against tens of millions of people had to be reviewed. "All false accusations and unjust sentences, irrespective of who is involved and at what level they were carried out, must be overturned," Hu declared.[28] He even formed a special group to review those cases in which Mao had personally pronounced the verdicts. He was truly an exceptional person.

Deng wholly supported Hu Yaobang, even though his protégé soon also began to reopen cases of "rightist elements" condemned in 1957 during the course of a repressive campaign led by Deng Xiaoping himself. One must give one's due to Deng; this time he was able to acknowledge his transgressions. At the same time, Deng reestablished a Political Research Office under the State Council. He assembled a group of major Marxist-Leninist theoreticians, under the leadership of Hu Qiaomu, to work on the theory of modernization. In late 1975 and 1976, when Deng was being criticized, all of these persons had been subjected to pressure from the leftists, and most of them, including Hu Qiaomu, had capitulated, even taking part in the persecution of their former chief. But Deng forgave them just as Zhou Enlai had once forgiven him.[29] There was no point in nursing grievances; one had to wage the struggle against the Whateverists.

The spring of 1978 brought new successes. In early March, Deng got one more post, albeit an honorary one. He became chair of the National Committee of the Chinese People's Political Consultative Conference (CPPCC),[30] the formal organization of the united front between the Communist party and eight tiny democratic parties that had consultative functions in the PRC. At the first session of the Fifth National People's Congress (NPC), taking place simultaneously, he was confirmed as deputy premier, the first among thirteen.

On March 5, under the chairmanship of Deng, the NPC adopted a new Constitution for the PRC, which, despite numerous changes, like the former Constitution of 1975 asserted, "Citizens enjoy freedom of speech, correspondence, the press, assembly, association, procession, demonstration and the freedom to strike, and have the right to 'speak out freely, air their views fully, hold great debates and write big-character posters'."[31] Ye Jianying, who delivered a report on the changes in the Constitution, drew particular attention to the fact that the new leaders of the PRC were preserving these rights, emphasizing that "we must energetically revive and carry forward our democratic tradition and fight against any encroachment on the people's democratic life or violations of the rights of citizens."[32]

The delegates chose Marshal Ye as chair of the NPC Standing Committee. Marshal Xu Xiangqian became the new minister of defense. Hua Guofeng, however, retained his positions, so Deng's struggle against him continued.

In March and April, at the All-China Conferences on Science and Education, Deng intensified his criticism of dogmatism. On May 10 the journal *Theoretical Trends* published a sharply polemical article under the title "Practice Is the Sole Criterion of Truth." Developing Deng's ideas, it said that every theory must be verified through practice. Hu Yaobang, who had edited the article written by a young Nanjing University philosophy professor and two staff persons from the Higher Party School, affirmed that the cult of reason had replaced the cult of faith in Chinese society.

Despite resistance from the conservatives, the article, which was reprinted in the central press over the next two days, provoked a very pointed discussion, not only in the party but in society, which did not quiet down all summer and fall. Hua Guofeng himself did not take part in it, but Wang Dongxing, who was overseeing ideology and propaganda in the CCP, was infuriated: "A party publication should reflect the party in character. . . . We did not read the article 'Practice Is the Sole Criterion of Truth' prior to its publication. . . . In essence it is aimed against Mao Zedong Thought. From what Central Committee did it issue? Our task is to defend and protect Mao Zedong Thought. We must conduct an investigation."[33]

Under pressure from Wang, *Red Flag*, the theoretical journal of the CC, refused to reprint the article. But Ye Jianying and Deng Xiaoping liked the article even though they also had not known about it beforehand. Both Ye and Deng stood foursquare in favor of its ideas. The marshal even proposed to the members of the Politburo Standing Committee that a conference on theory be convened to discuss the issues raised by the article, the text of which he suggested should be distributed throughout the country before the conference.[34] Deng, who asserted that there could be no retreat regarding theoretical matters, supported Ye's idea. "Giving in will lead to the loss of principle," he explained.[35]

On June 2, Deng spoke openly in defense of the article at a PLA conference on political work, coming down hard on Wang Dongxing. Although he did not refer to him by name, everyone knew what was afoot. "There are . . . comrades," Deng declared,

> who talk about Mao Zedong Thought every day, but who often forget, abandon or even oppose Comrade Mao's fundamental Marxist viewpoint and his method of seeking truth from facts, of always proceeding from reality and of integrating theory with practice. Some people even go further: they maintain that those who persist in seeking truth from facts, proceeding from reality and of integrating theory with practice are guilty of a heinous crime. . . . The principle of seeking truth from facts is the point of departure, the fundamental point, in Mao Zedong Thought.[36]

Deng bolstered his conclusion with an enormous number of excerpts and citations from Mao.

Following this many other veterans as well as the overwhelming majority of leading cadres from the central CCP apparatus, the State Council, local organs of power, and PLA generals came out in support of the article.[37] By mid-autumn it was clear that Deng, Ye Jianying, and Hu Yaobang had succeeded in "rocking the boat." The cadres began to overcome the ideology of Maoist communism. By now many were prepared to consciously adopt the policy proposed by Zhou and Deng of implementing the long-term program of the Four Modernizations: agriculture, industry, defense, and science and technology.

Deng struck while the iron was hot. In the spring through autumn of 1978, he was no longer speaking only of emancipating consciousness; he also began introducing important additions to the program of modernization, focusing attention on the need to combine restoration of order with expansion of the rights of enterprises in the domain of finance, foreign trade, and hiring and firing of labor. This signified a transition to economic accounting, strengthening the role of administrative-economic leaders and weakening control over them by party committees. It also meant adopting a policy of openness toward the outside world, including economic and technical exchanges abroad; borrowing foreign techniques, technology, and economic management experience; and attracting foreign capital to establish joint enterprises. "The world is developing," he said, "therefore, if we do not succeed in advancing technologically, to say nothing of any sort of overtaking others, we will simply be unable to catch up to others and will really be forced to lag behind."[38]

He considered it impossible "to lock our doors, refuse to use our brains and remain forever backward," but he was certainly not thinking of dismantling socialism, convinced as he was that "we must preserve . . . the socialist order . . . this is unshakable. We will not permit the appearance of a new bourgeoisie."[39]

Such modernization was somewhat reminiscent of the policy of "Self-strengthening" conducted in 1861–1894 by the Qing dynasty. They, too, recognizing China's backwardness, tried to modernize the country by borrowing foreign technology and pursuing rapid industrialization. They, too, did not change the existing socioeconomic system.

By this time serious changes had also occurred in Hua Guofeng's worldview. This uncharismatic man was not cut out to be a leader; he lacked experience in leading the party and the nation and therefore easily fell under the influence of more powerful personalities. Campaigning for the Two Whatevers, he followed the lead of Wang Dongxing, but under Marshal

Ye's influence he rehabilitated Deng. On economic issues, by early 1978 he had begun to rely on Li Xiannian and other leading economists, such as Yu Qiuli and Gu Mu, who had worked with Zhou Enlai in the past.[40] They finally convinced him of the need to reexamine the most odious of the Maoist directives.

In February 1978, at the first session of the Fifth National People's Congress, Hua delivered a revolutionary report that differed greatly from his speech at the Eleventh Congress. He warmly supported the program of the Four Modernizations—in essence, lining up with Deng Xiaoping. He affirmed the importance of economic reform, expanding trade with the West, borrowing foreign techniques and technology, and even increasing material work incentives. Yet he continued to insist strongly on a new Great Leap, although by now he wanted to secure it by attracting Western and Japanese credits and importing foreign equipment. Hua spoke of constructing 120 large industrial enterprises by 1985 and increasing steel production threefold, from 20 to 60 million tons, and production of oil by three and a half times, from 100 to 350 million tons. Although this would require colossal capital investments, no less than during the thirty preceding years of the PRC, he was confident of success.[41]

As time passed, Hua was increasingly convinced of the need for rapid modernization. His first foreign trip abroad, in the latter half of August 1978, made an enormous impression on him. (This was only the third trip abroad of a Chinese leader in the entire history of the PRC, after Mao's two trips to the USSR in 1949–50 and 1957.) Hua visited Romania, Yugoslavia, and Iran. He was especially struck by Yugoslavia, where foreign currency was freely convertible, Western techniques and technology had been successfully assimilated, and enterprises even worked jointly with Western investors. Yet Yugoslavia remained a socialist country and maintained its complete independence. The people lived much better than in China, where rationing was still in effect.[42]

Following Hua, other party leaders recognized the need for reform. Many of them also made their first trips abroad in 1978, expanding their understanding of China's place in the world. That year, thirteen officials of the rank of deputy premier went abroad as well as several hundred other high-ranking cadres. Mao had not allowed them to travel, but now their eyes were opened. "We thought capitalist countries were backward and decadent," one of them recalled. "When we left our country and took a look, we realized things were completely different." In October 1978, Deng himself traveled to Japan for a week and spent most of his time analyzing the possibilities for expanding economic ties with that country. "The more we see [of the world], the more we realize how backward we are," he summed up the results of his trips.[43]

In Hua's words, all the Politburo members, including Deng, then began talking about accelerated modernization, especially since the state security organs regularly provided reports about the flight of tens of thousands of young peasants and workers from Guangdong province to neighboring Hong Kong and Macao. People were fleeing because "Hong Kong and Macao were wealthy and the PRC was poor," Hua recalled. "And we decided to change the situation and make the PRC wealthy."[44]

In July to September 1978, after initial reports from high-ranking cadres on their trips abroad, the State Council convened a special theoretical conference on modernization at which Li Xiannian and other leaders affirmed the need to attract foreign capital to the PRC and borrow Western technology, equipment, and management expertise. The conference also discussed a proposal to establish an export processing zone on the border with Hong Kong, where Chinese workers could assimilate Western techniques and technology, through manufacturing products for overseas markets.[45] In mid-September Deng, who was following the work of the conference, noted that "economics must submit to the action of economic laws."[46]

On November 6, Hua convened a meeting of the Politburo, which decided to shift the center of gravity of all party work to modernization as of January 1979. Four days later, the CC held a work conference to discuss economic problems and draft resolutions for the forthcoming Third Plenum of the Eleventh Central Committee, scheduled for late December. The meeting was supposed to determine how to effect this transformation, and discuss four documents: "Resolution on Several Questions of Accelerating the Development of Agriculture," "An Experimental Model of Statutes Concerning the Work of Agricultural People's Communes," the economic plan for 1979–80, and the text of a speech by Li Xiannian on the State Council's theoretical conference on modernization.[47]

Deng was not present at the Politburo meeting, having departed on November 5 for a nine-day visit to Thailand, Malaysia, and Singapore. Of course, he knew of the forthcoming decisions, which obviously reflected his views. Moreover, it was he who suggested that the Politburo shift the center of gravity of party work to modernization as of January 1979.[48]

Deng and his supporters prepared seriously for the work conference, which was attended by more than two-hundred leading party officials. Among the latter only 63 percent were members or candidate members of the Eleventh Central Committee; most of the others were veterans recently rehabilitated thanks to Hu Yaobang. This shaped the character of the conference, stretching over thirty-six days until December 15. The atmosphere at the conference was "lively."[49] From the outset the forum took a different direction from what Hua Guofeng had intended, discussing political rather than economic problems after deciding at the beginning to break with the past, that is, to correct leftist errors committed by Mao Zedong himself.

Naturally, it was the veterans who touched off the row. On November 11, Tan Zhenlin, Deng's friend and former deputy in the CC Secretariat, spoke in favor of reassessing the events on Tiananmen Square. He was supported by seven others, including the old generals Chen Zaidao and Lü Zhengcao.[50] At once Marshal Ye Jianying met with Hua Guofeng and advised him to heed what was going on at the conference; otherwise he might lose his post.[51]

On November 12, Chen Yun, evidently completely recovered from the "illness" from which he had "suffered" ever since Mao attacked him for supporting the family contract system in 1962, dashed into the fray. He asserted that prior to discussing how to shift the center of gravity to modernization, the CC first had to resolve six issues of party history. Four of these concerned rehabilitation of well-known party figures who had been repressed not only during the Cultural Revolution but earlier, including Peng Dehuai. Chen Yun's fifth question concerned the events on Tiananmen Square, which he called "a great mass movement"; his sixth was an assessment of the activity of the adviser to the Cultural Revolution Group, Kang Sheng, whom Chen Yun accused of committing "monstrous crimes."[52]

The veterans' speeches were like an exploding bomb. Hua Guofeng, Wang Dongxing, and the other Whateverists were subjected to a withering attack, the agenda was discarded, and one speaker after another talked about the need to emancipate consciousness, and to provide an objective assessment of the Cultural Revolution and other events in the history of the CCP in order to correct leftist errors.

Soon things heated up not only at the conference but outside as well. The day after Chen Yun's speech, the new mayor of Beijing, Lin Hujia, convened an enlarged session of the capital's municipal party committee at which, following the revered Chen, and on his own responsibility, without the consent of the Politburo, he asserted that the demonstration on Tiananmen had been "revolutionary."[53] On November 14, the municipal newspaper *Beijing Daily* reported this, and on November 15 the news was disseminated by *People's Daily*, the Xinhua News Agency, and *Enlightenment Daily*. Hua and Wang Dongxing had lost control over events.

On the evening of November 14, when Deng returned from Southeast Asia, Marshal Ye briefed him and said it was time for Deng to become the head of the party and the nation. He proposed that Hua Guofeng remain the formal chairman of the CC, the Military Commission, and premier of the State Council, but that Deng, relying on collective leadership, become the de facto leader.[54] Marshal Ye opposed dismissing Hua from power entirely, saying he could not betray Mao, who before his death had supposedly entrusted Ye with "supporting" his successor. More likely, however, he was dissembling, and Mao had actually said nothing of the sort. At least, Mao Yuanxin, who had been present at Mao's last meeting with Ye Jianying, denied this had happened. The marshal seemed to be maneuvering to enhance his own power. By strengthening Deng while preserving Hua, he was positioning himself as an arbiter, a kind of higher authority in the party and the state to whom both Hua and Deng would be indebted.

Deng assented, realizing he had to accept this compromise. Afterward Ye Jianying informed Hua, who also had to agree. Frightened by the possibility of a split and his forcible removal from power, this weak man, lacking personal connections either with the leading generals or with the central and provincial party leadership, capitulated. On November 25, he spoke again at the conference, accepting all the proposals of Chen Yun and the other veterans. Thus the demonstrations on Tiananmen were officially recognized as "revolutionary," and all of the participants in the "disorders" of 1976 were rehabilitated.[55] To be sure, by then ten of them had already been executed. This occurred in 1977, after Mao's death and the arrest of the Gang of Four.[56]

The former mayor of Beijing, Wu De, then made a self-criticism. Wang Dongxing alone was unwilling to make any concessions, so he was openly criticized by participants in the forum.[57]

The question of Wang was exacerbated by a new outburst of popular dissatisfaction in the latter half of November 1978, provoked by his diehard Whateverist position. Two months before the conference, Wang, who oversaw questions of ideology and propaganda, banned distribution of the entire first issue of the journal of the Communist Youth League, *Zhongguo qingnian* (*Chinese Youth*), on grounds that the editors had been disrespectful to the memory of Mao Zedong. They had not reprinted newly discovered verses of the Great Helmsman, not begun the issue with what was then an obligatory Mao quotation, and in one article even called for an end to the "new superstition," deification of the deceased chairman. The chairman's former bodyguard could not let this pass. Despite the prohibition, on November 19, five days after publication in *Beijing Daily* of the reassessment of the events on Tiananmen, the editors of *Chinese Youth* posted the entire contents of the first issue on one of the city walls of Beijing, two steps from the intersection of Chang'an Avenue and Xidan Street. This was a lively place, close to downtown, and therefore hundreds and thousands of Beijingers and visitors could read the new *dazibao*.

The step taken by the editors of *Chinese Youth* led to spontaneous development of a new democratic movement, a kind of "wall newspaper rebellion," as a contemporary described it.[58] The internet did not exist then, and the eleven-and-a-half-foot-high, two-hundred-foot-long gray brick wall became a genuine "Democracy Wall." That's what the people called it. Soon people began to post *dazibao*, sharing their innermost thoughts. Beijing was crowded with people from all over the country hoping for rehabilitation after the long years of terror. The CC Organization Department addressed cases involving cadres and had neither time nor energy to deal with ordinary citizens. So people who had come to the capital seeking justice began posting their stories, attacking the Cultural Revolution. Soon other *dazibao* appeared on the wall, demanding the dismissal of Hua and other Whateverists and supporting Deng.[59] The pro-Deng leaflets grew particularly popular after it became known that on November 26, meeting with the chairman of the Japanese Democratic Socialist Party, Deng declared, "Our Constitution permits the writing of *dazibao*. We do not have the right to refute or criticize the masses for supporting democracy and posting *dazibao*. We need to allow the masses to express their dissatisfaction if it has accumulated. Not all of the comments are well-thought out, but we cannot demand perfection. And there is nothing to be afraid of."[60]

Encouraged by Deng's statement, people began posting even more critical *dazibao*, calling for further liberalization. A *dazibao* written by a twenty-eight-year-old electrician at the Beijing Zoo, Wei Jingsheng, produced a real furor. "The Fifth Modernization: Democracy" was posted on the night of December 5 by one of his friends. This was truly an unusual poster, a real political essay that, in surprising fashion, reflected the views of many Western critics of totalitarian communism, such as Bruno Rizzi and Milovan Djilas, with whose works the young man from Beijing could simply not have been familiar. Wei spoke out against the Gang of Four and the Whateverists and as well subjected the entire ruling bureaucratic class in China to a devastating critique, demanding reform of the entire political system of the PRC, even comparing the CCP dictatorship to Hitler's totalitarianism. "We want to be the masters of our own destiny," he wrote. "We do not want to serve as mere tools of dictators with personal ambitions for carrying out modernization. . .

. Do not be fooled again by dictators who talk of 'stability and unity.' Fascist totalitarianism can bring us nothing but disaster.... In achieving modernization, the Chinese people must first put democracy into practice and modernize China's social system."[61]

How the young Chinese electrician had been able to write such a *dazibao* is unknown, but Wei Jingsheng instantly became the hero of Democracy Wall.

Many participants in the CC work conference visited the Xidan crossroads several times, interested in acquainting themselves with the will of the people, and Marshal Ye Jianying and Hu Yaobang, like Deng, spoke out in support of Democracy Wall notwithstanding Wei Jingsheng's *dazibao*. Ye Jianying, for example, told conference participants, "The Third Plenum of the party [will become] the model for intra-party democracy while the Xidan Democracy Wall is the model of popular democracy."[62] It seemed that an era of openness had arrived in the country, and influential forces in the party along with the liberal intelligentsia and youth began to advance the cause of the democratic transformation of China.

In response to pressure from inside and outside the party, Wang Dongxing decided to retire. On December 13, he presented a written statement:

> At the conference comrades have made many good criticisms of my mistakes.... I really did commit errors in word and deed during the Cultural Revolution and after the downfall of the "Gang of Four"....
> I am deeply convinced that the posts I hold exceed my ability, and I am unworthy of these posts. For this, I sincerely request that the Party Central Committee should remove me from these posts.[63]

The work conference handed the case of Wang Dongxing to be taken up for consideration by the Third Plenum of the Eleventh Central Committee.

Thus, the CC work conference in November and December 1978 turned out to be the point at which Deng became the generally recognized leader of the Chinese communist movement. Although he did not occupy the highest rung in the formal hierarchy, no one doubted his preeminence in all affairs of the party, the army, and the state.

On December 13, Deng delivered the concluding speech. Hu Qiaomu had prepared the text several weeks prior to the conference, but after returning from Southeast Asia on November 14 and being apprised of what had transpired, Deng decided to change it. He turned to Hu Yaobang, who assembled a group of speech writers. Deng instructed them to emphasize democracy. "In order to develop the economy, we must have democratic elections, democratic management, and democratic oversight. . . . The reality of democracy must be stabilized in legal form."[64] Everyone was enthusiastic and composed a text that Deng ultimately approved.

The participants in the conference listened to him with bated breath. This was his "speech from the throne." "Today, I mainly want to discuss one question," he said:

> Namely, how to emancipate our minds, use our heads, seek truth from facts and unite as one in looking to the future. . . . In political life within the Party and among the people we must use democratic means and not resort to coercion or attack. The rights of citizens, Party members and Party committee members are respectively stipulated by the Constitution of the People's Republic and the Constitution [Statutes] of the Communist Party. . . . The masses should be encouraged to offer criticisms.

He even declared, "There is nothing to worry about even if a few malcontents take advantage of democracy to make trouble. . . . One thing a revolutionary party does need to worry about is its inability to hear the voice of the people. The thing to be feared most is silence."

He called for expansion of democracy in the economic sphere, again speaking against excessive centralism, in favor of enterprise and labor activity and restoration of the principle of material incentives. He even declared that from the perspective of economic policy it was acceptable for some regions and enterprise, and some workers and peasants, to take the lead in increasing their standard of living (that is, to become rich) before others. This would enable "the whole national economy to advance wave upon wave." We need to apply ourselves "to three subjects: economics, science and technology, and management," he noted.

Moreover, Deng called for continuing to resolve problems left over from the past so that "every wrong should be righted." He emphasized the need to assess both Mao Zedong and the Cultural Revolution "scientifically and in historical perspective," noting that the "great contributions of Comrade Mao in the course of long revolutionary struggles will never fade."[65]

Understandably, for all the revolutionary character of the times, Deng, like Hua, did not want to be known as "the Chinese Khrushchev." Shortly after the conference, Deng Nan asked him directly, "Isn't it true that you're afraid of being pegged like Khrushchev?" But Deng only smiled and said nothing in reply to his daughter.[66]

His speech made a strong impression on the participants in the conference. It was his speech, rather than Hua's at the opening of the forum, that was viewed as the basic document. It was decided to transmit his speech to the members of the Third Plenum, scheduled for December 18–22, which had already in purely formal terms adopted the course set forth by Deng. The plenum transmitted the decisions of the work conference, a closed meeting, to the Chinese and world publics.

Thus, in December 1978 the CCP shifted its center of gravity from propagandizing class struggle and organizing political campaigns to economic construction, thereby abandoning the revolution under the dictatorship of the proletariat.

The Third Plenum dismissed the most odious Whateverist, Wang Dongxing, from leadership of ideological-propaganda work and added such firm supporters of Deng as Chen Yun, Hu Yaobang, Zhou Enlai's widow Deng Yingchao, and Wang Zhen to the Politburo as well as Chen Yun to the Politburo Standing Committee. It established the Central Discipline Inspection Commission to conduct a purge of those party members who, from the perspective of Deng and his supporters, "did not want to abandon factionalism," that is, who did not accept the CC's new course. Chen Yun was appointed first secretary, Deng Yingchao second secretary, and Hu Yaobang third. The secretariat of the commission also included Huang Kecheng, the former chief of the PLA General Staff who had suffered on account of his support for Peng Dehuai in 1959.

Most importantly, the plenum confirmed Deng Xiaoping's de facto supreme power over the party and the state. China entered a new period of development, under the banners of economic reform and democracy.

The changes in the PRC evoked heightened interest in countries everywhere. Naturally, Deng Xiaoping himself attracted the greatest attention. This diminutive but strikingly strong man, who had sprung out like a genie from a bottle after his triple disgrace, inspired millions of people to hope that China would finally embark on a civilized path. The popular American journalist Robert D. Novak, who had secured a two-hour interview with Deng at the end of November 1978, informed the whole world that "China's dominant figure today . . . heartily endorses free speech."[67] On January 1, 1979, *Time* magazine proclaimed Deng Xiaoping Man of the Year. A depiction of Deng appeared on the front cover of the magazine against a traditional Chinese backdrop of mountains, forests, and clouds. Deng appeared calm, with a slightly ironic look on his face. But at the same time inscrutable: a kind of Chinese Sphinx whose riddle the world had yet to decipher.

The Cardinal Principles

IN LATE DECEMBER 1978, Deng spoke at a memorial ceremony where the ashes of Peng Dehuai were reinterred in the cemetery for revolutionary heroes. Without referring to the conflict between Marshal Peng and Mao Zedong, he noted that "Comrade P'eng Te-huai [Peng Dehuai] . . . was brave. . . . He was known for his honesty and integrity. He was concerned for the people, had no thought for himself, [and] defied difficulties."[1] Deng was apparently apologizing for having taken part in the persecution of Peng in 1959.

Soon after that, an important Politburo meeting was held at which Wang Dongxing was removed from most of his remaining posts, including director of the CC General Office. The new director was Yao Yilin, who had spent his whole life on economic and financial matters and was two years younger than Hu Yaobang. At the same time, Hu Yaobang was given the newly restored position of CC secretary. His deputies were Hu Qiaomu, Deng's chief speech writer, and the very same Yao Yilin. Hu Yaobang concurrently headed the daily work of the CC as well as the Propaganda Department. Deng's old friend Song Renqiong replaced Hu Yaobang as director of the Organization Department.[2]

Meanwhile, the movement for democracy gathered force and, in January 1979, spread from Beijing to other large cities, where Democracy Walls also appeared. At the same time, autonomous organizations not controlled by the party or the Communist Youth League formed. Activists began publishing handwritten journals in hundreds of copies. A group calling itself the Enlightenment Society posted a *dazibao* criticizing Mao Zedong right on one of the walls of his mausoleum. But the epicenter of political life remained Democracy Wall at Xidan, where people from all over the country streamed to "inhale the air of democracy in Beijing."[3]

The liberal changes in China inevitably impressed U.S. president Jimmy Carter, who had proclaimed himself a defender of human rights throughout the world. State Department China expert J. Stapleton Roy informed Carter that Deng "not only permitted but inspired the wall poster campaign denouncing hard-liners in the government in order to solidify control over the bureaucracy."[4] From Deng's interview with the conservative columnist Robert Novak, Carter knew that the "wise and dynamic" Deng was hastening to create "a rational economic and political system" and establish an alliance with the United States against Moscow. He also read Deng's call for stronger U.S.-China ties and a united front against Moscow in Deng's interview with the American journalists Hedley Donovan and Marsh Clark prepared for *Time* magazine.[5] The latter consideration was significant. The president viewed the USSR as Enemy Number One. All of this facilitated Sino-American rapprochement.

By mid-December 1978, the United States and China were ready to establish diplomatic relations. Both Carter and Deng strived to accelerate the process. Normalization of relations with the world's largest industrialized country could bring China palpable benefits with regard to achieving the Four Modernizations.[6] During several rounds of top-secret negotiations that took place in Beijing from late May 1978, the two sides finally reached a mutual understanding with regard to the Taiwan question. The Americans agreed to annul the 1954 Mutual Defense Treaty with Taiwan, withdraw all their military personnel from Taiwan, and sever diplomatic relations with the Guomindang regime. The Chinese grudgingly tolerated the continued supply of American weapons to Taiwan and did not contest an American statement regarding the need to resolve the problem of Taiwan by peaceful means, although they considered this "interference in the domestic affairs of the PRC."[7]

On December 15, 1978 (December 16 in Beijing), Carter and Hua Guofeng presented a joint communiqué regarding mutual recognition and establishment of diplomatic relations as of January 1, 1979.

This was a great surprise for the whole world, especially Taiwan. Leery of the Taiwan lobby in Congress, Carter had not informed Chiang Ching-kuo, president of the Republic of China and son of Chiang Kai-shek (who had died in 1975), of the negotiations with the communists. Just seven hours prior to the announcement of the communiqué, when it was 2:00 a.m. in Taipei, the U.S. ambassador aroused the flabbergasted Chiang Ching-kuo from his bed and conveyed the news. Chiang cried.[8] Had Deng known this, he would have been very happy.

Normalization of relations with the United States enabled Deng to fulfill his longstanding wish to visit the United States. Back in May 1978, when greeting Carter's National Security Adviser Zbigniew Brzezinski, Deng had said that he wanted to see America. Brzezinski responded immediately, inviting Deng to visit his home in Washington. Deng, smiling, agreed.[9] In December an official invitation from the president arrived and on January 28, 1979, along with Zhuo Lin and several assistants Deng set off across the ocean. "His visit vividly symbolizes the two principal thrusts of Chinese policy under his leadership—modernization and opposition to the Soviet Union," Secretary of State Cyrus Vance wrote to the president.[10]

Deng was met at Andrews Air Force Base by Vice President Walter Mondale and Secretary Vance, who were radiating cordiality. They escorted him to Blair House, the luxurious residence on Pennsylvania Avenue renowned for its splendid interior furnishings, elegant furniture, expensive carpets, and marvelous paintings. Everything Deng saw impressed him: the broad, straight avenues, the tall and massive buildings, the Capitol, the Mall, and the Washington Monument thrusting up into the sky, reminiscent of the Monument to the People's Heroes on Tiananmen Square, only much taller.

Several hours after their arrival, their "old friend" Brzezinski came to escort them to the small reception he had arranged for them in his home. In addition to the hosts and their three teenage children and the Deng couple, only Vance, Foreign Minister Huang Hua, and a few others were present at what was essentially a private dinner.[11] The following day there began a whirlwind of official meetings, trips, and speeches continuing until Deng's departure from the United States on February 5. There were many exclamations, smiles, and even tears of emotion. Deng shook the hands of politicians, businessmen, and athletes, kissed children who sang songs for him in Chinese, visited the Senate, the House of Representatives, scientific centers, including the Houston Space Center, the Ford and Boeing plants, a Texas rodeo, and, of course, the White House. The president was ecstatic. "I was favorably impressed with Deng," he wrote in his diary on January 29. "He's small, tough, intelligent, frank, courageous, personal, self-assured, friendly, and it's a pleasure to negotiate with him."[12] Deng, too, it seems, was satisfied.[13]

Agreements were signed on scientific-technological and cultural cooperation, student exchanges, and extending most-favored-nation trade status to the PRC. Deng was even presented an honorary doctor of laws degree from Temple University in Philadelphia and a ten-gallon cowboy hat during a rodeo in Simonton, Texas. As Vance later said, "Deng's visit was an extravaganza, and understandably so."[14]

Thus Deng was able to depict his U.S. visit as the start of an historic rapprochement between the two powers. In reality, of course, the PRC and the United States remained irreconcilable antagonists, but it was vitally important for Deng at the time to demonstrate their "alliance" in order to resolve serious geopolitical issues connected with his struggle against "Soviet hegemonism." The first arena was in Southeast Asia, where the USSR, in opposition to the PRC, was allied to Vietnam, which by then had turned from a one-time devoted friend of China into a fervent adversary.

Soon after his arrival, Deng had spoken about the USSR and Vietnam in Brzezinski's home, seething with indignation when the conversation touched upon the Soviets. Responding to a question of what China would do if attacked by the USSR, he replied that the PRC could administer a crushing blow in response, since it had sufficient nuclear weapons to reduce the Bratsk Dam, Novosibirsk, and possibly even Moscow itself to powder and ashes. Ironically, the conversation occurred while the guests were sipping Russian vodka, a present from Soviet Ambassador Anatolii Dobrynin to Brzezinski. Probably that is why Deng was so flushed in the face. On parting, he solemnly informed Brzezinski that he wanted to speak to the president and his most trusted aides about Vietnam in utmost confidence.[15]

He repeated this request to Carter himself the next day during their White House meeting. There in the Oval Office, Deng met Carter, Vice President Mondale, Vance, and Brzezinski—and in a somber but firm voice informed them of his decision to attack Vietnam.[16] Deep inside, the Americans probably felt happy that their long-time foe would now be punished by the very same China that had formerly stood on the side of North Vietnam, sending arms and even troops to Vietnam.[17] Now the communists were not only fighting each other, but also discussing their war plans with the imperialists.

On the surface, however, Carter remained calm and even tried to dissuade Deng. Although not expressing overt opposition, he voiced concern that world opinion and many members of the U.S. Congress would brand the PRC an aggressor. The next morning, meeting tête-à-tête with Deng, with only the interpreter Ji Chaozhu present, he even read him a special handwritten statement repeating his warning to Deng that the armed conflict he was undertaking "would cause serious concern in the United States concerning the general character of China and the future peaceful settlement of the Taiwan Issue." Carter also worried about a possible forceful Soviet reaction to a Chinese-Vietnamese conflict. Overall, he said that the invasion "will be a serious mistake."[18]

But Deng, smoking one cigarette after another, held firm to his decision, explaining that if China did not teach Vietnam a short-term lesson, then the Soviet Union, having consolidated its position in Vietnam, would strive to encircle the PRC by invading neighboring Afghanistan.[19] (He said this just eleven months prior to the Soviet intervention.) Carter made no reply, but Deng, having said his piece, calmed down at once.[20] It seemed he had come to Washington precisely to inform the Americans of the imminent war in Vietnam.

How did it happen that Deng had now formed what was essentially an alliance with America, not only against the "degenerate" USSR but also against the "heroic" Vietnamese, who only recently, at the end of April 1975, had been unified under the communists after a sixteen-year-long civil war aggravated by American intervention? Did he really fear that the Soviet Union would encircle the PRC with military bases along its entire border, from the north, the south, and the west, and then strike a nuclear blow? Possibly so. After all, border conflicts between China and the USSR had occurred in the very recent past. Probably, he also could not forgive the Vietnamese leaders, who, until the late 1960s, had maneuvered between the USSR and the PRC and then gradually gone over to the side of the Soviet "hegemonists" mainly because during the Cultural Revolution the Chinese, unlike the Soviets, could not provide them with substantial aid.

The situation with Vietnam was particularly annoying. In the early 1970s, feeling that they were losing Vietnam, Mao, Zhou, and Deng—all of whom were deeply offended—had switched over to another partner in Indochina, the Cambodian communists (Khmer Rouge), who did not demand the enormous investments that Vietnam required.[21] Soon after the Khmer Rouge came to power in April 1975, Cambodian relations with Vietnam also quickly deteriorated. After the end of the war in Indochina, the Vietnamese easily brought Laos under their influence and tried their utmost to draw Cambodia (at that timed named Kampuchea) into their orbit. The Cambodian leadership, however, reacted irritably to Vietnamese regional hegemonism, especially because in 1977 Vietnam had made two naval bases available to the Soviet Union, an action that infuriated both the Chinese and the Cambodians. Armed clashes occurred along the Sino-Vietnamese and Vietnamese-Cambodian borders, and territorial disputes flared. On December 31, 1977, the Khmer Rouge severed diplomatic relations with Vietnam.

In 1978, the situation continued to deteriorate. In the spring of 1978, the Vietnamese communists began large-scale expropriation of the property of many local Chinese as part of socialist reforms. As soon as the reforms began, many of the roughly 1.5 million Chinese emigrants living in South Vietnam, most of whom were small businesspeople, sought to flee to their historic homeland. In just the six weeks from the beginning of April to the middle of May 1978, more than 50,000 refugees crossed over from Vietnam into China, where they were greeted as martyrs by the leaders of the PRC, who stirred up a patriotic campaign in defense of their "innocently suffering" fellow countrymen. By July 1978, the number of Chinese refugees from Vietnam had reached 170,000, most of whom had fled not even from the south, but from the north of Vietnam.[22]

By the autumn it was clear that Vietnam intended to seize Cambodia and was only awaiting the start of the dry season to send in its troops. In November, it concluded a Treaty of Friendship and Cooperation with the Soviet Union as a means of protecting itself in the event of a backlash from China.

The Chinese leadership was outraged. Not all of its members, however, considered it wise to attack Vietnam, even if it invaded Cambodia. The actions of former friends certainly evoked bitter feelings, but to launch a full-scale war against a one-time fraternal country seemed excessive. Moreover, the Chinese army and its equipment were deficient. The PLA, though much larger, was significantly inferior to the Vietnamese army in both weaponry and battlefield experience.[23] There were also concerns about the possible reaction from the USSR. Would the Soviet leader, Leonid Brezhnev, suddenly decide to help Vietnam by raining rockets onto North China?

Deng's old mentor, Marshal Ye Jianying, openly opposed the war. He did not believe there was a danger of encirclement of China by the Soviet Union with the aid of Vietnam. Rather he thought it necessary first to strengthen the northern border of the PRC against a possible attack on the part of the USSR.[24] But Deng ignored him; he craved a war with Vietnam. It seemed as if his personal fate would depend on whether or not China attacked Vietnam. And not by chance: some observers in China believed that Deng, who was then the chief of the General Staff of the PLA, insisted on war and then directed the entire operation only so he could establish his own total control over the military in order to gain unlimited power.[25]

From September 1978—that is, from the moment war preparations began—Deng assumed de facto supreme command of the army. He directed planning for the operation and appointed his energetic friend General Xu Shiyou as the direct executor of the plans. By December 21, the redeployment of troops had been completed. According to various estimates, from 330,000 to 600,000 Chinese officers and troops were concentrated along the eight-hundred-mile border with Vietnam.[26] At the same time, PLA troops on the border with the Soviet Union were placed on full battle alert.

Meanwhile, with the USSR backing them, on December 25, 1978, the armed forces of Vietnam invaded Kampuchea, and by January 7, 1979, they had captured the capital, Phnom Penh. The Khmer Rouge regime fell, replaced by pro-Vietnamese forces that established a new government. But retreating to the jungles, the Khmer Rouge fought on until 1989.[27]

The capture of Phnom Penh meant a loss of face for China. Vietnam and the USSR turned out to be stronger than Kampuchea and China. Now an attack against Vietnam became a "matter of honor" for Deng.

But he had to secure diplomatic support for his war. In September he had visited Burma, Nepal, and North Korea, and in November Thailand, Malaysia, and Singapore. However, only the Thai leaders—seriously concerned that following Kampuchea they would be the next to face a Vietnamese attack—supported him. Yet, the heads of the other countries did not voice any strong objections, which satisfied Deng. Now Deng was informing the Americans, explaining to Carter that he needed their "moral support."[28] That Carter did not try too hard to dissuade him was very important for Deng. In essence, Carter gave implied consent. That, at least, is how it looked from the outside,[29] and this was what Deng needed.[30] By starting the war right after his visit to the United States, Deng might convince Brezhnev that he was acting in concert with the Americans, thereby reducing the temptation for Moscow to get involved in the conflict.

Deng was right. When, on Deng's order, two hundred thousand Chinese troops crossed the Vietnamese border at dawn on February 17, 1979, Brezhnev was really flummoxed. He even phoned Carter on the hot line to ascertain whether the Chinese were acting with tacit American approval. Carter tried to persuade him otherwise. Then, via Soviet Ambassador Dobrynin, Carter informed Brezhnev that he had warned Deng against such action, but the Soviet leader did not believe him.[31] In the end, Brezhnev did not respond with force.

The war continued for twenty-nine days, basically in the Sino-Vietnamese border region. Chinese troops were unable to penetrate more than twenty miles. On March 16, Deng withdrew his forces, leaving behind ruined cities and burnt villages.[32] According to various estimates some twenty-five thousand Chinese soldiers and ten thousand Vietnamese, both servicemen and peaceful inhabitants, died in the conflict.[33] Deng was unable to teach Vietnam a lesson; China's losses were two and half times those of the Vietnamese. This was no well-aimed blow.

But it was a great domestic victory for Deng. During the war Deng asserted himself as the authentic, authoritative leader of the party and the country. Marshal Ye was weakened and Hua Guofeng had long since ceased to be a threat. Only Chen Yun remained a strong figure within the leadership, and Deng was always able to reach agreement with him. Although Chen was jealous of him, he was essentially satisfied with the role of second-ranking person in the party hierarchy. Moreover, Chen wholly supported Deng in his struggle for power against Hua Guofeng.

From the end of 1978, Deng even began to rely on the respected party elder Chen for advice on economic problems, an area in which he himself was not well versed. To be sure, he was experienced at disentangling the knots of political intrigue, but he lacked the patience to work out economic problems methodically. "I am a layman in the field of economics," he said. "I know very little indeed."[34] Chen, on the contrary, loved to work on economic matters and was rightly considered the main economic specialist among party veterans.

Born on June 13, 1905, Chen was orphaned at the age of four and joined the CCP in 1925. He began to study economics seriously, albeit exclusively from the works of Marx, Engels, Lenin, and Stalin, in Moscow at the International Lenin School in 1935–36.[35] After the founding of the PRC he focused on the economics of socialism in practice.[36] After returning to the political arena following a prolonged "political illness," in early December 1978, at a CC work conference Chen made a series of proposals on matters of economic development. He unequivocally condemned Hua Guofeng's line of a new Great Leap Forward, instead calling for "moving forward gradually." He said the greatest attention should be paid to development of agriculture, light industry, housing construction, and tourism, and only after that to heavy industry.[37]

Striving to discredit Hua Guofeng, the main proponent of a new Great Leap, Deng quickly reoriented himself and supported Chen, abandoning his own prior views on accelerated modernization. He probably acted this way for political reasons.[38] Starting in January 1979, Deng, following Chen, began criticizing the erroneous economic policies of the Politburo and the State Council, which, as before, were formally headed by Hua Guofeng. "Comrade Chen Yun believes that . . . it is possible to reduce the indicators and curtail the number of construction projects. This is very important," he declared.[39]

In March 1979, Chen Yun, by now one of the deputy chairs of the CC, launched an all-out assault against Hua's economic policies. On March 21, at a Politburo meeting, Chen lambasted "comrades" who "returning from travel abroad, spread the news . . . that one must only invest a few hundred millions, and we will achieve acceleration." These "comrades," Chen Yun declared, obviously hinting at Hua, do not "take into account the actual [features] of our own country." But in China at present "in many places the problem of providing food for the people has not yet been solved," and masses of peasants teeter on the edge of starvation. This was right; people in almost 1.5 million of the five million or so production brigades received around 50 yuan, that is, US$30, a year, and some even less than that, and in another 2.5 million production brigades from 50 to 100 yuan. Overall, more than two hundred and fifty million peasants suffered from hunger.[40] Chen Yun called for balancing the basic branches of the economy so that in the field of heavy industry there would be "slow forward progress," while priority was given to agriculture. Only thus would it be possible to increase economic productivity and achieve a gradual upsurge in the entire economy.[41] Chen echoed Deng's speech at the close of the CC work conference when he spoke about "wave upon wave" advance.

Chen Yun even began to contemplate an economic system that combined socialist planning with reliance on the market to satisfy the basic needs of the people. He considered developing both the planned economy as well as market regulation "during the entire period of socialism." He lamented that "the share of the nonplan economy in agriculture is still too small."[42] No one at the time had dared to make such statements. On March 23, the Politburo approved the policy of "readjustment" according to the formula proposed by Chen Yun: "In order to unite Marxism with the practice of the Chinese revolution, we have to place the branches of the economy in the following order: agriculture in first place, then light industry and only after heavy industry."[43] Under Chen's leadership a new special Financial-Economic Commission was established within the State Council to work out and implement the innovative policy.[44]

Deng spoke at the same meeting of the Politburo and wholly supported the policy of readjustment. Although he said nothing about developing the market economy, he emphasized that China needed "modernization with Chinese characteristics." "By the end of the century we will be able more or less to achieve the level that advanced countries were at in the 1970s. The average incomes of the people cannot be raised drastically," he affirmed.[45] From then he would speak about this rather often, explaining to partisans of accelerated modernization, "We must take one step back in order to take two steps forward."[46]

It is striking how quickly Deng changed his point of view. Starting in 1975, he had consistently advocated that China should catch up with the advanced countries by the end of the twentieth century. But only a skillful politician could act like that. Deng may have been wrong in the past, but now Hua's authority was disintegrating.

Finally Deng was able to complete the reorganization of party leadership. Now it was entirely up to him how much longer Hua would remain within the structure of power. He could now also resolve another problem, that of the Democracy Wall in the center of Beijing; he no longer needed any liberalism. Now that he himself was in power, he no longer intended to allow any criticism.

On March 30, 1979, Deng delivered an important speech at a special party conference on questions of theory that was taking place in Beijing under the aegis of the Propaganda Department of the CC and the Chinese Academy of Social Sciences.

This forum was convened in January in response to a proposal by Marshal Ye to discuss the article "Practice Is the Sole Criterion of Truth."[47] In the initial stage of the forum, from January 18 to February 15, the tone was set by the intraparty liberals grouped around Hu Yaobang. At the outset, Hu called on all 160 participants "to emancipate consciousness . . . freely express one's thoughts, fully restore and develop intraparty democracy . . . distinguish truth from lies and to strengthen the unity of all ideologists and propagandists."[48] There was nothing that smacked of dissent in his words. Deng himself was then affirming democracy.

Many participants began to raise sharp questions: about genuine democracy, about the nature of transition to socialism in backward China, about the personal responsibility of Mao for the Great Leap and the Cultural Revolution, about the liquidation of the cult of personality, and so forth. Some even asserted that Mao was a worse criminal than Jiang Qing, saying one should speak not of the Gang of Four but of the Gang of Five. Under pressure from the liberals, one of the well-known conservatives, Wu Lengxi, was even forced to engage in self-criticism twice.[49] Other conservatives tried to make themselves inconspicuous.

When Deng returned from his trip to the United States on February 8, Hu Qiaomu, a generally moderate conservative, complained about the "arbitrariness" of the liberals. He himself had strongly opposed the Two Whatevers, but excessive liberalization sickened him. After listening attentively, Deng suddenly, for the first time since his return to power, expressed disapproval of Hu Yaobang's actions. He compared the democratic movement inside and outside the party with the "right opportunist threat" of 1957, and he even called it "more dangerous."[50] He asked Hu Qiaomu to prepare a text of his speech to deliver at the conference.

After the war in Vietnam wound down, Deng returned to the question of liberalism. On March 16, reporting on the results of the war at a CCP CC special meeting, Deng suddenly launched into a tirade against those who believed in freedom of speech. "We are developing democracy," he asserted. "But new problems have arisen for us. . . . In our articles we must defend the great banner of Chairman Mao, and no one should blacken it in any way whatsoever. . . . The main thing now is stability. . . . And the question of how to evaluate the Cultural Revolution can be deferred for now."[51]

Deng concluded it was time to tighten the screws. On March 27, he summoned Hu Yaobang and Hu Qiaomu and, countenancing no objections, declared, "We must firmly uphold the Four Cardinal Principles: defend the socialist path, the dictatorship of the proletariat, the leadership of the party, and Marxism-Leninism and Mao Zedong Thought."[52]

This was his theme in his important March 30 speech, which occurred two days after the start of the second phase of the conference (March 28 to April 3).[53] The majority of the veterans, including Chen Yun and Li Xiannian, enthusiastically supported him. Only Marshal Ye disliked the speech, but he had already begun his departure from the political stage.[54] The liberals were disappointed, of course, especially since Deng subjected them to devastating criticism: "A handful of people in society at large are spreading ideas which are against them [the Four Cardinal Principles]. . . . Facts show that they can do great damage to our cause and that they have already done so . . . we must . . . struggle unremittingly against currents of thoughts which throw doubts on the four cardinal principles."

He also explained what sort of democracy Chinese society needed: "It can only be socialist democracy, people's democracy, and not bourgeois democracy, individualist democracy. People's democracy is inseparable from dictatorship over the enemy and from centralism based on democracy."[55]

The brief period of Chinese openness was coming to an end. It was incompatible with "people's democracy." At the end of the conference, Hu Yaobang was compelled to agree with Deng. "Comrade Xiaoping's important speech in the name of the Central Committee facilitated a rather successful conclusion to the work of our conference," he said.[56]

The political situation had already begun to change after Deng's report of March 16, in which he called for curtailing democracy. On March 29, one day prior to Deng's important speech at the conference, the authorities in Beijing issued a directive prohibiting dissemination of "slogans, posters, books, magazines, photographs, and other materials that oppose socialism, the dictatorship of the proletariat, the leadership of the Communist Party, and Marxism-Leninism and Mao Zedong Thought," that is, the Four Cardinal Principles.[57] Neither the municipal authorities nor Deng was pleased with the fact that from the outset of the Vietnam war, antiwar broadsheets expressing sympathy for the Vietnamese and condemning the "reactionary clique" of CCP leaders had been posted on Democracy Wall.[58] Several hours after the pronouncement of the order, the police arrested Wei Jingsheng. The pretext was his last *dazibao*, titled, "Do We Want Democracy or a New Dictatorship?" It was directed personally against Deng Xiaoping. In it Wei angrily criticized Deng's report on the results of the war in Vietnam, calling Deng a "fascist dictator" and comparing him to Mao Zedong and the Gang of Four.[59] According to various sources, Deng personally gave the order for his arrest.[60]

In October 1979, Wei was sentenced to fifteen years' imprisonment. Neither his family members nor his lawyer was allowed into the courtroom.[61] No fewer than one hundred persons were taken into custody.[62] Deng flatly accused the dissidents of plotting sabotage and forging clandestine links with the Guomindang secret service and political forces in Taiwan and abroad.[63] Democracy Wall was stripped of *dazibao*, and it was forbidden to post anything there.

Obviously, this latest provocation, for which Deng was directly responsible, was in the best traditions of Chairman Mao. Chinese intellectuals again were shamelessly and cynically manipulated in the service of high politics. In the context of a democratic upsurge, Hua Guofeng and Wang Dongxing were overthrown, and Deng was greeted in the United States as almost a prophet of freedom in mainland China. Carter tacitly supported his aggression in Vietnam, and now the voice of the people could be silenced.

Deng achieved everything he wanted without regard for the many victims left strewn along his path to power. For him the end always justified the means—during the revolutionary years, the land reform, the struggle for socialism, and in the post-Mao struggle to establish his own authority. People were important only as instruments for achieving his goals.

He even sacrificed his family members if, from his perspective, the cause required it. From the very beginning, he devoted himself entirely to the political struggle. He abandoned his father and mother, never returned to the native places of his youth, and lived only for the interests of the organization. Only by immersing himself in his work did he feel himself a fish in water; he cracked jokes, he mixed freely with others, he easily struck up friendships. He gave the impression of being a "regular guy." But at home, worn out, he sat silently for hours on end. He was a tough and strong man, a brilliant politician and organizer; however, concepts such as humanism and morality were not in his lexicon. Even Ezra F. Vogel, a writer sympathetic to Deng, was forced to acknowledge, "Deng treated people like useful tools. . . . He was a comrade for the overall cause, not a friend whose loyalty went beyond organizational needs."[64]

After consolidating his power, Deng could celebrate victory. He did this in the best traditions of the Great Helmsman, who, it will be recalled, loved to startle his subordinates. Deng did not swim across any rivers, but in mid-July 1979, despite his seventy-five years, he climbed Huangshan, the famous mountain in Anhui province that from antiquity had been considered "the most beautiful under Heaven." He did not ascend to the topmost peak (6,150 feet), but he did make it to nearly 5,000 feet above sea level. He did so along difficult trails cut into the cliffs and rickety wooden bridges stretched along the mountain, with breathtaking views in every direction. Those accompanying him begged Deng to be careful, but he just waved them away. "You're still trying to instruct me! I have more experience than you. During the Long March many people hurried and fell by the wayside, but the farther I went the stronger I became." He spent three days on the mountain, looking around and seeing everything he could, and enjoying the picturesque views. After descending, he said to Wan Li, the first secretary of the Anhui Provincial Party Committee, "The lesson of Huangshan is that I am fully up to the standards."[65]

His ascent, needless to say, had enormous significance. He really had reached the summit and was still healthy and full of energy. This is what he wanted to tell the world.

But there were still many tasks ahead of him. He needed to continue the reforms, remove Hua and his supporters from all their positions in the structure of power, and sum up the experience of the history of the party since it had taken power in 1949. Without this, Deng's ascent to power would not be historically grounded. Like Mao back in 1945, he had to settle accounts with the past in order to secure his place in the future.

20

"Let Some People Get Rich First"

ASCENDING TO THE summit, Deng, like any authoritarian leader, immediately began to enlarge and strengthen his own bureaucratic elite. In other words, he began to plant everywhere people on whom he could rely. He always remembered the Chairman's thought, which Mao had borrowed from Stalin: "Cadres are a decisive factor, once the political line is determined."[1]

Arriving in Qingdao, a PLA naval base, on July 29, 1979 he gave a speech on the proper selection and assignment of cadres at a navy party committee reception. "Taking the country as a whole and considering the major issues, we can say that the debate over the thesis that practice—as opposed to the 'two whatevers'—is the sole criterion for testing truth has pretty definitely settled the question of what our ideological line should be," he said. "The Party's ideological line and political line have been established. What question remains to be settled, then? The extremely important question of organizational line." He called on all veterans who endorsed the idea of modernization "to select healthy young people to take over from us," right away, "while we are still around, because it will be hard for others to do so after we've left the scene." "We'll be ashamed to go to face Marx, if we fail to solve this problem well," he added. In this connection, for the first time since his agreement with Marshal Ye regarding dividing functions with Hua, he again severely criticized the Whateverists, whom he even compared to Lin Biao and the Gang of Four.[2] Evidently, Deng intended to deliver a knockout blow to his already defeated opponent.

Deng himself intended to retire in 1985, and he had already chosen Hu Yaobang as his successor, although Hu was too liberal from his perspective. Nevertheless, he entrusted Hu with the daily management of party-political affairs. Preferring to work at home, he only rarely visited Zhongnanhai.

Deng planned to divide management of the sphere of economics, Chen Yun's bailiwick, between two other "younger leaders," hopefully with Elder Chen's blessing. The two Deng had selected were sixty-three-year-old Wan Li, the secretary of the Anhui Party Committee, and the sixty-year-old secretary of the Sichuan Party Committee, Zhao Ziyang. Both had distinguished themselves as active proponents of modernization as far back as 1975. In 1977, they had begun to introduce experimental policies in their provinces.

Wan Li was the first to excel. This tall and stately native of Shandong was sharp and hot-tempered. As early as November 1977, struck by the incredible poverty of the Anhui peasants, he openly proposed returning to the family contract system that had been practiced in the early 1960s, at least in the poorest locales. By that time, poor peasants in Guzhen County of Anhui Province had already begun to experiment with family farming in the spring of 1977.[3] It will be recalled that under such a contract peasants rented land from the production brigade, after which they handed over either the entire harvest to the state in exchange for payment in workdays, or the larger part, keeping the remainder for themselves, although without the right to sell it on the market. They were not permitted to decide for themselves what to plant; instead, they received instructions from the brigade leadership, which supplied them with tools, fertilizer, and seeds. Obviously, collective property in land did not suffer at all from this, but the material incentives of the peasants increased.

At the time, however, Wan's idea attracted almost no support. Many in the party remembered the cold shower Mao had poured over supporters of the family contract system in July 1962, and although a campaign of "emancipation of consciousness" was taking place in the CCP, people did not want to be known as out-and-out capitalist roaders. Even at the famous CC work conference in November–December 1978, the family contract system was condemned all around. Wan Li recalls:

> At the CC work conference in November 1978, during discussion of the draft document ["On Some Questions Concerning the Acceleration of Agricultural Development"] I expressed disagreement. The draft referred to the "Two Nevers" [never divide the land for individual farming and never fix production assignments to household]. . . . I did not agree . . . [but] the leaders in charge of preparing this document did not accept my point of view.[4]

The work conference presented a very moderate document for consideration by the Third Plenum, and the plenum approved it as a draft along with

"Regulations on the Work in the Rural People's Communes (Draft for Trial Use)." Both documents spoke only of strengthening financial autonomy at the level of the production brigade and at most permitting team contracts. In January 1979, the documents were distributed to the localities "for discussion and implementation on a trial basis."[5]

Then at the end of December 1978, a real peasant rebellion took place in Xiaogang village in Fengyang county, Anhui. To call it a rebellion may be a bit of an exaggeration, but here is what happened. One night representatives of eighteen households (twenty-one persons), who had gathered in a hay shed, decided to divide up the land of their production team among themselves on a completely individual basis. This contract implied that they were no longer willing to work for payment in workdays. The standard method of payment on people's communes was calculated in workdays, that is, how many days different categories of workers had toiled on the collective fields, a measure that was then converted into payments in grain. Instead the peasants of Xiaogang proposed actually renting out the land that was the property of the brigade. The peasants decided to retain the excess production for themselves and did not exclude the possibility of selling on the market. They decided to determine themselves what crops were most advantageous to grow beyond the plan. They drafted a brief document that they not only signed but sealed, with personal seals or fingers marked with red mastic.

They could simply stand it no longer. During all the years of communist power, the inhabitants of this poor village had been unable to break loose from their poverty. During the years of the Great Famine (1958–1962), sixty-seven of the 120 persons then living in Xiaogang had died, and those who survived continued to balance on the edge of starvation. This was the condition of everyone living in Fengyang County, the poorest in all of East China for centuries. People survived largely by begging in the nearby cities.[6] Now they had taken extreme measures.

Fearing retribution, they swore to keep everything secret. But in the spring their "revisionist" action was revealed, and the brigade commander of the Xiaogang villagers was called on the carpet. To his surprise, the secretary of the county party committee did not rage at him. Evidently, the secretary could "see the clearing," which, in the language of party bureaucrats meant that he sensed the mood of his superiors. He knew that his direct boss, Wan Li, was pushing hard for the family contract system. Wan had so informed all county secretaries back in late 1977. Therefore the secretary permitted the brigade commander to adopt the contract system for the next three years.[7] Learning of the Xiaogang peasants' initiative, Wan Li visited their village in

June 1979, and encouraged by the prospects of a good harvest, he supported the peasants.[8]

He also approved the actions of members of one of the brigades in Feixi County. There production tasks were assigned by family two months earlier than in Xiaogang, in October 1978. But they went along the well-trodden path that had been approved in the early 1960s, which Wan Li, who was less courageous than the Xiaogang peasants, had himself fought for. The peasants simply divided the land of the brigade among themselves, decided to cultivate it individually, and delivered the entire harvest to the state in return for payment in workdays. Wan Li also approved the experiment in Guzhen County.[9]

Afterward Wan visited Chen Yun and informed him of the experiments. Chen apparently voted yes with both hands, but only privately. Deng, likewise, decided not to approve the family contract system openly, although he also let Wan know that he was acting on his responsibility and at his own risk.[10] Incidentally, Deng, who had long known Wan Li from when they worked together in the southwest region, had followed Wan's struggle over the family contract system from the beginning of 1978. At that time he had discussed the measures Wan Li was undertaking with Sichuan party secretary Zhao Ziyang, to whom he said in confidence, "We have to enlarge somewhat the paths [of development] of agriculture, emancipating consciousness. If the issue can't be solved in the old way, we need to solve it in a new way.... If [the current] system of property is not working, there's nothing to be afraid of! In both industry and agriculture—everywhere, we need to act this way."[11]

Meanwhile, encouraged by Chen Yun and Deng, Wan Li began to persuade the officials of the State Council to make changes in the draft document on agriculture adopted by the Third Plenum. At the very least, he wanted them to delete the "Two Nevers" from the resolution "On Some Questions Concerning the Acceleration of Agricultural Development." It was supposed to be adopted officially at the Fourth Plenum, but the bureaucrats in Beijing balked. The hot-headed Wan flew into a rage and called the deputy minister of agriculture a pig. "You have plenty to eat. The peasants are thin, because they do not have enough to eat. How can you tell the peasants they can't find a way to have enough to eat?"[12]

In September 1979, on the eve of the Fourth Plenum, he spoke with Hu Yaobang. Hu promised to help, but he was unable to do much, and perhaps did not want to. Like Deng and Chen, he was still cautious about these questions. The document approved by the plenum contained a compromise formula offered by Zhao Ziyang.[13] Instead of the second categorical "never" was written a softer "should not": "One must never divide the land for individual farming. Likewise one should not fix production assignments to households with the exception of certain villages engaged in the production of especially important sideline products or located in distant mountain regions with poor means of communication."[14]

By this time, in early 1979, the State Council, by decision of the Politburo, had raised the purchase price of agricultural commodities on the plan by nearly 25 percent and by 50 percent on above-plan commodities.[15] Taxes were lowered and subsidies and credits increased, which also served to stimulate the development of agriculture. Overall grain production in 1979 rose by more than 27 million tons compared to 1978, an 8 percent increase.[16] But in Xiaogang, hitherto the poorest of the poor, during the same period the family contract system produced a sixfold increase in grain production and the peasants average income grew eighteenfold, from 22 yuan to 400. For the first time since collectivization was implemented, Xiaogang peasants were able to deliver 15,000 tons of grain to the state.[17]

The superiority of the family contract system became widely evident. In different forms, it gradually began to spread through the efforts of peasants and local cadres. It produced good results everywhere. But for some time Deng and his supporters in Beijing remained cautious, not wanting to hand Hua and his supporters a weapon to strike them. Thus, throughout 1979 and even into early 1980, the radical reform of the countryside proceeded from below. In 1992 Deng recalled, "It was the peasants who invented the household contract responsibility system with remuneration linked to output. Many of the good ideas in rural reform came from people at the grass roots."[18]

In the spring of 1979, Zhao Ziyang, first secretary of the Sichuan Party Committee, actively supported the reforms. Starting in 1977, he had experimented at the level of team contracts, also permitting commune members to develop their household plots and sell on the market, but later he approved division of collective land and assignment of tasks by household. By 1980, Zhao too had achieved significant success in grain production.[19] Thereafter, a jingle was composed in China:

Yao chi mi, zhao Wan Li
Yao chi liang, Zhao Ziyang.

(If you want to eat rice, Wan Li is nice,
If you want to eat wheat, Ziyang is neat.)

Zhao, an energetic, businesslike, and bold organizer, just like Wan Li, was unafraid of taking on responsibilities. Deng had known him since the spring of 1945, when Zhao, then secretary of a local party committee in the Hebei-Shandong-Henan border region, had carried out the New Democratic land reform under his leadership.

By this time the tall young man, the son of a prosperous peasant family from Henan province who bore a striking resemblance to the youthful Zhou Enlai, had traveled a hard path. He had joined the Communist Youth League in 1932 at the age of thirteen, and in 1937, when the Japanese attacked China, he abandoned his high school studies. In the following year, he joined the CCP. On the party's recommendation, he went to study in the party school of the CCP Northern Bureau, located in the Taihang Mountains, territory controlled by Liu Bocheng and Deng. After studying there for a year, he worked for the party and was active in the anti-Japanese war. Deng took an immediate liking to him, and their acquaintanceship flourished. Zhao continued to serve under Deng until the founding of the PRC. Then Mao transferred him to Guangdong, under the command of Ye Jianying, who was in charge of CCP work in South China. Zhao also made a favorable impression on the future marshal. There in Guangdong, Zhao was able to make quite a career for himself despite the fact that after the Great Leap, like Liu Shaoqi, Chen Yun, and Deng, he had temporarily supported the family contract, which in Guangdong was called the "production responsibility system." In 1965, Mao appointed him first secretary of the Guangdong Party Committee. Zhao did not remain in this position very long, however. In September 1966, the Red Guards began to criticize him, and in January 1967 they kidnapped him and held him under arrest on the campus of Sun Yat-sen University in Canton. Zhao remained a prisoner until April 1971, undergoing humiliation and insults just like Deng, Hu Yaobang, and other victims of the Cultural Revolution. In 1971, Mao transferred him to party work in Inner Mongolia but a year later returned him to Guangdong as secretary of the revolutionary committee. In 1973 Zhao became a member of the Central Committee and in 1974 was reappointed first secretary of the Guangdong Party Committee. At the end of 1975, with Mao's blessing, Zhou and Deng sent him to Sichuan, one of the most densely populated provinces and one that required particularly close attention. There Zhao achieved success in many fields, not just agriculture. Impressing people as a skilled organizer, he was able to curtail the rate of provincial population growth to 0.67 percent—the lowest in the country—by restricting births. This helped reduce pressure on the food supply. At the First Plenum of the Eleventh Central Committee in August 1977, Zhao was elected a candidate member of the Politburo.

In January 1979, following Chen Yun and Deng, Zhao began to speak up about the need for "readjustment," pointing to "serious imbalances" in the economy. He insisted on accelerating reforms in industry, demanding that entrepreneurs be given greater autonomy, including permission for them to retain a share of the profits, and almost, like respected Elder Chen, discussing the utility of combining plan and market. No less ardently than Deng, he stood for an "open door" policy, that is, China's full integration into the world economic system.[20]

Deng intended that Zhao become premier with Wan Li as his deputy in charge of reforming agriculture. More than 80 percent of the workforce was employed in agriculture, the main sector of the economy. On September 28, 1979, at the Fourth Plenum of the Eleventh Central Committee, he made Zhao a full member of the Politburo, and seven months later, in April 1980, Zhao and Wan Li were co-opted into the State Council as deputies to Hua Guofeng. Soon the willful Zhao was acting as the de facto premier. The demoralized Hua submitted.

Like Hu Yaobang, both Zhao and Wan Li were men of liberal views, but within limits. They did not oppose the Four Cardinal Principles. Hu Yaobang, too, remained a communist, and his ideal at best was socialism with a human face. At the same time, conservatives joined Deng's team: among them were Hu Qiaomu and another of Deng's speech writers, the vice president of the Chinese Academy of Social Sciences, Deng Liqun. Although not objecting to reform, these people tried in every way to preserve the purity of Marxism-Leninism. They were also relatively young.

After assembling his team, Deng maintained a balance between the factions no less skillfully than Mao. Yet he did not abandon a strategic course of reform and opening to the outside world, although he supported Chen Yun regarding the pace of growth. "We loudly proclaim that we will achieve the Four Modernizations by the end of this century. Then we will turn down the heat and begin speaking about Chinese-style modernization, that is, to lower expectations," he declared, continuing at the same time to promote the idea of attracting foreign capital and expanding overseas exchanges.[21] He also spoke in favor of effectively combining plan and market throughout the period of socialism. "It is wrong to assert that . . . there is only a capitalist market economy," he told foreign guests from the United States and Canada. "Why can't it be developed under socialism? A market economy is not a synonym for capitalism. The planned economy is our foundation and exists in combination with the market, however, this is a socialist market economy."[22] His guests might have been surprised, but they made no objections.

The development of a market economy in 1979 touched not only the countryside but also the cities. By the early 1980s small entrepreneurs were active
in all large and small Chinese cities. By this time, masses of youths who had
been sent down to the people's communes during the Cultural Revolution
literally flooded into the cities from the countryside. In 1978–79, the urban
population grew by six and a half million people, and in the early 1980s by
another twenty million. What could be done with this labor force if state
enterprises were unable to provide jobs for all of them? Small-scale urban
businesses had to be permitted—individual household enterprises operating
on the market. So that no one in the party could object to such a zigzag,
Deng's supporters dug out of the fourth volume of Marx's *Capital* the story
of a capitalist who exploited eight workers. "If Marx spoke precisely of eight,
it means that the hiring of seven would not make one a capitalist," they logically concluded. "And if the boss himself will be working, then what sort of
capitalism could this possibly be?" Deng liked this "scholarly" argument, so
on his initiative the leadership of the CC and the State Council permitted
individual household enterprises with no more than seven workers. There
was an immediate explosion in the sphere of daily service enterprises: small
private restaurants, shoe repair and tailor shops, barber shops, and others like
it began to grow like wild mushrooms. The problem of employment was eased
for a time.[23]

Deng soon cloaked this new approach in a characteristically Chinese
form. He said that by the end of the twentieth century China could not
yet become a *fuli guojia* (a country with universal prosperity), but it could
achieve a state of *xiaokang* (moderate prosperity or relatively well-off). He
saw this as a "special kind of Chinese modernization." "Our concept of the
Four Modernizations does not coincide with yours," he explained to Prime
Minister Ohira of Japan. "It is the concept of '*xiaokang zhi jia*' [that is, a
modestly prosperous family]." Even if the PRC dashes forward, he explained,
by the end of the twentieth century the per capita income "will still be low
in comparison with the West" and it "will still remain backward as before."[24]
In propounding Chinese-style modernization, namely *xiaokang*, Deng acted
wisely. He grounded Chinese backward socialism in a system "of traditional
national values" because an idea of *xiaokang* has roots in Confucius's teaching. That enabled him to attract many overseas fellow countrymen (*huaqiao*)
to contribute to China's industrialization.

It was precisely such persons, along with former merchants and industrialists who had been dispossessed of their wealth in the 1950s, whom Deng
proposed to be allowed to establish enterprises in China. Only later did he

explain that attracting capital from *huaqiao* would pose less of a threat to Chinese socialism, since "the overwhelming majority of our countrymen abroad are motivated by concern for the well-being of their socialist father-land and the desire to cooperate in its development, and this is quite unlike foreign investments in the literal meaning of this word." Yet he favored creat-ing joint-stock companies with real foreigners, stressing that "utilizing for-eign capital is a very important policy that, I think, we should continue to follow."[25]

On July 15, 1979, the CC and the State Council even adopted a resolu-tion to establish special regions or zones on an experimental basis in the cit-ies of Shenzhen (on the border with Hong Kong), Zhuhai (next to Macao), Shantou in Guangdong province, and Xiamen in Fujian province. These four zones were established to attract investments from overseas Chinese as well as foreigners who wished to construct new industrial enterprises in China or to invest in existing Chinese enterprises.[26] The foreign or joint enterprises were initially restricted to producing products only for export and had to operate according to the laws of the market. Generally speaking, the special zones were established as market enclaves in the still socialist Chinese economy. They were separated from the rest of the country by well-guarded borders that were no less secure than the PRC itself was from other countries.[27]

Deng was a fervent supporter of these new special regions, and it was he who suggested the name, which was reminiscent of the communist-run Shaanxi-Gansu-Ningxia Special Region during the anti-Japanese war. The analogy was deeply flawed, however, as the wartime regions and the special zones had little in common, if anything. The special zones were officially inaugurated on August 26, 1979, and in May 1980, on Chen Yun's sugges-tion, they were rechristened SEZ, that is, Special *Economic* Zones. Chen was worried that some persons might wonder whether the Chinese communists intended to introduce special *political* arrangements in several places in the country. Deng did not object to the change in nomenclature as he, too, did not support political changes in the PRC.

The first enterprise established on the territory of an SEZ (in Shenzhen) was the branch of a Hong Kong company involved in ship recycling. But this was only the start. Deng appointed Gu Mu, a well-known supporter of reform, to oversee the new State Import and Export Administration Commission and State Foreign Investment Administration Commission to be in charge of SEZs. He also received full support from the party leaders of Guangdong and Fujian. Things went into high gear. All four of the SEZs began to develop at a rapid clip, not only on account of the *huaqiao*, although their money made up the bulk of the capital investments, but also thanks to the businesslike activity of the Japanese and "hairy foreign devils," that is, Western investors. That the latter began exploiting the inhabitants of these zones apparently bothered Deng not at all. On the contrary, he openly and rather cynically observed that China's "advantage consisted in the comparative cheapness of our labor force."[28]

On this latter issue, incidentally, he was much more radical than the ultra-cautious Chen Yun.[29] But Deng did not enter into polemics with respected Elder Chen, who continued to be very influential and really had a good grasp of economics. Deng still needed Chen in his battle against Hua Guofeng.

The next step in squeezing Hua from power was ousting his four main comrades-in-arms from the Politburo and stripping them of all their positions inside and outside the party. This was accomplished in February 1980, at the Fifth Plenum of the Central Committee when the careers of Wang Dongxing and Wu De as well as the commander of the Beijing Military District, General Chen Xilian, and deputy premier Ji Dengkui were ended. Deng had made this decision in principle in October 1979 in a private conference with Hu Yaobang, Yao Yilin, and Deng Liqun.[30]

At the same plenum, Hu Yaobang and Zhao Ziyang became members of the Standing Committee. Moreover, an eleven-member Secretariat of the Central Committee was reestablished—Wan Li became the secretary for agriculture—and the position of general secretary, which Deng had held until 1966, was restored. Hu Yaobang became the new general secretary. The plenum also took the historic decision to rehabilitate Liu Shaoqi.[31]

The question of Liu, naturally, was directly tied to an assessment of the Cultural Revolution as well as of Mao Zedong himself. By this time, according to incomplete data, more than 2.9 million victims of political repression had been rehabilitated. (These were only persons who had been charged as criminals.[32]) For the time being Liu remained *persona non grata*. On September 29, 1979, Marshal Ye Jianying, speaking in the name of the CC, the NPC Standing Committee, and the State Council on the thirtieth anniversary of the PRC, had nothing good to say about Liu Shaoqi. Yet that he also had nothing bad to say was noteworthy in itself. Moreover, for the first time, blame for the mistakes committed in the anti-Rightist campaign in 1957, the Great Leap, and the Cultural Revolution was not laid upon "antiparty elements" such as Lin Biao or the Gang of Four, but on the entire leadership of the party, including, in essence, Chairman Mao.[33] From there it was not far to rehabilitating Liu Shaoqi and offering a revised version of CCP history in the period after the founding of the PRC.

Right after the marshal's speech, Deng formed a small group headed by Hu Yaobang, Hu Qiaomu, and Deng Liqun to prepare a new official version of the history of the party over the past thirty years, the "Resolution on Certain Questions in the History of Our Party Since the Founding of the People's Republic of China." In November 1979, after discussing the relevant materials with Chen Yun, Zhou Enlai's widow Deng Yingchao, and Hu Yaobang, he made a decision regarding the matter of Liu Shaoqi.[34] In mid-January 1980, one month before the Fifth Plenum, he informed party officials of the forthcoming rehabilitation of the Number One Capitalist Roader. He also spoke of the resolution that was being prepared.[35] Yet, to block any liberal interpretation of the past, he proposed, in the name of the CC, deleting from the Constitution the clause about citizens having the right to "speak out freely, air their views fully, hold great debates and write big-character posters."[36] At its Fifth Plenum the following month the CC wholly supported him, and later, at the Third Session of the Fifth NPC in September, the Constitution was amended in the name of "the Exaltation of Democracy."[37]

Meanwhile, Liu's widow, Wang Guangmei, who had been released from prison in 1978, received the ashes of her beloved husband. On May 17, 1980, a ceremony to honor the memory of "the great proletarian revolutionary" was held in Beijing. Deng himself delivered a funeral speech. Then, squeezing the hands of Wang Guangmei, with great feeling, he said, "This is good! This is a victory!"[38]

In the changing political situation, Deng was now able to express himself publicly on the family contract system. Receiving President Sekou Touré of Guinea on May 5, 1980, he informed his guest that "in the past one to two years we have begun to stress the need for the countryside to proceed from concrete conditions and to fix the system of production responsibility to work teams and individual peasant households. This has yielded noteworthy results and helped increase production severalfold."[39] On May 31, he praised the peasants of Feixi and Fengyang counties in Anhui who had shifted to family contracts. "Some comrades are worried," he said to Hu Qiaomu and Deng Liqun, "that this practice may have an adverse effect on the collective economy. I think their fears are unwarranted. . . . Where farm output quotas are fixed by household, the production teams still constitute the main economic units. . . . The key task is to expand the productive forces."[40]

Deng's speeches were not published at the time, but they were quickly circulated to a wide circle of cadres via intraparty channels and greatly stimulated the growth of family contracts. Local officials who were afraid of appearing willful in the eyes of their superiors took the words of the leader as a call to action. Land began to be divided everywhere, as they say in China, "with one stroke of the knife," according to the number of family members, the amount per person depending on the quality of the parcel of land. By the end of 1981, almost 98 percent of the production brigades had shifted to one form or another of family contract. Half a year later, the number was approaching 100 percent. In June 1982, 67 percent of the brigades were on the "full contract" system compared to only 5 percent in December 1980. From 1978 to 1982, overall peasant income doubled.[41]

Meanwhile, several academic economists began to think that China should move toward lowering "the level of collectivization that had been achieved earlier, in accordance with the actual state of production forces."[42] In other words, they began suggesting a return from the people's communes and brigades with their collective property, not to the contract system but to the New Democratic model of a mixed economy based on the individual peasant household. They called on the leadership of the CCP to heed the historical experience of building socialism in the USSR and other socialist countries, insisting on the need to revisit the Leninist concept of the New Economic Policy.

Back in July 1979, one of the most liberally inclined philosophers and economists, vice president of the Chinese Academy of Social Sciences (CASS), Yu Guangyuan, who was close to Deng and to Hu Yaobang, established a special Institute on Marxism-Leninism and Mao Zedong Thought at CASS. Researchers there began a serious study of the Yugoslav and Hungarian experiences in building socialism and of Eurocommunism, but their main attention was devoted to the Bolsheviks' NEP and the works of Nikolai Bukharin, its greatest theoretician. That Bukharin had been repressed by Stalin bothered them not at all. On the contrary, it only increased their interest in his works and in his person. Having lived through the Cultural Revolution, the intelligentsia hated any kind of terror, the Stalinist variety included.

Interest in Bukharin was stimulated by the presence of Yu Guangyuan's deputy, the well-known historian and economist Su Shaozhi, former editor of the theory department of *People's Daily*, at an international conference on Bukharin organized by the Gramsci Institute in Italy and funded by the Italian Communist Party. Su was simply stunned by what he heard in Rome from Western and East European scholars. On his return to China, he informed the leadership of just what a stupendous theoretician Bukharin had been.[43] Su's report provoked a very lively response. Yu Guangyuan decided to convene a national scholarly symposium on Bukharin. Preparations took half a year, but finally, in September 1980 the forum was held, on the outskirts of Beijing. About sixty social scientists gathered and over many weeks discussed the theory of NEP, trying to understand why it was not fully implemented in the USSR and how applicable it is to China. At the conclusion of the sessions, acting on a proposal by Yu Guangyuan, an All-China Scholarly Council to Study the Works of Bukharin was created, headed by Su Shaozhi. It included thirty social scientists who knew foreign languages, including Lin Ying, who had been a pupil in the International Orphanage in the Soviet city of Ivanovo. She had been born in Moscow in 1937 and was the daughter of one of the Chinese staff of the Comintern who would later pass through the Stalinist camps for seventeen years. When her father was arrested on spurious espionage charges in 1938, she was one year old and was sent to the International Orphanage. She came to China after the 1949 revolution.[44] Lin Ying had become known in intellectual circles a year earlier when, together with the deputy director of the Institute of the USSR and Eastern Europe, Zhao Xun, she translated Roy Medvedev's *Let History Judge,* a dissident Soviet historian's powerful, critical analysis of Stalinism. Lin Ying was chosen as one of Su Shaozhi's deputies. Hu Yaobang allotted the entire upper floor of the Beijing Party School to the council.

The members of the council displayed exceptional energy, immediately undertaking the preparation of two volumes consisting of thirty-seven translated foreign works under the distinctive titles *Bukharin and Bukharin's Thought* and *A Study of Bukharin's Thought.* They also began translating the major biography of Bukharin, published in 1973, by the American Sovietologist Stephen F. Cohen.[45] They became acquainted with it both in the original and in the Russian translation done by Soviet emigrants in 1980.

Several Chinese Bukharin specialists began to give lectures at the newly established Department of Foreign Socialist Studies at the Higher Party School, and Lin Ying even traveled around the country lecturing on Bukharin. Within intellectual circles, there was enormous interest in her lectures. The venerable Lin recalls, "The halls were jam packed. People sat on the window sills, and everybody wanted to hear something new."[46]

At the same time, staff members of the History of the International Workers' Movement section of the Central Committee's Bureau of Translation of the Works of Marx, Engels, Lenin, and Stalin were also studying Bukharin's works. In 1981, they dedicated a special edition, almost three hundred pages, of their *Materials on the Study of History of the International Communist Movement* entirely to Bukharin.[47]

Moreover, in 1981 Chinese scholars began publishing their own articles on Bukharin. Over a period of two years, no fewer than thirty-six articles appeared in various PRC journals on his life and works.[48] One of the first articles, by the historian Zheng Yifan, a 1959 graduate of Leningrad University, which was published in the first issue of *Shijie lishi* (*World History*), caused quite a stir. Zheng flatly stated that Bukharin was a Marxist theorist and economist, and that everything Stalin had said about him was false. In this connection, he noted in particular the truth of Bukharin's slogan addressed to Russian peasants: "Enrich yourselves, accumulate, develop your farms." Understandably, he did not compare this slogan with Deng's well-known idea that it was good to be rich, but everyone knew what he meant.

Naturally, the majority of articles addressed Bukharin's economic views. Chinese social scientists recognized that they "were relevant today." They appreciated Bukharin's acknowledgment that socialism in the USSR was "backward in form," his defense of prosperous peasants, his insistence that the growth of industry directly depended on the growth of agriculture, his support of the harmonious combination of planned and market regulations, and his recognition of the important role of the law of value in commodity-financial relations under socialism.[49]

Meanwhile, another vice president of CASS, the veteran communist Song Yiping, who in 1933–38 had worked in the CCP delegation to the Comintern and, like Chen Yun, studied at the International Lenin School,[50] organized the first conference in China dedicated to the history of Stalinist repression against Chinese living in the USSR in the 1930s. The famous economist Sun Yefang, honorary director of the Institute of Economics, who had also studied and worked in Moscow (1925–30), delivered a brilliant speech in memory of the victims of Stalinism. Afterward, CASS began to translate the Soviet dissident historian Abdurakhman Avtorkhanov and to publish the memoirs of surviving Chinese victims of Stalin's Gulag.[51] Su Shaozhi published a lengthy review of a book by the French historian Jean Elleinstein, *The Stalin Phenomenon*, in which, paraphrasing the author, he informed Chinese readers what a terrible despot Mao Zedong's teacher had been. "The Stalin phenomenon must be abolished," Su concluded, "Elleinstein . . . has raised a problem worth thinking through in depth."[52]

Deng followed all of this closely and, like Hu Yaobang, was supportive. Unlike Wei Jingsheng and his friends, the staff members of CASS and the Higher Party School did not encroach on the Four Cardinal Principles. The books they wrote and translated were published in small editions with the stamp "For official use," so they could not exert much influence on the masses. Deng found this useful. It will be recalled that he himself had studied Marxism from the works of the Bolshevik leaders who had propounded NEP. It is obvious that he drew on ideas from NEP when he spoke of his own reforms. In 1985, he openly acknowledged that "perhaps" the most correct model of socialism was the New Economic Policy of the USSR.[53]

Thus Deng naturally supported, and perhaps also stimulated, the resurrection of the chief theoretician of NEP. This was especially so since, if one examines the philosophical roots of his own ideas as well as the thoughts of Chen Yun, they traced back to Bukharin more than to Lenin. Although Lenin had approved the shift to NEP, he associated the market with capitalism. While acknowledging the need for regulation by the market, he spoke of the presence of state capitalism, that is, capitalism under the control of the state, in the economy of Soviet Russia of state capitalism.[54] Bukharin, on the contrary, thought that "the essence of capitalism ... was 'capitalist property,' not market relations alone." He told Lenin directly, "I think you are misusing the word 'capitalism'."[55] Bukharin's approach, obviously, meshed with that of Chen Yun and Deng, who said that "a market economy is not a synonym for capitalism." In discussing the draft "Resolution on Certain Questions in the History of Our Party Since the Founding of the People's Republic of China," Deng specifically drew his comrades' attention to the need to criticize "the misunderstanding, dogmatic interpretation and erroneous application of Lenin's statement that small production engenders capitalism and the bourgeoisie daily, hourly, and on a mass scale."[56]

The only difference, though a crucial one, between Bukharin and the Chinese reformers was that Bukharin, like Lenin and all the other Bolsheviks, defined NEP as a transitional period toward socialism, while Deng and Chen spoke of combining the plan and the market under conditions of socialism itself. At the same time, they insisted that despite the complete triumph of the contract system, collective property was preserved in the countryside. Otherwise they would have had to repudiate all of their own political activity starting from 1955, that is, from the start of collectivization.

Meanwhile, in September 1980, under pressure from Deng Xiaoping, Hua Guofeng resigned the premiership and was replaced by Zhao Ziyang. Deng used the opportunity to refresh the leadership. He himself relinquished his duties as deputy premier and several other "oldsters" followed his example, among them Li Xiannian, Chen Yun, and Wang Zhen. This metamorphosis was presented as "Opening the path to the young!" (Of course, the retirement of Deng, Chen Yun, Li Xiannian, and Wang Zhen from their government posts meant nothing since they continued to occupy key positions in the party hierarchy.)

Afterward, in November and December, the Politburo resolved that the question of Hua's retirement from his other posts as chairman of the Central Committee and of the Central Military Commission would be addressed at the Sixth Plenum. Ye Jianying and several other leaders tried to defend Hua, but they got nowhere. Bowing to pressure from Deng, the Politburo agreed not only to remove Hua but also to criticize him in the "Resolution on Certain Questions in the History of Our Party Since the Founding of the People's Republic of China" for the Two Whatevers as well as for his plans for a new Great Leap.[57]

Admitting defeat, the marshal, following the traditions of the Chinese Communist Party, was forced to engage in self-criticism.[58] Afterward, he stopped working; went to Canton, where his son served as mayor; and visited Beijing rarely. In June 1981, he attended the opening of the Sixth Plenum but quickly departed, apparently not wishing to have a hand in the removal of Hua.[59] But Hua was dismissed without him and Hu Yaobang was unanimously elected chairman of the CC. (The post of general secretary was temporarily abolished.) Deng became chair of the Central Military Commission.[60] This latter position was critical; political power in China continued to come from the barrel of the gun.

The Sixth Plenum also adopted the "Resolution on Certain Questions in the History of Our Party Since the Founding of the People's Republic of China," which it had taken a year and a half to prepare. Deng personally supervised the working group, meeting with it sixteen times, attentively reading all of its drafts, repeatedly making corrections, and consulting with other veterans. He wanted to create a balanced document that, on one hand, would repudiate all the "leftist" mistakes and, on the other, would not divide but unite a society in which Maoist sentiment remained strong. The key problem, of course, was the assessment of Mao Zedong.[61] Khrushchev's ghost haunted Deng. In August 1980, in a way that would leave no one in doubt, in an interview with the famous Italian journalist Oriana Fallaci, Deng said he would not permit the complete debunking of Chairman Mao. Total de-Maofication, from his perspective, might undermine the foundations of the socialist order in the PRC and cast a shadow over all the revolutionaries of the older generation, including himself (Deng), since not only Mao but all of them had made mistakes.[62]

In October 1980, Deng decided to open the draft resolution for discussion by a broad circle of higher-level cadres. In all, fifty-six hundred people took part, including fifteen hundred students from the Higher Party School. Some considered Mao a tyrant, while others defended him unreservedly. But in the end Deng was able to achieve a consensus. Mao Zedong was said to be a "great Marxist and a great proletarian revolutionary, strategist and theorist," and his thought "the valuable spiritual asset of the Party." It was acknowledged that Mao had made mistakes from the late 1950s, especially during the period of the Cultural Revolution, but that they were of "secondary" importance in his life and activity.[63] Mao's achievements and mistakes were in a ratio of 70:30.

During the preparation of the resolution, a show trial was held in Beijing from November 1980 to January 1981 of those whom Deng and other leaders deemed the main culprits of the Cultural Revolution: Mao's widow, Jiang Qing, as well as Zhang Chunqiao, Wang Hongwen, Yao Wenyuan, Chen Boda, and five former generals who had been close comrades-in-arms of Lin Biao. Ten people were in the dock, eight of whom had been Politburo members under Mao. They were accused of numerous counterrevolutionary crimes, including persecution of party and state leaders with the aim of overthrowing the dictatorship of the proletariat and of mass repression. Lin Biao's supporters, moreover, were accused of preparing an attempt on Chairman Mao's life, and the Gang of Four of planning an armed uprising in Shanghai after the death of the Great Helmsman. All of them were found guilty, even though Jiang Qing cried out, "My arrest and trial are an insult to Chairman Mao!" Zhang Chunqiao also rejected the accusations, albeit without histrionics. Yao Wenyuan and former PLA Chief of the General Staff Huang Yongsheng did not admit to all of the charges. But Wang Hongwen, Chen Boda, and the overwhelming majority of the generals "surrendered." On January 25, they were all sentenced to varying prison terms, from a life sentence for Wang Hongwen to sixteen years for former Deputy Chief of the General Staff Qu Huizuo. Jiang Qing and Zhang Chunqiao were sentenced to death with a two-year delay of execution.[64] In 1983, however, their death sentences were commuted to life imprisonment.

Typically, Deng publicly expressed his certainty of Jiang Qing's guilt prior to the trial. Replying to Fallaci's questions in August 1980—"How would you assess Jiang Qing? What score would you give her?"—he replied in a tone that did not allow any objections: "Below zero. A thousand points below zero." "Jiang Qing did evil things. . . . Jiang Qing is rotten through and through. Whatever sentence is passed on the Gang of Four won't be excessive. They brought harm to millions upon millions of people," he explained.[65] In his world there was no presumption of innocence, and he made no secret of this.

The crimes of Jiang Qing, Lin Biao, and the others (including Kang Sheng) were condemned in the "Resolution on Certain Questions in the History of Our Party Since the Founding of the People's Republic of China." On the other hand, the document emphasized that "a crucial turning point of far-reaching significance in the history of our Party since the birth of the People's Republic" was "the Third Plenary Session of the Eleventh Central Committee in December 1978."[66] In this way, Deng's role was anchored in history, since everyone knew it was he who had brought about this "crucial turning point."

As for Ye Jianying, the elderly marshal who had done so much for Deng, the new ruler of China no longer maintained close connections with him. He never visited him even once, right up to Ye Jianying's death on October 22, 1986, although he knew that in April 1984, the marshal had become very ill. He was diagnosed with cerebral thrombosis and chronic pneumonia.[67] Deng no longer needed him. Now only great deeds stirred the charismatic leader.

One Country, Two Systems

IT IS DOUBTFUL that Deng took much pleasure in exacting his revenge on Hua, who by the early 1980s was a political corpse. At the Sixth Plenum of the Central Committee, Deng appointed Hua deputy to Hu Yaobang. This was just a formality, of course, until the CCP's forthcoming Twelfth Congress, which was scheduled for September 1982. Hua was listed last of the six deputy chairmen of the CC.

Very little change occurred in Deng's life. He spent almost all his time at home, avoiding the lengthy party "talk fests" in Zhongnanhai. He read party and state papers; received visitors, including Hu Yaobang and Premier Zhao; took his breakfast, lunch, and dinner; slept; watched television; looked through no fewer than fifteen newspapers a day; played bridge with his friends once a week; and daily took long walks in his courtyard. He almost never visited the Central Committee building, and when Zhao Ziyang once asked him why he did not even convene a meeting of the Standing Committee, Deng replied, "And what would two deaf people talk about?" (Like him, Chen Yun was also hard of hearing.) He also added: "As for me, I visit Chen Yun's house only once a year."[1]

His life was like that of a wise Chinese emperor following the traditional Daoist-Confucian principle of *wuwei* (noninterference in the eternally established order of things). As he had done during his exile in Jiangxi, he arose exactly at 6:30 a.m., did exercises, and washed himself with a cold, wet towel. He breakfasted at 8:00, and from 9:00 on he sat in his study, reading documents. Zhuo Lin continued to act as one of his personal secretaries, along with the devoted Wang Ruilin. Wang helped him prepare materials and drafts of resolutions. After working for an hour and a half, Deng usually went outside for some fresh air and then returned to his office. He lunched at

noon, then rested, and afterward again read documents if there were no official meetings.[2] He thought he was barely working. "I have much less energy
than I used to," he told his comrades in the party. "I can manage two activities
a day—one in the morning and one in the afternoon—but arrange another in
the evening and it's too much."[3]

The loyal Wang represented him at various party meetings, including
Politburo sessions, as did the secretaries of Chen Yun and several other party
veterans. In effect, both Hu Yaobang and Zhao Ziyang played the role of
assistants to Deng. But unlike Wang Ruilin, they enjoyed much greater lati-
tude since they were the main executors of the Patriarch's will. Once in place,
this mechanism of power worked meticulously.

Although Deng tired by the end of the day, he still felt very well. He did
not complain about his health even though he smoked two packs of cigarettes a day. To be sure, he smoked special Panda brand cigarettes with lower
nicotine content. Zhuo Lin suffered more from his bad habit than he did,
since Deng was constantly dropping ashes either on his trousers or his jacket,
igniting them; and she had to make sure he looked neat.[4] They had become so
accustomed to each other that it seemed they could not survive without each
other for even a day. Their children and grandchildren were touched by the
old couple's affection. In their honor they named two small pine trees growing close together in the courtyard in their honor "the Dragon Tree couple."
(As we remember, both Deng and Zhuo were born in the Year of the Dragon,
although separated by twelve years.)

Their home, a two-story detached house with a semicircular glassed-in
terrace and a large balcony, was surrounded by greenery. It was located on a
quiet lane behind a high wall. The noise of the city barely penetrated there.
Deng and his family lived as if in a country setting. The gray brick building under a gray brick roof still stands in the same place. It is rather large,
but Deng's family itself was by no means small and had grown even larger.
In addition to their granddaughter from Deng Nan, Mianmian, who was
almost ten years old, and their grandson from Deng Lin, Mengmeng, who
was eight, Deng and Zhuo Lin now had another granddaughter, from
Deng Rong, Yangyang. She was three. Next door, in one of the wings, lived
Wang Ruilin and the members of his household, the guard, chauffeur, and
other service personnel who had long since become almost like a part of the
family.[5]

Deng lived his last twenty years in this home under the shade of the pines.
Here he decided the fate of the country, the party, and the people. In the first
six months of 1982, he was mostly occupied with preparations for the Twelfth

Party Congress, which had enormous significance for him. This was the first congress of the CCP that would take place under his leadership.

From the fall of 1981, it seemed that Chen Yun had begun to irritate him. Like Marshal Ye, he had performed his role and Deng no longer needed him. Hua Guofeng and the other Whateverists had been overthrown. Deng was the universally acknowledged leader, and he had his own, young team. Consequently, of what use was Chen Yun now? Yet the know-it-all economist believed he had the right to give advice all the time and interfere in Deng's reforms. Thus, at the very end of December 1981, panicked by the rapid development of the family contract system in its full-blown form, he had expressed the fear that "the so-called freedom of 800 million peasants will overturn the state plan." After all, "we need [not only] to feed 800 million peasants," he explained to the first secretaries of the provinces, autonomous regions, and cities under central supervision, "but also to achieve socialist construction." Therefore, "agriculture must depend upon the plan as the foundation and utilize market regulation as a supplement."[6] Deng had no objections to socialist construction, but he perceived no threat from the universal contract system.

A disagreement between Chen and Deng over the development of the SEZs also emerged at the same conference of first secretaries. "At present we can only permit these [four zones]," Chen said. "We cannot increase their number . . . we cannot establish special zones in provinces [for example] such as Jiangsu."[7] Why? Because this would undermine the national currency and would encourage "bad people." (By the latter, Chen had in mind corrupt party officials who were taking advantage of the opening of SEZs to enrich themselves.)

On January 5, 1982, in his capacity as head of the Central Discipline Inspection Commission, Chen sent Deng, Hu Yaobang, Zhao Ziyang, and Li Xiannian a short report on disgraceful happenings in Guangdong. On the first page he wrote, "I believe that several of those who have committed the most serious economic crimes should be severely punished, for especially heinous acts the death sentence should be carried out and publicly announced. Otherwise, it will be impossible to rectify the party style."[8]

Not wishing an open conflict, Deng tabled a resolution, "To give priority to the problem swiftly and decisively and not to weaken our resolve."[9] On January 11, in concert with him, Hu Yaobang convened a special meeting of the CC Secretariat devoted to the corruption of Guangdong officials. On Deng's initiative, four members of the Politburo traveled to south China to investigate the problem.[10]

Just three days later, however, at a new session of the Secretariat, Hu presented a voluminous report defending the Central Committee's foreign economic policy. "Certain problems have arisen with respect to several concrete problems," he observed, "but from this we must not draw the mistaken conclusion that we should retreat rather than boldly and even more actively developing economic ties with the outside world. . . . It is impossible to think that the economic crimes are directly linked to the policy of openness. There is no indisputable causal relationship between them."[11] Afterward Deng himself went to Guangdong to inform provincial officials they had nothing to fear while working to develop the SEZs. (In order not to irritate Chen Yun he spoke to the first secretary of the Guangdong Party Committee in a private meeting.[12])

Meanwhile, Chen continued interfering in the work of modernizing Guangdong and even called the first secretary and the governor on the carpet, but he got nowhere. He was able to draw to his side only the conservative members of Deng's team—Hu Qiaomu and Deng Liqun—who began planting the thought in Deng's mind that the SEZs were turning into foreign settlements of the sort that had existed in China's accursed past. But Deng decisively supported Hu Yaobang, who with the help of researchers in the Chinese Academy of Social Sciences provided a Marxist-Leninist foundation for the SEZs. "For us this is something new," Hu said, "but in the Soviet Union [during Lenin's NEP] half a century ago . . . a system of concessions developed . . . in the concessionary enterprises, of which there were more than two hundred for a long time, foreigners were permitted to invest several tens of millions of rubles. Was that not a bold step!"[13]

Chen Yun, Hu Qiaomu, and Deng Liqun could not quarrel with Lenin, but they did not welcome "the construction of capitalism" in China. "All the provinces want to establish special zones, all want to open dikes," grumbled Chen. "If things go that way, then foreign capitalists and domestic investors will break loose from the cage. The only thing that will grow is speculation. Therefore, it must not be done."[14]

The rate of national economic growth also occasioned serious disagreement. After supporting Chen's program of "regulation" in 1979, basically from political considerations, Deng had no intention of following it his whole life. He understood that for objective reasons it was impossible to achieve universal abundance in China; yet he did not retreat from the idea of *xiaokang*, and he intended that by the beginning of the twenty-first century, per capita income in China would reach about US$1,000. (Later he lowered this to $800.[15]) This would be much less than, for example, Switzerland (almost $18,000), Hong

Kong (almost $6,000), Singapore (about $5,000), or Taiwan ($4,500). But it would be good for China. In the early 1980s, the Chinese per capita income for a population that had crossed the billion mark equaled $260;[16] consequently, more than a fourfold increase in production would be required to reach $1,000 or even $800 per capita, assuming, naturally, strict controls on the birth rate. Chen Yun's regulation did not jibe at all with this dream.

One cannot say that Chen Yun—this Doubting Thomas, as one of his biographers called him[17]—was opposed to improving the lives of the people, but he really disliked haste. He always worried about inflation, sectoral imbalance, and overheating of the economy.

At the same time, Deng and Chen demonstrated complete agreement on limiting the birth rate. Both Deng's notion of *xiaokang* and Chen's regulation depended on lowering the rate of population growth. Everyone in the CCP leadership agreed. Deng had raised the issue on March 23, 1979, at a Politburo meeting, demanding that the rate of population growth be lowered to 1 percent and that the new demographic policy be codified in law. Three months later, Hua Guofeng expounded this idea at the Second Session of the Fifth NPC, suggesting that by 1985 the population growth rate be lowered to 0.5 percent annually. In September 1980, the Third Session of the NPC considered a proposal from the State Council of an immediate shift to a policy of planned birth, with no more than one child per family so that by the end of the twentieth century the Chinese population would not exceed 1.2 billion. On September 25, the Central Committee sent an open letter to communists and CYL members calling on them to help propagandize the policy of limiting births according to the principle of one child per family. On January 4, 1981, a resolution followed obligating party and administrative organs to take all measures "to encourage couples to have one child."[18] All these documents aimed at lowering the growth in the number of Han Chinese and did not apply to national minorities.

There was a hostile reception to the policy in the countryside, where the land was divided up according to the number of persons in a family. A single-child policy was not in the interest of peasants, particularly if the single child was a girl. Everyone wanted an heir to carry on the family line, and additional male hands were welcome in the field. Thus from the very beginning the success of the new policy depended on the urban population. (Nevertheless, it would succeed, although a significant price was paid in terms of the sacrifice of personal freedom and enforcement through intrusive, and not infrequently coercive, means. In the year 2000, the population of the PRC would be just slightly more than 1.2 billion.)

Meanwhile, the Twelfth Congress of the CCP took place in Beijing from September 1 to 12, 1982, attended by 1,600 voting and 149 nonvoting delegates representing more than thirty-nine million Communist party members. Deng was in the driver's seat. He opened the congress and formulated the main strategic goals facing the Chinese people in the 1980s: "To accelerate socialist modernization, to strive for China's reunification and particularly for the return of Taiwan to the motherland, and to oppose hegemonism and work to safeguard world peace." He also provided a brief theoretical foundation for the cause of modernization, saying for the first time that the CCP and the Chinese people were constructing not just any kind of socialism but "a socialism with Chinese characteristics." What this was he did not explain, but he emphasized that "in carrying out our modernization programme we must proceed from Chinese realities. . . . We must integrate the universal truth of Marxism with the concrete realities of China, [and] blaze a path of our own."[19]

Both the delegates and many other Chinese likely understood what the leader had in mind. The ideas and goals of reform had been explained many times; only the label of "socialism with Chinese characteristics" had been missing. Everyone knew about China's great economic and cultural backwardness, the enormous population, most of them living in the countryside, and the limited amount of arable land. Everyone had heard of the concept of *xiaokang*, of the need to combine the plan and the market throughout the period of socialism and to strictly follow the Four Cardinal Principles. These were the earmarks of Chinese socialism.

Deng created his theory gradually, step by step, "crossing the river by feeling for the stones," as the Chinese expression has it. Not all of the ideas originated with him, but he embraced them and creatively reworked them. It is interesting to note that U.S. President Gerald R. Ford, who met with Deng during his own brief visit to China in late 1975, characterized him as "a doer—more pragmatic than theoretical."[20] He obviously underestimated Deng.

Hu Yaobang, who delivered the main report, basically expounded Deng's ideas. The main one was to increase industrial and agricultural output fourfold over the next twenty years. Hu also called for developing many forms of management over a long period of time, and although he noted that cooperatives would remain the main form he praised the system of production responsibility, that is, the household contract. He even spoke of the need to encourage the development of individual, which is to say private, economic enterprises, not only in the countryside in the form of the contract system but also in the cities, emphasizing that a portion of commodities could be produced and distributed "not according to the plan but to the market." Speaking about technical-economic exchanges with abroad, he specifically noted, "We must attract foreign capital for the needs of construction to the maximum possible extent. . . . We must borrow advanced technological achievements from other countries, adapting them to our conditions, especially those that help in the technological reconstruction of enterprises, assimilate them conscientiously, and in this way improve and stimulate production and construction here in China." Starting from Deng's theory of constructing "socialism with Chinese characteristics," Hu concluded, "socialist society in our country is still in a primary stage of its development."[21] It was a forward-looking report and Deng was pleased with it, especially since he himself had edited it.

The Twelfth Congress again elected Deng a member of the CC and also made him a member of the newly established Central Advisory Commission. In the new statutes adopted at the congress, the commission was defined as political assistant and consultant to the CC,[22] but Deng deemed it a transitional organizational structure affording an opportunity for leaders of the older generation who did not wish to retire to withdraw from affairs honorably while preserving face. Deng himself was in no hurry to retire, but he headed the commission, as if offering an example to the veterans who were clinging to their positions.[23]

At the CC plenum on September 2, he was again elected to the Politburo and its Standing Committee and confirmed as chair of the Military Commission. There were five others besides him in the highest party organ: Hu Yaobang, Ye Jianying, Zhao Ziyang, Li Xiannian, and Chen Yun. Hu Yaobang again was allotted the position of general secretary, a post that had been reestablished while that of chairman of the Central Committee was abolished, and Chen Yun remained head of the Central Disciplinary Inspection Commission.[24] Hua Guofeng was removed from both the Standing Committee and the Politburo but remained a member of the Central Committee.

Chen Yun did not spar with anyone at the congress, but after the sessions wrapped up he continued to interfere in the course of reform. In the words of Zhao Ziyang, "New issues emerged as we moved forward, but Chen Yun's ideas remained unchanged . . . [it was] impossible to persuade him to change his view."[25] From the beginning of November 1982, he constantly compared the plan with a cage and the market with a bird. He had initially started speaking of a cage in January 1982 when he suggested confining all the investors in the SEZs in it, but he did not at the time call such persons birds. Now he presented the concept rather clearly, although he stated that he was not its author. Huang Kecheng, secretary of the Central Disciplinary

Inspection Commission, had come up with the image in August 1982, on the eve of the Twelfth Congress, in conversation with Chen to emphasize the need for order in economic construction. Chen liked the image and began employing it. Thus, on December 2, talking with fellow Shanghainese who were delegates to the Fifth NPC, he said:

> We need to continue the policy of reviving the economy, display-ing the role of market regulation. But we have to put a stop to the tendency to reject the state plan. . . . The economy will revive if it is guided by the plan, not when the plan is disavowed. This is like the situation with a bird and a cage. It's impossible to hold the bird in your hand or it will die, but if you release it, it will fly off. Instead, the bird may be allowed to fly in the cage. . . . The bird is the flourish-ing lively economy, the plan is the cage. Of course, the "cage" may be made larger or smaller, let it be bigger. . . . But in any circumstances the "cage" is necessary.[26]

By this time, however, Deng and his closest associates, Hu Yaobang, Zhao Ziyang, Wan Li, and Gu Mu, were actively expanding the sphere of market regulation, whose superiority was clear to them. However, they still did not think either of completely abandoning the plan or of privatizing the state sector. It was only a question of reducing the part of the economy that was regulated by the plan to the maximum extent allowed by communist ideol-ogy in order to bring about a powerful breakthrough in the modernization of the country with the help of proven market mechanisms.

The bird-in-the-cage analogy did not fit. Deng and his colleagues acknowl-edged that peasants should grow a part of their harvest in accordance with the state plan, just as a certain volume of industrial production should be turned out according to directives from above. Otherwise, as everyone feared, there might be a shortage in food production as well as in other goods. But they did not intend the entire economy to be confined to a cage, however large it might be. The Twelfth Congress supported a "partial connection between planning and market mechanisms."[27] In other words, the economy resembled not a single bird but a flock of birds, among which the largest could really sit in the cage while the others had to be set free. The reformers wanted to construct two economic systems in the country, both a planned economy and a market economy. The most important question for them was how to combine these two systems optimally. "How should we handle the relation between planning and the market?" Deng posed the question before young economists. "If we handle it properly, it will help greatly to promote economic development; if we don't, things will go badly."[28]

It was by expanding the sphere of market regulation that Deng thought to achieve "a wavelike forward motion," allowing some people and regions to become well off before others. "It is only fair that people who work hard should prosper," he instructed. "To let some people and some regions become prosperous first is a new policy that is supported by everyone."[29]

Meanwhile, the Fifth Session of the Fifth National People's Congress, which took place under the dominant influence of the reformers, hammered the last nail into the coffin of the people's communes. Article 30 of the new Constitution of the PRC, adopted at the session, established that counties and autonomous counties henceforth would be divided not into communes and towns but into townships, nationality townships, and towns. In other words, communes ceased to exist as basic administrative units.[30] They were still mentioned in the Constitution as a form of the cooperative economy (Article 8), but no longer as one of the constituent elements of the three-tiered system of property in the countryside. The production brigades and production teams were also abolished.

To determine the degree to which the development of the market should be allowed to proceed, Deng and other reformers tried to stimulate discussion among Chinese economists and social scientists. Zhao was particularly energetic in this connection, establishing two scholarly centers under the aegis of the State Council, on agriculture and on structural reform. A sober-minded man, he first wanted to grasp everything in order to push economic modernization forward. Unexpectedly he encountered problems from Hu Yaobang.

The lively and impulsive Hu, who was nicknamed "Cricket" by his ill-wishers in the party leadership because he reminded them of a diminutive, fast-moving, and unpredictable ball used in the game of cricket,[31] was completely unlike the calm and composed Zhao, who it seemed was better able than anyone to settle the differences between Deng and Chen Yun. Hu was loath to wait while the "egghead" economists on Zhao's team tried to sort things out. He strived to expand the market as much as possible to accelerate the tempo of growth. Zhao recalled that Hu Yaobang and he "had differences on specific steps, approaches, and methods—especially on the question of speed. Yaobang was even more aggressive than Deng. . . . The difference of opinion emerged as early as 1982."[32] Everywhere he went, Hu, who loved to travel around the country on inspection tours (by the end of 1986 he had visited more than sixteen hundred of the two thousand counties in the PRC[33]), encouraged people to overfulfill the plan and develop market relations. In

January 1983, while Zhao was visiting Africa, Hu called for introducing the contract system in all commercial and industrial enterprises. In Zhao's words, this quickly led to the growth of speculation. The large Beijing department stores that shifted to the contract system began selling goods wholesale to private traders in order to make quick profits, and they in turn sold them retail at inflated prices. After returning from Africa, Zhao quickly opposed such a policy. On March 15, 1983, Deng intervened in the conflict, summoning Zhao and Hu to his home for talks. After hearing out both sides, Deng supported Zhao and admonished Hu for imprudence.[34]

The split in the reformers' camp played into the hands of Chen Yun and other conservatives. Of all the liberals the one they disliked the most was the "adventurist" Hu. He reciprocated their enmity. Thus, in spring 1982, while inspecting work in the provinces, he repeatedly criticized Chen Yun, without considering that Chen's well-wishers would inform him immediately.[35] Chen and his supporters threw their full support behind Zhao, and Hu found himself in a real bind.

Two days after the conversation at Deng's house, Chen Yun attacked Hu at a joint meeting of the Politburo Standing Committee and the Secretariat, accusing him of not understanding "historical materialism." All of his long-festering animus against the liberals finally burst out. Hu was caught completely off-guard, panicked, and made a self-criticism, following which Deng forbade him from intervening in the affairs of the State Council.[36]

After winning this round in the struggle against the chief liberal, the party conservatives stepped up their offensive on the ideological front. Deng was sensitive about anything that struck him as a retreat from the Four Cardinal Principles. Ever since March 1979, he had consistently stressed the need to intensify the ideological education of the masses, and from the early 1980s he repeatedly affirmed the need to combine reform and openness with the building of a so-called socialist spiritual culture. In the summer of 1983, Hu Qiaomu and Deng Liqun, who a year earlier had become head of the CC's Propaganda Department, were able to play on this skillfully, convincing Deng to launch a new ideological campaign against "spiritual pollution." They told him that in March the well-known cultural figure Zhou Yang, in a speech commemorating the hundredth anniversary of Marx's death, focused his remarks on humanism and alienation. (According to Marx, under capitalism workers were alienated from the work itself, from the product, from themselves, and from other people since they were working not for themselves but for the capitalist.) Zhou, who had suffered a lot during the Cultural Revolution, hinted at the existence of alienation in socialist society too, and he stressed the transcendent significance of humane relations among people. The meeting, incidentally, was organized by Su Shaozhi, who had replaced Yu Guangyuan in 1982 as director of the Institute of Marxism, Leninism, and Mao Zedong Thought. The liberals in attendance warmly greeted this idea. Many of the old conservatives, such as Deng's friend Wang Zhen, simply did not understand and therefore pretended that they also liked the report. But Hu Qiaomu and Deng Liqun, who understood everything very well, tried unsuccessfully to block publication of the report. Then they came to see Deng. He also understood nothing but asked, "Just what is alienation?" Without delving into details, Hu Qiaomu and Deng Liqun simply said, "It is against socialism."

Deng was indignant. In his old age he had become irritable and very authoritarian. "The literature, art, and theoretical circles should not produce spiritual pollution," he growled and ordered Hu Qiaomu to draft a speech for him on this subject.[37] He delivered the speech on October 12, 1983, at the Second Plenum of the Central Committee. He raged and fulminated, criticizing not only the members of the creative associations but also the leadership of the ideological front, that is, in essence, Hu Yaobang. He stressed the need to struggle against both left and right deviations, accusing those who did not do so of "weakness and laxity" and calling on the "engineers of the souls," the Stalinist term for writers and intellectuals, to hold high the banner of Marxism and socialism. He attacked "some comrades" who, from his perspective, had gone so far as to be "interested in discussing humanism, the value of the human being, and alienation." Things had come to such a pass, he complained, that "a few [artists even] produce pornography."[38]

After the plenum a real mass campaign unfolded against "spiritual (or mental) pollution," by which was meant "the spread of the corrupt and decadent ideas of the bourgeoisie and other exploiting classes and the spread of distrust of socialism, communism and leadership by the Communist Party."[39] Meanwhile, "idolizers of the West" were exposed, criticized, and fired not only for liberal thoughts but also for fashionable dress, stylish hairdos, and love of foreign music.

But the tepid liberal reformers, including Hu Yaobang and Zhao, would not give in and rallied together against such obscurantism. "Another Cultural Revolution almost seemed to be on the horizon," recalled Zhao Ziyang, "strong enough to threaten economic policies and reform."[40] Zhao, Wan Li, and other leaders of the State Council, as well as the General Political Administration of the PLA, prohibited the campaign from being conducted in the countryside, industrial enterprises, scientific and technological

institutions, and the army. In less than a month (in twenty-eight days) it fiz-
zled out. On February 11, 1984, Hu Yaobang declared that although Deng was
unquestionably correct in raising the problem, the methods of implementing
his "wise instructions" at the ground level were deficient and resulted in the
failure of the entire campaign.[41] "Deng was not happy with this kind of talk
from Yaobang. Even though he did not say anything at the time, he did not
back down an inch from his previous stand," Zhao noted.[42]

The brief truce among the liberals ended right after the conclusion of the
campaign. On May 26, 1984, Zhao wrote Deng a private letter saying he could
not work with Hu Yaobang. It is good that "both you and Comrade Chen
Yun [are] still energetic and in good health," he exclaimed, asking him to do
something to ensure that the party leadership remain stable and strong.[43] He
sent a copy to Chen Yun.

Deng made no reply, but instead of settling the relations between the two
most powerful members of his team, he shelved the letter. He was beginning to contemplate removing Hu Yaobang at the forthcoming Thirteenth
Congress of the CCP in 1987.

Meanwhile, reform continued to deepen, and leading economists were
increasingly active in developing new ideas. Some began talking about the
importance of a transition to a "dual-track economy," by which was meant
the need for some sort of "mutual penetration" of plan and market. And some
proffered even more liberal ideas, for example, the "organic" unity of regulation according to the plan at the macroeconomic level and market regulation
at the microeconomic level. The idea of developing guided planning rather
than command planning was also bruited, that is, a softer type of planning in
which only the direction of development would be indicated.[44]

At the same time, Chinese leaders invited foreign academics and businesspersons to listen to their points of view regarding problems of reform
in the PRC. Foreign economists, including from the World Bank, carried
out investigations and offered valuable suggestions, including not to pursue rapid privatization and to introduce a dual price system, one for the
planned economy and one for the market. They were also firmly convinced
that by the end of the twentieth century China would be able to quadruple its annual industrial and agricultural output. This latter conclusion
delighted Deng.[45]

In 1984 liquidation of the people's communes rapidly accelerated. In 1982,
on the eve of the Fifth Session of the Fifth NPC, which adopted the historic
decision to disband the communes, there were 54,300 of these rudiments of
Maoism; in 1983 there were 40,100; but by the end of 1984 only 249 remained.

By the spring of 1985, all of the communes were gone.[46] The production brigades and production teams were likewise disbanded.

Two documents, both bearing the number one—the first published in early 1983, the second in early 1984—and both drafted by the State Council's Center for Agricultural Development, had an enormous influence on the Chinese countryside. The first, adopted by the Politburo on December 23, 1982, allowed peasants to hire labor, albeit under the euphemism of "helpers and interns," but according to the same principle as small urban enterprises. Rural dwellers also received the right to purchase machine tools, implements to process agricultural products, small tractors, motorized boats, and motor vehicles. Moreover, peasants were allowed to engage in wholesale trade, that is, to purchase grain and other goods from their neighbors to sell on the market. The second document authorized long periods for family contracts (fifteen years and more) and encouraged the "gradual concentration of land in the hands of skillful landholders," that is, "kulaks." It also authorized subcontracts, permitting the transfer of contracts from one peasant to another. It included the proviso that even in households where the number of hired laborers exceeded the statutory limit of seven, this should not be viewed as capitalist.[47]

This latter provision also affected township and village enterprises, which had begun to develop very rapidly with the liquidation of people's communes. They were considered collectives, so the number of workers was not limited even if the managers had contracted the enterprises for their own services. These enterprises developed especially quickly. Most of the surplus labor freed up as a result of the dissolution of the brigades was absorbed by them. As the reforms deepened, the peasant market demanded an ever-increasing quantity of industrial goods. Consequently, from 1978 to 1985 the number of persons employed in township and village enterprises increased from twenty-eight million to seventy million.

In the cities, small businesses continued to proliferate. More than seven million persons were engaged in private enterprises, but this did not bother Deng. Informed of what was going on, he asked "what people were afraid of—that it would harm socialism?"[48] He thereby gave a green light to the development of urban entrepreneurship.

The special economic zones also flourished. Observing their rapid growth, even Chen Yun felt compelled to attenuate his criticism. By the end of 1982, he acknowledged, "We need to establish special zones. We need constantly to sum up their experience, but this needs to be done so that they will work."[49] Afterward, other conservatives also indicated positive aspects of the SEZs.

Deng was satisfied. "Now people are increasingly praising the special zones," he said after a while. "They are [really] working not badly."[50] In late January and early February 1984, he visited three of the four zones: Shenzhen, Zhuhai, and Xiamen. Favorably impressed, he proudly declared, "It was I who proposed creating the SEZs."[51] These once-backward territories had turned into urban showplaces, and he was convinced of the need to "manage the special economic zones in such a way as to achieve better and faster results."[52] At a meeting on February 24, with a number of leaders, Deng summed up his trips: "In establishing special economic zones and implementing an open policy, we must make it clear that our guideline is just that—to open and not to close." He explained, "I was impressed by the prosperity of the Shenzhen Special Economic Zone during my stay here. . . . A special economic zone is . . . a window for our foreign policy. Through the special economic zones we can import foreign technology, obtain knowledge, and learn management, which is also a kind of knowledge." He suggested allowing "free flow of capital [in and out of the SEZs]" and opening up "more port cities, such as Dalian and Qingdao" as well as the island of Hainan.[53] Hearing this, Hu Yaobang gave the cue: "I think we need to open seven or eight maritime cities; this is not dangerous."[54]

In late March and early April, the CC Secretariat and the State Council convened a conference with the leaders of several maritime cities and on May 4 adopted a resolution to establish SEZs in fourteen port cities, among them Shanghai, Tianjin, and Canton. These cities were given the name "Economic and Technological Development Zones" (ETDZ), but their essence did not change too much from the SEZs. The most favorable conditions for attracting foreign capital were created in all of them; in particular, taxes on profits were lowered to 15 percent.[55] To be sure, the ETDZs were not separated from the rest of China by checkpoints.

Even state-owned enterprises were actively drawn into the market economy, receiving ever-greater freedom with regard to their above-plan production. At the same time, banks acquired the right to engage in commercial activity and shifted to providing credit to enterprises. This also expanded the sphere of market regulation.[56] From the fall of 1984, state-owned enterprises were allowed to use a dual price system, for market production and production according to the plan.[57]

Overall the market quickly began to conquer economic space, which demanded that further thought be given to the course of reform. On September 9, 1984, Zhao Ziyang sent a letter to Hu Yaobang, Deng Xiaoping, Li Xiannian, and Chen Yun in which, on the basis of suggestions from economists, he sketched a new conception of the mutual relationship between plan and market regulation. He emphasized the need to methodically replace commands with guided planning, which should mainly be regulated by economic methods. "Socialist economy," he said in the letter,

> is a planned commodity economy on the basis of public ownership. . . . The expression of planning first, the law of value second, is not exact, should no longer be used. The two should be unified rather than separated or set against each other. . . . The planned economy of the Chinese style should be one of development in the light of and by virtue of the law of value.[58]

In sum, Zhao proposed to liberalize the entire economic system, converting it into a market economy. (It was purely for tactical reasons that he referred to "commodity" rather than "market" economy.)

Zhao's letter, which Deng found persuasive, sketched an organic unity between planning (at the macro level) and market regulation (at the micro level). The other members of the Standing Committee also approved—even Chen Yun, who however could not have been pleased since he had always insisted on something entirely different, namely, the plan as the foundation and the market as auxiliary. Apparently, Chen, viewing Zhao as an ally in his struggle against Hu Yaobang, simply did not want to quarrel with him.

In October 1984, this letter was the basis for a resolution of the Third Plenum of the Twelfth Central Committee, "The Decision on Reform of the Economic Structure," which provided a new impetus to the development of the market economy and its harmonious combination with the planned economy. In precise conformity with Bukharin (whom, to be sure, no one mentioned), it stressed that "the difference between socialist and capitalist economy, as far as a commodity economy and the law of value are concerned, lies not in whether these are still functioning, but in the difference in ownership."[59] Zhao recalled:

> The Decision on Economic Reform . . . stressed the importance of the natural laws of supply and demand and the power of the market. It defined the economy of socialism as that of the "commodity economy." Deng thought highly of this decision, and even regarded it as a "new theory of political economy. . . ." Even though he said different things at different times, he was always inclined toward a commodity economy, the laws of supply and demand, and the free market.[60]

By this time, the reforms had brought tangible results. From 1978 to 1984, a steady growth in GDP had occurred, averaging 8.8 percent per year (66 percent for the whole period). The PRC had not previously experienced such growth. During the same period the annual volume of industrial production grew by more than 78 percent, notably 66 percent in heavy industry, and almost 98 percent in light industry. The share of foreign capital investment in the volume of overall investment was still small (about 4 percent in 1984), but what the foreigners built was done quickly, reliably, and of good quality. Moreover, it was at a high level of technology. In 1984 a record grain harvest was achieved: over 407 million tons, which was more than 100 million tons above 1978. At that moment even the reformers were in a tizzy. No one knew what to do with such a colossal amount of grain. There were not enough granaries or sufficient funds to settle accounts with the peasants. Therefore, on January 1, 1985, the State Council declared that from now on the state would not assume the obligation to purchase grain produced in excess of the plan. This led to a slight decline in grain production (by a little over 28 million tons in 1985), but simultaneously it facilitated further development of monetized commodity relations in the countryside. By 1985, the median income of the rural population had increased by more than one and half times, and the average wages of workers and employees by roughly 60 percent. To be sure, 125 million peasants, or 15 percent, remained in the category of "absolutely poor," but Deng had never said that everyone would become well-to-do at once.[61] Nevertheless, the number of those suffering from hunger was cut in half.

By 1985 the reform policy had also brought about a notable success for the government in regard to the most sensitive question for Chinese national consciousness, national unification. In January 1979, Deng had presented a plan to unify mainland China with Taiwan, Hong Kong, and Macao on the basis of the principle of "one country, two systems." He guaranteed that after the return of Hong Kong and Macao to the People's Republic of China, as well as unification of the PRC with Taiwan, on all three territories for an extended period (somewhat later the figure of fifty years was given), the existing socioeconomic and even political systems would be preserved—that is, democratic capitalism. He even promised Taiwan that the PRC would not intervene in the domestic affairs of Taiwan, which could actually maintain its own armed forces. All he wanted from Taiwan was Beijing's right to speak in the name of one China in the international arena. Obviously, on the question of unification he was prepared to interpret the principle of "one country, two systems" much more broadly than with regard to his own SEZs.

The question of Taiwan was by no means a simple one, as Taiwan's president, Chiang Ching-kuo, did not even want to listen to proposals from Deng, his fellow student at Sun Yat-sen University in Moscow. Like his father Chiang Kai-shek, Chiang Ching-kuo insisted that his regime was the only lawful government of China.

The questions of Hong Kong and Macao were easier, although they too posed their own difficulties, particularly Hong Kong. There was no need to worry about Macao since the Portuguese themselves had repeatedly offered to return the island to the PRC and in 1979 even reached an appropriate understanding with the Chinese, which, to be sure, was kept secret. Deng was waiting for a propitious moment to announce it. But he did not succeed in quickly resolving the problem with the British. Prime Minister Margaret Thatcher of the United Kingdom thought that Hong Kong was "a unique example of successful Sino-British co-operation," and that a declaration about returning it to the PRC would have a "disastrous effect" since the people in the colony feared the communists and would immediately take their capital out.[62] Unlike the Chinese Nationalists on Taiwan, the British position was weak. In 1997 the ninety-nine-year lease on the greater part of Hong Kong, known as the New Territories, would expire. This region was the agricultural appendage of Hong Kong, and without it the multimillion-population city simply could not exist.

Knowing this, Deng was very tough in his negotiations with Thatcher in September 1982. "We shall face the disaster squarely and make a new policy decision," he noted, not without humor, thereby signaling China's resolve to reclaim Hong Kong whether or not the British agreed to hand it over. With this ill-concealed threat, he asserted that the Chinese could enter Hong Kong in a few hours, whenever they pleased.[63]

Thatcher retained the most unpleasant memories of Deng. In addition to his peremptory manner, like many Chinese of his generation who were inveterate smokers he was constantly spitting into a nearby brass spittoon. (He habitually did this, not only with Thatcher, although he knew it was impolite. "I have three vices," he said in a frank moment, "I drink, I spit, and I smoke."[64]) The Iron Lady was so shaken by what she had heard and seen that, when exiting the NPC building where the negotiations were held, and obviously upset, she suddenly slipped and fell on her left knee. TV cameramen recorded her fall, and broadcast this embarrassing episode to the whole world, accompanied by caustic comments such as "Obviously, Thatcher suffered a crushing defeat in the negotiations."[65]

This was an accurate assessment. By the end of September 1984, the Chinese and British diplomats had worked out all the details, and in mid-December Thatcher, who had returned to China, signed with Zhao Ziyang the so-called Joint Declaration on the question of Hong Kong, which indicated the return of the city to China in 1997, precisely on Deng's terms. Citizens of the PRC warmly greeted this first step in the unification of their homeland. Deng himself was happy. At the end of October 1984 he shared his joy with the veterans, telling them that in this year he had accomplished two things: first, he had opened fourteen maritime cities to foreign investment, and second, he had settled the question of Hong Kong according to the principle of "one country, two systems."[66]

Two months prior to his meeting with the veterans, Deng had celebrated his eightieth birthday within the circle of his large family. The only ones missing were his youngest son, Fei Fei, and daughter-in-law, Liu Xiaoyuan, who were far away in New York studying at the University of Rochester.[67] Zhuo Lin, Deng's daughters, and the servants laid out two large tables. On one of them was an enormous eight-layer cake topped with a cream icing. Around its perimeter were eighty peaches, eighty candles, and the character *shou* (long life) written in cream eighty times, symbolizing the birthday jubilee. To general laughter and with the help of his grandchildren, Deng blew out the candles on several tries. Everyone cried, "Happy Birthday!" Then they feasted on the cake. Deng was happy.[68] Not only did China enter 1985 renewed, but its leader demonstrated an enviable spiritual and physical health, even though this was the year he had planned on retiring.

Reforms and Democracy

THE YEAR 1985 turned out to be difficult, and Deng had to put off his retirement. Early in the year he again felt threatened by the creative intelligentsia. The Fourth Congress of Chinese Writers was taking place and free elections for the leadership were held, resulting in election of the liberal commentator Liu Binyan as deputy chairman. Many intellectuals viewed this as the start of profound ideological changes, especially since Hu Yaobang welcomed the congress in the name of the Central Committee, and writers spoke out in defense of "freedom of expression."[1] Deng, who had no understanding of "socialism with a human face," considered free elections as synonymous with capitalism.

He expressed his dissatisfaction to Hu Yaobang, whom he held responsible, and in March at the All-China Conference on Problems of Science and Technology he again raised the issue of ideals and discipline.[2] Thereafter he repeatedly emphasized that a constant struggle against "bourgeois liberalization" was necessary. He was convinced that "bourgeois liberalization will plunge our society into turmoil and make it impossible for us to proceed with the work of construction."[3]

But Hu Yaobang, apparently ignoring him, soon reignited Deng's anger. On May 10, Hu gave a two-hour interview to a certain Lu Keng, a Hong Kong journalist and publisher of the biweekly *Baixing* (*Common People*). When Deng learned of the interview, he simply exploded. Lu Keng had praised Hu as the greatest liberal in the CCP leadership and hailed him as the future leader. He also posed a provocative question: "Why wouldn't you [right away] take over the work of Mr. Deng in the Military Commission and become the chairman of the Military Commission while he [Deng] is still in good health?" In other words, Lu was hinting that Hu Yaobang should hasten to take all power into his own hands.

Instead of rebuking the journalist, Hu tried to be witty. He said that Deng enjoyed such great respect in the army that he only needed to utter a single sentence to have it implemented while it took him and Zhao Ziyang five. He added that the chairmanship of the Military Commission was not so onerous, and therefore Deng was simply sparing Hu and Zhao time to focus on more important matters.[4]

On June 28, Deng summoned a member of the Secretariat, Hu Qili, who was close to Hu Yaobang, requesting that he convey his unhappiness to Hu Yaobang because the latter was not adhering firmly to the Four Cardinal Principles. Hu Qili did so immediately, but Hu Yaobang did not respond, probably considering himself innocent.

Then on July 14, Deng again summoned Hu Qili and irritably said, "Someone [he had in mind Lu Keng and other bourgeois liberals] is egging on Yaobang and using his name to attack our domestic and foreign policy." He demanded that Hu Yaobang focus on the struggle against liberalism. But still Hu did not comply.[5]

Hearing of this, Zhao Ziyang, despite his friction with the general secretary, advised Hu to indulge Deng by convening a special meeting of the Secretariat on the struggle against bourgeois liberalization. "At that time, it was impossible to take a position opposed to Deng Xiaoping's," he recalled.[6] Hu still balked, refusing to act against his conscience. Unlike Deng, he was actually trying to build socialism with a human face in China.

Deng could not retire before he settled on a successor, and Hu, obviously, no longer suited him. He impatiently awaited the Thirteenth Congress of the CCP to replace Hu with someone more compliant.

Meanwhile, the discontented Patriarch was pondering whether to convene the Thirteenth Congress two years earlier, but other leaders were not supportive. Instead, it was decided to hold an all-China conference and two plenums in the fall of 1985 to effect radical renovation of the entire party and state leadership. Younger people from forty to fifty would replace a large number of veterans.

Deng, however, did not want to raise the question of Hu at a conference or a plenum. The retirement of the general secretary is a very serious matter; it might evoke unwanted discussions among the public. Therefore, it would be better to leave this for the regular party congress, where his retirement could be presented as a transition to another assignment. Deng was inclined to make Hu the chairman of the PRC or have Hu replace him as chairman of the Military Commission, but only if he vacated the post of general secretary. (Now Deng looked forward to retiring at the Thirteenth Congress in the fall of 1987,[7] especially since from the mid-1980s he had begun to manifest symptoms of Parkinson's disease.[8])

In mid-September the Fourth Plenum of the CC was convened, at which 131 veterans asked, and were granted permission, to retire.[9] Two days later, speaking at the party conference, Hu Yaobang declared that in place of those who were retiring, the CC was recommending co-option of a roughly equivalent number of new members, all of whom were approved by the assembled delegates.[10] Deng was satisfied. "A satisfactory job has been done," he said. "A number of veteran cadres have taken the lead in abolishing the system of life tenure in leading posts, furthering the reform of the cadre system. This deserves special mention in the annals of our Party."[11]

The Fifth Plenum of the CC, which convened immediately thereafter, chose six new Politburo members, who began to be referred to as the future leaders of the third generation (counting Mao and Deng as the first generation and Hu and Zhao as the second). Outstanding among them were fifty-six-year-old Hu Qili, a liberal, and Li Peng, a conservative who was Zhao's fifty-seven-year-old deputy. Hu Qili was close to Hu Yaobang—many in the party looked upon him as the future successor to Hu as general secretary—and Li Peng was the adopted son of Zhou Enlai and Deng Yingchao and was eyeing the premiership. Li Peng maintained ties with many veterans who were mostly conservative, and who influenced Li's thinking. He felt at ease in their company because many of them remembered his genuine father and especially his famous uncle (Zhao Shiyan), who had both perished as heroes for the revolution. It was said that Elder Sister Deng (this is how Zhou Enlai's widow was referred to by the leadership), who was half a year older than Deng Xiaoping, issued an ultimatum when hints were dropped that she should retire, "Good, I'll go, but Li Peng should take my place in the Politburo."[12] Naturally, no one disputed her; even without this, little Li's fate had long since been determined.

During the conference, to spite Hu Yaobang, whom he could not forgive, Deng began publicly praising Zhao Ziyang, not only for his successful reforms but also for firmly upholding the Four Cardinal Principles. Many took the hint that Deng was thinking of replacing Hu with Zhao. That is essentially what happened. Bypassing Hu Yaobang, Deng turned to Zhao to prepare the basic documents for the Thirteenth Party Congress. A while later, in May 1986, he informed Hu Yaobang that he intended to retire from the Politburo Standing Committee and the chairmanship of the Military Commission at the Thirteenth Congress in 1987. Hu politely replied that he too would retire. Deng did not try to dissuade him, as Hu Yaobang had apparently expected, but merely noted that it was not yet time for such a young person to retire completely; somewhat lighter work could be found for him. Deng suggested that Hu would "partly retire," that is, he would resign from the post of general secretary but would be elected either head of the Military Commission or chair of the People's Republic of China. Hu agreed.[13]

Hu Yaobang should have been able to read the writing on the wall and use the time before the congress to regain the trust of the Patriarch, but he did not, despite the fact that in 1986 Deng gave him what was probably his last chance, namely, to oversee preparation of a draft resolution for the forthcoming Sixth Plenum of the CC in September, "On the Guiding Principles for Building a Socialist Society with an Advanced Culture and Ideology." This resolution was intended to conclusively shut up the liberals, who were expecting not only economic growth but also profound transformation of the political system. Deng was prepared to reorganize the structure, but not the system, of power.[14] Such reorganization would have a positive impact on developing the economy, freeing it from excessive oversight by party organs, enabling factory directors to manage the economy more effectively, and empowering the masses to take a more active role in the production process.[15] But such a reform could not satisfy the nonparty dissenting intellectuals. Some party members also expressed disagreement. Such well-known communists as the astrophysicist Fang Lizhi and the public intellectuals Liu Binyan and Wang Ruowang repeatedly declared that China should take the American and West European path in developing democracy.[16] Deng advised Hu Yaobang to expel all three of them from the party, but Hu kept putting off a decision. This was why Deng wanted to adopt a resolution concerning creation of a socialist society with "an advanced culture and ideology."

As expected, Hu Yaobang also failed this final test. In August 1986, at a conference in Beidaihe, conservatives criticized the draft resolution prepared by Hu's Secretariat as fundamentally flawed because it did not include language about the struggle against bourgeois liberalization. A fistful of party veterans immediately attacked Hu Yaobang, demanding that he include this point. A majority, including Zhao, supported them, and Hu reluctantly made this correction.

Deng was terribly dissatisfied. After the conference he told Hu Yaobang that when he (Deng) retired from all his posts, it would be better for Hu not to head the Military Commission but rather the Central Advisory Commission. Then he shared his discontent concerning Hu with Yang Shangkun and Bo Yibo. "If I have made a mistake in life, then it is that I judged Hu Yaobang incorrectly," he said to Yang Shangkun, barely containing his rage. After discussing the situation, the veterans fully supported Deng's decision to replace Hu Yaobang.[17] Anger clouded Deng's judgment. Speaking of what a gentleman should bear in mind, Confucius had said, "when angry, to ponder the consequences."[18] Deng failed to do this. Four years later he would have reason to wish that he had.

Meanwhile, the Sixth CC Plenum opened on September 28. Several liberal supporters of Hu, including former head of the CC CCP propaganda department Lu Dingyi and the former leader of Anhui Wan Li, proposed deleting from the draft resolution the directive to struggle against bourgeois liberalization, but the majority resolutely opposed this. Hu Yaobang, who was chairing the plenum, took an evasive position.[19] Then Deng spoke and ended the discussion: "With regard to the question of opposing bourgeois liberalization, I am the one who has talked about it most often and most insistently ... [because] liberalization itself is bourgeois in nature—there is no such thing as proletarian or socialist liberalization. . . . Our current politics demands that we use it in the resolution, and I am in favor of it."[20] Deng said he was ready to continue the struggle against liberalization for ten or twenty years, and then he added, "So someone didn't like it. Okay, let's add on fifty years or more, seventy years altogether, so that now we'll oppose liberalism until the middle of the next century."[21]

After the plenum the veterans continued to criticize Hu on all fronts. "His work as a leader had already become very difficult," wrote an eyewitness.[22] On Deng's instructions, Zhao Ziyang began to work on the reform of the political structure. All the veterans supported him; they had already decided to make him general secretary at the Thirteenth Congress.

Just then events occurred in China that hastened the fall of Hu Yaobang. In Hefei in mid-December, student demonstrations demanding the very liberalization that Deng feared so much took place. They were supported by students in nearby Shanghai and Nanjing. The ideological inspiration and main organizer of these demonstrations was the astrophysicist Fang Lizhi, who had crossed swords with the authorities as far back as 1955 while a student in the Physics Department at Peking University. Later he was persecuted thrice. By the mid-1980s, his ideas and political outlook had matured. Although he was a member of the party, Fang fought for freedom of expression and praised Andrei Sakharov, the Soviet nuclear physicist and a leading dissident. In 1984 he became the vice president of the University of Science and Technology (UST) in Hefei and began to promote an atmosphere of freedom of thought in this institution. Fang lectured not only at UST but also in a number of higher educational institutions in Shanghai and Nanjing.

Wang Ruowang, another popular dissident who was deputy editor-in-chief of the journal *Shanghai wenxue* (*Shanghai Literature*), also often lectured in various venues in Shanghai. He too had endured a lot in his lifetime, imprisoned by the Guomindang and twice by the Maoists. Liu Binyan as well had been repeatedly persecuted in the late 1950s and 1960s. His articles about the corruption of those in power were widely admired. Thus, it was not surprising that disturbances, starting in Hefei in November, soon spread to other cities. Students came out on the streets chanting "Freedom or death!" They demanded honest elections for municipal assemblies, freedom of speech, and other democratic rights. The demonstrations rolled through some seventeen cities, and students from 150 colleges and universities took part.[23]

To a significant degree, the students, of course, were imitating the young South Koreans and Filipinos who several months earlier had held demonstrations in their countries demanding the overthrow of dictatorships. In the Philippines, their actions in late February 1986 had led to the downfall of the regime of Ferdinand Marcos. News from Taiwan that on September 28, 1986, the first opposition party—the Democratic Progressive Party—had been founded also provided a powerful impetus to the movement.

The upwelling of discontent with the dictatorship of the Communist party was natural, especially since during the previous year there had been a significant deterioration in the economic situation of students, and the part of the urban population that had been unable to gain its footing in the new economy. Rising prices and inflation, the inevitable side effects of market reforms, were taking their toll. Prices began to rise sharply in the first half of 1985: in six months they shot up 14 percent, while inflation was 16 percent.[24] In the second half of 1985 and in 1986 the situation did not improve.

Many ordinary people were extremely upset with official corruption. Not only did bureaucrats take bribes in the most flagrant manner but they also became involved in economic activities directly and through their relatives. This was natural since in Chinese clan-based society, *guanxi* (relations, connections) continued to play a central role. Only those who had relatives or friends in high positions were able to make their way in the world. It was no accident that Deng's younger son, Fei Fei, and his wife were among the first to study in the United States. Returning in the mid-1980s, they began to do business in the Hong Kong market. In 1985, Deng's eldest son, Pufang, became head of the All-China Association of Invalids; in 1979 his daughter Deng Nan suddenly rose to political prominence in the State Science Commission. At the same time, Deng Nan's husband became the general manager of one of the largest military companies. Another of Deng's daughters, Maomao, initially helped her father as his confidential secretary, and later along with her husband she succeeded in the business world. (Stubborn rumors circulate in China that all of Deng's children, with the exception of his eldest daughter, Deng Lin, were less than honest, but who knows if these accusations are true?[25])

Thus Chinese students in late 1986 had many reasons to express dissatisfaction. Their tribune Fang Lizhi suggested, "What kind of modernization is required. . . . We need complete modernization, not just modernization in a few chosen aspects. . . . I personally agree with the 'complete Westernizers.' . . . Orthodox socialism from Marx and Lenin to Stalin and Mao Zedong has been a failure."[26] When, at the end of November, the former leader of Anhui, Wan Li, came to UST to extinguish the still-developing movement and said that he had granted the students quite a lot of freedom and democracy, Fang Lizhi responded sharply, "It's not up to any single person to hand out democracy." Several days later at a student meeting, he declared, "Democracy is not conferred from above, but achieved in open struggle."[27]

Student ferment continued throughout December. In Shanghai in mid-December some workers joined them. In the center of the city, literally overflowing with demonstrations, as many as sixty thousand people may have taken to the streets. Fang Lizhi gave a brilliant speech in which he castigated the antidemocratic leadership of the CCP. The Shanghai party boss, Jiang Zemin, asked the students to return to their campuses but was ignored. Ultimately, Jiang resorted to force, but before doing so he issued a strict order labeling the demonstrations illegal.[28] Just then, in a mark of solidarity with their fellows in Shanghai, on December 24 students in Beijing tried marching to Tiananmen Square but were stopped by police. The Beijing Municipal Council also banned demonstrations, but on January 1 and 2 students organized demonstrations on Tiananmen Square. In early January, Tianjin students lay down on railways as a sign of protest. In a few days, the demonstrations gradually died down in all the cities. Again democracy was the loser.

Deng was enraged. He blamed the spinelessness of Hu Yaobang. On December 30, he invited Hu, Zhao, Wan Li, Hu Qili, Li Peng, and the deputy chairman of the State Education Commission, He Dongchang, to his home and declared, "Firm measures must be taken. . . . A disturbance . . . is the result of failure over the past several years to take a firm, clear-cut stand against bourgeois liberalization." He demanded the urgent dismissal of Fang Lizhi, Wang Ruowang, and Liu Binyan from the party,[29] but his main blow was directed against Hu Yaobang. He virtually accused Hu of taking "a laissez-faire attitude towards bourgeois liberalization."[30]

Hu was deeply dispirited. Two days after New Year he wrote Deng a letter of resignation in which he regretted not having shown sufficient firmness
in upholding the Four Cardinal Principles and having unwittingly served as
the "patron" of bad people. Contrary to party norms, Deng now decided to
replace the general secretary right away, not waiting for the forthcoming congress. On January 4, Deng gathered the old guard (Bo Yibo, Wang Zhen,
Yang Shangkun, Chen Yun, and Peng Zhen) at his home and also invited the
"youngsters" Zhao Ziyang and Wan Li. Without saying a word, he handed
them Hu Yaobang's letter. After everyone had read it, in an icy tone he said,
"We need to approve the retirement." No one objected. Deng installed Zhao
Ziyang as head of the Standing Committee. He added that they should tread
lightly with Hu Yaobang: summon him to a "party life meeting"—a kind of
party tribunal—but after criticizing him allow him to remain a member of
the Politburo Standing Committee.[31]

The party life meeting took place from January 10 to 15. Deng did not
attend it and let others do his dirty work for him. With Bo Yibo presiding,
Hu made two self-criticisms and was the target of unremitting criticism.
He was accused of violating the principles of collective leadership, failing to
maintain discipline, not understanding economics, being conceited, practic-
ing liberalism, and even attempting to overthrow Deng Xiaoping. Hu could
not control himself and burst out sobbing. But his tears could not move the
steely communists. What was most painful for Hu was that even his close
friends took part in tormenting him.[32] Only Wan Li took pity on the victim
of intraparty savagery. Knowing that Hu Yaobang loved dog meat, that very
same evening he sent his man over to bring him roast dog.[33]

The next day, January 16, an enlarged meeting of the Politburo under
Deng's chairmanship wrote finis to the Hu Yaobang affair. At the end of the
meeting everyone unanimously approved the resolution "To accept Comrade
Hu Yaobang's request to resign from the post of general secretary of the CC;
to appoint Zhao Ziyang as acting general secretary."[34] Zhao, in the Chinese
fashion, declared that he was "unworthy," but he did not resist for long.[35]
There was work to do, reforms to implement, the congress to prepare—and
all of this under very difficult circumstances.

Right after the Politburo meeting, Deng, supported by the conservatives,
launched a new mass campaign to struggle against bourgeois liberalism. All
the opponents of market reforms immediately raised their heads, making life
very difficult for Zhao to pursue economic reforms. Deng could not calm
down. He "suggested compiling a list of liberals and punishing them one after
another."[36] Soon the conservatives began to attack well-known reformers,
especially those who had helped Zhao push reforms.

Finally, Zhao requested a meeting with Deng, who received him on April 28. Complaining that "certain people were using the campaign to resist reform," the new general secretary doubted whether, under the circumstances, it would be possible to hold a successful Thirteenth Congress, at which it was intended to adopt a series of measures aimed at accelerating and deepening economic reform.[37] Deng himself realized he had gone too far. He began to stress the danger from the left and threw his support to Zhao.[38] In May 1987, the Chinese press began to emphasize pushing forward economic reforms.

From then on, preparations for the Thirteenth Congress proceeded smoothly. With the aid of his staff, Zhao prepared an extremely progressive report, which Deng approved. But the economic sections of the report, which underlined Zhao's commitment to market reforms as integral to the development of a socialist commodity economy, provoked Chen Yun's displeasure. Knowing that Deng liked the report, Chen Yun neither criticized nor supported it, but at the congress itself Chen Yun suddenly arose and stalked out at the very start of Zhao's presentation. Zhao understood he had acquired an additional enemy.[39]

The Thirteenth Congress of the CCP convened from October 25 to November 1, 1987, attended by 1,936 voting delegates and sixty-one nonvoting "specially invited delegates." By this time the CCP had grown to almost forty-six million members. As the acknowledged top leader, Deng, looking hale and hearty, opened the forum with a brief opening statement. Everyone stood to sing the *Internationale*. After the singing and a moment of silence in memory of Mao Zedong, Zhou Enlai, Liu Shaoqi, Zhu De, and other deceased revolutionaries of the older generation, Deng turned the podium over to Zhao.

After first sketching recent achievements, Zhao praised Deng Xiaoping for his "significant contributions" to the formation and development of the CCP's correct, Marxist line, "his courage in developing Marxist theory, his realistic approach, his rich experience and his foresight and sagacity."[40] Deng had never previously been so highly praised from the tribunal of a party congress. Zhao spoke even more enthusiastic words about the Patriarch in his report to the First Plenum of the Thirteenth Central Committee on November 2, revealing that he and all the other leaders consulted with Deng on all the most important questions, since Deng, as the party's main leader, had the right to make the ultimate decision. The plenum unanimously approved this, instructing Zhao and the others to obey Deng, and giving Deng the right to convene leadership meetings at his discretion.[41]

Back in March 1987, in a private conversation with Zhao, Deng had finally expressed his intention to retire from the CC, the Politburo, and its Standing

Committee. At the request of Zhao and other liberals, he agreed to remain chair of the Military Commission in order to keep the conservatives in check and preserve stability. Deng referred to this jokingly as "semiretirement." He wanted to retain power, but be relieved of the multitude of formal obligations. They arrived at a resolution: Zhao would praise Deng, and Deng would retire, but at Zhao's request the CC plenum would leave him as the supreme leader, regarding him in the role of "mother-in-law" (that is the term they used, naturally as a joke, referring to the informal head of the family, in this case the Politburo Standing Committee).[42] In early July it was decided that two more veteran political heavyweights, Chen Yun and Li Xiannian, would also go into semiretirement. Both would resign from the Central Committee and the Politburo, but Chen would become chair of the Central Advisory Commission and Li Xiannian chair of the National Committee of the Chinese People's Political Consultative Conference.

At the start of the Thirteenth Congress, Zhao paid his due to Mother-in-law Deng and then delivered his full report, which contained many innovations, including the definition of the current stage of development of the PRC as "the primary stage of socialism." This phase, in his words, should last for not less than one hundred years.[43] Many years later, Zhao acknowledged that he had laid particular stress on this term and grounded it theoretically in order to gratify the conservatives. He himself understood very well that China was a long way from socialism, but to say so would have aroused the ire of the veterans. "The primary stage of socialism" was thus the optimal formula. On one hand, it did not deny the achievements in socialist construction, and on the other hand Zhao and his liberal reformers "were totally freed from the restrictions of orthodox socialist principles."[44]

This verbal sleight of hand enabled Zhao Ziyang to advance many new ideas, in particular commercialization of production; transfer of the property rights of a number of small enterprises to collectives and individuals; separation of ownership from management in state enterprises; development of contracts, leases, and a stock market; enlargement of the market in the means of production, services, and finance; transition to market prices for the majority of goods and services; strengthening of the role of banks in the system of macroeconomic regulation; and even encouraging the private economy on the basis of hired labor.[45]

Obviously, Chen Yun had good reason to stalk out of the hall during Zhao's report. Zhao was not too worried, though, and after the congress he started saying that in two or three years the sphere of planning would be reduced from 60 percent to 30 percent of the economy.[46]

At the conclusion of the congress, elections were held for the CC. As had been agreed, Deng was not on the ballot, yet he was again designated chairman of the Military Commission. Hu Yaobang remained on the Politburo but was removed from the Standing Committee, which, in addition to Zhao Ziyang, included Yao Yilin, Li Peng, Hu Qili, and Qiao Shi, a veteran party member with responsibilities in intelligence and security affairs. Included in the Politburo were the Shanghai "hero" Jiang Zemin, who had successfully pacified the students; and Li Tieying, the son of Deng Xiaoping's former wife, Jin Weiying, who soon became the chairman of the State Commission on Economic Reform and, one year later, of the State Education Committee.[47] Zhao was confirmed as general secretary of the CC. Subsequently, he relinquished the post of premier, and Li Peng was appointed in his place.

Deng was ecstatic. Everything was going according to his plan. He didn't much care for Li Peng, but Chen Yun and Li Xiannian pressed the case for Zhou Enlai's foster son. Deng ultimately agreed, demanding that Li Peng publicly denounce the Soviet hegemonists. (For some reason Deng considered Li Peng pro-Soviet, most likely because he had studied for a long time in the USSR in the late 1940s and early 1950s.) Li complied and became premier.[48]

The new year of 1988 seemed to promise further successes on all fronts; instead it became the most difficult of all the years of reforms. New attempts to liberalize the economy led to a sharp rise in prices. In May rumors spread that Zhao planned to free prices on a majority of goods and services in the near future. This quickly led to a jump in market prices exceeding an annualized rate of 50 percent. Prices for alcohol and cigarettes shot up 200 percent![49] In early July inflation stood at 40 percent.

But the worst happened in August, after *People's Daily* published the Politburo's resolution on the reform of prices and wages.[50] Although it said that prices would be freed over a period of five years and not at once, people panicked, removed money from their bank accounts, and swept everything they could off the store shelves, from soap to rice to the most expensive electronic goods.[51] Forced to retreat, Deng and Zhao declared that the price reform would be delayed for five years or longer. But people were unable to calm down.

Meanwhile, Deng's bogeyman of liberalization began to grow stronger again, this time strengthened from late 1987 on by the wind of freedom and *glasnost* reaching China from the USSR. Intellectuals and many city folk as well, avidly imbibed the news from Moscow. Mikhail Gorbachev instantly became the most popular figure. University students hurried to learn Russian. On learning that foreigners were Russian, Chinese would signal with a raised thumb, *"Geerbaqiaofu hao!"* (Gorbachev is good!) Bus drivers placed photographs of the Soviet leader in their front windows. Many people hoped that Deng would follow Gorbachev's path.[52]

But Chinese leaders, and Deng himself, had mixed feelings about the reforms in the Soviet Union. They feared *glasnost* but reacted positively to the changes in Soviet foreign policy. Of course, the long years of enmity could not be quickly forgotten. Moreover, Gorbachev still retained a million troops along the border of the PRC, including in Mongolia. His forces were still in Afghanistan, and he supported Vietnam, which was occupying Cambodia. Thus, from Deng's perspective the USSR was still threatening China. Deng demanded that the USSR remove the so-called Three Obstacles on the path to normalization: resolve the border, Afghan, and Vietnam-Cambodia questions on terms favorable to the PRC. Only then would he be ready to normalize Soviet-Chinese relations.

Gorbachev too dreamed of restoring good relations with China. He addressed this issue in Vladivostok on July 28, 1986, even expressing his willingness to discuss the Three Obstacles.[53] Deng responded positively in an interview with the American journalist Mike Wallace on September 2, 1986.[54] Then on February 26, 1987, at a Politburo session, Gorbachev declared that "we must work . . . toward China," adding that it would be good to "try to induce Deng Xiaoping to come to Moscow."[55]

In February, lengthy negotiations commenced at the level of deputy foreign ministers, dealing initially with border issues and then the Vietnam-Cambodia question. Under pressure from Gorbachev, who yielded on all points, the two sides eventually reached complete mutual understanding. On July 30, 1987, Gorbachev suggested publishing the works of Deng Xiaoping in Russian as a signal of Moscow's willingness to start a serious dialogue with Beijing. His Politburo colleagues responded enthusiastically.[56] In early 1988, a collection of Deng's speeches and talks was published and a favorable review printed in *Pravda*.[57]

Exchanges of visits by the Chinese and Soviet foreign ministers followed, and by February 1989 agreement was reached to hold a summit meeting. The eighty-four-year-old Deng, of course, would not go to Moscow; he graciously consented to receive Mikhail Gorbachev. The visit was set for May 15–17, 1989.[58]

Deng was ready for Gorbachev's visit. In spite of the economic problems, China was still on the rise and the Communist Party's dictatorship seemed to be unshakable. So did Deng's authority.

The Tiananmen Tragedy

THEN THE ROOF caved in. Something entirely unexpected overshadowed both the inflation that was running rampant through the country and the preparations for Gorbachev's visit that were consuming the Chinese leaders in Beijing. At a Politburo meeting on the morning of April 8, 1989, Hu Yaobang suddenly felt unwell. He turned pale, rose from his seat, and waved at general secretary Zhao Ziyang who was chairing the meeting.

"Comrade Ziyang. May I be excused?"
Then he fell to the floor unconscious.
Zhao cried out, "Does anyone have nitroglycerin?"
"I do," Jiang Zemin quickly replied, "but I don't know how to use it. I've never had heart problems."

Someone quickly placed two tablets under Hu's tongue. They called the nearest hospital, no. 305, which was across the street from Zhongnanhai, but forgot to notify the guards. Ten minutes passed before the doctors were allowed in. When the ambulance finally arrived, the doctors diagnosed a heart attack. Hu was taken to hospital, where the doctors tried their best to save him; but a week later he died. He was only seventy-three.[1]

Soon thereafter, when the whole country learned of Hu's death, people cried on hearing the news. Regarded by many as the soul of the nation and an honest communist, Hu was particularly beloved by intellectuals, who believed he had suffered undeservedly from having supported the students in late 1986. There were calls for Deng to publicly rehabilitate Comrade Hu.

On the evening of April 15, the news broke, and the following day students gathered on campuses in Beijing. "He who should have lived has died," they proclaimed, adding, "he who should have died lives."[2] Some of the students trekked to the Monument to the People's Heroes in Tiananmen Square at the Gate of Heavenly Peace to place wreaths of white flowers in Hu's memory.[3] Shortly afterward a spontaneous movement erupted. On April 18, three days after Hu's death, several hundred students presented a list of political demands to the Standing Committee of the National People's Congress: "Freedom and democracy; Completely repudiate efforts to 'eliminate spiritual pollution'; Lift all bans on newspapers and implement freedom of the press; Require officials to resign for serious mistakes; Make the Central Government subject to popular votes of confidence; Publicize the incomes of leaders and their children; Release political prisoners unconditionally."[4]

Then, on the following evening, a crowd of two thousand gathered in front of Zhongnanhai, the compound inside which most of China's top leaders lived. "Hu Yaobang is not dead!" they shouted. "Down with Li Peng!" One of the impassioned students shouted, "Down with the Communist party!" At one point some students tried to break into the compound. When they failed they sat down on the ground, refusing to disperse. Police began beating them, shoving some into specially mustered buses. A riot ensued. It was a long night. Order was not restored until 5:00 a.m., but, as it turned out, only for a short time. On April 20 and 21, many students again gathered in the center of Beijing demanding the political rehabilitation of Hu Yaobang, an intensified fight against corruption, an end to business founded on *guanxi* (personal connections), and freedom to all Chinese citizens. As the days passed, the size of the demonstrations increased. On April 22, ten thousand people gathered in front of the Great Hall of the People on Tiananmen Square. Inside, a forty-minute memorial service for Hu Yaobang was taking place and the students were orderly, listening to the broadcast in bitter silence.[5]

Deng reacted calmly to the death of his former comrade. He had long since lost interest in him. In 1987, he still invited him to play bridge but did not conduct any serious talks. After December 30, 1987, Deng and Hu cut even these formal "card relations." Deng did not even visit Hu in the hospital, though Yang Shangkun and other Politburo members asked him twice to do so. "I am not a physician," Deng snapped.[6] Reviewing Zhao Ziyang's draft funeral speech on April 20, while student demonstrators filled the capital's squares, Deng deleted the phrase "great Marxist". Making a sour face, he said, "There's already too much about his merits. We won't raise the question of his dismissal, [but] none of us, including me, can be called a 'great Marxist'. When I die, don't call me that either."[7] Following his wife's advice, however, Deng attended the funeral service in the Great Hall of the People on April

22, expressing his condolences to Hu's widow and children. But he seemed unmoved, and he did not make a speech.

The Paramount Leader was most worried about student demonstrations in the center of the capital and their "impudent" demands. He was always inclined to use force to resolve such matters, but Zhao, who visited him on April 19, assured him that everything was under control. Deng bided his time, but he did not calm down. On April 23, Zhao left on a long-scheduled official visit to North Korea. He asked Premier Li Peng to fill in for him as head of the Politburo Standing Committee, but at the same time he assigned his trusted secretary, Bao Tong, to keep tabs on the situation.[8]

Meanwhile, the disturbances on campuses and in the city center continued unabated; the students began to organize, and leaders emerged. They were joined by students in more than twenty other cities; a genuine democratic student movement was springing to life around the country. Anxious and concerned by developments in the streets, Li Peng and Yang Shangkun asked to see Deng. They met with him on the morning of April 25 and gave him a report from Li Ximin, the first secretary of the Beijing Municipal Party Committee, and Chen Xitong, Beijing's mayor. It described the student demonstrations as antisocialist, and among other things it also pointed out that the students were attacking Deng Xiaoping by name. Li Peng deemed this a manifestation of "bourgeois liberalism."[9]

Not surprisingly, Deng was enraged. In his old age, he had become hypersensitive and suspicious, to the point where he could not abide any criticism. "This is not an ordinary student movement; this is a rebellion," Deng asserted.

> We need to raise the pure banner and take effective measures to suppress these disorders. We need to act quickly to gain time. . . . The goal of these people is to overthrow the leadership of the Communist party and rob the country and the people of the future. . . . This is a rebellion—a well-planned plot. . . . We must do everything possible to avoid bloodletting, but we should understand that it will probably be impossible to avoid it completely.[10]

In Pyongyang, on being informed of Deng's words, Zhao thought it best to express his "full agreement," which he relayed to Deng and other leaders in a telegram.[11] Li Peng then directed *People's Daily* to publish an editorial responding to the students. The editorial was composed by a staff member of the CC under the supervision of Hu Qili who would later feel sorry for this.[12] It repeated Deng's words verbatim, but without indicating their authorship.[13]

Whether Li Peng anticipated it or not, he could have thought of nothing worse. The editorial enraged a majority of the students. They were motivated by patriotism, not by a desire to destroy the party and the socialist system. In fact, they wanted to help the CCP become a genuine party of the people, and to express their sorrow at the loss of the one leader who, it seemed, had understood them.

On April 27, in Beijing alone, some fifty thousand people took part in a protest demonstration. Convinced that the government would try to violently break up the protest, several students wrote their testaments and farewell letters. They were ready to die. The students' fears were well founded. Yang Shangkun had received Deng's approval to deploy five hundred soldiers from the capital military district to assist the police. The students marched in solid ranks along the streets of the city, chanting, "Mother! We have done nothing wrong!" Beijing citizens shouted their support, and some joined in. In many districts even the police expressed their sympathy.

Hearing what was happening on the streets of the capital, the veteran party leaders panicked. Li Xiannian quickly phoned Deng, "We must make a decision and be prepared to arrest hundreds of thousands of people!" Wang Zhen was in complete agreement.[14] But Deng temporized. Gorbachev was arriving in two weeks, and Deng did not want to stain the streets of the capital with blood. For the moment, the students felt safe. They celebrated their victory and expressed their readiness to renew their battle. They felt the party leaders were frightened and ready to capitulate to their demands. Five weeks later, they would learn just how mistaken that assessment was.

The students were not entirely off-base. Deng was increasingly nervous. He understood that many Chinese citizens no longer viewed him as a father-benefactor but instead as a tyrant-suppressor, and he was terribly upset when he learned that Li Peng had not only referred to Deng's decision but even paraphrased his words when he instructed the editor-in-chief of *People's Daily* to publish the notorious editorial. Deng preferred to remain in the shadows; even while issuing strict orders, he still did not want his name bandied about in public. (That such conduct was immoral probably never even entered his head.)

Deng's immediate family members were also concerned about his reputation. Maomao, Deng's daughter, for example, called Bao Tong, Zhao Ziyang's personal secretary, who was drafting Zhao's speech for the forthcoming celebration of the seventieth anniversary of the May 4 Movement of 1919, requesting a paragraph in the speech about how Deng Xiaoping had been concerned about China's youth throughout his whole life. Bao complied after receiving permission from Zhao upon his return from North Korea.[15]

Nevertheless, the general secretary's speech, which Zhao delivered on May 3, greatly increased tension among the party leadership. Although Zhao spoke about historical topics, the parallel between the two patriotic youth movements—that of 1919 and that of 1989—was self-evident. Most importantly, the general secretary, desperately trying to resolve the problem peacefully, provided an assessment of the student disturbances that differed essentially from the editorial that had appeared in *People's Daily*. Not only did Zhao say nothing about the struggle against bourgeois liberalization, but he acknowledged that the young people were acting correctly by striving for democracy and condemning corruption.[16]

Zhao's speech the following day at a meeting of Asian Development Bank leaders went even further. "These students do not oppose our underlying system," Zhao said at the bank meeting, "but they do demand that we eliminate the flaws in our work."[17]

Deng was enraged by Zhao's remarks. He could not forgive Zhao for disavowing Deng's own assessment of the movement. Other veterans, including Li Peng, were similarly indignant. On May 11, Deng told Yang Shangkun that the students' talk about corruption was no more than "smoke. Their real goal was to overthrow the CCP and the socialist system." He then condemned Zhao.

During Deng's conversation with Yang, the name of Jiang Zemin, the Shanghai leader, came up. Two weeks earlier, Jiang Zemin had shut down a local newspaper that was encouraging the people to demonstrate. Although this had aroused a stormy protest among journalists all over China, Deng told Yang Shangkun that Chen Yun and Li Xiannian were ecstatic. It seemed that Deng, too, admired Jiang Zemin's fidelity to the Four Cardinal Principles. Yang Shangkun agreed, adding that the Shanghai boss not only knew how to handle waves of protest but was strikingly well informed about Marxism: "He recited passages from Marx in English," Yang noted.[18] At the end of their talk Deng asked Yang Shangkun to bring Zhao to him.

Two days later, Zhao and Yang Shangkun appeared before Deng. Deng wanted to know why Zhao had suddenly "betrayed" him. After all, as recently as April 25, Zhao had dispatched a telegram from Korea expressing his "complete agreement" with Deng's point of view. Why the sudden about-face? Zhao explained:

I've noticed that . . . the student slogans all support the Constitution; they favor democracy and oppose corruption. These demands are basically in line with what the Party and the government advocate, so we cannot reject them out of hand. . . . The number of demonstrators and supporters is enormous, and they include people from all parts of society. So I think we have to keep an eye on the majority and give approval to the mainstream view of the majority if we want to calm this thing down.

But Deng would have none of it: "We can't be led around by the nose. This movement's dragged on too long, almost a month now. The senior comrades are getting worried. . . . We have to be decisive. I've said over and over that we need stability if we're going to develop. . . . These people want to overthrow our Party and state."[19]

The conversation ended abruptly. Even though he was general secretary of the Party, nominally the highest position, Zhao had made a serious political miscalculation. He failed to understand that in totalitarian China, even thirteen years after the death of Mao, only one opinion could be correct, that of the Leader. Although Deng himself had previously battled against unquestioning adherence to the thoughts and policies of Mao Zedong—the Two Whatevers—he considered his own point of view beyond dispute. An eyewitness recalls, "Deng Xiaoping . . . listened to nobody's opinion. . . . Whatever he decided was hard to change."[20] Like many elderly leaders, he stubbornly believed in his own infallibility.

How quickly everything changed. From that day on, Deng ceased to trust Zhao Ziyang. Zhao was about to become a victim of the very same system that had already crushed Hu Yaobang. As good communists, both Hu and Zhao knew if they followed the established go-along, get-along rules of the party they would have no problems, but at some point their consciences began to torment them and they felt compelled to speak out. Zhao did so at a particularly inopportune time. At this point only two people in the leadership shared his views: Wan Li and Hu Qili.[21]

Meanwhile, Gorbachev's visit was fast approaching. Despite Zhao's speech, offering some hint that some members of the party leadership were sympathetic to their views, many students did not want to back down. The student movement renewed momentum. Demonstrations broke out in fifty-one cities across China. On May 11, some students in Beijing conceived the idea of a massive protest hunger strike in Tiananmen Square to attract the attention of Gorbachev, hoping that the "empathetic" Soviet leader might then intercede on their behalf with Deng. At 2:00 p.m. on May 13, about a thousand students occupied Tiananmen, pitched their tents, and began their hunger strike. "Mother China! Look at your children," they wrote on *dazibao* (big-character posters) that they had hung on a number of campuses the pre-vious evening. "Can you not be moved when you see death approach us?"[22] Now they were basically demanding just one thing from the government: that it admit the hardline April 26 editorial in *People's Daily* was mistaken. But Deng would not budge. It would have meant a serious loss of face for him.

On May 15, the day Gorbachev arrived, two thousand students were already fasting in Tiananmen; the next day there were three thousand. Ten thousand more students surrounded the hunger strikers, expressing their sympathy. Many of them loudly cursed Deng, demanding his retirement. Meanwhile, Deng's meeting with the Soviet general secretary was scheduled to take place in the Great Hall of the People, adjacent to the tent city of the hunger strikers.

For Deng, a hypersensitive eighty-four-year-old, this was a trying moment. Things started out well. Looking cheerful, Deng met with Gorbachev on the morning of May 16, and the two leaders held a two-and-a-half-hour conver-sation "in a free and unconstrained manner." Deng immediately suggested to Gorbachev, "Let bygones be bygones and open the door to the future," and Gorbachev agreed, a first step in normalizing relations between the two countries. Deng then acknowledged that he himself had played "a by no means insignificant role" in the "bitter polemics" between the two parties, saying that, "both sides had contributed a lot of empty talk." But at the same time, Deng reminded his guest how many cruel injustices China had suffered at the hands of Russia in the past. A consummate statesman, Gorbachev replied that we cannot rewrite history, but we can acknowledge the mistakes we committed in the recent past.[23]

During the visit, all the students waited to see whether Gorbachev would come out to meet them. They gathered signatures on an appeal, asking him to address them. A crowd assembled in front of the Soviet embassy, chant-ing, "Gorbachev! Come out!" But he never appeared, especially since he was not staying at the embassy, but in the luxurious Diaoyutai Guest House at the other end of the city. Moreover, he did not want to burden his trip with unnecessary complications.

Consequently, Gorbachev was very surprised when, on the evening of May 16, Zhao suddenly brought up the subject of the student disturbances. Zhao told him, first, that the CCP and the students lacked mutual under-standing; second, that in the future the question of introducing a multiparty system might arise in China; and third, that his guest should know that Deng was in charge of everything in China, that it was Deng who had headed the party and the country ever since the Third Plenum of the Central Committee of the Chinese Communist Party in December 1978. In other words, Zhao placed responsibility for everything that might happen in China in the near future on Deng.[24]

After his talk with Gorbachev, Zhao made another bold but politically ill-advised move. He convened a meeting of the leadership at which he demanded publication of a statement in support of the students and repudiation of the article in *People's Daily*. Li Peng jumped up, saying, "the key phrases of the April 26 editorial were drawn from Comrade Xiaoping's remarks. . . . They cannot be changed." Yang Shangkun supported Li. He "warned that revising the April 26 editorial would damage Deng Xiaoping's image."[25]

After the sparring session, both sides hastened to call Deng. He demanded they all come to see him the next morning, May 17. It would be a decisive and fateful day. At the meeting, only Hu Qili supported Zhao Ziyang. Exasperated, Deng repeated everything he had already said many times about the students, that their goal was to "set up a bourgeois republic on the Western model," and "if our one billion people jumped into multiparty elections, we'd get chaos like the 'all-out civil war' we saw during the Cultural Revolution." "If things continue like this," Deng added, "we could even end up under house arrest." Then he delivered his decision: "I've concluded that we should bring in the People's Liberation Army and declare martial law in Beijing, more precisely in Beijing's urban districts. [In addition to five urban districts in metropolitan Beijing, there are also five rural districts.] The aim of martial law will be to suppress the turmoil once and for all and to return things quickly to normal."[26] Acting on Deng's instructions, Li Peng, Yang Shangkun, and Qiao Shi formed a triumvirate to introduce martial law. Zhao refused to take part in suppressing the students, and that same evening he sent the Central Committee his request to retire. (The next day, under Yang Shangkun's pressure he retracted it, but this changed nothing. By then Deng had already removed him from power.[27])

Within hours, rumors began circulating throughout the city about the imminent imposition of martial law. By the afternoon, about 1.2 million people were in the streets—students, teachers, civil servants, and workers—all expressing solidarity with the hunger strikers on the square and condemning Deng. Placards appeared, "You are old, Xiaoping! When a person turns eighty he turns stupid! Old-man government is due for retirement! Oppose the cult of personality!"[28]

Realizing that his career was over, Zhao Ziyang openly sided with the students. He arrived in a minibus at Tiananmen early on the morning of May

19 to meet with the hunger strikers. Li Peng tried to stop him, but once he understood he couldn't, he joined him, not wishing to turn Zhao into a hero in the eyes of the students. Li Peng quickly withdrew, however, and Zhao addressed the students through a small megaphone. Looking exhausted, he said with great compassion, "We have come too late, forgive us, forgive us. You have the right to criticize us." He pleaded with the students to end their hunger strike, promising to resolve all their problems, perhaps not right away, but gradually.[29] He knew very well, of course, he had no power to do this.

Many in the crowd started crying, and at the end of Zhao's speech they even applauded. Deng, who saw everything on television (Zhao's remarks were broadcast), was unable to control his irritation. Summoning Yang Shangkun, he asked, "Did you hear what he [Zhao] said? Tears were streaming down his face [in reality Zhao did not cry, and why Deng said this is unknown] and he really tried to look mistreated. He's flouted Party principles here—very undisciplined." Yang, Deng's old friend, of course, wholly agreed, and then he suggested that Deng move to Zhongnanhai in the interest of security. But Deng refused.[30]

At 10:00 a.m. on May 20, Li Peng proclaimed martial law in the urban districts of Beijing. By May 26, four hundred thousand troops from military districts all around the country had been deployed around the city.[31]

The students and their sympathizers were indignant. Everywhere one could hear the cries, "Down with the puppet Li Peng! Down with Deng Xiaoping!"[32] Some three hundred thousand people gathered on Tiananmen Square. In various districts around the city, people began to erect barricades to block army units from entering. Events were inexorably moving toward a bloody dénouement.

Meanwhile, late on the night of May 27, Deng assembled seven veteran Party elders at his home—Yang Shangkun, Chen Yun, Li Xiannian, Peng Zhen, Deng Yingchao, Wang Zhen, and Bo Yibo—to discuss who should be the new general secretary. Everyone, of course, was interested in Deng's opinion. He said, "After long and careful comparison, the Shanghai Party secretary, Comrade Jiang Zemin, does indeed seem a proper choice."[33] The others agreed. Several days later, on May 31, while talking to Li Peng and Yao Yilin, Deng declared that he himself was "resolved to withdraw," and as soon as the new leadership headed by Jiang Zemin was in place, he would not interfere in its affairs.[34]

Meanwhile, the students continued to prepare for the final battle. As early as May 24, one of their leaders, Wang Dan, a frail youth wearing large eyeglasses, had called on everyone to defend the square against "the forces of darkness." The students and their supporters began to arm themselves with whatever they could, but of course, they would prove no match for the troops and tanks still gathering around the city. Meanwhile, to lift their spirits, the students and teachers of the Central Art Institute of Beijing erected a plaster statue of the Goddess of Democracy, resembling the Statue of Liberty, on Tiananmen Square. Gradually, however, the number of protesters diminished. By the end of May, only seven to ten thousand demonstrators remained.[35] They were the ones who faced the army on the night of June 4.

The troops forced their way into the city despite the barricades. On the afternoon of June 3, bloody clashes took place on the approaches to Tiananmen. Tanks opened the way, driving straight into the crowds followed by soldiers firing directly at the people. In response, angry demonstrators threw Molotov cocktails at the military vehicles and lynched individual soldiers and officers who strayed from their columns. Within a short time, the streets and avenues leading to the square were stained with blood, the bodies of the dead lay everywhere, and the moans of the wounded filled the air. Smoke billowed from trucks and armored transports that had been torched. Eventually the defenders of the square were forced to retreat. Around 1:30 a.m. on the night of June 4, the troops forced their way into Tiananmen and surrounded it. Over the course of more than three hours, using loudspeakers, the army repeatedly ordered the students to vacate the square. The majority of the students did so by 5:00 a.m. But several hundred remained there. They crowded together in the center of the square at the Monument to the People's Heroes and began singing the *Internationale*. Within forty minutes, they too were forced out by the army tanks. Wiping away tears, mustering all the strength they could, the students shouted at the soldiers, "Fascists! Down with fascism! Bandits! Bandits!" The soldiers did not assault them; instead they concentrated on demolishing the tent city and toppling the statue of the Goddess of Democracy. The whole square was occupied. Meanwhile, other military servicemen combed the campuses and the streets, dispersing crowds and arresting activists. Over the next three days, shooting was audible in several districts of the city. Without warning, soldiers opened fire on any small group of people.[36]

Deng could celebrate another victory, but this time it was a victory over the youth of his own country. According to various estimates, between 220 and 3,000 people died in Beijing from June 3 to June 6. The exact number is in dispute and may never be known. Among the victims was a nine-year-old child.

24

A Retired Patriarch

ON JUNE 4, a light rain fell throughout the day. But on June 5, the sun reappeared and with it the humidity. On Chang'an Avenue, the main thoroughfare, and on neighboring streets lay the blackened skeletons of burned vehicles, chunks of concrete, stones, bicycles, and paving blocks that had been used to construct barricades. Splinters of glass glistened in the sunlight. Already the bodies of the dead were nowhere to be seen, but bloodstains blackened the gray asphalt: yesterday's drizzle had failed to wash them entirely off.

Most residents of Beijing stayed at home, but those who dared to appear on the streets looked depressed. Many of them cried, and swallowing their tears, whispered, "We will not forgive you! Deng Xiaoping, you killed children!"[1]

On June 5, a statement from the Central Committee and the State Council was broadcast on radio and television about the suppression in the capital of a "counterrevolutionary rebellion." Nothing was said about the events in the other cities, although youth demonstrations had taken place in 181 cities. They died down only around June 10.[2]

Deng, too, did not leave his house on either June 4 or June 5, and he saw no one. Only after "order was established," on June 6, did he receive several of the veterans in his home, as well as Li Peng, Yao Yilin, and Qiao Shi. He was very agitated and repeatedly assured everyone that even if foreigners applied sanctions, the "Chinese people" would not turn from their chosen path. He was anxious that the events that had just taken place not hinder the economic reforms that had slowed down after the Black August of 1988.[3] Then it had been necessary to forget about reducing the sphere of planning from 60 percent to 30 percent of the economy. Li Peng, supported by many of the veterans, had adopted a series of measures designed to constrict the market. No one referred any longer to the organic unity of planning and market regulation that Zhao had posited at the Thirteenth Congress. The economy continued to move on two tracks, of which planning was considered primary and the market auxiliary. Mutual penetration of the plan and the market remained basically fragmentary. In September 1988, Li Peng, Yao Yilin, and other members of the State Council had worked out a program of new regulations that the Third Plenum of the Thirteenth Central Committee adopted right away.[4]

Now Bloody June threatened to throw Deng's reforms even farther back. He understood that many in the party, especially the veterans, saw the market reforms as the cause of all the disasters. They said it opened China to the "rotten West," through which "bourgeois liberalization" "contaminated" the minds of the youth. Over and over again, he agonized over how to adhere to a reasonable balance between economic reforms and the Four Cardinal Principles. But no answer to this fundamental question was forthcoming.

On June 9, Deng addressed the command staff of the military units that had taken part in suppressing the student demonstrations. He expressed his gratitude to the military for their efforts and his condolences regarding the soldiers and officers who "had died heroically" in the "struggle" against "counterrevolutionary rebellion." At his suggestion, everyone stood to honor the memory of the fallen fighters and commanders. He reiterated his analysis of what had transpired in April through early June but stressed there would be no return to the previous, leftist policies. Reform would remain on course, and it was simply necessary to conduct educational work among the population.[5] The commanders all applauded, but whether they agreed with the deepening of market reforms is unknown.

A week later, Deng met with the top leaders of the party and the state. Jiang Zemin, Li Peng, Yang Shangkun, Wan Li, and several others were present. Deng repeated his message of May 31 to Li Peng and Yao Yilin, namely, that Jiang Zemin would become the new general secretary and that he (Deng) would soon retire. "Of course, if you want to consult me, I'm not going to turn you down, but it won't be the way it used to be. . . . You must be responsible for everything," he added, after which once again he spoke about developing the economy. "Economic development should not slow down," he declared, calling on the younger comrades to take measures so that the development of the country would be "steady and sustained" and external economic ties as broad as possible.[6]

An enlarged session of the Politburo followed on June 19–21, at which the matter of Zhao was examined. As with Hu Yaobang two and a half years earlier, everyone in concert subjected their former comrade to savage criticism, but unlike the emotional Hu, Zhao not only refused to acknowledge any fault but stubbornly defended his position. In violation of party regulations, Deng allowed everyone present to vote, whether or not they were members of the Politburo, and the majority, naturally, raised their hands in favor of the dismissal of the "renegade" from the post of general secretary and his expulsion from the CC, the Politburo, and its Standing Committee. Only one person, Zhao himself, voted no. He said, "I do not take issue with being dismissed from my positions, but I do not agree with the . . . accusations."[7] Neither Deng nor Li Peng, who was presiding over the session, nor anyone else responded.

Soon, on June 23–24, the Fourth Plenum of the CC confirmed the decision of the enlarged Politburo meeting regarding Zhao. Li Peng delivered the main report on Zhao Ziyang, depicting the former general secretary in the worst light. Materials from the CC General Office were distributed to the members of the plenum in which Zhao was presented as "a conspirator and representative of counterrevolutionary forces in the country and overseas aimed at overthrowing the Chinese Communist Party and Deng."[8] After the plenum, Zhao was placed under house arrest, and an investigation of him was initiated. It lasted for three years, until October 1992, but a verdict was not revealed, apparently because the leaders did not want to stir up the past. However, they acquainted Zhao himself with the lengthy document, which contained thirty accusations; they took no supplemental measures with respect to the prisoner.[9] Zhao remained under house arrest until his death on January 17, 2005.[10]

As the veterans had already determined, the plenum chose Jiang Zemin to replace Zhao—unanimously, of course. They also sacked Hu Qili from the Secretariat, the Politburo, and its Standing Committee because he had steadfastly supported Zhao during the Tiananmen events.[11] No sanctions were applied against Wan Li; at the decisive moment he had stood with Deng.

It seemed that everything had worked out well for Deng, but his agitation did not abate. All summer and fall he continued to emphasize the need to continue the reforms, but his appeals fell on deaf ears. It was not just the old guard, but the new as well (Jiang Zemin, Li Peng, and others) who remained passive. The Tiananmen events probably undermined Deng's authority not only among the people but in the party leadership as well. As early as the enlarged session of the Politburo on June 19–21, several leading members of the CCP in reality condemned Deng's reforms under the guise of criticizing Zhao.[12] Despite the Patriarch's appeals, the reforms stalled. Deng, who had a poor grasp of economics, now had no one on whom to depend. On such questions Jiang Zemin and Li Peng were oriented toward Chen Yun and Li Xiannian, whose influence grew. An active struggle against "bourgeois liberalization" resumed while the pace of economic growth slackened.

In mid-August 1989, just before he turned eighty-five, Deng firmly decided: I will retire once and for all. On August 17, he informed Yang Shangkun and Wang Zhen. (All three were vacationing near the Yellow Sea at Beidaihe.[13]) He supposed that Li Xiannian and Chen Yun would also fully retire; to leave both conservatives in power would jeopardize reform. But they absolutely refused, stubbornly holding on to their prestigious positions. (They would pass away on the job, Li in 1992 and Chen Yun in 1995.) So Deng had to retire by himself. On September 4, he made his intentions known to Jiang Zemin, Li Peng, and other leaders of the younger generation. His parting words were, "China must have a leading collective with the image of people who favor the policies of reform and opening to the outside world. I hope you will pay special attention to this point. We cannot abandon those policies."[14] At the same time, he submitted his request to the Politburo to retire from the post of chair of the Central Military Commission.[15]

In early November, the Fifth Plenum of the Thirteenth Central Committee approved his request, emphasizing that the full retirement of the "outstanding leader of the Chinese people" was not caused at all by deterioration in his health; it only bore witness to "the broad-mindedness of a great proletarian revolutionary."[16] Jiang Zemin was chosen as chair of the Central Military Commission in Deng's place. Deng handed him and Li Peng the reins of government.

FROM THEN ON, Deng spent all his days within the circle of his family. As before, he frequently strolled about in his courtyard, usually with Zhuo Lin, who had also grown old. They walked arm in arm, taking several turns around the path that encircled the park. They both supported themselves on canes and walked in silence as Deng did not much like talking with his family members. He simply walked and thought his own thoughts. His staff joked that "Grandfather decides the fate of China on this narrow footpath." Everyone called him "Grandfather"—not only his grandchildren, but also Zhuo Lin, his children, and his servants.[17] Although he no longer made many decisions, to the members of his household he remained the most important person. During his strolls he loved to walk to a small pond in the center of the park, beautifully encircled by stone masonry in the guise of flowers. He would gaze for a long time at the goldfish cavorting in the water. He would crumble pieces of bread that they, with gaping mouths, greedily devoured.

Everything took its course. Every evening the family members seated themselves at the round table in the dining room. Deng loved to eat well, but he no longer did any cooking. Like other honored party leaders, he had a chef who knew his boss's tastes. In his old age, Deng still preferred very spicy and fatty food: pork with red peppers and roast brisket. He would not allow leftovers to be discarded: "Anyone who throws out leftovers is a fool," he said, with a smile. "One can braise them and eat them the next day."[18]

His passion for bridge did not desert him, and he continued to play even more often than before. He also loved billiards, but had not picked up a cue since the time he had broken his femoral bone in 1959, after slipping while playing a game. He was very proud when, in July 1988, he was chosen as honorary president of the All-China Association of Bridge Players. But he swelled up with pride even more when five years later, in 1993, he received an official certificate from the head of the World Bridge Association "for developing and promoting" bridge throughout the world.

Soccer was another of his passions. He himself had never played it, but he adored watching it on television and in the stadium. If for whatever reason he missed a television broadcast, he always asked his bodyguard Zhang Baozhong to videotape it for him.[19]

During the summer months, Deng and his family went to the seashore, either to Beidaihe or to Qingdao, where they stayed in the CC guest house near the shore. He loved to swim, not in sheltered swimming pools but in the open, to experience the freedom. In his eighties he swam for an hour a day with his children and bodyguards.[20]

Of course, he could not give up work entirely. Every day party and government documents were brought to him; he read them over, made comments, and gave them to his secretary. He continued to read many newspapers and kept up with events. His study was in perfect order; he loved tidiness and made sure that everything was in its place. On his big desk near the lamp were children's porcelain toys, gifts from his grandchildren—a mouse, a little tiger, a lamb, and a calf. Each represented one of his four grandchildren: the mouse his granddaughter Mianmian, the tiger his grandson Mengmeng, the lamb his granddaughter Yangyang, and the calf his grandson Xiaodi. Behind them was a small woven basket with a tall handle in which stood two darling fat piglets wearing glasses. One was sporting a small man's fedora on its head, the other a bow. These were Deng Xiaoping and Zhuo Lin. In the basket were five piglets: Deng and Zhuo's children, Deng Lin, Pufang, Deng Nan, Deng Rong, and Zhifang. This was the idea of the grandchildren.[21]

Deng loved these little beasts a lot, but most of all, of course, the ones that reminded him of his grandsons and granddaughters. He spent a lot more time with his grandchildren now. In the winter he built snowmen with them in the courtyard; in the summer they rode out to the countryside. He said jokingly, "In our country we have the Four Cardinal Principles, and in my family there are also four. Our family's cardinal principles are my four grandsons and granddaughters."[22] Under the desk in his study, he always had several colored boxes in which he kept toys for his grandchildren.

In retirement, even while he was working he didn't want to be alone, so when he went to his study after breakfast he usually took little Xiaodi with him. The child immediately crawled under his grandfather's desk, and grandfather and grandson each attended to his own business. Zhuo Lin also frequented her husband's study to look in on Xiaodi, who, naturally, might be making a lot of noise. But Deng was not bothered by his grandson. Deng sank into a soft armchair, stretched his legs out on a low hassock, and immersed himself in reading. Sometimes he crossed over to a couch against the wall, lay down, and continued to read under a lampshade. As he grew older, his eyesight deteriorated; his close vision was poor, which forced him to wear large, thick glasses.[23] He loved to leaf through dictionaries, especially the voluminous Chinese dictionary *Cihai* (Sea of Words). Encountering an unfamiliar Chinese character, he took pleasure in deciphering its meaning. He often reread the famous "Records of the Grand Historian" by Sima Qian, who lived during the Han epoch, the second to first centuries BCE, as well as the Song dynasty historian Sima Guang (eleventh century CE) "Comprehensive Mirror to Aid in Government." His favorite work of literature was by Pu Songling (Liao Zhai) (1640–1715), a brilliant writer and author of a collection of fairy tales, *Strange Tales from a Chinese Studio*, who lived at the time of the Manchu conquest of China. He and Zhuo Lin also often listened to recordings of Peking opera.[24]

From time to time, he received foreign guests who had indicated they wanted to meet with him. Abroad he was still viewed as the charismatic leader of the PRC, so it is not surprising that many political figures wanted to speak with him, although they knew he was responsible for the bloody Tiananmen suppression. Business is business. In October 1989, he met with former U.S. president Richard M. Nixon, to whom he complained that after June 4 the Americans "keep denouncing China." But for no good reason, he added; "China has done nothing to harm the United States," while "the recent disturbances and counterrevolutionary rebellion that took place in Beijing were fanned by international anticommunism and antisocialism." He asked Nixon to tell President George H. W. Bush, whom he had known since 1974 when Bush headed the American Liaison Office in Beijing, that it was necessary to put "the past behind us."[25]

He repeated this to Bush's National Security Advisor, Brent Scowcroft, in December 1989. "I hope as special envoy you will tell President Bush that there is a retired old man in China who is concerned about the improvement of Sino-U.S. relations," he smiled. His daughter Maomao, who was serving as the interpreter, also smiled.[26]

Sometimes he also met with Jiang Zemin, Li Peng, and other leaders, usually at his home. He might give them some advice or praise, but generally he did not intervene in daily issues of the party. Overall he was enjoying his retirement.

Only once, at the end of 1990, did he indulge himself by delivering a lecture on the market economy to Jiang Zemin and Li Peng. It seemed that he increasingly disliked the conservative approach of the new leadership. "We must understand theoretically that the difference between capitalism and socialism is not a market economy as opposed to a planned economy," he explained again. "Socialism has regulation by market forces, and capitalism has control through planning. . . . You must not think that if we have some market economy we shall be taking the capitalist road. That's simply not true. Both a planned economy and a market economy are necessary. . . . Don't be afraid of taking a few risks."[27] Yang Shangkun participated in the meeting and fully supported Deng.

Although retirement had its pleasures, Deng remained a politician. He was still concerned about China's problems. In early January 1991, during the preparations for celebrating the Chinese New Year holiday, he traveled to Shanghai, not only to relax but to engage in inspections. During a meeting with city leaders, he advised them to engage "without hesitation" in developing the semi-deserted Pudong district on the opposite bank of the Huangpu River directly across from the Bund. He suggested that they attract foreign investors for this purpose. The idea itself was not his; it was first expressed by a wealthy American Overseas Chinese in conversation with Zhao Ziyang in late 1986 or early 1987. Zhao told Deng, who was enthusiastic, but Chen Yun and other conservatives were opposed, and the project was put off.[28] Now Deng seized it and expounded it as if it were his own (without any reference to Zhao, of course). He explained that "so long as we keep our word and act in accordance with international practice . . . foreign entrepreneurs will choose to invest in Shanghai. That is the right way to compete." He also reminded the municipal leaders that a planned economy does not mean socialism, nor a market economy capitalism, and he expressed the wish that all Shanghai people would "further emancipate their minds, be more daring and move ahead faster."[29]

Six months later, he again raised the issue of the tempo of growth with Jiang Zemin, Li Peng, and minister of foreign affairs Qian Qichen, once again accompanied by Yang Shangkun. "It is right to stress stability," he again suggested to the new leaders, "but if we overdo it, we may let opportunities slip by.... Stability alone cannot solve all problems."[30] Apparently they paid little heed to what he said.

Now he began to have grave doubts that the new leaders, preoccupied with the struggle against spiritual pollution, might not achieve the goal he had posited many years earlier of quadrupling China's gross domestic product by the end of the century. The growth rate of GDP caused anxiety. If in 1986–88 it had grown by more than 35 percent, in 1989–91 growth was only 18 percent. Deng was cheered by the fact that growth in exports had not slackened and that foreign direct investment had grown rapidly. If in 1985–88 foreign businesspersons had invested about US$9 billion in the Chinese economy, then in 1989–91 the figure had increased to more than US$11 billion.[31] World public opinion, of course, expressed profound indignation at the cruel suppression of student demonstrations in China,[32] but the economic benefits of stabilizing the situation in China outweighed all moral considerations.

Deng felt he needed to intervene to provide a new impetus to reform, since the international situation was favorable. The Tiananmen tragedy had receded into the past. Now it was possible to dial back the antiliberal campaign and switch the whole country over to economic construction in the spirit of the Thirteenth Congress of the CCP.

On January 17, 1992, three weeks before the lunar New Year, the eighty-seven-year-old Patriarch set out from the Beijing Railroad Station to the south, via Wuchang and Changsha, to the special economic zones of Shenzhen and Zhuhai. He was accompanied by his wife, four of his children (all but Zhifang), his grandchildren, Yang Shangkun, and the faithful Wang Ruilin. He also planned to visit Shanghai again. The goal of his journey, which lasted more than a month, was to reinvigorate the new forces in the CCP, pointing the party and its leadership onto the path of accelerated marketization, by visiting the places that had come to symbolize his reforms. He had thought it through carefully. Deng used the same maneuver repeatedly employed by the Great Helmsman: he appealed directly to the masses over the heads of the leaders in Beijing, and like Mao, he was successful.

The local cadres and ordinary citizens supported him wholeheartedly with regard to the matter of reform, and Jiang Zemin and Li Peng could no longer ignore him, especially since, everywhere he went, Deng declared, "Any one who attempted to change the line, principles and policies adopted since the Third Plenary Session of the Eleventh Central Committee would not be countenanced by the people; he would be toppled." He met with local heads, engineers, technicians, and other persons, speaking openly of the need to make every effort to advance reconstruction, accelerate the tempo of growth, and expand the sphere of market regulation. This was the first time since his retirement that he had engaged in such strenuous public activity.

"We should be bolder than before in conducting reform and opening up to the outside and have the courage to experiment," he said repeatedly. "We should not act like women with bound feet." He appealed for the creation of the largest possible number of joint enterprises, and, in general "to draw on the achievements of all cultures and to learn from other countries, including the developed capitalist countries, all advanced methods of operation and techniques of management." He openly ridiculed those who were afraid to develop a market economy, and who dismissed "reform and the open policy as means of introducing capitalism," as persons who "lack basic knowledge." He got so worked up he even declared that presently in China "leftist" views are the most deeply rooted and the ones against which everyone needs to struggle. After all, "in the history of the Party, those ['Left'] tendencies have led to dire consequences. Some fine things were destroyed overnight." At the same time, as in the past, he stressed the need to adhere firmly to the Four Cardinal Principles, emphasizing that all the reforms were ultimately directed toward building advanced socialism.[33]

After such words were spoken in public, the leaders in Beijing indeed had to snap to attention. Although Deng had lost some of his influence, he was still the "head of the family."

In brief, the Patriarch's Southern Tour exerted an enormous influence on the mood of the party. At the end of February 1992, the Central Committee transmitted the content of Deng's conversations and speeches during his trip to all the members of the CCP. On March 9–10, Jiang Zemin convened a meeting of the Politburo, in essence to resolve once again to shift the center of gravity of party work to economic construction, following the policy of reform and opening. The meeting acknowledged the need to use Deng's latest speeches as the basis of the documents being prepared for the forthcoming Fourteenth Congress of the CCP.[34]

Everything had gone according to Deng's plan. His last appearance before the people was the Patriarch's farewell to the nation. Deng Xiaoping exited the stage; his valedictory to the party and the people was to continue reform, emancipate consciousness, and boldly advance on the path of opening to the outside world.

The Fourteenth Congress of the CCP took place from October 12 to 18, 1992. Deng attended as a "specially invited" delegate. Forty-six such delegates, all of whom had joined the party prior to 1927, were in attendance. There were 1,989 official delegates, representing an enormous army of more than fifty-one million communists. Deng listened to the entire report by Jiang Zemin, after which he shared his impressions in the corridors, "Not bad at all. I fully approve this report."[35] He was not dissembling. The report not only reflected the essence of his conversations and speeches in southern China but also meshed with the spirit of the resolutions of the Thirteenth Congress. It posited the task of constructing a so-called socialist market economy in China, based on the concept of an organic unity between plan and market. A two-track development model had to be rejected. Following after Zhao Ziyang, whom Jiang, naturally, did not mention, the new general secretary emphasized that China was "still in the primary stage of socialism," after which he appealed for a reorientation of the economy toward export, to open China up even wider to the outside world, to achieve modernization and to "accelerate the pace of reform."[36]

Following the congress, market reforms got a second wind. In the cities the number of owners of private enterprises rapidly increased; by the year 2000 it was 39.5 million. GDP began to grow at a rapid rate. Between 1991 and 1995, the increase was 78.3 percent, or average annual growth of 12.2 percent.[37] China again demonstrated the vitality of "socialism with Chinese characteristics."

Deng could celebrate yet again; he no longer doubted that by the end of the twentieth century China's GDP would be quadruple what it had been in 1980. (Jumping forward, we can say that he was not mistaken, and that everything he foresaw came to pass.) Now he could relax. From late 1992 on, he spent less and less time working. He met very rarely with Jiang Zemin. During the winter months he left Beijing, not to go on inspections but just to rest. The cold northern climate began to tire him. He and Zhuo Lin spent late December 1992 and early January 1993 in Hangzhou, on the shore of the breathtakingly beautiful West Lake, which Mao Zedong too had loved. They spent the rest of January and part of February in Shanghai. A year later they again spent almost two months in Shanghai.

His old comrades dropped off one after another: Deng Yingchao, Li Xiannian, Wang Zhen. Chen Yun was extremely ill and also spent winters in Shanghai. But Deng was still in high spirits, although Parkinson's disease was inexorably exacting its due. He had severe tremors in his hands and head, and he walked with a shuffle, unable to lift his feet off the floor. On August 22, 1994, he celebrated his ninetieth birthday in the circle of his family. There was a large cake, everyone wished Grandfather good health and a long life, and everyone made merry.

By the end of 1994, however, Deng was feeling very poorly. Tests revealed he was suffering from a serious lung infection, and on December 22 he was hospitalized, in an excellent PLA clinic. There he remained for a month and a half, until February 7. On the eve of the Chinese New Year, at the end of January, Jiang Zemin visited him at the hospital. Deng shook his hand, and asked Jiang to convey his heartfelt holiday greetings to the Chinese people.[38]

On April 10, he learned of the passing of Chen Yun; one of the last of the veterans whom Deng had been close to, now gone forever. Only Peng Zhen, Bo Yibo, and, of course, his old friend Yang Shangkun remained. All of them were already senile but for now still firmly holding on to life. (They passed away after Deng's death: Peng Zhen in April 1997, Yang Shangkun just over a year later, and Bo Yibo in 2007.)

In 1996, the Parkinson's progressed rapidly. On December 12, he was admitted to the same clinic, his old illness complicated by another serious lung infection. Thus, he greeted 1997 in his hospital bed, terribly emaciated and fatigued. He was extremely weak; nevertheless, on January 1, he watched part one of a new television film about himself. He seemed pleased, although he could barely hear by this time, and the nurses had to constantly repeat the voice-over to him. Over the next eleven days he viewed the entire series.[39]

In early February, Jiang Zemin came to see him again to wish him a happy New Year. Deng again sent his greetings to all the peoples of the country, expressing his hope that in this year the party Central Committee, united around Jiang, would successfully achieve two historic tasks: extending the sovereignty of the PRC over Hong Kong and convening the Fifteenth Congress of the CCP. (The official handover ceremony of Hong Kong to the PRC was scheduled for July 1, 1997; the Fifteenth Congress two months later, in September.)

He wanted very much to live to see the reunion of Hong Kong with the PRC and even dreamed about visiting the city. But fate decided otherwise. By mid-February, Deng's condition deteriorated badly. He was quickly losing his ability to breathe. Zhuo Lin and the children realized this was the end. Deng was dying, and the doctors could do nothing to help him. On February 15, Zhuo Lin and the children wrote a letter to Jiang Zemin and the CC regarding funeral arrangements. From Deng's own wish that the party leaders keep his funeral ceremony simple,[40] they requested there be no elaborate funeral and that his body not be put on display. The memorial gathering should take place before the urn with the ashes of the deceased,[41] placed underneath his portrait. After the ceremony, Deng's ashes were to be scattered over the waves of the Yellow Sea.[42] This was his testament.

The great revolutionary and reformer passed away on February 19, 1997, at 9:08 p.m. in his ninety-third year.

THE FUNERAL WAS arranged precisely according to his wishes. On February 24, party and state leaders said their farewells to him in the clinic where he had died. Afterward his body was transported to the crematorium of the cemetery of revolutionary heroes. Tens of thousands of people lined up along Chang'an Avenue to see him off on his final journey. What brought them out on the street? Was it sympathy, curiosity, love? Who knows? Most Beijing residents stayed home. The next day a memorial gathering was held in the Great Hall of the People where Jiang Zemin delivered a speech. The more than ten thousand persons in the hall honored Deng's memory with a minute of silence.

Six days later, on March 2, Zhuo Lin, accompanied by Politburo Standing Committee member Hu Jintao, the future fourth-generation leader of the CCP and the PRC, scattered the ashes of her husband on the broad waters of the Yellow Sea.[43]

Epilogue

ON EVERY RETURN visit, China is virtually unrecognizable. Beijing, Shanghai, Chongqing, Xi'an, and many other cities change at fantastic speed. There is new construction everywhere. Hotels, apartment houses, offices, everything thrusts upward; Mercedes and BMWs speed along the new boulevards; old districts are being reconstructed; people are increasingly well dressed. Street life is vibrant, stores are bursting with goods, couples in love kiss out on the streets. No one follows after foreigners any longer or surrounds them in a tight circle to ogle or touch them, although some twenty years ago almost all Chinese did so. Chinese now do business with the "hairy foreign devils"; foreigners are partners, not exhibits in museums of colonial history. One can sense the changes even in the interior, in villages in the northwest and southwest, though the changes there are not so dramatic as in the cities. But Deng never said the entire population would immediately become well-to-do and civilized.

Shanghai is particularly impressive. This ultracontemporary megalopolis is colorful, businesslike, and energetic, and on the go from morning until late at night. Upscale foreign stores, from Versace to Macy's, strung out along the main commercial arteries, Nanjing Road and Huaihai Road, are crowded with people. The old-style jackets that Mao and Deng wore have long since gone out of style; everyone wants to dress fashionably, in Western styles. Women purchase expensive cosmetics, wear colorful dresses, and sport elegant hats. Across the Huangpu River, in the business district of Pudong, tens of thousands of businesspersons are making money hand over fist. Branches of the largest foreign firms are located here, including the headquarters of Sony and a multitude of Chinese firms. From Monday through Friday, Pudong is the Chinese Wall Street, but on weekends it is almost deserted. The empty skyscrapers keep silent watch on the occasional tourists who come to gawk at the transformation of what, not along ago, was undeveloped land.

From the twentieth-story window of a hotel, Shanghai is spread out below. Beyond the smooth surface of the Huangpu lies the silent mass of Pudong, but here, in downtown Shanghai, the pulse of life is beating ever faster. In the European district close by Huaihai Road, foreign cafes and small restaurants quickly fill with young people. The young men and young women drink coffee and eat ice cream. They are animated and full of life. By 6:00 p.m. the sky darkens and the city is flooded with waves of advertisements. McDonald's and Coca-Cola, Volvo and Panasonic. Multicolored lights of every hue lure one onto the street.

Walking along the brightly lit avenues and looking at the happy young people, we involuntarily think of Hong Kong, a former British colony that is now a Special Administrative Region of the PRC. It is lively and colorful like Shanghai, with young people no less attractive and in love with life. Then we think how a few months earlier, on June 4, 2014, the young people of Hong Kong went out on the streets to honor the memory of the fallen defenders of Tiananmen Square. Tens of thousands of people filled the streets and the squares to express their sorrow and their anger. They have demonstrated and lit candles every year on this day for a quarter of a century. Nothing like this has occurred in any other city in Mainland China.

It is not so much a matter of fear before the all-powerful authoritarian regime. In the PRC, few actually keep the tragedy of Tiananmen in their thoughts. Deng raised overall standards of living and gave many people a real chance to get rich. Contemporary Shanghai, Pudong, and Beijing, filled with happy young people, are the best monument to him. "Socialism with Chinese characteristics" turned out to be viable.

Of course, the other monument to Deng is a powerful authoritarian machine, run by the Communist party, that he deliberately strengthened throughout his life. It is due to his efforts, in particular after Mao's death, that China in the twenty-first century remains the only large communist country whose leaders still pay loyalty not only to Marx and Lenin but also even to Stalin and to Mao Zedong. The Communist party dictatorship in mainland China has withstood the efforts of those who sought to transform it into a democratic state. The Chinese people in the PRC, unlike those in Taiwan, have never enjoyed civil liberties. Deng's Four Cardinal Principles, the pillars of the communist dictatorship, still frame and restrict the everyday lives of average Chinese citizens.

The PRC is unusual in the contemporary world. Its politics and ideology are a species of authoritarian socialism. Yet its current prosperity is based on a market economy, albeit one in which the state continues to play a commanding role. This is a living symbiosis created by Deng Xiaoping, who combined Marxism, Stalinism, Maoism, and pragmatism into a unique model of Chinese socialism.

Deng revitalized China's economy, but he did not become China's Gorbachev, a Russian Westernizer who was profusely praised by the likes of Ronald Reagan and Margaret Thatcher for promoting liberalism in Russia around the same time Deng Xiaoping was massacring liberal students. But should we simply blame Deng for this? Could he have become China's Gorbachev?

No, he could not. It was not only because Deng himself was unlike Gorbachev, but more importantly because the country he ruled was significantly different from the Soviet Union. To the end of his life, Deng characterized Gorbachev with just two words: "very stupid" (*hen chun*).[1] However, he was quite wrong. Things in both countries were not that simple. China is not Russia; therefore, it could not have followed a Russian path to reform or transformation.

First, in the PRC, as we have seen, agrarian reform was initiated spontaneously from below, and Deng supported it only a year and a half later. The situation was entirely different in the Soviet Union. When Gorbachev started reforms in 1985, he, like Deng, began with the emancipation of consciousness. However, he could not proceed to divide up the land as the Chinese did. Unlike Chinese peasants, Russian farmers themselves did not want this division. They were not dying of hunger; they grew everything they wanted on their private plots, both for themselves and for the local markets; they raised their own poultry and cattle, and they stole whatever they could from the collective farms.

Second, the situation in cities was likewise different. In the Chinese SEZs, it was *huaqiao* (overseas Chinese) who were the primary investors. Chinese have a clan consciousness; for them the motherland is not simply an object of patriotic feelings but a concrete expression of family. Therefore, for *huaqiao* investing in the economy of the PRC means helping both the country and their own extended family. It was their money that made Shenzhen, Zhuhai, and other SEZs grow. Could the Russians have established special economic zones even had Gorbachev desired to do so? It seems highly improbable. The relationship of the various waves of Russian emigrants to the motherland is entirely different from that of Chinese *huaqiao*.

Third, at the foundation of the Chinese miracle has been the extraordinary cheapness of Chinese labor. Even at the time of Deng's death, the average wage of a Chinese worker was just over 2 percent of that in the United

States and 5 percent of that in Taiwan.[2] Soviet workers even at the beginning of reform refused to work for such pitiful compensation.

Fourth, even the cadres in China were different from the Soviets. Till the end of his days, the tyrant Mao kept the cadres in check. Perhaps strange to say, the nightmare that was the Cultural Revolution at least had the positive effect of restraining the potential for self-indulgence of the Chinese ruling elite. The Chinese *ganbu* under Mao was not corrupted to nearly the degree that the rotten Soviet *nomenklatura* was during Brezhnev's rule. It was precisely the *nomenklatura* that destroyed the Soviet Union, pilfering the national wealth and making themselves, and only themselves, superrich.

Finally, one should also not underestimate the factor of the Cold War. At the start of Gorbachev's *perestroika*, in 1985, the Soviets were spending 40 percent of their budget on defense while the Chinese at the beginning of their reform in 1978 were spending 15 percent.[3] The economy of the USSR collapsed under the burden of military expenditures. This situation virtually compelled Gorbachev to sit down at the table with Reagan to negotiate arms limitations, and to accept the American demands that he improve the human rights situation in the USSR. This is exactly why Gorbachev returned head of the Soviet dissident movement Andrei Sakharov from exile to Moscow and initiated *glasnost*. At this same time, Deng was skillfully playing on the contradictions between the two superpowers, using the Americans to develop the economy of the PRC.

Therefore, Deng had a much easier time than Gorbachev in developing a market economy. Consequently, when he determined to crush the liberal opposition he could count on receiving solid support from the army, the *ganbu*, the fast-growing middle class, and well-to-do peasants.

As a result the majority of Chinese, satisfied with the great economic progress in their country, passively accept the official assessment of the Tiananmen incident as a "suppression of a counterrevolutionary rebellion." By the same token they also accept the luminous praise of Deng Xiaoping provided by Jiang Zemin:

> If not for Comrade Deng Xiaoping, the Chinese people would not have their present new life, China would not have the new situation of reform and opening, and wonderful prospects for socialist modernization. Comrade Deng Xiaoping is recognized by our whole party, army, and the peoples of our country as an outstanding leader who enjoys the highest authority, a great Marxist, a great proletarian revolutionary, a political and military leader, diplomat, a battle-hardened fighter

for the cause of communism, the chief architect of socialist reform, opening, and modernization, the creator of the theory of building socialism with Chinese characteristics.[4]

Was Deng really so good? Our study provides a clear answer to this question by recording all his accomplishments, as well as his undeniable and large-scale crimes, to create a nuanced and multifaceted portrait of the man.

In sum, Deng was definitely an outstanding revolutionary leader, a great economic and social reformer, a talented strategist and tactician, and a skillful political organizer. But he was also a bloody dictator who, along with Mao, was responsible for the deaths of millions of innocent people, thanks to the terrible social reforms and unprecedented famine of 1958–62. After Mao's death, Deng incurred everlasting shame as the murderer of China's young fighters for democracy on the streets of Beijing in June 1989.

IRONICALLY, DENG HIMSELF calculated that he "could be rated fifty-fifty in merits and demerits." Therefore, he requested in vain that future leaders not call him a great Marxist. Several years before his death, he even said he would never agree to publication of his biography. "If a biography is written, it should include both good and bad things, even the mistakes one has made," he noted.[5] In his own words, he had done a lot of wrong things.

So far the Chinese people could at least accept Deng's self-assessment. But in the future, following the development of the global economy and the spread of Western values all over the world, when the concepts of freedom and civil rights will someday be embraced by most Chinese, the new generation of Chinese people will definitely find a more appropriate place for Deng Xiaoping in their long and tortuous history. And the ghosts of Marx and Mao will never tell anyone what they are saying about Deng Xiaoping between themselves.

APPENDIX I

Deng Xiaoping's Chronology

1904   *August 22*—A son named Xiansheng is born into the family of a wealthy land-owner, Deng Wenming, and his wife, neé Dan, in the village of Yaoping (Paifang), Wangxi township (now Xiexing), Guan'an county, Sichuan Province.

1919   *September*—Enters the Chongqing preparatory school for students wishing to take part in a work-study program in France.

1920   *October 19*—Arrives in France, where over the next four and a half years he studies, works, and is engaged in political activities.

1921   *July 23 to 31*—The First Congress of the Chinese Communist Party is held in Shanghai and Jiaxing.

1923   *June*—Joins the European branch of the Chinese Socialist Youth League and soon severs ties with his parents.

1925   *April*—Joins the European branch of the CCP.

1926   *January 7*—Leaves Paris for Moscow, where, on January 17, he matriculates at the Communist University of the Toilers of the East (KUTV).

       January 29—Transfers to the Sun Yat-sen University of the Toilers of China (UTK).

1926   Deng's mother dies of tuberculosis.

1927   *January 12*—Not having finished his studies, he leaves for China to engage in political work in the Nationalist Army of Marshal Feng Yuxiang, an ally of the communists in the anti-imperialist front.

       Late March—Feng Yuxiang appoints Deng head of the Political Department of the Sun Yat-sen Military Academy in Xi'an.

       Late June—Feng Yuxiang breaks with the communists and requests they leave his army.

Early July—Deng arrives in Wuhan, where he becomes technical secretary of the Central Committee of the CCP. Changes his name to Deng Xiaoping.

August 7—Takes part in the emergency conference of the CC CCP in Hankou. Meets Mao Zedong for the first time.

Late September or early October—Moves to Shanghai with the CC and in December becomes head of the Secretariat of the CC CCP.

1928   *spring*—Marries Zhang Xiyuan (born October 28, 1907).

1929   *August*—Designated CC representative in Guangxi province to organize an anti-Guomindang uprising.

December 11—A communist uprising takes place in the city of Bose, resulting in the formation of the 7th Corps of the Red Army.

1930   *January*—Birth of first child, a daughter. Zhang Xiyuan and the daughter both die. CC soon appoints Deng political commissar of the 7th Corps.

February 1—A communist uprising takes place in the city of Longzhou, resulting in the formation of the 8th Corps of the Red Army. The CC appoints Deng political commissar of this unit as well.

April and May—Engages in building a soviet area in Donglang in northwest Guangxi.

1931   *February 8*—The 7th Corps departs for Jiangxi province, after which Deng leaves to report in Shanghai.

Early August—Assigned by the CC to work in the Central Soviet Area, he arrives there. He marries "Goldie" Jin Weiying (born in the autumn of 1904).

Mid-August 1931 to early May 1933—Works consecutively as CCP secretary in Ruijin county, Huichang, Xunwu, and Anyuan counties and director of the Department of Propaganda of the Jiangxi Party Committee.

1933   *February to May*—Subjected to direct criticism by party leaders as a "Maoist," that is, a supporter of Mao Zedong's purely guerrilla defensive tactics. His wife leaves him.

July—Appointed editor-in-chief of the journal *Hongxing* (*Red Star*), the official organ of the Central Military Revolutionary Committee.

1934   *October*—Leaves on the Long March with Red Army troops.

December—Again appointed head of the Secretariat of the CC CCP.

1935   *January 15 to 17*—Attends the enlarged Politburo conference in Zunyi.

1935   *late June to early January 1938*—Consecutively occupies a series of military and political leadership positions in the Red Army (from August 1937, the 8th Route Army).

1936   Deng's father dies.

1937   *July 7*—Japan launches a broadscale war against China.

1938   *January 5*—Appointed political commissar and chief of the political department of the 129th Division of the 8th Route Army.

1939   *late August*—Marries Zhuo Lin (born April 6, 1916).

1941   *September 11*—Daughter Deng Lin is born.

1942 *through 1944*—Leads a broadscale party purge (*zhengfeng*), inspired by Mao Zedong, in the Shanxi-Hebei-Shandong-Henan border region in the Japanese rear.

1944 *April*—Birth of son Pufang.

1945 *April 23 to June 11*—The Seventh Congress of the CCP takes place in Yan'an. Deng is elected to the Central Committee.

   August 14 (15)—Japan surrenders.

   September and October—Conducts a successful operation against Guomindang troops, initiating a new civil war.

   October—Birth of daughter Deng Nan.

1946 *June*—Start of large-scale offensive by the Nationalist Army against positions occupied by CCP forces.

1947 *May 15*—Mao appoints Deng secretary of the CC Bureau for the Central Plains.

   June—Deng's troops cross the Yellow River and begin a new stage in the civil war, a communist counteroffensive.

   August—Deng's troops execute a forced march to Chiang Kai-shek's rear and establish a "liberated area" in the mountains on the Central Plains.

1948 *November, through January 1949*—Deng and Liu Bocheng command communist troops in the Huaihai Campaign.

1949 *April 20*—Deng's troops cross the Yangzi River, occupy Nanjing on April 23 and Shanghai on May 27.

   August 1—Mao appoints Deng first secretary of the newly established Southwest Bureau of the CC CCP.

   September 30—Chosen as a member of the Central People's Government.

   October 1—Mao Zedong proclaims the founding of the People's Republic of China.

   Early December—Appointed mayor of Chongqing.

   December 10—Chiang Kai-shek flees from Chengdu, the capital of Sichuan, to Taiwan.

1950 *January 25*—Birth of daughter Deng Rong.

1950 *October, through October 1951*—Deng's troops along with He Long's army "liberate" Tibet.

1950 *through 1952*—Suppresses "counterrevolutionary elements" and carries out radical agrarian reform in Southwest China.

1951 *August*—Birth of son Zhifang.

1952 *July*—Mao transfers Deng to Beijing as a deputy premier of the State Administrative Council.

1953 *summer*—Appointed first deputy chairman of the Financial-Economic Council and minister of finance of the PRC.

1953 *December, to February 1954*—On Mao's instructions, handles the Gao Gang, Rao Shushi affair.

1954 *April*—Appointed head of the Secretariat and the Organization Department of the CC CCP.

September—Confirmed as deputy premier of the State Council at the First Session of the NPC.

1955   *April*—Elected a member of the Politburo of the CC CCP.

1956   *February 11 to March 1*—Visits the Soviet Union as deputy head of the CCP delegation to the Twentieth Congress of the CPSU.

September 15 to 27—The Eighth Congress of the CCP takes place in Beijing. Deng reports on changes in the Party Statutes and is elected a member of the CC. At the First Plenum of the CC after the congress, becomes a member of the Politburo, the Politburo Standing Committee, and general secretary of the CC CCP.

October 23 to 31—In connection with the events in Poland and Hungary, he visits Moscow with a CCP delegation, where he negotiates with a CPSU delegation headed by Khrushchev.

1957   *February through September*—On Mao's orders, he oversees a purge of the party and the national campaign "Let a Hundred Flowers Bloom, Let a Hundred Schools of Thought Contend," after which he heads a campaign of repression against the intellectuals.

November 2 to 21—Accompanies Mao to the Soviet Union for the fortieth anniversary of the October Revolution. Takes part in conferences of representatives of communist and workers' parties and of leaders of the communist parties of socialist countries.

1958   *February 18*—Takes part in an enlarged Politburo session that proclaims the policy of "more, faster, better, and more economical" as the new general line of the party in socialist construction. Three months later, the Second Session of the Eighth CCP Congress confirms this line. The Great Leap Forward, which Deng fervently supports, commences.

July 31 to August 3—Takes part in negotiations between Mao and Khrushchev in Beijing. Growing tension in Sino-Soviet relations.

Winter—Beginning of mass famine as a result of the Great Leap.

1960   *April*—Start of public polemics between the CCP and the CPSU.

September through early December—*As head of the CCP delegation, he takes part in negotiations with a CPSU delegation in Moscow, after which he participates in the work of an editorial commission of a new conference of representatives of communist and workers' parties and in the conference itself.*

1961   *May*—Supports Liu Shaoqi, who criticizes the Great Leap.

December—On Mao's instructions, he reports on the struggle against Soviet "revisionism" at a CC CCP work conference.

1962   *January and February*—Takes part in an enlarged CC plenum of seven thousand cadres in Beijing at which Mao makes a self-criticism.

Late June to early July—*Characterizes the development of the household contract system in the countryside with the statement "It doesn't matter if the cat is black or yellow, as long as it can catch mice it is a good cat."*

July—Mao unleashes a struggle in the party against "moderates," including Deng.

1963 *July 5 to 20*—Leads a CCP delegation at a conference in Moscow with representatives of the CPSU. Relations between the two parties are essentially broken.

1965 *November 10*—The Shanghai newspaper *Wenhui bao* (*Literary Reports*) publishes a critical article by Yao Wenyuan on the play by Beijing's deputy mayor Wu Han, "The Dismissal of Hai Rui from Office."

1966 *May 16*—On Mao's initiative, an enlarged meeting of the Politburo, in the name of the CC, adopts the text of a special message to all party organizations in China in which it calls on them to hold high the banner of the Great Proletarian Cultural Revolution.

August—The post of general secretary of the CC CCP, which Deng occupies, is abolished.

October 23—Makes a self-criticism at a work conference of the CC CCP.

December 25—Students and teachers at Tsinghua University organize a demonstration in Beijing at which, for the first time, they openly attack Liu Shaoqi and Deng Xiaoping.

1967 *April 1*—*Renmin ribao* (*People's Daily*) and *Hongqi* (*Red Flag*) publish an article in which for the first time in the open press Deng is referred to as the "second [after Liu Shaoqi] most important person in power in the party who is taking the capitalist road."

July 29—The Rebels in Zhongnanhai drag Deng and Zhuo Lin to a "criticism and struggle" meeting during which they are humiliated in every way and even beaten, and then are placed under house arrest.

1968 *July 5*—Deng presents his "confession" to the "Group on the Special Case of Deng Xiaoping."

1969 *April*—At the Ninth Congress of the CCP, Mao asserts that "a distinction should be drawn between Deng Xiaoping and Liu Shaoqi."

October 22—Deng, his wife, and his stepmother are transferred from Beijing to Nanchang and placed under house arrest in the former Nanchang Infantry Academy of the Fuzhou Military District, which has been converted into a so-called May 7 school. Deng spends three and a half years there.

1973 *February 22*—On Mao's decision, Deng returns to Beijing with his family.

March 9—Mao again appoints Deng deputy premier of the State Council.

December—On Mao's proposal, Deng is inducted into the Politburo of the CC.

1974   *April 10*—Speaks at a session of the UN General Assembly in New York, set-
        ting forth Mao's "Three Worlds" theory, after which he holds talks with
        Henry Kissinger.

        October—Mao appoints Deng deputy chair of the Central Military
        Commission and chief of the General Staff of the PLA.

1975   *January*—At Mao's suggestion, a CC CCP plenum chooses Deng Xiaoping as
        one of the deputy chairs of the CC and a member of the Politburo Standing
        Committee. Afterward a session of the NPC confirms Deng as first deputy
        premier and Deng starts to work on restoring the economy and confirming
        the policy of the Four Modernizations.

1976   *March 19 to April 5*—Massive demonstrations in Tiananmen Square in connec-
        tion with the death of Zhou Enlai. Acting on reports by Jiang Qing and her
        supporters, Mao blames Deng for this "counterrevolutionary uprising."

        April 7—Mao dismisses Deng from all his positions and appoints Hua
        Guofeng first deputy chairman of the CC and premier of the State Council.
        Deng is again put under house arrest.

        September 9—Mao dies.

        October 6—Hua Guofeng, Ye Jianying, and Wang Dongxing arrest Jiang
        Qing and other members of the Gang of Four. The next day Hua Guofeng
        becomes chairman of the CC and of the Central Military Commission.

        October 10—Writes a letter to Hua Guofeng expressing his joy at the arrest of
        the Gang of Four.

1977   *February 7*—Hua Guofeng expounds the concept of the "Two Whatevers."
        Deng opposes it.

        February—General Xu Shiyou writes a letter to Hua Guofeng demanding
        Deng's rehabilitation.

        March—At a CC work conference Chen Yun, Wang Zhen, and several other
        veterans demand that Deng be rehabilitated.

        July 17—A CC plenum restores Deng to his positions as a member of the CC
        and of the Politburo and its Standing Committee, deputy chair of the CC
        and Central Military Commission, deputy premier of the State Council, and
        chief of the General Staff of the PLA. Deng calls on communists "to seek
        truth from facts."

1978   *May 10*—The journal *Lilun dongtai* (*Theoretical Trends*) publishes the article
        "Practice Is the Sole Criterion of Truth." Deng uses the article in his strug-
        gle against Hua Guofeng.

        November and December—At a CC work conference Deng's supporters are
        victorious over Hua Guofeng's group.

        December 18 to 22—The Third Plenum of the Eleventh Central Committee
        shifts the center of gravity of party work from class struggle to economic
        construction.

Late December—*Peasants from Xiaogang village in Fengyang County, Anhui Province, adopt the "full contract" system.*

1978 **late, to early 1979**—The rise of the democratic movement among youths.

1979 *January*—Puts forward a plan to reunify Mainland China with Taiwan, Hong Kong, and Macao on the principle of "One country, two systems."

January 28 to February 6—Visits the United States, holds talks with President Jimmy Carter.

February 17 to March 16—Wages war against the Socialist Republic of Vietnam.

March 30—*Gives a speech about the Four Cardinal Principles; around this time he crushes the democratic movement.*

Mid-July—Climbs Huangshan Mountain.

August 26—Opens the first four Special Economic Zones.

December 6—Sets forth the concept of moderate prosperity (*xiaokang*).

1980 *February*—At a CC plenum, Deng removes the main supporters of Hua Guofeng and adds Hu Yaobang and Zhao Ziyang to the Standing Committee. The plenum adopts a resolution to rehabilitate Liu Shaoqi.

May—Speaks in favor of the family contract system.

September—Resigns his position of deputy premier and forces Hua Guofeng to cede the position of premier to Zhao Ziyang.

1981 *June*—A CC plenum adopts the "Resolution on Certain Questions in the History of Our Party Since the Founding of the People's Republic of China." Hua Guofeng is dismissed from high party posts. Deng is elected chair of the Central Military Commission.

1982 *September*—Chosen as chair of the newly established Central Advisory Commission.

1983 *November, through February 1984*—Conducts a campaign against "spiritual pollution."

1984 *May 4*—On Deng's initiative a decision is taken to open fourteen economic and technological development zones.

October—With Deng's support, a CC plenum adopts "The Decision on Reform of the Economic Structure."

1985 *January*—Starts a campaign to combat "bourgeois liberalization."

1986 *December, and January 1987*—The rise of a new democratic movement among youths.

December 30—Blames Hu Yaobang for the student unrest.

1987 *January 16*—On Deng's suggestion, an enlarged session of the Politburo elects Zhao Ziyang general secretary of the CC CCP.

October 25 to November 1—At the Thirteenth Congress of the CCP resigns as a member of the CC, the Politburo, and its Standing Committee; and as chair of the Central Advisory Commission.

1989   *April 15 to June 4*—Development of a new democratic youth movement in Beijing and other cities.

       May 16—Meets with Mikhail S. Gorbachev in the Great Hall of the People. Normalizes Sino-Soviet relations.

       May 17—Decides to impose martial law in urban districts of Beijing.

       May 27—At a meeting of veterans, decides to appoint Jiang Zemin as general secretary of the CC CCP.

       June 4—Crushes the student democratic movement in Beijing.

       September 4—submits request to Politburo to retire from post of chairman of the Central Military Commission.

1992   *January and February*—Makes tour of Wuchang, Changsha, Shenzhen, Zhuhai, and Shanghai, stressing the need to deepen market reforms.

1994   *December 22, to February 7, 1995*—Undergoes treatment for Parkinson's disease, aggravated by a lung infection, in a PLA hospital.

1996   *December 12*—Again hospitalized with the same diagnosis.

1997   *February 19, 9:08 p.m.*—Deng dies.

Deng Xiaoping's Genealogy

PARENTS

Father (eighteenth generation of the Deng clan named "shao," "continue")—Deng
  Shaochang (Deng Wenming) (1886–1936)
Mother—neé Dan (1884–1926)

WIVES

First wife—Zhang Xiyuan (October 28, 1907–January 1930); married in the spring
  of 1928
Second wife—Jin Weiying (autumn of 1904–1941); married in August or September
  1931
Third wife—Zhuo Lin (April 6, 1916–July 29, 2009); married in the late summer
  of 1939

CHILDREN

First child (from his first wife)—a daughter (born and died January 1930)
Second child (from his third wife)—a daughter, Deng Lin (born September 11, 1941)
Deng Lin's husband—Wu Jianchang (born 1939)
Third child (from his third wife)—a son, Deng Pufang (twentieth generation of the
  Deng clan named "xing," "model") (born April 16, 1944)
Deng Pufang's wife—Gao Suning (born?)
Fourth child (from his third wife)—a daughter, Deng Nan (born October 1945)
Deng Nan's husband—Zhang Hong (born?)

Fifth child (from his third wife)—a daughter, Deng Rong (Maomao) (born January 25, 1950)

Deng Rong's husband—He Ping (born 1946)

Sixth child (from his third wife)—a son, Deng Zhifang (twentieth generation of the Deng clan named "xing," "model") (born August 1951)

Deng Zhifang's wife—Liu Xiaoyuan (born?)

GRANDCHILDREN

Granddaughter (from Deng Nan)—Mianmian (Deng Zhuorui) (born November 1972)

Grandson (from Deng Lin)—Mengmeng (Deng Zhuosu) (April 1974–March 26, 2014)

Granddaughter (from Deng Rong)—Yangyang (Deng Zhuoyue) (born 1979)

Yangyang's husband—Feng Bo (born?)

Grandson (from Deng Zhifang)—Xiaodi (David Zhuo, Deng Zhuodi) (twenty-first generation of the Deng clan named "pei," "cultivate") (born 1985)

SIBLINGS

Elder sister—Deng Xianlie (1902–1997)

Younger brother—Deng Xianxiu (Deng Ken) (nineteenth generation of the Deng clan named "xian," "surpass") (born 1910 or 1911)

Younger brother—Deng Xianzhi (Deng Shuping) (nineteenth generation of the Deng clan named "xian," "surpass") (1912–March 15, 1967)

Younger sister—Deng Xianzhen (1913–1923)

Younger brother—Deng Xianqing (nineteenth generation of the Deng clan named "xian," "surpass") (born 1927)

Younger sister—Deng Xianrong (1930?–1940?)

Younger sister—Deng Xianqun (born December 1935)

GREAT-GRANDDAUGHTER

Great-granddaughter (from Yangyang)—? (born 2009)

FOSTER SISTER

Younger sister—Deng Xianfu (born?)

Notes

INTRODUCTION

1. Lao Tsu, *Tao Te Ching*, trans. Ralph Alan Dale (London: Watkins, 2002), 157.
2. Ibid., 145.
3. Confucius, *The Analects of Confucius*, trans. Simon Leys (New York: Norton, 1997), 64, 100.
4. See, for instance, critical reviews by Christian Caryl (*Foreign Policy*, Sept. 13, 2011), Jonathan Mirsky (*New York Times*, Oct. 21, 2011), Pete Sweeney (*China Economic Review*, Nov. 1, 2011), John Garnaut (*The Sydney Morning Herald,* Nov. 5, 2011), Clarissa Sebag-Montefiore (*The Independent*, Dec. 2, 2011), Andrew Nathan (*New Republic*, Feb. 22, 2012), Charles Horner (*Claremont Review of Books*, Summer 2012), and many others. See also reviews by the famous Chinese dissidents Fang Lizhi (*New York Review of Books*, Nov. 10, 2011) and Wang Dan (*Taipei Times*, Jan. 29, 2012).
5. Pete Sweeney, "Burying Deng: Ezra Vogel Lets Deng Xiaoping off the Hook," *China Economic Review*, vol. 22, no. 11 (Nov. 1, 2011): 62.

CHAPTER I

1. See Deng Maomao, *Deng Xiaoping: My Father* (New York: Basic Books, 1995), 13; Alexander V. Pantsov's notes made during his field trip to the former Paifang Village, June 24, 2010.
2. *Dizhu* literally means "master of the land" and is conventionally translated as "landlord," which is not wholly accurate because it did not constitute a separate social category as in Europe. *Dizhu*, or wealthy landholders, differed from other peasants (*nong* or *nongmin*) only in the level of their material wealth. Peasants were categorized as poor peasants (*pinnong*), middle peasants (*zhongnong*), and rich peasants (*funong*).

3. See *Lichnoe delo Den Sisiana (Dozorova)* (Personal File of Deng Xixian [Dozorov]), *Rossiiskii gosudarstvennyi arkhiv sotsial'no-politicheskoi istorii* (Russian State Archive of Social and Political History, hereafter RGASPI), collection 495, inventory 225, file 1629, sheets 2, 4, 5.

4. Deng, *Deng Xiaoping*, 34.

5. Deng Ken, "Deng Ken tan Deng Xiaoping" (Deng Ken Speaks About Deng Xiaoping), in Liu Jintian, ed., *Huashuo Deng Xiaoping* (Stories About Deng Xiaoping) (Beijing: Zhongyang wenxian chubanshe, 2004), 3.

6. See M. I. Sladkovskii, ed., *Informatsionnyi biulleten'. Seriia A. "Kulturnaia revoliutsiia" v Kitae. Dokumenty i materialy (perevod s kitaiskogo), Vypusk 2: "Hunveibinskaia pechat' o Den Siaopine, Pen Chzhene, Yan Shankune i Khe Lune* (Information Bulletin: Series A: "The "Cultural Revolution" in China. Documents and Materials Translated from Chinese: The 2nd Installment. Red Guard Press on Deng Xiaoping, Peng Zhen, Yang Shangkun, and He Long (Moscow: IDV AN SSSR, 1968), 4.

7. Benjamin Yang, *Deng: A Political Biography* (Armonk, NY: Sharpe, 1998), 10, 11.

8. See *Shiji xiange, bainian chuanxiang: Sichuan da xuexiao shizhan (1896–2006)* (Instrumental Song of a Centenary Echoes for a Hundred Years: History of Universities in Sichuan) (Chengdu: Sichuan daxue chubanshe, 2007), 51.

9. See Deng, *Deng Xiaoping*, 35; *Deng Xiaoping, 1904–1997* (Chengdu: Sichuan chuban jituan/Sichuan renmin chubanshe, 2009), 18.

10. See *Deng Xiaoping yu xiandai Zhongguo* (Deng Xiaoping and Contemporary China) (Beijing: Xiandai chubanshe, 1997), 3; *Deng Xiaoping, 1904–1997*, 17–18; Robert S. Ramsay, *The Languages of China* (Princeton, NJ: Princeton University Press, 1987), 33.

11. See Sladkovskii, *Informatsionnyi biulleten'. Seriia A. Vypusk 2* (Information Bulletin: Series A: 2nd Installment), 82–83; Deng, *Deng Xiaoping*, 20–22.

12. Deng, *Deng Xiaoping*, 40.

13. Mencius, *Mencius*, trans. Irene Bloom (New York: Columbia University Press, 2009), 63–64.

14. See Deng Xiaoping, *Deng Xiaoping zishu* (Autobiographical Notes of Deng Xiaoping) (Beijing: Jiefangjun chubanshe, 2004), 3–4.

15. See ibid., 2.

16. See ibid., 3.

17. See Uli Franz, *Deng Xiaoping*, trans. Tom Artin (Boston: Harcourt Brace Jovanovich, 1987), 10; Richard Evans, *Deng Xiaoping and the Making of Modern China*, rev. ed. (London: Penguin Books, 1997), 4.

18. See Deng, *Deng Xiaoping*, 12.

19. See Jin Xiaoming et al., "'Deng jia lao yuanzi' de lao gushi" (Old Stories of "The Deng Family Old Household"), *Renmin ribao* (*People's Daily*), Aug. 22, 2004; "Deng Xiaoping yi jiade gushi" (Stories of Deng Xiaoping's Family), *Xin lang* (*New Wave*), Sept. 7, 2006; Deng, *Deng Xiaoping*, 40.

20. Alexander V. Pantsov's interview with Professor of the PRC Academy of Social Sciences Institute of Modern History Li Yuzhen in Beijing, June 27, 2004.

21. See Deng, *Deng Xiaoping*, 40; Yang Shengqun and Yan Jianqi, eds., *Deng Xiaoping nianpu: 1904–1974* (Chronological Biography of Deng Xiaoping: 1904–1974), vol. 1 (Beijing: Zhongyang wenxian chubanshe, 2010), 3. According to some other sources, it happened two years later. See Jin, "'Deng jia lao yuanzi' de lao gushi" (Old Stories of "The Deng Family Old Household"); "Deng Xiaoping yi jiade gushi" (Stories of Deng Xiaoping's Family).

22. See in detail Alexander V. Pantsov with Steven I. Levine, *Mao: The Real Story* (New York: Simon & Schuster, 2012), 15, 20. It was no accident when, in Moscow several years later, in the autobiography he wrote for the Instructional Department of the Sun Yat-sen University of the Toilers of China, Deng, for some reason quoting one of Mencius' famous phrases, "There are three things that are unfilial, and the greatest of them is to have no posterity," ascribed it to Confucius. See RGASPI, collection 530, inventory 2, file 5, sheet 175; Deng, *Deng Xiaoping zishu* (Autobiographical Notes of Deng Xiaoping), 3. This was an unforgivable error for an educated Chinese.

23. Quoted from Deng, *Deng Xiaoping*, 34.

24. See in detail Robert A. Kapp, *Szechwan and the Chinese Republic: Provincial Militarism and Central Power, 1911–1938* (New Haven: Yale University Press, 1973), 8–10.

25. See Deng, *Deng Xiaoping zishu* (Autobiographical Notes of Deng Xiaoping), 2; Deng, "Deng Ken tan Deng Xiaoping" (Deng Ken Speaks About Deng Xiaoping), 3–4; [Deng Ken], "Gege wei geming bu huijia" (Elder Brother Did Not Return Home for the Sake of the Revolution), *Zhongguo ribao* (*China Newspaper*), Sept. 28, 2008.

26. See Yue Fei, "Man jiang hong" (The River Is Dyed Red), in Yue Fei, *Jingzhong Yue Fei quanji* (Collected Works of the Extremely Dedicated Patriot Yue Fei) (Taipei: Hansheng chubanshe, 1976), 155.

27. Quoted from Franz, *Deng Xiaoping*, 22.

28. See in detail Daria A. Spichak, *Kitaitsy vo Frantsii* (Chinese in France) (manuscript), 9–12.

29. See ibid., 23–24.

30. See Yang and Yan, *Deng Xiaoping nianpu: 1904–1974* (Chronological Biography of Deng Xiaoping: 1904–1974), vol. 1, 7; Jiang Zemin, "Liu Fa, Bi qingong jianxue huiyi" (Recollections on the Diligent Work, Frugal Study in France and Belgium), in *Fu Fa qingong jianxue yundong shiliao* (Materials on the History of the Diligent Work, Frugal Study Movement in France), vol. 3 (Beijing: Beijing chubanshe, 1981), 448–49.

31. Jiang, "Liu Fa, Bi qingong jianxue huiyi" (Recollections on the Diligent Work, Frugal Study in France and Belgium), 448.

32. See Deng, *Deng Xiaoping*, 70.

33. See in detail Kapp, *Szechwan and the Chinese Republic*, 8, 14, 17–23.

34. See in detail *Wusi yundong zai Sichuan* (May 4th Movement in Sichuan) (Chengdu: Sichuan daxue chubanshe, 1989), 103–18, 235–63, 188–322, 355–71; Wen Xianmei and Deng Shouming, *Wusi yundong yu Sichuan jiandang* (May 4th

Movement and Party Building in Sichuan) (Chengdu: Sichuan renmin chuban-she, 1985), 10–29.

35. See Jiang, "Liu Fa, Bi qingong jianxue huiyi" (Recollections on the Diligent Work, Frugal Study in France and Belgium), 448.

36. See Jin, " 'Deng jia lao yuanzi' de lao gushi" (Old Stories of "The Deng Family Old Household").

37. See Deng, *Deng Xiaoping zishu* (Autobiographical Notes of Deng Xiaoping), 3; [Deng], "Gege wei geming bu huijia" (Elder Brother Did Not Return Home for the Sake of the Revolution); Deng, *Deng Xiaoping*, 60.

38. Quoted from "Deng Xiaoping yi jiade gushi" (Stories of Deng Xiaoping's Family).

CHAPTER 2

1. The chapter is written with assistance of Daria Alexandrovna Arincheva (Spichak).

2. See Luo Zhengkai et al., eds., *Deng Xiaoping zaoqi geming huodong* (Deng Xiaoping's Early Revolutionary Activity) (Shenyang: Liaoning renmin chubanshe, 1991), 54.

3. See Ibid., 56.

4. Quoted from Yang, *Deng*, 29.

5. See "Liner André Lebon," http://www.frenchlines.com/ship_en_1018.php.

6. See Jiang, "Liu Fa, Bi qingong jianxue huiyi" (Recollections on the Diligent Work, Frugal Study in France and Belgium), 449–50; Luo, *Deng Xiaoping zaoqi geming huodong* (Deng Xiaoping's Early Revolutionary Activity), 63–64.

7. Twenty student groups totaling 1,449 persons came to France from China in 1919–20. The first arrived on March 17, 1919, and the last on December 15, 1920.

8. See Zi Hui, "Liu Fa jianxue qingong liang nian laizhi jingguo ji xianzhuang" (The Two-year History and Present Development of the Frugal Study, Diligent Work [movement] in France), in *Fu Fa qingong jianxue yundong shiliao* (Materials on the History of the Diligent Work, Frugal Study Movement in France), vol. 1 (Beijing: Beijing chubanshe, 1981), 85–94; Huang Jinping and Zhang Li, *Deng Xiaoping zai Shanghai* (Deng Xiaoping in Shanghai) (Shanghai: Shanghai ren-min chubanshe, 2004), 17, 18.

9. Deng, *Deng Xiaoping*, 60. The students had to be back in the dormitory by 8:00 p.m. and lights out was at 9:00 p.m. The students were made to arise at 6:00 a.m. Classes ran from 8:00 to 11:00 in the morning and from 2:00 to 4:00 in the afternoon.

10. See Deng, *Deng Xiaoping*, 60; Yang and Yan, *Deng Xiaoping nianpu: 1904–1974* (Chronological Biography of Deng Xiaoping: 1904–1974), vol. 1, 10.

11. Yang and Yan, *Deng Xiaoping nianpu: 1904–1974* (Chronological Biography of Deng Xiaoping: 1904–1974), vol. 1, 8.

12. See Deng, *Deng Xiaoping*, 61–62.

13. Chen Yi, "Wo liang nian lai liu Fa qingong jianxuede shigan" (My Two-year Impressions from the Diligent Work, Frugal Study in France), in *Fu Fa qingong*

jianxue yundong shiliao (Materials on the History of the Diligent Work, Frugal Study Movement in France), vol. 3, 47, 53.

14. Chen Yi, "Wo liang nian lai liu Fa de tong ku" (My Two-year Sufferings from Sojourning in France), ibid., 57.

15. "Fatherland of Liberty" is what Zhou Enlai, the future premier of the PRC, called France in his verses.

16. See ibid.

17. Li Huang, *Xuedun shi huiyilu* (Reminiscences of an Uneducated Scholar in His Study Room) (Taipei: Chuanji wenxue chubanshe, 1973), 69.

18. See Marilyn A. Levine and Chen San-ching, *The Guomindang in Europe: A Sourcebook of Documents* (Berkeley: University of California Press, 2000), 11.

19. Quoted from Deng, *Deng Xiaoping*, 60.

20. See Li, *Xuedun shi huiyilu* (Reminiscences of an Uneducated Scholar in His Study Room), 70.

21. See Paul J. Bailey, "The Chinese Work-Study Movement in France," *China Quarterly*, vol. 115 (September 1988): 458; Marilyn A. Levine, *The Found Generation: Chinese Communists in Europe During the Twenties* (Seattle: University of Washington Press, 1993), 126.

22. See Deng, *Deng Xiaoping*, 69.

23. For more details, see Levine, *The Found Generation*, 121–31; Nora Wang, *Émigration et Politique: Les Étudiants-Ouvriers Chinois en France (1919–1925)* (Emigration and Politics: Chinese Worker-Students in France [1919–1925]) (Paris: Indes savantes, 2002), 213–28, 238–40; Nie Rongzhen, *Inside the Red Star: The Memoirs of Marshal Nie Rongzhen* (Beijing: New World Press, 1983), 18.

24. For more details, see Zheng Chaolin, *An Oppositionist for Life: Memoirs of the Chinese Revolutionary Zheng Chaolin*, trans. Gregor Benton (Atlantic Highlands, NJ: Humanities Press, 1997), 25–26; Zheng Chaolin, "Zheng Chaolin tan Deng Xiaoping" (Zheng Chaolin Speaks About Deng Xiaoping), in Liu Jintian, ed., *Huashuo Deng Xiaoping* (Stories About Deng Xiaoping) (Beijing: Zhongyang wenxian chubanshe, 2004), 10.

25. Quoted from Deng, *Deng Xiaoping*, 72.

26. Zheng, "Zheng Chaolin tan Deng Xiaoping" (Zheng Chaolin Speaks About Deng Xiaoping), 11.

27. See Wen and Deng, *Wusi yundong yu Sichuan jiandang* (May 4th Movement and Party Building in Sichuan), 40–41.

28. See Zheng, *An Oppositionist for Life*, 17–18; Nie, *Inside the Red Star*, 25–26.

29. See *Zhou Enlai nianpu (1898–1949)* (Chronological Biography of Zhou Enlai [1898–1949]), rev. ed. (Beijing: Zhongyang wenxian chubanshe, 1997), 45, 48; Liao Gailong et al., eds., *Zhongguo gongchandang lishi da cidian. Zengdingben. Zonglun. Renwu* (Great Dictionary of the History of the Chinese Communist Party. Expanded ed. General Section. Personnel) (Beijing: Zhonggong zhongyang dangxiao chubanshe, 2001), 198.

30. See Zheng, *An Oppositionist for Life*, 22; Liao Gailong et al., eds., *Zhongguo gongchandang lishi da cidian: Chuangli shiqi fenqi* (Great Dictionary of the History of the Chinese Communist Party: Foundation Period Section) (Beijing: Zhonggong zhongyang dangxiao chubanshe, 1989), 205.

31. See Zheng, *An Oppositionist for Life*, 25; Sun Qiming, "Chen Yannian," in Hu Hua, ed., *Zhonggong dangshi renwu zhuan* (Biographies of Persons in CCP History), vol. 12 (Xi'an: Shaanxi renmin chubanshe, 1983), 7.

32. See Daria A. Spichak, *Kitaiskii avangard Kremlia: Revoliutsionery Kitaia v moskovskikh shkolakh Kominterna (1921–1939)* (The Chinese Vanguard of the Kremlin: Revolutionaries of China in Moscow Comintern Schools [1921–1939]) (Moscow: "Veche," 2012), 91–92.

33. See *Zhou Enlai nianpu (1898–1949)* (Chronological Biography of Zhou Enlai [1898–1949]), 56; Zheng, *An Oppositionist for Life*, 27–29; Peng Chengfu, "Zhao Shiyan," in Hu Hua, ed., *Zhonggong dang shi renwu zhuan* (Biographies of Persons in CCP History), vol. 7 (Xi'an: Shaanxi renmin chubanshe, 1983), 13–14.

34. See Liao, *Zhongguo gongchandang lishi da cidian: Chuangli shiqi fenqi* (Great Dictionary of the History of the Chinese Communist Party: Foundation Period Section), 205.

35. Deng, *Deng Xiaoping*, 73.

36. See Edgar Snow, *Random Notes on Red China (1936–1945)* (Cambridge, MA: East Asian Research Center, Harvard University, 1957), 137.

37. Deng, *Deng Xiaoping*, 73.

38. *Lichnoe delo Den Sisiania (Dozorova)* (Personal File of Deng Xixian [Dozorov]), 4, 5.

39. Deng, *Deng Xiaoping zishu* (Autobiographical Notes of Deng Xiaoping), 13.

40. Ibid., 10; *Lichnoe delo Den Sisiania (Dozorova)* (Personal File of Deng Xixian [Dozorov]), 4–5.

41. On Chen Duxiu's and the Central Executive Committee of the Chinese Socialist Youth League's demand to change the name of the European organization of the Chinese communist youth.

42. See Deng, *Deng Xiaoping*, 80–81; Deng, *Deng Xiaoping zishu* (Autobiographical Notes of Deng Xiaoping), 16; Letter from Xiao Jing Wang, a grandson of Wang Zekai, the man who recommended Deng to the CSYL, to Alexander V. Pantsov of December 2, 2012. Later, in his old age, Deng would tell his daughter that he joined the Chinese Socialist Youth League in the summer of 1922. See Deng, *Deng Xiaoping*, 80. But this does not accord with the facts. In 1926 in Moscow, in various questionnaires and in his own handwritten autobiography, he repeatedly indicated that he had become a member of the Youth League in June 1923. See *Lichnoe delo Den Sisiania (Dozorova)* (Personal File of Deng Xixian [Dozorov]), 2 reverse side, 4, 5, 10 reverse side, 12 reverse side; *Lichnoe delo Deng Sisiania* (Personal File of Deng Xixian), RGASPI, collection 495, inventory 225, file 2574, sheet 3; Deng, *Deng Xiaoping zishu* (Autobiographical Notes of Deng Xiaoping), 11, 14, 31. See

also Yang and Yan, *Deng Xiaoping nianpu: 1904–1974* (Chronological Biography of Deng Xiaoping: 1904–1974), vol. 1, 18.

43. Deng, *Deng Xiaoping zishu* (Autobiographical Notes of Deng Xiaoping), 4; Deng, "Deng Ken tan Deng Xiaoping" (Deng Ken Speaks About Deng Xiaoping), 6–7.

44. Deng, *Deng Xiaoping zishu* (Autobiographical Notes of Deng Xiaoping), 4.

45. See Deng, "Deng Ken tan Deng Xiaoping" (Deng Ken Speaks About Deng Xiaoping), 7; [Deng], "Gege wei geming bu huijia" (Elder Brother Did Not Return Home for the Sake of the Revolution).

46. In Japan, Zhou just studied Japanese, if only for a brief time, from late 1917 to early 1918, in the East Asia Senior Preparatory School in the Kanda district of Tokyo.

47. Cai Chang, "Tan qingong jianxue he shehuizhuyi qingniantuan lü Ou zhibu" (On the Diligent Work, Frugal Study in France and the European Branch of the Socialist Youth League), *Gongchanzhuyi xiaozu* (Communist Cells), vol. 2 (Beijing: Zhonggong dangshi ziliao chubanshe, 1987), 947.

48. Quoted from Deng, *Deng Xiaoping*, 88. See also Deng Xiaoping, *Selected Works of Deng Xiaoping*, vol. 2 *(1975–1982)*, 2nd ed. (Beijing: Foreign Languages Press, 1995), 329.

49. Li, *Xuedun shi huiylu* (Reminiscences of an Uneducated Scholar in His Study Room), 89.

50. See Alexander V. Pantsov and Gregor Benton, "Did Trotsky Oppose Entering the Guomindang 'From the First'?" *Republican China*, vol. 19, no. 2 (April 1994): 52–66.

51. See *Zhou Enlai nianpu (1898–1949)* (Chronological Biography of Zhou Enlai [1898–1949]), 62.

52. The assertion by Deng's daughter that Deng supposedly became a member of the Communist party in 1924 is obviously far-fetched. It is based on the supposition that her father's election to the Executive Committee of the European branch of the CSYL automatically signified his admission into the party. See Deng, *Deng Xiaoping*, 87.

53. See *Lichnoe delo Den Sisiania (Dozorova)* (Personal File of Deng Xixian [Dozorov]), 2 reverse, 4, 5, 10 reverse, 12 reverse; *Lichnoe delo Den Sisiania* (Personal File of Deng Xixian), 3; Deng, *Deng Xiaoping zishu* (Autobiographical Notes of Deng Xiaoping), 1, 31.

54. See *Lichnoe delo Den Sisiania* (Personal File of Deng Xixian), 3.

55. See Yang and Yan, *Deng Xiaoping nianpu: 1904–1974* (Chronological Biography of Deng Xiaoping: 1904–1974), vol. 1, 24.

56. For more details, see Nora Wang, "Deng Xiaoping: The Years in France," *China Quarterly*, vol. 92 (December 1982): 701–705; Wang, *Émigration et Politique* (Emigration and Politics), 280–83; Deng, *Deng Xiaoping*, 92–97.

57. Yang Pinsun would come to study in Moscow only in the fall of 1926. By that time he had become a member of the CCP in Paris. See *Lichnoe delo Maikova*

(Yan Pinsunia) (Personal File of Maikov [Yang Pinsun]), RGASPI, collection 495, inventory 225, file 1994.

58. Quoted from Wang, *Émigration et Politique* (Emigration and Politics) 281; Deng, *Deng Xiaoping*, 97.

59. See Alexander Pantsov, *The Bolsheviks and the Chinese Revolution, 1919–1927* (Honolulu: University of Hawai'i Press, 2000), 282.

60. For more details, see Spichak, *Kitaiskii avangard Kremlia* (The Chinese Vanguard of the Kremlin), 43–44.

61. See ibid., 43, 45.

62. More than two hundred of the three hundred members of the European branches of the CCP and CCYL were then studying in Moscow. See Deng, *Deng Xiaoping zishu* (Autobiographical Notes of Deng Xiaoping), 23.

63. See *Lichnoe delo Den Sisiania* (Personal File of Deng Xixian), 1–4.

64. Zheng, *An Oppositionist for Life*, 48, 54.

65. Ren Zhuoxuan, "Liu E ji gui guo hou de huiyi" (Reminiscences of Life in Russia and After Returning to the Motherland), in *Liushi nian lai zhongguo liu E xuesheng zhi fengxian diaoku* (Reminiscences of Chinese Students About Their Sojourns in Russia Sixty Years Ago) (Taibei: Zhonghua shuju chubanshe, 1988), 74.

66. Deng, *Deng Xiaoping zishu* (Autobiographical Notes of Deng Xiaoping), 28.

67. See Spichak, *Kitaiskii avangard Kremlia* (The Chinese Vanguard of the Kremlin), 77.

68. See Pantsov, *The Bolsheviks and the Chinese Revolution, 1919–1927*, 282; *Deng Xiaoping*, 31; Sheng Yueh, *Sun Yat-sen University in Moscow and the Chinese Revolution: A Personal Account* (Lawrence: University of Kansas, 1971), 88.

69. See RGASPI, collection 530, inventory 1, file 16, not paginated; S. A. Dalin, *Kitaiskie memuary: 1921–1927* (Chinese Memoirs: 1921–1927) (Moscow: Nauka, 1975), 176.

70. See "V universitete trudiashchikhsia Sun Yat-sena" (In Sun Yat-sen University of Toilers), *Pravda*, Mar. 11, 1926. Starting in the second half of 1926, the schedule was eight hours from Monday through Wednesday and six hours from Thursday through Saturday. See RGASPI, collection 530, inventory 1, file 17, sheet 53.

71. RGASPI, collection 530, inventory 2, file 5, sheet 175; Deng, *Deng Xiaoping zishu* (Autobiographical Notes of Deng Xiaoping), 26–27.

72. Sheng, *Sun Yat-sen University in Moscow and the Chinese Revolution*, 87–88.

73. See Deng, *Deng Xiaoping*, 106.

74. Karl Marx, "Critique of the Gotha Programme," in Karl Marx and Frederick Engels, *Collected Works*, vol. 24, trans. Richard Dixon and others (New York: International, 1989), 87.

75. V. I. Lenin, "The Tax in Kind," in V. I. Lenin, *Collected Works*, vol. 32 (Moscow: Progress Publishers, 1965), 344.

76. J. V. Stalin, "The Fourteenth Congress of the C.P.S.U.(B.). December 18–31, 1925," in J. V. Stalin, *Works*, vol. 7 (Moscow: Foreign Languages Publishing House, 1954), 374.

77. N. I. Bukharin, *Selected Writings on the State and the Transition to Socialism*, trans., ed., and introduced Richard B. Day (Armonk, NY: Sharpe, 1982), 189, 197.

78. See RGASPI, collection 495, inventory 225, file 1629, unpaginated; Sheng, *Sun Yat-sen University in Moscow and the Chinese Revolution*, 69–70; Leng Rong and Yan Jianqi, eds., *Deng Xiaoping huazhuan* (Pictorial Biography of Deng Xiaoping vol. 1) (Chengdu: Sichuan chuban jituan and Sichuan renmin chubanshe, 2004), 26.

79. Quoted from L. Yu Miin-ling, *Sun Yat-sen University in Moscow, 1925–1930*, PhD dissertation (New York, 1995), 179.

80. See ibid., 175.

81. See RGASPI, collection 530, inventory 2, file 33, sheets 28–30.

82. See ibid., 31–32.

83. See ibid., inventory 1, file 42, unpaginated; Sun Yefang, "Guanyu Zhonggong liu Mo zhibu" (On the Moscow Branch of the CCP), *Zhonggong dangshi ziliao* (Materials on the History of the CCP), no. 1 (1982): 180–83; Sheng, *Sun Yat-sen University in Moscow and the Chinese Revolution*, 111–12.

84. See Yu, *Sun Yat-sen University in Moscow, 1925–1930*, 172–73.

85. See ibid., 175.

86. RGASPI, collection 530, inventory 2, file 15, sheet 42 reverse.

87. Quoted from Deng, *Deng Xiaoping*, 107–8.

88. *Lichnoe delo Den Sisiania (Dozorova)* (Personal File of Deng Xixian [Dozorov]), 18.

89. Ibid., 9.

90. *Lichnoe delo Dogadovoi* (Personal File of Dogodova), RGASPI, collection 495, inventory 225, file 1669; Leng and Yan, *Deng Xiaoping huazhuan* (Pictorial Biography of Deng Xiaoping), vol. 1, 41.

91. For more details, see Pantsov, *The Bolsheviks and the Chinese Revolution, 1919–1927*, 84–98.

92. For more details, see Pantsov with Levine, *Mao*, 153–56.

93. See RGASPI, collection 17, inventory 162, file 3, sheet 55; M. L. Titarenko et al., eds., *VKP(b), Komintern i Kitai: Dokumenty* (The AUCP[b], the Comintern, and China: Documents), vol. 2 (Moscow: AO "Buklet," 1996), 202.

94. See Titarenko, et al. *VKP(b), Komintern i Kitai: Dokumenty* (The AUCP[b], the Comintern, and China. Documents), vol. 2, 228, 281.

95. See George T. B. Davis, *China's Christian Army: A Story of Marshal Feng and His Soldiers* (New York: Christian Alliance, 1925), 7; Marshall Broomhall, *General Feng: A Good Soldier of Christ Jesus* (London: China Inland Mission, 1923), 11; Marcus Ch'eng, *Marshal Feng—The Man and His Work* (Shanghai: Kelly & Walsh, 1926), 9; Feng Lida, *Wo de fuqin Feng Yuxiang jiangjun* (My Father General Feng Yuxiang) (Chengdu: Sichuan renmin chubanshe, 1984), 92.

96. See Feng Yuxiang, *Feng Yuxian riji* (Diary of Feng Yuxiang), vol. 2 (Nanjing: Jiangsu guji chubanshe, 1992), 177–215; Lars T. Lih et al., eds., *Stalin's Letters to Molotov, 1925–1936*, trans. Catherine A. Fitzpatrick (New Haven: Yale University Press, 1995), 103–18; Meng Xinren and Cao Shusheng, *Feng Yuxiang zhuan* (Biography of Feng Yuxiang) (Hefei: Anhui renmin chubanshe, 1998), 118; *Lichnoe delo Sobinovoi* (Personal File of Sobinova), RGASPI, collection 495, inventory 225, file 1341; *Lichnoe delo Nezhdanovoi* (Personal File of Nezhdanova), ibid., file 2034; *Lichnoe delo Kalganskogo* (Personal File of Kalganskii), ibid., file 1818. See also personal file of KUTV student Zeng Yongquan (Nikolai Petrovich Nakatov), who, on assignment from the Executive Committee of the Comintern (ECCI), served as Feng Yuxiang's interpreter during his sojourn in the USSR (ibid., file 2051).

97. See Feng, *Feng Yuxiang riji* (Diary of Feng Yuxiang), vol. 2, 177–215; Feng Yuxiang, *Wo de shenghuo* (My Life) (Harbin: Heilongjiang renmin chubanshe, 1984), 461–82; Titarenko, et al. *VKP(b), Komintern i Kitai: Dokumenty* (The AUCP[b], the Comintern, and China: Documents), vol. 2, 241, 242; Sheng, *Sun Yat-sen University and the Chinese Revolution*, 133–43; Jin Yanshi et al., "Liu Bojian," in Hu Hua, ed., *Zhonggong dangshi renwu zhuan* (Biographies of Persons in the History of the CCP History), vol. 4 (Xi'an: Shaanxi renmin chubanshe, 1982), 267–68.

98. See Pang Xianzhi, ed., *Mao Zedong nianpu, 1893–1949* (Chronological Biography of Mao Zedong, 1893–1949), vol. 1 (Beijing: Renmin chubanshe and Zhongyang wenxian chubanshe, 2002), 169–72; M. F. Yuriev, *Revoliutsiia 1925–1927 gg. v Kitae* (The Revolution of 1925–1927 in China) (Moscow: Nauka, 1968), 416; Vera Vladimirovna Vishniakova-Akimova, *Two Years in Revolutionary China 1925–1927*, trans. Steven I. Levine (Cambridge, MA: Harvard University Press, 1971), 243–71; Chang Kuo-t'ao, *The Rise of the Chinese Communist Party, 1921–1927*, vol. 1 (Lawrence: University Press of Kansas, 1972), 532–72.

99. See James E. Sheridan, *Chinese Warlord: The Career of Feng Yu-hsiang* (Stanford, CA: Stanford University Press, 1966), 203–9.

100. Titarenko, et al. *VKP(b), Komintern i Kitai: Dokumenty* (The AUCP[b], the Comintern, and China. Documents), vol. 2, 449.

101. For a photocopy of the document, see Deng, *Deng Xiaoping zishu* (Autobiographical Notes of Deng Xiaoping), 28; Leng and Yan, *Deng Xiaoping huazhuan* (Pictorial Biography of Deng Xiaoping), vol. 1, 42.

102. See *Lichnoe delo Den Sisiania* (Personal File of Deng Xixian), 9.

CHAPTER 3

1. Quoted from Deng, *Deng Xiaoping*, 112. See also Deng, *Deng Xiaoping zishu* (Autobiographical Notes of Deng Xiaoping), 27; Yang and Yan, *Deng Xiaoping nianpu: 1904–1974* (Chronological Biography of Deng Xiaoping: 1904–1974), vol. 1, 32.

2. On Feng, see V. M. Primakov, *Zapiski volontera: Grazhdanskaia voina v Kitae* (Notes of a Volunteer: The Civil War in China) (Moscow: Nauka, 1967), 36–37.

3. A Chinese saying has it that "A wise person should speak softly and should be afraid of spilling the cup of wisdom."

4. See Gao Kelin, "Gao Kelin tan Deng Xiaoping" (Gao Kelin Speaks About Deng Xiaoping); in Liu Jintian, ed., *Huashuo Deng Xiaoping* (Stories About Deng Xiaoping) (Beijing: Zhongyang wenxian chubanshe, 2004), 19.

5. See Zhang Junhua and Wang Shaomin, "Shi Kexuan," in Hu Hua, ed., *Zhonggong dangshi renwu zhuan* (Biographies of Persons in CCP History), vol. 26 (Xi'an: Shaanxi renmin chubanshe, 1985), 104, 111–15.

6. Quoted from Deng, *Deng Xiaoping*, 113.

7. See ibid.; Gao, "Gao Kelin tan Deng Xiaoping" (Gao Kelin Speaks About Deng Xiaoping), 19; Deng Maomao, *Wode fuqin Deng Xiaoping* (My Father Deng Xiaoping) (Beijing: Zhongyang wenxian chubanshe, 1997), 157.

8. See Deng, *Deng Xiaoping*, 113; Luo, *Deng Xiaoping zaoqi geming huodong* (Early Revolutionary Activities of Deng Xiaoping), 130. The other secretary, whether before or after him is unknown, was his subordinate in the Political Department, the chief of the Organization Bureau, Gao Kelin. See Gao, "Gao Kelin tan Deng Xiaoping" (Gao Kelin Speaks About Deng Xiaoping), 20; Zhang and Wang, "Shi Kexuan", 114–15.

9. See Yang and Yan, *Deng Xiaoping nianpu: 1904–1974* (Chronological Biography of Deng Xiaoping), vol. 1, 33.

10. See Gao, "Gao Kelin tan Deng Xiaoping" (Gao Kelin Speaks About Deng Xiaoping), 20.

11. See Deng, *Deng Xiaoping*, 113.

12. RGASPI, collection 17, inventory 162, file 4, sheets 71–72. See also Titarenko, et al. *VKP(b), Komintern i Kitai. Dokumenty* (The AUCP[b], the Comintern, and China. Documents), vol. 2, 632–33. [Italics in original.]

13. Chang, *The Rise of the Chinese Communist Party*, vol. 1, 606.

14. See Feng, *Wo de shenghuo* (My Life), 535. Earlier, prior to the proclamation of the Republic on January 1, 1912, the residence of the head of Shaanxi province was called the People's House. Harry Alverson Franck, *Wandering in Northern China* (New York: Century, 1923), 383.

15. See Zhang and Wang, "Shi Kexuan," 117.

16. See Feng, *Feng Yuxiang riji* (Feng Yuxiang's Diary), vol. 2, 333–34; Sheridan, *Chinese Warlord*, 224.

17. Quoted from Sheridan, *Chinese Warlord*, 227.

18. See ibid., 225–26.

19. Quoted from ibid., 232.

20. Quoted from ibid., 228.

21. See Feng, *Wo de shenghuo* (My Life), 563; Feng, *Feng Yuxiang riji* (Feng Yuxiang's Diary), vol. 2, 337; *Deng Xiaoping*, 35; Jin, "Liu Bojian," 275; Luo, *Deng Xiaoping*

zaoqi geming huodong (Early Revolutionary Activities of Deng Xiaoping), 132; Meng and Cao, *Feng Yuxian zhuan* (Biography of Feng Yuxiang), 144–45.

22. Quoted from Yang, *Deng Xiaoping*, 55.

23. See Zhang and Wang, "Shi Kexuan," 119.

24. See *Deng Xiaoping*, 35–36; Luo, *Deng Xiaoping zaoqi geming huodong* (Early Revolutionary Activities of Deng Xiaoping), 132; Gao, "Gao Kelin tan Deng Xiaoping" (Gao Kelin Speaks About Deng Xiaoping), 20.

25. See Zheng, *An Oppositionist for Life*, 127, 130–31.

26. See Deng, *Deng Xiaoping*, 118.

27. RGASPI, collection 17, inventory 162, file 5, sheet 30. This telegram was first published in 1996. See Titarenko, et al. *VKP(b), Komintern i Kitai: Dokumenty* (The AUCP[b], the Comintern, and China: Documents), vol. 2, 763–64.

28. Titarenko, et al. *VKP(b), Komintern i Kitai: Dokumenty* (The AUCP[b], the Comintern, and China: Documents), vol. 2, 814, 823.

29. Ibid., 843.

30. Quoted from Chang, *The Rise of the Chinese Communist Party*, vol. 1, 715.

31. Zheng, *An Oppositionist for Life*, 129.

32. See Patricia Stranahan, *Underground: The Shanghai Communist Party and the Politics of Survival, 1927–1937* (Lanham, MD: Rowman & Littlefield, 1998), 23.

33. Chang, *The Rise of the Chinese Communist Party*, vol. 1, 669–70.

34. Stuart R. Schram, ed., *Mao's Road to Power: Revolutionary Writings, 1912–1949* vol. 3 (Armonk, NY: Sharpe, 1995), 30–33; *Baqi huiyi* (The August 7 Conference), Beijing: Zhonggong dangshi ziliao chubanshe, 1986), 73.

35. Quoted from Leng Buji, *Deng Xiaoping zai Gannan* (Deng Xiaoping in South Jiangxi) (Beijing: Zhongyang wenxian chubanshe, 1995), 85.

36. In addition to Mao, the Provisional Politburo, selected by Lominadze, included fifteen persons: nine members and six candidate members, among them Qu Qiubai, Deng Zhongxia, Zhou Enlai, Zhang Guotao, and Li Lisan.

37. For more details see Pantsov with Levine, *Mao*, 194–98.

38. See Zheng, *An Oppositionist for Life*, 133; Titarenko et al., eds., *VKP(b), Komintern i Kitai: Dokumenty* (The AUCP[b], the Comintern, and China: Documents), vol. 3, 126–27.

39. For more details see A. M. Grigoriev, *Kommunisticheskaia partiia Kitaia v nachal'nyi period sovetskogo dvizheniia (iul' 1927g.–sentiabr' 1931g.)* (The Communist Party of China in the Initial Period of the Soviet Movement [July 1927–September 1931]) (Moscow: IDV AN SSSR, 1976), 37–46.

40. Sun Yat-sen's Three Principles of the People (Nationalism, Democracy, People's Livelihood), the core of the Guomindang's program, were intended to lay the groundwork for a future democratic Chinese state based on cooperation among all classes.

41. See Frederic Wakeman, Jr., *Policing Shanghai, 1927–1937* (Berkeley: University of California Press, 1995), 58, 133.

42. See Stranahan, *Underground*, 17.

43. See Pantsov with Levine, *Mao*, 205.

44. See Chang, *The Rise of the Chinese Communist Party*, vol. 2, 39.

45. See *Deng Xiaoping*, 37; Yang and Yan, *Deng Xiaoping nianpu: 1904–1974* (Chronological Biography of Deng Xiaoping: 1904–1974), vol. 1, 39.

46. See Leng and Yan, *Deng Xiaoping huazhuan* (Pictorial Biography of Deng Xiaoping), vol. 1, 49.

47. See Huang Zeran, "Huang Zeran tan Deng Xiaoping" (Huang Zeran Speaks About Deng Xiaoping), in Liu Jintian, ed., *Huashuo Deng Xiaoping* (Stories About Deng Xiaoping) (Beijing: Zhongyang wenxian chubanshe, 2004), 21.

48. See Deng, *Deng Xiaoping*, 135.

49. Quoted from ibid., 132.

50. See Zheng, *An Oppositionist for Life*, 215.

51. See Luo, *Deng Xiaoping zaoqi geming huodong* (Early Revolutionary Activities of Deng Xiaoping), 134.

52. See Sladkovskii, *Informatsionnyi biulleten'. Seriia A. Vypusk 2* (Information Bulletin: Series A: 2nd Installment), 4.

53. Alexander Pantsov's personal impressions from visiting the hamlet of Xiexing, June 24, 2010.

54. Franz, *Deng Xiaoping*, 13–14.

55. Quoted from Deng, *Deng Xiaoping*, 136–37.

56. See *Ren Bishi nianpu: 1904–1950* (Chronological Biography of Ren Bishi: 1904–1950) (Beijing: Zhongyang wenxian chubanshe, 2004), 95.

57. M. I. Sladkovskii, ed., *Dokumenty po istorii Kommunisticheskoi partii Kitaia 1920–1949 (v chetyrekh tomakh)* (Documents on the History of the Communist Party of China, 1920–1949. In four volumes), vol. 1 (Moscow: IDV AN SSSR, 1981), 180–81; vol. 2, 26, 30.

58. Pavel Mif, ed., *Strategiia i taktika Kominterna v natsional'no-kolonial'noi revoliutsii na primere Kitaia* (Strategy and Tactics of the Comintern in National and Colonial Revolutions: The Case of China) (Moscow: IWEIP Press, 1934), 236–44.

59. See Titarenko et al., *VKP(b), Komintern i Kitai: Dokumenty* (The AUCP[b], the Comintern, and China: Documents), vol. 3, 603. See also Yang and Yan, *Deng Xiaoping nianpu: 1904–1974* (Chronological Biography of Deng Xiaoping: 1904–1974), vol. 1, 49.

60. For more details on Gong Yinbing, see Gong Youzhi, "Gong Yinbing," in Hu Hua, ed., *Zhonggong dangshi renwu zhuan* (Biographies of Persons in CCP History), vol. 34 (Xi'an: Shaanxi renmin chubanshe, 1987), 261–70.

61. See Deng, *Deng Xiaoping*, 159.

62. Quoted from Leng and Yan, *Deng Xiaoping huazhuan* (Pictorial Biography of Deng Xiaoping), vol. 1, 50.

CHAPTER 4

1. See Nie, *Inside the Red Star*, 84–85; Liao Gailong, *Zhongguo gongchandang lishi da cidian. Zengdingben. Zonglun. Renwu* (Great Dictionary of the History of the Chinese Communist Party. Expanded edition. General. Personnel), 177.

2. See Nie, *Inside the Red Star*, 84–85; Yang and Yan, *Deng Xiaoping nianpu: 1904–1974* (Chronological Biography of Deng Xiaoping: 1904–1974), vol. 1, 50–51; Gong Chu, *Wo yu hongjun* (The Red Army and I) (Hong Kong: Nan feng chubanshe, 1954), 165–67.

3. See Gong, *Wo yu hongjun* (The Red Army and I), 167.

4. See Diana Lary, *Region and Nation: The Kwangsi Clique in Chinese Politics, 1925–1937* (London: Cambridge University Press, 1974), 103.

5. Ibid., 183–200; Gong, *Wo yu hongjun* (The Red Army and I), 173; *Dangshi yanjiu ziliao* (Study Materials on Party History), series 5 (Chengdu: Sichuan renmin chubanshe, 1985), 496–97.

6. See Chen Xinde, "Wei Baqun," in Hua, ed., *Zhonggong dangshi renwu zhuan* (Biographies of Persons in CCP History), vol. 12, 183–200. According to other data, Wei Baqun became a member of the CCP at the end of 1928. See *Zhuangzu jianshi* (Short History of the Zhuang) (Nanning: Guangxi renmin chubanshe, 1980), 149; Huang Xianfan, *Zhuangzu tongshi* (Comprehensive History of the Zhuang) (Nanning: Guangxi renmin chubanshe, 1988), 788.

7. Titarenko et al., *VKP(b), Komintern i Kitai: Dokumenty* (The AUCP[b], the Comintern, and China: Documents), vol. 3, 732.

8. Quoted from Deng, *Deng Xiaoping*, 144.

9. Ibid.

10. Ibid., 146.

11. *Zuo you jiang geming genjudi* (Revolutionary Bases in the Zuojiang and Youjiang Areas), vol. 1 (Beijing: Zhonggong dangshi ziliao chubanshe, 1989), 79. For information that the report at the congress was delivered by He Chang, see *Zhang Yunyi dajiang huazhuan* (Pictorial Biography of General Zhang Yunyi) (Chengdu: Sichuan renmin chubanshe, 2009), 66.

12. Regarding Lei Jingtian, see Wang Linmao, "Lei Jingtian," in Hu Hua, ed., *Zhonggong dangshi renwu zhuan* (Biographies of Persons in CCP History), vol. 20 (Xi'an: Shaanxi renmin chubanshe, 1984), 346–60.

13. See Deng, *Deng Xiaoping zishu* (Autobiographical Notes of Deng Xiaoping), 40.

14. See Leng and Yan, *Deng Xiaoping huazhuan* (Pictorial Biography of Deng Xiaoping), vol. 1, 52; Yang and Yan, *Deng Xiaoping nianpu: 1904–1974* (Chronological Biography of Deng Xiaoping: 1904–1974), vol. 1, 50.

15. See Gong, *Wo yu hongjun* (The Red Army and I), 168–69.

16. See ibid., 171–72; Yang and Yan, *Deng Xiaoping nianpu: 1904–1974* (Chronological Biography of Deng Xiaoping: 1904–1974), vol. 1, 51; *Zhang Yunyi dajiang huazhuan* (Pictorial Biography of General Zhang Yunyi), 66.

17. See Deng, *Deng Xiaoping*, 145.

18. Gong, *Wo yu hongjun* (The Red Army and I), 173–74.

19. H. G. W. Woodhead, ed., *China Year Book 1931* (Nendeln/Liechtenstein: Kraus Reprint, 1969), 595. On the opium trade in this region, see also Harry A. Franck, *China: A Geographical Reader* (Dansville, NY: F. A. Owen, 1927), 212–13.

20. See Deng, *Deng Xiaoping*, 148–49; Yang and Yan, *Deng Xiaoping nianpu: 1904–1974* (Chronological Biography of Deng Xiaoping: 1904–1974), vol. 1, 51; Zhang Yunyi, "Bose qiyi yu hong qi jun de jianli" (The Uprising in Bose and the Establishment of the 7th Corps of the Red Army), in *Guangxi geming huiyilu* (Reminiscences of the Revolution in Guangxi) (Nanning: Guangxi zhuangzu zizhiqu renmin chubanshe, 1959), 6.

21. See [Deng Xiaoping] "Baogao" (Report) [January 1930], in *Zuo you jiang geming genjudi* (Revolutionary Bases in the Zuojiang and Youjiang Areas), vol. 1, 175.

22. Harry A. Franck, *Roving Through Southern China* (New York: Century, 1925), 356, 357.

23. For this letter see *Zuo you jiang geming genjudi* (Revolutionary Bases in the Zuojiang and Youjiang Areas), vol. 1, 76–92.

24. See Zhang, "Bose qiyi yu hong qi junde jianli" (The Bose Uprising and Establishment of the 7th Corps of the Red Army), 9–10; Chen Daomin [Chen Haoren], "Qi jun qianwei baogao (1930 nian 1 yue) (Report of the Front Committee of the 7th Corps, January 1930), in *Zuo you jiang geming genjudi* (Revolutionary Bases in the Zuojiang and Youjiang Areas), vol. 1, 158.

25. [Deng], "Baogao" (Report), 176–77; Chen Haoren, "Qi jun gongzuo zong baogao (1931 nian 3 yue 9 ri) (General Report on the Work of the 7th Corps, Mar. 9, 1931), in *Zuo you jiang geming genjudi* (Revolutionary Bases in the Zuojiang and Youjiang Areas), vol. 1, 361; Deng, *Deng Xiaoping*, 155–56.

26. See Yang and Yan, *Deng Xiaoping nianpu: 1904–1974* (Chronological Biography of Deng Xiaoping: 1904–1974), vol. 1, 53; Huang Rong, "Huang Rong tan Deng Xiaoping" (Huang Rong Speaks About Deng Xiaoping), in Liu Jintian, ed., *Huashuo Deng Xiaoping* (Stories About Deng Xiaoping) (Beijing: Zhongyang wenxian chubanshe, 2004), 24.

27. See Chen, "Qi jun gongzuo zong baogao" (General Report on the Work of the 7th Corps), 360.

28. Lary, *Region and Nation*, 102. See also Katherine Palmer Kaup, *Creating the Zhuang: Ethnic Politics in China* (Boulder, CO, and London: L. Reiner, 2000), 94–100; Lan Handong and Lan Qixun, *Wei Baqun* (Beijing: Zhongguo qingnian chubanshe, 1986), 93; Franz, *Deng Xiaoping*, 77–78.

29. See Mary S. Erbaugh, "The Secret History of the Hakkas: The Chinese Revolution as a Hakka Enterprise," in Susan D. Blum and Lionel M. Jensen, eds., *China off Center: Mapping the Migrants of the Middle Kingdom* (Honolulu: University of Hawai'i Press, 2002), 187, 189; Eugene W. Levich, *The Kwangsi Way in Kuomintang China, 1931–1939* (Armonk, NY: Sharpe, 1993), 179.

30. See Kaup, *Creating the Zhuang*, 96; Pavel Mif, ed., *Sovety v Kitae: Sbornik doku-mentov i materialov* (Soviets in China: A Collection of Documents and Materials) (Moscow: Partizdat TsK VKP[b], 1934), 196.

31. See Kaup, *Creating the Zhuang*, 95.

32. See Lary, *Region and Nation*, 103.

33. See [Deng], "Baogao" (Report), 178.

34. For more details on Wei's efforts in this direction, see Kaup, *Creating the Zhuang*, 96–99.

35. See ibid., 104.

36. "The local inhabitants speak various entirely different languages," Deng Xiaoping reported to the CC CCP in January 1930, after he was acquainted with the situa-tion. [Deng], "Baogao" (Report), 175.

37. See also Yang and Yan, *Deng Xiaoping nianpu: 1904–1974* (Chronological Biography of Deng Xiaoping: 1904–1974), vol. 1, 54, 55; Deng, *Deng Xiaoping*, 152–53.

38. See *Zuo you jiang geming genjudi* (Revolutionary Bases in the Zuojiang and Youjiang Areas), vol. 1, 97, 99; Deng, *Deng Xiaoping zishu* (Autobiographical Notes of Deng Xiaoping), 41; Deng Xiaoping, *Wode zishu (Zhailu)* (My Autobiographical Notes [Excerpts]), June 20–July 5, 1968, http://blog. smthome.net/article-htm-tid-993.html; Yang and Yan, *Deng Xiaoping nianpu: 1904–1974* (Chronological Biography of Deng Xiaoping: 1904–1974), vol. 1, 53–54.

39. See [Deng], "Baogao" (Report), 175.

40. Quoted from Deng, *Deng Xiaoping*, 153.

41. Chen, "Qi jun gongzuo zong baogao" (General Report on the Work of the 7th Corps), 360.

42. Ibid.

43. See [Deng], "Baogao" (Report), 178.

44. Ibid.

45. See also ibid., 175–76, 179, 363.

46. Chen, "Qi jun gongzuo zong baogao" (General Report on the Work of the 7th Corps), 360.

47. Deng Xiaoping, "Deng Xiaoping qicaode 'Qi jun gongzuo baogao'" ("Report on the Work on the 7th Corps, Written by Deng Xiaoping"), in Deng, *Deng Xiaoping zishu* (Autobiographical Notes of Deng Xiaoping), 50–51.

48. See Chen, "Qi jun gongzuo zong baogao" (General Report on the Work of the 7th Corps), 360.

49. See Deng, "Deng Xiaoping qicaode 'Qi jun gongzuo baogao'" ("Report on the Work on the 7th Corps Written by Deng Xiaoping"), 67–69.

50. See Wang Fukun, ed., *Hong qi jun hong ba jun zong zhihui Li Mingrui* (Li Mingrui, Commander-in-chief of the 7th and 8th Corps of the Red Army) (Nanning: Guangxi renmin chubanshe, 2008), 123–26.

51. See Yang and Yan, *Deng Xiaoping nianpu: 1904–1974* (Chronological Biography of Deng Xiaoping: 1904–1974), vol. 1, 56–57.

52. See Chen, "Qi jun qianwei baogao (1930 nian 1 yue)" ("Report of the Front Committee of the 7th Corps, January 1930), 159–60; Yang and Yan, *Deng Xiaoping nianpu: 1904–1974* (Chronological Biography of Deng Xiaoping: 1904–1974), vol. 1, 55–58; [Deng Xiaoping], "Buchong baogao" (Supplementary Report), in *Zuo you jiang geming genjudi* (Revolutionary Bases in the Zuojiang and Youjiang Areas), vol. 1, 180.

53. See [Deng], "Baogao" (Report), 178.

54. See Deng, "Deng Xiaoping qicaode 'Qi jun gongzuo baogao'" ("Report on the Work of the 7th Corps" Written by Deng Xiaoping), 65; Chen, "Qi jun gongzuo zong baogao" (General Report on the Work of the 7th Corps), 375.

55. See *Zuo you jiang geming genjudi* (Revolutionary Bases in the Zuojiang and Youjiang Areas), vol. 1, 105–6; Chen, "Qi jun qianwei baogao (1930 nian 1 yue)" (Report of the Front Committee of the 7th Corps, January 1930), 161.

56. Titarenko et al., *VKP(b), Komintern i Kitai: Dokumenty* (The AUCP[b], the Comintern, and China: Documents), vol. 3, 607.

57. Ibid., 621.

58. Rejecting these accusations, the Central Committee of the CCP sent a complaint to the Presidium of the ECCI in which it asserted that the criticism by the Far Eastern Bureau was "wholly unfounded slander." Ibid., 732.

59. *Pravda*, Dec. 29, 1929.

60. *Zuo you jiang geming genjudi* (Revolutionary Bases in the Zuojiang and Youjiang Areas), vol. 1, 180–98, 233. See also Yang Shengqun and Liu Jintian, eds., *Deng Xiaoping zhuan (1904–1974)* (Biography of Deng Xiaoping [1904–1974]), vol. 1 (Beijing: Zhongyang wenxian chubanshe, 2014), 137–40.

61. *Zuo you jiang geming genjudi* (Revolutionary Bases in the Zuojiang and Youjiang Areas), vol. 1, 179–80, 187–88.

62. See Deng, *Deng Xiaoping*, 158; Wang, *Hong qi jun hong ba jun zong zhihui—Li Mingrui* (Li Mingrui, Commander-in-chief of the 7th and 8th corps), 251.

63. See *Zuo you jiang geming genjudi* (Revolutionary Bases in the Zuojiang and Youjiang Areas), vol. 1, 198, 229, 233.

64. See [Deng], "Buchong baogao" (Supplementary report), 180; *Zuo you jiang geming genjudi* (Revolutionary Bases in the Zuojiang and Youjiang Areas), vol. 1, 105.

65. See *Zuo you jiang geming genjudi* (Revolutionary Bases in the Zuojiang and Youjiang Areas), vol. 1, 218–48.

66. See Deng, *Deng Xiaoping zishu* (Autobiographical Notes of Deng Xiaoping), 38; Yang and Yan, *Deng Xiaoping nianpu: 1904–1974* (Chronological Biography of Deng Xiaoping: 1904–1974), vol. 1, 60. Unfortunately, documentary evidence of this appointment is lacking.

67. Quoted from Yang and Yan, *Deng Xiaoping nianpu: 1904–1974* (Chronological Biography of Deng Xiaoping: 1904–1974), vol. 1, 61.

68. See ibid. 203–4; Deng, "Deng Xiaoping qicaode 'Qi jun gongzuo baogao'" ("Report on the Work of the 7th Corps Written by Deng Xiaoping"), 45–46.

69. See A. Ivin, *Sovetskii Kitai* (Soviet China) (Moscow: "Molodaia gvardiia," 1931), 151; Siao Lo (Xiao Luo), "Sovetskaia vlast' v Lunzhou (provintsiia Guansi)" (Soviet Power in Longzhou [Guangxi province]), in Pavel Mif, ed., *Sovety v Kitae: Sbornik dokumentov i materialov* (Soviets in China: A Collection of Documents and Materials), (Moscow: 4) 198; Deng, "Deng Xiaoping qicaode 'Qi jun gongzuo baogao'" ("Report on the Work of the 7th Corps Written by Deng Xiaoping"), 46–47.

70. For excerpts from the note, see *Zuo you jiang geming genjudi* (Revolutionary Bases in the Zuojiang and Youjiang Areas), vol. 1, 206.

71. See [Li] Lisan, "Chisede Longzhou" (Red Longzhou), in ibid., 251; Siao, "Sovetskaia vlast' v Lunzhou (provintsiia Guansi)" (Soviet Power in Longzhou [Guangxi Province]), 194.

72. Deng, *Deng Xiaoping,* 156.

73. See Ivin, *Sovetskii Kitai* (Soviet China), 151; Siao, "Sovetskaia vlast' v Lunzhou (provintsiia Guansi)" (Soviet Power in Longzhou [Guangxi Province]), 194–99; Snow, *Random Notes on Red China (1936–1945),* 138.

74. See Yang and Yan, *Deng Xiaoping nianpu: 1904–1974* (Chronological Biography of Deng Xiaoping: 1904–1974), vol. 1, 62–63.

75. Yang, *Deng,* 63.

76. Deng, "Deng Xiaoping qicaode 'Qi jun gongzuo baogao'" ("Report on the Work of the 7th Corps Written by Deng Xiaoping"), 48.

77. Deng, *Deng Xiaoping zishu* (Autobiographical Notes of Deng Xiaoping), 40.

78. See ibid., 43.

79. Quoted from Deng, *Deng Xiaoping,* 166.

80. See Lan and Lan, *Wei Baqun,* 139–40; Chen, "Wei Baqun," 201.

81. See Deng, *Deng Xiaoping,* 166.

82. *Zuo you jiang geming genjudi* (Revolutionary Bases in the Zuojiang and Youjiang Areas), vol. 1, 265–66; Yang and Yan, *Deng Xiaoping nianpu: 1904–1974* (Chronological Biography of Deng Xiaoping: 1904–1974), vol. 1, 64–65.

83. Siao, "Sovetskaia vlast' v Lunzhou (provintsiia Guansi)" (Soviet Power in Lonzhou [Guangxi Province]), 198.

84. See Deng, "Deng Xiaoping qicaode 'Qi jun gongzuo baogao'" ("Report on the Work of the 7th Corps Written by Deng Xiaoping"), 65–66. See also Huang, "Huang Rong tan Deng Xiaoping" (Huang Rong Speaks About Deng Xiaoping), 26; Chen, "Wei Baqun," 206–7.

85. See Ivin, *Sovetskii Kitai* (Soviet China), 149.

86. See Woodhead, *China Year Book 1931,* 595.

87. Quoted from Deng, *Deng Xiaoping,* 170. See also Deng, *Deng Xiaoping zishu* (Autobiographical Notes of Deng Xiaoping), 41.

88. See *Lichnoe delo Den Gana* (Personal File of Deng Gang), RGASPI, collection 495, inventory 225, file 2956. In 1928, UTK was renamed KUTK, i.e. Communist University of the Toilers of China.

89. Quoted from Wang Jianmin, *Zhongguo gongchandang shigao* (A Draft History of the Chinese Communist Party), vol. 2 (Taipei: Author Press, 1965), 77.

90. See Yang and Yan, *Deng Xiaoping nianpu: 1904–1974* (Chronological Biography of Deng Xiaoping: 1904–1974) vol. 1, 69–70.

91. See ibid., 70. An eyewitness of the events, Gong Chu, it is true, asserts that on the contrary Deng was a fervent supporter of attacking the large cities, and that he himself was a strong opponent. See Gong, *Wo yu hong jun* (The Red Army and I), 198. This claim, however, is not confirmed by other information.

92. See Deng, "Deng Xiaoping qicaode 'Qi jun gongzuo baogao'" (Report on the Work of the 7th Corps Written by Deng Xiaoping), 54.

93. See Chen Jinyuan, "Wei Baqun tougu chutu jishu" (True Story of the Exhumation of Wei Baqun's Skull), *Wenshi chunqiu* (*Literary and Historical Chronicle*), no. 5 (2004): 5–25; Lan and Lan, *Wei Baqun*, 215–18; Levich, *The Kwangsi Way in Kuomintang China, 1931–1939*, 58.

94. See Deng, "Deng Xiaoping qicaode 'Qi jun gongzuo baogao'" (Report on the Work of the 7th Corps Written by Deng Xiaoping), 57–58; Yang and Yan, *Deng Xiaoping nianpu: 1904–1974* (Chronological Biography of Deng Xiaoping: 1904–1974), vol. 1, 75.

95. Mif, *Strategiia i taktika Kominterna v natsional'no-kolonial'noi revoliutsii na primere Kitaia* (Strategy and Tactics of the Comintern in National and Colonial Revolutions: The Case of China), 283–90.

96. See *Zuo you jiang geming genjudi* (Revolutionary Bases in the Zuojiang and Youjiang Areas), vol. 1, 513–14.

97. For more details, see Deng, "Deng Xiaoping qicaode 'Qi jun gongzuo baogao'" (Report on the Work of the 7th Corps Written by Deng Xiaoping), 61–63; Mo Wenhua, *Huiyi hong qi jun* (Reminiscences of the Red 7th Corps), 3rd rev. ed. (Nanning: Guangxi renmin chubanshe, 1979), 85–106; Huang, "Huang Rong tan Deng Xiaoping" (Huang Rong Speaks About Deng Xiaoping), 26.

98. Deng, *Wode zishu (Zhailu)* (My Autobiographical Notes [Excerpts]).

99. Quoted from Yang, *Deng*, 65–66. See also Yang and Yan, *Deng Xiaoping nianpu, 1904–1974* (Chronological Biography of Deng Xiaoping: 1904–1974), vol. 1, 81; Deng, *Deng Xiaoping*, 185–86; Franz, *Deng Xiaoping*, 87–88.

100. See the first two editions of General Mo's memoirs of the 7th Corps. Mo Wenhua, *Huiyi hong qi jun* (Remembering the 7th Corps) (Nanning: Guangxi renmin chubanshe, 1961 and 1962). Only in the third revised edition, published in 1979, shortly after Deng came to power, was there mention of the "party's decision" in March 1931 to send Deng to Shanghai. See Mo Wenhua, *Huiyi hong qi jun* (Remembering the 7th Corps), 3rd rev. ed., 106.

101. Sladkovskii, *Informatsionnyi biulleten'. Seriia A. Vypusk 2* (Information Bulletin: Series A: 2nd Installment), 7.

102. Deng, *Wode zishu (Zhailu)* (My Autobiographical Notes [Excerpts]); Deng, "Deng Xiaoping gei Mao zhuxide xin (1972 nian 8 yue 3 ri)" (Deng Xiaoping's Letter to Chairman Mao, Aug. 3, 1972), http://www.sinovision.net/blog/index/php?act=details&id=12850&bcode=xinwu.

103. See Deng, "Deng Xiaoping qicaode 'Qi jun gongzuo baogao'" (Report on the Work of 7th Corps Written by Deng Xiaoping), 72.

CHAPTER 5

1. In Deng's words, "He left quietly after a battle without telling anyone, and no one knew where he had gone." Quoted from Deng, *Deng Xiaoping*, 181.

2. Chen, *Qi jun gongzuo zong baogao* (General Report on the Work of the 7th Corps), 378.

3. Yan Heng, *Yan Heng tongzhi guanyu di qide baogao (1931 nian 4 yue 4 ri)* (Comrade Yan Heng's Report on the 7th Corps, April 4, 1931), in *Zuo you jiang geming genjudi* (Revolutionary Bases in the Zuojiang and Youjiang Areas), vol. 1, 382–84.

4. Titarenko et al., *VKP(b), Komintern i Kitai: Dokumenty* (The AUCP[b], the Comintern, and China: Documents), vol. 3, 1357.

5. Deng, "Deng Xiaoping qicao de 'Qi jun gongzuo baogao'" (Report on the Work of the 7th Corps Written by Deng Xiaoping), 72.

6. Deng, *Deng Xiaoping,* 219.

7. Zhang Xiyuan's remains were reinterred, under her own name, in the Cemetery for Revolutionary Heroes in Shanghai in 1969.

8. Deng had met his younger brother in mid-May 1931 after reading his announcement in the newspaper *Shishi xinbao* (*New Newspaper of Facts*): "Attention elder brother Deng Xixian. Younger brother has arrived in Shanghai and hopes to see you." *New Newspaper of Facts*, May 2, 1931.

9. See *Lichnoe delo Ttszin Veiyin (Lizy)* (Personal File of Jin Weiying [Liza]), RGASPI, collection 495, inventory 225, file 428, sheets 28–31; Xu Zhujin, *Jin Weiying zhuan* (Biography of Jin Weiying) (Beijing: Zhonggong dangshi chubanshe, 2004), 6–86, 330–33.

10. Quoted from Xu, *Jin Weiying zhuan* (Biography of Jin Weiying), 95.

11. See Leng, *Deng Xiaoping zai Gannan* (Deng Xiaoping in South Jiangxi), 31–32, 35.

12. See ibid., 30.

13. For more details, see Stephen C. Averill, "The Origins of the Futian Incident," in Tony Saich and Hans J. van de Ven, eds., *New Perspectives on the Chinese Communist Revolution* (Armonk, NY: Sharpe, 1995), 79–115; Pantsov with Levine, *Mao*, 239–45.

14. Deng, "Deng Xiaoping qicao de 'Qi jun gongzuo baogao'" (Report on the Work of the 7th Corps Written by Deng Xiaoping), 71.

15. Deng, *Wode zishu (Zhailu)* (My Autobiographical Notes [Excerpts]). See also Yang and Yan, *Deng Xiaoping nianpu: 1904–1974* (Chronological Biography of Deng Xiaoping: 1904–1974), vol. 1, 84–85; Leng, *Deng Xiaoping zai Gannan* (Deng Xiaoping in South Jiangxi), 32–37; Feng Du, "Suqu 'jingguan' Deng Xiaoping" (Deng Xiaoping, Head of the "Capital" of the Soviet Area), http://cpc.people.com.cn/GB/64162/64172/64915/4670788.html.

16. See Yang and Yan, *Deng Xiaoping nianpu: 1904–1974* (Chronological Biography of Deng Xiaoping: 1904–1974), vol. 1, 86.

17. See Leng, *Deng Xiaoping zai Gannan* (Deng Xiaoping in South Jiangxi), 38–42.

18. Schram, *Mao's Road to Power*, vol. 3, 256, 257, 504.

19. See Hsiao Tso-liang, *Power Relations Within the Chinese Communist Movement, 1930–1934* (Seattle: University of Washington Press, 1967), vol. 2, 382–89.

20. See "Beseda [G. I.] Mordvinova st. Chzhou En'laem 4 marta 1940 g. (Conversation between [G. I.] Mordvinov and Zhou Enlai, Mar. 4, 1940), RGASPI, collection 495, inventory 225, file 71, vol. 1, sheet 32.

21. Pantsov with Levine, *Mao*, 255.

22. The Chinese Soviet Republic (CSR) was proclaimed by the First Congress of Soviets, held in Ruijin from Nov. 7 to 20, 1931.

23. Quoted from Leng, *Deng Xiaoping zai Gannan* (Deng Xiaoping in South Jiangxi), 41–42.

24. In December 1931, the Land Law of the Chinese Soviet Republic was unveiled in the CSR. According to it, kulaks were given the worst land and "landlords" generally nothing. See L. M. Gudoshnikov, ed., *Sovetskie raiony Kitaia. Zakonodatel'stvo Kitaiskoi Sovetskoi Respubliki, 1931–1934* (Soviet Areas of China: Codes of Laws of the Chinese Soviet Republic, 1931–1934), trans. Z. E. Maistrova (Moscow: Nauka, 1983), 80–81. In December 1932, an analogous law was adopted by the Soviet government in Jiangxi. See *Liu da yilai: Dangnei mimi wenxian* (After the Sixth Congress: Secret Intra-party Documents), vol. 1 (Beijing: Renmin chubanshe, 1989), 309–12. Deng, of course, could not ignore these.

25. Schram, *Mao's Road to Power*, vol. 3, 155–56.

26. Titarenko et al., *VKP(b), Komintern i Kitai: Dokumenty* (The AUCP[b], the Comintern, and China: Documents), vol. 4, 194, 225, 227.

27. See Leng, *Deng Xiaoping zai Gannan* (Deng Xiaoping in South Jiangxi), 85.

28. See Bo Gu, *Moia predvaritel'naia ispoved'* (My Preliminary Confession), RGASPI, collection 495, inventory 225, file 2847, sheet 48.

29. See Wang Jianying, ed., *Zhongguo gongchandang zuzhi shi ziliao huibian—lingdao jigou yange he chengyuan minglu* (Collection of Documents on the Organizational History of the Chinese Communist Party—The Evolution of Leading Organs and Name List of Personnel) (Beijing: Hongqi chubanshe, 1983), 188; Zhang Peisen, ed., *Zhang Wentian nianpu* (Chronological Biography of Zhang Wentian), vol. 1 (Beijing: Zhonggong dangshi chubanshe, 2000), 190.

30. See Leng, *Deng Xiaoping zai Gannan* (Deng Xiaoping in South Jiangxi), 76.

31. He expressed his disagreements at the time when the Red Army prepared to repel Chiang Kai-shek's fourth punitive expedition. The fourth punitive expedition began at the end of February 1933 and wound up a month later with a new defeat for Guomindang troops. See for more detail Luo Ming, *Luo Ming huiyilu* (Reminiscences of Luo Ming) (Fuzhou: Fujian renmin chubanshe, 1991).

32. See *Liu da yilai* (After the Sixth Congress), vol 1, 330–48; Li Xing and Zhu Hongzhao, eds., *Bo Gu, 39 suide huihuang yu beizhuang* (Bo Gu, Brilliant Rise and Tragic End at 39) (Shanghai: Xuelin chubanshe, 2005), 215–24; Leng, *Deng Xiaoping zai Gannan* (Deng Xiaoping in South Jiangxi), 77.

33. See Yang and Yan, *Deng Xiaoping nianpu: 1904–1974* (Chronological Biography of Deng Xiaoping: 1904–1974), vol. 1, 94; Leng, *Deng Xiaoping zai Gannan* (Deng Xiaoping in South Jiangxi), 80.

34. *Liu da yilai* (After the Sixth Congress), vol. 1, 349–50.

35. For the basic content of this report, see *Liu da yilai* (After the Sixth Congress), vol. 1, 362–68. For Li Weihan's unseemly role in fabricating the "Deng, Mao, Xie, and Gu" Affair, see the letter from Mao Zemin, brother of Mao Zedong and Mao Zetan, to the ECCI of Aug. 26, 1939 (Titarenko et al., *VKP[b], Komintern i Kitai: Dokumenty* [The AUCP[b], the Comintern, and China: Documents], vol. 4, 1136–38); and Bo, "Moia predvaritel'naia ispoved' " (My Preliminary Confession), 68–69.

36. Quoted from Yang and Yan, *Deng Xiaoping nianpu: 1904–1974* (Chronological Biography of Deng Xiaoping: 1904–1974), vol. 1, 96.

37. See Mao Zedong, *Report from Xunwu*, trans. and with an introduction and notes Roger R. Thomson (Stanford, CA: Stanford University Press, 1990), 28.

38. See Deng, *Wo de zishu. (Zhailu)* (My Autobiographical Notes. [Excerpts]).

39. Quoted from Wu Lengxi, *Yi Mao zhuxi: Wo qinshen jingli de ruogan zhongda lishi shijian pianduan* (Remembering Chairman Mao: Several Important Events from My Own Life) (Beijing: Xinhua chubanshe, 1995), 157–58.

40. During the Cultural Revolution, Red Guards claimed that Ajin lost her mind as the result of an obsession, namely, that Li Weihan had supposedly decided to "get rid of her" by sending her to Moscow.

41. Deng Yingchao, "Guanyu Jin Weiying qingkuang (Li Tieying tongzhi de muqin)" (Regarding Jin Weiying [Comrade Li Tieying's Mother]), in Xu, *Jin Weiying zhuan* (Biography of Jin Weiying), 319–20.

42. See *Lichnoe delo Tszin Veiyin (Lizy)* (Personal File of Jin Weiying [Liza]), 30–32. Sladkovskii, *Informatsionnyi biulleten'. Seriia A. Vypusk 2* (Information Bulletin: Series A: 2nd Installment), 10.

43. Mao Zedong, *Jianguo yilai Mao Zedong wengao* (Manuscripts of Mao Zedong from the Founding of the PRC), vol. 13 (Beijing: Zhongyang wenxian chubanshe, 1998), 308.

44. Deng, *Deng Xiaoping zishu* (Autobiographical Notes of Deng Xiaoping), 76.

45. Titarenko et al., *VKP(b), Komintern i Kitai: Dokumenty* (The AUCP[b], the Comintern, and China: Documents), vol. 4, 1146.

46. See Yang and Yan, *Deng Xiaoping nianpu: 1904–1974* (Chronological Biography of Deng Xiaoping: 1904–1974), vol. 1, 99–111; Deng, *Deng Xiaoping,* 222.

47. See Titarenko et al., *VKP(b), Komintern i Kitai: Dokumenty* (The AUCP[b], the Comintern, and China: Documents), vol. 4, 602, 613.

48. For details, see Pantsov with Levine, *Mao*, 276–77.

49. On the Long March, see in detail Otto Braun, *A Comintern Agent in China, 1932–1939*, trans. Jeanne Moore (Stanford, CA: Stanford University Press, 1982); Harrison E. Salisbury, *The Long March: The Untold Story* (New York: Harper & Row, 1985); Charlotte Y. Salisbury, *Long March Diary: China Epic* (New York: Walker, 1986); Ed Jocelyn and Andrew McEwen, *The Long March and the True Story Behind the Legendary Journey that Made Mao's China* (London: Constable, 2006); and Sun Shuyun, *The Long March: The True History of Communist China's Founding Myth* (New York: Doubleday, 2006).

50. Quoted from Deng, *Deng Xiaoping*, 241.

51. Alexander V. Pantsov's personal impressions on visiting Zunyi, June 21, 2010.

52. Braun, *A Comintern Agent in China, 1932–1939*, 99–102; *Zunyi huiyi wenxian* (Documents of the Zunyi Conference) (Beijing: Renmin chubanshe, 1985), 116–17; Jin Chongji, ed., *Mao Zedong zhuan (1893–1949)* (Biography of Mao Zedong [1893–1949]) (Beijing: Zhongyang wenxian chubanshe, 2004), 353–54; Yang Shangkun, *Yang Shangkun huiyilu* (Memoirs of Yang Shangkun) (Beijing: Zhongyang wenxian chubanshe, 2002), 117–21.

53. See *Zunyi huiyi wenxian* (Documents of the Zunyi Conference), 117. Many years later, in October 1966, Mao, recalling the Zunyi conference, particularly noted the "positive" role that Zhou Enlai and Zhu De played: "Things would have gone badly at that time without them." O. Borisov (O. B. Rakhmanin) and Titarenko, eds., *Vystupleniia Mao Tsze-duna, ranee ne publikovavshiesia v kitaiskoi pechati* (Mao Zedong's Speeches Previously Unpublished in the Chinese Press), series 5 (Moscow: Progress, 1976), 120.

54. See Zhang Wentian, *Zhang Wentian xuanji* (Selected Works of Zhang Wentian) (Beijing: Renmin chubanshe, 1985), 37–59.

55. See *Zunyi huiyi wenxian* (Documents of the Zunyi Conference), 42–43, 132–36.

56. See ibid., 134.

57. See *Lichnoe delo Chzhu Zhuia* (Personal File of Zhu Rui), RGASPI, collection 495, inventory 225, file 1285.

58. Quoted from Deng, *Deng Xiaoping*, 246–47.

59. Quoted from ibid., 244.

60. For more details, see Pantsov with Levine, *Mao*, 285–88.

61. See Jocelyn and McEwen, *The Long March*, 326–27.

62. Deng, *Deng Xiaoping*, 252.

63. Ibid., 264.

64. See Franz, *Deng Xiaoping*, 15–17; Yang and Yan, *Deng Xiaoping nianpu: 1904–1974* (Chronological Biography of Deng Xiaoping: 1904–1974), vol. 1, 140. On Dai Wang see Richard Wilhelm, ed., *The Chinese Fairy Book* (New York: Frederick A. Stokes, 1921), 131–37.

CHAPTER 6

1. The Guomindang government followed the example of the first ruler of the Ming dynasty, which established its capital at Nanjing (Southern capital) and renamed the former capital Beiping (Northern peace).

2. See Mif, *Sovety v Kitae* (Soviets in China), 454–56; Schram, *Mao's Road to Power*, vol. 4, 209–14.

3. See Liu Chongwen and Chen Shaochou, eds., *Liu Shaoqi nianpu: 1898–1969* (Chronological Biography of Liu Shaoqi: 1898–1969), vol. 1 (Beijing: Zhongyang wenxian chubanshe, 1998), 145.

4. See *Zhou Enlai nianpu (1898–1949)* (Chronological Biography of Zhou Enlai [1898–1949]), 366–67: Chang, *The Rise of the Chinese Communist Party*, vol. 2, 517–20.

5. See Chang, *The Rise of the Chinese Communist Party*, vol. 2, 517–20.

6. Chang Kuo-t'ao, "Introduction," in Liu Shaoqi, *Collected Works of Liu Shao-ch'i Before 1944* (Hong Kong: Union Research Institute, 1969), i.

7. See the reminiscences about him by Sidney Rittenberg; Sidney Rittenberg and Amanda Bennett, *The Man Who Stayed Behind* (New York: Simon & Schuster, 1993), 313.

8. See Liu and Chen, *Liu Shaoqi nianpu: 1898–1969* (Chronological Biography of Liu Shaoqi: 1898–1969), vol. 1, 178–84; Pang, *Mao Zedong nianpu: 1893–1949* (Chronological Biography of Mao Zedong: 1893–1949), vol. 1, 672–80.

9. See Yang and Yan, *Deng Xiaoping nianpu: 1904–1974* (Chronological Biography of Deng Xiaoping: 1904–1974), vol. 1, 144–45; Li Jingtian, ed., *Yang Shangkun nianpu: 1907–1998* (Chronological Biography of Yang Shangkun: 1907–1998), vol. 1 (Beijing: Zhonggong dangshi chubanshe, 2008), 265.

10. Quoted from Deng, *Deng Xiaoping*, 269.

11. It was renamed the 18th Army Group on Sept. 11, 1937.

12. See Yang and Yan, *Deng Xiaoping nianpu: 1904–1974* (Chronological Biography of Deng Xiaoping: 1904–1974), vol. 1, 150–51; P. P. Vladimirov, *Osobyi raion Kitaia, 1942–1945* (Special Region of China, 1942–1945) (Moscow: APN, 1975), 239–40.

13. See Yang and Yan, *Deng Xiaoping nianpu: 1904–1974* (Chronological Biography of Deng Xiaoping: 1904–1974), vol. 1, 150, 153.

14. See Liu Bocheng, "Women zai Taihangshan" (We are in the Taihang Mountains), in Liu Bocheng, *Liu Bocheng huiyilu* (Reminiscences of Liu Bocheng), vol. 1 (Shanghai: Shanghai wenyi chubanshe, 1981), 16; Nie, *Inside the Red Star*, 295.

15. See Wang Shi, ed., *Zhongguo gongchandang lishi jianbian* (Short History of the Chinese Communist Party) (Shanghai: Shanghai renmin chubanshe, 1959), 178–79; Zhang, *Zhang Wentian nianpu* (Chronological Biography of Zhang Wentian), vol. 1, 488–90; Schram, *Mao's Road to Power*, vol. 6, 11, 12, 14.

16. Mao Zedong, *Mao Zedong wenji* (Works of Mao Zedong), vol. 2 (Beijing: Renmin chubanshe, 1993), 8–10.

17. Schram, *Mao's Road to Power*, vol. 6, 11, 12, 14; See also Vladimirov, *Osobyi Raion Kitaia, 1942–1945* (Special Region of China, 1942–1945), 519, 600.

18. See Schram, *Mao's Road to Power*, vol. 6, 11, 12; Braun, *A Comintern Agent in China, 1932–1939*, 212.

19. Quoted from Pang Xianzhi, ed., *Mao Zedong nianpu: 1893–1949* (Chronological Biography of Mao Zedong: 1893–1949), vol. 2 (Beijing: Renmin chubanshe and Zhongyang renmin chubanshe, 2002), 18–19.

20. See Nie, *Inside the Red* Star, 310–24; A. V. Pantsov, "Obrazovanie opornykh baz 8-i Natsional'no-revoliutsionnoi armii v tylu iaponskikh voisk v Severnom Kitae" (Establishment of Base Areas of the 8th National Revolutionary Army in the Rear of Japanese Troops in North China), in M. F. Yuriev, ed., *Voprosy istorii Kitaia* (Problems of Chinese history) (Moscow: Izdatel'stvo MGU, 1981), 39, 41, 42.

21. Mao Zedong, *Selected Works of Mao Tse-tung*, vol. 2 (Peking: Foreign Languages Press, 1967), 62; Schram, *Mao's Road to Power*, vol. 6, 144, 146, 149.

22. See Yang and Yan, *Deng Xiaoping nianpu: 1904–1974* (Chronological Biography of Deng Xiaoping: 1904–1974), vol. 1, 167.

23. Quoted from Jack Belden, *China Shakes the World* (New York: Harper, 1949), 48.

24. Quoted from Deng, *Deng Xiaoping*, 280.

25. Deng Xiaoping, "Diao Liu Bocheng" (To the Memory of Liu Bocheng), in Liu Bocheng, *Liu Bocheng huiyilu* (Reminiscences of Liu Bocheng), vol. 3 (Shanghai: Shanghai wenyi chubanshe, 1987), 5.

26. See ibid., 8–9.

27. Ibid., 5; see also *Lichnoe delo Liu Bochena* (Personal File of Liu Bocheng), RGASPI, collection 495, inventory 225, file 171.

28. See Yang and Yan, *Deng Xiaoping nianpu: 1904–1974* (Chronological Biography of Deng Xiaoping: 1904–1974), vol. 1, 168–230.

29. Evans Fordyce Carlson, *Twin Stars of China: A Behind-the-Scenes Story of China's Valiant Struggle for Existence by a U.S. Marine Who Lived and Moved with the People* (New York: Dodd, Mead & Company, 1940), 252.

30. Deng Xiaoping, *Selected Works of Deng Xiaoping (1938–1965)* (Beijing: Foreign Languages Press, 1992), 11.

31. Ibid., 40–41, 42.

32. See Zhang, *Zhang Wentian xuanji* (Selected Works of Zhang Wentian), 66–70; Zhang, *Zhang Wentian nianpu* (Chronological Biography of Zhang Wentian), vol. 1, 278–79, 286–87; Mao, *Mao Zedong wenji* (Works of Mao Zedong), vol. 1 (Beijing: Renmin chubanshe, 1993), 374–75.

33. See Sidney L. Greenblatt, ed., *The People of Taihang: An Anthology of Family Histories* (White Plains, NY: International Arts and Sciences Press, 1976), xiv.

34. See Pantsov, *Obrazovanie opornykh baz 8-i Natsional'no-revoliutsionnoi armii v tylu iaponskikh voisk v Severnom Kitae* (Establishment of Base Areas of the 8th National Revolutionary Army in the Japanese Rear in North China), 43.

35. See Yang and Yan, *Deng Xiaoping nianpu: 1904–1974* (Chronological Biography of Deng Xiaoping: 1904–1974), vol. 1, 206–27; Schram, *Mao's Road to Power*, vol. 6, 267–68.

36. See Wang, *Zhongguo gongchandang zuzhi shi ziliao huibian -lingdao jigou yange he chengyuan minglu* (Collection of Documents on the Organizational History of the Chinese Communist Party—The Evolution of Leading Organs and Name List of Personnel), 330; Zhang Heng and Jiang Fei, eds., *Zhonggong zhongyang zuzhi renshi jianming tupu* (Brief Chronological Tables of the Organizational Composition of the CC CCP) (Beijing: Zhongguo guangbo dianshi chubanshe, 2003), 17.

37. Schram, *Mao's Road to Power*, vol. 6, 539.

38. Quoted from Yang and Yan, *Deng Xiaoping nianpu: 1904–1974* (Chronological Biography of Deng Xiaoping: 1904–1974), vol. 1, 230.

39. See ibid., 233.

40. Quoted from ibid., 231.

41. See Deng, *Selected Works of Deng Xiaoping (1938–1965)*, 318–19.

42. The New 4th Army was formed in the National Revolutionary Army in October 1937 from communist detachments in Southeast China.

43. Quoted from Pang, *Mao Zedong nianpu: 1893–1949* (Chronological Biography of Mao Zedong: 1893–1949), vol. 2, 134.

44. For details on Stalin's role in initiating this matter, see Pantsov with Levine, *Mao*, 316, 319, 332.

45. See Schram, *Mao's Road to Power*, vol. 7, 279–306, 330–69, 526.

46. See Yang and Yan, *Deng Xiaoping nianpu: 1904–1974* (Chronological Biography of Deng Xiaoping: 1904–1974), vol. 1, 449.

47. See Deng, *Selected Works of Deng Xiaoping (1938–1965)*, 320. See also Deng Xiaoping's telegraphic report to Mao Zedong from Aug. 24, 1944, published in Song Yuxi and Mo Jiaolin, *Deng Xiaoping yu kangri zhanzheng* (Deng Xiaoping and the Anti-Japanese War) (Beijing: Zhongyang wenxian chubanshe, 2005), 318–20.

48. Ibid., 83, 84, 88.

49. See Deng, *Deng Xiaoping*, 345.

50. Quoted from ibid., 293.

51. See Carlson, *Twin Stars of China*, 162.

52. Zhuo Lin, "Zhuo Lin tan Deng Xiaoping" (Zhuo Lin Speaks About Deng Xiaoping), in Liu Jintian, ed., *Huashuo Deng Xiaoping* (Stories About Deng Xiaoping) (Beijing: Zhongyang wenxian chubanshe, 2004), 387–88; *Yongyuande Xiaoping: Zhuo Lin dengren fangtanlu* (The Unforgettable Xiaoping: Interviews with Zhuo Lin and others) (Chengdu: Sichuan chubanshe, 2004), 22–23; Wu Shihong, *Deng Xiaoping yu Zhuo Lin* (Deng Xiaoping and Zhuo Lin) (Beijing: Tuanjie chubanshe, 2006), 32; Deng, *Deng Xiaoping zishu* (Autobiographical Notes of Deng Xiaoping), 101–2.

53. Deng, *Deng Xiaoping*, 312.
54. *Yongyuande Xiaoping* (The Unforgettable Xiaoping), 25; Deng, *Deng Xiaoping zishu* (Autobiographical Notes of Deng Xiaoping), 103; Wu, *Deng Xiaoping yu Zhuo Lin* (Deng Xiaoping and Zhuo Lin), 37.
55. Quoted from Wu, *Deng Xiaoping yu Zhuo Lin* (Deng Xiaoping and Zhuo Lin), 65.
56. See Deng, *Deng Xiaoping*, 328.
57. See in detail Wu, *Deng Xiaoping yu Zhuo Lin* (Deng Xiaoping and Zhuo Lin), 48–51.
58. See ibid., 362.
59. See Zhang and Jian, *Zhonggong zhongyang zuzhi renshi jianming tupu* (Brief Chronological Tables of the Organizational Composition of the CC CCP), 20.
60. See Pantsov with Levine, *Mao*, 333–34.
61. See Wu, *Deng Xiaoping yu Zhuo Lin* (Deng Xiaoping and Zhuo Lin), 51.
62. On Deng's view of Mao, see Deng, *Selected Works of Deng Xiaoping (1938–1965)*, 90–96.
63. Liu Shao-chi, *On the Party* (Peking: Foreign Languages Press, 1950), 157.
64. That Mao drew up the list of Central Committee members for the Seventh Congress is noted in Vladimirov, *Osobyi Raion Kitaia, 1942–1945* (Special Region of China, 1942–1945), 607–8.

CHAPTER 7

1. See Deng, *Deng Xiaoping zishu* (Autobiographical Notes of Deng Xiaoping), 114; Yang and Yan, *Deng Xiaoping nianpu: 1904–1974* (Chronological Biography of Deng Xiaoping: 1904–1974), vol. 1, 562–63; Deng, *Deng Xiaoping*, 358.
2. See Dieter Heinzig, *The Soviet Union and Communist China, 1945–1950: The Arduous Road to the Alliance* (Armonk, NY: Sharpe, 2004), 51–125.
3. See Pantsov with Levine, *Mao*, 345–47; Chiang Chung-cheng (Chiang Kai-shek), *Soviet Russia in China: Summing-Up at Seventy*, trans. under the direction of Madame Chiang Kai-shek, rev., enlarged ed., with maps (New York: Farrar, Straus and Cudahy, 1958), 143–44; Vladislav Zubok, "The Mao-Khrushchev Conversations, July 31–August 3, 1958, and October 2, 1959," *Cold War International History Project* (hereafter *CWIHP*) *Bulletin*, nos. 12–13 (Fall–Winter 2001): 255.
4. Private archives of Igor Vasilievich Yurchenko (Yuzhin), Stalin's emissary at Mao's headquarters in Yan'an, 1941–43.
5. Quoted from *Zhu De nianpu* (Chronological Biography of Zhu De) (Beijing: Renmin chubanshe, 1986), 274.
6. Chiang, *Soviet Russia in China*, 137.
7. See Suzanne Pepper, *Civil War in China: The Political Struggle, 1945–1949*, 2nd ed. (Lanham, MD: Rowman & Littlefield, 1999), xi.
8. Quoted from *Zhu De nianpu* (Chronological Biography of Zhu De), 276.
9. See Pepper, *Civil War in China*, xi.

10. Quoted from Deng, *Deng Xiaoping zishu* (Autobiographical Notes of Deng Xiaoping), 111.

11. For more details, see Christopher R. Lew, *The Third Chinese Revolutionary Civil War, 1945–1949: An Analysis of Communist Strategy and Leadership* (London and New York: Routledge, 2009), 23–24.

12. Deng, *Deng Xiaoping zishu* (Autobiographical Notes of Deng Xiaoping), 113.

13. Mao Zedong, "Mao Tszedun o kitaiskoi politike Kominterna i Stalina" (Mao Zedong on the China Policy of the Comintern and Stalin), *Problemy Dal'nego Vostoka* (Far Eastern Affairs), no. 5 (1994), 107.

14. Quoted from Jonathan Fenby, *Chiang Kai-shek: China's Generalissimo and the Nation He Lost* (New York: Carroll & Graf, 2004), 454.

15. Mao, *Selected Works of Mao Tse-tung*, vol. 4, 54.

16. See Dean Acheson, "Letter of Transmittal," in *United States Relations with China: With Special Relations to the Period 1944–1949* (New York: Greenwood Press, 1968), ix–x; Dieter Heinzig, *The Soviet Union and Communist China, 1945–1950*, 79–82, 86–97; *Peng Zhen nianpu, 1902–1997* (Chronological Biography of Peng Zhen, 1902–1997), vol. 1 (Beijing: Zhongyang wenxian chubanshe, 2002), 281–307.

17. See Yang and Yan, *Deng Xiaoping nianpu: 1904–1974* (Chronological Biography of Deng Xiaoping: 1904–1974), vol. 1, 577.

18. Quoted from Deng, *Deng Xiaoping*, 365.

19. *Pis'mo I. V. Stalina V. M. Molotovu, L. P. Berii, G. M. Malenkovu i A. I. Mikoianu* (Letter of J. V. Stalin to V. M. Molotov, L. P. Beria, G. M. Malenkov, and A. I. Mikoyan), RGASPI, collection 558, inventory 11, file 98, sheet 81.

20. See Chiang, *Soviet Russia in China*, 179–81.

21. See O. Arne Westad, *Cold War and Revolution: Soviet-American Rivalry and the Origins of the Chinese Civil War, 1944–1946* (New York: Columbia University Press, 1993), 152.

22. See Heinzig, *The Soviet Union and Communist China, 1945–1950*, 98–101; Westad, *Cold War and Revolution*, 161.

23. See Steven I. Levine, *Anvil of Victory: The Communist Revolution in Manchuria, 1945–1948* (New York: Columbia University Press, 1987), 78–79.

24. Quoted from O. Arne Westad, *Decisive Encounters: The Chinese Civil War, 1946–1950* (Stanford, CA: Stanford University Press, 2003), 35.

25. Quoted from Pang Xianzhi, ed., *Mao Zedong nianpu: 1893–1949* (Chronological Biography of Mao Zedong: 1893–1949), vol. 3 (Beijing: Renmin chubanshe/ Zhongyang wenxian chubanshe, 2002), 92–93.

26. Acheson, "Letter of Transmittal," xv.

27. Quoted from Deng, *Deng Xiaoping*, 384.

28. Acheson, "Letter of Transmittal," vi.

29. Quoted from Douglas J. Macdonald, *Adventures in Chaos: American Intervention for Reform in the Third World* (Cambridge, MA: Harvard University Press, 1992), 107–8.

30. Ibid., 110. That many soldiers of the CCP armies were armed with modern American weapons (Thompson automatics) seized from Guomindang troops is attested to by an eyewitness. See Noel Barber, *The Fall of Shanghai* (New York: Coward, McCann & Geoghegan, 1979), 146.

31. See Acheson, "Letter of Transmittal," xv.

32. Deng, *Deng Xiaoping*, 452.

33. See Deng Rong, *Deng Xiaoping and the Cultural Revolution: A Daughter Recalls the Critical Years*, trans. Sidney Shapiro (Beijing: Foreign Languages Press, 2002), 146, 203, 204; Salisbury, *The Long March*, 137.

34. See *Taihang geming genjudi shigao, 1937–1949* (Draft History of the Taihang Revolutionary Base Area, 1937–1949) (Taiyuan: Shanxi renmin chubanshe, 1987), 298–304; William Hinton, *Fanshen: A Documentary of Revolution in a Chinese Village* (New York: Monthly Review Press, 2008), 131–38.

35. Quoted from Wu, *Deng Xiaoping yu Zhuo Lin* (Deng Xiaoping and Zhuo Lin), 39.

36. Quoted from ibid., 52–53.

37. Quoted from Deng, *Deng Xiaoping*, 400.

38. See Yang and Yan, *Deng Xiaoping nianpu: 1904–1974* (Chronological Biography of Deng Xiaoping: 1904–1974), vol. 1, 614–15.

39. See Mao Zedong, *Mao Zedong wenji* (Works of Mao Zedong), vol. 4 (Beijing: Renmin chubanshe, 2001), 241.

40. See Yang and Yan, *Deng Xiaoping nianpu: 1904–1974* (Chronological Biography of Deng Xiaoping: 1904–1974), vol. 2 (Beijing: Zhongyang wenxian chubanshe, 2010), 666–67.

41. Westad, *Decisive Encounters*, 168.

42. Quoted from Deng, *Deng Xiaoping*, 395. See also Yang and Yan, *Deng Xiaoping nianpu: 1904–1974* (Chronological Biography of Deng Xiaoping: 1904–1974), vol. 2, 670–71.

43. See Deng, *Deng Xiaoping zishu* (Autobiographical Notes of Deng Xiaoping), 118.

44. See Mao, *Mao Zedong wenji* (Works of Mao Zedong), vol. 4, 274–75.

45. *The Holy Bible* (King James version) (Iowa Falls, IA: World Bible, 1990), 47. [Exodus 14:21, 26, 27].

46. Deng, *Deng Xiaoping zishu* (Autobiographical Notes of Deng Xiaoping), 119.

47. Deng, *Selected Works of Deng Xiaoping (1938–1965)*, 97.

48. Deng, *Deng Xiaoping zishu* (Autobiographical Notes of Deng Xiaoping), 119.

49. *Vazhneishie dokumenty ob osvoboditel'noi voine kitaiskogo naroda v poslednee vremia* (The Most Important Documents of the Chinese People's Liberation War in the Most Recent Period) (Harbin: Izd-vo Severo-Vostoka Kitaia, 1948), 3–4.

50. A. V. Meliksetov, *Pobeda kitaiskoi revoliutsii: 1945–1949* (The Victory of the Chinese Revolution: 1945–1949) (Moscow: Nauka, 1989), 112.

51. For more details, see ibid., 110–20.

52. See Jin Chongji, ed., *Liu Shaoqi zhuan: 1898–1969* (Biography of Liu Shaoqi: 1898–1969), vol. 1 (Beijing: Zhongyang wenxian chubanshe, 2008), 538–45.

53. Mao Zedong, *Mao Zedong wenji* (Works of Mao Zedong), vol. 5 (Beijing: Renmin chubanshe, 2001), 17.

54. Quoted from Yang and Yan, *Deng Xiaoping nianpu, 1904–1974* (Chronological Biography of Deng Xiaoping: 1904–1974), vol. 2, 712.

55. Mao, *Mao Zedong wenji* (Works of Mao Zedong), vol. 5, 18.

56. Quoted from Yang and Yan, *Deng Xiaoping nianpu: 1904–1974* (Chronological Biography of Deng Xiaoping: 1904–1974), vol. 2, 716.

57. Quoted from Pang, *Mao Zedong nianpu, 1893–1949* (Chronological Biography of Mao Zedong: 1893–1949), vol. 3, 282.

58. Deng, *Selected Works of Deng Xiaoping (1938–1965)*, 107.

59. Ibid., 110–16.

60. Ibid., 110; Pang, *Mao Zedong nianpu, 1893–1949* (Chronological Biography of Mao Zedong, 1893–1949), vol. 3, 319.

61. Acheson, "Letter of Transmittal," vii, xi.

62. See Li Zhisui, *The Private Life of Chairman Mao: The Memoirs of Mao's Personal Physician*, trans. Tai Hung-chao (New York: Random House, 1994), 37.

63. See A. V. Meliksetov, ed., *Istoriia Kitaia* (History of China) (Moscow: Izdatel'stvo MGU, 1998), 582–88; Jonathan D. Spence, *The Search for Modern China*, 2nd ed. (New York: Norton, 1999), 473–80.

64. Acheson, "Letter of Transmittal," xiv.

65. See Wu Qinjie, ed., *Mao Zedong guanghui licheng dituji* (Atlas of Mao Zedong's Glorious Historical Path) (Beijing: Zhongguo ditu chubanshe, 2003), 81.

66. See Pang, *Mao Zedong nianpu: 1893–1949* (Chronological Biography of Mao Zedong: 1893–1949), vol. 3, 343–44.

67. Quoted from Yang and Yan, *Deng Xiaoping nianpu: 1904–1974* (Chronological Biography of Deng Xiaoping: 1904–1974), vol. 2, 780.

68. Quoted from Deng, *Deng Xiaoping*, 456.

69. See ibid., 422–23.

70. See Borisov and Titarenko, *Vystupleniia Mao Tsze-duna, ranee ne publikovavshie-sia v kitaiskoi pechati* (Mao Zedong's Speeches Previously Unpublished in the Chinese Press), series 2, 181.

71. Mao, *Mao Zedong wenji* (Works of Mao Zedong), vol. 5, 140–41, 145.

72. Liu Shaoqi, "Guanyu xinminzhuyi de jianshe wenti" (On the Question of New Democratic Construction), in *Gongheguo zouguode lu—jianguo yilai zhongyao wenxian zhuanti xuanji (1949–1952 nian)* (The Path the Republic Has Taken—Thematic Collection of Selected Important Documents from the Time of the Founding of the PRC [1949–1952]) (Beijing: Zhongyang wenxian chubanshe, 1991), 24. See also Yang Kuisong, "Mao Zedong weishemma fangqi xinminzhu-zhuyi?—Guanyu Eguo moshide yingxiang wenti" (Why Did Mao Zedong Abandon New Democracy? On the Influence of the Russian Model), *Jindaishi yanjiu* (Studies in Modern History), no. 4 (1997): 177.

73. Deng, *Selected Works of Deng Xiaoping (1938–1965)*, 104–5, 116.

74. See Pang, *Mao Zedong nianpu: 1893–1949* (Chronological Biography of Mao Zedong: 1893–1949), vol. 3, 437.

75. Deng, *Deng Xiaoping*, 445–46.

76. Deng, *Selected Works of Deng Xiaoping (1938–1965)*, 139.

77. Deng, *Deng Xiaoping*, 449.

78. See Wu, *Deng Xiaoping yu Zhuo Lin* (Deng Xiaoping and Zhuo Lin), 60–61.

79. Deng, *Selected Works of Deng Xiaoping (1938–1965)*, 137.

80. Ibid., 141.

81. See Deng, *Deng Xiaoping*, 454.

82. See *Obrazovanie Kitaiskoi Narodnoi Respubliki: Dokumenty i materialy* (Establishment of the People's Republic of China: Documents and Materials) (Moscow: Gospolitizdat, 1950), 64–66.

83. Quoted from Pang Xianzhi and Jin Chongji, ed., *Mao Zedong zhuan (1949–1976)* (Biography of Mao Zedong [1949–1976]), vol. 1 (Beijing: Zhongyang wenxian chubanshe, 2003), 3.

CHAPTER 8

1. C. Martin Wilbur, ed., *The Communist Movement in China: An Essay Written in 1924 by Ch'en Kung-po* (New York: East Asian Institute of Columbia University, 1960), 126.

2. See Yang and Yan, *Deng Xiaoping nianpu: 1904–1974* (Chronological Biography of Deng Xiaoping: 1904–1974), vol. 2, 831.

3. See ibid., 831, 832, 845–46. The full complement of the Southwest Bureau would be formed later, at the end of November.

4. *Yongyuande Xiaoping* (The Unforgettable Xiaoping), 28.

5. Ibid.

6. Quoted from Thomas Laird, *The Story of Tibet: Conversations with the Dalai Lama* (New York: Grove Press, 2006), 295, 298.

7. Mao, *Jianguo yilai Mao Zedong wengao* (Manuscripts of Mao Zedong from the Founding of the PRC), vol. 1, 226, 209.

8. Quoted from Yang and Yan, *Deng Xiaoping nianpu: 1904–1974* (Chronological Biography of Deng Xiaoping: 1904–1974), vol. 2, 860.

9. For more details, see Melvyn C. Goldstein, *A History of Modern Tibet, 1913–1951: The Demise of the Lamaist State* (Berkeley: University of California Press, 1989), 638–87; Tang Peiji ed., *Zhongguo lishi dashi nianbiao: Xiandaishi juan* (Chronology of Events in Chinese History: Contemporary History Volume) (Shanghai: Shanghai cishu chubanshe, 1997), 668–69.

10. An eyewitness, the English radio engineer Robert Ford, who was then the only European working in the Tibetan government, gives a rather amusing description of the auditors' reactions to these words. "There was a buzz of conversation among the Tibetans. They were completely bewildered, for I was the only foreign devil

most of them had ever seen. They could not imagine where all the other foreigners were that needed such a large army to turn them out." Robert Ford, *Captured in Tibet* (Hong Kong: Oxford University Press, 1990), 138–39.

11. Quoted from Laird, *The Story of Tibet*, 305. Ford had similar recollections: "The Communists were clever. . . . They soon had the monks thanking the gods for their deliverance. . . . No Chinese troops in Tibet had ever behaved so well before." Ford, *Captured in Tibet*, 139.

12. *The Question of Tibet and the Rule of Law* (Geneva: International Commission of Jurists, 1959), 140.

13. Quoted from Laird, *The Story of Tibet*, 312.

14. See Melvyn C. Goldstein, *The Snow Lion and the Dragon: China, Tibet, and the Dalai Lama* (Berkeley: University of California Press, 1997), 51–52; Goldstein, *A History of Modern Tibet*, 698–813.

15. See Deng Xiaoping, *Deng Xiaoping xinan gongzuo wenji* (Works of Deng Xiaoping on His Work in the Southwest) (Beijing/Chongqing: Zhongyang wenxian chubanshe/Chongqing chubanshe, 2006), 340.

16. At the time, the new authorities of the PRC had only a vague idea of the size of their own population. They supposed it was about 475 million, when in fact it was 541.6 million. See M. L. Titarenko, ed., *Istoriia Kommunisticheskoi partii Kitaia* (History of the Communist Party of China), vol. 1 (Moscow: IDV AN SSSR, 1987), 48–49. Regarding the population of the Southwest, in February 1951 Deng figured it at 70 million, but in May 1951 he gave the figure of 80 million. See Deng, *Deng Xiaoping xinan gongzuo wenji* (Works of Deng Xiaoping on His Work in the Southwest), 342; Deng, *Selected Works of Deng Xiaoping (1938–1965)*, 177. According to data in Richard Evans's biography of Deng, in the early 1950s, 150 million people lived in this region. Evans, *Deng Xiaoping and the Making of Modern China*, 109.

17. See *Zhonghua renmin gongheguo dashi (1949–2004)* (Chronicle of Major Events in the People's Republic of China [1949–2004]), vol. 1 (Beijing: Renmin chubanshe, 2004), 9; Mao, *Selected Works of Mao Tse-tung*, vol. 5, 40.

18. See *Obrazovanie Kitaiskoi Narodnoi Respubliki: Dokumenty i materialy* (Establishment of the People's Republic of China: Documents and Materials), 35.

19. Quoted from Meliksetov, *Istoriia Kitaia* (History of China), 619.

20. *Eighth National Congress of the Communist Party of China*, vol. 1 (Peking: Foreign Languages Press, 1956), 90.

21. In April 1952, Deng proposed establishing a Military Administrative Committee in Tibet, but Mao did not agree. See Mao, *Selected Works of Mao Tse-tung*, vol. 5, 73, 74.

22. See Deng, *Selected Works of Deng Xiaoping (1938–1965)*, 162, 330–31; Deng Xiaoping, *Deng Xiaoping wenxuan* (Selected Works of Deng Xiaoping), vol. 1 (Beijing: Renmin chubanshe, 1994), 370; Dorothy J. Solinger, *Regional Government and Political Integration in Southwest China, 1949–1954: A Case Study* (Berkeley: University of California Press, 1977), 180.

23. Deng always devoted a lot of attention to propaganda. "The pen is a major tool for exercising leadership," he said. In this connection, like every communist, he had no doubt that the press should be completely under the control of the Communist party. Deng, *Selected works of Deng Xiaoping (1938–1965)*, 146–47.

24. Karl Marx. "Capital. Vol. 1. The Process of Production of Capital," in Karl Marx and Friedrich Engels. *Collected Works*, vol. 35 [trans. Richard Dixon and others] (New York: International, 1996), 739.

25. Mao, *Selected Works of Mao Tse-tung*, vol. 5, 29.

26. See Shi Ch'eng-chih, *People's Resistance in Mainland China* (Hong Kong: Union Research Institute, 1956), 1.

27. Cited from Yang Kuisong, "Xin zhongguo 'zhenya fangeming' yundong yanjiu" (A Study of New China's Campaign to "Suppress Counter-revolutionaries"), http://www.chinese-thought.org/shgc/007682.htm.

28. Deng, *Deng Xiaoping zishu* (Autobiographical Notes of Deng Xiaoping), 130.

29. The personal notes and reports of Mao's Russian doctor L. Mel'nikov, preserved in the archives, eloquently attest to Mao's illness at the time. See RGASPI, collection 495, inventory 225, file 71, vol. 1, sheets 185, 187–87 reverse side.

30. Quoted from *Eighth National Congress of the Communist Party of China*, vol. 2, 119.

31. See Deng, *Selected Works of Deng Xiaoping (1938–1965)*, 155, 157.

32. For more details, see Solinger, *Regional Government and Political Integration in Southwest China, 1949–1954*, 177–78.

33. See Yang, "Xin Zhongguo 'zhenya fangeming' yundong yanjiu" (A study of New China's Campaign to "Suppress Counter-revolutionaries").

34. See Mao, *Jianguo yilai Mao Zedong wengao* (Manuscripts of Mao Zedong from the Founding of the PRC), vol. 2, 267.

35. See Frank Dikötter, *The Tragedy of Liberation: A History of the Chinese Revolution, 1945–1957* (New York: Bloomsbury Press, 2013), 88, 90, 309.

36. Mao, *Jianguo yilai Mao Zedong wengao* (Manuscripts of Mao Zedong from the Founding of the PRC), vol. 2, 267.

37. See Yang, "Xin zhongguo 'zhenya fangeming' yundong yanjiu" (A Study of New China's Campaign to "Suppress Counter-revolutionaries").

38. See Stéphane Courtois et al., *The Black Book of Communism: Crimes, Terror, Repression*, trans. Jonathan Murphy and Mark Kramer (Cambridge, MA: Harvard University Press, 1999), 481; Maurice Meisner, *Mao's China and After: A History of the People's Republic of China*, 3rd. ed. (New York: Free Press, 1999), 72.

39. See *Eighth National Congress of the Communist Party of China*, vol. 2, 119–20.

40. Mao, *Selected Works of Mao Tse-tung*, vol. 5, 33.

41. Ibid., 24.

42. See A. S. Mugruzin, *Agrarnye otnosheniia v Kitae v 20-40-x godakh XX veka* (Agrarian Relations in China in the 1920s–1940s) (Moscow: Nauka, 1970), 18, 197.

43. Deng, *Selected Works of Deng Xiaoping (1938–1965)*, 178. See also Deng, *Deng Xiaoping xinan gongzuo wenji* (Works of Deng Xiaoping on His Work in the Southwest), 371, 407.

44. Mao, *Selected Works of Mao Tse-tung*, vol. 5, 34.

45. Mao, *Jianguo yilai Mao Zedong wengao* (Manuscripts of Mao Zedong from the Founding of the PRC), vol. 2, 303, 304; Deng, *Selected Works of Deng Xiaoping (1938–1965)*, 177.

46. See Ezra F. Vogel, *Deng Xiaoping and the Transformation of China* (Cambridge, MA: Belknap Press of Harvard University Press, 2011), 42.

47. Deng, *Selected Works of Deng Xiaoping (1938–1965)*, 169. For more details on agrarian reform in the nationality regions, see Solinger, *Regional Government and Political Integration in Southwest China, 1949–1954*, 180–82.

48. See Deng, *Selected works of Deng Xiaoping (1938–1965)*, 169; Solinger, *Regional Government and Political Integration in Southwest China, 1949–1954*, 184, 187.

49. Deng, *Deng Xiaoping xinan gongzuo wenji* (Works of Deng Xiaoping on His Work in the Southwest), 544.

50. See ibid., 407, 447, 508, 544.

51. For more details see K. V. Shevelev, *Formirovaniie sotsial'no-ekonomicheskoi politiki rukovodstva KPK v 1949–1956 godakh (rukopis')* (The Formation of the CCP's Socio-economic Policy in 1949–1956) (manuscript), IV-6.

52. Mao, *Selected Works of Mao Tse-tung*, vol. 5, 77.

53. See Deng, *Deng Xiaoping xinan gongzuo wenji* (Works of Deng Xiaoping on His Work in the Southwest), 466–70, 481–93, 504–11, 514–17, 520–21, 524–40, 542–45.

54. See Mao, *Jianguo yilai Mao Zedong wengao* (Manuscripts of Mao Zedong from the Founding of the PRC), vol. 2, 513; Mao, *Selected Works of Mao Tse-tung*, vol. 5, 64–69. For more details see Wang Shoujun and Zhang Fuxing, *Fanfu fengbao—Kaiguo sutan di yi zhan* (The Hurricane Aimed Against Corruption—The First Battle after the Founding of the PRC to Liquidate Corruption) (Beijing: Zhonggong dangshi chubanshe, 2009); *Sanfan wufan yundong wenjian huibian* (Collection of Documents from the Three Anti and Five Anti Movements) (Beijing: Renmin chubanshe, 1953).

55. Quoted from Bo Yibo, *Ruogan zhongda juece yu shijiande huigu* (Recollections of Several Important Decisions and Their Implementation), vol. 1 (Beijing: Zhonggong zhongyang dangxiao chubanshe, 1991), 167.

56. See Yang, "Mao Zedong weishemma fangqi xinminzhuyi?" (Why did Mao Zedong Abandon New Democracy?), 182–83; Pang and Jin, *Mao Zedong zhuan (1949–1976)* (Biography of Mao Zedong [1949–1976]), vol. 1, 236.

57. Evans, *Deng Xiaoping and the Making of Modern China*, 112.

58. Deng, *Selected Works of Deng Xiaoping (1938–1965)*, 153.

59. Ibid., 158.

60. Sladkovskii, *Informatsionnyi biulleten'. Seriia A. Vypusk 2* (Information Bulletin: Series A: 2nd Installment), 22.

61. Quoted from Deng, *Deng Xiaoping*, 453. See also Gao Yi, ed., *Fengbei—Deng Xiaoping guju chenleguan* (A Monument to Deng Xiaoping) (Chengdu: Sichuan chubanshe, 2004), 95.

62. Deng, *Deng Xiaoping*, 465.

63. See *Yongyuande Xiaoping* (The Unforgettable Xiaoping), 78.

64. Sending her off to the academy, he joked, "And you, madam, need to have your brain washed, undergo ideological reconstruction, and learn how monkeys turned into human beings." Ibid., 79.

65. Sladkovskii, *Informatsionnyi biuletten'. Seriia A. Vypusk 2* (Information Bulletin: Series A: 2nd Installment), 22.

CHAPTER 9

1. See Frederick C. Teiwes, *Politics at Mao's Court: Gao Gang and Party Factionalism* (Armonk, NY: Sharpe, 1990), 100.

2. Deng, *Deng Xiaoping*, 463.

3. Bo, *Ruogan zhongda juece yu shijiande huigu* (Recollections of Several Important Political Decisions and Their Implementation), vol. 1, 318.

4. For more details, see Pantsov with Levine, *Mao*, 390–91.

5. See Jin *Liu Shaoqi zhuan: 1898–1969* (Biography of Liu Shaoqi: 1898–1969), vol. 2, 671.

6. See K. V. Shevelev, *Formirovaniie sotsial'no-ekonomicheskoi politiki rukovdostva KPK v 1949–1956 godakh* (The Formation of the CCP's Socioeconomic Policy in 1949–1956), V–4.

7. See Mao, *Selected Works of Mao Tse-tung*, vol. 5, 71; M. I. Sladkovskii, ed., *Informatsionnyi biulleten'. Seriia A. "Kul'turnaia revoliutsiia v Kitae. Dokumenty i materialy. Vypusk 1: "Hunveibinovskaia" pechat' o Liu Shaotsi"* (Information Bulletin: Series A: The Cultural Revolution in China. Trans. from Chinese: The 1st installment: The Red Guard Press on Liu Shaoqi) (Moscow: IDV AN SSSR, 1968), 73–74.

8. Shevelev, *Formirovaniie sotsial'no-ekonomicheskoi politiki rukovdostva KPK v 1949–1956 godakh* (The Formation of the CCP's Socio-economic Policy in 1949–1956), IV–14.

9. See J. V. Stalin, *Sochineniia* (Works), vol. 18 (Tver': Informatsionno-izdatel'skii tsentr "Soiuz," 2006), 587.

10. Quoted from Wu, *Deng Xiaoping yu Zhuo Lin* (Deng Xiaoping and Zhuo Lin), 85–86.

11. Quoted from Jin, *Liu Shaoqi zhuan: 1898–1969* (Biography of Liu Shaoqi: 1898–1969), vol. 2, 664; *Dnevnik sovtskogo posla v Kitae V. V. Kuznetsova. Zapis' besedy s Liu Shaoqi, 9 noiabra 1953 g.* (Diary of Soviet Ambassador to China V. V.

Kuznetsov. Notes of a Conversation with Liu Shaoqi. November 9, 1953), Archive of the Foreign Policy of the Russian Federation (hereafter AVP RF), collection 0100, inventory 46, file 12, folder 362, sheet 185.

12. See Philip Short, *Mao: A Life* (New York: Holt, 1999), 442.

13. See Bo, *Ruogan zhongda juece yu shijiande huigu* (Recollections of Several Important Political Decisions and Their Implementation), vol. 1, 240; Jin Chongji, ed., *Zhou Enlai zhuan: 1898–1976 (Biography* of Zhou Enlai: 1898–1976), vol. 2 (Beijing: Zhongyang wenxian chubanshe, 2009), 987–88.

14. See Yang and Yan, *Deng Xiaoping nianpu: 1904–1974* (Chronological Biography of Deng Xiaoping: 1904–1974), vol. 2, 1078–79.

15. See Mao, *Jianguo yilai Mao Zedong wengao* (Manuscripts of Mao Zedong from the Founding of the PRC), vol. 4, 27.

16. Mao, *Selected Works of Mao Tse-tung*, vol. 5, 105; Bo, *Ruogan zhongda juece yu shijiande huigu* (Recollections of Several Important Political Decisions and Their Implementation), vol. 1, 234–35.

17. See Bo, *Ruogan zhongda juece yu shijiande huigu* (Recollections of Several Important Political Decisions and Their Implementation), vol. 1, 242; Jin, *Zhou Enlai zhuan 1898–1976* (Biography of Zhou Enlai 1898–1976), vol. 2, 989.

18. Gao Gang, *Izbrannoe* (Selected Works) (Moscow: IDV AN SSSR, 1989), 226–31.

19. See Jin, *Liu Shaoqi zhuan: 1898–1969* (Biography of Liu Shaoqi: 1898–1969), vol. 2, 680; Bo, *Ruogan zhongda juece yu shijiande huigu* (Recollections of Several Important Political Decisions and Their Implementation), vol. 1, 218.

20. See Pang and Jin, *Mao Zedong zhuan (1949–1976)* (Biography of Mao Zedong [1949–1976]), vol. 1, 252.

21. Mao, *Selected Works of Mao Tse-tung*, vol. 5, 93.

22. See Paul Wingrove, "Mao's Conversations with the Soviet Ambassador, 1953–1955," *CWIHP Working Paper*, no. 36 (April 2002), 40; Bo, *Ruogan zhongda juece yu shijiande huigu* (Recollections of Several Important Political Decisions and Their Implementation), vol. 1, 241, 311; Teiwes, *Politics at Mao's Court*, 242.

23. Teiwes, *Politics at Mao's Court*, 163.

24. Quoted from Bo, *Ruogan zhongda juece yu shijiande huigu* (Recollections of Several Important Political Decisions and Their Implementation), vol. 1, 247.

25. See Mao, *Selected Works of Mao Tse-tung*, vol. 5, 103–11; Zhou Enlai, "Rech' na Vsekitaiskom finansovo-ekonomicheskom soveshchanii" (Speech at the All-China Financial-Economic Conference), AVP RF, collection 0100, inventory 46, file 374, folder 121, sheets 8–19; Bo, *Ruogan zhongda juece yu shijiande huigu* (Recollections of Several Important Political Decisions and Their Implementation), vol. 1, 247–48; A. M. Ledovskii, *Delo Gao Gana-Rao Shushi* (The Gao Gang, Rao Shushi Affair) (Moscow: IDV AN SSSR, 1990), 99.

26. Zhou Enlai, "Rech' na Vsekitaiskom finansovo-ekonomicheskom soveshchanii" (Speech at the All-China Financial-Economic Conference), 18.

27. Quoted from Bo, *Ruogan zhongda juece yu shijiande huigu* (Recollections of Several Important Political Decisions and Their Implementation), vol. 1, 251.

28. See ibid., 252.

29. Mao, *Selected Works of Mao Tse-tung*, vol. 5, 103, 104, 110.

30. See Teiwes, *Politics at Mao's Court*, 6–7, 93–96, 101–11, 221–27.

31. Deng, *Selected Works of Deng Xiaoping*, vol. 2 *(1975–1982)*, 278–79.

32. See Teiwes, *Politics at Mao's Court*, 94.

33. Deng, *Selected Works of Deng Xiaoping*, vol. 2 *(1975–1982)*, 278.

34. See Yang and Yan, *Deng Xiaoping nianpu: 1904–1974* (Chronological Biography of Deng Xiaoping: 1904–1974), vol. 2, 1129–35.

35. For more details, see Teiwes, *Politics at Mao's Court*, 44–47.

36. Quoted from ibid., 85.

37. See ibid., 308–9. For Confucius's quotation see Confucius, *The Analects of Confucius*, 15.

38. Quoted from Teiwes, *Politics at Mao's Court*, 229.

39. See ibid., 117.

40. Liu Shaoqi, *Liu Shaoqi xuanji* (Selected Works of Liu Shaoqi), vol. 2 (Beijing: Renmin chubanshe, 1985), 125–31.

41. Zhou Enlai, "Comrade Zhou Enlai's Speech Outline at the Discussion Meeting on the Gao Gang Question (February 1954)," in Teiwes, *Politics at Mao's Court*, 240–45.

42. I. V. Kovalev, "Zapiska I. V. Kovaleva ot 24 dekabria 1949 g." (I. V. Kovalev's Note of December 24, 1949), *Novaia i noveishaia istoriia* (*Modern and Contemporary History*), no. 1 (2004), 132–39; I. V. Kovalev, "Dialog Stalina s Mao Tszedunom" (Stalin's Dialogue with Mao Zedong), *Problemy Dal'nego Vostoka* (*Far Eastern Affairs*), no. 6 (1991): 89, 91; I. V. Kovalev, "Rossiia v Kitae (S missiei v Kitae)" (Russia in China [My Mission to China]), *Duel*, Nov. 19, 1997; N. S. Khrushchev, *Memoirs of Nikita Khrushchev*, trans. George Shriver, vol. 3 (University Park: Pennsylvania State University Press, 2004), 412–14; Bo, *Ruogan zhongda juece yu shijiande huigu* (Recollections of Several Important Political Decisions and Their Implementation), vol. 1, 40–41; Ye Zilong, *Ye Zilong huiyilu* (Memoirs of Ye Zilong) (Beijing: Zhongyang wenxian chubanshe, 2000), 201; Chen Aifei and Cao Zhiwei, *Zouchu guomende Mao Zedong* (Mao Zedong Abroad) (Shijiazhuang: Hebei renmin chubanshe, 2001), 88–91; Heinzig, *The Soviet Union and Communist China, 1945–1950*, 157, 158, 285–86, 296–97.

43. Deng Xiaoping, Chen Yi, and Tan Zhenlin, "Report of Deng Xiaoping, Chen Yi, and Tan Zhenlin Concerning the Discussion Meeting on the Rao Shushi Question (March 1, 1954)," in Teiwes, *Politics at Mao's Court*, 245–52.

44. For more details, see Zhao Jialiang and Zhang Xiaoji, *Banjie mubei xia de wangshi: Gao Gang zai Beijing* (A Story Dug from Underneath a Half-destroyed Tombstone: Gao Gang in Beijing) (Hong Kong: Dafeng chubanshe, 2008), 203–16, 238–45.

45. See Short, *Mao*, 442, 444, 737.
46. See Ruan Ming, *Deng Xiaoping: Chronicle of an Empire*, trans. and ed. Nancy Liu, Peter Rand, and Lawrence R. Sullivan (Boulder, CO: Westview Press, 1992), 55.
47. N. G. Sudarikov, ed., *Konstitutsiia i osnovnye zakonodatel'nye akty Kitaiskoi Narodnoi Respubliki* (The Constitution and Founding Legislative Acts of the People's Republic of China) (Moscow: Izdatel'stvo inostrannoi literatury, 1955), 31.
48. See Deng Xiaoping, "Report on the Gao Gang, Rao Shushi Anti-Party Alliance (March 21, 1955)," in Teiwes, *Politics at Mao's Court*, 254–76.
49. See Yang Shangkun, *Yang Shangkun riji* (Diary of Yang Shangkun), vol. 1 (Beijing: Zhongyang wenxian chubanshe, 2001), 180, 181, 184.
50. Quoted in Teiwes, *Politics at Mao's Court*, 26.

CHAPTER 10

1. See O. Arne Westad, ed., *Brothers in Arms: The Rise and Fall of the Sino-Soviet Alliance, 1945–1963* (Stanford, CA: Stanford University Press, 1998), 16, 39; Khrushchev, *Memoirs of Nikita Khrushchev*, vol. 3, 420–27; D. T. Shepilov, "Vospominaniia" (Reminiscences), *Voprosy istorii* (*Problems of History*), no. 9 (1998), 18–33, no. 10 (1998), 3–31; K. I. Koval', "Moskovskiie peregovory I. V. Stalina s Chzhou En'laem v 1953 g. i N. S. Khrushcheva s Mao Tzedunom v 1954 g." (J. V. Stalin's Moscow Negotiations with Zhou Enlai in 1953 and N. S. Khrushchev's with Mao Zedong in 1954), *Novaia i noveishaia istoriia* (*Modern and Contemporary History*), no. 5 (1989), 113–18; Shi Zhe, *Feng yu gu—Shi Zhe huiyilu* (Summit and Abyss—Reminiscences of Shi Zhe) (Beijing: Hongqi chubanshe, 1992), 106–15; Zhihua Shen and Yafeng Xia, "Between Aid and Restrictions: Changing Soviet Policies Toward China's Nuclear Weapons Program, 1954–1960," *Nuclear Proliferation International History Project Working Paper*, no. 2 (May 2012), 1–80.
2. Quoted from Yang and Yan, *Deng Xiaoping nianpu: 1904–1974* (Chronological Biography of Deng Xiaoping: 1904–1974), vol. 1, 1272.
3. *Stenograficheskii otchet XX s"ezda KPSS* (Stenographic Record of the Twentieth Congress of the CPSU), vol. 1 (Moscow: Gospolitizdat, 1956), 230.
4. Quoted from Yang and Yan, *Deng Xiaoping nianpu: 1904–1974* (Chronological Biography of Deng Xiaoping: 1904–1974), vol. 1, 1273.
5. Ibid., 1274.
6. Quoted from Shi Zhe, *Zai lishi juren shenbian* (By the Side of Historical Titans) (Beijing: Zhongyang wenxian chubanshe, 1995), 595.
7. See N. S. Khrushchev, *Speech of Nikita Khrushchev Before a Closed Session of the XXth Congress of the Communist Party of the Soviet Union on February 25, 1956* (Washington, DC: U.S. Government Printing Office, 1957).

8. Quoted from Wu Lengxi, *Shi nian lunzhan: Zhongsu guanxi huiyilu (1956–1966)* (The Ten-Year Debate: Reminiscences of Sino-Soviet Relations [1956–1966]), vol. 1 (Beijing: Zhongyang wenxian chubanshe, 1999), 4–5.

9. Quoted from Shi, *Zai lishi juren shenbian* (By the Side of Historical Titans), 596; Wu, *Shi nian lunzhan* (The Ten-Year Debate), vol. 1, 5.

10. See Pang and Jin, *Mao Zedong zhuan (1949–1976)* (Biography of Mao Zedong [1949–1976]), vol. 2, 495.

11. See Mao Zedong, "Mao Tszedun o kitaiskoi politike Kominterna i Stalina" (Mao Zedong on the China Policy of the Comintern and Stalin), *Problemy Dal'nego Vostoka (Far Eastern Affairs)*, no. 5 (1998) 103; M. S. Kapitsa, *Sovetsko-kitaiskie otnosheniia* (Soviet-Chinese Relations) (Moscow: Gospolitizdat, 1958), 357, 364; *Zhanhou zhongsu guanxi zouxiang (1945–1960)* (The Development of Soviet-Chinese Relations After the War [1945–1960]) (Beijing: Shehui kexue wenhua chubanshe, 1997), 78.

12. See K. Aimermakher, ed., *Doklad N. S. Khrushcheva o kul'te lichnosti Stalina na XX s'ezde KPSS: Dokumenty.* (N. S. Khrushchev's Report on Stalin's Cult of Personality at the 20th CPSU Congress: Documents) (Moscow: ROSSPEN, 2002), 24, 37, 252–53. See also Vittorio Vidali, *Diary of the Twentieth Congress of the Communist Party of the Soviet Union*, trans. Nell Amter Cattonar and A. M. Elliot (Westport, CT, and London: Lawrence Hill and Journeyman Press, 1974), 26–27.

13. See A. A. Fursenko, ed., *Prezidium TsK KPSS: 1954–1964* (Presidium of the CC CPSU: 1954–1964), vol. 1. *Chernovye protokol'nye zapisi zasedanii, stenogramy, postanovleniia* (Draft Protocol Minutes of the Sessions, Stenographic Records, and Resolutions) (Moscow: ROSSPEN, 2003), 106–7; Yang and Yan, *Deng Xiaoping nianpu: 1904–1974* (Chronological Biography of Deng Xiaoping: 1904–1974), vol. 1, 1275; Shi, *Zai lishi juren shenbian* (By the Side of Historical Titans), 597.

14. Quoted from Li, *The Private Life of Chairman Mao*, 115.

15. See Wu, *Shi nian lunzhan* (The Ten-Year Debate), vol. 1, 6–7; Liu Chongwen and Chen Shaochu, eds, *Liu Shaoqi nianpu: 1898–1969* (Chronological Biography of Liu Shaoqi: 1898–1969), vol. 2 (Beijing: Zhongyang wenxian chubanshe, 1998), 363. According to other sources this was an enlarged meeting of the Politburo of the CC, taking place on March 12. Quoted from Pang and Jin Chongji, eds., *Mao Zedong zhuan (1949–1976)* (Biography of Mao Zedong [1949–1976]), vol. 2 (2003), 363.

16. See Pang and Jin, *Mao Zedong zhuan (1949–1976)* (Biography of Mao Zedong [1949–1976]), vol. 2, 496.

17. Quoted from Wu, *Shi nian lunzhan* (The Ten-Year Debate), vol. 1, 8.

18. Quoted from ibid.

19. Wang Ming was the pseudonym of Chen Shaoyu, beginning in 1931.

20. Quoted from ibid., 11.

21. Quoted from ibid., 14–15.

22. See ibid., 15.

23. For more details, see Pantsov with Levine, *Mao*, 415–21.

24. See Wu, *Shi nian lunzhan* (The Ten-Year Debate), vol. 1, 16–19.

25. For the corrections and additions made in the text by Mao himself, see ibid., 59–67. See also Wu, *Yi Mao zhuxi* (Remembering Chairman Mao), 2–7.

26. Borisov and Titarenko, *Vystupleniia Mao Tsze-duna, ranee ne publikovavshiesia v kitaiskoi pechati* (Mao Zedong's Speeches Previously Unpublished in the Chinese Press), series 1, 93.

27. See Mao, *Selected Works of Mao Tse-tung*, vol. 5, 284–307. See also Stuart Schram, ed., *Chairman Mao Talks to the People: Talks and Letters, 1956–1971* (New York: Pantheon Books, 1974), 81–82; Borisov and Titarenko, *Vystupleniia Mao Tsze-duna, ranee ne publikovavshiesia v kitaiskoi pechati* (Mao Zedong's Speeches Previously Unpublished in the Chinese Press), series 1, 66–86.

28. Borisov and Titarenko, *Vystupleniia Mao Tsze-duna, ranee ne publikovavshiesia v kitaiskoi pechati* (Mao Zedong's Speeches Previously Unpublished in the Chinese Press), series 2, 122; Li, *Private Life of Chairman Mao*, 181, 183, 192.

29. See Yang, *Deng Xiaoping*, 134.

30. *The Case of Peng Dehuai, 1959–1968* (Hong Kong: Union Research Institute, 1968), 445.

31. See Deng, *Deng Xiaoping zishu (Zhailu)* (Autobiographical Notes of Deng Xiaoping. [Excerpts]).

32. See Zhihua Shen, "Zhonggong bada weishemma bu ti 'Mao Zedong sixiang'?" (Why Did the Eighth CCP Congress Not Raise "Mao Zedong Thought"?), *Lishi jiaoxue* (Teaching history), no. 5 (2005), 6. See also Mao Zedong, *Mao Zedong wenjii* (Works of Mao Zedong), vol. 6 (Beijing: Renmin chubanshe, 1999), 387.

33. See Deng, *Deng Xiaoping and the Cultural Revolution*, 53.

34. Liu, *On the Party*, 157; *Eighth National Congress of the Communist Party of China*, vol. 1, 137.

35. *Eighth National Congress of the Communist Party of China*, vol. 1, 200.

36. Deng, *Wode zishu (Zhailu)* (My Autobiographical Notes [Excerpts]).

37. *Eighth National Congress of the Communist Party of China*, vol. 2, 199–200.

38. Mao Zedong, *Mao Zedong wenji* (Works of Mao Zedong), vol. 7 (Beijing: Renmin chubanshe, 1999), 111–12. See also Mao Zedong, *Jianguo yilai Mao wengao* (Manuscripts of Mao Zedong from the Founding of the PRC), vol. 6, 165; Wingrove, "Mao's Conversations with the Soviet Ambassador, 1953–1955," 36.

39. Quoted from Mao, *Mao Zedong wenji* (Works of Mao Zedong), vol. 7, 111–12. This took place on September 13, 1956, at the third meeting of the Seventh plenum of the Seventh CCP Central Committee. See in detail Yang Shengqun and Liu Jintian, eds., *Deng Xiaoping zhuan (1904–1974)* (Biography of Deng Xiaoping [1904–1974]), vol. 2 (Beijing: Zhongyang wenxian chubanshe, 2014), 993–96.

CHAPTER 11

1. Deng, *Deng Xiaoping and the Cultural Revolution*, 4.

2. See ibid., 37, 44–45, 46, 50–51; Wu, *Deng Xiaoping yu Zhuo Lin* (Deng Xiaoping and Zhuo Lin), 71.

3. Fursenko, *Presidium TsK KPSS: 1954–1964* (Presidium of the CC CPSU: 1954–1964), vol. 1, 173.

4. For more details, see Paul E. Zinner, ed., *National Communism and Popular Revolt in Eastern Europe: A Selection of Documents on Events in Poland and Hungary* (New York: Columbia University Press, 1956), 9–262; Mark Kramer, "New Evidence on Soviet Decision-Making and the 1956 Polish and Hungarian Crisis," *CWIHP Bulletin*, nos. 8–9 (1996–97): 360-61.

5. See Vladislav M. Zubok, "Look What Chaos in the Beautiful Socialist Camp! Deng Xiaoping and the Sino-Soviet Split, 1956–1963," *CWIHP Bulletin*, no. 10 (March 1998): 153.

6. Quoted from Wu, *Shi nian lunzhan* (The Ten-Year Debate), vol. 1, 35.

7. Ibid., 39–40.

8. *Istoricheskii arkhiv* (Historical Archive), nos. 4–5 (1996): 184–85; Fursenko, *Prezidium TsK KPSS: 1954–1964* (Presidium of the CC CPSU: 1954–1964), vol. 1, 174–75; A. A. Fursenko, *Prezidium TsK KPSS: 1954–1964* (Presidium of the CC CPSU: 1954–1964), vol. 2. *Postanovleniia: 1954–1958* (Resolutions of 1954–1958) (Moscow: ROSSPEN, 2006), 471–72.

9. *Vozniknovenie i razvitie raznoglasii mezhdu rukovodstvom KPSS i nami: Po povodu otkrytogo pis'ma TsK KPSS* (The Origin and Development of Disagreements Between the Leadership of the CPSU and Us: On the Open Letter of the CC CPSU) (Beijing: Izdatel'stvo literatury na inostrannykh iazykakh, 1963), 12; See also Wu, *Shi nian lunzhan* (The Ten-Year Debate), vol. 1, 42–45; "Records of Meeting of the CPSU and CCP Delegations, Moscow, July 5–20, 1963," in Westad, *Brothers in Arms*, 378.

10. Sándor Petöfi, *Rebel or Revolutionary: Sándor Petöfi as Revealed by His Diary, Letters, Notes, Pamphlets and Poems*, trans. Edwin Morgan (Budapest: Corvina Press, 1974), 196.

11. For more details, see Zinner, *National Communism and Popular Revolution*, 398–434; Kramer, "New Evidence on Soviet Decision-Making and the 1956 Polish and Hungarian Crisis," 362–69.

12. See Fursenko, *Prezidium TsK KPSS: 1954–1964* (Presidium of the CC CPSU: 1954–1964), vol. 1, 178–79, 187–88; Yang and Yan, *Deng Xiaoping nianpu: 1904–1974* (Chronological Biography of Deng Xiaoping: 1904–1974), vol. 2, 1322; Xu Zehao, ed., *Wang Jiaxiang nianpu: 1906–1974* (Chronological Biography of Wang Jiaxiang: 1906–1974) (Beijing: Zhongyang wenxian chubanshe, 2001, 439–40.

13. See Pang and Jin, *Mao Zedong zhuan (1949–1976)* (Biography of Mao Zedong [1949–1976]), vol. 1, 602–3; Shi Zhe and Li Haiwen, *Zhong-su guanxi jianzheng lu* (Eyewitness Notes of Sino-Soviet Relations) (Beijing: Dangdai Zhongguo chubanshe, 2005), 225; *Vozniknovenie i razvitie raznoglasii mezhdu rukovodstvom KPSS*

i nami: Po povodu otkrytogo pis'ma TsK KPSS (The Origins and Development of Disagreements Between the Leadership of the CPSU and Us: On the Open Letter of the CC CPSU), 12; Wu, *Shi nian lunzhan* (The Ten-Year Debate), vol. 1, 45.

14. Fursenko, *Prezidium TsK KPSS: 1954–1964* (Presidium of the CC CPSU: 1954–1964), vol. 1, 178. See also Shi Zhe and Shi Qiulang, *Wode yisheng—Shi Zhe zishu* (My Life—Autobiographical Notes of Shi Zhe) (Beijing: Renmin chubanshe, 2002), 470–71.

15. Khrushchev, *Memoirs of Nikita Khrushchev*, vol. 3, 430, 488, 489.

16. See William Taubman, *Khrushchev: The Man and His Era* (New York: Norton, 2003), 297.

17. Fursenko, *Prezidium TsK KPSS: 1954–1964* (Presidium of the CC CPSU: 1954–1964), vol. 1, 188; Wu, *Shi nian lunzhan* (The Ten-Year Debate), vol. 1, 52.

18. Fursenko, *Prezidium TsK KPSS: 1954–1964* (Presidium of the CC CPSU: 1954–1964), vol. 1, 188.

19. Quoted from Shi and Li, *Zhong-su guanxi jianzheng lu* (Eyewitness Notes of Sino-Soviet Relations), 235; Zubok, "Look What Chaos in the Beautiful Socialist Camp!" 153.

20. Quoted from Shi and Li, *Zhong-su guanxi jianzheng lu* (Eyewitness Notes of Sino-Soviet Relations), 234.

21. I. F. Kurdiukov et al., eds., *Sovetsko-kitaiskie otnosheniia, 1917–1957: Sbornik dokumentov* (Soviet-Chinese Relations, 1917–1957: A Documentary Collection) (Moscow: Izd-vo vostochnoi literatury, 1959), 319. See also Fursenko, *Prezidium TsK KPSS: 1954–1964* (Presidium of the CC CPSU: 1954–1964), vol. 1, 191.

22. Fursenko, *Prezidium TsK KPSS: 1954–1964* (Presidium of the CC CPSU: 1954–1964), vol. 1, 191.

23. Khrushchev, *Memoirs of Nikita Khrushchev*, vol. 3, 651. See also the explication of Liu Shaoqi's speech on this issue at the Second Plenum of the Eighth CC CCP (Nov. 10, 1956), in Pang and Jin, *Mao Zedong zhuan (1949–1976)* (Biography of Mao Zedong [1949–1976]), vol. 1, 603–5.

24. See G. F. Krivosheev, ed., *Grif sekretnosti sniat: Poteri Vooruzhennykh Sil SSSR v voinakh, boevykh deistviiakh i voennykh konfliktakh: Statisticheskoe issledovanie* (The Stamp of Secrecy Is Removed: Losses of the Armed Forces of the USSR in Wars, Battles, and Armed Conflicts: A Statistical Analysis) (Moscow: Voennoye izdatel'stvo, 1993), 397; Micheal Clodfelter, *Warfare and Armed Conflict: A Statistical Encyclopedia of Casualty and Other Figures, 1494–2007*, 3rd. ed. (Jefferson, NC: McFarland, 2008), 576–77.

25. Quoted from Xiao Denglin, *Wushi nian guoshi jiyao: Waijiao juan* (Draft History of State Affairs for the Past Fifty Years: Foreign Affairs Volume) (Changsha: Hunan renmin chubanshe, 1999), 194–95.

26. Wu, *Shi nian lunzhan* (The Ten-Year Debate), vol. 1, 59.

27. See *People's Daily*, Dec. 29, 1956.

28. Quoted from Yang and Yan, *Deng Xiaoping nianpu: 1904–1974* (Chronological Biography of Deng Xiaoping: 1904–1974), vol. 2, 1323.

29. For more details, see Mao, *Jianguo yilai Mao Zedong wengao* (Manuscripts of Mao Zedong from the Founding of the PRC), vol. 6, 120–21; Roderick MacFarquhar, *The Hundred Flowers Campaign and the Chinese Intellectuals* (New York: Praeger, 1960), 6–9; [Robert R. Bowie and John K. Fairbank, eds.,] *Communist China, 1955–1959: Policy Documents with Analysis* (Cambridge, MA: Harvard University Press, 1962), 5–7.

30. See Yang and Yan, *Deng Xiaoping nianpu: 1904–1974* (Chronological Biography of Deng Xiaoping: 1904–1974), vol. 2, 1321; Li Ping and Ma Zhisun, eds., *Zhou Enlai nianpu (1949–1976)* (Chronological Biography of Zhou Enlai [1949–1976]), vol. 1 (Beijing: Zhongyang wenxian chubanshe, 1997), 628.

31. Quoted from Yang and Yan, *Deng Xiaoping nianpu: 1904–1974* (Chronological Biography of Deng Xiaoping: 1904–1974), vol. 2, 1327.

32. See Sladkovskii, *Informatsionnyi biulleten'. Seriia A. Vypusk 2* (Information Bulletin: Series A: 2nd Installment), 33; Mao, *Selected Works of Mao Tse-tung*, vol. 5, 353.

33. See Mao, *Selected Works*, vol. 5, 408–14.

34. Quoted from Sladkovskii, *Informatsionnyi biulleten'. Seriia A. Vypusk 2* (Information Bulletin: Series A: 2nd Installment), 35. See also Deng, *Selected Works of Deng Xiaoping*, vol. 2 *(1975–1982)*, 282–83.

35. In the PRC, in addition to the ruling CCP there have been eight minuscule so-called democratic parties that formed a united front with the communists.

36. *People's Daily*, June 8, 1957.

37. *CWIHP Bulletin*, no. 10 (2001), 165.

38. Quoted from V. N. Berezhkov, *Riadom so Stalinym* (By Stalin's Side) (Moscow: Vagrius, 1998), 443–44.

39. Quoted from Jonathan Fenby, *The Penguin History of Modern China: The Fall and Rise of a Great Power, 1850–2009* (London: Penguin Books, 2009), 392. See also Yang, *Deng Xiaoping*, 141.

40. Quoted from Fenby, *The Penguin History of Modern China*, 393. On the scale of arrests, see Meliksetov, *Istoriia Kitaia* (History of China), 649.

41. Deng Xiaoping, "Report on the Rectification Campaign, 1955–1959," [Bowie and Fairbank,] *Communist China, 1955–1959: Policy Documents with Analysis*, 341, 344.

42. Deng, *Selected Works of Deng Xiaoping*, vol. 2 *(1975–1982)*, 262–63, 279.

43. Quoted from Li Yueran, *Waijiao wutai shang de xin Zhongguo lingxiu* (Leaders of New China in the Diplomatic Arena) (Beijing: Waiyu jiaoxue yu yanjiu chubanshe, 1994), 143; Khrushchev, *Memoirs of Nikita Khrushchev*, vol. 3, 439, 488; N. S. Khrushchev, *Vremia, Liudi, Vlast': Vospominaniia* (Time, People, Power: Memoirs), vol. 3 (Moscow: Moskovskiie novosti, 1999), 58, 104–5.

44. Quoted from Li, *Waijiao wutai shang de xin Zhongguo lingxiu* (Leaders of New China in the Diplomatic Arena), 143.

45. Quoted from Khrushchev, *Memoirs of Nikita Khrushchev*, vol. 3, 439; Li, *Waijiao wutai shang de xin Zhongguo lingxiu* (Leaders of New China in the Diplomatic Arena), 143–44.

46. See Fursenko, *Prezidium TsK KPSS: 1954–1964* (Presidium of the CC CPSU: 1954–1964), vol. 1, 224, 274, 991, 1017; vol. 2, 540, 1003; Yang and Yan, *Deng Xiaoping nianpu: 1904–1974* (Chronological Biography of Deng Xiaoping: 1904–1974), vol. 3, 1401. Mao, to be sure, later asserted that Khrushchev had proposed convening the conference and adopting the declaration. See Mao Zedong, *Mao Zedong on Diplomacy* (Beijing: Foreign Languages Press, 1998), 251. But his assertion is contradicted by documentary materials.

47. See N. S. Khrushchev, *Report of the Central Committee of the Communist Party of the Soviet Union to the 20th Party Congress, February 14, 1956* (Moscow: Foreign Languages Publishing House, 1956), 38–47.

48. See the explication of Mao's speech on this issue at an enlarged Politburo session on Mar. 12, 1956, published in Wu, *Yi Mao zhuxi* (Remembering Chairman Mao), 4–5, as well as Mao's speech at the Second Plenum of the Eighth Central Committee in mid-November 1956, Mao, *Selected Works of Mao Tse-tung*, vol. 5, 341, 342.

49. Mao, *Mao Zedong on Diplomacy*, 252; Yang and Yan, *Deng Xiaoping nianpu: 1904–1974* (Chronological Biography of Deng Xiaoping: 1904–1974), vol. 3, 1401.

50. *Modern China*, 393. See Yang and Yan, *Deng Xiaoping nianpu: 1904–1974* (Chronological Biography of Deng Xiaoping: 1904–1974), vol. 3, 1402–16; Wu, *Shi nian lunzhan* (The Ten-Year Debate), vol. 1, 96–98; Yang, *Yang Shangkun riji* (Diary of Yang Shangkun), vol. 1, 286–95.

51. "Tezisy mnenii po voprosu o mirnom perekhode (10 noiabria 1957 g.)" (Theses of Opinions on the Issue of Peaceful Transition [November 10, 1957]), in *Polemika o general'noi linii mezhdunarodnogo kommunisticheskogo dvizheniia* (Polemic on the General Line of the International Communist Movement) (Beijing: Izdatel'stvo literatury na inostrannykh iazykakh, 1965), 112–15.

52. *Dokumenty soveshchanii predstavitelei kommunisticheskikh i rabochikh partii, sostoiavshikhsia v Moskve v noiabre 1957 goda* (Documents from the Meetings of Representatives of Communist and Workers' Parties That Took Place in Moscow in November 1957) (Moscow: Gospolitizdat, 1957), 18–22; See also, Wu, *Shi nian lunzhan* (The Ten-year Debate), vol. 1, 98, 127–41; Yang, *Yang Shangkun riji* (Diary of Yang Shangkun), vol. 1, 285–96; Yang and Yan, *Deng Xiaoping nianpu: 1904–1974* (Chronological Biography of Deng Xiaoping: 1904–1974), vol. 3, 1402–7; Fursenko, *Prezidium TsK KPSS: 1954–1964* (Presidium of the CC CPSU: 1954–1964), vol. 1, 279–81; vol. 2, 720–31, 1004; Yan Mingfu, "Yan Mingfu tan Deng Xiaoping" (Yan Mingfu Speaks About Deng Xiaoping), in Liu Jintian, ed., *Huashuo Deng Xiaoping* (Stories About Deng Xiaoping) (Beijing: Zhongyang wenxian chubanshe, 2004), 164–65.

53. See Yang and Yan, *Deng Xiaoping nianpu: 1904–1974* (Chronological Biography of Deng Xiaoping: 1904–1974), vol. 3, 1408; Wu, *Shi nian lunzhan* (The Ten-Year Debate), vol. 1, 153–55.

54. Quoted from Wu, *Shi nian lunzhan* (The Ten-Year Debate), vol. 1, 100. See also Mao, *Mao Zedong on Diplomacy*, 251.

55. See Li, *Waijiao wutai shang de xin Zhongguo lingxiu* (Leaders of New China in the Diplomatic Arena), 130–47.

56. Quoted from ibid., 137.

57. See Yang, *Yang Shangkun riji* (Diary of Yang Shangkun), vol. 1, 285, 291.

58. Borisov and Titarenko, *Vystupleniia Mao Tsze-duna, ranee ne publikovavshie-sia v kitaiskoi pechati* (Mao Zedong's Speeches Previously Unpublished in the Chinese Press), series 1, 94. Mao said essentially the same thing at a meeting with the foreign minister of the USSR Gromyko on Nov. 19, 1957. See A. A. Gromyko, *Pamiatnoe* (Remembered), vol. 2 (Moscow: Politizdat, 1988), 131.

59. *Pravda*, Nov. 7, 1957.

60. See Chen Jian and Yang Kuisong, "Chinese Politics and the Collapse of the Sino-Soviet Alliance," in Westad, *Brothers in Arms*, 265.

61. Deng, *Selected Works of Deng Xiaoping*, vol. 2 *(1975–1982)*, 281.

62. Borisov and Titarenko, *Vystupleniia Mao Tsze-duna, ranee ne publikovavshiesia v kitaiskoi pechati* (Mao Zedong's Speeches Previously Unpublished in the Chinese Press), series 2, 112, 123; Li Ping, *Kaiguo zongli Zhou Enlai* (Zhou Enlai: The First Premier) (Beijing: Zhonggong zhongyang dangxiao chubanshe, 1994), 359.

63. Quoted from Li, *Kaiguo zongli Zhou Enlai* (Zhou Enlai, the First Premier), 361.

64. See ibid., 362–63.

65. Borisov and Titarenko, *Vystupleniia Mao Tsze-duna, ranee ne publikovavshiesia v kitaiskoi pechati* (Mao Zedong's Speeches Previously Unpublished in the Chinese Press), series 2, 134–55.

66. Deng, *Wode zishu (Zhailu)* (My Autobiographical Notes [Excerpts]).

67. See Chen Yungfa, "Jung Chang and Jon Halliday. 'Mao: The Unknown Story'," *Twentieth Century China*, vol. 33, no 1 (2007): 111.

68. Li, *The Private Life of Chairman Mao*, 277.

69. Quoted from Yang and Yan, *Deng Xiaoping nianpu: 1904–1974* (Chronological Biography of Deng Xiaoping: 1904–1974), vol. 3, 1405.

70. Borisov and Titarenko, *Vystupleniia Mao Tsze-duna, ranee ne publikovavshiesia v kitaiskoi pechati* (Mao Zedong's Speeches Previously Unpublished in the Chinese Press), series 2, 156, 158.

71. Quoted from Yang and Yan, *Deng Xiaoping nianpu: 1904–1974* (Chronological Biography of Deng Xiaoping: 1904–1974), vol. 3, 1421.

72. *CWIHP Bulletin*, no. 10 (March 1998), 167.

73. See *Vtoraia sessiia VIII Vsekitaiskogo s"ezda Kommunisticheskoi partii Kitaia* (Second Session of the Eighth Congress of the Chinese Communist Party)

(Peking: Izdatel'stvo literatury na inostrannykh iazykakh, 1958), 70–81; Yang and Yan, *Deng Xiaoping nianpu: 1904–1974* (Chronological Biography of Deng Xiaoping: 1904–1974), vol. 3, 1426.

74. *Vtoraia sessiia VIII Vsekitaiskogo s"ezda Kommunisticheskoi partii Kitaia* (Second Session of the Eighth Congress of the Chinese Communist Party), 68.

75. See Borisov and Titarenko, *Vystupleniia Mao Tsze-duna, ranee ne publikovavshie-sia v kitaiskoi pechati* (Mao Zedong's Speeches Previously Unpublished in the Chinese Press), series 2, 264, 275, 281; Roderick MacFarquhar, *The Origins of the Cultural Revolution*, vol. 2: *The Great Leap Forward, 1958–1960* (New York: Columbia University Press, 1983), 85, 90.

76. See Yang and Yan, *Deng Xiaoping nianpu: 1904–1974* (Chronological Biography of Deng Xiaoping: 1904–1974), vol. 2, 1318–19.

77. See Mao, *Mao Zedong on Diplomacy*, 247; B. N. Vereshchagin, *V starom i novom Kitae: Iz vospominanii diplomata* (In Old and New China: Reminiscences of a Diplomat) (Moscow: IDV RAN, 1999), 119–20; Shu Guang Zhang, "Sino-Soviet Economic Cooperation," in Westad, *Brothers in Arms*, 207; Zhang Shu Guang and Chen Jian, "The Emerging Disputes Between Beijing and Moscow: Ten Newly Available Chinese Documents, 1956–1958," *CWIHP Bulletin*, nos. 6–7 (1995–96), 154–59, 162–63.

78. Mao, *Mao Zedong on Diplomacy*, 250–58; Vereshchagin, *V starom i novom Kitae* (In Old and New China), 128.

79. Khrushchev, *Memoirs of Nikita Khrushchev*, vol. 3, 455.

80. Ibid., 456.

81. Quoted from Yan, "Yan Mingfu tan Deng Xiaoping," (Yan Mingfu Speaks About Deng Xiaoping), 165–66. See also Yan Mingfu's interview with the American journalist Harrison Salisbury on Apr. 29, 1988, in Harrison E. Salisbury, *The New Emperors: China in the Era of Mao and Deng* (Boston: Little, Brown, 1992), 155–58.

82. See Zubok, "The Mao-Khrushchev Conversations, July 31–August 3, 1958, and October 2, 1959," 244–72.

83. Of the stenographic records of the four conversations at the highest level that took place in Beijing between July 31 and Aug. 3, 1958, only the first and the last are available, so we don't know for certain who spoke at the second and the third meetings. It might have been Deng. For a short exposition of all the conversations, see Wu, *Shi nian lunzhan* (The Ten-Year Debate), vol. 1, 162–74. Wu Lengxi, however, says nothing about Deng's speeches.

84. Quoted from Salisbury, *The New Emperors*, 156.

85. Quoted from Yan, "Yan Mingfu tan Deng Xiaoping" (Yan Mingfu Speaks About Deng Xiaoping), 166.

86. Quoted from Li, *Private Life of Chairman Mao*, 261.

87. See Yang and Yan, *Deng Xiaoping nianpu: 1904–1974* (Chronological Biography of Deng Xiaoping: 1904–1974), vol. 3, 1448.

88. Borisov and Titarenko, *Vystupleniia Mao Tsze-duna, ranee ne publikovavshiesia v kitaiskoi pechati* (Mao Zedong's Speeches Previously Unpublished in the Chinese Press), vol. 2, 311.

89. Deng Xiaoping, "Velikoe splochenie kitaiskogo naroda i velikoe splochenie narodov mira" (The Great Unity of the Chinese People and the Great Unity of the Peoples of the World), *Pravda*, Oct. 1, 1959.

90. Peng Dehuai, "Comrade Peng Dehuai's Letter to Chairman Mao (July 14, 1959)," in Peng Dehuai, *Memoirs of a Chinese Marshal: The Autobiographical Notes of Peng Dehuai*, trans. Zheng Longpu (Beijing: Foreign Languages Press, 1984), 515.

91. Quoted from Yang and Yan, *Deng Xiaoping nianpu: 1904–1974* (Chronological Biography of Deng Xiaoping: 1904–1974), vol. 3, 1453–68; MacFarquhar, *Origins of the Cultural Revolution*, vol. 2, 85, 121.

92. See MacFarquhar, *Origins of the Cultural Revolution*, vol. 2, 127.

93. Alexander V. Pantsov's interview with a citizen of Beijing, Oct. 28, 2004.

94. Quoted from Yang and Yan, *Deng Xiaoping nianpu: 1904–1974* (Chronological Biography of Deng Xiaoping: 1904–1974), vol. 3, 1462, 1467.

95. See Yu Guangren, "Deng Xiaoping qiushi yu fansi jingshen" (The Spirit of Deng Xiaoping: Seek the Truth and Reflect It), *Yanhuang chunqiu* (*History of China*), no. 4 (2002): 2–8.

96. Deng, *Selected Works of Deng Xiaoping*, vol. 2 *(1975–1982)*, 328.

97. See Borisov and Titarenko, *Vystupleniia Mao Tsze-duna, ranee ne publikovavshiesia v kitaiskoi pechati* (Mao Zedong's Speeches Previously Unpublished in the Chinese Press), series 2, 348–407; Yang and Yan, *Deng Xiaoping nianpu: 1904–1974* (Chronological Biography of Deng Xiaoping: 1904–1974), vol. 3, 1468–69, 1471.

98. See *Materialy 6-go plenuma Tsentral'nogo Komiteta Kommunisticheskoi partii Kitaia vos'mogo sozyva* (Materials of the Sixth Plenum of the Eighth Central Committee of the Chinese Communist Party) (Beijing: Izdatel'stvo literatury na inostrannykh iazykakh, 1959), 13–54.

99. Quoted from Yang and Yan, *Deng Xiaoping nianpu: 1904–1974* (Chronological Biography of Deng Xiaoping: 1904–1974), vol. 3, 1472–73.

100. See *Materialy 6-go plenuma Tsentral'nogo Komiteta Kommunisticheskoi partii Kitaia vos'mogo sozyva* (Materials of the Sixth Plenum of the Eighth Central Committee of the Chinese Communist Party), 55.

101. Quoted from Frank Dikötter, *Mao's Great Famine: The History of China's Most Devastating Catastrophe, 1958–1962* (New York: Walker, 2010), 80.

102. See ibid., 89; Jasper Becker, *Hungry Ghosts: China's Secret Famine* (New York: Free Press, 1996), 85.

CHAPTER 12

1. Mao, *Jianguo yilai Mao Zedong wengao* (Manuscripts of Mao Zedong from the Founding of the PRC), vol. 8, 42.
2. Quoted from Yang and Yan, *Deng Xiaoping nianpu: 1904–1974* (Chronological Biography of Deng Xiaoping: 1904–1974), vol. 3, 1490.
3. See ibid.
4. See Li, *Private Life of Chairman Mao*, 295.
5. Borisov and Titarenko, *Vystupleniia Mao Tsze-duna, ranee ne publikovavshiesia v kitaiskoi pechati* (Speeches of Mao Zedong Previously Unpublished in the Chinese Press), series 2, 419, 420; series 3, 67.
6. See Yang and Yan, *Deng Xiaoping nianpu: 1904–1974* (Chronological Biography of Deng Xiaoping: 1904–1974), vol. 3, 1478–87.
7. See MacFarquhar, *Origins of the Cultural Revolution*, vol. 2, 162–63, 169–70.
8. Mao, *Mao Zedong wenji* (Works of Mao Zedong), vol. 7, 117; Yang and Yan, *Deng Xiaoping nianpu: 1904–1974* (Chronological Biography of Deng Xiaoping: 1904–1974), vol. 3, 1490.
9. Mao employed a Chinese idiom referencing an historical event from the Warring States period of ancient China.
10. Quoted from Yang and Yan, *Deng Xiaoping nianpu: 1904–1974* (Chronological Biography of Deng Xiaoping: 1904–1974), vol. 3, 1501. See also Mao, *Jianguo yilai Mao Zedong wengao* (Manuscripts of Mao Zedong from the Founding of the PRC), vol. 8, 196.
11. Peng, "Comrade Peng Dehuai's Letter to Chairman Mao (July 14, 1959)," 510–20.
12. See Dikötter, *Mao's Great Famine*, 92.
13. Sladkovskii, *Informatsionnyi biulleten'. Seriia A. Vypusk 2* (Information Bulletin: Series A: 2nd Installment), 45.
14. See Li, *Private Life of Chairman Mao*, 314–15.
15. For more details, see Li Rui, *Lushan huiyi shilu* (The True Record of the Lushan Plenum) (Beijing: Chunqiu chubanshe/Hunan jiaoyu chubanshe, 1989); *The Case of Peng Dehuai, 1959–1968*, 1–121, 405–46.
16. See Li Xinzhi and Wang Yuezong, eds., *Weida de shijian, guanghui de sixiang—Deng Xiaoping geming huodong dashiji* (Great Practice, Glorious Ideology—Chronicle of Basic Events in the Revolutionary Activity of Deng Xiaoping) (Beijing: Hualing chubanshe, 1990), 117.
17. See Deng, "Velikoe splochenie kitaiskogo naroda i velikoe splochenie narodov mira" (The Great Unity of the Chinese People and the Great Unity of the Peoples of the World).
18. See Wu, *Deng Xiaoping yu Zhuo Lin* (Deng Xiaoping and Zhuo Lin), 153–54, 157.
19. Fursenko, *Prezidium TsK KPSS: 1954–1964* (Presidium of the CC CPSU: 1954–1964), vol. 1, 337.
20. See Wu, *Shi nian lunzhan* (The Ten-Year Debate), vol. 1, 191.

21. Quoted from Roxane Witke, *Comrade Chiang Ch'ing* (Boston: Little, Brown, 1977), 272.

22. *Stenograficheskii otchet XXI s"ezda Kommunisticheskoi partii Sovetskogo Soiuza* (Stenographic Record of the Twenty-first Congress of the Communist Party of the Soviet Union), vol. 1 (Moscow: Gospolitizdat, 1959), 93–110.

23. Khrushchev, *Memoirs of Nikita Khrushchev*, vol. 3, 450–51.

24. See "Records of the Meeting of the CPSU and CCP Delegations, Moscow, July 5–20, 1963," 379; MacFarquhar, *Origins of the Cultural Revolution*, vol. 2, 225–26; Zhang Shu Guang, "Between 'Paper' and 'Real Tigers': Mao's View of Nuclear Weapons," in John Lewis Gaddis et al., eds., *Cold War Statesmen Confront the Bomb: Nuclear Diplomacy Since 1945* (New York: Oxford University Press, 1999), 208.

25. Khrushchev, *Memoirs of Nikita Khrushchev*, vol. 3, 480–81.

26. Quoted from MacFarquhar, *Origins of the Cultural Revolution*, vol. 2, 226.

27. See Wu, *Shi nian lunzhan* (The Ten-Year Debate), vol. 1, 208.

28. See Yang and Yan, *Deng Xiaoping nianpu: 1904–1974* (Chronological Biography of Deng Xiaoping: 1904–1974), vol. 3, 1518.

29. Zubok, "The Mao-Khrushchev Conversations, July 31–August 3, 1958, and October 2, 1959," 267–69; See also Li, *Waijiao wutai shang de xin Zhongguo lingxiu* (Leaders of New China in the International Arena), 161–64; Wu, *Shi nian lunzhan* (The Ten-Year Debate), vol. 1, 226–27.

30. Quoted from Li, *Waijiao wutai shang de xin Zhongguo lingxiu* (Leaders of New China in the International Arena), 164.

31. Fursenko, *Prezidium TsK KPSS: 1954–1964* (Presidium of the CC CPSU: 1954–1964), vol. 1, 390. By some sort of miracle, the record was preserved.

32. Quoted from Wu, *Shinian lunzhan* (The Ten-Year Debate), vol. 1, 227, 231–34; Mao, *Jianguo yilai Mao Zedong wengao* (Manuscripts of Mao Zedong from the Founding of the PRC), vol. 8, 599–602. See also Yang and Yan, *Deng Xiaoping nianpu: 1904–1974* (Chronological Biography of Deng Xiaoping: 1904–1974), vol. 3, 1520.

33. See Wu, *Shi nian lunzhan* (The Ten-Year Debate), vol. 1, 251.

34. Quoted from ibid., 251–52.

35. Quoted from ibid., 254–55; Deng, *Selected Works of Deng Xiaoping (1938–1965)*, 259–60.

36. See *Red Flag*, no. 8 (1960); *People's Daily*, Apr. 22, 1960; *Pravda*, Apr. 23, 1960.

37. See Glenn W. LaFantasie, ed., *Foreign Relations of the United States: 1958–1960*, vol. 19: *China* (Washington, DC: U.S. Government Printing Office, 1996), 710.

38. See Zubok, "Look What Chaos in the Beautiful Socialist Camp!" 156–57.

39. Fursenko, *Prezidium TsK KPSS: 1954–1964* (Presidium of the CC CPSU: 1954–1964), vol. 1, 443.

40. Quoted from Pantsov with Levine, *Mao*, 474|.

41. Quoted from Lorenz Lüthi, *The Sino-Soviet Split: Cold War in the Communist World* (Princeton, NJ: Princeton University Press, 2008), 173.

42. Westad, *Brothers in Arms*, 361–62.

43. See Lüthi, *Sino-Soviet Split*, 183–84; Yang and Yan, *Deng Xiaoping nianpu: 1904– 1974* (Chronological Biography of Deng Xiaoping: 1904–1974), vol. 3, 1571–73; Yang, *Yang Shangkun riji* (Diary of Yang Shangkun), vol. 1, 536–37.

44. Quoted from Li, *Waijiao wutai shang de xin Zhongguo lingxiu* (Leaders of New China in the International Arena), 167.

45. Yang, *Yang Shangkun riji* (Diary of Yang Shangkun), vol. 1, 541.

46. Li, *Waijiao wutai shang de xin Zhongguo lingxiu* (Leaders of New China in the International Arena), 167. See also Yang, *Yang Shangkun riji* (Diary of Yang Shangkun), vol. 1, 546.

47. Quoted from Li, *Waijiao wutai shang de xin Zhongguo lingxiu* (Leaders of New China in the International Arena), 172–74. See also Deng Xiaoping, "Deng Xiaoping's Talks with the Soviet Ambassador and Leadership, 1957–1963," *CWIHP Bulletin*, no. 10 (March 1998): 172–73.

48. Quoted from Li Yueran, "Li Yueran tan Deng Xiaoping" in (Li Yueran Speaks About Deng Xiaoping), Liu, Jintian, ed. *Huashuo Deng Xiaoping* (Stories About Deng Xiaoping) (Beijing: Zhongyang wenxian chubanshe, 2004), 176. See also Yang, *Yang Shangkun riji* (Diary of Yang Shangkun), vol. 1, 546.

49. Quoted from Li, *Waijiao wutai shang de xin Zhongguo lingxiu* (Leaders of New China in the International Arena), 168.

50. Quoted from ibid., 169–72.

51. Quoted from Yang and Yan, *Deng Xiaoping nianpu: 1904–1974* (Chronological Biography of Deng Xiaoping: 1904–1974), vol. 3, 1579.

52. See Yang, *Yang Shangkun riji* (Diary of Yang Shangkun), vol. 1, 551–77; Cui Ji, *Wo suo qinlide zhongsu da lunzhan* (The Great Polemic Between the USSR and the PRC as Part of My Own History) (Beijing: Renmin ribao chubanshe, 2009), 88–89.

53. Quoted from Li, *Waijiao wutai shang de xin Zhongguo lingxiu* (Leaders of New China in the Diplomatic Arena), 175–76; Liu Xiao, *Chushi Sulian ba nian* (Eight Years as Ambassador to the USSR) (Beijing: Zhonggong dangshi chubanshe, 1998), 121.

54. See Liu and Chen, *Liu Shaoqi nianpu: 1898–1969* (Chronological Biography of Liu Shaoqi: 1898–1969), vol. 2, 496–99; Yang and Yan, *Deng Xiaoping nianpu: 1904–1974* (Chronological Biography of Deng Xiaoping: 1904–1974), vol. 3, 1592–1603; Yang, *Yang Shangkun riji* (Diary of Yang Shangkun), vol. 1, 580–629.

55. Quoted from Westad, *Brothers in Arms*, 366.

56. See Lüthi, *Sino-Soviet Split*, 159.

57. See Roderick MacFarquhar, *The Origins of the Cultural Revolution*, vol. 3: *The Coming of the Cataclysm, 1961–1966* (New York: Columbia University Press, 1997), 323.

58. Quoted from Westad, *Brothers in Arms*, 371.

59. Confucius, *The Analects of Confucius*, 70.

60. See MacFarquhar, *Origins of the Cultural Revolution*, vol. 3, 324; Li and Ma, *Zhou Enlai nianpu (1949–1976)* (Chronological Biography of Zhou Enlai [1949–1976]), vol. 2, 366.

61. See David Wolff, "'One Finger's Worth of Historical Events': New Russian and Chinese Evidence on the Sino-Soviet Alliance and Split, 1948–1959," *CWIHP Working Paper*, no. 30 (August 2000), 63–64; MacFarquhar, *Origins of the Cultural Revolution*, vol. 3, 202.

62. See Li, *Private Life of Chairman Mao*, 339, 340.

63. See Yang Jisheng, *Mubei: Zhongguo liushi nian dai da jihuang jishi* (Tombstone: Unforgettable Facts About the Great Famine of the 1960s), vol. 2 (Hong Kong: Tian di tushu youxian gongsi, 2008), 875; Lüthi, *Sino-Soviet Split*, 158.

64. See Dikötter, *Mao's Great Famine*, x, 325. A Chinese researcher gives a more "modest" figure: thirty-six million. See Yang Jisheng, *The Great Chinese Famine, 1958–1962*, trans. Stacy Mosher and Guo Jian (New York: Farrar, Straus and Giroux, 2012), 430. Some other people give different figures: from twenty to thirty million. See in detail Pantsov with Levine, *Mao*, 475.

65. Borisov and Titarenko, *Vystupleniia Mao Tsze-duna, ranee ne publikovavshiesia v kitaiskoi pechati* (Speeches of Mao Zedong Previously Unpublished in the Chinese Press), series 3, 268, 272.

66. See Yang and Yan, *Deng Xiaoping nianpu: 1904–1974* (Chronological Biography of Deng Xiaoping: 1904–1974), vol. 3, 1621–23, 1628; Dikötter, *Mao's Great Famine*, 118–19.

67. Quoted from Wu, *Deng Xiaoping yu Zhuo Lin* (Deng Xiaoping and Zhuo Lin), 73.

68. Quoted from Yang and Yan, *Deng Xiaoping nianpu: 1904–1974* (Chronological Biography of Deng Xiaoping: 1904–1974), vol. 3, 1636–37.

69. Quoted from Li and Ma, *Zhou Enlai nianpu (1949–1976)* (Chronological Biography of Zhou Enlai [1949–1976]), vol. 2, 409. See also *Zhu De nianpu* (Chronological Biography of Zhu De), 478.

70. Mao, *Jianguo yilai Mao Zedong wengao* (Manuscripts of Mao Zedong from the Founding of the PRC), vol. 8, 273.

71. *Liu, Shaoqi xuanji* (Selected Works of Liu Shaoqi), vol. 2, 337.

72. Quoted from Yang and Yan, *Deng Xiaoping nianpu: 1904–1974* (Chronological Biography of Deng Xiaoping: 1904–1974), vol. 3, 1642.

73. Mao Zedong, *Mao Zedong wenji* (Works of Mao Zedong), vol. 8 (Beijing: Renmin chubanshe, 1999), 273.

74. Quoted from Li, *The Private Life of Chairman Mao*, 380.

75. Deng, *Selected Works of Deng Xiaoping*, vol. 2 *(1975–1982)*, 327–28.

CHAPTER 13

1. See MacFarquhar, *Origins of the Cultural Revolution*, vol. 3, 217.

2. Quoted from Bo Yibo, *Ruogan zhongda juece yu shijiande huigu* (Recollections of Several Important Decisions and Their Implementation), vol. 2 (Beijing: Zhongggong zhongyang dangxiao chubanshe), 1080.

3. Quoted from ibid.

4. Quoted from ibid., 1026–27.

5. Quoted from Sladkovskii, *Informatsionnyi biulleten'. Seriia A. Vypusk 2* (Information Bulletin: Series A: 2nd Installment), 184.

6. Liu, *Liu Shaoqi xuanji* (Selected Works of Liu Shaoqi), vol. 2, 419, 420–21. See also V. N. Usov, *KNR: Ot "bol'shogo skachka" k "kul'turnoi revoliutsii" (1960–1966)* (The PRC: From the Great Leap to the Cultural Revolution [1960–1966]), part 1 (Moscow: IDV RAN, 1998), 78; Huang Lingjun, "Liu Shaoqi yu dayuejin" (Liu Shaoqi and the Great Leap)," *Zhongguo xiandaishi* (*Contemporary History of China*), no. 7 (2003), 10.

7. Borisov and Titarenko, *Vystupleniia Mao Tsze-duna, ranee ne publikovavshie-sia v kitaiskoi pechati* (Speeches of Mao Zedong Previously Unpublished in the Chinese Press), series 4 (Moscow: Progress, 1976), 12, 19, 20, 29.

8. Deng, *Selected Works of Deng Xiaoping (1938–1965)*, 269–86. See also Bo, *Ruogan zhongda juece yu shijiande huigu* (Recollections of Several Important Decisions and Their Implementation), vol. 2, 1028.

9. Quoted from Gao Wenqian, *Zhou Enlai: The Last Perfect Revolutionary: A Biography* (New York: PublicAffairs, 2007), 96.

10. See Li, *Private Life of Chairman Mao*, 386.

11. See ibid., 386–87.

12. Borisov and Titarenko, *Vystupleniia Mao Tsze-duna, ranee ne publikovavshie-sia v kitaiskoi pechatii* (Speeches of Mao Zedong Previously Unpublished in the Chinese Press), series 4, 114.

13. See Pang and Jin, *Mao Zedong zhuan (1949–1976)* (Biography of Mao Zedong [1949–1976]), vol. 2, 1207–8, 1218; Zhu Jiamu, ed., *Chen Yun nianpu: 1905–1995* (Chronological Biography of Chen Yun: 1905–1995), vol. 3 (Beijing: Zhongyang wenxian chubanshe, 2000), 107–10; Becker, *Hungry Ghosts*, 156.

14. See Deng, *Selected Works of Deng Xiaoping (1938–1965)*, 293; Bo, *Ruogan zhongda juece yu shijiande huigu* (Recollections of Several Important Decisions and Their Implementation), vol. 2, 1078.

15. See Peng Dehuai, *Memuary marshala* (Memoirs of a Marshal), trans. A. V. Pantsov, V. N. Usov, and K. V. Shevelev (Moscow: Voenizdat, 1988), 16.

16. Quoted from Ma Qibin et al., eds., *Zhongguo gongchandang zhizheng sishi nian (1949–1989): Zengdingben* (Forty Years of the Leadership of the CCP [1949–1989]), rev. ed. (Beijing: Zhonggong dangshi chubanshe, 1991), 217.

17. Quoted from Li, *Private Life of Chairman Mao*, 390–91.

18. Quoted from Bo, *Ruogan zhongda juece yu shijiande huigu* (Recollections of Several Important Decisions and Their Implementation), vol. 2, 1084.

19. Quoted from ibid.

20. Quoted from Ma, *Zhongguo gongchandang zhizheng sishi nian (1949–1989): Zengdingben* (Forty Years of the Leadership of the CCP [1949–1989]), 217.

21. Quoted from Bo, *Ruogan zhongda juece yu shijiande huigu* (Recollections of Several Important Decisions and Their Implementation), vol. 2, 1084.

22. See Ma, *Zhongguo gongchandang zhizheng sishi nian (1949–1989): Zengdingben* (Forty Years of the Leadership of the CCP [1949–1989]), 217.

23. Deng, *Selected Works of Deng Xiaoping (1938–1965)*, 292–93.

24. Ibid., 306.

25. Quoted from Gao, *Zhou Enlai*, 98.

26. Quoted from Bo, *Ruogan zhongda juece yu shijiande huigu* (Recollections of Several Important Decisions and Their Implementation), vol. 2, 1086.

27. Quoted from Li, *The Private Life of Chairman Mao*, 392.

28. See Zhu, *Chen Yun nianpu: 1905–1995* (Chronological Biography of Chen Yun: 1905–1995), vol. 3, 120.

29. See Pang and Jin, *Mao Zedong zhuan (1949–1976)* (Biography of Mao Zedong [1949–1976]), vol. 2, 1232–33.

30. See Bo, *Ruogan zhongda juece yu shijiande huigu* (Recollections of Several Important Decisions and Their Implementation), vol. 2, 1086–87.

31. Ibid., 1086.

32. See MacFarquhar, *Origins of the Cultural Revolution*, vol. 3, 268.

33. Quoted from Bo, *Ruogan zhongda juece yu shijiande huigu* (Recollections of Several Important Decisions and Their Implementation), vol. 2, 1087; Yang, *Yang Shangkun riji* (Diary of Yang Shangkun), vol. 2 (Beijing: Zhongyang wenxian chubanshe, 2001), 196.

34. Quoted from Pang and Jin, *Mao Zedong zhuan (1949–1976)* (Biography of Mao Zedong [1949–1976]), vol. 2, 1234.

35. Borisov and Titarenko, *Vystupleniia Mao Tsze-duna, ranee ne publikovavshiesia v kitaiskoi pechati* (Speeches of Mao Zedong Previously Unpublished in the Chinese Press), series 4, 38–40.

36. Quoted from Lüthi, *Sino-Soviet Split*, 189.

37. Quoted from Khrushchev, *Memoirs of Nikita Khrushchev*, vol. 3, 502.

38. Fursenko, *Prezidium TsK KPSS: 1954–1964* (Presidium CC CPSU: 1954–1964), vol. 1, 498, 1088.

39. Quoted from Wu, *Shi nian lunzhan* (The Ten-Year Debate), vol. 1, 460.

40. Quoted from Lüthi, *Sino-Soviet Split*, 208.

41. Quoted from B. T. Kulik, *Sovetsko-kitaiskii raskol: Prichiny i posledstviia* (The Sino-Soviet Split: Causes and Consequences) (Moscow: IDV RAN, 2000), 317.

42. *XXII s"ezd Kommunisticheskoi partii Sovetskogo Soiuza: 17-31 oktiabria 1961 goda: Stenograficheskii otchet* (Twenty-second Congress of the Communist Party of the Soviet Union: Oct. 17–31, 1961: Stenographic Record), vol. 3 (Moscow: Gospolitizdat, 1962), 362.

43. Quoted from Wu, *Shi nian lunzhan* (The Ten-Year Debate), vol. 1, 480.

44. See Zhu Ruizhen, "Zhong-su fenliede genyuan" (Causes of the Sino-Soviet Split), in *Zhanhou zhongsu guanxi zouxiang (1945–1960)* (The Development of Sino-Soviet Relations after the War [1945–1960]), 99–100; Niu Jun, "1962: The

Eve of the Left Turn in China's Foreign Policy," *CWIHP Working Paper*, no. 48 (October 2005), 28–29; Lüthi, *Sino-Soviet Split*, 212–13.

45. Borisov and Titarenko, *Vystupleniia Mao Tsze-duna, ranee ne publikovavshiesia v kitaiskoi pechati* (Speeches of Mao Zedong Previously Unpublished in the Chinese Press), series 4, 38, 39.

46. Ibid., 47.

47. Mao Zedong, *Oblaka v snegu: Stikhotvoreniia v perevodakh Aleksandra Pantsova* (Clouds in the Snow: Poems in [Russian] Translation by Alexander Pantsov) (Moscow: "Veche," 2010), 85.

48. See Wu, *Shi nian lunzhan* (The Ten-Year Debate), vol. 2, 537–38; Bo, *Ruogan zhongda juece yu shijiande huigu* (Recollections of Several Important Decisions and Their Implementation), vol. 2, 1146.

49. Georgi Arbatov, *Zhizn', sobytiia, liudi: Avtobiografiia na fone istoricheskikh peremen* (Life, Events, People: An Autobiography Against the Background of Historical Changes) (Moscow: Liubimaia Rossiia, 2008), 99.

50. Georgi Arbatov, *Zatianuvsheesia vyzdorovlenie (1953–1985): Svidetel'stvo sovremennika* (A Lengthy Convalescence [1953–1985]: Testimony of a Contemporary) (Moscow: Mezhdunarodnye otnosheniia, 1991), 93. See also Georgii Arbatov, *The System: An Insider's Life in Soviet Politics* (New York: Times Books, 1992), 97–98.

51. It was not until October 16, 1964, that the Chinese conducted a successful test of a nuclear weapon.

52. See Wu, *Shi nian lunzhan* (The Ten-Year Debate), vol. 2, 602.

53. *Stenogramma vstrechi delegatsii Kommunisticheskoi partii Sovetskogo Soiuza i Kommunisticheskoi partii Kitaia 5–20 iulia 1963 g.* (Stenographic Record of the Meeting Between a Delegation of the Communist Party of the Soviet Union and the Communist Party of China, July 5–20, 1963). Moscow, part 1, *Former Archives of the Central Committee of the Socialist Unity Party of Germany*, 93. (We are thankful to V. M. Zubok who kindly presented us a copy of the document.).

54. Ibid., part 2, 294. See also Yang, *Yang Shangkun riji* (Diary of Yang Shangkun), vol. 2, 294–301; Wu, *Shi nian lunzhan* (The Ten-Year Debate), vol. 2, 601–23; Li, *Waijiao wutai shang de xin* Zhongguo *lingxiu* (Leaders of New China in the Diplomatic Arena), 206–11.

55. *Stenogramma vstrechi delegatsii Kommunisticheskoi partii Sovetskogo Soiuza i Kommuniticheskoi partii Kitaia 5–20 iulia 1963 g. Zhongguo* (Stenogram of the Meeting Between a Delegation of the Communist Party of the Soviet Union and the Communist Party of China, July 5–20, 1963), part 2, 317.

56. Ibid., 317, 318.

57. Ibid., 329. See the communiqué of the negotiations in *Za splochenost' mezhdunarodnogo kommunistichekogo dvizheniia: Dokumenty i materialy* (For the Unity of the International Communist Movement: Documents and Materials) (Moscow: Politizdat, 1964), 66.

58. See Yan, "Yan Mingfu tan Deng Xiaoping" (Yan Mingfu Speaks About Deng Xiaoping), 170; Yang, *Yang Shangkun riji* (Diary of Yang Shangkun), vol. 2, 301; Yang and Yan, *Deng Xiaoping nianpu: 1904–1974* (Chronological Biography of Deng Xiaoping: 1904–1974), vol. 3, 1763–66.

59. Borisov and Titarenko, *Vystupleniia Mao Tsze-duna, ranee ne publikovavshiesia v kitaiskoi pechati* (Speeches of Mao Zedong Previously Unpublished in the Chinese press), series 4, 170.

60. See Yang, *Yang Shangkun riji* (Diary of Yang Shangkun), vol. 2, 294–301; Yan, "Yan Mingfu tan Deng Xiaoping" (Yan Mingfu Speaks About Deng Xiaoping), 170–71; Wu, *Shi nian lunzhan* (The Ten-Year Debate), vol. 2, 623.

61. See *Otkrytoe pis'mo Tsentral'nogo Komiteta Kommunisticheskoi partii Sovetskogo Soiuza partiinym organizatsiiam, vsem kommunistam Sovetskogo Soiuza* (Open Letter of the Central Committee of the Communist Party of the Soviet Union to All Party Organizations and Communists in the Soviet Union) (Moscow: Gospolitizdat, 1963).

62. Li, *Waijiao wutai shang de xin Zhongguo lingxiu* (Leaders of New China in the Diplomatic Arena), 211. See also Yang and Yan, *Deng Xiaoping nianpu: 1904–1974* (Chronological Biography of Deng Xiaoping: 1904–1974), vol. 3, 1766–67.

63. Fursenko, *Prezidium TsK KPSS: 1954–1964* (Presidium of the CC CPSU: 1954–1964), vol. 1, 696.

CHAPTER 14

1. See Richard Baum and Frederick C. Teiwes, *Ssu-Ch'ing: The Socialist Education Movement of 1962–1966* (Berkeley: University of California Press), 1968, 58–71.

2. Deng, *Wode zishu (Zhailu)* (My Autobiographical Notes [Excerpts]).

3. Quoted by Baum and Teiwes, *Ssu-ch'ing*, 77.

4. See MacFarquhar, *Origins of the Cultural Revolution*, vol. 3, 344–48, 426, 606.

5. Borisov and Titarenko, *Vystupleniia Mao Tsze-duna, ranee ne publikovavshiesia v kitaiskoi pechati* (Speeches of Mao Zedong Previously Unpublished in the Chinese Press), series 5, 198.

6. Ibid., series 4, 183–184.

7. Ibid., series 5, 133.

8. See *History of the Chinese Communist Party—A Chronology of Events (1919–1990)* (Beijing: Foreign Languages Press, 1991), 311.

9. See Wu, *Yi Mao zhuxi* (Remembering Chairman Mao), 148.

10. See Baum and Teiwes, *Ssu-ch'ing*, 102–17.

11. Borisov and Titarenko, *Vystupleniia Mao Tsze-duna, ranee ne publikovavshiesia v kitaiskoi pechati* (Speeches of Mao Zedong Previously Unpublished in the Chinese Press), series 4, 183–200.

12. Quoted from Bo, *Ruogan zhongda juece yu shijiande huigu* (Recollections of Several Important Decisions and Their Implementation), vol. 2, 1131; MacFarquhar,

Origins of the Cultural Revolution, vol. 3, 423; Jin, *Liu Shaoqi zhuan* (Biography of Liu Shaoqi), vol. 2, 890.

13. Mao Zedong, *Miscellany of Mao Tse-tung Thought (1949–1968)*, part 2 (Springfield, VA: Joint Publications Research Service, 1974), 427; Yang, *Yang Shangkun riji* (Diary of Yang Shangkun), vol. 1, 476.

14. Borisov and Titarenko, *Vystupleniia Mao Tsze-duna, ranee ne publikovavshiesia v kitaiskoi pechati* (Speeches of Mao Zedong Previously Unpublished in the Chinese Press), series 4, 206–7; Li, *Private Life of Chairman Mao*, 416–17; Bo, *Ruogan zhongda juece yu shijiande huigu* (Recollections of Several Important Decisions and Their Implementation), vol. 2, 1131; Pang and Jin, *Mao Zedong zhuan (1949–1976)* (Biography of Mao Zedong [1949–1976]), vol. 2, 1266–1375; MacFarquhar, *Origins of the Cultural Revolution*, vol. 3, 424–25.

15. Quoted from Baum and Teiwes, *Ssu-ch'ing*, 120.

16. Edgar Snow, *The Long Revolution* (New York: Random House, 1972), 17.

17. Sladkovskii, *Informatsionnyi biulleten'. Seriia A. Vypusk 2* (Information Bulletin: Series A: 2nd Installment), 62; Witke, *Comrade Chiang Ch'ing*, 310, 332.

18. See Sladkovskii, *Informatsionnyi biulleten'. Seriia A. Vypusk 2* (Information Bulletin: Series A: 2nd Installment), 68; Franz, *Deng*, 180.

19. See MacFarquhar, *Origins of the Cultural Revolution*, vol. 3, 252–56, 443–47.

20. Quoted from V. N. Usov, *KNR: Ot "bol'shogo skachka" k "k'ul'turnoi revoliutsii" (1960–1966)* (The PRC: From the Great Leap to the Cultural Revolution, 1960–1966), part 2, 186.

21. Borisov and Titarenko, *Vystupleniia Mao Tsze-duna, ranee ne publikovavshie-sia v kitaiskoi* pechati (Speeches of Mao Zedong Previously Unpublished in the Chinese Press), series 5, 153; Snow, *The Long Revolution*, 169.

22. Borisov and Titarenko, *Vystupleniia Mao Tsze-duna, ranee ne publikovavshiesia v kitaiskoi pechati* (Speeches of Mao Zedong Previously Unpublished in the Chinese Press), series 4, 154, 194–95.

23. See Roderick MacFarquhar and Michael Schoenhals, *Mao's Last Revolution* (Cambridge, MA: Belknap Press of Harvard University Press, 2006), 17.

24. Sladkovskii, *Informatsionnyi biulleten'. Seriia A. Vypusk 2* (Information Bulletin: Series A: 2nd Installment), 68. See also *Velikaia proletarskaia kul'turnaia revoliutsiia (vazhneishie dokumenty)* (The Great Proletarian Cultural Revolution [Key Documents]) (Beijing: Izdatel'stvo literatury na inostrannykh iazykakh, 1970), 99.

25. Quoted from Andrew Hall Wedeman, *The East Wind Subsides: Chinese Foreign Policy and the Origins of the Cultural Revolution* (Washington, DC: Washington Institute Press, 1988), 176.

26. Quoted from Pang and Jin, *Mao Zedong zhuan (1949–1976)* (Biography of Mao Zedong [1949–1976]), vol. 2, 1395.

27. Quoted from Deng, *Deng Xiaoping and the Cultural Revolution*, 3.

Notes to Pages 241–245

501

28. Quoted from Pang and Jin, *Mao Zedong zhuan (1949–1976)* (Biography of Mao Zedong [1949–1976]), vol. 2, 1399.

29. Borisov and Titarenko, *Vystupleniia Mao Tsze-duna, ranee ne publikovavshiesia v kitaiskoi pechati* (Speeches of Mao Zedong Previously Unpublished in the Chinese Press), series 5, 154.

30. Quoted from Deng, *Deng Xiaoping and the Cultural Revolution*, 3–4.

31. Quoted from Pang and Jin, *Mao Zedong zhuan (1949–1976)* (Biography of Mao Zedong [1949–1976]), vol. 2, 1399.

32. Quoted from MacFarquhar and Schoenhals, *Mao's Last Revolution*, 18.

33. Sladkovskii, *Informatsionnyi biulleten'. Seriia A. Vypusk 2* (Information Bulletin: Series A: 2nd Installment), 68.

34. See MacFarquhar and Schoenhals, *Mao's Last Revolution*, 18; Wedeman, *The East Wind Subsides*, 223–24.

35. Sladkovskii, *Informatsionnyi biulleten'. Seriia A. Vypusk 2* (Information Bulletin: Series A: 2nd Installment), 68.

36. Quoted from MacFarquhar and Schoenhals, *Mao's Last Revolution*, 28.

37. Borisov and Titarenko, *Vystupleniia Mao Tsze-duna, ranee ne publikovavshiesia v kitaiskoi pechati* (Speeches of Mao Zedong Previously Unpublished in the Chinese Press), series 5, 195.

38. See Wu, *Mao Zedong guanghui licheng dituji* (Atlas of Mao Zedong's Glorious Historical Path), 122, 125. According to another source, Mao arrived in Wuhan on Jan. 5, 1966. See Pang and Jin, *Mao Zedong zhuan (1949–1976)* (Biography of Mao Zedong [1949–1976]), vol. 2, 1402.

39. M. I. Sladkovskii, ed., *Informatsionnyi biulleten'. Seriia A. "Kul'turnaia revoliutsiia v Kitae" (perevod s kitaisogo). Vypusk 12: Dokumenty. Sbornik, fevral' 1966—fevral' 1967 gg.* (Information Bulletin. Series A: The Cultural Revolution in China. The 12th installment: Documents, Collection: February 1966–February 1967) (Moscow: IDV AN SSSR, 1972), 1, 5, 7. For the text of the theses, see also Sladkovskii, *Informatsionnyi biulleten'. Seriia A. Vypusk 2* (Information Bulletin: Series A: 2nd Installment), 157–63.

40. Quoted from Li, *Private Life of Chairman Mao*, 448. See also *History of the Chinese Communist Party—A Chronology of Events (1919–1990)*, 320.

41. Quoted from Pang and Jin, *Mao Zedong zhuan (1949–1976)* (Biography of Mao Zedong [1949–1976]), vol. 2, 1402.

42. See MacFarquhar and Schoenhals, *Mao's Last Revolution*, 31.

43. Borisov and Titarenko, *Vystupleniia Mao Tsze-duna, ranee ne publikovavshiesia v kitaiskoi pechati* (Speeches of Mao Zedong Previously Unpublished in the Chinese Press), series 5, 62–63, 66, 68.

44. Quoted from Wu, *Yi Mao zhuxi* (Remembering Chairman Mao), 152.

45. Quoted from Pang and Jin, *Mao Zedong zhuan (1949–1976)* (Biography of Mao Zedong [1949–1976]), vol. 2, 1404; See also MacFarquhar and Schoenhals, *Mao's Last Revolution*, 32, 491.

46. See MacFarquhar and Schoenhals, *Mao's Last Revolution*, 32.

47. See Chen Qingquan and Song Guangwei, *Lu Dingyi zhuan* (Biography of Lu Dingyi) (Beijing: Zhonggong dangshi chubanshe, 1999), 496–508.

48. See *Lichnoe delo Mao Tszeduna* (Personal File of Mao Zedong), RGASPI, collection 495, inventory 225, file 71, vol. 3, sheet 77; *History of the Chinese Communist Party—A Chronology of Events (1919–1990)*, 324–25; Chen Boda, *Chen Boda zuihou koushu huiyi* (The Last Oral Reminiscences of Chen Boda), rev. ed. (Hong Kong: Xingke'er chubanshe youxian gongsi, 2005), 305; Chen Boda, *Chen Boda yi gao: Yuzhong zishu ji qita* (Manuscripts of Chen Boda: Autobiographical Notes from Prison and Other [Materials] (Hong Kong: Tiandi tushu youxian gongsi, 1998), 87–88.

49. *CCP Documents of the Great Proletarian Cultural Revolution, 1966–1967* (Hong Kong: Union Research Institute, 1968), 27.

50. Ibid., 28.

51. O. Arne Westad et al., eds. "77 Conversations Between Chinese and Foreign Leaders on the Wars in Indochina, 1964–1977" *CWIHP Working Paper*, no. 22 (May 1998), 130–31.

52. Nie Yuanzi et al., "Song Shuo, Lu Ping, Peng Peiyuan zai wenhua gemingzhong jiujing gan shenma?" (What Are Song Shuo, Lu Ping, and Peng Peiyuan Really Doing with Respect to the Cultural Revolution?), *People's Daily*, June 2, 1966.

53. See Deng, *Deng Xiaoping and the Cultural Revolution*, 8.

54. Quoted from ibid.

55. Ibid., 6, 15.

56. Sladkovskii, *Informatsionnyi biulleten'. Seriia A. Vypusk 2* (Information Bulletin: Series A: 2nd Installment), 73.

57. See Liu and Chen, *Liu Shaoqi nianpu: 1898–1967* (Chronological Biography of Liu Shaoqi: 1898–1967), vol. 2, 640; MacFarquhar and Schoenhals, *Mao's Last Revolution*, 65, 66.

58. See Barbara Barnouin and Yu Changgen, *Ten Years of Turbulence: The Chinese Cultural Revolution* (London: Kegan Paul International, 1993), 75; Lowell Dittmer, *Liu Shao-ch'i and the Chinese Revolution: The Politics of Mass Criticism* (Berkeley: University of California Press, 1974), 81. See also Liu and Chen, *Liu Shaoqi nianpu: 1898–1969* (Chronological Biography of Liu Shaoqi: 1898–1969), vol. 2, 641.

59. Quoted from Pang and Jin, *Mao Zedong zhuan (1949–1976)* (Biography of Mao Zedong [1949–1976]), vol. 2, 1415.

60. See M. I. Sladkovskii, ed., *Informatsionnyi Biulleten'. Seriia A. "Kul'turnaia revoliutsiia" v Kitae. Dokumenty i materialy (perevod s kitaisogo). Vypusk 7: Vystupleniia Chzhou En'-laia v period "kul'turnoi revoliutsii" (1966)* (Information Bulletin. Series A. The Cultural Revolution in China. Documents and Materials Translated from Chinese. The 7th installment: Speeches of Zhou Enlai during the Cultural Revolution [1966]) (Moscow: IDV AN SSSR, 1971), 6.

61. Quoted from MacFarquhar and Schoenhals, *Mao's Last Revolution*, 77.

62. Quoted from Deng, *Deng Xiaoping and the Cultural Revolution*, 16. See also Liu and Chen, *Liu Shaoqi nianpu: 1898–1969* (Chronological Biography of Liu Shaoqi: 1898–1969), vol. 2, 645.

63. Borisov and Titarenko, *Vystupleniia Mao Tsze-duna, ranee ne publikovavshiesia v kitaiskoi pechati* (Speeches of Mao Zedong Previously Unpublished in the Chinese Press), series 5, 84.

64. Ibid., 84, 85.

65. Ibid., 129, 130. See also MacFarquhar and Schoenhals, *Mao's Last Revolution*, 84.

66. Deng, *Deng Xiaoping and the Cultural Revolution*, 17.

67. Quoted from ibid., 18.

68. Rittenberg and Bennett, *The Man Who Stayed Behind*, 313.

69. See Yang and Yan, *Deng Xiaoping nianpu: 1904–1974* (Chronological Biography of Deng Xiaoping: 1904–1974), vol. 3, 1926.

70. *CCP Documents of the Great Proletarian Cultural Revolution, 1966–1967*, 42.

71. See Pang and Jin, *Mao Zedong zhuan (1949–1976)* (Biography of Mao Zedong [1949–1976]), vol. 2, 1428–29; Liu and Chen, *Liu Shaoqi nianpu: 1898–1969* (Chronological Biography of Liu Shaoqi: 1898–1969), vol. 2, 649.

72. Westad et al., "77 Conversations Between Chinese and Foreign Leaders on the Wars in Indochina," 133.

73. See MacFarquhar and Schoenhals, *Mao's Last Revolution*, 94.

74. See *Lichnoe delo Mao Tszeduna* (Personal File of Mao Zedong), RGASPI, collection 495, inventory 225, file 71, vol. 3, sheets 104–5; Liao Gailong et al. eds., *Mao Zedong baike quanshu* (Encyclopedia of Mao Zedong), vol. 6 (Beijing: Guangming ribao chubanshe, 2003), 3215; *History of the Chinese Communist Party—A Chronology of Events (1919–1990)*, 329; Pang and Jin, *Mao Zedong zhuan (1949–1976)* (Biography of Mao Zedong [1949–1976]), vol. 2, 1429.

75. Deng, *Deng Xiaoping and the Cultural Revolution*, 22.

76. See Yang and Yan, *Deng Xiaoping nianpu: 1904–1974* (Chronological Biography of Deng Xiaoping: 1904–1974), vol. 3, 1930.

77. Quoted from ibid., 1932; Liao, *Mao Zedong baike quanshu* (Encyclopedia of Mao Zedong), vol. 6, 3219; *History of the Chinese Communist Party—A Chronology of Events (1919–1990)*, 331.

78. Quoted from MacFarquhar and Schoenhals, *Mao's Last Revolution*, 138.

79. Deng, *Deng Xiaoping and the Cultural Revolution*, 28.

80. Quoted from ibid.

81. Borisov and Titarenko, *Vystupleniia Mao Tsze-duna, ranee ne publikovavshiesia v kitaiskoi pechati* (Speeches of Mao Zedong Previously Unpublished in the Chinese Press), series 5, 126.

82. Quoted from Yang and Yan, *Deng Xiaoping nianpu: 1904–1974* (Chronological Biography of Deng Xiaoping: 1904–1974), vol. 3, 1934.

83. See Letter from Ezra F. Vogel to Alexander V. Pantsov, Mar. 17, 2011.

84. See Yang and Yan, *Deng Xiaoping nianpu: 1904–1974* (Chronological Biography of Deng Xiaoping: 1904–1974), vol. 3, 1935.

85. Confucius, *The Analects of Confucius*, 43.

CHAPTER 15

1. Quoted from Wu, *Deng Xiaoping yu Zhuo Lin* (Deng Xiaoping and Zhuo Lin), 103.

2. Quoted from ibid.

3. Deng, *Deng Xiaoping and the Cultural Revolution*, 28.

4. Ibid., 40, 81.

5. See MacFarquhar and Schoenhals, *Mao's Last Revolution*, 124–25; Pang and Jin, *Mao Zedong zhuan (1949–1976)* (Biography of Mao Zedong [1949–1976]), vol. 2, 1438.

6. Quoted from MacFarquhar and Schoenhals, *Mao's Last Revolution*, 110.

7. Quoted from ibid., 126.

8. *CCP Documents of the Great Proletarian Cultural Revolution, 1966–1967*, 50.

9. Quoted from *History of the Chinese Communist Party—A Chronology of Events (1919–1990)*, 334.

10. See MacFarquhar and Schoenhals, *Mao's Last Revolution*, 165.

11. Mao, *Jianguo yilai Mao Zedong wengao* (Manuscripts of Mao Zedong from the Founding of the PRC), vol. 12, 186–87; Pang and Jin, *Mao Zedong zhuan (1949–1976)* (Biography of Mao Zedong [1949–1976]), vol. 2, 1466.

12. See Yang and Yan, *Deng Xiaoping nianpu: 1904–1974* (Chronological Biography of Deng Xiaoping: 1904–1974), vol. 3, 1936; Deng Maomao, *Wode fuqin Deng Xiaoping: "Wenge" suiyue* (My Father Deng Xiaoping: Years of the Cultural Revolution) (Beijing: Zhongyang wenxian chubanshe, 2000), 40.

13. Quoted from Deng, *Deng Xiaoping and the Cultural Revolution*, 36.

14. See ibid., 37; Yang and Yan, *Deng Xiaoping nianpu: 1904–1974* (Chronological Biography of Deng Xiaoping: 1904–1974), vol. 2, 1937.

15. See Deng, *Deng Xiaoping and the Cultural Revolution*, 37; Yang and Yan, *Deng Xiaoping nianpu: 1904–1974* (Chronological Biography of Deng Xiaoping: 1904–1974), vol. 3, 1937.

16. See Deng, *Deng Xiaoping and the Cultural Revolution*, 42–43.

17. See Yang and Yan, *Deng Xiaoping nianpu: 1904–1974* (Chronological Biography of Deng Xiaoping: 1904–1974), vol. 3, 1938.

18. Quoted from Deng, *Deng Xiaoping and the Cultural Revolution*, 44.

19. Quoted from Pang and Jin, *Mao Zedong zhuan (1949–1976)* (Biography of Mao Zedong [1949–1976]), vol. 2, 1490.

20. Quoted from Deng, *Deng Xiaoping and the Cultural Revolution*, 39.

21. See Yang and Yan, *Deng Xiaoping nianpu: 1904–1974* (Chronological Biography of Deng Xiaoping: 1904–1974), vol. 3, 1938–42, 1944, 1946–47.

22. Deng, *Deng Xiaoping and the Cultural Revolution*, 45–46.

23. See Yang and Yan, *Deng Xiaoping nianpu: 1904–1974* (Chronological Biography of Deng Xiaoping: 1904–1974), vol. 3, 1939.

24. See Franz, *Deng Xiaoping*, 201.

25. See Wu, *Deng Xiaoping yu Zhuo Lin* (Deng Xiaoping and Zhuo Lin), 111; Deng, *Deng Xiaoping and the Cultural Revolution*, 57, 150.

26. Quoted from Deng, *Deng Xiaoping and the Cultural Revolution*, 53.

27. Quoted from ibid.

28. Quoted from Yang and Yan, *Deng Xiaoping nianpu: 1904–1974* (Chronological Biography of Deng Xiaoping: 1904–1974), vol. 3, 1944.

29. Deng, *Wode zishu (Zhailu)* (My Autobiographical Notes [Excerpts]).

30. Quoted from Yang and Yan, *Deng Xiaoping nianpu: 1904–1974* (Chronological Biography of Deng Xiaoping: 1904–1974), vol. 3, 1946.

31. Quoted from *Velikaia proletarskaia kul'turnaia revoliutsiia (vazhneishie dokumenty)* (The Great Proletarian Cultural Revolution [Key Documents]), 167.

32. Quoted from Yang and Yan, *Deng Xiaoping nianpu: 1904–1974* (Chronological Biography of Deng Xiaoping: 1904–1974), vol. 3, 1946.

33. Quoted from ibid., 1947.

34. Quoted from ibid., 1948; Deng, *Deng Xiaoping and the Cultural Revolution*, 101.

35. Quoted from Deng, *Deng Xiaoping and the Cultural Revolution*, 103.

36. Quoted from ibid., 81.

37. For more details see ibid., 103–5, 108, 109.

38. *Yongyuande Xiaoping* (The Unforgettable Xiaoping), 46.

39. See Yang and Yan, *Deng Xiaoping nianpu: 1904–1974* (Chronological Biography of Deng Xiaoping: 1904–1974), vol. 3, 1948; Deng, *Xiaoping and the Cultural Revolution*, 124.

40. See *Geroi ostrova Damanskii* (Heroes of Damansky Island) (Moscow: "Molodaia gvardiia," 1969); Christian F. Osterman, "East German Documents on the Border Conflict, 1969," *CWIHP Bulletin*, nos. 6–7, (1995–96), 188–90; Krivosheev, *Grif sekretnosti snyat* (The Stamp of Secrecy Is Removed), 398; Clodfelter, *Warfare and Armed Conflict*, 676; D. S. Riabushkin, *Mify Damanskogo* (Myths of Damansky) (Moscow: AST, 2004), 73–75, 78–81.

41. Borisov and Titarenko, *Vystupleniia Mao Tsze-duna, ranee ne publikovavshiesia v kitaiskoi pechati* (Speeches of Mao Zedong Previously Unpublished in the Chinese Press), series 6 (Moscow: Progress, 1976), 266.

42. See Barnouin and Yu, *Ten Years of Turbulence*, 91.

43. See Liu Shaoqi, *Liu Shaoqi zishu* (Autobiographical Notes of Liu Shaoqi) (Beijing: Jiefangjun wenyi chubanshe, 2002), 179–254; Wang Guangmei and Liu Yuan, *Ni suo bu zhidaode Liu Shaoqi* (The Unknown Liu Shaoqi) (Zhengzhou: Henan renmin chubanshe, 2000); Liu and Chen, *Liu Shaoqi nianpu: 1898–1969* (Chronological Biography of Liu Shaoqi: 1898–1969), vol. 2, 661; Yen Chia-chi and Kao Kao, *The Ten-Year History of the Chinese Cultural Revolution* (Taipei: Institute of Current China Studies, 1988), 168.

44. Quoted from Deng, *Deng Xiaoping and the Cultural Revolution*, 109–10.
45. There were so many goods that the pilots could take only half; the plane could not set off with such a heavy load.
46. Ibid., 108.
47. See ibid., 127–32; Wu, *Deng Xiaoping yu Zhuo Lin* (Deng Xiaoping and Zhuo Lin), 107–11; *Yongyuande Xiaoping* (The Unforgettable Xiaoping), 40–52; Yang and Yan, *Deng Xiaoping nianpu: 1904–1974* (Chronological Biography of Deng Xiaoping: 1904–1974), vol. 3, 1949–54; *Deng Xiaoping yu xiandai Zhongguo* (Deng Xiaoping and Contemporary China), 94–99; Xiong Min and Mei Biao, "Huiyi Deng Xiaoping zai Jiangxi Xinjian de yiduan rizi—fangwen Luo Peng tanhualu" (Remembering the Days Spent with Deng Xiaoping in Xinjian [County] of Jiangxi: Notes of a Conversation with Luo Peng), in Wei Renzheng, ed., *Deng Xiaoping zai Jiangxi derizi* (The Days Deng Xiaoping Spent in Jiangxi) (Beijing: Zhonggong dangshi chubanshe, 1997), 134–38.
48. Quoted from Deng, *Deng Xiaoping and the Cultural Revolution*, 130.
49. See ibid., 130, 149–51, 165–66, 173, 198–200; Yang and Yan, *Deng Xiaoping nianpu: 1904–1974* (Chronological Biography of Deng Xiaoping: 1904–1974), vol. 3, 1950, 1953–55, 1958–59.
50. Deng, *Deng Xiaoping and the Cultural Revolution*, 179–80.
51. On the fall of Chen Boda, see Pantsov with Levine, *Mao*, 549.
52. For more details see ibid., 547–51.
53. Quoted from Deng, *Deng Xiaoping and the Cultural Revolution*, 184.
54. Quoted from ibid., 184–87.
55. Ibid., 69, 184.
56. Quoted from ibid., 193.
57. Quoted from ibid., 201.
58. Deng, *Deng Xiaoping gei Mao zhuxi xin (1972 nian 8 yue 3 ri)* (Deng Xiaoping's Letter to Chairman Mao [Aug. 3, 1972]).
59. Mao, *Jianguo yilai Mao Zedong wengao* (Manuscripts of Mao Zedong from the Founding of the PRC), vol. 13, 308.
60. Witke, *Comrade Chiang Ch'ing*, 362, 363.
61. See Deng, *Deng Xiaoping and the Cultural Revolution*, 238; Xu and Mei, "Huiyi Deng Xiaoping zai Jiangxi Xinjian deyiduan rizi—fangwen Luo Peng tanhualu" (Remembering the Days Spent with Deng Xiaoping in Xinjian [County] of Jiangxi: Notes of a Conversation with Luo Peng), 138.
62. Quoted from Deng, *Deng Xiaoping and the Cultural Revolution*, 226.

CHAPTER 16

1. Deng, *Deng Xiaoping and the Cultural Revolution*, 240.
2. Quoted from ibid., 220.

3. See Mao, *Jianguo yilai Mao Zedong wengao* (Manuscripts of Mao Zedong from the Founding of the PRC), vol. 13, 347–48; Yang and Yan, *Deng Xiaoping nianpu: 1904–1974* (Chronological Biography of Deng Xiaoping: 1904–1974), vol. 3, 1972.

4. Quoted from Yang and Yan, *Deng Xiaoping nianpu: 1904–1974* (Chronological Biography of Deng Xiaoping: 1904–1974), vol. 3, 1973.

5. Quoted from Henry A. Kissinger, *White House Years* (Boston: Little, Brown, 1979), 1492.

6. See Franz, *Deng Xiaoping*, 225–26; Yang, *Deng Xiaoping*, 174.

7. See Deng, *Deng Xiaoping and the Cultural Revolution*, 245.

8. See Gao, *Zhou Enlai*, 235–36, 260–62; Zhang Yufeng, "Neskol'ko shtrikhov k kartine poslednikh let zhizni Mao Tszeduna, Chzhou En'laia" (Some Brush Strokes Toward a Picture of the Last Years of Mao Zedong and Zhou Enlai), in Yu. M. Galenovich, *Smert' Mao Tszeduna* (The Death of Mao Zedong) (Moscow: Izd-vo "Izograf," 2005), 81.

9. For more details, see Wang Ting, *Chairman Hua: Leader of the Chinese Communists* (Montreal: McGill-Queen's University Press, 1980); Robert Weatherley, *Mao's Forgotten Successor: The Political Career of Hua Guofeng* (New York: Palgrave Macmillan, 2010).

10. Mao, *Jianguo yilai Mao Zedong wengao* (Manuscripts of Mao Zedong from the Founding of the PRC), vol. 13, 356–57.

11. See Gao, *Zhou Enlai*, 239.

12. See *History of the Chinese Communist Party—A Chronology of Events (1919–1990)*, 385.

13. See *The Tenth National Congress of the Communist Party of China (Documents)* (Peking: Foreign Languages Press, 1973); *Lichnoe delo Mao Tszeduna* (Personal File of Mao Zedong), RGASPI, collection 495, inventory 225, file 71, vol. 6, sheets 257–60.

14. See Yang and Yan, *Deng Xiaoping nianpu: 1904–1974* (Chronological Biography of Deng Xiaoping: 1904–1974), vol. 3, 1978.

15. Quoted from Deng, *Deng Xiaoping and the Cultural Revolution*, 252.

16. See William Burr, ed., *The Kissinger Transcripts: The Top Secret Talks with Beijing and Moscow* (New York: New Press, 1998), 166–216; Li and Ma, *Zhou Enlai nianpu (1949–1976)* (Chronological Biography of Zhou Enlai [1949–1976])), vol. 3, 632–34; Gao, *Zhou Enlai*, 239–42.

17. Burr, *The Kissinger Transcripts*, 205.

18. Quoted from Gao, *Zhou Enlai*, 241.

19. Quoted from Yang and Yan, *Deng Xiaoping nianpu: 1904–1974* (Chronological Biography of Deng Xiaoping: 1904–1974), vol. 3, 1990; Gao, *Zhou Enlai*, 246.

20. Quoted from Deng, *Deng Xiaoping and the Cultural Revolution*, 256.

21. Gao, *Zhou Enlai*, 244.

22. Quoted from ibid.

23. Deng, *Selected Works of Deng Xiaoping*, vol. 2 *(1975–1982)*, 329–30.

24. See Li and Ma, *Zhou Enlai nianpu (1949–1976)* (Chronological Biography of Zhou Enlai [1949–1976]), vol. 3, 634–35.

25. Quoted from Yang and Yan, *Deng Xiaoping nianpu: 1904–1974* (Chronological Biography of Deng Xiaoping: 1904–1984), vol. 3, 1991–92. Also see Deng, *Deng Xiaoping and the Cultural Revolution*, 259, for a slightly different translation.

26. Borisov and Titarenko, *Vystupleniia Mao Tsze-duna, ranee ne publikovavshie-sia v kitaiskoi pechati* (Speeches of Mao Zedong Previously Unpublished in the Chinese Press), series 6, 283; Yang and Yan, *Deng Xiaoping nianpu: 1904–1974* (Chronological Biography of Deng Xiaoping: 1904–1974), vol. 3, 1993.

27. *Vypiska iz materialov posol'stva SSSP v Kitae, vkh. no. 05220 ot 11 fevralia 1975 g. (Zapis' besedy s poslom DRV v KNR Nguyen Chan Vinem i sovetnikom-poslannikom posol'stva DRV Nguyen T'enom 30. V. 1975 g.* (Excerpt from Materials of the USSR Embassy in the PRC, no. 05220, Feb. 11, 1975 [Notes of a Conversation with DRV Ambassador Nguyen Chang Vinh and DRV Minister Counselor Nguyen Tien, May 30, 1975]), RGASPI, collection 495, inventory 225, file 2, vol. 3, sheet 12; *Vypiska iz materialov posol'stva SSSR v SShA, vkh. no. 16203, 26. IV. 1974 g. (Zapis' besedy s nauchnym sotrudnikom "Rend korporeishen' W. Whitsonom 16. IV. 1974 g.* (Excerpt from Materials of the USSR Embassy in the U.S.A., no. 16203, Apr. 26, 1974 [Notes of a Conversation with Rand Corporation Researcher W. Whitson, Apr. 16, 1974]), ibid., 28. See also Gao, *Zhou Enlai*, 245.

28. See *Lichnoe delo Chzhou En'laia* (Personal File of Zhou Enlai), RGASPI, collection 495, inventory 225, file 2, vol. 3, sheet 17.

29. See Yang and Yan, *Deng Xiaoping nianpu: 1904–1974* (Chronological Biography of Deng Xiaoping: 1904–1974), vol. 3, 2004.

30. *Vypiska iz soobshcheniia sovposla v Pekine (vkh. no. 010324 ot 5 aprelia 1974 g.)* (Excerpt from a Report by the Soviet Ambassador in Beijing. [No. 010324, Apr. 5, 1974]), RGASPI, collection 495, inventory 225, file 2, vol. 3, sheet 31.

31. Mao, *Jianguo yilai Mao Zedong wengao* (Manuscripts of Mao Zedong from the Founding of the PRC), vol. 13, 373.

32. See Mao, *Mao Zedong wenji* (Works of Mao Zedong), vol. 8, 441–42; Mao, *Jianguo yilai Mao Zedong wengao* (Manuscripts of Mao Zedong from the Founding of the PRC), vol. 13, 379–82.

33. Alexander V. Pantsov's interview with Steven I. Levine in Columbus, OH, Jan. 25, 2012.

34. See Mao, *Jianguo yilai Mao Zedong wengao* (Manuscripts of Mao Zedong from the Founding of the PRC), vol. 13, 386.

35. Deng Xiaoping, *Speech by Chairman of Delegation of the People's Republic of China, Teng Hsiao-p'ing, at the Special Session of the U.N. General Assembly* (Peking: Foreign Languages Press, 1974), 2.

36. Burr, *The Kissinger Transcripts*, 273.

37. Ibid., 270, 272, 275, 317.

38. Henry A. Kissinger, *Years of Renewal* (New York: Simon & Schuster, 1999), 164.

39. See Vogel, *Deng Xiaoping and the Transformation of China*, 85–86.

40. Confucius, *The Analects of Confucius*, 6.

41. See Yang and Yan, *Deng Xiaoping nianpu: 1904–1974* (Chronological Biography of Deng Xiaoping: 1904–1974), vol. 3, 2015; Deng, *Deng Xiaoping and the Cultural Revolution*, 269; Salisbury, *The Long March,* 137.

42. See Li and Ma, *Zhou Enlai nianpu (1949–1976)* (Chronological Biography of Zhou Enlai [1949–1976]), vol. 3, 671.

43. See Li, *Private Life of Chairman Mao*, 581–82.

44. Mao, *Jianguo yilai Mao Zedong wengao* (Manuscripts of Mao Zedong from the Founding of the PRC), vol. 13, 394–96.

45. Quoted from Yang and Yan, *Deng Xiaoping nianpu: 1904–1974* (Chronological Biography of Deng Xiaoping: 1904–1974), vol. 3, 2058; Deng, *Deng Xiaoping zishu* (Autobiographical Notes of Deng Xiaoping), 167; Deng, *Deng Xiaoping and the Cultural Revolution*, 277.

46. Quoted from *A Great Trial in Chinese History: The Trial of Lin Biao and Jiang Qing Counter-Revolutionary Cliques, Nov. 1980–Jan. 1981* (Oxford: Pergamon Press, 1981), 47, 159.

47. Quoted from Pang and Jin, *Mao Zedong zhuan (1949–1976)* (Biography of Mao Zedong [1949–1976]), vol. 2, 1704.

48. Quoted from Yang and Yan, *Deng Xiaoping nianpu: 1904–1974* (Chronological Biography of Deng Xiaoping: 1904–1974), vol. 3, 2066; Deng, *Deng Xiaoping and the Cultural Revolution*, 281.

49. See Barnouin and Yu, *Ten Years of Turbulence*, 276–77; V. G. Gel'bras, *Ekonomika Kitaiskoi Narodnoi Respubliki: Vazhneishie etapy razvitiia, 1949–2008: Kurs lektsii: v 2 ch.* (Economy of the People's Republic of China: Key Stages of Development 1949–2008: Lecture Series. In two parts) (Moscow: Rubezhi XXI veka, 2010), 90, 94–97.

50. See Yang and Yan, *Deng Xiaoping nianpu: 1904–1974* (Chronological Biography of Deng Xiaoping: 1904–1974), vol. 3, 2053–54, 2061, 2064.

51. Quoted from ibid., 2060.

52. Mao, *Jianguo yilai Mao Zedong wengao* (Manuscripts of Mao Zedong from the Founding of the PRC), vol. 13, 402.

53. Ibid., 410.

54. Quoted from Yang and Yan, *Deng Xiaoping nianpu: 1904–1974* (Chronological Biography of Deng Xiaoping: 1904–1974), vol. 3, 2066; Deng, *Deng Xiaoping and the Cultural Revolution*, 281.

55. Quoted from Yang and Yan, *Deng Xiaoping nianpu: 1904–1974* (Chronological Biography of Deng Xiaoping: 1904–1974), vol. 3, 2076; Deng, *Deng Xiaoping and the Cultural Revolution*, 285.

56. Mao, *Jianguo yilai Mao Zedong wengao* (Manuscripts of Mao Zedong from the Founding of the PRC), vol. 13, 413–14; Borisov and Titarenko, *Vystupleniia Mao Tszeiduna, ranee ne publikovavshiesia v kitaiskoi pechati* (Mao Zedong's Speeches Previously Unpublished in the Chinese Press), series 6, 288.

57. See Gel'bras, *Ekonomika Kitaiskoi Narodnoi Respubliki* (Economy of the People's Republic of China), 85–86.

58. Quoted from Deng, *Deng Xiaoping and the Cultural Revolution*, 283. See also Deng Xiaoping, *Selected Works of Deng Xiaoping*, vol. 3 *(1982–1992)* (Beijing: Foreign Languages Press, 1994), 369.

59. See Deng, *Selected Works of Deng Xiaoping*, vol. 2, 11–13.

60. Ibid., 14.

61. Ibid., 19.

62. Quoted from Leng Rong and Wang Zuoling, eds., *Deng Xiaoping nianpu: 1975–1997* (Chronological Biography of Deng Xiaoping: 1975–1997), vol. 1 (Beijing: Zhongyang wenxian chubanshe, 2004), 50.

63. See ibid., 63–64; Pang and Jin, *Mao Zedong zhuan (1949–1976)* (Biography of Mao Zedong [1949–1976]), vol. 2, 1739; Yu Guangyuan, *Wo yi Deng Xiaoping* (I Remember Deng Xiaoping) (Hong Kong: Shi dai guo chuban youxian gongsi, 2005), 2–9; Deng, *Deng Xiaoping and the Cultural Revolution*, 329.

64. Empiricism referred to acting without theoretical grounding, capitulationism to surrendering one's position to enemies. See *Kaizhan dui "Shuihu" de pinglun* (Develop Criticism of [the Novel] *Water Margin*) (Xi'an: [n.p.], 1975).

65. *Lichnoe delo Chzhou En'laia* (Personal File of Zhou Enlai), RGASPI, collection 495, inventory 225, file 2, vol. 3, sheet 47.

66. See Yu, *Wo yi Deng Xiaoping* (I Remember Deng Xiaoping), 5.

67. See Barnouin and Yu, *Ten Years of Turbulence*, 274; Zhang, "Neskol'ko shtrik-hov k kartine poslednikh let zhizni Mao Tszeduna, Chzhou En'laia" (Some Brush Strokes Toward a Picture of the Last Years of Mao Zedong and Zhou Enlai), 95.

68. Westad et al., "77 Conversations Between Chinese and Foreign Leaders on the Wars in Indochina," 193. See also Deng, *Deng Xiaoping and the Cultural Revolution*, 300, for a slightly different quotation.

69. Westad et al., "77 Conversations Between Chinese and Foreign Leaders on the Wars in Indochina," 194.

70. Quoted from Leng and Wang, *Deng Xiaoping nianpu: 1975–1997* (Chronological Biography of Deng Xiaoping: 1975–1997), vol. 1, 125; Deng, *Deng Xiaoping and the Cultural Revolution*, 352.

71. Mao, *Jianguo yilai Mao Zedong wengao* (Manuscripts of Mao Zedong from the Founding of the PRC), vol. 13, 486.

72. Ibid.

CHAPTER 17

1. See Mao, *Jianguo yilai Mao Zedong wengao* (Manuscripts of Mao Zedong from the Founding of the PRC), vol. 13, 488.

2. Quoted from Deng, *Wode fuqin Deng Xiaoping: "Wenge" suiyue* (My Father Deng Xiaoping: The Cultural Revolution Years), 427.

3. Mao, *Jianguo yilai Mao Zedong wengao* (Manuscripts of Mao Zedong from the Founding of the PRC), vol. 13, 488.

4. See Deng, *Deng Xiaoping and the Cultural Revolution*, 364–69.

5. See ibid., 272.

6. Ibid., 360.

7. Quoted from ibid., 347.

8. See Zhou Bingde, *Moi diadia Chzhou Enlai* (My Uncle Zhou Enlai) (Beijing: Foreign Languages Press, 2008), 285; Deng, *Deng Xiaoping and the Cultural Revolution*, 373.

9. See James Palmer, *Heaven Cracks, Earth Shakes: The Tangshan Earthquake and the Death of Mao's China* (New York: Basic Books, 2012), 8.

10. See Leng and Wang, *Deng Xiaoping nianpu: 1975–1997* (Chronological Biography of Deng Xiaoping: 1975–1997), vol. 1, 143.

11. Deng, *Deng Xiaoping and the Cultural Revolution*, 381.

12. Quoted from Leng and Wang, *Deng Xiaoping nianpu: 1975–1997* (Chronological Biography of Deng Xiaoping: 1975–1997), vol. 1, 145–47.

13. Quoted from Pang and Jin, *Mao Zedong zhuan (1949–1976)* (Biography of Mao Zedong [1949–1976]), vol. 2, 1767.

14. Quoted from Leng and Wang, *Deng Xiaoping nianpu: 1975–1997* (Chronological Biography of Deng Xiaoping: 1975–1997), vol. 1, 147.

15. See ibid., 147–48; Pang and Jin, *Mao Zedong zhuan (1949–1976)* (Biography of Mao Zedong [1949–1976]), vol. 2, 1771–72; *History of the Chinese Communist Party—A Chronology of Events (1919–1990)*, 374–75.

16. Quoted from Leng and Wang, *Deng Xiaoping nianpu: 1975–1997* (Chronological Biography of Deng Xiaoping: 1975–1997), vol. 1, 148; Deng, *Deng Xiaoping and the Cultural Revolution*, 386.

17. Mao, *Jianguo yilai Mao Zedong wengao* (Manuscripts of Mao Zedong from the Founding of the PRC), vol. 13, 527.

18. See *Rethinking the "Cultural Revolution"* (Beijing: Foreign Languages Press, 1987), 22–23; Yen and Kao, *The Ten-Year History of the Cultural Revolution*, 553; Palmer, *Heaven Cracks, Earth Shakes*, 95; MacFarquhar and Schoenhals, *Mao's Last Revolution*, 420–30; Witke, *Comrade Chiang Ch'ing*, 15, 469.

19. Quoted from Qing Wu and Fang Lei, *Deng Xiaoping zai 1976* (Deng Xiaoping in 1976), vol. 1 (Shenyang: Chunfeng wenyi chubanshe, 1993), 178, 180.

20. Quoted from Pang and Jin, *Mao Zedong zhuan (1949–1976)* (Biography of Mao Zedong [1949–1976]), vol. 2, 1776; Deng, *Deng Xiaoping and the Cultural*

Revolution, 398. The text of Mao Yuanxin's report is in Qing and Fang, *Deng Xiaoping zai 1976* (Deng Xiaoping in 1976), vol. 1, 180–83.

21. Quoted from Pang and Jin, *Mao Zedong zhuan (1949–1976)* (Biography of Mao Zedong [1949–1976]), vol. 2, 1776–77.

22. Quoted from ibid., 1977.

23. Mao, *Jianguo yilai Mao Zedong wengao* (Manuscripts of Mao Zedong from the Founding of the PRC), vol. 13, 538.

24. Quoted from ibid., 530.

25. See Leng and Wang, *Deng Xiaoping nianpu: 1975–1997* (Chronological Biography of Deng Xiaoping: 1975–1997), vol. 1, 150.

26. See Deng, *Deng Xiaoping and the Cultural Revolution*, 399.

27. Quoted from ibid., 409.

28. See Chi Hsin, *The Case of Gang of Four: With First Translation of Teng Hsiaoping's "Three Poisonous Weeds"* (Hong Kong: Cosmos Books, 1977), 201–2.

29. Rittenberg and Bennett, *The Man Who Stayed Behind*, 425–26.

30. Deng, *Deng Xiaoping and the Cultural Revolution*, 419.

31. Ibid., 422–23.

32. Borisov and Titarenko, *Vystupleniia Mao Tsze-duna, ranee ne publikovavshiesia v kitaiskoi pechati* (Speeches of Mao Zedong Previously Unpublished in the Chinese Press), series 6, 274.

33. *People's Daily*, Sept. 19, 1976.

34. See Leng and Wang, *Deng Xiaoping nianpu: 1975–1997* (Chronological Biography of Deng Xiaoping: 1975–1997), vol. 1, 151.

35. Deng, *Selected Works of Deng Xiaoping*, vol. 2 *(1975–1982)*, 264, 287.

36. Deng, *Deng Xiaoping and the Cultural Revolution*, 440–41.

37. Quoted from Qing Wu and Fang Lei, *Deng Xiaoping zai 1976* (Deng Xiaoping in 1976), vol. 2 (Shenyang: Chunfeng wenyi chubanshe, 1993), 378. See also James T. Myers et al., eds., *Chinese Politics: Documents and Analysis*, vol. 3 (Columbia: University of South Carolina Press, 1995), 174–75.

38. Quoted from Liu Jixian, ed., *Ye Jianying nianpu (1897–1986)* (Chronological Biography of Ye Jianying [1897–1986]), vol. 2 (Beijing: Zhongyang wenxian chubanshe, 2007), 1110–13; Deng, *Deng Xiaoping and the Cultural Revolution*, 434.

39. Quoted from Deng, *Deng Xiaoping and the Cultural Revolution*, 437.

40. Quoted from MacFarquhar and Schoenhals, *Mao's Last Revolution*, 443; Liu, *Ye Jianying nianpu (1897–1986)* (Chronological Biography of Ye Jianying [1897–1986]), vol. 2, 1111.

41. Quoted from Liu, *Ye Jianying nianpu (1897–1986)* (Chronological Biography of Ye Jianying [1897–1986]), vol. 2, 1112–13.

42. See ibid., 1114.

43. Zhang Yaoci, *Zhang Yaoci huiyilu—zai Mao zhuxi shenbian rizi* (Reminiscences of Zhang Yaoci—Days at the Side of Chairman Mao) (Beijing: Zhonggong dangshi chubanshe, 2008), 271–72. See also Fan Shuo, *Ye Jianying zai guanjian shike*

(Ye Jianying in a Critical Period of Time) (Changchun: Liaoning renmin chuban-she, 2011), 294–306; Qing and Fang, *Deng Xiaoping zai 1976* (Deng Xiaoping in 1976), vol. 2, 282–331.

44. Quoted from Liu, *Ye Jianying nianpu (1897–1986)* (Chronological Biography of Ye Jianying [1897–1986]), vol. 2, 1114–15.

45. See ibid., 1116.

46. Quoted from Leng and Wang, *Deng Xiaoping nianpu: 1975–1997* (Chronological Biography of Deng Xiaoping: 1975–1997), vol. 1, 156. See also *History of the Chinese Communist Party—A Chronology of Events (1919–1990)*, 378.

47. Quoted from Ruan, *Deng Xiaoping*, 19–20.

48. Quoted from *Zhonggong dangshi dashi nianbiao* (Chronology of Major Events in the History of the CCP) (Beijing: Renmin chubanshe, 1987), 405.

49. Quoted from Leng and Wang, *Deng Xiaoping nianpu: 1975–1997* (Chronological Biography of Deng Xiaoping: 19751997), vol. 1, 153.

CHAPTER 18

1. See Ruan, *Deng Xiaoping*, 20–21.

2. *People's Daily*, Feb. 7, 1977.

3. Leng and Wang, *Deng Xiaoping nianpu: 1975–1997* (Chronological Biography of Deng Xiaoping: 1975–1997), vol. 1, 155; Deng, *Deng Xiaoping zishu* (Autobiographical Notes of Deng Xiaoping), 177.

4. Deng, *Selected Works of Deng Xiaoping*, vol. 2 *(1975–1982)*, 51.

5. See Meliksetov, *Istoriia Kitaia* (History of China), 699–700.

6. Chen Yun, *Chen Yun wenxuan: 1956–1985* (Selected Works of Chen Yun: 1956–1985) (Beijing: Renmin chubanshe, 1986), 207.

7. Quoted from Ruan, *Deng Xiaoping*, 21; Chen Zhongyuan, Wang Yuxiang, and Li Zhenghua, *1976–1981 niande Zhongguo* (China in 1976–1981) (Beijing: Zhongyang wenxian chubanshe, 2008), 43–45.

8. Quoted from Leng and Wang, *Deng Xiaoping nianpu: 1975–1997* (Chronological Biography of Deng Xiaoping: 1975–1997), vol. 1, 156. See also Ruan, *Deng Xiaoping*, 21.

9. Myers, *Chinese Politics: Documents and Analysis*, vol. 3, 175–76; Deng Xiaoping, *Deng Xiaoping shouji xuan* (Selected Manuscripts of Deng Xiaoping), vol. 3 (Beijing: Zhongguo dang'an chubanshe/Daxiang chubanshe, 2004), 32, 143; Deng, *Selected Works of Deng Xiaoping*, vol. 2 *(1975–1982)*, 52, 55. See also Leng and Wang, *Deng Xiaoping nianpu: 1975–1997* (Chronological Biography of Deng Xiaoping: 1975–1997), vol. 1, 157.

10. Deng, *Selected Works of Deng Xiaoping*, vol. 2 *(1975–1982)*, 51; Ruan, *Deng Xiaoping*, 29–30.

11. Deng, *Selected Works of Deng Xiaoping*, vol. 2 *(1975–1982)*, 52.

12. Deng, *Deng Xiaoping zishu* (Autobiographical Notes of Deng Xiaoping), 174.

13. See *History of the Chinese Communist Party—A Chronology of Events (1919–1990)*, 382.

14. *People's Daily*, May 1, 1977.

15. Deng, *Selected Works of Deng Xiaoping*, vol. 2 *(1975–1982)*, 58–59, 81, 141; Ruan, *Deng Xiaoping*, 40.

16. Deng, *Selected Works of Deng Xiaoping*, vol. 2 (1975–1982), 59.

17. Deng, *Deng Xiaoping zishu* (Autobiographical Notes of Deng Xiaoping), 171–72.

18. Ruan, *Deng Xiaoping*, 40.

19. *The Eleventh National Congress of the Communist Party of China: Documents* (Beijing: Foreign Languages Press, 1977), 192.

20. Ibid., 8, 52, 86.

21. Deng, *Deng Xiaoping zishu* (Autobiographical Notes of Deng Xiaoping), 178, 180. For others of Deng's speeches on developing science and education, see Deng, *Selected Works of Deng Xiaoping*, vol. 2 *(1975–1982)*, 61–86, 101–16, 119–26.

22. *Great Historic Victory: In Warm Celebration of Chairman Hua Kuo-feng's Becoming Leader of the Communist Party of China, and of the Crushing of the Wang-Chang-Chiang-Yao Anti-Party Clique* (Peking: Foreign Languages Press, 1976), 34, 41.

23. See Lu Keng, *Hu Yaobang fangwen ji* (Interview with Hu Yaobang) (New York: Niuyue huayu jigou, 1985), 8–9; Hu Deping, *Zhongguo weishemma yao gaige—siyi fuqin Hu Yaobang* (Why Should China Reform? Thoughts and Reflections on My Father Hu Yaobang) (Beijing: Renmin chubanshe, 2011), 3–77; Zheng Zhongbing, ed., *Hu Yaobang nianpu ziliao changbian* (Large Collection of Materials for a Chronological Biography of Hu Yaobang), vol. 1 (Hong Kong: Shidaiguo ji chuban youxian gongsi, 2005), 1–286; Yang Zhongmei, *Hu Yaobang: A Chinese Biography*, trans. William A. Wycoff (Armonk, NY: Sharpe, 1988), 3–126; Sladkovskii, *Informatsionnyi biulleten'. Seriia A. Vypusk 2* (Information Bulletin: Series A: 2nd Installment), 24.

24. See Zheng, *Hu Yaobang nianpu ziliao changbian* (Large Collection of Materials for a Chronological Biography of Hu Yaobang), vol. 1, 286.

25. Ruan, *Deng Xiaoping*, 24. See also Li Rui, "Yaobang qushi qiande tanhua" (Talks with [Hu] Yaobang Before His Death), *Dangdai Zhongguo yanjiu* (*Modern China Studies*), issue, no. 4 (2001), 23–45.

26. *People's Daily*, Oct. 7, 1977.

27. See *History of the Chinese Communist Party—A Chronology of Events (1919–1990)*, 387.

28. Quoted from Ruan, *Deng Xiaoping*, 36.

29. See Vogel, *Deng Xiaoping and the Transformation of China*, 152, 197–98, 724, 726; Frederick C. Teiwes and Warren Sun, *The End of the Maoist Era: Chinese Politics During the Twilight of the Cultural Revolution, 1972–1976* (Armonk, NY: Sharpe, 2007), 423–25.

30. See *History of the Chinese Communist Party—A Chronology of Events (1919–1990)*, 387.

31. *Documents of the First Session of the Fifth National People's Congress of the People's Republic of China* (Peking: Foreign Languages Press, 1978), 166.

32. Ibid., 190–91.

33. Quoted from Zheng, *Hu Yaobang nianpu ziliao changbian* (Large Collection of Materials for a Chronological Biography of Hu Yaobang), vol. 1, 316; Ruan, *Deng Xiaoping*, 33.

34. See Leng and Wang, *Deng Xiaoping nianpu: 1975–1997* (Chronological Biography of Deng Xiaoping: 1975–1997), vol. 1, 357, 401–02, 544; Deng, *Selected Works of Deng Xiaoping*, vol. 2 *(1975–1982)*, 197; Liu, *Ye Jianying nianpu (1897–1986)* (Chronological Biography of Ye Jianying [1897–1986]), vol. 2, 1145, 1152; Zheng, *Hu Yaobang nianpu ziliao changbian* (Large Collection of Materials for a Chronological Biography of Hu Yaobang), vol. 1, 318; Yu Guangyuan, *Deng Xiaoping Shakes the World: An Eyewitness Account of China's Party Work Conference and the Third Plenum (November–December 1978)* trans. Steven I. Levine (Norwalk, CT: EastBridge, 2004), 15–16.

35. Quoted from Yu, *Deng Xiaoping Shakes the World*, 18.

36. Deng, *Selected Works of Deng Xiaoping*, vol. 2 *(1975–1982)*, 128.

37. See *History of the Chinese Communist Party—A Chronology of Events (1919–1990)*, 389.

38. Deng Xiaoping, *Deng Xiaoping wenxuan* (Selected Works of Deng Xiaoping), vol. 2 (Beijing: Renmin chubanshe, 1994), 129.

39. Deng, *Selected Works of Deng Xiaoping*, vol. 2 *(1975–1982)*, 143. Deng, *Deng Xiaoping wenxuan* (Selected Works of Deng Xiaoping), vol. 2, 133.

40. See Vogel, *Deng Xiaoping and the Transformation of China*, 187, 189.

41. See *Documents of the First Session of the Fifth National People's Congress of the People's Republic of China*, 35–66; Meliksetov, *Istoriia Kitaia* (History of China), 702.

42. See Vogel, *Deng Xiaoping and the Transformation of China*, 189–90.

43. Quoted from ibid., 223, 218.

44. Quoted from *Li Xiannian zhuan: 1949–1992* (Biography of Li Xiannian: 1949–1992), vol. 2 (Beijing: Zhongyang wenxian chubanshe, 2009), 1048.

45. See ibid., 1048–71.

46. Deng, *Deng Xiaoping wenxuan,* (Selected Works of Deng Xiaoping), vol. 2, 130.

47. See Yu, *Deng Xiaoping Shakes the World*, 23, 25; Liu, *Ye Jianying nianpu (1897–1986)* (Chronological Biography of Ye Jianying [1897–1986]), vol. 2, 1155.

48. See Zhu, *Chen Yun nianpu: 1905–1995* (Chronological Biography of Chen Yun: 1905–1995), vol. 3, 226.

49. Deng, *Selected Works of Deng Xiaoping*, vol. 2 *(1975–1982)*, 151.

50. See Ye Xuanji, "Ye shuai zai shi yi di san zhongquanhui qianhou: Du Yu Guangyuan zhu '1978: Wo qinlide naci lishi da zhuanzhe yugan'" (Marshal Ye Before and

After the Third Plenum of the Eleventh Central Committee: Impressions from Yu Guangyuan's Work *1978: The Great Historical Turning Point That I Personally Witnessed*), *Nanfang zhoumo* (*Southern Weekly*), Oct. 30, 2008.

51. See Vogel, *Deng Xiaoping and the Transformation of China*, 233.

52. Chen, *Chen Yun wenxuan: 1956–1985* (Selected Works of Chen Yun: 1956–1985), 208–10.

53. See Vogel, *Deng Xiaoping and the Transformation of China*, 235.

54. See Ibid., 240.

55. See Yu, *Deng Xiaoping Shakes the World*, 74–76; Liu, *Ye Jianying nianpu (1897–1986)* (Chronological Biography of Ye Jianying [1897–1986]), vol. 2, 1157.

56. See Ruan, *Deng Xiaoping*, 21–22.

57. See Yu, *Deng Xiaoping Shakes the World*, 80–83, 90–92, 97.

58. Robert D. Novak, *The Prince of Darkness: 50 Years Reporting in Washington* (New York: Crown Forum, 2007), 324.

59. For more details, see Roger Garside, *Coming Alive: China After Mao* (New York: McGraw-Hill, 1981), 212–39; Alexander Pantsov's interview with Wei Jingsheng in Washington, DC, Oct. 21, 2012.

60. Deng's interview was published in *People's Daily* on Nov. 28, 1978.

61. Wei Jingsheng, *The Courage to Stand Alone: Letters from Prison and Other Writings*, ed. and trans. Kristina Torgeson (New York: Viking, 1997), 208–9.

62. Quoted from Hu Jiwei, "Hu Yaobang yu Xidan minzhu qiang" (Hu Yaobang and Democracy Wall), http://www.boxun.com/news/gb/z_special/2004/04/200404220644.shtml.

63. Quoted from Yu, *Deng Xiaoping Shakes the World*, 163–65.

64. Quoted from Ruan, *Deng Xiaoping*, 7.

65. Deng, *Selected Works of Deng Xiaoping*, vol. 2 *(1975–1982)*, 151–65.

66. Quoted from Ruan, *Deng Xiaoping*, 13.

67. Novak, *The Prince of Darkness*, 327.

CHAPTER 19

1. Quoted from Myers, *Chinese Politics: Documents and Analysis*, vol. 3, 361.

2. See Zheng, *Hu Yaobang nianpu ziliao changbian* (Large Collection of Materials for a Political Biography of Hu Yaobang), vol. 1, 134; Yu, *Deng Xiaoping Shakes the World*, 207.

3. Ruan, *Deng Xiaoping*, 47; See also James D. Seymour, ed., *The Fifth Modernization: China's Human Rights Movement, 1978–1979* (Stanfordville, NY: Human Rights, 1980); Stephen C. Angle and Marina Svensson, eds., *The Chinese Human Rights Reader: Documents and Commentary, 1900–2000* (Armonk, NY: Sharpe, 2001), 253–72; Maurice Meisner, *The Deng Xiaoping Era: An Inquiry into the Fate of Chinese Socialism, 1978–1994* (New York: Hill and Wang, 1996), 110–14.

4. Novak, *The Prince of Darkness*, 330–31.

5. Ibid., 327, 328. "An Interview with Teng Hsiao-p'ing Calling for Stronger U.S.-China Ties and a United Front Against Moscow," *Time*, vol. 113, no. 6 (Feb. 5, 1979): 32–35; David P. Nickles and Adam M. Howard, eds., *Foreign Relations of the United States, 1977–1980*, vol. 13: *China* (Washington, DC: U.S. Government Printing Office, 2013), 743.

6. See Kissinger, *Years of Renewal*, 868–69.

7. See Huang Hua, *Memoirs* (Beijing: Foreign Languages Press, 2008), 347–50; Zbigniew Brzezinski, *Power and Principle: Memoirs of the National Security Advisor, 1977–1981* (New York: Farrar, Straus and Giroux, 1985), 209–33; Jimmy Carter, *Keeping Faith: Memoirs of a President* (Fayetteville: University of Arkansas Press, 1995), 199–203; Jimmy Carter, *White House Diary* (New York: Farrar, Straus and Giroux, 2010), 85, 170, 265.

8. See Patrick Tyler, *A Great Wall: Six Presidents and China: An Investigative History* (New York: PublicAffairs, 1999), 271.

9. See Huang, *Memoirs*, 347–48; Brzezinski, *Power and Principle*, 215.

10. Nickles and Howard, *Foreign Relations of the United States 1977–1980*, vol. 13: *China*, 729.

11. See Huang, *Memoirs*, 352; Brzezinski, *Power and Principle*, 405–6; Ji Chaozhu, *The Man on Mao's Right: From Harvard Yard to Tiananmen Square: My Life Inside China's Foreign Ministry* (New York: Random House, 2008), 298–99.

12. Carter, *White House Diary*, 283.

13. See Carter, *Keeping Faith*, 207; Ji, *The Man on Mao's Right*, 299–301.

14. Cyrus Vance, *Hard Choices: Critical Years in America's Foreign Policy* (New York: Simon & Schuster, 1983), 121.

15. Nickles and Howard, *Foreign Relations of the United States, 1977–1980*, vol. 13: *China*, 738–41. See also Huang, *Memoirs*, 352; Brzezinski, *Power and Principle*, 405–6.

16. For his speech, see Nickles and Howard, *Foreign Relations of the United States 1977–1980*, vol. 13: *China*, 767–70.

17. According to various sources, in the period from June 1965 to August 1973 there were no fewer than 320,000 Chinese "volunteers" who rotated through Vietnam.

18. Nickles and Howard, *Foreign Relations of the United States, 1977–1980*, vol. 13: *China*, 770–71. See also Carter, *White House Diary*, 284, 285; Carter, *Keeping Faith*, 211, 213; Brzezinski, *Power and Principle*, 409–10; Henry A. Kissinger, *On China* (New York: Penguin Press, 2011), 365–67.

19. See Brzezinski, *Power and Principle*, 410; Kissinger, *On China*, 367.

20. See Carter, *Keeping Faith*, 211–13.

21. See Zhai Qiang, "China and the Cambodian Conflict, 1970–1975," in Priscilla Roberts, ed., *Behind the Bamboo Curtain: China, Vietnam, and the World Beyond Asia* (Washington, DC, and Stanford, CA: Woodrow Wilson Center Press and Stanford University Press, 2007), 391–92.

22. See Robert S. Ross, *The Indochina Tangle: China's Vietnam Policy, 1975–1979* (New York: Columbia University Press, 1988), 176–89; Steven J. Hood, *Dragons Entangled: Indochina and the China-Vietnam War* (Armonk, NY: Sharpe, 1992), 136–50.

23. See Ross, *The Indochina Tangle*, 230–31.

24. See Weatherley, *Mao's Forgotten Successor*, 153–54; Vogel, *Deng Xiaoping and the Transformation of China*, 532.

25. Alexander V. Pantsov's interview with Wei Jingsheng in Washington, DC, Oct. 21, 2012; Vogel, *Deng Xiaoping and the Transformation of China*, 528.

26. See King C. Chen, *China's War with Vietnam, 1979: Issues, Decisions, and Implications* (Stanford, CA: Hoover Institution Press, 1987), 102; John Pilger, *Heroes* (Cambridge, MA: South End Press, 2001), 248; Stein Tønnesson and Christopher E. Goscha, "Le Duan and the Break with China," in Priscilla Roberts, ed., *Behind the Bamboo Curtain: China, Vietnam, and the World Beyond Asia* (Washington, DC, and Stanford, CA: Woodrow Wilson Center Press and Stanford University Press, 2006), 462.

27. For further details, see Stephen J. Morris, *Why Vietnam Invaded Cambodia: Political Culture and the Causes of War* (Stanford, CA: Stanford University Press, 1999); Benjamin E. Kringer, "The Third Indochina War: A Case Study on the Vietnamese Invasion of Cambodia," in Ross A. Fisher, John Norton Moore, and Robert F. Turner, eds., *To Oppose Any Foe: The Legacy of U.S. Intervention in Vietnam* (Durham, NC: Carolina Academic Press, 2006), 275–326; Clodfelter, *Warfare and Armed Conflict*, 669.

28. Quoted from Brzezinski, *Power and Principle*, 409.

29. See Kissinger, *On China*, 365–66.

30. Before Deng departed from Washington, Brzezinski even underlined "Presidential support" to him (Brzezinski, *Power and Principle*, 410–11). This, naturally, gladdened the lofty Chinese guest.

31. See Vance, *Hard Choices*, 121–22; Elizabeth Wishnick, *Mending Fences: The Evolution of Moscow's China Policy from Brezhnev to Yeltsin* (Seattle: University of Washington Press, 2001), 63–64.

32. See *Chinese War Crimes in Vietnam* (Hanoi: Vietnam Courier, 1979).

33. The Chinese asserted that Vietnam had lost fifty-seven thousand officers and soldiers killed and wounded, but this does not correspond to reality. See Zhang Xiaoming, "China's 1979 War with Vietnam: A Reassessment," *China Quarterly*, vol. 184 (December 2005): 866; Clodfelter, *Warfare and Armed Conflict*, 669.

34. Deng, *Selected Works of Deng Xiaoping*, vol. 3 (*1982–1992*), 85.

35. See Spichak, *Kitaiskii avangard Kremlia* (The Chinese Vanguard of the Kremlin), 134.

36. See *Lichnoe delo Chen' Yunia* (Personal File of Chen Yun), RGASPI, collection 495, inventory 225, file 157.

37. Chen, *Chen Yun wenxuan, 1956–1985* (Selected Works of Chen Yun, 1956–1985), 213. Chen Yun had also raised these issues earlier, including in a letter to Li Xiannian in the summer of 1978 during a theoretical conference on modernization. But no one listened to him then. See Vogel, *Deng Xiaoping and the Transformation of China*, 427.

38. See Yang, *Deng*, 209–10.

39. Quoted from Leng and Wang, *Deng Xiaoping nianpu: 1975–1997* (Chronological Biography of Deng Xiaoping: 1975–1997), vol. 1, 466.

40. See V. V. Azhaeva, *Evoliutsiia politiki KNR v oblasti sel'skogo khoziaistva: Nauchno-analiticheskii obzor* (Evolution of PRC Agricultural Policy: A Scholarly Analysis) (Moscow: INION AN SSSR, 1983), 5; Gel'bras, *Ekonomika Kitaiskoi Narodnoi Respubliki* (Economy of the People's Republic of China), 110.

41. Chen, *Chen Yun wenxuan, 1956–1985* (Selected Works of Chen Yun, 1956–1985), 224–31.

42. Ibid., 221, 222.

43. Ibid., 222–23.

44. See ibid., 232–34; *History of the Chinese Communist Party—A Chronology of Events (1919–1990)*, 399–400.

45. Quoted from Leng and Wang, *Deng Xiaoping nianpu: 1975–1997* (Chronological Biography of Deng Xiaoping: 1975–1997), vol. 1, 497.

46. See *Deng, Selected Works of Deng Xiaoping*, vol. 2 *(1975–1982)*, 169.

47. See Liu, *Ye Jianying nianpu (1897–1986)* (Chronological Biography of Ye Jianying [1897–1986]), vol. 2, 1145.

48. See Zheng, *Hu Yaobang nianpu ziliao changbian* (Large Collection of Materials for a Chronological Biography of Hu Yaobang), vol. 1, 359.

49. See Vogel, *Deng Xiaoping and the Transformation of China*, 259.

50. Quoted from Richard Baum, *Burying Mao: Chinese Politics in the Age of Deng Xiaoping* (Princeton, NJ: Princeton University Press, 1994), 80.

51. Quoted from Leng and Wang, *Deng Xiaoping nianpu: 1975–1997* (Chronological Biography of Deng Xiaoping: 1975–1997), vol. 1, 493.

52. Quoted from ibid., 499.

53. See Deng, *Selected Works of Deng Xiaoping*, vol. 2 *(1975–1982)*, 172.

54. See Vogel, *Deng Xiaoping and the Transformation of China*, 260, 783.

55. Deng, *Selected Works of Deng Xiaoping*, vol. 2 *(1975–1982)*, 174, 183.

56. Zheng, *Hu Yaobang nianpu changbian* (Large Collection of Materials for a Chronological Biography of Hu Yaobang), vol. 1, 387.

57. Quoted from Wei, *The Courage to Stand Alone*, 255.

58. See Hemen Ray, *China's Vietnam War* (New Delhi: Radiant, 1983), 111.

59. Myers, *Chinese Politics: Documents and Analysis*, vol. 3, 401–6; *Democracy Wall Prisoners: Xu Wenli, Wei Jingsheng and Other Jailed Prisoners of the Chinese Pro-Democracy Movement* (New York: Asia Watch, 1993), 38–42.

60. See Hu, "Hu Yaobang yu Xidan minzhu qiang" (Hu Yaobang and the Xidan Democracy Wall), 27; Wei, *The Courage to Stand Alone*, xii; Alexander V. Pantsov's interview with Wei Jingsheng in Washington, DC, Oct. 21, 2012; Alexander V. Pantsov's interview with former research fellow of the PRC Academy of Social Sciences, Lin Ying in Columbus, OH, Apr. 30, 2012.

61. See Alexander V. Pantsov's interview with Wei Jingsheng in Washington, DC, Oct. 21, 2012. See also Wei, *The Courage to Stand Alone*, 257.

62. See Wei, *The Courage to Stand Alone*, 256.

63. See Deng, *Selected Works of Deng Xiaoping*, vol. 2 *(1975–1982)*, 182.

64. Vogel, *Deng Xiaoping and the Transformation of China*, 383.

65. Quoted from Leng and Wang, *Deng Xiaoping nianpu: 1975–1997* (Chronological Biography of Deng Xiaoping: 1975–1997), vol. 1, 355. See also *Deng Xiaoping yu xiandai Zhongguo* (Deng Xiaoping and Contemporary China), 145–46.

CHAPTER 20

1. Mao, *Selected Works of Mao Tse-tung*, vol. 2, 202.

2. Deng, *Selected Works of Deng Xiaoping*, vol. 2 *(1975–1982)*, 196–99.

3. See Wu Xiang, Zhang Guangyou, and Han Gang, "Wan Li tan shiyi jie san zhongquanhui qianhoude nongcun gaige" (Wan Li Speaks About Rural Reform Before and After the Third Plenum of the Eleventh Central Committee), in Yu Guangyuan et al. *Gaibian Zhongguo mingyunde 41 tian—Zhongyang gong-zuo huiyi, shiyi ji zhongquanhui qin liji* (41 Days That Changed China's Fate: Reminiscence of the Central Committee Work Conference and the Third Plenum of the Eleventh Central Committee) (Shenzhen: Haitian chubanshe, 1998), 282–83; Chen, Wang, and Li, *1976–1981 niande Zhongguo* (China in 1976–1981), 358; Daniel Kelliher, *Peasant Power in China: The Era of Rural Reform, 1979–1989* (New Haven: Yale University Press, 1992), 60.

4. Wu, Zhang, and Han, "Wan Li tan shiyi jie san zhongquanhui qianhoude nongcun gaige" (Wan Li Speaks About Rural Reform Before and After the Third Plenum of the Eleventh Central Committee), 286–87.

5. Deng, *Selected Works of Deng Xiaoping*, vol. 2 *(1975–1982)*, 406; *History of the Chinese Communist Party—A Chronology of Events (1919–1990)*, 397.

6. See Wu Nanlan, "The Xiaogang Village Story", http://www.china.org.cn/china/features/content_11778487.htm; Chen, Wang, and Li, *1976–1981 niande Zhongguo* (China in 1976–1981), 366; William Hinton, "A Trip to Fengyang County: Investigating China's New Family Contract System," *Monthly Review*, vol. 35, no. 6 (1983): 1–28; Becker, *Hungry Ghosts*, 130–49; Zhang Deyuan and He Kaiying, *Bianqian: Anhui nongcun gaige shulun* (Changes: On the Reform in the Anhui Countryside) (Hefei: Anhui daxue chubanshe, 2004), 12–13.

7. Wu, "The Xiaogang Village Story."

8. See Meliksetov, *Istoriia Kitaia* (History of China), 708.

9. See Chen, Wang, and Li, *1976–1981 niande Zhongguo* (China in 1976–1981), 364–65; Kelliher, *Peasant Power in China*, 61–62.

10. See Vogel, *Deng Xiaoping and the Transformation of China*, 439.

11. Quoted from Chen, Wang, and Li, *1976–1981 niande Zhongguo* (China in 1976–1981), 359.

12. Quoted from Vogel, *Deng Xiaoping and the Transformation of China*, 439.

13. See Wu, Zhang, and Han, "Wan Li tan shiyi ji zhongquanhui qianhoude nongcun gaige" (Wan Li Talks About Rural Reform Before and After the Third Plenum of the Eleventh Central Committee), 287.

14. *San zhongquanhui yilai—zhongyang wenxian xuanbian* (Collection of Selected Key Documents Since the Third Plenum), vol. 1 (Beijing: Renmin chubanshe, 1982), 172.

15. See *History of the Chinese Communist Party—A Chronology of Events (1919–1990)*, 398; Azhaeva, *Evoliutsiia politiki KNR v oblasti sel'skogo khoziastva* (Evolution of PRC Agricultural Policy), 9.

16. See Gel'bras, *Ekonomika Kitaiskoi Narodnoi Respubliki* (Economy of the People's Republic of China), 128.

17. See Wu, "The Xiaogang Village Story."

18. Deng *Selected Works of Deng Xiaoping*, vol. 3 *(1982–1992)*, 369–70.

19. See Zhao Wei, *The Biography of Zhao Ziyang*, trans. Chen Shibin (Hong Kong: Educational & Cultural Press, 1989), 219–30; David L. Shambaugh, *The Making of a Premier: Zhao Ziyang's Provincial Career* (Boulder, CO: Westview Press, 1984), 81, 99.

20. See David Bachman, "Differing Visions of China's Post-Mao Economy: The Ideas of Chen Yun, Deng Xiaoping, and Zhao Ziyang," *Asian Survey*, vol. 26, no. 3 (1986): 311–21.

21. Deng. *Xiaoping wenxuan* (Selected Works of Deng Xiaoping), vol. 2, 194.

22. Ibid., 236.

23. For more details, see Vogel, *Deng Xiaoping and the Transformation of China*, 447–49.

24. Deng, *Deng Xiaoping wenxuan* (Selected Works of Deng Xiaoping), vol. 2, 237, 259.

25. Ibid., 156–57, 198, 235.

26. See ibid., 443; Wang Shuo, "Teshi teban: Hu Yaobang yu jingji tequ" (Special Things Done in Special Ways: Hu Yaobang and Special Economic Zones), *Yanhuang chunqiu* (*History of China*), no. 4 (2008): 36; *Huiyi Deng Xiaoping* (Remembering Deng Xiaoping), vol. 2 (Beijing: Zhongyang wenxian chubanshe, 1998), 383.

27. Alexander Pantsov's personal impressions from visiting the special zones of Zhuhai and Shenzhen, Dec. 2, 1987, and Feb. 13, 1988.

28. Deng, *Deng Xiaoping wenxuan* (Selected Works of Deng Xiaoping), vol. 2, 199.

29. See for example, Chen, *Chen Yun wenxuan: 1956–1985* (Selected Works of Chen Yun: 1956–1985), 236–37.

30. See Leng and Wang, *Deng Xiaoping nianpu: 1975–1997* (Chronological Biography of Deng Xiaoping: 1975–1997), vol. 1, 574.

31. See Wang, *Zhongguo gongchandang zuzhi shi ziliao huibian—lingdao jigou yange he chengyuan minglu* (Collection of Materials on the Organizational History of the CCP—Evolution of the Leading Organs and Name List of Personnel), 654.

32. See Deng, *Selected Works of Deng Xiaoping*, vol. 2 *(1975–1982)*, 228.

33. See *People's Daily*, Sept. 30, 1979.

34. See Huang Zheng, *Wang Guangmei fang tan lu* (Notes on Conversations with Wang Guangmei) (Beijing: Zhongyang wenxian chubanshe, 2006), 438.

35. See Deng, *Selected Works of Deng Xiaoping*, vol. 2 *(1975–1982)*, 228–30.

36. Ibid., 241–42.

37. Quoted from Chang Chen-pang, Hsiang Nai-kuang, and Yin Ching-yao, *Mainland Situation Viewed from the Third Session of the Fifth "National People's Congress"* (Taipei: World Anti-Communist League, China Chapter/Asian Peoples' Anti-Communist League, 1980), 12.

38. Quoted from Huang, *Wang Guangmei fang tan lu* (Notes on Conversations with Wang Guangmei), 441.

39. Deng, *Deng Xiaoping wenxuan* (Selected Works of Deng Xiaoping), vol. 2, 313.

40. Deng, *Selected Works of Deng Xiaoping*, vol. 2 *(1975–1982)*, 297.

41. See Hinton, "A Trip to Fengyang County," 2–3; Azhaeva, *Evoliutsiia politiki KNR v oblasti sel'skogo khoziastva* (Evolution of PRC Agricultural Policy), 34; Vogel, *Deng Xiaoping and the Transformation of China*, 443.

42. O. N. Borokh, *Kontseptsii ekonomicheskogo razvitiia Kitaia (1978–1982): Avtoreferat dissertatsiii na soiskanie uchenoi stepeni kandidata economicheskih nauk* (Concepts of Economic Development in China [1978–1982]: Abstract of Dissertation Submitted for PhD in Economics) (Moscow: IDV AN SSSR, 1985), 8.

43. See Su Shaozhi, "A Decade of Crisis at the Institute of Marxism-Leninism-Mao Zedong Thought, 1979–1989," *China Quarterly*, vol. 134 (June 1993): 335–51.

44. See Sin-Lin (Lin Ying), *Shattered Families, Broken Dreams: Little-Known Episodes from the History of the Persecution of Chinese Revolutionaries in Stalin's Gulag: Rescued Memoirs and Archival Revelations*, trans. Steven I. Levine (Portland, ME: MerwinAsia, 2012).

45. See Stephen F. Cohen, *Bukharin and the Bolshevik Revolution: A Political Biography, 1888–1938* (New York: Knopf, 1973).

46. Alexander V. Pantsov's interview with former senior research fellow of the PRC Academy of Social Sciences Lin Ying, in Columbus, OH, May 27, 2012.

47. See *Guoji gongyun shi yanjiu ziliao: Buhalin zhuanji* (Materials on the Study of History of the International Communist Movement: Special Collection on Bukharin) (Beijing: Renmin chubanshe, 1981).

48. See Yin Xuyi and Zheng Yifan, "Bukharin in the People's Republic of China," in Theodor Bergmann, Gert Schaefer, and Mark Selden, eds., *Bukharin in Retrospect* (Armonk, NY: Sharpe, 1994), 58.

49. Ibid., 59.

50. See *Lichnoe delo Sun Yipina* (Personal File of Song Yiping), RGASPI, collection 495, inventory 225, file 2807.

51. Alexander V. Pantsov's interview with former senior research fellow of the PRC Academy of Social Sciences Lin Ying in Columbus, OH, May 27, 2012.

52. Su Shaozhi, *Democratization and Reform* (Nottingham: Spokesman, 1988), 36–38.

53. Deng, *Selected Works of Deng Xiaoping*, vol. 3 *(1982–1992)*, 143.

54. See, for example, Lenin, "The Tax in Kind," 329–54.

55. N. I. Bukharin, "Otvet na zapisku V. I. Lenina" (Reply to V. I. Lenin's Note), in L. B. Kamenev, ed., *Leninskii sbornik* (Lenin's Collection), vol. 4 (Moscow: Gosizdat, 1925), 384. See also Cohen, *Bukharin*, 139.

56. Deng, *Selected Works of Deng Xiaoping*, vol. 2 *(1975–1982)*, 296.

57. See ibid., 295–96; Deng, *Deng Xiaoping wenxuan* (Selected Works of Deng Xiaoping), vol. 2, 441–42; *Resolution on CPC History (1949–81)* (Beijing: Foreign Languages Press, 1981), 48–49. See also Hu Yaobang's speech criticizing Hua at the Politburo session of Nov. 19, 1980, in Zheng, *Hu Yaobang nianpu ziliao changbian* (Large Collection of Materials for a Chronological Biography of Hu Yaobang), vol. 1, 504–5.

58. See Liu, *Ye Jianying nianpu (1897–1986)* (Chronological Biography of Ye Jianying [1897–1986]), vol. 2, 1196.

59. See Vogel, *Deng Xiaoping and the Transformation of China*, 372.

60. See Wang, *Zhongguo gongchandang zuzhi shi ziliao huibian—lingdao jigou yange he chengyuan minglu* (Collection of Materials on the Organizational History of the Chinese Communist Party—Evolution of Leading Organs and Name List of Personnel), 654–55.

61. See Deng, *Selected Works of Deng Xiaoping vol. 2 (1975–1982)*, 276–96.

62. See ibid., 326–27.

63. *Resolution on CPC History (1949–81)*, 56, 72.

64. See *A Great Trial in Chinese History*, 18–26, 102, 108–9, 111, 114, 115, 118, 119, 122–25, 127, 128, 233.

65. Deng, *Selected Works of Deng Xiaoping*, vol. 2 *(1975–1982)*, 334.

66. *Resolution of CPC History (1949–81)*, 49.

67. See Liu, *Ye Jianying nianpu (1897–1986)* (Chronological Biography of Ye Jianying [1897–1986]), vol. 2, 1228.

CHAPTER 21

1. Quoted from Vogel, *Deng Xiaoping and the Transformation of China*, 380; Li, "Yaobang qushi qiande tanhua" (Talks with [Hu] Yaobang Before His Death), 42.

2. See Vogel, *Deng Xiaoping and the Transformation of China*, 378.

3. Deng, *Selected Works of Deng Xiaoping*, vol. 2 *(1975–1982)*, 214.

4. Alexander Pantsov's personal impressions from visiting the Museum of Deng Xiaoping in his former village of Paifang, June 24, 2010; Zhang Weiwei, "My

Personal Memoirs as Deng Xiaoping's Interpreter: From Oriana Fallaci to Kim Il-sung to Gorbachev," http://huffingtonpost.com/zhang-weiwei/deng-xiaoping-remembered_b_5706143.html.

5. See *Yongyuande Xiaoping* (The Unforgettable Xiaoping), 3.

6. Chen, *Chen Yun wenxuan: 1956–1985* (Selected Works of Chen Yun: 1956–1985), 275–77.

7. Ibid., 276–77.

8. Quoted from Zhu, *Chen Yun nianpu: 1905–1995* (Chronological Biography of Chen Yun: 1905–1995), vol. 3, 287.

9. Quoted from Leng and Wang, *Deng Xiaoping nianpu: 1975–1982* (Chronological Biography of Deng Xiaoping: 1975–1982), vol. 2, 796.

10. See Wang, "Teshi teban: Hu Yaobang yu jingji tequ" (Special Things Done in Special Ways: Hu Yaobang and Special Economic Zones), 37; Zheng, *Hu Yaobang nianpu ziliao changbian* (Large Collection of Materials for a Chronological Biography of Hu Yaobang), vol. 2, 648; Zhu, *Chen Yun nianpu: 1905–1995* (Chronological Biography of Chen Yun: 1905–1995), vol. 3, 287–88.

11. Zheng, *Hu Yaobang nianpu ziliao changbian* (Large Collection of Materials for a Chronological Biography of Hu Yaobang). vol. 2, 650; Wang, "Teshi teban: Hu Yaobang yu jingji tequ" (Special Things Done in Special Ways: Hu Yaobang and Special Economic Zones), 36–37.

12. See Leng and Wang, *Deng Xiaoping nianpu: 1975–1997* (Chronological Biography of Deng Xiaoping: 1975–1997), vol. 2, 799; Vogel, *Deng Xiaoping and the Transformation of China*, 415.

13. Zheng, *Hu Yaobang nianpu ziliao changbian* (Large Collection of Materials for a Chronological Biography of Hu Yaobang), vol. 2, 653.

14. Chen, *Chen Yun wenxuan: 1956–1985* (Selected Works of Chen Yun: 1956– 1985), 280.

15. See Deng, *Selected Works of Deng Xiaoping*, vol. 2 *(1975–1982),* 223–24; Deng, *Deng Xiaoping zishu* (Autobiographical Notes of Deng Xiaoping), 189, 259; Deng, *Selected Works of Deng Xiaoping*, vol. 3 *(1982–1992),* 67, 74.

16. See Li Songchen, ed., *Gaige dang'an (1976–1999)* (Archive of Reform [1976–1999]), vol. 1 (Beijing: Dangdai Zhongguo chubanshe, 2000), 429; Deng, *Selected Works of Deng Xiaoping*, vol. 2 *(1975–1982),* 383.

17. Bachman, "Differing Visions of China's Post-Mao Economy," 321.

18. See *Zhongguo gongchandang xin shiqi lishi dashiji (zengdingben) (12, 1978–3, 2008)* (Chronology of CCP History in the New Period: Expanded edition [in between 12, 1978 and 3, 2008]) (Beijing: Zhonggong dangshi chubanshe, 2009), 11, 45; *People's Daily*, June 19, 1979; Susan Greenhalgh, *Just One Child: Science and Policy in Deng's China* (Berkeley: University of California Press, 2008), 298–302; Vogel, *Deng Xiaoping and the Transformation of China*, 435.

19. Deng, *Selected Works of Deng Xiaoping*, vol. 3 *(1982–1992),* 14–15.

20. Gerald R. Ford, *A Time to Heal: The Autobiography of Gerald R. Ford* (New York: Harper & Row, 1979), 337.

21. *Dvenadtsatyi Vsekitaiskii s"ezd Kommunisticheskoi partii Kitaia (dokumenty)* (Twelfth National Congress of the Communist Party of China [Documents]) (Beijing: Foreign Languages Press, 1982), 20, 30–33, 37, 40.

22. *Zhongguo gongchandang di shier ci quanguo daibiao dahui wenjian huibian* (Collection of Documents from the Twelfth National Congress of the Communist Party of China) (Beijing: Renmin chubanshe, 1982), 110.

23. See Deng, *Selected Works of Deng Xiaoping*, vol. 3 *(1982–1992)*, 17, 18–19.

24. See *Dvenadtsatyi Vsekitaiskii s"ezd Kommunisticheskoi partii Kitaia (dokumenty)* (Twelfth National Congress of the Communist Party of China [Documents]), 161–65.

25. Zhao Ziyang, *Prisoner of the State: The Secret Journal of Premier Zhao Ziyang*, trans. Bao Pu et al. (New York: Simon & Schuster, 2009), 93, 122.

26. Chen, *Chen Yun wenxuan: 1956–1985* (Selected Works of Chen Yun: 1956–1985), 287. See also Zhu, *Chen Yun nianpu: 1905–1995* (Chronological Biography of Chen Yun: 1905–1995), vol. 3, 311–12.

27. O. N. Borokh, *Razvitie kitaiskoi ekonomicheskoi nauki v period reform* (Development of Chinese Economic Science During the Reform Period), part 1 (Moscow: IDV RAN, 1997), 99–100.

28. Deng, *Selected Works of Deng Xiaoping*, vol. 3 *(1982–1992)*, 26–27.

29. Ibid., 33.

30. See *Fifth Session of the Fifth National Congress (Main Documents)* (Beijing: Foreign Languages Press, 1982), 12, 20–21; *Documents of the First Session of the Fifth National People's Congress of the People's Republic of China*, 155.

31. Quoted from Vogel, *Deng Xiaoping and the Transformation of China*, 569.

32. Zhao, *Prisoner of the State*, 92, 114.

33. See Ruan, *Deng Xiaoping*, 109.

34. See Zhao, *Prisoner of the State*, 116; Zheng, *Hu Yaobang nianpu ziliao changbian* (Large Collection of Materials for a Chronological Biography of Hu Yaobang), vol. 2, 778–79, 801–2.

35. See Zhao, *Prisoner of the State*, 97.

36. Ibid., 179–80; Zheng, *Hu Yaobang nianpu ziliao changbian* (Large Collection of Materials for a Chronological Biography of Hu Yaobang), vol. 2, 799–802; Zhu, *Chen Yun nianpu: 1905–1995* (Chronological Biography of Chen Yun: 1905–1995), vol. 3, 322–23.

37. Quoted from Su, "A Decade of Crisis at the Institute of Marxism-Leninism-Mao Zedong Thought, 1979–1989," 343.

38. Deng, *Selected Works of Deng Xiaoping*, vol. 3 *(1982–1992)*, 48, 50, 51, 53.

39. Ibid., 51.

40. Zhao, *Prisoner of the State*, 163. Hu Yaobang recalled: "Zhao Ziyang and I blocked this campaign." Quoted from Li, "Yaobang qushi qiande tanhua" (Talks with [Hu] Yaobang Before His Death), 43.

41. See Zheng, *Hu Yaobang nianpu ziliao changbian* (Large Collection of Materials for a Chronological Biography of Hu Yaobang), vol. 2, 901.

42. Zhao, *Prisoner of the State*, 164.

43. Ibid., 177.

44. Borokh, *Razvitie kitaiskoi ekonomicheskoi nauki* (Development of Chinese Economic Science), 99–101.

45. See Vogel, *Deng Xiaoping and the Transformation of China*, 454–64.

46. See Gel'bras, *Ekonomika Kitaiskoi Narodnoi Respubliki* (Economy of the People's Republic of China), 115; Wu Li, ed., *Zhongguo renmin gongheguo jingji shi* (Economic History of the PRC), vol. 2 (Beijing: Zhongguo jingji chubanshe, 1999), 58.

47. See L. D. Boni, ed., *Ekonomicheskaia reforma v KNR: Preobrazovaniia v derevne: 1978–1988: Dokumenty* (Economic Reform in the PRC: Reform in Villages: 1978–1988: Documents) (Moscow: Nauka, 1993), 81–82, 128–30.

48. Quoted from Vogel, *Deng Xiaoping and the Transformation of China*, 449.

49. Quoted from Wang, "Teshi teban: Hu Yaobang yu jingji tequ" (Special Things Done in Special Ways: Hu Yaobang and Special Economic Zones), 37.

50. Ibid., 38.

51. Quoted from Leng and Wang, *Deng Xiaoping nianpu: 1975–1997* (Chronological Biography of Deng Xiaoping: 1975–1997), vol. 3, 954.

52. Deng, *Selected Works of Deng Xiaoping*, vol. 3 *(1982–1992)*, 61.

53. Ibid., 61–62.

54. Quoted from Wang, "Teshe teban: Hu Yaobang yu jingji tequ" (Special Things Done in Special Ways: Hu Yaobang and Special Economic Zones), 39.

55. *Shiyi jie san zongquanhui yilai zhongyao wenxian xuandu* (A Reader of Important Documents Since the Third Plenum of the Eleventh Central Committee), vol. 2 (Beijing: Renmin chubanshe, 1987), 735–46.

56. For more details, see Gel'bras, *Ekonomika Kitaiskoi Narodnoi Respubliki* (Economy of the People's Republic of China), 125–26, 130–31, 137.

57. See Vogel, *Deng Xiaoping and the Transformation of China*, 465.

58. Quoted from Zhao, *The Biography of Zhao Ziyang*, 241–42. See also Zhao, *Prisoner of the State*, 121.

59. *Major Documents of the People's Republic of China: Selected Important Documents Since the Third Plenary Session of the Eleventh Central Committee of the Communist Party of China, December 1978–November 1989* (Beijing: Foreign Languages Press, 1991), 407.

60. Zhao, *Prisoner of the State*, 119–20.

61. See Wu, *Zhonghua renmin gongheguo jingji shi* (Economic History of the PRC), vol. 2, 109, 127, 131, 141, 143; Gel'bras, *Ekonomika Kitaiskoi Narodnoi Respubliki*

(Economy of the People's Republic of China), 122–23, 128, 138, 140; Vogel, *Deng Xiaoping and the Transformation of China*, 444–45.

62. Margaret Thatcher, *The Downing Street Years* (New York: HarperCollins, 1993), 260; Deng, *Selected Works of Deng Xiaoping*, vol. 3 *(1982–1992)*, 25.

63. Deng, *Selected Works of Deng Xiaoping*, vol. 3 *(1982–1992)*, 25; Thatcher, *The Downing Street Years*, 262.

64. Quoted from Mark Roberti, *The Fall of Hong Kong: China's Triumph and Britain's Betrayal* (New York: Wiley, 1996), 192.

65. The video of Thatcher's fall is available on YouTube.

66. Deng, *Selected Works of Deng Xiaoping*, vol. 3 *(1982–1992)*, 91.

67. Fei Fei and his wife were among the first from China to go overseas, at the beginning of the 1980s, soon after Deng and Carter had agreed to a student exchange. Their son, Xiaodi ("Little Heir"), born in America in 1985 and thus an American citizen, would change his name to David Zhuo, go to work on Wall Street after graduating from Duke University, live a millionaire's life, and be involved in a sex scandal before finally returning to China. Grandpa Deng would not have been happy.

68. Wu, *Deng Xiaoping yu Zhuo Lin* (Deng Xiaoping and Zhuo Lin), 183; *Yongyuande Xiaoping* (The Unforgettable Xiaoping), 121; Yang, *Deng*, 126.

CHAPTER 22

1. See Liu Binyan. *A Higher Kind of Loyalty: A Memoir by China's Foremost Journalist*, trans. Zhu Hong (New York: Pantheon Books, 1990), 247.

2. See Vogel, *Deng Xiaoping and the Transformation of China*, 567; Deng, *Selected Works of Deng Xiaoping*, vol. 3 *(1982–1992)*, 116–19.

3. Deng, *Selected Works of Deng Xiaoping*, vol. 3 *(1982–1992)*, 130.

4. See Lu, *Hu Yaobang fangwen ji* (Interview with Hu Yaobang), 31–33, 37–42.

5. Quoted from Zhao, *Prisoner of the State*, 164–69.

6. Ibid., 165–66.

7. See ibid., 171.

8. See *Yongyuande Xiaoping* (The Unforgettable Xiaoping), 158.

9. See M. V. Karpov, *Ekonomicheskie reformy i politicheskaia bor'ba v KNR (1984–1989)* (Economic Reforms and Political Struggle in the PRC [1984–1989]) (Moscow: ISAA of MGU Press, 1997), 41.

10. See Zheng, *Hu Yaobang nianpu ziliao changbian* (Large Collection of Materials for a Chronological Biography of Hu Yaobang), vol. 2, 1044.

11. Deng, *Selected Works of Deng Xiaoping*, vol. 3 *(1982–1992)*, 148.

12. Alexander V. Pantsov's interview with former senior research fellow of the PRC Academy of Social Sciences Lin Ying in Columbus, OH, Apr. 24, 2012.

13. See Li, "Yaobang qushi qiande tanhua" (Talks with [Hu] Yaobang Before His Death), 43.

14. See Deng, *Selected Works of Deng Xiaoping*, vol. 3 *(1982–1992)*, 178–79.

15. See Karpov, *Ekonomicheskie reformy i politicheskaia bor'ba v KNR (1984–1989)* (Economic Reforms and Political Struggle in the PRC [1984–1989]), 66.

16. See Gregor Benton and Alan Hunter, eds., *Wild Lily, Prairie Fire: China's Road to Democracy: From Yan'an to Tian'anmen, 1942–1989* (Princeton, NJ: Princeton University Press, 1995), 307–32; Merle Goldman, *Sowing the Seeds of Democracy in China: Political Reform in the Deng Xiaoping Era* (Cambridge, MA: Harvard University Press, 1994), 191–203; Fang Lizhi, *Fang Lizhi zizhuan* (The Autobiography of Fang Lizhi) (Taipei: Tianxia yuanjian chuban gufen youxian gongsi, 2013).

17. See Zhao, *Prisoner of the State*, 166, 168–69; Ruan, *Deng Xiaoping*, 162–63.

18. Confucius, *The Analects of Confucius*, 83.

19. See Zhao, *Prisoner of the State*, 166; Li, "Yaobang qushi qiande tanhua" (Talks with [Hu] Yaobang Before His Death), 40.

20. Deng, *Selected Works of Deng Xiaoping*, vol. 3 *(1982–1992)*, 182–83.

21. Quoted from Ruan, *Deng Xiaoping*, 163.

22. Zhao, *Prisoner of the State*, 170.

23. See Goldman, *Sowing the Seeds of Democracy in China*, 200–201.

24. See Karpov, *Ekonomicheskie reformy i politicheskaia bor'ba v KNR (1984–1989)* (Economic Reforms and Political Struggle in the PRC [1984–1989]), 29.

25. See Seth Faison, "Condolences Calls Put Rare Light on Deng's Family," *New York Times*, Feb. 22, 1997; Bao Tong, "Bao Tong zai xuechao he dongluan qijian yanxing de 'jiaodai': 1989 nian 9 yue 25 ri yu Qincheng jianyu" ("Explanations" of Bao Tong's Words and Actions During the Student Movement and Disturbances: September 25, 1989, the Qincheng Municipal Prison), in Wu Wei, *Zhongguo bashi niandai zhengzhi gaigede taiqian muhou* (On Stage and Backstage: China's Political Reform in the 1980s) (Hong Kong: Xin shiji chubanshe, 2013), 628–29. "China's Former 'First Family': Deng Children Enjoy Privilege, Jealous Attention," http://www.cnn.com/SPECIALS/1999/china.50/inside.china/profiles/deng.xiaoping/children/.

26. Fang Lizhi, *Bringing Down the Great Wall: Writings on Science, Culture, and Democracy in China*, trans. James H. Williams and others (New York: Knopf, 1991), 158, 160.

27. Quoted from Goldman, *Sowing the Seeds of Democracy*, 200; Karpov, *Ekonomicheskie reformy i politicheskaia bor'ba v KNR (1984–1989)* (Economic Reforms and Political Struggle in the PRC [1984–1989]), 80. See also Fang, *Fang Lizhi zizhuan* (The Autobiography of Fang Lizhi), 367–68.

28. See Robert Lawrence Kuhn, *The Man Who Changed China: The Life and Legacy of Jiang Zemin* (New York: Crown, 2004), 126–34; Goldman, *Sowing the Seeds of Democracy in China*, 201–2; Karpov, *Ekonomicheskie reformy i politicheskaia bor'ba v KNR (1984–1989)* (Economic Reforms and Political Struggle in the PRC [1984–1989]), 81–83.

29. All three were expelled in January 1987, but unlike Wei Jingsheng they were not imprisoned. In the spring of 1988, Liu Binyan was even allowed to go on a lecture tour to the United States. Fang Lizhi and Wang Ruowang left for the United States after the suppression of the new student disturbances in June 1989.

30. Deng, *Selected Works of Deng Xiaoping*, vol. 3 *(1982–1992)*, 194–97. See also Fang, *Fang Lizhi zizhuan* (The Autobiography of Fang Lizhi), 370–77; Li, "Yaobang qushi qiande tanhua" (Talks with [Hu] Yaobang Before His Death), 41.

31. Zhao, *Prisoner of the State*, 172–73; Zheng, *Hu Yaobang nianpu ziliao changbian* (Large Collection of Materials for a Chronological Biography of Hu Yaobang), vol. 2, 1182. He also requested that Hu's mistakes not be characterized as an anti-party line, that he not be accused of factionalism, and that his personal character not be discussed.

32. See Zhao, *Prisoner of the State*, 164, 174–75; Zheng, *Hu Yaobang nianpu ziliao changbian* (Large Collection of Materials for a Chronological Biography of Hu Yaobang), vol. 2, 1182–86. Li, "Yaobang qushi qiande tanhua" (Talks with [Hu] Yaobang Before His Death), 43, 44.

33. See Zheng, *Hu Yaobang nianpu ziliao changbian* (Large Collection of Materials for a Chronological Biography of Hu Yaobang), vol. 2, 1186.

34. Quoted from ibid., 1187.

35. See Zhao, *Prisoner of the State*, 176.

36. Ibid., 190.

37. Ibid., 194.

38. See Deng, *Selected Works of Deng Xiaoping*, vol. 3 *(1982–1992)*, 223.

39. See Zhao, *Prisoner of the State*, 122–23.

40. *Documents of the Thirteenth National Congress of the Communist Party of China (October 25–November 1, 1987)* (Beijing: Foreign Languages Press, 1987), 7–8.

41. See Zhao, *Prisoner of the State*, 46–47, 210.

42. Deng's role may be compared to that of Empress Ci Xi, who also ruled from behind the screen, but no one was bold enough to suggest this.

43. *Documents of the Thirteenth National Congress of the Communist Party of China (October 25–November 1, 1987)*, 9–18.

44. Zhao, *Prisoner of the State*, 206.

45. See *Documents of the Thirteenth National Congress of the Communist Party of China (October 25–November 1, 1987)*, 18–42.

46. See Richard Baum, "Zhao Ziyang and China's 'Soft Authoritarian' Alternative," in Guoguang Wu and Helen Lansdowne, eds., *Zhao Ziyang and China's Political Future* (London: Routledge, 2008), 111–12; Zhao, *Prisoner of the State*, 220.

47. After the selection of Li Tieying, rumors began circulating around the country that he was Deng's illegitimate son. People were persuaded that during the Long March in 1935, supposedly behind the back of her new husband Li Weihan, Jin Weiying—recalling her previous love—somehow yielded to Deng. This gossip, however, was certainly untrue. As we know, to the end of his days Deng could

not forgive his wife, who had betrayed him. But he had good relations with Li Tieying.

48. See Zhao, *Prisoner of the State*, 211.

49. The prices for alcohol and cigarettes rose especially high because the state actually did free prices. State prices on other goods did not change, so that the market price increase was entirely due to the public hullabaloo.

50. See *Zhongguo gongchandang xin shiqi lishi dashiji (zengdingben) (12, 1978–3, 2008)* (Chronology of CCP History in the New Period: Expanded edition [December 1978–March 2008]) Beijing: 182–83.

51. See Vogel, *Deng Xiaoping and the Transformation of China*, 470; Karpov, *Ekonomicheskie reformy i politicheskaia bor'ba v KNR (1984–1989)* (Economic Reforms and Political Struggle in the PRC [1984–1989]), 106; Victor Shih, *Factions and Finance in China: Elite Conflict and Inflation* (New York: Cambridge University Press, 2008), 124–36.

52. Alexander V. Pantsov's reminiscences of his 1987–88 visit to China.

53. See *Pravda*, July 29, 1986.

54. See Deng, *Selected Works of Deng Xiaoping*, vol. 3 *(1982–1992)*, 170–77.

55. A. S. Cherniaev et al., eds., *V Politburo TsK KPSS . . . Po zapisiam Anatoliia Cherniaeva, Vadima Medvedeva, Georgiia Shakhnazarova (1985–1991)* (In the CC CPSU Politburo . . . from The Notes Taken by Anatolii Cherniaev, Vadim Medvedev, Georgii Shakhnazarov [1985–1991]) (Moscow: Alphina Biznes Buks, 2006), 152.

56. See ibid., 216.

57. See Deng Xiaoping, *Osnovnye voprosy sovremennogo Kitaia* (Fundamental Issues of Contemporary China) (Moscow: Politizdat, 1988).

58. For details, see Huang, *Memoirs*, 493–518; Qian Qichen, *Ten Episodes in China's Diplomacy* (New York: HarperCollins, 2005), 1–28; V. P. Fedotov, *Polveka vmeste s Kitaem: Vospominaniia, zapisi, razmyshleniia* (A Half a Century Together with China: Reminiscences, Notes, Thoughts) (Moscow: ROSSPEN, 2005), 482–613; Wishnick, *Mending Fences*, 98–103, 107–15.

CHAPTER 23

1. Li Peng, "Guanjian shike—Li Peng riji" (The Crucial Moment—Li Peng's Diary), in Zhang Ganghua, *Li Peng liu si riji zhenxiang* (A True Nature of Li Peng's June 4th Diary) (Hong Kong: Aoya chuban youxian gongsi, 2010), 55–56; Zheng, *Hu Yaobang nianpu ziliao changbian* (Large Collection of Materials for a Chronological Biography of Hu Yaobang), vol. 2, 1216–17; Andrew J. Nathan and Perry Link, eds., *The Tiananmen Papers*, compiled Zhang Liang (New York: PublicAffairs, 2002), 20–21; Lo Ping, "The Last Eight Days of Hu Yaobang," in Michel Oksenberg, Lawrence R. Sullivan, and Marc Lambert, eds., *Beijing Spring, 1989: Confrontation and Conflict: The Basic Documents* (Armonk, NY: Sharpe,

1990), 195–203; Pang Pang, *The Death of Hu Yaobang*, trans. Si Ren (Honolulu: Center for Chinese Studies, 1989), 9–49.

2. Quoted from Karpov, *Ekonomicheskie reformy i politicheskaia bor'ba v KNR (1984–1989)* (Economic Reforms and Political Struggle in the PRC [1984–1989]), 168.

3. See Li, "Guanjian shike—Li Peng riji" (The Crucial Moment—Li Peng's Diary), 59–62.

4. Nathan and Link, *The Tiananmen Papers*, 34.

5. See Li, "Guanjian shike—Li Peng riji" (The Crucial Moment—Li Peng's Diary), 73, 77; Zhao, *Prisoner of the State*, 4; Nathan and Link, *The Tiananmen Papers*, 29–31; David Turnley, *Beijing Spring* (New York: Stewart, Tabori & Chang, 1989), 29–31, 38–44.

6. Quoted from Yang Shangkun, "Yang Shangkun riji: Deng Xiaoping jujue kanwang linzhongde Hu Yaobang" (Yang Shangkun's Diaries: Deng Xiaoping Refused to Visit Dying Hu Yaobang), http://qzxy.blog.epochtimes.com/article/show?articleid=28779. See also Li, "Yaobang qushi qiande tanhua" (Talks with [Hu] Yaobang Before His Death), 43, 44.

7. Quoted from Zheng, *Hu Yaobang nianpu ziliao changbian* (Large Collection of Materials for a Chronological Biography of Hu Yaobang), vol. 2, 1220. See also Li, "Guanjian shike—Li Peng riji" (The Crucial Moment—Li Peng's Diary), 71.

8. See Zhao, *Prisoner of the State*, 5–6, 8–9, 50, 63–64.

9. See ibid., 9–10; Nathan and Link, *The Tiananmen Papers*, 53–54, 57–60; Leng and Wang, *Deng Xiaoping nianpu: 1975–1997* (Chronological Biography of Deng Xiaoping: 1975–1997), vol. 2, 1272.

10. Quoted from Leng and Wang, *Deng Xiaoping nianpu: 1975–1997* (Chronological Biography of Deng Xiaoping: 1975–1997), vol. 2, 1272–74; Oksenberg, Sullivan, and Lambert, *Beijing Spring, 1989*, 203–6.

11. Nathan and Link, *The Tiananmen Papers*, 74; Zhao, *Prisoner of the State*, 11.

12. See Bao, "Bao Tong zai xuechao he dongluan qijian yanxing de 'jiaodai': 1989 nian 9 yue 25 ri yu Qincheng jianyu" ("Explanations" of Bao Tong's Words and Actions During the Student Movement and Disturbances: September 25, 1989, the Qincheng Municipal Prison), 626.

13. See Oksenberg, Sullivan, and Lambert, *Beijing Spring, 1989*, 206–8.

14. Quoted from Zhao, *Prisoner of the State*, 13. Zhao added, however, "I admit I can't attest to the accuracy of this."

15. See ibid., 16; Zhao Ziyang, "Make Further Efforts to Carry Forward the May 4th Spirit in the New Age of Construction and Reform," in Oksenberg, Sullivan, and Lambert, *Beijing Spring, 1989*, 249; Bao, "Bao Tong zai xuechao he dongluan qijian yanxing de 'jiaodai': 1989 nian 9 yue 25 ri yu Qincheng jianyu" ("Explanations" of Bao Tong's Words and Actions during the Student Movement and Disturbances: September 25, 1989, the Qincheng Municipal Prison), 624–25.

16. See Zhao, "Make Further Efforts to Carry Forward the May 4th Spirit in the New Age of Construction and Reform," 248.

17. Nathan and Link, *The Tiananmen Papers*, 115. This speech was also composed by Bao Tong, but Zhao orally shaped all main ideas to him. According to Bao Tong, Zhao himself contrasted his views to the "collective decision" of the Standing Committee. See Bao, "Bao Tong zai xuechao he dongluan qijian yanxing de 'jia-odai': 1989 nian 9 yue 25 ri yu Qincheng jianyu" ("Explanations" of Bao Tong's Words and Actions During the Student Movement and Disturbances: September 25, 1989, the Qincheng Municipal Prison), 625.

18. Ibid., 143.

19. Ibid., 147–49.

20. John Garnaut's interview with Hu Shiying, a son of Hu Qiaomu, Beijing, February 2013.

21. See ibid., 19–22.

22. Nathan and Link, *The Tiananmen Papers*, 154. See also Philip J. Cunningham, *Tiananmen Moon: Inside the Chinese Student Uprising of 1989* (Lanham, MD: Rowman & Littlefield, 2009), 59–85.

23. Mikhail Gorbachev, *Memoirs* (New York: Vantage Press, 1996), 488–89; Deng, *Selected Works of Deng Xiaoping*, vol. 3 *(1982–1992)*, 284–87; Qian, *Ten Episodes in China's Diplomacy*, 29–30; Fedotov, *Polveka vmeste s Kitaem* (A Half a Century Together with China), 616–18.

24. See Gorbachev, *Memoirs*, 490; Oksenberg, Sullivan, and Lambert, *Beijing Spring, 1989*, 261; Wu, *Zhongguo bashi niandai zhengzhi gaigede taiqian muhou* (On Stage and Backstage: China's Political Reform in the 1980s), 438, 621–23, 626. Some people close to the party leadership later would claim that Zhao did it because he drank too much during the reception. See ibid., 627.

25. Nathan and Link, *The Tiananmen Papers*, 181; Zhao, *Prisoner of the State*, 27.

26. Nathan and Link, *The Tiananmen Papers*, 188–89.

27. Zhao, *Prisoner of the State*, 29, 68–69. Yang Shangkun worried that Zhao's resignation would fuel the students' "disturbances." See Bao, "Bao xuechao he dongluan qijian yanxing de 'jiaodai': 1989 nian 9 yue 25 ri yu Qincheng jianyu" ("Explanations" of Bao Tong's Words and Actions During the Student Movement and Disturbances: September 25, 1989, the Qincheng Municipal Prison), 627.

28. Nathan and Link, *The Tiananmen Papers*, 194.

29. Oksenberg, Sullivan, and Lambert, *Beijing Spring, 1989*, 288–90.

30. Nathan and Link, *The Tiananmen Papers*, 217–19.

31. See Oksenberg, Sullivan, and Lambert, *Beijing Spring, 1989*, 309–16; Karpov, *Ekonomicheskie reformy i politicheskaia bor'ba v KNR (1984–1989)* (Economic Reforms and Political Struggle in the PRC [1984–1989]), 148.

32. Nathan and Link, *The Tiananmen Papers*, 238–39.

33. Ibid., 309.

34. Deng, *Selected Works of Deng Xiaoping*, vol. 3 *(1982–1992)*, 292.

35. See Karpov, *Ekonomicheskie reformy i politicheskaia bor'ba v KNR (1984–1989)* (Economic Reforms and Political Struggle in the PRC [1984–1989]), 148.

36. See Nathan and Link, *The Tiananmen Papers*, 377–85, 421–22, 436–37; David J. Firestein, *Beijing Spring 1989: An Outsider's Inside Account* (Austin, TX: Banner Press, 1990), 147–56; Chen Yizi, *Chen Yizi huiyilu* (Memoirs of Chen Yizi) (Hong Kong: New Century, 2013), 626–28; Latin American Diplomat Eyewitness Account of June 3–4 Events in "Tiananmen Square," https://wikileaks.org/cable/1989/07/89BEIJING8828/html.

CHAPTER 24

1. Alexander V. Pantsov's interview with a Chinese citizen, June 4 and 5, 1989.
2. See *Major Documents of the People's Republic of China*, 828–31; Nathan and Link, *The Tiananmen Papers*, 392–96, 398–416.
3. See Nathan and Link, *The Tiananmen Papers*, 420–24.
4. See Zhao, *Prisoner of the State*, 231–36.
5. Deng, *Selected Works of Deng Xiaoping*, vol. 3 *(1982–1992)*, 294–99.
6. Ibid., 301, 303. See also Leng and Wang, *Deng Xiaoping nianpu: 1975–1997* (Chronological Biography of Deng Xiaoping: 1975–1997), vol. 2, 1281–82.
7. Zhao, *Prisoner of the State*, 41.
8. Ibid., 42; Nathan and Link, *The Tiananmen Papers*, 438–41.
9. For the text of the verdict, see Zhao, *Prisoner of the State*, 63–70.
10. Several years prior to his death, Zhao began to dictate his reminiscences onto a tape recorder. He hid the cassettes in empty boxes among his grandsons' toys. After the demise of the former general secretary, members of his family took the cassettes to Hong Kong. The simultaneous publication in Hong Kong, Taipei, and New York of his reminiscences under the title *Prisoner of the State: The Secret Diaries of Zhao Ziyang* produced a sensation.
11. See *Major Documents of the People's Republic of China*, 840–43.
12. See Nathan and Link, *The Tiananmen Papers*, 432–36.
13. See Leng and Wang, *Deng Xiaoping nianpu: 1975–1997* (Chronological Biography of Deng Xiaoping: 1975–1997), vol. 2, 1286.
14. Deng, *Selected Works of Deng Xiaoping*, vol. 3 *(1982–1992)*, 307–8.
15. See ibid., 312–13.
16. *Major Documents of the People's Republic of China*, 878.
17. *Yongyuande Xiaoping* (The Unforgettable Xiaoping), 15, 17.
18. Ibid., 39.
19. See ibid., 147, 177; Wu, *Deng Xiaoping yu Zhuo Lin* (Deng Xiaoping and Zhuo Lin), 153–55.
20. See Deng, *Selected Works of Deng Xiaoping*, vol. 3 *(1982–1992)*, 314; Wu, *Deng Xiaoping yu Zhuo Lin* (Deng Xiaoping and Zhuo Lin), 152.
21. See Wu, *Deng Xaoping yu Zhuo Lin* (Deng Xiaoping and Zhuo Lin), 198; *Yongyuande Xiaoping* (The Unforgettable Xiaoping), 12, 15, 159.
22. Quoted from Wu, *Deng Xiaoping yu Zhuo Lin* (Deng Xiaoping and Zhuo Lin), 185.

23. See *Yongyuande Xiaoping* (The Unforgettable Xiaoping), 13, 18, 179.
24. See ibid., 159; Wu, *Deng Xiaoping yu Zhuo Lin* (Deng Xiaoping and Zhuo Lin), 148–51.
25. Deng, *Selected Works of Deng Xiaoping*, vol. 3 *(1982–1992)*, 320–21.
26. Ibid., 339; George Bush and Brent Scowcroft, *A World Transformed* (New York: Knopf, 1998), 176.
27. Deng, *Selected Works of Deng Xiaoping*, vol. 3 *(1982–1992)*, 457.
28. See Zhao, *Prisoner of the State*, 109–10.
29. Deng, *Selected Works of Deng Xiaoping*, vol. 3 *(1982–1992)*, 353–55.
30. Ibid., 356.
31. See Gel'bras, *Ekonomika Kitaiskoi Narodnoi Respubliki* (Economy of the People's Republic of China), 161, 177–78, 187–89.
32. On world reaction to the events on Tiananmen Square, see, for example, Nathan and Link, *The Tiananmen Papers*, 416–18; Gorbachev, *Memoirs,* 492–93; Bush and Scowcroft, *A World Transformed*, 86–89, 97–99, 101, 106–11, 115, 128, 174.
33. Deng, *Selected Works of Deng Xiaoping*, vol. 3 *(1982–1992)*, 358–70.
34. See Leng and Wang, *Deng Xiaoping nianpu: 1975–1997* (Chronological Biography of Deng Xiaoping: 1975–1997), vol. 2, 1341, 1345–46.
35. Quoted from ibid., 1355.
36. See Jiang Zemin, *Izbrannoye* (Selected Works), vol. 1 (Beijing: Izdatel'stvo literatury na inostrannykh iazykakh, 2010), 247, 252–75.
37. See Gel'bras, *Ekonomika Kitaiskoi Narodnoi Respubliki* (Economy of the People's Republic of China), 206, 230.
38. See Leng and Wang, *Deng Xiaoping nianpu: 1975–1997* (Chronological Biography of Deng Xiaoping: 1975–1997), vol. 2, 1367–71.
39. See *Yongyuande Xiaoping* (The Unforgettable Xiaoping), 159; Gao Xiaolin, ed., *Zoujin Deng Xiaoping* (Together with Deng Xiaoping) (Beijing: Dangdai Zhongguo chubanshe, 2004), 197.
40. See for example, Deng, *Selected Works of Deng Xiaoping*, vol. 3 *(1982–1992)*, 307.
41. According to Deng's wish, only his body was to be cremated. He wanted his corneas and internal organs given to medical specialists for research.
42. See Leng and Wang, *Deng Xiaoping nianpu: 1975–1997* (Chronological Biography of Deng Xiaoping: 1975–1997), vol. 2, 1374–75.
43. Zhuo Lin would outlive Deng Xiaoping by twelve and a half years, almost the number of years she was his junior. She died on July 29, 2009, after a prolonged illness.

EPILOGUE

1. After his meeting with Gorbachev, Deng said to his translator, "Gorbachev may look very smart, but in fact is very stupid." [Zhang Weiwei], "Fangyiyuan huiyi Deng Xiaoping: Qiangdiao renhe shiqing dou yao qin zi shijian" (Interpreter Remembers Deng Xiaoping: One Must Definitely Go from Practice in All Things),

news.qq.com/2/20140818/009294.htm. See also Vogel, *Deng Xiaoping and the Transformation of China*, 423.

2. See Gel'bras, *Ekonomika Kitaiskoi Narodnoi Respubliki* (Economy of the People's Republic of China), 288.

3. See M. S. Gorbachev, *Zhizn' i reformy* (Life and Reforms), vol. 2 (Moscow: Novosti, 1995), 334; Barry Naughton, *Growing out of the Plan: Chinese Economic Reform, 1978–1993* (Cambridge: Cambridge University Press, 1995), 261; M. L. Titarenko, ed., *40 let KNR* (Forty Years of the PRC) (Moscow: Nauka, 1989), 531–32.

4. Jiang, *Izbrannoye* (Selected Works), vol. 1, 727.

5. Deng, *Selected Works of Deng Xiaoping*, vol. 2 (1975–1982), 349; *vol. 3 (1982–1992)*, 175.

Bibliography

PRIMARY SOURCES

I. Archival Sources

Russian State Archive of Social and Political History (RGASPI in Russian Abbreviation)

Collection 17. Inventory 2. Plenums of the Central Committee of the Russian Communist Party (Bolsheviks) and the All-Union Communist Party (Bolsheviks). 1918–1941.

Collection 17. Inventory 3. Minutes of Sessions of the Politburo of the Central Committee of the Russian Communist Party (Bolsheviks) and the All-Union Communist Party (Bolsheviks).

Collection 17. Inventory 162. Special Papers of the Politburo of the Central Committee of the Russian Communist Party (Bolsheviks) and the All-Union Communist Party (Bolsheviks).

Collection 146. Inventory 2. File 3. The Diary of Georgii Dimitrov (Mar. 9, 1933–Feb. 6, 1949).

Collection 495. Inventory 65a. Personal Files of Employees of the Executive Committee of the Communist International Apparatus.

Collection 495. Inventory 225. File 71. Dossier to the Personal File of Mao Zedong. 5 vols.

Collection 495. Inventory 225. File 71. Personal File of Mao Zedong. 10 vols.

Collection 495. Inventory 225. File 428. Personal file of Jin Weiying (Liza). [Deng Xiaoping's second wife.]

Collection 495. Inventory 225. File 1629. Personal File of Deng Xixian (Dozorov). [Deng Xiaoping.]

Collection 495. Inventory 225. File 1669. Personal File of Dogadova. [Deng Xiaoping's first wife.]

Collection 495. Inventory 225. File 2574. Personal File of Deng Xixian. [Deng Xiaoping.]

Collection 495. Inventory 225. Personal Files of 3,323 Members of the Chinese
     Communist Party and the Guomindang.

Collection 505. International Control Commission of the Communist International.

Collection 514. Central Committee of the Chinese Communist Party.

Collection 514. Inventory 3. Collection of Mao Zedong's Documents of 1923–1940.

Collection 530. Communist University of the Toilers of China.

Collection 531. International Lenin School.

Collection 532. Communist University of the Toilers of the East and the
     Research Institute of National and Colonial Problems.

Collection 558. Joseph Vissarionovich Stalin. Collection of unsorted documents.

Archive on the Foreign Policy of the Russian Federation (AVP RF in Russian
     Abbreviation)

Collection 0100. Inventory 46. File 12. Folder 362. The Diary of Soviet
     Ambassador to China Vasily Vasilevich Kuznetsov. Miscellaneous papers.

Collection 0100. Inventory 46. File 374. Folder 121. Zhou Enlai Speech at the
     All-China Financial-Economic Conference.

Former Archive of the Central Committee of the Socialist Unity Party of Germany.

Stenographic Record of the Meeting Between a Delegation of the Communist
     Party of the Soviet Union and the Communist Party of China, July 5–20,
     1963. Moscow. [2 parts.]

Bureau of Investigation of the Ministry of Legislation on Taiwan

Miscellaneous papers on Chinese Communist movement.

Private Archives

Archives of Alexander V. Pantsov. Miscellaneous papers.

Archives of Igor Vasilievich Yurchenko (Yuzhin), Stalin's Emissary at Mao's
     Headquarters in Yan'an, 1941–1943. Miscellaneous papers.

II. PRINTED DOCUMENTS

Acheson, Dean. "Letter of Transmittal." In *United States Relations with China: With
     Special Reference to the Period 1944–1949.* New York: Greenwood Press, 1968, iii–xvii.

Aimermakher, K., ed. *Doklad N. S. Khrushcheva o kul'te lichnosti Stalina na XX s"ezde
     KPSS: Dokumenty* (N. S. Khrushchev's Report on Stalin's Cult of Personality at
     the 20th CPSU Congress: Documents). Moscow: ROSSPEN, 2002.

"'All Under the Heaven Is Great Chaos': Beijing, the Sino-Soviet Clashes, and the Turn to Sino-American Rapprochement, 1968–69." *CWIHP Bulletin*, no. 11 (March 1998): 155–75.

Angle, Stephen C., and Marina Svensson, eds. *The Chinese Human Rights Reader: Documents and Commentary, 1990–2000.* Armonk, NY: Sharpe, 2001.

Bao Tong. "Bao Tong zai xuechao he dongluan qijian yanxing de 'jiaodai': 1989 nian 9 yue 25 ri yu Qincheng jianyu" ("Explanations" of Bao Tong's Words and Actions During the Student Movement and Disturbances: September 25, 1989, the Qincheng Municipal Prison). In Wu Wei, *Zhongguo bashi niandai zhengzhi gaigede taiqian muhou* (On Stage and Backstage: China's Political Reform in the 1980s). Hong Kong: Xin shiji chubanshe, 2013, 624–30.

Baqi huiyi (August 7 Conference). Beijing: Zhonggong dangshi ziliao chubanshe, 1986.

Baum, Richard, and Frederick C. Teiwes. *Ssu-Ch'ing: The Socialist Education Movement of 1962–1966.* Berkeley: University of California Press, 1968.

Benton, Gregor, and Alan Hunter, eds. *Wild Lily, Prairie Fire: China's Road to Democracy: From Yan'an to Tian'anmen, 1942–1989.* Princeton, NJ: Princeton University Press, 1995.

Boni, L. D., ed. *Ekonomicheskaia reforma v KNR: Preobrazovaniia v derevne: 1978–1988: Dokumenty* (Economic Reform in the PRC: Reform in Villages: 1978–1988: Documents). Moscow: Nauka, 1993.

Borisov, O. [Rakhmanin O. B.], and M. Titarenko, eds. *Vystupleniia Mao Tsze-duna, ranee ne publikovavshiesia v kitaiskoi pechati* (Mao Zedong's Speeches Previously Unpublished in the Chinese Press.) 6 series. Moscow: Progress, 1975–76.

[Bowie, Robert R., and John K. Fairbank, eds.] *Communist China, 1955–1959: Policy Documents with Analysis.* Cambridge, MA: Harvard University Press, 1962.

Bukharin, N. I. "Otvet na zapisku V. I. Lenina" (Reply to V. I. Lenin's Note). In L. B. Kamenev, ed. *Leninskii sbornik* (Lenin's Collection). Vol. 4. Moscow: Gosizdat, 1925, 384–85.

Bukharin, N. I. *Selected Writings on the State and the Transition to Socialism.* Translated, edited, and introduced by Richard B. Day. Armonk, NY: Sharpe, 1982.

Burr, William, ed. *The Kissinger Transcripts: The Top Secret Talks with Beijing and Moscow.* New York: New Press, 1998.

Carter, Jimmy. *White House Diary.* New York: Farrar, Straus and Giroux, 2010.

The Case of Peng Dehuai: 1959–1968. Hong Kong: Union Research Institute, 1968.

CCP Documents of the Great Proletarian Cultural Revolution, 1966–1976. Hong Kong: Union Research Institute, 1968.

Chen Jian. "Deng Xiaoping, Mao's 'Continuous Revolution,' and the Path Towards the Sino-Soviet Split: A Rejoinder." *CWIHP Bulletin*, no. 10 (March 1998): 162–64.

Chen Yun. *Chen Yun wenxuan: 1926–1949* (Selected Works of Chen Yun: 1926–1949). Beijing: Renmin chubanshe, 1984.

Chen Yun. *Chen Yun wenxuan: 1949–1956* (Selected Works of Chen Yun: 1949–1956). Beijing: Renmin chubanshe, 1984.

Chen Yun. *Chen Yun wenxuan: 1956–1985* (Selected Works of Chen Yun: 1956–1985). Beijing: Renmin chubanshe, 1986.

Cherniaev, A. S., et al., eds. *V Politburo TsK KPSS . . . Po zapisiam Anatoliia Cherniaeva, Vadima Medvedeva, Georgiia Shakhnazarova (1985–1991)* (In the CC CPSU Politburo . . . from the Notes Taken by Anatolii Cherniaev, Vadim Medvedev, Georgii Shakhnazarov). Moscow: Alphina Biznes Buks, 2006.

Chi Hsin. *The Case of Gang of Four: With First Translation of Teng Hsiao-ping's "Three Poisonous Weeds."* Hong Kong: Cosmos Books, 1977.

Chinese War Crimes in Vietnam. Hanoi: Vietnam Courier, 1979.

Chou En-lai. "Report on the Proposals for the Second Five-Year Plan for Development of the National Economy." In *Eighth National Congress of the Communist Party of China.* Vol. 1: *Documents.* Peking: Foreign Languages Press, 1956, 261–328.

Deng Xiaoping. "Deng Xiaoping gei Mao zhuxide xin (1972 nian 8 yue 3 ri)" (Deng Xiaoping's Letter to Chairman Mao [August 3, 1972]), http://www.sinovision.net/blog/index/php?act=details&id=12850&bcode=xinwu.

Deng Xiaoping. "Deng Xiaoping qicaode 'Qi jun gongzuo baogao'" (Report on the Work of the 7th Corps Written by Deng Xiaoping). In Deng Xiaoping. *Deng Xiaoping zishu* (Autobiographical Notes of Deng Xiaoping). Beijing: Jiefangjun chubanshe, 2004, 45–74.

Deng Xiaoping. *Deng Xiaoping shouji xuan* (Selected Manuscripts of Deng Xiaoping). 4 vols. Beijing: Zhongguo dang'an chubanshe/Daxiang chubanshe, 2004.

Deng Xiaoping. *Deng Xiaoping wenxuan* (Selected Works of Deng Xiaoping). 3 vols. Beijing: Renmin chubanshe, 1994.

Deng Xiaoping. *Deng Xiaoping xinan gongzuo wenji* (Works of Deng Xiaoping on His Work in the Southwest). Beijing/Chongqing: Zhongyang wenxian chubanshe/Chongqing chubanshe, 2006.

Deng Xiaoping. "Deng Xiaoping's Talks with the Soviet Ambassador and Leadership, 1957–1963." *CWIHP Bulletin,* no. 10 (March 1998): 165–82.

Deng Xiaoping. *Osnovnye voprosy sovremennogo Kitaia* (Fundamental Issues of Contemporary China). Moscow: Politizdat, 1988.

Deng Xiaoping. "Report on the Rectification Campaign, 1955–1959." In [Bowie, Robert R., and John K. Fairbank, eds.] *Communist China, 1955–1959: Policy Documents with Analysis.* Cambridge, MA: Harvard University Press, 1962, 341–63.

Deng Xiaoping. *Selected Works of Deng Xiaoping (1938–1965)* Beijing: Foreign Languages Press, 1992.

Deng Xiaoping. *Selected Works of Deng Xiaoping.* Vol. 2 *(1975–1982).* Beijing: Foreign Languages Press, 1995.

Deng Xiaoping. *Selected Works of Deng Xiaoping.* Vol. 3 *(1982–1992).* Beijing: Foreign Languages Press, 1994.

Deng Xiaoping. *Speech by Chairman of Delegation of the People's Republic of China, Teng Hsiao-p'ing, at the Special Session of the U.N. General Assembly.* Beijing: Foreign Languages Press, 1974.

Deng Xiaoping. "Velikoe splochenie kitaiskogo naroda i velikoe splochenie narodov mira" (The Great Unity of the Chinese People and the Great Unity of the Peoples of the World). *Pravda (Truth)*, Oct. 1, 1959.

IX Vsekitaiskii s"ezd Kommunisticheskoi partii Kitaia (dokumenty) (Ninth Congress of the Communist Party of China [Documents]). Beijing: Izdatel'stvo literatury na inostrannykh iazykakh, 1969.

Documents of the First Session of the Fifth National People's Congress of the People's Republic of China. Beijing: Foreign Languages Press, 1978.

Documents of the National Conference of the Communist Party of China: March 1955. Peking: Foreign Languages Press, 1955.

Documents of the Thirteenth National Congress of the Communist Party of China (October 25–November 1, 1987). Peking: Foreign Languages Press, 1987.

"Doklad delegatsii iz Guansi na I Vsekitaiskoi konferentsii predstavitelei Sovetskikh raionov: Mai 1930 g." (Report of the Guangxi Delegation at the First All-China Conference of the Soviet Areas' Representatives: May 1930). In Pavel Mif, ed. *Sovety v Kitae: Sbornik dokumentov i materialov* (Soviets in China: A Collection of Documents and Materials). Moscow: Partizdat TsK VKP(b), 1934, 195–200.

Dokumenty soveshchaniia predstavitelei kommunisticheskikh i rabochikh partii, sostoiavshikhsia v Moskve v noiabre 1957 goda (Documents from the Meetings of Representatives of Communist and Workers' Parties that Took Place in Moscow in November 1957). Moscow: Gospolitizdat, 1957.

Dokumenty VIII Plenuma Tsentral'nogo Komiteta Kommunisticheskoi partii Kitaia vos'mogo sozyva (Documents of the Eighth Plenum of the Eighth Central Committee of the Communist Party of China). Beijing: Izdatel'stvo literatury na inostrannykh iazykakh, 1959.

Dvenadtsatyi Vsekitaiskii s"ezd Kommunisticheskoi partii Kitaia (dokumenty) (Twelfth National Congress of the Communist Party of China [Documents]). Beijing: Foreign Languages Press, 1982.

XXII s"ezd Kommunisticheskoi partii Sovetskogo Soiuza: 17–31 oktiabria 1961: Stenograficheskii otchet (Twenty-second Congress of the Communist Party of the Soviet Union: October 17–31, 1961: Stenographic Record). 3 vols. Moscow: Gospolitizdat, 1962.

Eighth National Congress of the Communist Party of China. 2 vols. Peking: Foreign Languages Press, 1956.

The Eleventh National Congress of the Communist Party of China: Documents. Beijing: Foreign Languages Press, 1977.

"The Emerging Disputes Between Beijing and Moscow: Ten Newly Available Chinese Documents, 1956–1958." *CWIHP Bulletin*, nos. 6–7 (1995–96): 148–63.

"Excerpt from the Communiqué of the Fourth Plenum (February 18, 1954)." In Frederick C. Teiwes. *Politics at Mao's Court: Gao Gang and Party Factionalism.* Armonk, NY: Sharpe, 1990, 236–37.

Fang Lizhi. *Bringing Down the Great Wall: Writings on Science, Culture, and Democracy in China.* Translated by James H. Williams and others. New York: Knopf, 1991.

Feng Yuxiang, *Wo de shenghuo* (My Life). Harbin: Heilongjiang renmin chubanshe, 1984.

Feng Yuxiang. *Feng Yuxian riji* (Diary of Feng Yuxiang). 2 vols. Nanjing: Jiangsu guji chubanshe, 1992.

Fifth Session of the Fifth National Congress (Main Documents). Beijing: Foreign Languages Press, 1982.

Fu Fa qingong jianxue yundong shiliao (Materials on the History of the Diligent Work, Frugal Study Movement in France). 3 vols. Beijing: Beijing chubanshe, 1981.

Fursenko, A. A., ed. *Prezidium TsK KPSS: 1954–1964* (Presidium of the CC CPSU: 1954–1964). Vol. 1. *Chernovye protokol'nye zapisi zasedanii, stenogramy, post-anovleniia* (Draft Protocol Minutes of the Sessions, Stenographic Records, and Resolutions). Moscow: ROSSPEN, 2003.

Fursenko, A. A., ed. *Prezidium TsK KPSS: 1954–1964* (Presidium of the CC of the CPSU: 1954–1964). Vol. 2. *Postanovleniia 1954-1958* (Resolutions of 1954–1958). Moscow: ROSSPEN, 2006.

Fursenko, A A., ed. *Prezidium TsK KPSS: 1954–1964* (Presidium of the CC of the CPSU: 1954–1964). Vol. 3. *Postanovleniia 1959-1964* (Resolutions of 1959–1964). Moscow: ROSSPEN, 2008.

Gao Gang. *Izbrannoe* (Selections). Moscow: IDV AN SSSR, 1989.

Gao Yi, ed. *Fengbei—Deng Xiaoping guju chenleguan* (A Monument to Deng Xiaoping). Chengdu: Sichuan chubanshe, 2004.

Geroi ostrova Damanskii (Heroes of Damansky Island). Moscow: "Molodaia gvardiia," 1969.

Gongchan xiaozu (Communist Cells). 2 vols. Beijing: Zhonggong dangshi ziliao chubanshe, 1987.

Gongheguo zouguode lu—jianguo yilai zhongyao wenxian zhuanti xuanji (1949–1952 nian) (The Path the Republic Has Taken—Thematic Collection of Selected Important Documents from the Time of the Founding of the PRC [1949–1952]). Beijing: Zhongyang wenxian chubanshe, 1991.

The Great Cultural Revolution in China. Rutland, VT: Tuttle, 1968.

Great Historic Victory: In Warm Celebration of Chairman Hua Kuo-feng's Becoming Leader of the Communist Party of China, and of the Crushing of the Wang-Chang-Chiang-Yao Anti-Party Clique. Beijing: Foreign Languages Press, 1976.

The Great Socialist Cultural Revolution in China. 1–6. Peking: Foreign Languages Press, 1966.

A Great Trial in Chinese History: The Trial of the Lin Biao and Jiang Qing Counter-Revolutionary Cliques, Nov. 1980–Jan. 1981. Oxford: Pergamon Press, 1981.

Han Minzhu, ed. *Cries for Democracy: Writings and Speeches from the 1989 Chinese Democracy Movement*. Princeton, NJ: Princeton University Press, 1990.

Ho Chi Minh. "The Last Testament of Ho Chi Minh." *Antioch Review*. Vol. 29, no. 4 (1969–1970): 497–99.

Hsiao Tso-liang. *Power Relations Within the Chinese Communist Movement, 1930–1934*. Vol. 2. Seattle: University of Washington Press, 1967.

Huang Jinping, and Zhang Li. *Deng Xiaoping zai Shanghai* (Deng Xiaoping in Shanghai). Shanghai: Shanghai renmin chubanshe, 2004.

"An Interview with Teng Hsiao-p'ing: Calling for Stronger U.S.-China Ties and a United Front Against Moscow." *Time, v*ol. 113, no. 6 (Feb. 5, 1979): 32–35.

Jiang Zemin, Izbrannoye (Selected Works), vol. 1. Beijing: Izdatel'stvo literatury na inostrannykh iazykakh, 2010.

Jinggangshan geming genjudi shiliao xuanbian (Collection of Selected Materials on the Revolutionary Base Area in the Jinggang Mountains). Nanchang: Jiangxi renmin chubanshe, 1986.

Kaizhan dui "Shuihu" de pinglun (Develop Criticism of [the Novel] *Water Margin*). Xi'an: [n.p.], 1975.

Kau, Michael Y. M., ed. *The Lin Piao Affair: Power Politics and Military Coup*. White Plains, NY: International Arts and Sciences Press, 1975.

Khrushchev, N. S. *Report of the Central Committee of the Communist Party of the Soviet Union to the 20th Party Congress*, February 14, 1956. Moscow: Foreign Languages Publishing House, 1956.

Khrushchev, N. S. *Speech of Nikita Khrushchev Before a Closed Session of the XXth Congress of the Communist Party of the Soviet Union on February 25, 1956*. Washington, DC: U.S. Government Printing Office, 1957.

"Khrushchev's Nuclear Promise to Beijing During the 1958 Crisis." *CWIHP Bulletin*, nos. 6–7 (1995–96): 219, 226–27.

Kovalev, I. V. "Zapiska I. V. Kovaleva ot 24 dekabria 1949 g." (I. V. Kovalev's Note of December 24, 1949). *Novaia i noveishaia istoriia* (*Modern and Contemporary History*), no. 1 (1998): 132–39.

Kramer, Mark. "New Evidence on Soviet Decision-Making and the 1956 Polish and Hungarian Crisis." *CWIHP Bulletin*, nos. 8–9 (1996–97): 358–84.

Kramer, Mark. "The USSR Foreign Ministry's Appraisal of Sino-Soviet Relations on the Eve of the Split, September 1959." *CWIHP Bulletin*, nos. 6–7 (1995–96): 170–85.

Kurdiukov, I. F., et al., eds. *Sovetsko-kitaiskie otnosheniia, 1917–1957: Sbornik dokumentov* (Soviet-Chinese Relations, 1917–1957: A Documentary Collection). Moscow: Izd-vo vostochnoi literatury, 1959.

LaFantasie, Glenn W., ed. *Foreign Relations of the United States: 1958–1960*. Vol. 19: *China*. Washington, DC: U.S. Government Printing Office, 1996.

Laird, Thomas. *The Story of Tibet: Conversations with the Dalai Lama*. New York: Grove Press, 2006.

Laoyibei gemingjia shuxin xuan (Selected Letters of the Old Generation Revolutionaries). Changsha: Hunan renmin chubanshe, 1984.

Latin American Diplomat Eyewitness Account of June 3–4 Events in "Tiananmen Square." https://wikileaks.org/ cable/1989/07/89BEIJING8828/html.

"Le Duan and the Break with China." *CWIHP Bulletin*, nos. 12–13 (Fall–Winter 2001), 273–88.

Lenin, V. I. *Collected Works.* 45 vols. Moscow: Progress Publishers, 1972.

Lenin, V. I. *Polnoe sobranie sochinenii* (Complete Collected Works). 55 vols. Moscow: Politizdat, 1963–1978.

Levine, Marilyn A., and Chen San-ching. *The Guomindang in Europe: A Sourcebook of Documents.* Berkeley: University of California Press, 2000.

Li Fu-ch'un. "Report on the First Five-Year Plan, 1953–1957, July 5–6, 1955." In [Robert R. Bowie and John K. Fairbank, eds.] *Communist China, 1955–1959: Policy Documents with Analysis.* Cambridge, MA: Harvard University Press, 1962, 43–91.

Li Songchen, ed. *Gaige dang'an (1976–1999)* (Archive of Reform [1976–1999]). 2 vols. Beijing: Dangdai Zhongguo chubanshe, 2000.

Li Xiannian. *Li Xiannian wenxuan: 1935–1988* (Selected Works of Li Xiannian). Beijing: Renmin chubanshe, 1989.

Lih, Lars T., et al., eds. *Stalin's Letters to Molotov, 1925–1936.* Translated by Catherine A. Fitzpatrick. New Haven: Yale University Press, 1995.

Liu da yilai: Dangnei mimi wenxian (After the Sixth Congress: Secret Intra-party Documents). 2 vols. Beijing: Renmin chubanshe, 1989.

Liu Shao-chi. *On the Party.* Peking: Foreign Languages Press, 1950.

Liu Shaoqi. "Guanyu xinminzhuyi de jianshe wenti" (On the Question of New Democratic Construction). In *Gongheguo zouguode lu—jianguo yilai zhongyao wenxian zhuanti xuanji (1949–1952 nian)* (The Path the Republic Has Taken—Thematic Collection of Selected Important Documents from the Time of the Founding of the PRC [1949–1952]). Beijing: Zhongyang wenxian chubanshe, 1991, 17–26.

Liu Shaoqi. *Liu Shaoqi xuanji* (Selected Works of Liu Shaoqi). 2 vols. Beijing: Renmin chubanshe, 1985.

Liu Shaoqi. *Selected Works of Liu Shaoqi.* 2 vols. Beijing: Foreign Languages Press, 1984.

Lu Keng. *Hu Yaobang fangwen ji* (Interview with Hu Yaobang). New York: Niuyue huayu jigou, 1985.

MacFarquhar, Roderick, ed. *The Secret Speeches of Chairman Mao: From the Hundred Flowers to the Great Leap Forward.* Cambridge, MA: Council on East Asian Studies/Harvard University, 1989.

Major Documents of the People's Republic of China: Selected Important Documents Since the Third Plenary Session of the Eleventh Central Committee of the Communist Party of China, December 1978–November 1989. Beijing: Foreign Languages Press, 1991.

Mao Zedong. *Jianguo yilai Mao Zedong wengao* (Manuscripts of Mao Zedong from the Founding of the PRC). 13 vols. Beijing: Zhongyang wenxian chubanshe, 1987–1998.

Mao Zedong. "Mao Tszedun o kitaiskoi politike Kominterna i Stalina" (Mao Zedong on the China Policy of the Comintern and of Stalin). *Problemy Dal'nego Vostoka* (*Far Eastern Affairs*), no. 5 (1998): 101–10.

Mao Zedong. *Mao Zedong on Diplomacy*. Beijing: Foreign Languages Press, 1998.

Mao Zedong. *Mao Zedong shuxin xuanji* (Selected Letters of Mao Zedong). Beijing: Renmin chubanshe, 1983.

Mao Zedong. *Mao Zedong sixiang wansui* (Long Live Mao Zedong Thought). 2 vols. Beijing: S.N.I., 1967–69.

Mao Zedong. *Mao Zedong wenji* (Works of Mao Zedong). 8 vols. Beijing: Renmin chubanshe, 1993–99.

Mao Zedong. *Mao Zedong xuanji* (Selected Works of Mao Zedong). Vols. 1–5. Beijing: Renmin chubanshe, 1951–1977.

Mao Zedong. *Mao Zedong zai qidade baogao he jianghua ji* (Collection of Reports and Speeches of Mao Zedong at the 7th Congress). Beijing: Zhangyang wenxian chubanshe, 2000.

Mao Zedong. *Miscellany of Mao Tse-tung Thought (1949–1968)*. 2 parts. Springfield, VA: Joint Publications Research Service, 1974.

Mao Zedong. *Oblaka v snegu. Stikhotvoreniia v perevodakh Aleksandra Pantsova* (Clouds in the Snow: Poems in [Russian] Translation by Alexander Pantsov). Moscow: "Veche," 2010.

Mao Zedong. "Qida gongzuo fangzhen" (Work Report at the Seventh Congress). *Hongqi (Red Flag)*, no. 11 (1981): 1–7.

Mao Zedong. *Report from Xunwu*. Translated, with an introduction and notes by Roger R. Thomson. Stanford, CA: Stanford University Press, 1990.

Mao Zedong. *Selected Works of Mao Tse-tung*. 5 vols. Peking: Foreign Languages Press, 1967–1977.

Mao Zedong shenghuo dang'an (Archives of Mao Zedong's Life). 3 vols. Beijing: Zhonggong dangshi chubanshe, 1999.

Materialy 6-go plenuma Tsentral'nogo Komiteta Kommunisticheskoi partii Kitaia vos'mogo sozyva (Materials of the Sixth Plenum of the Eighth Central Committee of the Chinese Communist Party). Beijing: Izdatel'stvo literatury na inostran- nykh iazykakh, 1959.

Materialy VIII Vsekitaiskogo s"ezda Kommunisticheskoi partii Kitaia (Materials from the 8th Congress of the Communist Party of China). Moscow: Gospolitizdat, 1956.

"Memo, PRC Foreign Ministry to the USSR Embassy in Beijing, March 13, 1957." *CWIHP Bulletin*, nos. 6–7 (1995–96): 159–60.

"Meeting Between Zhou Enlai and Kosygin at the Beijing Airport." http://www. fmprc.gov.cn/eng/56920%l.html.

Mif, Pavel, ed. *Sovety v Kitae: Materialy i dokumenty: Sbornik vtoroi* (Soviets in China: Materials and Documents. Collection Two). Moscow: Partizdat TSK VKP(b), 1935. Unpublished proofs.

Mif, Pavel, ed. *Sovety v Kitae: Sbornik materialov i dokumentov* (Soviets in China: Collection of Materials and Documents). Moscow: Partizdat, 1934.

Mif, Pavel, ed. *Strategiia i taktika Kominterna v natsional'no-kolonial'noi revoliutsii na primere Kitaia* (Strategy and Tactics of the Comintern in National and Colonial Revolution: The Case of China). Moscow: IWEIP Press, 1934.

"Minutes, Mao's Conversation with a Yugoslavian Communist Union Delegation, Beijing, [undated] September, 1956." *CWIHP Bulletin*, nos. 6–7 (1995–96): 148–52.

Myers, James T., et al., eds. *Chinese Politics: Documents and Analysis*. 4 vols. Columbia: University of South Carolina Press, 1986.

Nathan, Andrew J., and Perry Link, eds. *The Tiananmen Papers*. Compiled by Zhang Liang. New York: PublicAffairs, 2002.

"A New 'Cult of Personality': Suslov's Secret Report on Mao, Khrushchev, and Sino-Soviet Tensions, December 1959." *CWIHP Bulletin*, nos. 8–9 (1996–97): 244, 248.

Nickles, David P., and Adam M. Howard, eds. *Foreign Relations of the United States, 1977–1980*. Vol. 13: *China*. Washington, DC: U.S. Government Printing Office, 2013.

Nie Yuanzi, et al. "Song Shuo, Lu Ping, Peng Peiyuan zai wenhua gemingzhong jiujing gan shenma" (What Are Song Shuo, Lu Ping, and Peng Peiyuan Really Doing with Respect to the Cultural Revolution). *Renmin ribao* (*People's Daily*), June 2, 1966.

The Ninth National Congress of the Communist Party of China (Documents). Peking: Foreign Languages Press, 1969.

Obrazovanie Kitaiskoi Narodnoi Respubliki: Dokumenty i materialy (Establishment of the Chinese People's Republic: Documents and Materials). Moscow: Gospolitizdat, 1950.

Ogden, Suzanne, et al., eds. *China's Search for Democracy: The Student and the Mass Movement of 1989*. Armonk, NY: Sharpe, 1992.

Oksenberg, Michel, Lawrence R. Sullivan, and Marc Lambert, eds. *Beijing Spring, 1989: Confrontation and Conflict: The Basic Documents*. Armonk, NY: Sharpe, 1990.

Ostermann, Christian F. "East German Documents on the Border Conflict, 1969." *CWIHP Bulletin*, nos. 6–7 (1995–96): 186–93.

Otkrytoe pis'mo Tsentral'nogo Komiteta Kommunisticheskoi partii Sovetskogo Soiuza partiinym organizatsiiam, vsem kommunistam Sovetskogo Soiuza (Open Letter of the Central Committee of the Communist Party of the Soviet Union to all Party Organizations and Communists in the Soviet Union). Moscow: Gospolitizdat, 1963.

Peng Dehuai. "Comrade Peng Dehuai's Letter to Chairman Mao (July 14, 1959)." In Peng Dehuai. *Memoirs of a Chinese Marshal: The Autobiographical Notes of Peng Dehuai (1898–1974)*. Translated by Zheng Longpu. Beijing: Foreign Languages Press, 1984, 510–20.

The Polemic on the General Line of the International Communist Movement. Peking: Foreign Languages Press, 1965.

Polemika o general'noi linii mezhdunarodnogo kommunisticheskogo dvizheniia (Polemic on the General Line of the International Communist Movement). Beijing: Izdatel'stvo literatury na inostrannykh iazykakh, 1965.

Politburo TSK VKP(b) i Sovet ministrov SSSR 1945–1953 (The Politburo of the CC of the AUCP[b] and the USSR Council of Ministers 1945–1953). Moscow: ROSSPEN, 2002.

The Question of Tibet and the Rule of Law. Geneva: International Commission of Jurists, 1959.

"Record of Conversation, Mao Zedong and Soviet Ambassador to Beijing Pavel Yudin, July 22, 1958." In O. Arne Westad, ed., *Brothers in Arms: The Rise and Fall of the Sino-Soviet Alliance, 1945–1963.* Stanford, CA: Stanford University Press, 1998, 347–56.

Resolution on CPC History (1949–81). Beijing: Foreign Languages Press, 1981.

Saich, Tony, ed. *The Rise to Power of the Chinese Communist Party: Documents and Analysis.* Armonk, NY: Sharpe, 1996.

Sanfan wufan yundong wenjian huibian (Collection of Documents from the Three Anti and Five Anti Movements). Beijing: Renmin chubanshe, 1953.

San zhongquanhui yilai—zhongyang wenxian xuanbian (Collection of Selected Key Documents Since the Third Plenum). 2 vols. Beijing: Renmin chubanshe, 1982.

Schell, Orville. *Mandate of Heaven: A New Generation of Entrepreneurs, Dissidents, Bohemians, and Technocrats Lays Claim to China's Future.* New York: Simon & Schuster, 1994.

Schell, Orville, and David Shambaugh, eds. *The China Reader: The Reform Era.* New York: Vintage Books, 1999.

Schoenhals, Michael, ed. *China's Cultural Revolution, 1966–1969: Not a Dinner Party.* Armonk, NY: Sharpe, 1996.

Schram, Stuart, ed. *Chairman Mao Talks to the People: Talks and Letters, 1956–1971.* New York: Pantheon Books, 1974.

Schram, Stuart R., ed. *Mao's Road to Power: Revolutionary Writings, 1912–1949.* 7 vols. Armonk, NY: Sharpe, 1992–2005.

Seymour, James D., ed. *The Fifth Modernization: China's Human Rights Movement, 1978–1979.* Stanfordville, NY: Human Rights, 1980.

Shi Ch'eng-chih. *People's Resistance in Mainland China.* Hong Kong: Union Research Institute, 1956.

Shiyi jie san zhongquanhui yilai zhongyao wenxian xuandu (A Reader of Important Documents Since the Third Plenum of the Eleventh Central Committee). 2 vols. Beijing: Renmin chubanshe, 1987.

Siao Lo (Xiao Luo). "Sovetskaia vlast' v Lunzhou (provintsiia Guansi)" (Soviet Power in Longzhou [Guangxi Province]). In Pavel Mif, ed. *Sovety v Kitae: Sbornik dokumentov i materialov* (Soviets in China: A Collection of Documents and Materials). Moscow: Partizdat TsK VKP(b), 1934, 192–95.

The Sino-Soviet Dispute. New York: Scribner, 1969.

Sladkovskii, M. I., ed. *Dokumenty po istorii Kommunisticheskoi partii Kitaia 1920–1949 (v chetyrekh tomakh)* (Documents on the History of the Communist Party of China, 1920–1949. 4 vols.). Moscow: IDV AN SSSR, 1981.

Sladkovskii, M. I., ed. *Informatsionnyi biulleten': Seriia A: "Kulturnaia revoliutsiia" v Kitae: Dokumenty i materialy (perevod s kitaiskogo)* (Information Bulletin. Series A: The "Cultural Revolution" in China. Documents and Materials [Translated from Chinese]). 12 installments. Moscow: IDV AN SSSR, 1968–72.

Stalin, J. V. *Sochineniia (Works)*. Vol. 18. Tver': Informatsionno-izdatel'skii tsentr "Soiuz," 2006.

Stalin, J. V. *Works*. 13 vols. Moscow: Foreign Languages Publishing House, 1954.

"Stalin's Conversations with Chinese Leaders: Talks with Mao Zedong, 1949–January 1950, and with Zhou Enlai, August–September 1952." *CWIHP Bulletin*, nos. 6–7 (1995–96): 5–19.

Stenograficheskii otchet XX s"ezda KPSS (Stenographic Record of the Twentieth Congress of the CPSU). 2 vols. Moscow: Gospolitizdat, 1956.

Stenograficheskii otchet XXI s"ezda Kommunisticheskoi partii Sovetskogo Soiuza (Stenographic Record of the Twenty-first Congress of the Communist Party of the Soviet Union). 2 vols. Moscow: Gospolitizdat, 1959.

Sudarikov, N. G., ed. *Konstitutsiia i osnovnye zakonodatel'nye akty Kitaiskoi Narodnoi Respubliki* (The Constitution and Founding Legislative Acts of the People's Republic of China). Moscow: Izdatel'stvo inostrannoi literatury, 1955.

Sun Yat-sen. *Izbrannye proizvedeniia* (Selected Works), 2nd ed., revised and expanded. Moscow: Nauka, 1985.

Sun Yat-sen. *Zhongshan quanji* (Complete works of [Sun] Yatsen). 2 vols. Shanghai: Lianyou tushuguan yinshu gongsi, 1931.

The Tenth National Congress of the Communist Party of China (Documents). Peking: Foreign Languages Press, 1973.

Tikhvinsky, S. L., ed. *Rossiisko-kitaiskiie otnosheniia v XX veke* (Russo-Chinese Relations in the 20th Century). Vol. 5. 2 books. Moscow: Pamiatniki istoricheskoi mysli, 2005.

Titarenko, M. L., ed. *Kommunisticheskii Internatsional i kitaiskaia revoliutsiia: Dokumenty i materialy* (The Communist International and the Chinese Revolution: Documents and Materials). Moscow: Nauka, 1986.

Titarenko, M. L., et al., eds., *VKP (b), Komintern i Kitai: Dokumenty* (The AUCP[b], the Comintern, and China: Documents). 5 vols. Moscow: AO "Buklet," 1994–2007.

Unger, Jonathan, ed. *The Pro-Democracy Protests in China: Reports from the Provinces*. Armonk, NY: Sharpe, 1991.

United States Relations with China: With Special Reference to the Period 1944–1949. New York: Greenwood Press, 1968.

"V universitete trudiashchikhsia Sun Yat-sena" (In Sun Yat-sen University of Toilers). *Pravda (Truth)*. March 11, 1926.

Vazhneishie dokumenty ob osvoboditel'noi voine kitaiskogo naroda v poslednee vremia (The Most Important Documents of the Chinese People's Liberation War in the Most Recent Period). Harbin: Izd-vo Severo-Vostoka Kitaia, 1948.

Velikaia proletarskaia kul'turnaia revoliutsiia (vazhneishie dokumenty) (The Great Proletarian Cultural Revolution [Key Documents]). Beijing: Izdatel'stvo literatury na inostrannykh iazykakh, 1970.

Vladimirov, P. P. *Osobyi raion Kitaia, 1942–1945* (Special Region of China, 1942–1945). Moscow: APN, 1975.

Vidali, Vittorio. *Diary of the Twentieth Congress of the Communist Party of the Soviet Union.* Translated by Nell Amter Cattonar and A. M. Elliot. Westport, CT, and London: Lawrence Hill and Journeyman Press, 1974.

Vozniknovenie i razvitie raznoglasii mezhdu rukovodstvom KPSS i nami: Po povodu otkrytogo pis'ma TsK KPSS (The Origin and Development of Disagreements Between the Leadership of the CPSU and Us: On the Open Letter of the CC CPSU). Beijing: Izdatel'stvo literatury na inostrannykh iazykakh, 1963.

Vtoraia sessiia VIII Vsekitaiskogo s"ezda Kommunisticheskoi partii Kitaia (Second Session of the Eighth Congress of the Communist Party of China). Beijing: Izdatel'stvo literatury na inostrannykh iazykakh, 1958.

Wang Dongxing. *Wang Dongxing riji* (Diary of Wang Dongxing). Beijing: Zhongguo shehui kexue chubanshe, 1993.

Wang Ming. *Sobranie sochinenii* (Collected Works). 4 vols. Moscow: IDV AN SSSR, 1984–87.

Wei Jingsheng. *The Courage to Stand Alone: Letters from Prison and Other Writings.* Edited and translated by Kristina Torgeson. New York: Viking, 1997.

Westad, O. Arne, et al., eds. "77 Conversations Between Chinese and Foreign Leaders on the Wars in Indochina, 1964–1977." *CWIHP Working Paper*, no. 22 (May 1998).

Wilbur, C. Martin, ed. *The Communist Movement in China: An Essay Written in 1924 by Ch'en Kung-po.* New York: East Asian Institute of Columbia University, 1960.

Wingrove, Paul. "Mao's Conversations with the Soviet Ambassador, 1953–1955." *CWIHP Working Paper*, no. 36 (April 2002).

Wishnick, Elizabeth. "In the Region and in the Center: Soviet Reactions to the Border Rift." *CWIHP Bulletin*, nos. 6–7 (1995–96): 194–201.

Wishnick, Elizabeth. "Sino-Soviet Tensions, 1980: Two Russian Documents." *CWIHP Bulletin*, nos. 6–7 (1995–96): 202–6.

Wolff, David. "'One Finger's Worth of Historical Events': New Russian and Chinese Evidence on the Sino-Soviet Alliance and Split, 1948–1959." *CWIHP Working Paper*, no. 30 (August 2000).

Wusi shiqi qikan jieshao (Survey of May 4th Era Publications). 4 vols. Beijing: Shenghuo. Dushu. Xinzhi sanlian shudian, 1979.

Wusi yundong zai Sichuan (May 4th Movement in Sichuan). Chengdu: Sichuan daxue chubanshe, 1989.

Yang Shangkun. *Yang Shangkun riji* (Diary of Yang Shangkun). 2 vols. Beijing: Zhongyang wenxian chubanshe, 2001.

Yang Shangkun. "Yang Shangkun riji: Deng Xiaoping jujue kanwang linzhongde Hu Yaobang" (Yang Shangkun's Diaries: Deng Xiaoping Refused to Visit Dying Hu Yaobang), http://qzxy.blog.epochtimes.com/article/show?articleid=28779.

Za splochenost' mezhdunarodnogo kommunistichekogo dvizheniia: Dokumenty i materialy (For the Unity of the International Communist Movement: Documents and Materials). Moscow: Politizdat, 1964.

Zhang Shu Guang, and Chen Jian. "The Emerging Disputes Between Beijing and Moscow: Ten Newly Available Chinese Documents, 1956–1958." *CWIHP Bulletin*, nos. 6–7 (1995–96), 148–63.

Zhang Wentian. *Zhang Wentian xuanji* (Selected Works of Zhang Wentian). Beijing: Renmin chubanshe, 1985.

Zhang Yunhou, et al. *Wusi shiqi de shetuan* (Societies During the May 4th Era). 4 vols. Beijing: Shenghuo. Dushu. Xinzhi sanlian shudian, 1979.

Zhao Ziyang. *China's Economy and Development Principles: A Report by Zhao Ziyang.* Beijing: Foreign Languages Press, 1982.

Zhao Ziyang. "Make Further Efforts to Carry Forward the May 4th Spirit in the New Age of Construction and Reform." In Michel Oksenberg, Lawrence R. Sullivan, and Marc Lambert, eds. *Beijing Spring, 1989: Confrontation and Conflict: The Basic Documents.* Armonk, NY: Sharpe, 1990, 244–51.

Zheng Zhongbing, ed. *Hu Yaobang nianpu ziliao changbian* (Large Collection of Materials for a Chronological Biography of Hu Yaobang). 2 vols. Hong Kong: Shidaiguo ji chuban youxian gongsi, 2005.

Zhonggong zhongyang wenjian xuanji (Collection of CCP CC Selected Documents). 18 vols. Beijing: Zhonggong zhongyang dangxiao chubanshe, 1989.

Zhongguo gongchandang di shier ci quanguo daibiao dahui wenjian huibian (Collection of Documents from the Twelfth National Congress of the Communist Party of China). Beijing: Renmin chubanshe, 1982.

Zhou Enlai. *K voprosu ob intelligentsii. (Doklad na soveshchanii po voprosu ob intelligentsii, sozvannom TsK KPK 14 ianvaria 1956 g.)* (On the Issue of Intelligentsia: A Report at the Meeting on Intelligentsia Held by the CCP CC on January 14, 1956). Beijing: Izdatel'stvo literatury na inostrannykh iazykakh, 1956.

Zhou Enlai. *Selected works of Zhou Enlai.* 2 vols. Beijing: Foreign Languages Press, 1981.

Zhou Enlai. *Zhou Enlai xuanji* (Selected works of Zhou Enlai). 2 vols. Beijing: Renmin chubanshe, 1980.

Zhou Xun, ed. *The Great Famine in China, 1958–1962: A Documentary History.* New Haven: Yale University Press, 2012.

Zinner, Paul E. ed. *National Communism and Popular Revolt in Eastern Europe: A Selection of Documents on Events in Poland and Hungary.* New York: Columbia University Press, 1956.

Zubok, Vladislav. "'Look What Chaos in the Beautiful Socialist Camp!' Deng Xiaoping and the Sino-Soviet Split, 1956–1963." *CWIHP Bulletin*, no. 10 (March 1998): 152–62.

Zubok, Vladislav. "The Mao-Khrushchev Conversations, July 31–August 3, 1958, and October 2, 1959." *CWIHP Bulletin*, nos. 12–13 (Fall–Winter 2001): 244–72.

Zunyi huiyi wenxian (Documents of the Zunyi Conference). Beijing: Renmin chubanshe, 1985.

Zuo you jiang geming genjudi (Revolutionary Bases in the Zuojiang and Youjiang Areas). 2 vols. Beijing: Zhonggong dangshi ziliao chubanshe, 1989.

III. MEMOIRS

Aleksandrov-Agentov, A. M. *Ot Kollontai do Gorbacheva: Vospominaniia diplomata, sovetnika A. A. Gromyko, pomoshchnika L. I. Brezhneva, Iu. V. Andropova, K. U. Chernenko i M. S. Gorbacheva* (From Kollontai to Gorbachev: The Reminiscences of a Diplomat and Adviser to A. A. Gromyko, and Assistant to L. I. Brezhnev, Iu. V. Andropov, K. U. Chernenko, and M. S. Gorbachev). Moscow: Mezhdunarodnye otnosheniia, 1994.

Arbatov, Georgii. *The System: An Insider's Life in Soviet Politics.* New York: Times Books, 1992.

Arbatov, Georgii. *Zatianuvsheesia vyzdorovlenie (1953–1985): Svidetel'stvo sovremennika* (A Lengthy Convalescence [1953–1985]: Testimony of a Contemporary). Moscow: Mezhdunarodnye otnosheniia, 1991.

Arbatov, Georgii. *Zhizn', sobytiia, liudi: Avtobiografiia na fone istoricheskikh peremen* (Life, Events, People: An Autobiography Against the Background of Historical Changes). Moscow: Liubimaia Rossiia, 2008.

Barber, Noel. *The Fall of Shanghai.* New York: Coward, McCann & Geoghegan, 1979.

Belden, Jack. *China Shakes the World.* New York: Harper, 1949.

Berezhkov, V. N. *Riadom so Stalinym* (By Stalin's Side). Moscow: Vagrius, 1998.

Bo Yibo. *Ruogan zhongda juece yu shijiande huigu* (Recollections of Several Important Decisions and Their Implementation). 2 vols. Beijing: Zhonggong zhongyang dangxiao chubanshe, 1991.

Braun, Otto. *A Comintern Agent in China, 1932–1939.* Translated by Jeanne Moore. Stanford, CA: Stanford University Press, 1982.

Brezhnev, A. A. *Kitai: ternistyi put' k dobrososedstvu: vospominaniia i razmyshleniia* (China: The Arduous Way to Neighborliness: Reminiscences and Thoughts). Moscow: Mezhdunarodnye otnosheniia, 1998.

Broomhall, Marshall. *General Feng: A Good Soldier of Christ Jesus.* London: China Inland Mission, 1923.

Brzezinski, Zbigniew. *Power and Principle: Memoirs of the National Security Advisor, 1977–1981.* New York: Farrar, Straus and Giroux, 1985.

Bush, George, and Brent Scowcroft. *A World Transformed*. New York: Knopf, 1998.

Cai Chang. "Tan fu Fa qingong jianxue he shehuizhuyi qingniantuan lü Ou zhibu" (On the Diligent Work, Frugal Study in France and the European Branch of the Socialist Youth League). *Gongchanzhuyi xiaozu* (Communist Cells). Vol. 2. Beijing: Zhonggong dangshi ziliao chubanshe, 1987, 945–48.

Carlson, Evans Fordyce. *Evans F. Carlson on China at War, 1937–1941*. New York: China and Us, 1993.

Carlson, Evans Fordyce. *Twin Stars of China: A Behind-the-Scenes Story of China's Valiant Struggle for Existence by a U.S. Marine Who Lived and Moved with the People*. New York: Dodd, Mead & Company, 1940.

Carter, Jimmy. *Keeping Faith: Memoirs of a President*. Fayetteville: University of Arkansas Press, 1995.

Chang Kuo-t'ao. "Introduction." In Liu Shaoqi. *Collected Works of Liu Shao-ch'i Before 1944*. Hong Kong: Union Research Institute, 1969, i–x.

Chang Kuo-t'ao. *The Rise of the Chinese Communist Party. Volumes One & Two of Autobiography of Chang Kuo-t'ao*. Lawrence: University Press of Kansas, 1972.

Chen Boda. *Chen Boda yi gao: yuzhong zishu ji qita* (Manuscripts of Chen Boda: Autobiographical Notes from Prison and Other [Materials]). Hong Kong: Tiandi tushu youxian gongsi, 1998.

Chen Boda. *Chen Boda zuihou koushu huiyi* (The Last Oral Reminiscences of Chen Boda). Rev. ed. Hong Kong: Xingke'er chubanshe youxian gongsi, 2005.

Chen Yi. "Wo liang nian lai liu Fa de tong ku" (My Two-year Sufferings from Sojourning in France). In *Fu Fa qingong jianxue yundong shiliao* (Materials on the History of the Diligent Work, Frugal Study Movement in France). Vol. 3. Beijing: Beijing chubanshe, 1981, 54–57.

Chen Yi. "Wo liang nian lai liu Fa qingong jianxuede shigan" (My Two-year Impressions from the Diligent Work, Frugal Study in France). In *Fu Fa qingong jianxue yundong shiliao* (Materials on the History of the Diligent Work, Frugal Study Movement in France). Vol. 3. Beijing: Beijing chubanshe, 1981, 47–53.

Chen Yizi. *Chen Yizi huiyilu* (Memoirs of Chen Yizi). Hong Kong: New Century, 2013.

Ch'eng, Marcus. *Marshal Feng—The Man and His Work*. Shanghai: Kelly & Walsh, 1926.

Chiang Ching-kuo. *My Days in Soviet Russia*. [Taipei: [n.p.], 1963].

Chiang Chungcheng (Chiang Kai-shek). *Soviet Russia in China: Summing-Up at Seventy* Translated, under the direction of Madame Chiang Kai-shek. Rev., enlarged ed., with maps. New York: Farrar, Straus and Cudahy, 1958.

Cressy-Marcks, Violet. *Journey into China*. New York: Dutton, 1942.

Cui Ji. *Wo suo qinlide zhongsu da lunzhan* (The Great Polemic Between the USSR and the PRC as Part of My Own History). Beijing: Renmin ribao chubanshe, 2009.

Cunningham, Philip J. *Tiananmen Moon: Inside the Chinese Student Uprising of 1989*. Lanham, MD: Rowman & Littlefield, 2009.

Dalin, S. A. *Kitaiskie memuary: 1921–1927* (Chinese Memoirs: 1921–1927). Moscow: Nauka, 1975.

Davidson, Robert J., and Isaac Mason. *Life in West China Described by Two Residents in the Province of Sz-Chwan*. London: Headley Brothers, 1905.

Davis, George T. B. *China's Christian Army: A Story of Marshal Feng and His Soldiers*. New York: Christian Alliance, 1925.

Dedijer, Vladimir. *Tito Speaks*. London: Weidenfeld and Nicolson, 1953.

Deng Ken. "Deng Ken tan Deng Xiaoping" (Deng Ken Speaks About Deng Xiaoping). In Liu Jintian, ed. *Huashuo Deng Xiaoping* (Stories About Deng Xiaoping). Beijing: Zhongyang wenxian chubanshe, 2004, 3–9.

[Deng Ken]. "Gege wei geming bu huijia" (Elder Brother Did Not Return Home for the Sake of the Revolution). *Zhongguo ribao* (*China Newspaper*). Sept. 28, 2008.

Deng Maomao. *Deng Xiaoping: My Father*. New York: Basic Books, 1995.

Deng Maomao. *Wode fuqin Deng Xiaoping* (My Father Deng Xiaoping). Beijing: Zhongyang wenxian chubanshe, 1997.

Deng Maomao. *Wode fuqin Deng Xiaoping: "Wenge" suiyue* (My Father Deng Xiaoping: Years of the Cultural Revolution). Beijing: Zhongyang wenxian chubanshe, 2000.

Deng Rong. *Deng Xiaoping and the Cultural Revolution: A Daughter Recalls the Critical Years*. Translated by Sidney Shapiro. Beijing: Foreign Languages Press, 2002.

Deng Xiaoping. *Deng Xiaoping zishu* (Autobiographical Notes of Deng Xiaoping). Beijing: Jiefangjun chubanshe, 2004.

Deng Xiaoping. "Diao Liu Bocheng" (To the Memory of Liu Bocheng). In Liu Bocheng, *Liu Bocheng huiyilu* (Reminiscences of Liu Bocheng). Vol. 3. Shanghai: Shanghai wenyi chubanshe, 1987, 5–9.

Deng Xiaoping. *Wode zishu (Zhailu)* (My Autobiographical Notes [Excerpts]). June 20–July 5, 1968. http://blog.smthome.net/article-htm-tid-993.html.

Deng Yingchao, "Guanyu Jin Weiying qingkuang (Li Tieying tongzhi de muqin)" (Regarding Jin Weiying [Comrade Li Tieying's Mother]). In Xu Zhujin. *Jin Weiying zhuan* (Biography of Jin Weiying). Beijing: Zhonggong dangshi chubanshe, 2004, 319–20.

Djilas, Milovan. *Conversations with Stalin*. Translated by Michael B. Petrovich. New York: Harcourt, Brace & World, 1962.

Fang Lizhi. *Fang Lizhi zizhuan* (The Autobiography of Fang Lizhi). Taipei: Tianxia yuanjian chuban gufen youxian gongsi, 2013.

Fedotov, V. P. *Polveka vmeste s Kitaem: Vospominaniia, zapisi, razmyshleniia* (A Half a Century Together with China: Reminiscences, Notes, Thoughts). Moscow: ROSSPEN, 2005.

Feng Lida. *Wo de fuqin Feng Yuxiang jiangjun* (My Father General Feng Yuxiang). Chengdu: Sichuan renmin chubanshe, 1984.

Feng Yuxiang, Wo de shenghuo (My Life). Harbin: Heilongjiang renmin chubanshe, 1984.

Firestein, David J. *Beijing Spring 1989: An Outsider's Inside Account*. Austin, TX: Banner Press, 1990.

Ford, Gerald R. *A Time to Heal: The Autobiography of Gerald R. Ford*. New York: Harper & Row, 1979.

Ford, Robert. *Captured in Tibet*. Hong Kong: Oxford University Press, 1990.

Franck, Harry Alverson. *China: A Geographical Reader*. Dansville, NY: Owen, [1927].

Franck, Harry Alverson. *Roving Through Southern China*. New York: Century, 1925.

Franck, Harry Alverson. *Wandering in Northern China*. New York: Century, 1923.

Gao Kelin. "Gao Kelin tan Deng Xiaoping" (Gao Kelin Speaks About Deng Xiaoping). In Liu Jintian, ed. *Huashuo Deng Xiaoping* (Stories About Deng Xiaoping). Beijing: Zhongyang wenxian chubanshe, 2004, 17–20.

Gao Xiaolin, ed. *Zoujin Deng Xiaoping* (Together with Deng Xiaoping). Beijing: Dangdai Zhongguo chubanshe, 2004.

Garside, Roger. *Coming Alive: China after Mao*. New York: McGraw-Hill, 1981.

Geil, William Edgar. *Eighteen Capitals of China*. Philadelphia: Lippincott, 1911.

Geil, William Edgar. *A Yankee on the Yangtse: Being a Narrative of a Journey from Shanghai Through the Central Kingdom to Burma*. New York: A. C. Armstrong and Son, 1904.

Gong Chu. *Wo yu hongjun* (The Red Army and I). Hong Kong: Nan feng chubanshe, 1954.

Gorbachev, Mikhail. *Memoirs*. New York: Vantage Press, 1996.

Gorbachev, Mikhail. *Zhizn'i reformy* (Life and Reforms). 2 vols. Moscow: Novosti, 1995.

Greenblatt, Sidney L., ed. *The People of Taihang: An Anthology of Family Histories*. White Plains, NY: International Arts and Sciences Press, 1976.

Gromyko, A. A. *Pamiatnoe* (Remembered). 2 vols. Moscow: Politizdat, 1988.

Gromyko, A. A. *Pamiatnoe* (Remembered). 2 vols. 2nd, enlarged ed. Moscow: Politizdat, 1990.

Hu Deping. *Zhongguo weishemma yao gaige—siyi fuqin Hu Yaobang* (Why Should China Reform? Thoughts and Reflections on My Father Hu Yaobang). Beijing: Renmin chubanshe, 2011.

Hu Jiwei. "Hu Yaobang yu Xidan minzhu qiang" (Hu Yaobang and the Xidan Democracy Wall"), http://www.boxun.com/news/gb/z_special/2004/ 04/ 200404220644.shtml.

Huang Hua. *Memoirs*. Beijing: Foreign Languages Press, 2008.

Huang Rong. "Huang Rong tan Deng Xiaoping" (Huang Rong Speaks About Deng Xiaoping). In Liu Jintian, ed. *Huashuo Deng Xiaoping* (Stories About Deng Xiaoping). Beijing: Zhongyang wenxian chubanshe, 2004, 24–26.

Huang Zeran. "Huang Zeran tan Deng Xiaoping" (Huang Zeran Speaks About Deng Xiaoping). In Liu Jintian, ed. *Huashuo Deng Xiaoping* (Stories About Deng Xiaoping). Beijing: Zhongyang wenxian chubanshe, 2004, 21–23.

Huang Zheng. *Wang Guangmei fang tan lu* (Notes on Conversations with Wang Guangmei). Beijing: Zhongyang wenxian chubanshe, 2006.

Huiyi Deng Xiaoping (Remembering Deng Xiaoping). 3 vols. Beijing: Zhongyang wenxian chubanshe, 1998.

Ji Chaozhu. *The Man on Mao's Right: From Harvard Yard to Tiananmen Square, My Life Inside China's Foreign Ministry*. New York: Random House, 2008.

Jiang Zemin. "Liu Fa, Bi qingong jianxue huiyi" (Recollections on the Diligent Work, Frugal Study in France and Belgium). In *Fu Fa qingong jianxue yundong shiliao* (Materials on the History of the Diligent Work, Frugal Study Movement in France), vol. 3. Beijing: Beijing chubanshe, 1981, 448–68.

Kapitsa, M. S. *Na raznykh paralleliakh: Zapiski diplomata* (On Various Parallels: Notes of a Diplomat). Moscow: Kniga i biznes, 1996.

Khrushchev, Nikita S. *Memoirs of Nikita Khrushchev.* 3 vols. Translated by George Shriver. University Park: Pennsylvania State University Press, 2004–2008.

Khrushchev, Nikita S. *Vospominaniia: Izbrannye fragmenty* (Reminiscences: Selected Fragments). Moscow: Vagrius, 1997.

Khrushchev, Nikita S. *Vremia, Liudi, Vlast'. Vospominaniia* (Time, People, Power. Memoirs). 4 vols. Moscow: Moskovskie novosti, 1999.

Kissinger, Henry A. *On China.* New York: Penguin Press, 2011.

Kissinger, Henry A. *White House Years.* Boston: Little, Brown, 1979.

Kissinger, Henry A. *Years of Renewal.* New York: Simon & Schuster, 1999.

Kissinger, Henry A. *Years of Upheaval.* Boston: Little, Brown, 1982.

Koval', K. I. "Moskovskiie peregovory I. V. Stalina s Chzhou En'laem v 1953 g. i N. S. Khrushcheva s Mao Tszedunom v 1954 g. (J. V. Stalin's Negotiations in Moscow with Zhou Enlai in 1953 and N. S. Khrushchev's with Mao Zedong in 1954), *Novaia i noveishaia istoriia* (*Modern and Contemporary History*), no. 5 (1989): 104–19.

Kovalev, I. V. "Dialog Stalina s Mao Tszedunom" (Stalin's Dialogue with Mao Zedong). *Problemy Dal'nego Vostoka* (*Far Eastern Affairs*), no. 6 (1991): 83–93; nos. 1–3 (1992): 77–91.

Kovalev, I.V. "Rossiia v Kitae (S missiei v Kitae)" (Russia in China [My Mission to China]). *Duel'* (*Duel*). Nov. 5, 11, 19, 25, Dec. 3, 17, 1996, Jan. 14, Feb. 11, 25, Mar. 25, Apr. 8, 1997.

Krutikov, K. I. *Na kitaiskom napravleniu: Iz vospominanii diplomata* (Pointed Toward China: A Diplomat's Reminiscences). Moscow: IDV RAN, 2003.

Lee, Xiao Hong Lily, and A. D. Stefanowska, eds. Biographical Dictionary of Chinese Women: The Twentieth Century, 1912–2000. Hong Kong: Hong Kong University Press, 2003.

Li Huang. *Xuedun shi huiyilu* (Reminiscences of an Uneducated Scholar in His Study Room). Taipei: Chuanji wenxue chubanshe, 1973.

Li Peng. "Guanjian shike—Li Peng riji" (The Crucial Moment—Li Peng's Diary). In Zhang Ganghua, *Li Peng liu si riji zhenxiang* (A True Nature of Li Peng's June 4th Diary). Hong Kong: Aoya chuban youxian gongsi, 2010, 43–379.

Li Rui. *Lushan huiyi shilu* (The True Record of the Lushan Plenum). Beijing: Chunqiu chubanshe/Hunan jiaoyu chubanshe, 1989.

Li Rui. "Yaobang qushi qiande tanhua" (Talks with [Hu] Yaobang Before His Death), *Dangdai Zhongguo yanjiu* (*Modern China Studies*), no. 4 (2001), 23–45.

Li Weihan. *Huiyi yu yanjiu* (Reminiscences and Studies). 2 vols. Beijing: Zhonggong dangshi ziliao chubanshe, 1986.

Li Yueran. "Li Yueran tan Deng Xiaoping" (Li Yueran Speaks About Deng Xiaoping). In Liu Jintian, ed. *Huashuo Deng Xiaoping* (Stories About Deng Xiaoping). Beijing: Zhongyang wenxian chubanshe, 2004, 174–77.

Li Yueran. "Mao zhuxi di erci fangwen Sulian" (Chairman Mao's Second Visit to the Soviet Union). In Li Min, et al., eds. *Zhenshide Mao Zedong: Mao Zedong shenbian gongzuo renyuande huiyi* (The Real Mao Zedong: Recollections of People Who Worked with Mao Zedong). Beijing: Zhongyang wenxian chubanshe, 2004: 566–78.

Li Yueran. *Waijiao wutai shang de xin Zhongguo lingxiu* (Leaders of the New China in the Diplomatic Arena). Beijing: Waiyu jiaoxue yu yanjiu chubanshe, 1994.

Li Zhisui. *The Private Life of Chairman Mao: The Memoirs of Mao's Personal Physician.* Translated by Tai Hung-chao. New York: Random House, 1994.

Liu Binyan. *A Higher Kind of Loyalty: A Memoir by China's Foremost Journalist.* Translated by Zhu Hong. New York: Pantheon Books, 1990.

Liu Bocheng. *Liu Bocheng huiyilu* (Reminiscences of Liu Bocheng). 3 vols. Shanghai: Shanghai wenyi chubanshe, 1981.

Liu Jintian, ed. *Huashuo Deng Xiaoping* (Stories About Deng Xiaoping). Beijing: Zhongyang wenxian chubanshe, 2004.

Liu Shaoqi. *Liu Shaoqi zishu* (Autobiographical Notes of Liu Shaoqi). Beijing: Jiefangjun wenyi chubanshe, 2002.

Liu Xiao. *Chushi Sulian ba nian* (Eight Years as Ambassador to the USSR). Beijing: Zhonggong dangshi chubanshe, 1998.

Luo Ming. *Luo Ming huiyilu* (Reminiscences of Luo Ming). Fuzhou: Fujian renmin chubanshe, 1991.

Meng Qingshu. *Chen Shaoyu—Wan Min: Biografiia: Vospominania* (Chen Shaoyu—Wang Ming: A Biography. Memoirs). Translated and edited by Wang Danzhi. Moscow: BF "Ontopsikhologiia," 2011.

Mo Wenhua. *Huiyi hong qi jun* (Reminiscences of the Red 7th Corps). Nanning: Guangxi renmin chubanshe, 1961.

Mo Wenhua. *Huiyi hong qi jun* (Reminiscences of the Red 7th Corps). 2nd rev. ed. Nanning: Guangxi renmin chubanshe, 1962.

Mo Wenhua. *Huiyi hong qi jun* (Reminiscences of the Red 7th Corps). 3rd rev. ed. Nanning: Guangxi renmin chubanshe, 1979.

Nichols, Francis H. *Through Hidden Shensi.* London: G. Newnes, 1902.

Nie Rongzhen. *Inside the Red Star: The Memoirs of Marshal Nie Rongzhen.* Beijing: New World Press, 1983.

Nixon, Richard. *RN: The Memoirs of Richard Nixon.* New York: Grosset & Dunlap, 1978.

Novak, Robert D. *The Prince of Darkness: 50 Years Reporting in Washington.* New York: Crown Forum, 2007.

Peng Dehuai. *Memoirs of a Chinese Marshal: The Autobiographical Notes of Peng Dehuai (1898–1974).* Translated by Zheng Longpu. Beijing: Foreign Languages Press, 1984.

Peng Dehuai. *Memuary marshala* (Memoirs of a Marshal). Translated by A. V. Pantsov, V. N. Usov, and K. V. Shevelev. Moscow: Voenizdat, 1988.

Primakov, V. M. *Zapiski volontera: Grazhdanskaia voina v Kitae* (Notes of a Volunteer: The Civil War in China). Moscow: Nauka, 1967.

Pu Yi. *From Emperor to Citizen.* Translated by W. J. F. Jenner. Oxford: Oxford University Press, 1987.

Qian Qichen. *Ten Episodes in China's Diplomacy.* New York: HarperCollins, 2005.

Quan Yanchi. *Mao Zedong: Man, Not God.* Beijing: Foreign Languages Press, 1992.

Ren Zhuoxuan. "Liu E ji gui guo hou de huiyi" (Reminiscences of Life in Russia and After Returning to the Motherland). In *Liushi nian lai zhongguo liu E xuesheng zhi fengxian diaoku* (Reminiscences of Chinese Students About Their Sojourns in Russia Sixty Years Ago). Taibei: Zhonghua shuju chubanshe, 1988), 73–78.

Rittenberg, Sidney, and Amanda Bennett. *The Man Who Stayed Behind.* New York: Simon & Schuster, 1993.

Ruan Ming. *Deng Xiaoping: Chronicle of an Empire.* Translated and edited by Nancy Liu, Peter Rand, and Lawrence R. Sullivan. Boulder, CO: Westview Press, 1992.

Sheng Yueh. *Sun Yat-sen University in Moscow and the Chinese Revolution: A Personal Account.* Lawrence: University of Kansas, 1971.

Shepilov, D. T. "Vospominaniia" (Reminiscences). *Voprosy istorii* (*Problems of History*), no. 9 (1998): 18–33; no. 10 (1998): 3–31.

Shi Zhe. *Feng yu gu—Shi Zhe huiyilu* (Summit and Abyss—Reminiscences of Shi Zhe). Beijing: Hongqi chubanshe, 1992.

Shi Zhe. *Zai lishi juren shenbian* (By the Side of Historical Titans). Rev. ed. Beijing: Zhongyang wenxian chubanshe, 1995.

Shi Zhe, and Li Haiwen. *Zhong-su guanxi jianzheng lu* (Eyewitness Notes of Sino-Soviet Relations). Beijing: Dangdai Zhongguo chubanshe, 2005.

Shi Zhe, and Shi Qiulang. *Wode yisheng—Shi Zhe zishu* (My Life—Reminiscences of Shi Zhe Autobiographical Notes). Beijing: Renmin chubanshe, 2002.

Sin-Lin (Lin Ying). *Shattered Families, Broken Dreams: Little-Known Episodes from the History of the Persecution of Chinese Revolutionaries in Stalin's Gulag: Rescued Memoirs and Archival Revelations.* Translated by Steven I. Levine. Portland: MerwinAsia, 2012.

Snow, Edgar. *Journey to the Beginning.* New York: Random House, 1958.

Snow, Edgar. *The Long Revolution.* New York: Random House, 1972.

Snow, Edgar. *Random Notes on Red China (1936–1945).* Cambridge, MA: East Asian Research Center, Harvard University, 1957.

Snow, Edgar. *Red Star over China.* London: Victor Gollancz, 1937.

Snow, Helen Foster (Nym Wales). *The Chinese Communists: Sketches and Autobiographies of the Old Guard.* Westport, CT: Greenwood, 1972.

Snow, Helen Foster (Nym Wales). *Inside Red China.* New York: Da Capo Press, 1977.

Snow, Helen Foster (Nym Wales). *My China Years.* New York: Morrow, 1984.

Su Shaozhi. "A Decade of Crisis at the Institute of Marxism-Leninism-Mao Zedong Thought, 1979–89." *China Quarterly*, vol. 134 (June 1993): 335–51.

Sun Yefang. "Guanyu Zhonggong liu Mo zhibu" (On the Moscow Branch of the CCP). *Zhonggong dangshi ziliao (Materials on the History of the CCP)*, no. 1 (1982): 180–83.

Sun Yong. *Zai Mao zhuxi shenbian ershi nian* (Twenty Years at the Side of Chairman Mao). Beijing: Zhongyang wenxian chubanshe, 2010.

Teichman, Eric. *Travels of a Consular Officer in North-West China.* Cambridge: Cambridge University Press, 1921.

Thatcher, Margaret. *The Downing Street Years.* New York: HarperCollins, 1993.

Vance, Cyrus. *Hard Choices: Critical Years in America's Foreign Policy.* New York: Simon & Schuster, 1983.

Vereshchagin, B. N. *V starom i novom Kitae: Iz vospominanii diplomata* (In Old and New China: Reminiscences of a Diplomat). Moscow: IDV RAN, 1999.

Vishniakova-Akimova, Vera Vladimirovna. *Dva goda v vostavshem Kitae 1925–1927: Vospominaniia* (Two Years in Revolutionary China, 1925–1927: Memoirs). Moscow: Nauka, 1965.

Vishniakova-Akimova, Vera Vladimirovna. *Two Years in Revolutionary China, 1925–1927.* Translated by Steven I. Levine. Cambridge, MA: East Asian Research Center, Harvard University, 1971.

Wang Guangmei, and Liu Yuan. *Ni suo bu zhidaode Liu Shaoqi* (The Unknown Liu Shaoqi). Zhengzhou: Henan renmin chubanshe, 2000.

Witke, Roxane. *Comrade Chiang Ch'ing.* Boston: Little, Brown, 1977.

Wu Lengxi. *Shi nian lunzhan: Zhongsu guanxi huiyilu (1956–1966)* (The Ten-Year Debate: Reminiscences of Sino-Soviet Relations [1956–1966]). 2 vols. Beijing: Zhongyang wenxian chubanshe, 1999.

Wu Lengxi. *Yi Mao zhuxi: Wo qinshen jinglide ruogan zhongda lishi shijian pianduan* (Remembering Chairman Mao: Some Important Historical Events from My Own Life). Beijing: Xinhua chubanshe, 1995.

Wu Wei. *Zhongguo bashi niandai zhengzhi gaigede taiqian muhou* (On Stage and Backstage: China's Political Reform in the 1980s). Hong Kong: Xin shiji chubanshe, 2013.

Wu Xiang, Zhang Guangyou, and Han Gang. "Wan Li tan shiyi san zhong-quanhui qianhoude nongcun gaige" (Wan Li Speaks About Rural Reform Before and After the Third Plenum of the Eleventh Central Committee). In Yu Guangyuan et al. *Gaibian Zhongguo mingyunde 41 tian—Zhongyang gong-zuo huiyi, shiyi ji zhongquanhui qin liji* (41 Days That Changed China's Fate: Reminiscence of the Central Committee Work Conference and the Third Plenum of the Eleventh Central Committee). Shenzhen: Haitian chubanshe, 1998, 281–89.

Xiong Min and Mei Biao. "Huiyi Deng Xiaoping zai Jiangxi Xinjian de yiduan rizi—fangwen Luo Peng tanhualu" (Remembering the Days Spent with Deng Xiaoping

Bibliography

559

in Xinjian [County] of Jiangxi: Notes of a Conversation with Luo Peng). In Wei Renzheng, ed. *Deng Xiaoping zai Jiangxi de rizi* (The Days Deng Xiaoping Spent in Jiangxi). Beijing: Zhonggong dangshi chubanshe, 1997, 134–38.

Yan Mingfu. "Yan Mingfu tan Deng Xiaoping" (Yan Mingfu Speaks About Deng Xiaoping). In Liu Jintian, ed. *Huashuo Deng Xiaoping* (Stories About Deng Xiaoping). Beijing: Zhongyang wenxian chubanshe, 2004), 164–73.

Yang, Rae. *Spider Eaters: A Memoir.* Berkeley: University of California Press, 1997.

Yang Shangkun. *Yang Shangkun huiyilu* (Memoirs of Yang Shangkun). Beijing: Zhongyang wenxian chubanshe, 2001.

Ye Zilong. *Ye Zilong huiyilu* (Memoirs of Ye Zilong). Beijing: Zhongyang wenxian chubanshe, 2000.

Yongyuande Xiaoping: Zhuo Lin dengren fangtanlu (The Unforgettable Xiaoping: Interviews with Zhuo Lin and others). Chengdu: Sichuan chubanshe, 2004.

Yu Guangyuan. *Deng Xiaoping Shakes the World: An Eyewitness Account of China's Party Work Conference and the Third Plenum (November–December 1978).* Translated by Steven I. Levine. Norwalk, CT: EastBridge, 2004.

Yu Guangyuan. *Wo yi Deng Xiaoping* (I Remember Deng Xiaoping). Hong Kong: Shi dai guo chuban youxian gongsi, 2005.

Yu Guangyuan, et al. *Gaibian Zhongguo mingyunde 41 tian—Zhongyang gongzuo huiyi, shiyi ji zhongquanhui qin liji* (Forty-one Days That Changed China's Fate: Reminiscence of the Central Committee Work Conference and the Third Plenum of the Eleventh Central Committee). Shenzhen: Haitian chubanshe, 1998.

Zhao Ziyang. *Prisoner of the State: The Secret Journal of Premier Zhao Ziyang.* Translated by Bao Pu et al. New York: Simon & Schuster, 2009.

[Zhang Weiwei]. "Fangyiyuan huiyi Deng Xiaoping: Qiangdiao renhe shiqing dou yao qin zi shijian" (Interpreter Remembers Deng Xiaoping: One Must Definitely Go from Practice in All Things), news.qq.com/d/20140818/009294.htm.

Zhang Weiwei. "My Personal Memoirs as Deng Xiaoping's Interpreter: From Oriana Fallaci to Kim Il-sung to Gorbachev." http://www.huffingtonpost.com/zhang-weiwei/deng-xiaoping-remembered_b_5706143.html.

Zhang Yaoci. *Zhang Yaoci huiyilu—Zai Mao zhuxi shenbian de rizi* (Memoirs of Zhang Yaoci—Days at the Side of Chairman Mao). Beijing: Zhonggong dangshi chubanshe, 2008.

Zhang Yufeng. "Neskol'ko shtrikhov k kartine poslednikh let zhizni Mao Tszeduna, Chzhou En'laia" (Some Brush Strokes Toward a Picture of the Last Years of Mao Zedong and Zhou Enlai). In Yu. M. Galenovich, *Smert' Mao Tszeduna* (The Death of Mao Zedong). Moscow: Izd-vo "Izograf," 2005, 79–106.

Zhang Yunyi. "Bose qiyi yu hong qi jun de jianli" (The Uprising in Bose and the Establishment of the 7th Corps of the Red Army). In *Guangxi geming huiyilu* (Reminiscences of the Revolution in Guangxi). Nanning: Guangxi zhuangzu zizhiqu renmin chubanshe, 1959, 1–16.

Zheng Chaolin. *An Oppositionist for Life: Memoirs of the Chinese Revolutionary Zheng Chaolin.* Translated by Gregor Benton. Atlantic Highlands, NJ: Humanities Press, 1997.

Zhang Chaolin. *Zheng Chaolin huiyilu* (Memoirs of Zheng Chaolin). [Hong Kong], [n.p.], 1982.

Zhang Chaolin. "Zheng Chaolin tan Deng Xiaoping" (Zheng Chaolin Speaks About Deng Xiaoping). In Liu Jintian, ed. *Huashuo Deng Xiaoping* (Stories About Deng Xiaoping). Beijing: Zhongyang wenxian chubanshe, 2004, 10–12.

Zhou Bingde. *Moi diadia Chzhou Enlai* (My Uncle Zhou Enlai). Beijing: Foreign Languages Press, 2008.

Zhou Enlai. *Zhou Enlai zishu* (Autobiographical Notes of Zhou Enlai). Beijing: Jiefangjun wenyi chubanshe, 2002.

Zhuo Lin. "Zhuo Lin tan Deng Xiaoping" (Zhuo Lin Speaks About Deng Xiaoping), in Liu Jintian, ed. *Huashuo Deng Xiaoping* (Stories About Deng Xiaoping). Beijing: Zhongyang wenxian chubanshe, 2004, 387–92.

Zi Hui. "Liu Fa jianxue qingong liang nian laizhi jingguo ji xianzhuang" (The Two-year History and Present Development of the Frugal Study, Diligent Work [movement] in France). In *Fu Fa qingong jianxue yundong shiliao* (Materials on the History of the Diligent Work, Frugal Study Movement in France). Vol. 1. Beijing: Beijing chubanshe, 1981, 83–94.

IV. NEWSPAPERS AND JOURNALS

Asian Survey. Berkeley, CA, 1986.

Bainian chao (Century Tides). Beijing, 2001–2005.

Bulletin of Concerned Asian Scholars. Cambridge, MA., 1988.

China Economic Review. London/Hong Kong, 2011.

The China Quarterly. London, 1960–2009.

Claremont Review of Books. Claremont, 2012.

Dangdai Zhongguo yanjiu (Modern China Studies). Princeton, NJ, 2001–2014.

Dangshi yanjiu (Studies on Party History). Beijing, 1986–1987.

Dangshi yanjiu ziliao (Study Materials on Party History). Beijing, 1979–2009.

Duel' (Duel). Moscow, 1996–97.

Ershiyi shiji (The Twenty-first Century). Beijing, 2007.

Far Eastern Affairs, Moscow, 2011–2014.

Foreign Policy. Washington, 2011.

Guangming ribao (Enlightenment Daily). Beijing, 1988.

Hongqi (Red Flag). Beijing, 1958-1988.

The Independent. London, 2011.

Istoricheskii arkhiv (Historical Archive). Moscow, 1992–1996.

Izvestiia (News). Moscow, 1994.

Izvestiia TsK KPSS (News of the CPSU CC). Moscow, 1989–1991.

Jindaishi yanjiu (Studies in Modern History). Beijing, 1985–2009.

Jiefang ribao (Liberation Daily). Beijing, 2005.

Moskovskii komsomolets (Moscow Young Communist). Moscow, 2002.

Nanfang zhoumo (Southern Weekly). Canton, 2008.

Narody Azii i Afriki (Peoples of Asia and Africa). Moscow, 1972–1976.

New York Times. New York, 1997–2011.

The New Republic. Washington, DC, 2012.

New York Review of Books. New York, 2011.

Novaia i noveishaia istoriia (Modern and Contemporary History). Moscow, 1989–2011.

Pravda (Truth). 1917–2009.

Problemy Dal'nego Vostoka (Far Eastern Affairs). Moscow, 1972–2011.

Renmin ribao (People's Daily). Beijing, 1949–2014.

Renmin zhengxie bao (Newspaper of the Chinese People's Political Consultative Conference). Beijing, 2004.

Segodnia (Today). Ukraine, 1989.

Shishi xinbao (New Newspaper of Facts). Shanghai, 1931.

The Sydney Morning Herald. Sydney, 2011.

Taipei Times. Taipei, 2012.

Time. New York, 1978–1986.

Twentieth Century China. Columbus, OH, 2007.

Voprosy istorii (Problems of History). Moscow, 1990.

Voprosy istorii KPSS (Problems of History of the Communist Party of the Soviet Union). Moscow, 1958.

Wenshi chunqiu (Literary and Historical Chronicle). Nanning, 2004.

Xin lang (New Wave). Shanghai, 2006.

Xinmin wanbao (The Renovation of People Evening Newspaper). Beijing, 2004.

Yanhuang chunqiu (History of China). Beijing, 2002.

Za rubezhom (Abroad). Moscow, 1934.

Zhongguo ribao (China Newspaper). Beijing, 2008.

Zhongguo xiandaishi (Contemporary History of China). Beijing, 2003.

Zhuanji wenxue (Biographical Literature). Beijing, 2004–2008.

V. SECONDARY SOURCES

All About Shanghai and Environs: A Standard Guide Book: Historical and Contemporary Facts and Statistics. Shanghai: University Press, 1934.

Arincheva, Daria A., and Alexander V. Pantsov. "Mao Zedong's 'New Democracy' and Chiang Kai-shek's New Authoritarianism: Two Paradigms of China's Social Progress in the Middle of the 20th Century." *Problemy Dal'nego Vostoka (Far Eastern Affairs)* no. 1 (March 2014): 109–18.

Averill, Stephen C. "The Origins of the Futian Incident." In Tony Saich and Hans J. van de Ven, eds. *New Perspectives on the Chinese Communist Revolution.* Armonk, NY: Sharpe, 1995, 79–115.

Azhaeva, V. V. *Evoliutsiia politiki KNR v oblasti sel'skogo khoziaistva: Nauchno-analiticheskii obzor* (Evolution of PRC Agricultural Policy: A Scholarly Analysis). Moscow: INION AN SSSR, 1983.

Bachman, David. "Differing Visions of China's Post-Mao Economy: The Ideas of Chen Yun, Deng Xiaoping, and Zhao Ziyang." *Asian Survey.* Vol. 26, no. 3 (1986): 292–321.

Bailey, Paul J. "The Chinese Work-Study Movement in France." *China Quarterly,* vol. 115 (September 1988): 441–61.

Barnouin, Barbara, and Yu Changgen. *Ten Years of Turbulence: The Chinese Cultural Revolution.* London: Kegan Paul International, 1993.

Baum, Richard. *Burying Mao: Chinese Politics in the Age of Deng Xiaoping.* Princeton, NJ: Princeton University Press, 1994.

Baum, Richard. "Zhao Ziyang and China's 'Soft Authoritarian' Alternative." In Guoguang Wu and Helen Lansdowne, eds. *Zhao Ziyang and China's Political Future.* London: Routledge, 2008, 110–21.

Becker, Jasper. *Hungry Ghosts: Mao's Secret Famine.* New York: Free Press, 1996.

Bonavia, David. *Deng.* Hong Kong: Longman, 1989.

Bony, L. D. "Mekhanizm iz"iatiia tovarnogo zerna v KNR (50-e gody)" (The Mechanism of Grain Acquisition in the PRC in the 1950s). In L. P. Deliusin, ed. *Kitai: gosudarstvo i obshchestvo* (China: State and Society). Moscow: Nauka, 1977, 275–95.

Borokh, O. N. *Kontseptsii ekonomicheskogo razvitiia Kitaia (1978–1982): Avtoreferat dissertatsiii na soiskanie uchenoi stepeni kandidata economicheskih nauk* (Concepts of Economic Development in China [1978–1982]: Abstract of Dissertation Submitted for PhD in Economics). Moscow: IDV AN SSSR, 1985.

Borokh, O. N. *Razvitie kitaiskoi ekonomicheskoi nauki v period reform* (Development of Chinese Economic Science During the Reform Period). Moscow: IDV RAN, 1997.

Burlatskii, F. *Mao Zedong, Tsian Tsin i sovetnik Den* (Mao Zedong, Jiang Qing, and the Advisor Deng). Moscow: Eksmo-press, 2003.

Chang Chen-pang, Hsiang Nai-kuang, and Yin Ching-yao. *Mainland Situation Viewed from the Third Session of the Fifth "National People's Congress."* Taipei: World Anti-Communist League, China Chapter/Asian Peoples' Anti-Communist League, Republic of China, 1980.

Chao Feng, ed. *"Wenhua da geming" cidian* (Dictionary of the Great Cultural Revolution). Taibei: Taiwan donghua shuju gufen youxian gongsi, 1993.

Chen Aifei and Cao Zhiwei, *Zouchu guomende Mao Zedong* (Mao Zedong Abroad). Shijiazhuang: Hebei renmin chubanshe, 2001.

Chen Jian. "A Crucial Step Towards the Breakdown of the Sino-Soviet Alliance: The Withdrawal of Soviet Experts from China in July 1960." *CWIHP Bulletin*, nos. 8–9 (1996–97): 246, 249–50.

Chen Jian. *Mao's China and the Cold War*. Chapel Hill: University of North Carolina Press, 2001.

Chen Jian. "Deng Xiaoping, Mao's 'Continuous Revolution,' and the Path Towards the Sino-Soviet Split." *CWIHP Bulletin*, no. 10 (March 1998): 162–64.

Chen Jian, and Yang Kuisong. "Chinese Politics and the Collapse of the Sino-Soviet Alliance." In O. Arne Westad, ed., *Brothers in Arms: The Rise and Fall of the Sino-Soviet Alliance, 1945–1963*. Stanford, CA: Stanford University Press, 1998, 246–94.

Chen Jinyuan. "Wei Baqun tougu chutu jishu" (True Story of the Exhumation of Wei Baqun's Skull). *Wenshi chunqiu* (*Literary and Historical Chronicle*), no. 5 (2004): 5–25.

Chen, King C. *China's War with Vietnam, 1979: Issues, Decisions, and Implications*. Stanford, CA: Hoover Institution Press, 1987.

Chen Qingquan, and Song Guangwei. *Lu Dingyi zhuan* (Biography of Lu Dingyi). Beijing: Zhonggong dangshi chubanshe, 1999.

Chen Xinde. "Wei Baqun." In Hu Hua, ed., *Zhonggong dangshi renwu zhuan* (Biographies of Persons in CCP History). Vol. 12. Xi'an: Shaanxi renmin chubanshe, 1983, 183–200.

Chen Yungfa. "Jung Chang and Jon Halliday. 'Mao: The Unknown Story.'" *Twentieth Century China*, vol. 33, no. 1 (2007): 104–13.

Chen Yutang. *Zhonggong dangshi renwu bieming lu (zihao, biming, huaming)* (Collection of Pseudonyms of CCP Historical Personalities [Aliases, Pen names, Other Names]). Beijing: Hongqi chubanshe, 1985.

Chen Zhiling. "Li Fuchun." In Hu Hua, ed. *Zhonggong dangshi renwu zhuan* (Biographies of Persons in CCP History). Vol. 44. Xi'an: Shaanxi renmin chubanshe, 1990, 1–112.

Chen Zhongyuan, Wang Yuxiang, and Li Zhenghua. *1976–1981 niande Zhongguo* (China in 1976–1981). Beijing: Zhongyang wenxian chubanshe, 2008.

Cheng Bo. *Zhonggong "bada" juece neimu* (Behind the Scenes Decision-making at the Eighth Congress of the CCP). Beijing: Zhonggong dang'an chubanshe, 1999.

"China's Former 'First Family': Deng Children Enjoy Privilege, Jealous Attention.", http://www.cnn.com/SPECIALS/1999/china.50/inside.china/profiles/deng.xiaoping/children/.

Clodfelter, Micheal. *Warfare and Armed Conflict: A Statistical Encyclopedia of Casualty and Other Figures, 1494–2007*. 3rd. ed. Jefferson, NC: McFarland, 2008.

Cohen, Stephen F. *Bukharin and the Bolshevik Revolution: A Political Biography, 1888–1938*. New York: Knopf, 1973.

Confucius. *The Analects of Confucius*. Translated by Simon Leys. New York: Norton, 1997.

Cormack, J. G. *Chinese Birthday, Wedding, Funeral, and Other Customs.* Peking, Tientsin: La Librairie française, 1923.

Courtois, Stéphane, et al. *The Black Book of Communism: Crimes, Terror, Repression.* Translated by Jonathan Murphy and Mark Kramer. Cambridge, MA: Harvard University Press, 1999.

Democracy Wall Prisoners: Xu Wenli, Wei Jingsheng and Other Jailed Pioneers of the Chinese Pro-Democracy Movement. New York: Asia Watch, 1993.

Deng Xiaoping, 1904–1997. Chengdu: Sichuan chuban jituan/Sichuan renmin chubanshe, 2009.

"Deng Xiaoping yi jiade gushi" (Stories of Deng Xiaoping's Family). *Xin lang* (*New Wave*). Sept. 7, 2006.

Deng Xiaoping yu xiandai Zhongguo (Deng Xiaoping and Contemporary China). Beijing: Xiandai chubanshe, 1997.

Dikötter, Frank. *Mao's Great Famine: The History of China's Most Devastating Catastrophe, 1958–1962.* New York: Walker, 2010.

Dikötter, Frank. *The Tragedy of Liberation: A History of the Chinese Revolution, 1945–1957.* New York: Bloomsbury Press, 2013.

Dillon, Michael, ed. *China: A Cultural and Historical Dictionary.* Richmond, Surrey: Curzon Press, 1998.

Dillon, Michael. *Deng Xiaoping: A Political Biography.* London: I. B. Tauris, 2015.

Dittmer, Lowell. *Liu Shao-ch'i and the Chinese Revolution: The Politics of Mass Criticism.* Berkeley: University of California Press, 1974.

Ehrenburg, G. "K voprosu o kharaktere i osobennostiakh narodnoi demokratii v Kitae" (On the Nature and Characteristics of People's Democracy in China). In L. V. Simonovskaia and M. F. Yuriev, eds. *Sbornik statei po istorii stran Dal'nego Vostoka* (Collection of Articles on the History of the Countries of the Far East). Moscow: Izdatel'stvo MGU, 1952, 5–21.

Ehrenburg, G. "Mao Tszedun" (Mao Zedong). *Za Rubezhom* (*Abroad*), no. 31 (63) (1934): 15.

Ehrenburg, G. *Sovetskii Kitai* (Soviet China). Moscow: Partizdat, 1933.

Esherick, Joseph W. *Reform and Revolution in China: The 1911 Revolution in Hunan and Hubei.* Berkeley: University of California Press, 1976.

Erbaugh, Mary S. "The Secret History of the Hakkas: The Chinese Revolution as a Hakka Enterprise." In Susan D. Blum and Lionel M. Jensen, eds. *China off Center: Mapping the Migrants of the Middle Kingdom.* Honolulu: University of Hawai'i Press, 2002, 185–213.

Evans, Richard. *Deng Xiaoping and the Making of Modern China.* Rev. ed. London: Penguin Books, 1997.

Faison, Seth. "Condolences Calls Put Rare Light on Deng's Family." *New York Times.* Feb. 22, 1997.

Fan Shuo. *Ye Jianying zai guanjian shike* (Ye Jianying in a Critical Period of Time). Changchun: Liaoning renmin chubanshe, 2011.

Fenby, Jonathan. *Chiang Kai-shek: China's Generalissimo and the Nation He Lost.* New York: Carroll & Graf, 2004.

Fenby, Jonathan. *The Penguin History of Modern China: The Fall and Rise of a Great Power, 1850–2009.* London: Penguin Books, 2009.

Feng Du. "Suqu 'jingguan' Deng Xiaoping" (Deng Xiaoping—head of the "Capital" of the Soviet Area), http://cpc.people.com.cn/GB/64162/64172/64915/4670788.html.

Franz, Uli. *Deng Xiaoping.* Translated by Tom Artin. Boston: Harcourt Brace Jovanovich, 1987.

Galenovich, Yu. M. *Smert' Mao Tszeduna* (The Death of Mao Zedong). Moscow: Izd-vo "Izograf," 2005.

Gao, Mobo G. G. *Gao Village: A Portrait of Rural Life in Modern China.* Honolulu: Hawai'i University Press, 1999.

Gao Wenqian. *Zhou Enlai: The Last Perfect Revolutionary: A Biography.* New York: Public Affairs, 2007.

Gel'bras, V. G. *Ekonomika Kitaiskoi Narodnoi Respubliki: Vazhneishie etapy razvitiia, 1949–2008: Kurs llektsii. V 2 ch* (The Economy of the People's Republic of China: Key Stages of Development, 1949–2008: Lecture Series. In two parts). Moscow: Rubezhi XXI veka, 2010.

Goldman, Merle. *Sowing the Seeds of Democracy in China: Political Reform in the Deng Xiaoping Era.* Cambridge, MA: Harvard University Press, 1994.

Goldstein, Melvyn C. *A History of Modern Tibet, 1913–1951: The Demise of the Lamaist State.* Berkeley: University of California Press, 1989.

Goldstein, Melvyn C. *The Snow Lion and the Dragon: China, Tibet, and the Dalai Lama.* Berkeley: University of California Press, 1997.

Gong Youzhi. "Gong Yinbing." In Hu Hua, ed. *Zhonggong dangshi renwu zhuan* (Biographies of Persons in CCP History). Vol. 34. Xi'an: Shaanxi renmin chubanshe, 1987, 261–70.

Goodman, David S. G. *Deng Xiaoping and the Chinese Revolution: A Political Biography.* London: Routledge, 1994.

Greenhalgh, Susan. *Just One Child: Science and Policy in Deng's China.* Berkeley: University of California Press, 2008.

Grigoriev, A. M. *Kommunisticheskaia partiia Kitaia v nachal'nyi period sovetskogo dvizheniia (iul' 1927 g.–sentiabr' 1931 g.)* (The Communist Party of China in the Initial Soviet Period [July 1927–September 1931]). Moscow: IDV AN SSSR, 1976.

Guoji gongyun shi yanjiu ziliao: Bukhalin zhuanji (Materials on the Study of History of the International Communist Movement: Special Collection on Bukharin). Beijing: Renmin chubanshe, 1981.

Gudoshnikov, L. M., ed. Sovetskie raiony Kitaia: Zakonodatel'stvo Kitaiskoi Sovetskoi Respubliki, 1931–1934 (Soviet Areas of China: Codes of Laws of the Chinese Soviet Republic, 1931–1934). Translated by Z. E. Maistrova. Moscow: Nauka, 1983.

Han Wenfu. *Deng Xiaoping zhuan* (A Biography of Deng Xiaoping). 2 vols. Taipei: Shibao wenhua, 1993.

He Long nianpu (Chronological Biography of He Long). Beijing: Zhonggong zhong-yang dangxiao chubanshe, 1988.

Heinzig, Dieter. *The Soviet Union and Communist China, 1945–1950: The Arduous Road to the Alliance*. Armonk, NY: Sharpe, 2004.

Hinton, William. *Fanshen: A Documentary of Revolution in a Chinese Village*. New York: Monthly Review Press, 2008.

Hinton, William. "A Trip to Fengyang County: Investigating China's New Family Contract System." *Monthly Review*, vol. 35, no. 6 (1983): 1–28.

History of the Chinese Communist Party—A Chronology of Events (1919–1990). Beijing: Foreign Languages Press, 1991.

Hood, Steven J. *Dragons Entangled: Indochina and the China-Vietnam War*. Armonk, NY: Sharpe, 1992.

Hsiao Tso-liang. *Power Relations Within the Chinese Communist Movement, 1930–1934: A Study of Documents*. Seattle: University of Washington Press, 1967.

Hu Sheng et al. *Zhongguo gongchandang qishi nian* (Seventy Years of the Chinese Communist Party). Beijing: Zhonggong dangshi chubanshe, 1991.

Huang Lingjun. "Liu Shaoqi yu dayuejin" (Liu Shaoqi and the Great Leap Forward). *Zhongguo xiandaishi* (*Contemporary History of China*), no. 7 (2003): 107–11.

Huang Xianfan. *Zhuangzu tongshi* (Comprehensive History of the Zhuang). Nanning: Guangxi renmin chubanshe, 1988.

Jiang Boying et al. "Deng Zihui." In Hu Hua, ed. *Zhonggong dangshi renwu zhuan* (Biographies of Persons in CCP History). Vol. 7. Xi'an: Shaanxi renmin chuban-she, 1990, 296–380.

Jin Chongji, ed. *Liu Shaoqi zhuan: 1898–1969* (Biography of Liu Shaoqi: 1898–1969). 2 vols. Beijing: Zhongyang wenxian chubanshe, 2008.

Jin Chongji, ed. *Mao Zedong zhuan (1893–1949)* (Biography of Mao Zedong [1893–1949]). Beijing: Zhongyang wenxian chubanshe, 2004.

Jin Chongji, ed. *Zhou Enlai zhuan: 1898–1976* (Biography of Zhou Enlai: 1898–1976). 2 vols. Beijing: Zhongyang wenxian chubanshe, 2009.

Jin Qiu. *The Culture of Power: The Lin Biao Incident in the Cultural Revolution*. Stanford, CA: Stanford University Press, 1999.

Jin Xiaoming, et al. "'Deng jia lao yuanzi' de lao gushi" (Old Stories of "The Deng Family Old Household"). *Renmin ribao* (*People's Daily*), Aug. 22, 2004.

Jin Yanshi, et al. "Liu Bojian." In Hu Hua, ed. *Zhonggong dangshi renwu zhuan* (Biographies of Persons in CCP History). Vol. 4. Xi'an: Shaanxi renmin chuban-she, 1982), 255–94.

Jocelyn, Ed, and Andrew McEwen. *The Long March and the True Story Behind the Legendary Journey that Made Mao's China*. London: Constable, 2006.

Ivin, A. *Sovetskii Kitai* (Soviet China). Moscow: "Molodaia gvardiia," 1931.

Kapitsa, M. S. *Sovetsko-kitaiskie otnosheniia* (Soviet-Chinese Relations). Moscow: Gospolitizdat, 1958.

Kapp, Robert A. *Szechwan and the Chinese Republic: Provincial Militarism and Central Power, 1911–1938.* New Haven: Yale University Press, 1973.

Karpov, M. V. *Ekonomicheskie reformy i politicheskaia bor'ba v KNR (1984–1989)* (Economic Reforms and Political Struggle in the PRC [1984–1989]). Moscow: ISAA of MGU Press, 1997.

Kaup, Katherine Palmer. *Creating the Zhuang: Ethnic Politics in China.* Boulder, CO, and London: L. Reiner, 2000.

Kelliher, Daniel. *Peasant Power in China: The Era of Rural Reform, 1979–1989.* New Haven: Yale University Press, 1992.

Kenny, Henry J. "Vietnamese Perceptions of the 1979 War with China." In Mark A. Ryan, David M. Finkelstein, and Michael A. McDevitt, eds. *Chinese Warfighting: The PLA Experience Since 1949.* Armonk, NY: Sharpe, 2003, 217–40.

Klein, Donald, and Anne Clark. *Biographic Dictionary of Chinese Communism: 1921–1969.* 2 vols. Cambridge, MA: Harvard University Press, 1971.

Kratkaia Istoriia KPK (1921–1991) (A Short History of the CCP [1921–1991]). Beijing: Izdatel'stvo literatury na inostrannykh iazykakh, 1993.

Kringer, Benjamin E. "The Third Indochina War: A Case Study on the Vietnamese Invasion of Cambodia." In Ross A. Fisher, John Norton Moore, and Robert F. Turner, eds. *To Oppose Any Foe: The Legacy of U.S. Intervention in Vietnam.* Durham, NC: Carolina Academic Press, 2006, 275–326.

Krivosheev, G. F., ed. *Grif sekretnosti sniat: Poteri Vooruzhennykh Sil SSSR v voinakh, boevykh deistviiakh i voennykh konfliktakh: Statisticheskoe issledovanie* (The Stamp of Secrecy Is Removed: Losses of the Armed Forces of the USSR in Wars, Battles, and Armed Conflicts: A Statistical Analysis). Moscow: Voennoye izdatel'stvo, 1993.

Kuhn, Robert Lawrence. *The Man Who Changed China: The Life and Legacy of Jiang Zemin.* New York: Crown, 2004.

Kulik, B. T. *Sovetsko-kitaiskii raskol: Prichiny i posledstviia* (The Sino-Soviet Split: Causes and Consequences). Moscow: IDV RAN, 2000.

Lan Handong, and Lan Qixun. *Wei Baqun.* Beijing: Zhongguo qingnian chubanshe, 1986.

Lao Tsu. *Tao Te Ching.* Translated by Ralph Alan Dale. London: Watkins, 2002.

Lary, Diana. *Region and Nation: The Kwangsi Clique in Chinese Politics, 1925–1937.* London: Cambridge University Press, 1974.

Ledovskii, A. M. *Delo Gao Gana-Rao Shushi* (The Gao Gang, Rao Shushi Affair). Moscow: IDV AN SSSR, 1990.

Lee, Frederic E. *Currency, Banking, and Finance in China.* Washington, DC: U.S. Government Printing Office, 1926.

Leng Buji. *Deng Xiaoping zai Gannan* (Deng Xiaoping in South Jiangxi). Beijing: Zhongyang wenxian chubanshe, 1995.

Leng Rong and Wang Zuoling, eds. *Deng Xiaoping nianpu: 1975–1997* (Chronological Biography of Deng Xiaoping: 1975–1997). 2 vols. Beijing: Zhongyang wenxian chubanshe, 2004.

Leng Rong and Yan Jianqi, eds. *Deng Xiaoping huazhuan* (Pictorial Biography of Deng Xiaoping). 2 vols. Chengdu: Sichuan chuban jituan/Sichuan renmin chubanshe, 2004.

Lévesque, Léonard. *Hakka Beliefs and Customs.* Translated by J. Maynard Murphy. Taichung: Kuang Chi Press, 1969.

Levich, Eugene W. *The Kwangsi Way in Kuomintang China, 1931–1939.* Armonk, NY: Sharpe, 1993.

Levine, Marilyn A. *The Found Generation: Chinese Communists in Europe During the Twenties.* Seattle: University of Washington Press, 1993.

Levine, Steven I. *Anvil of Victory: The Communist Revolution in Manchuria, 1945–1948.* New York: Columbia University Press, 1987.

Lew, Christopher R. *The Third Chinese Revolutionary Civil War, 1945–1949: An Analysis of Communist Strategy and Leadership.* London and New York: Routledge, 2009.

Li Jingtian, ed. *Yang Shangkun nianpu, 1907–1998* (Chronological Biography of Yang Shangkun, 1907–1998). Vol. 1. Beijing: Zhonggong dangshi chubanshe, 2008.

Li Ping. *Kaiguo zongli Zhou Enlai* (Zhou Enlai, the First Premier). Beijing: Zhonggong zhongyang dangxiao chubanshe, 1994.

Li Ping and Ma Zhisun, eds. *Zhou Enlai nianpu (1949–1976)* (Chronological Biography of Zhou Enlai: [1949–1976]). 3 vols. Beijing: Zhongyang wenxian chubanshe, 1997.

Li Xiannian nianpu (Chronological Biography of Li Xiannian). 6 vols. Beijing: Zhongyang wenxian chubanshe, 2011.

Li Xiannian zhuan: 1949–1992 (Biography of Li Xiannian: 1949–1992). 2 vols. Beijing: Zhongyang wenxian chubanshe, 2009.

Li Xing and Zhu Hongzhao, eds. *Bo Gu, 39 suide huihuang yu beizhuang* (Brilliant Rise and Tragic End at 39). Shanghai: Xuelin chubanshe, 2005.

Li Xinzhi and Wang Yuezong, eds. *Weida de shijian, guanghui de sixiang—Deng Xiaoping geming huodong dashiji* (Great Practice, Glorious Ideology—Chronicle of Basic Events in the Revolutionary Activity of Deng Xiaoping). Beijing: Hualing chubanshe, 1990.

Li Ying, ed. *Cong yida dao shiliu da* (From the First to the Sixteenth Congress). 2 vols. Beijing: Zhongyang wenxian chubanshe, 2002.

Li Yuan, ed. *Mao Zedong yu Deng Xiaoping* (Mao Zedong and Deng Xiaoping). Beijing: Zhonggong dangshi chubanshe, 2008.

Liao Gailong et al., eds. *Mao Zedong baike quanshu* (Encyclopedia of Mao Zedong). 7 vols. Beijing: Guangming ribao chubanshe, 2003.

Liao Gailong, et al., eds. *Zhongguo gongchandang lishi da cidian: Chuangli shiqi fengqi* (Great Dictionary of the History of the Chinese Communist Party: Foundation Period Section). Beijing: Zhonggong zhongyang dangxiao chubanshe, 1989.

Liao Gailong, et al., eds. *Zhongguo gongchandang lishi da cidian. Zengdingben: Shehui geming shiqi* (Great Dictionary of the History of the Chinese Communist Party. Expanded edition: The Period of the Socialist Revolution). Rev. ed. Beijing: Zhonggong zhongyang dangxiao chubanshe, 2001.

Liao Gailong, et al., eds. *Zhongguo gongchandang lishi da cidian. Zengdingben: Xin minzhu zhuyi geming shiqi* (Great Dictionary of the History of the Chinese Communist Party. Expanded edition: The Period of the New Democratic Revolution). Rev. ed. Beijing: Zhonggong zhongyang dangxiao chubanshe, 2001.

Liao Gailong, et al., eds. *Zhongguo gongchandang lishi da cidian. Zengdingben. Zonglun: Renwu.* (Great Dictionary of the History of the Chinese Communist Party. Expanded edition. General section: Personnel). Rev. ed. Beijing: Zhonggong zhongyang dangxiao chubanshe, 2001.

Liao Gailong, et al., eds. *Zhongguo renwu da cidian* (Great Dictionary of China's Personalities). Shanghai, Shanghai cishu chubanshe, 1992.

"Liner André Lebon.", http:www.frenchlines.com/ship_en_1018.php.

Liu Binyan, with Ruan Ming, and Xu Gang. *"Tell the World": What Happened in China and Why.* Translated by Henry L. Epstein. New York: Pantheon Books, 1989.

Liu Chongwen and Chen Shaochou, eds. *Liu Shaoqi nianpu: 1898–1969* (Chronological Biography of Liu Shaoqi: 1898–1969). (2) vols. Beijing: Zhongyang wenxian chubanshe, 1998.

Liu Guokai. *A Brief Analysis of the Cultural Revolution.* Armonk, NY: Sharpe, 1987.

Liu Jixian, ed. *Ye Jianying nianpu (1897–1986)* (Chronological Biography of Ye Jianying [1897–1986]). 2 vols. Beijing: Zhongyang wenxian chubanshe, 2007.

Lo Ping. "The Last Eight Days of Hu Yaobang." In Michel Oksenberg, Lawrence R. Sullivan, and Marc Lambert, eds. *Beijing Spring, 1989: Confrontation and Conflict: The Basic Documents.* Armonk, NY: Sharpe, 1990, 195–203.

Lu Ren and Liu Qingxia. "Mao Zedong chong Heluxiaofu fahuo" (How Mao Got Angry at Khrushchev). *Zhuanji wenxue (Biographical Literature)*, no. 4 (2004): 21–28.

Lubetkin, Wendy. *Deng Xiaoping.* New York: Chelsea House, 1988.

Luo Shaozhi. "Cai mu Ge Jianhao" (Mama Cai, Ge Jianhao). In Hu Hua, ed. *Zhonggong dangshi renwu zhuan* (Biographies of Persons in CCP History). Vol. 6. Xi'an: Shaanxi renmin chubanshe, 1982, 47–57.

Luo Shaozhi et al. "Cai Hesen." In Hu Hua, ed. *Zhonggong dangshi renwu zhuan* (Biographies of Persons in CCP History). Vol. 6. Xi'an: Shaanxi renmin chubanshe, 1982, 1–46.

Luo Zhengkai et al., eds. *Deng Xiaoping zaoqi geming huodong* (Deng Xiaoping's Early Revolutionary Activity). Shenyang: Liaoning renmin chubanshe, 1991.

Lüthi, Lorenz M. *The Sino-Soviet Split: Cold War in the Communist World.* Princeton, NJ: Princeton University Press, 2008.

Ma Qibin et al., eds. *Zhongguo gongchandang zhizheng sishi nian (1949–1989): Zengdingben* (Forty Years of the Leadership of the CCP [1949–1989]). Rev. ed. Beijing: Zhonggong dangshi chubanshe, 1991.

Macdonald, Douglas J. *Adventures in Chaos: American Intervention for Reform in the Third World.* Cambridge, MA: Harvard University Press, 1992.

MacFarquhar, Roderick. *The Hundred Flowers Campaign and the Chinese Intellectuals.* New York: Praeger, 1960.

MacFarquhar, Roderick. *The Origins of the Cultural Revolution. Vol. 1: Contradictions Among the People, 1956–1957.* New York: Columbia University Press, 1974.

MacFarquhar, Roderick. *The Origins of the Cultural Revolution. Vol. 2: The Great Leap Forward, 1958–1960.* New York: Columbia University Press, 1983.

MacFarquhar, Roderick. *The Origins of the Cultural Revolution. Vol. 3: The Coming of the Cataclysm, 1961–1966.* New York: Columbia University Press, 1997.

MacFarquhar, Roderick, and Michael Schoenhals. *Mao's Last Revolution.* Cambridge, MA: Belknap Press of Harvard University Press, 2006.

Maliavin, V. V. *Kitaiskaia tsivilizatsiia* (Chinese Civilization). Moscow: Astrel', 2004.

Marx, Karl. "Capital. Vol. 1. The Process of Production of Capital." In Karl Marx and Friedrich Engels. *Collected Works.* Vol. 35. [Translated by Richard Dixon and others.] New York: International, 1996.

Marx, Karl. "Critique of the Gotha Program." In Karl Marx and Friedrich Engels. *Collected Works.* Vol. 24. [Translated by Richard Dixon and others]. New York: International, 1989.

McCord, Edward A. *The Power of the Gun: The Emergence of Modern Chinese Warlordism.* Berkeley: University of California Press, 1993.

Meisner, Maurice. *The Deng Xiaoping Era: An Inquiry into the Fate of Chinese Socialism, 1978–1994.* New York: Hill and Wang, 1996.

Meisner, Maurice. *Li Ta-chao and the Origins of Chinese Marxism.* New York: Atheneum, 1979.

Meisner, Maurice. *Mao's China and After: A History of the People's Republic.* 3rd ed. New York: Free Press, 1999.

Meliksetov, A. V., ed. *Istoriia Kitaia* (History of China). Moscow: Izdatel'stvo MGU, 1998.

Meliksetov, A. V. "'Novaia demokratiia'" i vybor Kitaem putei sotsial'no-ekonomicheskogo razvitiia (1949–1953)" ("New Democracy" and China's Choice of a Socio-economic Development Path in 1949–1953). *Problemy Dal'nego Vostoka (Far Eastern Affairs)*, no. 1 (1996): 82–95.

Meliksetov, A. V. *Pobeda kitaiskoi revoliutsii: 1945–1949* (The Victory of the Chinese Revolution: 1945–1949). Moscow: Nauka, 1989.

Meliksetov, A. V., and Alexander Pantsov. "Stalinization of the People's Republic of China." In William C. Kirby, ed. *Realms of Freedom in Modern China.* Stanford, CA: Stanford University Press, 2003, 198–233.

Mencius. *Mencius.* Translated by Irene Bloom. New York: Columbia University Press, 2009.

Meng Xinren, and Cao Shusheng. *Feng Yuxiang zhuan* (Biography of Feng Yuxiang). Hefei: Anhui renmin chubanshe, 1998.

Morris, Stephen J. "The Soviet-Chinese-Vietnamese Triangle in the 1970's: The View from Moscow." *CWIHP Working Paper*, no. 25 (April 1999).

Morris, Stephen J. *Why Vietnam Invaded Cambodia: Political Culture and the Causes of War*. Stanford, CA: Stanford University Press, 1999.

Mugruzin, A. S. *Agrarnye otnosheniia v Kitae v 20-40-kh godakh XX veka* (Agrarian Relations in China in the 1920s–1940s). Moscow: Nauka, 1970.

Niu Jun. "1962: The Eve of the Left Turn in China's Foreign Policy." *CWIHP Working Paper*, no. 48 (October 2005).

Niu Jun. "The Origins of the Sino-Soviet Alliance." In O. Arne Westad, ed. *Brothers in Arms: The Rise and Fall of the Sino-Soviet Alliance, 1945–1963*. Stanford, CA: Stanford University Press, 1998, 47–89.

North, Robert C. *Moscow and Chinese Communists*. Stanford, CA: Stanford University Press, 1953.

Naughton, Barry. *Growing out of the Plan: Chinese Economic Reform, 1978–1993*. Cambridge, UK: Cambridge University Press, 1995.

Palmer, James. *Heaven Cracks, Earth Shakes: The Tangshan Earthquake and the Death of Mao's China*. New York: Basic Books, 2012.

Pan Ling. *In Search of Old Shanghai*. Hong Kong: Joint Pub., 1983.

Pang Pang. *The Death of Hu Yaobang*. Translated by Si Ren. Honolulu: Center for Chinese Studies, School of Hawaiian, Asian, and Pacific Studies, University of Hawai'i, 1989.

Pang Xianzhi, ed. *Mao Zedong nianpu: 1893–1949* (Chronological Biography of Mao Zedong: 1893–1949). 3 vols. Beijing: Renmin chubanshe/Zhongyang wenxian chubanshe, 2002.

Pang Xianzhi and Jin Chongji, eds. *Mao Zedong zhuan (1949–1976)* (Biography of Mao Zedong [1949–1976]). 2 vols. Beijing: Zhongyang wenxian chubanshe, 2003.

Pantsov, Alexander V. *The Bolsheviks and the Chinese Revolution 1919–1927*. Honolulu: University of Hawai'i Press, 2000.

Pantsov, Alexander *Den Siaopin* (Deng Xiaoping). Moscow: "Molodaia gvardiia," 2013.

Pantsov, Alexander V. *Iz istorii ideinoi bor'by v kitaiskom revoliutsionom dvizhenii 20-40-x godov* (On the History of Ideological Struggle in the Chinese Revolutionary Movement, 1920s–1940s). Moscow: Nauka, 1985.

Pantsov, Alexander V. "Liubimets partii" (The Favorite of the Party). *The Primary Russian Magazine*, no. 20 (2013): 95–100.

Pantsov, Alexander V. *Mao Tszedun* (Mao Zedong). 2nd, rev. ed. Moscow: "Molodaia gvardiia," 2012.

Pantsov, Alexander V. "Obrazovanie opornykh baz 8-i Natsional'no-revoliutsionnoi armii v tylu iaponskikh voisk v Severnom Kitae" (Establishment of Base Areas of the 8th National Revolutionary Army in the rear of Japanese Troops in North China). In M. F. Yuriev, ed. *Voprosy istorii Kitaia* (Problems of Chinese History). Moscow: Izdatel'stvo MGU, 1981, 39–43.

Pantsov, Alexander V., and Daria A. Spichak. "Deng Xiaoping in Moscow (1926–27): Ideological Development of a Chinese Reformer." *Far Eastern Affairs*, no. 4 (November 2011): 153–64.

Pantsov, Alexander V., and Daria A. Spichak. "Light from the Russian Archives: Chinese Stalinists and Trotskyists at the International Lenin School, 1926–1938." *Twentieth-Century China*, no. 2 (2008): 29–50.

Pantsov, Alexander V., and Gregor Benton. "Did Trotsky Oppose Entering the Guomindang 'From the First'?" *Republican China*, vol. 19, no. 2 (April 1994): 52–66.

Pantsov, Alexander V., and Steven I. Levine. *Chinese Comintern Activists: An Analytic Biographic Dictionary.* (Manuscript.)

Pantsov, Alexander V., with Steven I. Levine. *Mao: The Real Story.* New York: Simon & Schuster, 2012.

Peng Chengfu. "Zhao Shiyan." In Hu Hua, ed. *Zhonggong dangshi renwu zhuan* (Biographies of Persons in CCP History). Vol. 7. Xi'an: Shaanxi renmin chubanshe, 1983, 1–48.

Peng Dehuai nianpu (Chronological Biography of Peng Dehuai). Beijing: Renmin chubanshe, 1998.

Peng Zhen nianpu (1902–1997) (Chronological Biography of Peng Zhen, 1902–1997). vol. 1 Beijing: Zhongyang wenxian chubanshe, 2002.

Pepper, Suzanne. *Civil War in China: The Political Struggle, 1945–1949.* 2nd ed. Lanham, MD: Rowman & Littlefield, 1999.

Perevertailo, A. S., et al., eds. *Ocherki istorii Kitaia v noveishee vremia* (An Outline History of Contemporary China). Moscow: Izd-vo vostochnoi literatury, 1959.

Perry, Elizabeth J., and Li Xun. *Proletarian Power: Shanghai in the Cultural Revolution.* Boulder, CO: Westview Press, 1997.

Pilger, John. *Heroes.* Cambridge, MA: South End Press, 2001.

Poston, Jr., Dudley L., and David Yaukey, eds. *The Population of Modern China.* New York: Plenum Press, 1992.

Qing Shi (Yang Kuisong). "Gongchan guoji yazhi Mao Zedong le ma?—Mao Zedong yu Mosike de enen yuanyuan" (Did the Comintern Suppress Mao Zedong? Concord and Discord in the Relations Between Mao Zedong and Moscow). *Bainian chao (Century Tides)*, no. 4 (1997): 21–33.

Qing Wu and Fang Lei. *Deng Xiaoping zai 1976* (Deng Xiaoping in 1976). 2 vols. Shenyang: Chunfeng wenyi chubanshe, 1993.

Ramsay, Robert S. *The Languages of China.* Princeton, NJ: Princeton University Press, 1987.

Ray, Hemen. *China's Vietnam War.* New Delhi: Radiant, 1983.

Ren Bishi nianpu, 1904–1950 (Chronological Biography of Ren Bishi, 1904–1950). Beijing: Zhongyang wenxian chubanshe, 2004.

Ren Jianshu. "Chen Duxiu." In Wang Qi and Chen Zhiling, eds. *Zhonggong dangshi renwu zhuan* (Biographies of Persons in the CCP History). Vol. 51. Xi'an: Shaanxi renmin chubanshe, 1992, 1–129.

Rethinking the "Cultural Revolution." Beijing: Beijing Review, 1987.

Riabushkin, D. S. *Mify Damanskogo* (Myths of Damansky). Moscow: AST, 2004.

Roberti, Mark. *The Fall of Hong Kong: China's Triumph and Britain's Betrayal.* New York: Wiley, 1996.

Roberts, Priscilla, ed. *Behind the Bamboo Curtain: China, Vietnam, and the World Beyond Asia.* Washington, DC, and Stanford, CA: Woodrow Wilson Center Press and Stanford University Press, 2006.

Ross, Robert S. *The Indochina Tangle: China's Vietnam Policy, 1975–1979.* New York: Columbia University Press, 1988.

Rue, John E. *Mao Tse-tung in Opposition: 1927–1935.* Stanford, CA: Stanford University Press, 1966.

Saich, Tony, and Hans J. van de Ven, eds. *New Perspectives on the Chinese Communist Revolution.* Armonk, NY: Sharpe, 1995.

Salisbury, Charlotte Y. *Long March Diary: China Epic.* New York: Walker, 1986.

Salisbury, Harrison E. *The Long March: The Untold Story.* New York: Harper & Row, 1985.

Salisbury, Harrison. *The New Emperors: China in the Era of Mao and Deng.* Boston: Little, Brown, 1992.

Sándor, Petöfi. *Rebel or Revolutionary: Sándor Petöfi as Revealed by His Diary, Letters, Notes, Pamphlets and Poems.* Translated by Edwin Morgan. Budapest: Corvina Press, 1974.

Schram, Stuart R. *Mao Tse-tung.* New York: Simon and Schuster, 1966.

Schram, Stuart R. *Mao Tse-tung.* Harmondsworth: Penguin, 1974.

Sergeant, Harriet. *Shanghai.* London: Jonathan Cape, 1991.

Shambaugh, David L. *The Making of a Premier: Zhao Ziyang's Provincial Career.* Boulder, CO: Westview Press, 1984.

Shen Zhihua. "Zhonggong bada weishemma buti 'Mao Zedong sixang?'" (Why Did the Eighth Congress Not Raise "Mao Zedong Thought?" *Lishi jiaoxue (Teaching of History)*, no. 5 (2005): 5–10.

Shen Zhihua and Yafeng Xia. "Between Aid and Restrictions: Changing Soviet Policies Toward China's Nuclear Weapons Program, 1954–1960." *Nuclear Proliferation International History Project Working Paper.* No. 2 (May 2012).

Sheridan, James E. *Chinese Warlord: The Career of Feng Yu-hsiang.* Stanford, CA: Stanford University Press, 1966.

Shevelev, K. V. *Formirovaniie sotsial'no-ekonomicheskoi politiki rukovodstva KPK v 1949–1956 godakh (rukopis')* (The Formation of the CCP's Socio-economic Policy in 1949–1956). (Manuscript.)

Shevelev, K. V. *Iz istorii obrazovaniia Kommunisticheskoi partii Kitaia* (From the History of the Establishment of the Communist Party of China). Moscow: IDV AN SSSR, 1976.

Shih, Victor. *Factions and Finance in China: Elite Conflict and Inflation.* New York: Cambridge University Press, 2008.

Shiji xiange, bainian chuanxiang: Sichuan da xuexiao shizhan (1896–2006) (Instrumental Song of a Centenary Echoes for a Hundred Years: History of Universities in Sichuan). Chengdu: Sichuan daxue chubanshe, 2007.

Short, Philip. *Mao: A Life*. New York: Holt, 1999.

Song Yuxi and Mo Jiaolin. *Deng Xiaoping yu kangri zhanzheng* (Deng Xiaoping and the Anti-Japanese War). Beijing: Zhongyang wenxian chubanshe, 2005.

Spence, Jonathan D. *Mao Zedong*. New York: Viking, 1999.

Spence, Jonathan D. *The Search for Modern China*. 2nd ed. New York: Norton, 1999.

Spichak, Daria A. *Kitaitsy vo Frantsii* (Chinese in France). (Manuscript.)

Spichak, Daria A. *Kitaiskii avangard Kremlia: Revoliutsionery Kitaia v moskovskikh shkolakh Kominterna (1921–1939)* (The Chinese Vanguard of the Kremlin: Revolutionaries of China in Moscow Comintern Schools [1921–1939]). Moscow: "Veche," 2012.

Solinger, Dorothy J. *Regional Government and Political Integration in Southwest China, 1949–1954: A Case Study*. Berkeley: University of California Press, 1977.

Stewart, Whitney. *Deng Xiaoping: Leader in a Changing China*. Minneapolis, MN: Lerner, 2001.

Stranahan, Patricia. *Underground: The Shanghai Communist Party and the Politics of Survival, 1927–1937*. Lanham, MD: Rowman & Littlefield, 1998.

Su Shaozhi. *Democratization and Reform*. Nottingham: Spokesman, 1988.

Sun Qiming. "Chen Yannian." In Hu Hua, ed. *Zhonggong dangshi renwu zhuan* (Biographies of Persons in CCP History). Vol. 12. Xi'an: Shaanxi renmin chubanshe, 1983, 1–38.

Sun Shuyun. *The Long March: The True History of Communist China's Founding Myth*. New York: Doubleday, 2006.

Sweeney, Pete. "Burying Deng: Ezra Vogel Lets Deng Xiaoping off the Hook." *China Economic Review*, vol. 22, no. 11 (November 2011): 62.

"A Symposium on Marxism in China Today: An Interview with Su Shaozhi, with Comments by American Scholars and a Response by Su Shaozhi." *Bulletin of Concerned Asian Scholars*, vol. 20, no. 1 (January–March 1988): 11–35.

Taihang geming genjudi shigao, 1937–1949 (Draft History of the Taihang Revolutionary Base Area, 1937–1949). Taiyuan: Shanxi renmin chubanshe, 1987.

Tang Chunliang. *Li Lisan quanzhuan* (A Complete Biography of Li Lisan). Hefei: Anhui renmin chubanshe, 1999.

Tang Chunliang. *Li Lisan zhuan* (Biography of Li Lisan). Harbin: Heilongjiang renmin chubanshe, 1984.

Tang Peiji, ed. *Zhongguo lishi da nianbiao: Xiandaishi juan* (Chronology of Events in Chinese History: Contemporary History Volume). Shanghai: Shanghai cishu chubanshe, 1997.

Tang Zhentang. *Jindai Shanghai fanhualu* (Lively Notes on Modern Shanghai). Beijing: Shangwu yinshuguan, 1993.

Taubman, William. *Khrushchev: The Man and His Era*. New York: Norton, 2003.

Taylor, Jay. *The Generalissimo: Chiang Kai-shek and the Struggle for Modern China*. Cambridge, MA: Belknap Press of Harvard University Press, 2009.

Teiwes, Frederick C. *Politics and Purges in China: Rectification and the Decline of Party Norms, 1950–1965.* 2nd ed. Armonk, NY: Sharpe, 1993.

Teiwes, Frederick C. *Politics at Mao's Court: Gao Gang and Party Factionalism.* Armonk, NY: Sharpe, 1990.

Teiwes, Frederick C., and Warren Sun. *The End of the Maoist Era: Chinese Politics During the Twilight of the Cultural Revolution, 1972–1976.* Armonk, NY: Sharpe, 2007.

Teiwes, Frederick C., and Warren Sun, eds. *The Politics of Agricultural Cooperativization in China: Mao, Deng Zihui and the "High Tide" of 1955.* Armonk, NY: Sharpe, 1993.

Terrill, Ross. *Madam Mao: The White-boned Demon.* Rev. ed. Stanford, CA: Stanford University Press, 1999.

Thomas, S. Bernard. *Season of High Adventure: Edgar Snow in China.* Berkeley: University of California Press, 1996.

Titarenko, M. L., ed. Istoriia Kommunisticheskoi partii Kitaia (History of the Communist Party of China). 2 vols. Moscow: IDV AN SSSR, 1987.

Titarenko, M. L. ed. *40 let KNR* (Forty Years of the PRC). Moscow: Nauka, 1989.

Titov, A. S. *Iz istorii bor'by i raskola v rukovodstve KPK, 1935–1936 gg.* (From the History of Struggle and Split in the Leadership of the CCP, 1935–1936). Moscow: Nauka, 1979.

Titov, A. S. *Materialy k politicheskoi biografii Mao Tsze-duna* (Materials for a Political Biography of Mao Zedong). 3 vols. Moscow: IDV AN SSSR, 1969.

Tønnesson, Stein, and Christopher E. Goscha. "Le Duan and the Break with China." In Priscilla Roberts, ed. *Behind the Bamboo Curtain: China, Vietnam, and the World Beyond Asia.* Washington, DC, and Stanford, CA: Woodrow Wilson Center Press and Stanford University Press, 2006, 453–86.

Turnley, David. *Beijing Spring.* New York: Stewart, Tabori & Chang, 1989.

Tyler, Patrick. *A Great Wall: Six Presidents and China: An Investigative History.* New York: PublicAffairs, 1999.

Usov, V. N. *KNR: Ot "bol'shogo skachka" k "kul'turnoi revoliutsii" (1960–1966)* (The PRC: From the Great Leap to the Cultural Revolution, 1960–1966). 2 parts. Moscow: IDV RAN, 1998.

Vogel, Ezra F. *Canton Under Communism: Programs and Politics in a Provincial Capital.* Cambridge, MA: Harvard University Press, 1969.

Vogel, Ezra F. *Deng Xiaoping and the Transformation of China.* Cambridge, MA: Belknap Press of Harvard University Press, 2011.

Wakeman, Jr., Frederic. *Policing Shanghai, 1927–1937.* Berkeley: University of California Press, 1995.

Wang Dong. "The Quarreling Brothers: New Chinese Archives and a Reappraisal of the Sino-Soviet Split, 1959–1962." *CWIHP Working Paper*, no. 36 (April 2002).

Wang Fukun, ed. *Hong qi jun hong ba jun zong zhihui Li Mingrui* (Li Mingrui, Commander-in-chief of the 7th and 8th Corps of the Red Army). Nanning: Guanxi renmin chubanshe, 2008.

Wang Jianmin. *Zhongguo gongchandang shigao* (A Draft History of the Chinese Communist Party). 3 vols. Taipei: Author Press, 1965.

Wang Jianying, ed. *Zhongguo gongchandang zuzhi shi ziliao huibian—lingdao jigou yange he chengyuan minglu* (Collection of Documents on the Organizational History of Chines Communist Party—The Evolution of Leading Organs and Name List of Personnel). Beijing: Hongqi chubanshe, 1983.

Wang Linmao. "Lei Jingtian." In Hu Hua, ed. *Zhonggong dangshi renwu zhuan* (Biographies of Persons in CCP History). Vol. 20. Xi'an: Shaanxi renmin chubanshe, 1984, 346–60.

Wang Meng. *Bolshevik Salute: A Modernist Chinese Novel*. Translated by Wendy Larson. Seattle: University of Washington Press, 1989.

Wang, Nora. "Deng Xiaoping: The Years in France." *China Quarterly*, vol. 92 (December 1982): 698–705.

Wang, Nora. *Émigration et Politique: Les Étudiants-Ouvriers Chinois en France (1919–1925)* (Emigration and Politics: Chinese Worker-Students in France [1919–1925]). Paris: Indes savantes, 2002.

Wang Shaoguang. *Failure of Charisma: The Cultural Revolution in Wuhan*. Hong Kong: Oxford University Press, 1995.

Wang Shi, ed. *Zhongguo gongchandang lishi jianbian* (Short History of the Chinese Communist Party). Shanghai: Shanghai renmin chubanshe, 1959.

Wang Shoujun and Zhang Fuxing. *Fanfu fengbao—Kaiguo sutan di yi zhan* (The Hurricane Aimed Against Corruption—The First Battle After the Founding of the PRC to Liquidate Corruption). Beijing: Zhonggong dangshi chubanshe, 2009.

Wang Shuo. "Teshi teban: Hu Yaobang yu jingji tequ" (Special Things Done in Special Ways: Hu Yaobang and Special Economic Zones). *Yanhuang chunqiu* (*History of China*), no. 4 (2008): 36–40.

Wang Ting. *Chairman Hua: Leader of the Chinese Communists*. Montreal: McGill-Queen's University Press, 1980.

Wang Xingfu. *Linshi sanxiongdi: Lin Yuying, Lin Yunan, Lin Biao* (The Three Lin Brothers: Lin Yuying, Lin Yunan, Lin Biao). Wuhan: Hubei renmin chubanshe, 2004.

Weatherley, Robert. *Mao's Forgotten Successor: The Political Career of Hua Guofeng*. New York: Palgrave Macmillan, 2010.

Wedeman, Andrew Hall. *The East Wind Subsides: Chinese Foreign Policy and the Origins of the Cultural Revolution*. Washington, DC: Washington Institute Press, 1988.

Wei, Betty Peh-t'i. *Old Shanghai*. Hong Kong: Oxford University Press, 1993.

Wei Renzheng, ed. *Deng Xiaoping zai Jiangxi rizi* (The Days Deng Xiaoping Spent in Jiangxi). Beijing: Zhonggong dangshi chubanshe, 1997.

Wen Xianmei and Deng Shouming. *Wusi yundong yu Sichuan jiandang* (May 4th Movement and Party Building in Sichuan). Chengdu: Sichuan renmin chubanshe, 1985.

Westad, Odd Arne, ed. *Brothers in Arms: The Rise and Fall of the Sino-Soviet Alliance, 1945–1963.* Stanford, CA: Stanford University Press, 1998.

Westad, Odd Arne. *Cold War and Revolution: Soviet-American Rivalry and the Origins of the Chinese Civil War, 1944–1946.* New York: Columbia University Press, 1993.

Westad, Odd Arne. *Decisive Encounters: The Chinese Civil War, 1946–1950.* Stanford, CA: Stanford University Press, 2003.

Westad, Odd Arne. "Fighting for Friendship: Mao, Stalin, and the Sino-Soviet Treaty of 1950." *CWIHP Bulletin,* nos. 8–9 (1996–97): 224–36.

Wilhelm, Richard, ed. *The Chinese Fairy Book.* New York: Frederick A. Stokes, 1921.

Wilson, Dick. *Zhou Enlai: A Biography.* New York: Viking, 1984.

Wishnick, Elizabeth. *Mending Fences: The Evolution of Moscow's China Policy from Brezhnev to Yeltsin.* Seattle: University of Washington Press, 2001.

Woodhead, H. G. W., ed. *China Year Book 1931.* Nendeln/Liechtenstein: Kraus Reprint, 1969.

Wu Guoguang and Helen Lansdowne, eds. *Zhao Ziyang and China's Political Future* London: Routledge, 2012.

Wu Li, ed. *Zhongguo renmin gongheguo jingji shi* (Economic History of the PRC). 2 vols. Beijing: Zhongguo jingji chubanshe, 1999.

Wu Nanlan. "The Xiaogang Village Story.", http://www.china.org.cn/china/feature-content_11778487.htm.

Wu Qinjie, ed. *Mao Zedong guanghui licheng dituji* (Atlas of Mao Zedong's Glorious Historical Path). Beijing: Zhongguo ditu chubanshe, 2003.

Wu Shihong. *Deng Xiaoping yu Zhuo Lin* (Deng Xiaoping and Zhuo Lin). Beijing: Tuanjie chubanshe, 2006.

Xiao Denglin. *Wushi nian guoshi jiyao: Waijiao juan* (Draft History of State Affairs for the Past Fifty Years: Foreign Affairs Volume). Changsha: Hunan renmin chubanshe, 1999.

Xiao Xiaoqin et al., ed. *Zhonghua renmin gongheguo sishi nian* (Forty Years of the People's Republic of China). Beijing: Beijing shifan xueyuan chubanshe, 1990.

Xu Yuandong et al. *Zhongguo gongchandang lishi jianghua* (Lectures on the History of the CCP). Beijing: Zhongguo qingnian chubanshe, 1982.

Xu Zehao, ed. *Wang Jiaxiang nianpu: 1906–1974* (Chronological Biography of Wang Jiaxiang: 1906–1974). Beijing: Zhongyang wenxian chubanshe, 2001.

Xu Zhujin. *Jin Weiying zhuan* (Biography of Jin Weiying). Beijing: Zhonggong dang-shi chubanshe, 2004.

Yang, Benjamin. *Deng: A Political Biography.* Armonk, NY: Sharpe, 1998.

Yang Jisheng. *Mubei: Zhongguo liushi niandai da jihuang jishi* (Tombstone: Unforgettable Facts About the Great Famine in the 1960s). 2 vols. Hong Kong: Tian di tushu youxian gongsi, 2008.

Yang Jisheng. *The Great Chinese Famine, 1958–1962.* Translated by Stacy Mosher and Guo Jian. New York: Farrar, Straus and Giroux, 2012.

Yang Kuisong. "Mao Zedong weishenma fangqi xinminzhuyi? Guanyu Eguo moshide yingxiang wenti" (Why Did Mao Zedong Discard New Democracy? On the Influence of the Russian Model). *Jindaishi yanjiu* (*Studies in Modern History*), no. 4 (1997): 139–83.

Yang Kuisong. "Xin zhongguo 'zhenya fangeming' yundong yanjiu" (A Study of New China's Campaign to "Suppress Counter-revolutionaries"), http://wenku.baidu.com/view/6a3d9b165f0e7cd18425362b.html

Yang Kuisong. *Zhonggong yu Mosike guanxi (1920–1960)* (Relations Between the CCP and Moscow [1920–1960]). Taibei: Sanmin shuju, 1997.

Yang Kuisong. *Zouxiang polie: Mao Zedong yu Mosike enen yuanyuan* (Heading for a Split: Concord and Discord in Relations Between Mao Zedong and Moscow). Hong Kong: Sanlian shudian, 1999.

Yang Shengqun and Liu Jintian, eds. *Deng Xiaoping zhuan (1904–1974)* (Biography of Deng Xiaoping [1904–1974]). 2 vols. Beijing: Zhongyang wenxian chubanshe, 2014.

Yang Shengqun and Yan Jianqi, eds. *Deng Xiaoping nianpu: 1904–1974* (Chronological Biography of Deng Xiaoping: 1904–1974). 3 vols. Beijing: Zhongyang wenxian chubanshe, 2010.

Yang Zhongmei. *Hu Yaobang: A Chinese Biography*. Translated by William A. Wycoff. Armonk, NY: Sharpe, 1988.

Ye Jianying zhuanlüe (Short Biography of Ye Jianying). Beijing: Junshi kexueyuan chubanshe, 1987.

Ye Xuanji. "Ye shuai zai shi yi di san zhongquanhui qianhou: Du Yu Guangyuan zhu '1978: Wo qinlide naci lishi da zhuanzhe yugan'" (Marshal Ye Before and After the Third Plenum of the Eleventh Central Committee: Impressions from Yu Guangyuan's Work *1978: The Great Historical Turning Point That I Personally Witnessed*), *Nanfang zhoumo* (*Southern Weekend*), Oct. 30, 2008.

Ye Yonglie. *Deng Xiaoping gaibian Zhongguo: Cong Hua Guofeng dao Deng Xiaoping* (Deng Xiaoping Transforms China: From Hua Guofeng to Deng Xiaoping). Chengdu: Sichuan renmin chubanshe, 2014.

Ye Yonglie. *Jiang Qing zhuan* (Biography of Jiang Qing). Beijing: Zuojia chubanshe, 1998.

Yen Chia-chi and Kao Kao. *The Ten-Year History of the Chinese Cultural Revolution*. Taipei: Institute of Current China Studies, 1988.

Yin Xuyi and Zheng Yifan. "Bukharin in the People's Republic of China." In Theodor Bergmann, Gert Schaefer, and Mark Selden, eds. *Bukharin in Retrospect*. Armonk, NY: Sharpe, 1994, 54–62.

Yu Guangren. "Deng Xiaoping qiushi yu fansi jingshen" (The Spirit of Deng Xiaoping: Seek the Truth and Reflect It). *Yanhuang chunqiu* (*History of China*), no. 4 (2002): 2–8.

Yu Miin-ling, L. *Sun Yat-sen University in Moscow, 1925–1930*. PhD dissertation. New York, 1995.

Yue Fei. "Man jiang hong" (The River Is Dyed Red). In Yue Fei. *Jingzhong Yue Fei quanji* (Collected Works of the Extremely Dedicated Patriot Yue Fei). Taipei: Hansheng chubanshe, 1976, 155.

Yuriev, M. F. *Revoliutsiia 1925–1927 gg. v Kitae* (The Revolution of 1925–1927 in China). Moscow: Nauka, 1968.

Zhai Qiang. "China and the Cambodian Conflict, 1970–1975." In Priscilla Roberts, ed. *Behind the Bamboo Curtain: China, Vietnam, and the World Beyond Asia.* Washington, DC, and Stanford, CA: Woodrow Wilson Center Press and Stanford University Press, 2006, 369–404.

Zhang Deyuan and He Kaiying. *Bianqian: Anhui nongcun gaige shulun* (Changes: On the Reform in the Anhui Countryside). Hefei: Anhui daxue chubanshe, 2004.

Zhang Heng and Jiang Fei, eds. *Zhonggong zhongyang zuzhi renshi jianmian tupu* (Brief Chronological Tables of the Organizational Composition of the CC CCP). Beijing: Zhongguo guangbo dianshi chubanshe, 2003.

Zhang Jingru et al. *Wusi yilai lishi renwu biming, bieming lu* (Collection of Pen names and Pseudonyms of Historical People Since the May 4 Movement). Xi'an: Shaanxi renmin chubanshe, 1986.

Zhang Junhua and Wang Shaomin. "Shi Kexuan." In Hu Hua, ed. *Zhonggong dangshi renwu zhuan* (Biographies of Persons in CCP History). Vol. 26. Xi'an: Shaanxi renmin chubanshe, 1985), 104–21.

Zhang Peisen, ed. *Zhang Wentian nianpu* (Chronological Biography of Zhang Wentian). 2 vols. Beijing: Zhonggong dangshi chubanshe, 2000.

Zhang Shu Guang. "Between 'Paper' and 'Real Tigers': Mao's View of Nuclear Weapons." In John Lewis Gaddis, et al., eds. *Cold War Statesmen Confront the Bomb: Nuclear Diplomacy Since 1945.* New York: Oxford University Press, 1999, 194–215.

Zhang Shu Guang. "Sino-Soviet Economic Cooperation." In O. Arne Westad, ed. *Brothers in Arms: The Rise and Fall of the Sino-Soviet Alliance, 1945–1963.* Stanford, CA: Stanford University Press, 1998, 189–225.

Zhang Xiaoming. "China's 1979 War with Vietnam: A Reassessment." *China Quarterly*, vol. 184 (December 2005): 851–74.

Zhang Yunyi dajiang huazhuan (Pictorial Biography of General Zhang Yunyi). Chengdu: Sichuan renmin chubanshe, 2009.

Zhanhou zhongsu guanxi zouxiang (1945–1960) (The Development of Sino-Soviet Relations After the War [1945–1960]). Beijing: Shehui kexue wenhua chubanshe, 1997.

Zhao Chang'an et al. *Lao gemingjiade lian'ai, hunyin he jiating shenghuo* (Love, Marriages, and Family Life of the Old Generation Revolutionaries). Beijing: Gongren chubanshe, 1985.

Zhao Jialiang and Zhang Xiaoji. *Banjie mubei xia de wangshi: Gao Gang zai Beijing* (A Story Dug from Underneath a Half-destroyed Tombstone: Gao Gang in Beijing). Hong Kong: Dafeng chubanshe, 2008.

Zhao Wei. *The Biography of Zhao Ziyang*. Translated by Chen Shibin. Hong Kong: Educational & Cultural Press, 1989.

Zhonggong dangshi dashi nianbiao (Chronology of Major Events in the History of the CCP). Beijing: Renmin chubanshe, 1987.

Zhongguo gongchandang lishi jiangyi (Lectures on CCP History). 2 vols. Changchun: Liaoning renmin chubanshe, 1981.

Zhongguo gongchandang lishi jiangyi (Lectures on CCP History). 2 vols. Jinan: Shandong renmin chubanshe, 1982.

Zhongguo gongchandang xin shiqi lishi dashiji (zengdingben) (12, 1978–3, 2008) (Chronology of CCP History in the New Period: Expanded edition [December 1978–March 2008]). Beijing: Zhonggong dangshi chubanshe, 2009.

Zhonghua renmin gongheguo dashi (1949–2004) (Chronicle of Major Events in the People's Republic of China [1949–2004]). 2 vols. Beijing: Renmin chubanshe, 2004.

Zhongguo renmin jiefangjun zuzhi yange he geji lingdao chengyuan minglu (Organizational Evolution and Personnel of the Leading Organs at All Levels of the PLA). Beijing: Junshi kexue chubanshe, 1987.

Zhou Enlai nianpu (1898–1949) (Chronological biography of Zhou Enlai [1898–1949]). Rev. ed. Beijing: Zhongyang wenxian chubanshe, 1998.

Zhou Guoquan et al. *Wang Ming nianpu* (Chronological Biography of Wang Ming). [Hefei]: Anhui renmin chubanshe, 1991.

Zhu De nianpu (Chronological Biography of Zhu De). Beijing: Renmin chubanshe, 1986.

Zhu Jiamu, ed. *Chen Yun nianpu: 1905–1995* (Chronological Biography of Chen Yun: 1905–1995). 3 vols. Beijing: Zhongyang wenxian chubanshe, 2000.

Zhu Ruizhen. "Zhong-su fenliede genyuan" (Causes of the Sino-Soviet Spilt). In *Zhanhou zhong-su guanxi zuoxiang (1945–1960)* (The Development of Sino-Soviet Relations After the War [1945–1960]). Beijing: Shehui kexue wenhua chubanshe, 1997, 91–116.

Zhuangzi. *The Complete Works of Chuang Tsu*. Translated by Burton Watson. New York: Columbia University Press, 1968.

Zhuangzu jianshi (Short History of the Zhuang). Nanning: Guangxi renmin chubanshe, 1980.

Zweig, David. "Context and Content in Policy Implementation: Household Contracts and Decollectivization, 1977–1983." In David M. Lampton, ed. *Policy Implementation in Post-Mao China*. Berkeley: University of California Press, 1987, 255–83.

Illustration Credits

The photographs reproduced in this book are from three sources. Photographs 4, 7, 9, and 11–20 come from the Associated Press. Photographs 6, 8, and 10 are preserved in the Russian State Archive of Social and Political History. Photographs 1–3 and 5 were taken by Alexander V. Pantsov during his visits to the People's Republic of China and Russia.

We express our gratitude to Matthew Lutts of the Associated Press Images Department and Valerii N. Shepelev, deputy director of the Russian State Archive of Social and Political History for granting us permission to reproduce their photographs.

Index

policy and, 6–7, 148, 288–90, 294,
336–37, 352–54, 360, 365–70, 372–73,
379–92, 388–91, 403–6, 409–12;
education of, 15–16, 17, 18–20, 34–36;
at 8th Congress of the CCP, 174–75;
80th birthday celebration of, 394; at
11th Congress of the CCP, 329–30;
ends-justifies-means philosophy of,
356–57; enlargement of support base,
359; executions ordered by, 8, 145; exile
and reeducation of, 264–70, 425; failed
attempt to find compromising material
on, 259–61; family contract system and,
217–18, 222–25, 232, 269, 364, 369–70,
425; family home of, 11–12, 569(figure);
family members assisted by, 150; family
relations severed by, 30–31, 421; as First
Army Group propaganda head, 98, 100;
as first deputy premier, 287–88, 426;
first political activities of, 27; Ford's
visit and, 382; in France (work and
study), 21–22, 23–30, 34–35, 421; France
visited by, 284–85; Gang of Four arrests
and, 304, 426; Gao Gang denounced
by, 159, 160, 161, 163, 423; Gorbachev's
visit and, 392, 399, 428, 534n1; Great
Leap Forward and, 189–97, 199–204,
252; Guangxi experiment and (see
Guangxi experiment); health problems
of, 308–9, 383, 413, 428; hearing
loss of, 251–52, 258, 304, 377, 413;
under house arrest, 257–59, 301, 425,
426; Hua Guofeng undermined by,
325–28, 333, 339, 356, 357, 368, 426, 427;
Huangshan Mountain climbed by, 357,
427; in Huichang, 90–93; "Hundred
Flowers" campaign and, 183–86, 424;
Hungarian-USSR relations and, 180,
181, 182–83; Hu Yaobang's death and,
393–95; Japan visited by, 336–37; Jiang
Qing and, 238–39, 259, 260, 269, 276,
282–83, 286–87, 290, 296, 297, 300–302,
305, 375–76, 426; Khrushchev and,
165–66, 181, 186, 192–94, 209–12, 234,
424; Kim Il Song's visit and, 290–91;
legacy of, 416–19; in Long March, 99,
100, 357, 422; Mao and (see under Mao
Zedong); marriage arranged for, 14;
marriage arrangement terminated by,

30–31; modernization and, 328–29,
330, 333–38, 352, 353, 366, 382; name at
birth (Xiansheng), 12; name changed in
childhood (Xixian), 15; name changed
to Xiaoping, 15, 50, 422; national
unification plan of, 392–93, 427; 90th
birthday celebration of, 413; in North
China Bureau, 111–12; Parkinson's
disease of, 383, 413, 428; patriotism of,
17–18; Peng Dehuai's memorial speech
delivered by, 345; people's communes
investigated by, 200, 213–16; personality
of, 18; photos of, 571(figure), 573(figure),
574(figure), 575(figure), 576(figure),
577(figure), 578(figure), 579(figure),
580(figure), 581(figure); in Politburo (see
under Politburo); in Politburo Standing
Committee (see under Politburo
Standing Committee); popular
support for, 300, 340; pragmatism
of, 32; propaganda used by, 76–77,
462–63n23; pseudonyms of, 35, 37, 62;
Rao Shushi denounced by, 161, 162, 163,
423; as Red Star editor-in-chief, 94,
96–97, 422; rehabilitation of, 307–9,
326–27, 336, 426; rehabilitation of
purge victims urged by, 221; renewed
movement against, 291–92, 293–302;
retirement of, 406–13; return to power,
268–70, 273–75; in Ruijin, 87–90;
self-criticism of, 37, 86, 93, 158, 161,
191, 220, 249, 250–51, 260, 294, 296,
425; semiretirement of, 389–90; 7th
Corps abandoned by, 75, 80–81, 85, 256,
259–60; shifting party relationships
and, 155–63; show trials and, 375–76;
small stature of, 18; smoking habit of,
378, 393; Socialist Education movement
and, 234, 235–36, 237; southeast Asia
visited by, 337; as Southwest Bureau
first secretary, 139, 142, 143, 423; as
Southwest region chief, 139–40, 142–51;
Soviet-Chinese relations and, 192–94,
203–12, 227, 228–32; in Soviet Union
(studies), 35–44; Soviet Union visited
by, 165–69, 186–89, 208–12, 424, 425;
special economic zones and, 379–80,
390, 410; spiritual pollution, campaign
against, 386–88, 410, 427; struggle